International Financial Management

International Financial Management

SEVENTH EDITION

Vyuptakesh Sharan
Former Emeritus Professor
Chandragupt Institute of Management Patna (CIMP)
and
Former Emeritus Fellow
South Asian Studies Division
School of International Studies
Jawaharlal Nehru University, New Delhi

Prof. Amit Kumar Singh
Department of Commerce
Faculty of Commerce and Business
Delhi School of Economics, University of Delhi

Dr. Rohit Kumar Shrivastav
Department of Commerce
Faculty of Commerce and Business
Delhi School of Economics, University of Delhi

PHI Learning Private Limited
Delhi-110092
2026

*In fond memory of **Shri Asoke K. Ghosh** (October 1942–February 2024), Founder Chairman and Managing Director of PHI Learning, whose vision endlessly inspires.*

The Legacy Continues....

Published by Pushpita Ghosh, PHI Learning Private Limited, Rimjhim House, 111, Patparganj Industrial Estate, Delhi-110092 and Printed by Multi Colour Services, 92, DSIDC Sheds, Okhla Industrial Area, Phase-I, New Delhi-110020.

₹1125.00

INTERNATIONAL FINANCIAL MANAGEMENT, Seventh Edition
Vyuptakesh Sharan, Amit Kumar Singh, and Rohit Kumar Shrivastav

© 2026 by PHI Learning Private Limited, Delhi. Previous editions © 2012, 2009, 2006, 2004, 2003, 2000.

All right reserved. This publication is protected by copyright and may not be reproduced, in whole or in part, in any form or by any electronic, mechanical, or other means, now known or hereafter invented, including photocopying, recording, or any information storage and retrieval system, OR to train artificial intelligence systems without permission in writing from the publisher.

ISBN-978-93-5443-933-9 (Print Book)
ISBN-978-93-5443-913-1 (e-Book)

The export rights of the book are vested solely with the publisher.

Dedicated to
My Parents
Smt. Kalyani Devi and Shri Hrishikesh Sharan

Contents

Preface

"The world of international finance is as dynamic as it is challenging. It is a field where opportunities abound, but only for those who understand its complexities."

— Anonymous

It is with great pleasure that we present the **7th Edition of International Financial Management** to readers worldwide. In today's interconnected and rapidly evolving global economy, understanding the intricacies of international financial management is not just a skill—it is a necessity. This book has been designed to provide students, professionals, and financial enthusiasts with the tools and knowledge needed to navigate the complexities of global finance effectively.

Over the past few decades, global trade, the rise of multinational corporations (MNCs), and transformations in international financial markets have reshaped the financial landscape. The complexities of exchange rates, foreign investments, risk management, and sustainability require both a solid theoretical foundation and practical strategies. This book seeks to strike that balance, offering insights that are as academically rigorous as they are practically applicable.

India's role in the global financial ecosystem is more pronounced than ever. As one of the fastest-growing economies, India is navigating profound transformations in trade policies, foreign investments, and currency dynamics. With its deeper integration into the global economy, there is an urgent need for Indian students and professionals to understand the challenges and opportunities of international finance this **7th Edition** highlights India's evolving role in global finance, covering topics such as market liberalization, the rise of Indian MNCs, and strategies for navigating global financial challenges.

This edition reflects contemporary developments, incorporating updates that ensure its relevance to today's economic realities. Key enhancements include:

- **Updated data and statistics for the current financial year** to provide readers with the most up-to-date insights.
- **Refreshed and newly added case studies**, offering real-world scenarios from both global and Indian perspectives to bridge theory and practice.

- **Expanded practical questions** and activities to prepare readers for real-life financial decision-making.
- **Three new chapters** that address the most pressing developments in global finance:
  - *Fintech and Digital Transformation*: Exploring the revolutionary impact of blockchain, digital payments, and cryptocurrencies.
  - *Global Financial Crisis*: Analyzing past crises to understand and mitigate future risks.
  - *Sustainable Finance and ESG Investing*: Reflecting the growing emphasis on environmental and social responsibility in financial decision-making.

To ensure the book remains relevant and forward-looking, outdated data and redundant material have been replaced with new dimensions that align with current trends. By integrating emerging themes such as sustainability, technology, and evolving monetary policies, this edition equips readers to thrive in an increasingly dynamic financial world.

We would like to extend our heartfelt gratitude to our students, colleagues, and readers for their invaluable feedback, which has shaped this book into a comprehensive and practical guide. Their insights and engagement have been instrumental in refining the content to meet the needs of today's learners and professionals.

Our hope is that this book not only deepens, their understanding of international financial management but also inspires them to actively engage with this dynamic field. As India and the world continue to face new financial challenges and opportunities, their ability to contribute meaningfully to this ever-changing landscape will be essential for fostering growth, innovation, and resilience in the global economy.

Vyuptakesh Sharan
Amit Kumar Singh
Rohit Kumar Shrivastav

Preface to the First Edition

With the growing acceptance of the policy of economic liberalisation and globalisation, there has been fast expansion in international trade, in the activities of the multinational corporations and in the international financial market. Recent times have witnessed remarkable growth in international transactions. To handle these transactions effectively, it is imperative to have qualified and trained personnel. In fact, this is one of the main reasons that the subject of international financial management has gained importance in the area of international financial dealings and in the curricula of business management courses all over the world and especially in the developing countries.

I have been teaching this subject not only at the Jawaharlal Nehru University (JNU), New Delhi, but I have also been delivering lectures on it at different institutions in the country as a visiting faculty. It is my students at different institutions who insisted and motivated me to write a textbook on this subject. So, the credit for this text goes to them.

Today, we find that though there are a few good textbooks on this subject, they lack some of the important perspectives of the developing countries. My effort has been to fill this gap and to shape this book to suit the interests of the readers of both the developed and the developing countries. I have tried to include almost all the topics that have been covered by the existing textbooks and to make the explanation lucid and intelligible even to a general reader who does not necessarily have a strong background of economics or commerce. The size of the book has been kept reasonable since the business management students get less than a month for one course on an average. If any student likes to delve deeper into a particular topic, he or she can do so through the Suggested Reading at the end of each chapter.

Quite a number of people—my colleagues and others—have helped me considerably during the preparation of this manuscript. I am grateful to Prof. I.N. Mukherji of the Jawaharlal Nehru University, and Prof. R.S. Nigam, Prof. Y.P. Singh and Prof. D.P.S. Varma of the Delhi School of Economics, University of Delhi, for their useful suggestions. I also wish to express my sincere thanks to my wife for the inspiration and encouragement she has provided for preparing this book.

I am sure, the readers will find this book both interesting and useful. Nevertheless, I expect comments from them in order to make the next edition still more useful.

Vyuptakesh Sharan

PART 1

International Financial and Monetary Environment

CHAPTER 1

International Financial Management— An Overview

Learning Objectives

The present chapter presents a bird's-eye view of international financial management (IFM). In particular, it:

- Explains the nature and scope of IFM.
- Describes the factors responsible for fast growth in international financial functions.
- Makes broad comparison between the domestic financial management and IFM.
- Outlines broad contours in which IFM is discussed in the present text.

International financial management (IFM) is concerned with the management of international business (IB)-related financial functions, commonly known as the international financial functions. The nature and scope of IFM will thus be clear if one tries to understand the nature and modes of international business, the forms of financial functions carried out by those participating in IB, and the complexities of international financial functions that differentiate them from domestic financial functions. Let us discuss these issues in brief so as to acquaint the readers with what IFM really means.

IFM is concerned with IB-related financial functions.

INTERNATIONAL BUSINESS AND ITS MODES

IB means carrying of business activities beyond national boundary. These activities include normally international trade of goods and services and also international production of goods and provision of services normally under the garb of foreign direct investment (FDI). To be precise, IB takes three modes: international trade; contractual entry mode, such as licensing, franchising, management contracts and turn-key projects; and foreign investment, especially FDI.

IB means international trade of goods and services and international production and provision of services.

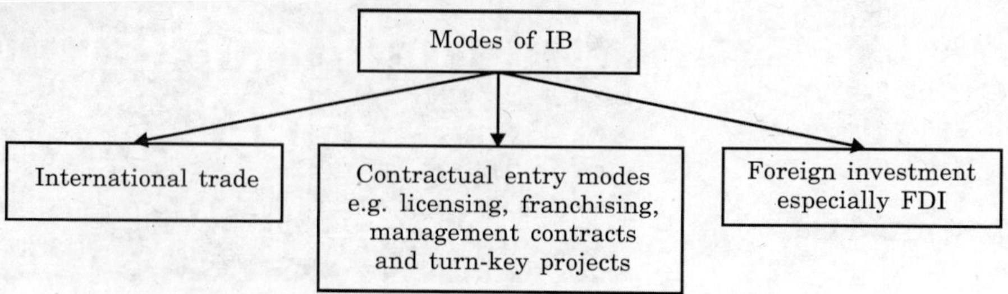

FIGURE 1.1 Modes of International Business.

It is now evident that international trade—export and import—is an important mode of IB. Export may be both direct and indirect. Direct export occurs when a company takes full responsibility for making its goods available in the target market by selling directly or through its agents. On the contrary, indirect export takes place when the exporting company sells its product to the end-users through intermediaries, such as export houses, etc.

Again, international trade is primarily multilateral in character, but bilateral trade does exist in many cases. Bilateral trade, often known as counter-trade is a sort of bartering of goods in different ways. Sometimes we find industrial counter-trade or the buy-back agreement that involves the sale of industrial equipment or turn-key plants in exchange for the products manufactured by the industrial plant so delivered.

Foreign investment is the other mode of IB. Foreign investment is classified as foreign portfolio investment (FPI) and foreign direct investment (FDI). FPI occurs when firms diversify their investment in international securities and often operate on the stock exchange in a foreign country with the sole objective of getting high return. It is nothing to do with the production of goods and provision of services abroad. On the other hand, FDI is very much concerned with the operation and ownership of host-country firms.

FDI takes broadly three forms: one is greenfield investment; the other is mergers and acquisitions (M&As) and still the other is brownfield investment. Greenfield investment can be made through opening of branch in a host-country or through making investment in the equity capital of the host-country firm. The latter is also known as *financial collaboration*. If the parent holds the entire equity of the host-country firm, the latter is called a wholly-owned subsidiary of the parent. If it is more than half, it is known as a subsidiary. Otherwise, it is simply an affiliate of the parent company.

M&As are either outright purchase of a running company abroad or an amalgamation with a running foreign company. While in the former, the acquiring company maintains its existence and the target company loses its existence; in the latter, both lose their existence in favour of a new company. M&As are either horizontal or vertical or conglomerate. Horizontal M&As are found in cases where two or more firms engaged in similar line of activities combine. On the contrary, vertical M&As occur among firms involved in different stages of production of a single final product. Merger of an oil exploration unit with a refining unit is vertical. Conglomerate merger involves two or more firms in unrelated activities, e.g. a financial company managing the financial functions of other companies in the group. Again, M&As may be either friendly or hostile. While hostile take-overs involve least of negotiations, friendly take-overs occur only after lot of negotiations.

Brownfield investment is a combination of greenfield investment and M&A. It exists when a company first goes for an international M&A and then makes huge investment for replacing plant and machinery in the target company.

Contractual entry mode does not involve any financial investment. So it is known as technical collaboration. It may take different forms, such as franchising, licensing, management contracts and turn-key project contracts. Franchising is a contract where the franchiser permits a foreign company to use its brand name for some amount of royalty. Licensing is a contract where technology is transferred to a foreign company for some amount of technical service fees. Management capabilities are transferred abroad in case of management contracts. Turn-key projects are those where a firm constructs the plant in a foreign location and hands over the key to the foreign partner for operation. In all these contracts, it is true that no investment flows abroad, but there is reverse flow of funds for the use of these facilities or services.

MULTINATIONAL CORPORATIONS: THE KEY PARTICIPANT IN INTERNATIONAL FINANCIAL FUNCTIONS

It is true that even small trading firms and small investors participate in IB. But it is the multinational corporations (MNCs) that are responsible for a lion's share of world trade and investment. The readers should know what speciality MNCs do have. An MNC is an enterprise that owns and controls production or service facilities outside the country in which it is based (United Nations, 1973). But for qualifying as an MNC, the number of countries where the firm operates must be at least six (Vernon, 1971; United Nations, 1978). At the same time, the firm must generate a sizeable proportion of its revenue from the foreign operation, although no exact percentage is agreed upon. All this means that the firm should be big enough to have its stronghold in many countries through branches and subsidiaries. MNCs' stronghold in the host countries is evident from the fact that in 2010, 64 per cent of the total sales, 62 per cent of the total assets and 56 per cent of the total employment in top 100 MNCs were accounted for by the host countries (United Nations, 2011).

> MNCs are normally big firms with stronghold in many host countries through branches and subsidiaries.

Something more will be clear if one goes through the behavioural definition of an MNC given by Vernon and Wells Jr. (1986). According to them, MNCs represent a cluster of affiliated firms located in different countries that: 1. are linked through common ownership, 2. draw upon a common pool of resources, and 3. respond to a common strategy. All this means a high degree of integration among different units of the firm.

Based on the strategic features, MNCs are grouped as ethnocentric, polycentric and geocentric (Perlmutter, 1969; Perlmutter and Heenan, 1974). Ethnocentric firms are those that adopt home-market-oriented policy and seldom distinguish between the domestic operation and the global operation policies. On the other extreme, polycentric firms operate in the foreign country just to cater to the demand in those countries. This means that they follow a host-market-oriented policy. Between these two extremes, the geocentric firms maintain a balance between the home-market and host-market oriented policies. They are in fact closer to real situation. Punnett and Ricks (1997) differentiate between a multi-domestic company and a global company. While the former is concerned more with the market of the host country where it operates, the latter is concerned with the global market. It finds the world as a single market and plans to cater it through integrated operations. Similarly, Bartlett and Ghoshal (1989) differentiate between a multinational company and a transnational company. In the former, decision-making is normally decentralised and the activities of the firm are not strongly co-ordinated. In the latter, the global business activities of the firm are perfectly configured, co-ordinated and controlled so as to achieve global competitiveness.

NATURE OF INTERNATIONAL FINANCIAL FUNCTIONS AND THE SCOPE OF IFM

It has already been mentioned that the entire gamut of financial functions related to IB forms the subject-matter of IFM. Let us discuss here the nature of these financial functions which will unravel the nature and scope of IFM. To begin with trade, an importer pays for the import usually in a convertible currency. The exporter converts the foreign currency of the export proceeds into its own currency. The exchange of currency has thus led to the emergence of a globally spread foreign exchange market. The discussion of the foreign exchange market and of the various activities therein forms the subject-matter of IFM.

When currencies are exchanged in the foreign exchange market, there arises another question as to what should be the exchange rate. In other words, the question is how many units of a foreign currency, a unit of the domestic currency would fetch. In some cases, the exchange rate between any two currencies is fixed as per the governmental announcement. But in many cases, it is floating, based on the market forces of supply and demand. In fact, it is the International Monetary Fund (IMF) that has laid down the norms and the procedures for different types of the exchange rate regimes. The member countries follow those norms and procedures. The IMF maintains surveillance over the functioning of the exchange rate regime; and over and above, it helps maintain international liquidity so as to ease the international monetary and financial transactions. Thus the functioning of IMF and the determination of exchange rate form an integral part of the study of IFM.

The foreign exchange market is supposed to be perfect where all information is easily available and where nobody can influence the exchange rate. But in real life, it is not perfect. Varying exchange rates exist in different markets at the same point of time. The arbitrageurs take advantage of this kind of disparity and make profits. Moreover, the market-determined exchange rates tend to oscillate putting in turn the traders to exchange rate exposure/risk. The traders hedge their risk in the foreign exchange market. Again, speculators are quite active in the foreign exchange market in order to make profits out of exchange rate oscillations. Hedging and speculations are frequent also in the market for derivatives, such as the market for currency futures and the market for currency options that have evolved and matured over time. IFM covers all these activities concerning arbitrage, hedging and speculation.

The IB-related financial functions are not limited to the foreign exchange market. A lot of such functions are involved in cross-border investment. The operation of financial companies at the stock exchanges abroad with the objective of maximising gains with a given level of risk or minimising risk with a given level of return is known as foreign portfolio investment and is an important segment of IFM. But more important are the financial activities of the MNCs that are related to FDI. First of all, an MNC selects a new proposal on the basis of its viability in terms of a positive net present value. If it aims at acquiring a running firm abroad, it finds out whether the gains are higher than the consideration value it is paying to the target company. In all the cases, political risk is taken into consideration. If the situation is favourable, the MNC makes actual investment. So the FDI involving long-term investment decision, often known as international capital budgeting forms a part of IFM.

International investment is possible only when the required funds are raised and are made available for this purpose. It is true that MNCs have an easy access to the international financial market. International financial market embraces variety of sources—beginning from the international development banks, such as the World Bank and International Finance Corporation, and regional development banks, such as Asian Development Bank, etc. to the eurocurrency market and international securities market. Whatever may be the source of funds, the MNC is very much careful of, firstly, the effective cost of funds that depends not only on the interest rate but also on the appreciation/depreciation of the currency; and secondly, the debt-equity norm that varies from one country to the other and that does influence the weighted average cost of capital. Sometimes the borrower does not get the desired currency. Sometimes it does not get funds at the desired type of interest rate meaning that it gets funds at floating interest rate instead of fixed interest rate or vice versa. In such cases, the borrower swaps the loan. The swap may be a currency swap or it may be an interest-rate swap. Again, the floating interest rate changes more frequently with the result that the lender/borrower is exposed to interest rate risk. In such cases, there are ways to hedge the interest rate risk and eliminate/minimise the losses on this account. Thus the international financial functions are related to the raising of funds from different windows of the international financial market and also to the related activities, such as financial swap and interest-rate risk management. The study of IFM covers all these activities.

The international financial functions spread even beyond long-term investment and funds raising decisions of international firms. After project is finalised and the fixed assets are created through the funds raised from the international financial market, the project starts operation. The current assets are created financed out of both the long-term funds and the short-term funds. In order to smoothen the operation, emphasis is given on the optimisation of the size of current assets and on a perfect ratio between the long-term and short-term liabilities for the purpose of financing of current assets so that the trade-off between liquidity and profitability is optimised. In case of the MNCs, special consideration is given to the management of cash in view of, first, large-scale intra-firm movement of cash vis-à-vis restrictions imposed by host governments on such movements and, second, the international cash positioning meant for the investment of the surplus cash during a specific period. IFM takes care of all such activities.

At the end of the financial year, the international firm tries to consolidate the financial statements of all the units so as to assess the global profit and global financial status. As far as global profit is concerned, it depends on the tax rates and tax rules that vary widely between home and host countries and among different host countries. International firms often resort to transfer pricing in order to siphon pre-tax profit from a high-tax country to a low-tax country and thereby to maximise the global profit despite close watch by the government authorities. IFM thus deals with international accounting and international tax strategy and all the related activities.

Last but not least, the government of different countries records all types of flow of funds on the debit and credit sides so as to know the net flow of funds into the economy or out of the economy. The statement recording the transactions is known as balance of payments in which the performance of the entire external sector is reflected. It happens in most of the cases that the flow of funds into the economy either on the trade account or on investment account falls short of the outflow. In such cases, borrowing is sought that often leads to unmanageable external debt burden and weakens the external sector and thereby the entire economy. IFM thus covers essentially the study of the balance of payments and external indebtedness.

In short, the broad areas of IB-related financial functions showing the scope of IFM can be outlined in the box below.

International Financial Functions Showing the Scope of IFM

- Foreign exchange market including the market for derivatives and all the different types of transactions concluded in these markets.
- Exchange rate—its determination and forecasting along with the factors influencing exchange rate.
- Exchange rate exposure—its assessment and management.
- International monetary system especially with a focus on the IMF designing the exchange rate regime and promoting international liquidity.
- Investment decision of the international firms including both FDI and FPI.
- International financial market including international and regional development banks, eurocurrency market, and international securities market and the entire range of transactions concluded therein.
- Assessment and management of interest rate exposure.
- MNCs' working capital management.
- International accounting and taxation strategy.
- Balance of payments analysis showing flow of funds following international financial transactions.
- International indebtedness and its management.

It is worth noting here that some of the aspects of IFM have more of macro-economic element, such as the functions of the IMF, preparation of the balance of payments, country's external indebtedness or so. On the contrary, the others have more of micro-economic element, such as arbitrage, hedging and speculative activities of the participants in the foreign exchange market, investment and working capital management of a particular MNC, and so. Thus the study of IFM presents a mix of the two.

Again, IFM analyses the IB-related financial functions not only in a theoretical setting, but also from the viewpoint of their real-life implications. And thus it would not be wrong to say that IFM is a behavioural science.

FACTORS LEADING TO FAST STRIDES IN INTERNATIONAL FINANCIAL FUNCTIONS

IB is not new, nor are new the IB-related international financial functions. But since the trade and foreign investment were found mostly between the empire and the colony till the first half of the twentieth century, the scope of such functions was very limited. It was only in the wake of the GATT's effort to reduce trade restrictions in the second half of the twentieth century and finally the establishment of the WTO in 1995 with its large functions and power that the world trade grew phenomenally.

> Growth in IB-related financial functions is attributed mainly to:
> 1. Growth in international trade,
> 2. Growth in foreign investment,
> 3. Structural change in the international financial market,
> 4. Adoption of floating exchange rate regime, and
> 5. Fast development in information technology.

It is not solely the international trade. FDI got growing since 1950s. The American MNC emerged fast on the map of the global economy since 1950s. Since 1960s, many European firms went multinational. In 1970s, MNCs came to be headquartered in Japan. The growth in Japanese MNCs coincided with the emergence of the MNCs in the newly industrialising countries.

The amount of world FDI inflows grew from US $ 117.106 billion in 2003 to US $ 288.131 billion in 2013. In 2018–2020, it was US $ 222.587 billion on an average. In 2021, it was US $ 475.805 billion that fell to US $ 408.982 billion in 2022, and to 348.784 billion in 2023.

TABLE 1.1 Growth in FDI Inflows/Outflows

(US $ billion)

	2003	*2013*	*2018–2020 average*	*2021*	*2022*	*2023*
FDI net outflows	195.218	392.796	175.993	341.954	388.510	454.084
FDI net inflows	117.106	288.131	222.587	475.805	408.982	348.784
FDI net (BoP)	–78.112	–104.665	46.594	133.851	20.472	–105.300

Source: World Investment Report, various issues.

IFM AND DOMESTIC FINANCIAL MANAGEMENT

IFM is, to a great extent, similar to domestic corporate financial management. A domestic company takes up a project for investment only when the net present value of cash flows is positive and it shapes the working capital policy in a way that maximises profitability and ensures desired liquidity. It is not different in case of MNCs. Again, the financing decisions, in respect of whether a domestic or an international company, aim at minimising the overall cost of capital and providing optimum liquidity.

However, IFM has a wider scope than domestic corporate finance and it is designed to cope with greater range of complexities than the latter. The reasons are as follows:

1. The MNCs operate in different economic, political, legal, cultural and tax environments.
2. They operate across and within varied ranges of product and factor markets which vary in regard to competition and efficiency.
3. They trade in a large number of currencies as a result of which their dependence on the foreign exchange market is quite substantial.
4. They have easy access not only to varying domestic capital markets but also to unregulated international capital markets which differ in terms of efficiency and competitiveness.

The greater the degree of involvement of the firm in the international economic environment or the greater the degree of differences among different segments of the international economic environment, the greater are the complexities. Naturally, when these firms make international investments, they also need to take into account the political relations between the home government and the host government. The capital budgeting technique also considers the intra-firm flows. A domestic company does not have to bother with these complexities.

Similarly, working capital management in an MNC is more complex because it involves cash movement and movement of raw material, semi-finished and finished goods from one political and tax jurisdiction to another. Cash positioning is thus an important decision in the working capital management of MNCs. Again, the dividend decision of an international firm is separated into subsidiary dividend paid to the parent company and the parent company's dividend paid to its shareholders. The former involves complexities and has many novel implications. Yet again, in an international firm, foreign exchange management is very crucial as the firm operates in different countries. The domestic firm has not to bother for it unless it goes for external capital or for international trade.

STRUCTURE OF THE BOOK

The present text-book deals with all the issues that are concerned with IB-related financial functions. The discussion is divided into seven parts. The first part discusses some basic international norms and practices. It explains how international financial transactions are recorded in the balance of payments, how the international monetary system, especially the IMF system works, and how exchange rates are determined.

The second part deals with how transactions take place in the foreign exchange market including also the market for derivatives. The third part discusses exchange rates forecast, and how the exchange rate exposure is assessed and managed.

The fourth part begins with the discussion of the investment decision of the MNCs—the basics of FDI, the evaluation of foreign investment proposals, the assessment and management of political risk and finally the international portfolio investment. Part V deals with how funds are raised to finance the investment projects. The sources of funds beginning from international development banks to eurocurrency market and international securities market are discussed. Financial swaps and interest rate exposure are especially dealt with in this context.

Part VI deals with the international working capital management. It also describes the foreign trade financing. Lastly, Part VII deals with international accounting, international indebtedness and international taxation.

REVIEW QUESTIONS

Objective-Type Questions

1. State whether true (T) or false (F):

(a) Global and multi-domestic firms are synonyms. ☐
(b) Ethnocentric firms have host-country-oriented policies. ☐
(c) Geocentric firms have host-country-oriented policies. ☐
(d) Direct trade is carried out through intermediaries. ☐
(e) Foreign portfolio investment is concerned with international production. ☐

2. Choose the correct answer:

(a) MNCs must operate at least in:
(i) four countries
(ii) six countries
(iii) ten countries

(b) International production is a function of:
(i) trade
(ii) FDI
(iii) FPI

(c) In 2000s, FDI has:
(i) consistently moved up.
(ii) experienced a downtrend.
(iii) been stagnant.

Short-Answer Questions

1. Distinguish between multinational corporations and transnational corporations.
2. Explain ethnocentric, polycentric and geocentric firms.

Long-Answer Questions

1. Name some of the complexities of international financial management compared to domestic financial management.
2. How has the growth in international trade and multinational corporations been responsible for growing importance of the study of international finance?
3. Discuss the nature and scope of international financial decision.

REFERENCES

Bartlett, C.A. and S. Ghoshal (1989), *Managing Across Borders: The Transnational Solution*, Boston: Harvard Business School Press.

Perlmutter, H.V. (1969), "The Tortuous Revolution of the Multinational Corporation", *Columbia Journal of World Business*, IV (Jan.–Feb.), 9–18.

Perlmutter, H.V. and D.A. Heenan (1974), "How Multinational Should Your Top Manager Be", *Harvard Business Review*, LII (Nov.–Dec.), 121–32.

Punnett, B.J. and D.A. Ricks (1997), *International Business*, Oxford: Blackwell Business.

United Nations (1973), *Multinational Corporations in World Development*, New York.

United Nations (1978), *Transnational Corporations in World Development: A Re-examination*, New York.

United Nations (2011), *World Investment Report: 2010*, New York.

Vernon, R. (1971), *Sovereignty at Bay: The Multinational Spread of United States Enterprises*, New York: Basic Books.

Vernon, R. and L.T. Wells, Jr. (1986), *Manager in the International Economy*, Englewood Cliffs: Prentice-Hall.

WTO (2011), *Annual Report, 2010*, Geneva.

SUGGESTED FURTHER READING

Daniels, J.D. and J. Bracker (1989), Profit Performance: Do foreign operations make a difference? *Management International Review*, I, 46–56.

Holland, John (1986), *International Financial Management*, Oxford: Basil Blackwell, Chap. 1.

CHAPTER 2

International Flow of Funds: Balance of Payments

Learning Objectives

The chapter acquaints the readers with the structure of, and with disequilibrium arising in, the balance of payments and also with the issue of liberalization in the capital account transactions. In particular, it attempts:

- To discuss the structure of balance of payments (BOP) with a focus on the current and capital account transactions.
- To explain BOP equilibrium and disequilibrium and to show how official reserves account is related to BOP disequilibrium.
- To discuss various approaches to BOP adjustment—beginning from the mercantilist view and classical approach to the elasticity approach, Keynesian approach and monetary approach.
- To evaluate various aspects of capital account liberalisation.

Let us begin with how the cross-border flow of funds is recorded by the monetary authorities in different countries in order to evaluate the strength of their external sector. The statement recording the flow is purely a macro-economic statement and is known as the balance of payments statement. The present chapter discusses the various aspects of the balance of payments.

STRUCTURE OF BALANCE OF PAYMENTS

Balance of payments is a statement listing receipts and payments in international transactions of a country. It is based on the concept of double-entry book-keeping where the credit balance shows the receipts of foreign exchange from abroad and the debit balance shows payments in foreign exchange to foreign residents; and debit and credit balances are equal if the various entries are properly made. Disequilibrium does occur but not from the accounting point of view. The concept of accounting equilibrium is discussed later in this chapter.

Current account and capital account are two compartments of BOP. While the former shows transfer of real income, the latter shows simply transfer of funds without effecting real income.

Again, receipts and payments are compartmentalised into two heads, namely current account and capital account. The basic distinction between the two is that the former represents transfer of real income, while the latter records only transfer of funds without effecting a shift in real income.

Current Account Transactions

The current account records the receipts and payments of foreign exchange in the following ways:

Current account receipts:

1. Export of goods
2. Invisibles
3. Non-monetary movement of gold

Current account payments:

1. Import of goods
2. Invisibles
3. Non-monetary movement of gold

Export of goods effects flow of foreign exchange into the country, while import of goods causes outflow of foreign exchange from the country. The difference between the two is known as the *balance of trade*. If export exceeds import, balance of trade turns surplus while excess of import over export results in a deficit balance of trade. Table 2.1 shows a deficit balance of trade of US $ 242.06 billion.

Invisibles include receipts and payments on account of (1) trade-in services such as travel and tourism, transport, etc. (2) investment income, such as interest and dividend, etc., and (3) unilateral transfers. Unilateral transfers include pensions, remittances, gifts, and other transfers for which no specific services are rendered. They are called unilateral transfers because they represent flow of funds only in one direction, that is the direction of payment. They are unlike the export or import where goods flow in one direction and the payment flows in the other direction.

Invisibles include non-merchandise trade, such as trade in services, investment income, unilateral transfers, etc.

The movement of gold may be monetary or non-monetary. Monetary movement is the sale or purchase that influences the international monetary reserves. Non-monetary sale and purchase of gold is done for industrial purposes that is shown in the current account either separately or along with the merchandise trade. Presently, it is shown as a part of merchandise trade. Suppose the credit side on account of these transactions, that is on account of the trade of goods and services, investment income, unilateral transfers and non-monetary movement of gold in the current account is greater than the debit side, the *balance of the current account* turns surplus. If the debit is greater than the credit, the balance of the current account shows a deficit. Table 2.1 shows a deficit for US $ 23.28 billion on the current account.

TABLE 2.1 Country A: Balance of Payments: 2023–24

(US $ billion)

	Credit	*Debit*	*Balance*
A. Current Account			
Merchandise import		683.54	
Merchandise export	441.48		
Balance of Trade			–242.06
Invisibles			
Services (net)	162.76		
Unilateral transfers (net)	104.78		
Investment income (net)			
Non-monetary movement of gold (net)	–	49.77	
Balance of current account			–23.28
B. Capital Account			
Foreign Investment:			
Direct investment abroad		16.67	
Direct foreign investment inflow	26.46		
Portfolio investment (net)	44.08		
Loans–official and private net of repayments	1.69		
Basic balance			53.87
Short-term:			
Holdings with banks	40.54		
Other short-term transactions		9.832	
Balance of capital account			86.27
C. Errors and Omissions			0.71
Overall balance (A + B + C)			63.7
D. Official Reserves			
SDR allocations	17.84		
Net official reserves	604.66		
Overall balance	–63.7		
Official reserves movement	63.7		

PROBLEM 2.1

Find out (a) the balance of trade and (b) balance of current account, if: Inflow on account of services: $ 1,500; outflow on account of services: $ 1,200; outflow of dividend, royalty, etc. $ 1,100; inflow of dividend, etc. $ 620; export of goods: $ 11,500; import of goods: $ 15,000; remittances: $ 1,200.

Solution

	$
Import	–15,000
Export	11,500
Balance of trade	–3,500
Services (net)	300
Investment income (net)	–480
Remittances (net)	1,200
Balance of current account:	–2,480

Capital Account Transactions

Capital account transactions, on the other hand, comprise long-term and short-term inflow and outflow of funds under the capital account receipt and payment heads. Long-term transactions involve maturity periods of over one year, while short-term flows are effected for one year or less. The credit side records the official and private borrowing from abroad net of repayments, direct and portfolio investments, and short-term investments into the country. It records also the bank balances of the non-residents held in the country. The debit side includes dis-investment of capital invested into the country, the country's investment abroad, loans given to a foreign government or a foreign party and the bank balances held abroad. When the credit side of the current account along with the credit side of the long-term capital account transactions is compared with the transactions on the debit side of the current account plus the long-term capital account, the difference is known as the *basic balance* which may be negative or positive. As shown in Table 2.1, the basic balance indicates a surplus of US $ 53.87 billion. However, in India and in many other countries, basic balance is not shown in the balance of payments statement.

Balancing of the capital account is not complete with the basic balance. The debit and credit sides of the short-term capital account transactions are added to their respective sides and then the capital account is balanced.

PROBLEM 2.2

Find out the balance of the capital account, if: inflow of loans: $ 2,500; repayment of loan: $ 2,050; FDI inflow: $ 9,000; FDI outflow: $ 2,500; FIIs' investment in India: $ 700; short-term movement of funds: –200.

Solution

Loan	$ –450
FDI	$ 6,500
FIIs' investment	$ 700
Short-term funds	$ –200
Balance of capital account	$ 6,550

After balancing the capital account, errors and omissions are mentioned. Finally, the two sides are compared. The difference is known as the overall balance. Table 2.1 shows an overall balance of payments surplus for US $ 63.7 ($ 64 approx.) billion.

Errors and omissions, collectively termed as "statistical discrepancy" arise for different reasons. The first may be related to difficulties involved in collecting balance of payments data. There may be different sources of data that sometimes differ in their approach. In India, the trade figures compiled by the Reserve Bank of India differ from those compiled by the Director-General of Commercial Intelligence and Statistics. Also, the movements of capital may precede or follow the transactions that they are supposed to finance. For example, payments for goods shipped in March may be received in April. If figures are compiled on 31 March based on the shipment, these will differ from those which are based on the actual payment. Such differences lead to the emergence of statistical discrepancy. Again, certain figures are based on estimates. For example, figures for earning in the travel and tourism account are estimated on the basis of sample cases. If the sample is defective, there is every possibility for the emergence of errors and omissions. Lastly, errors and omissions are explained by unrecorded illegal transactions that may be either on the debit side or on the credit side or on both. Only the net amount is written on the balance of payments. When the country is politically or economically stable, a credit balance is normally found due to unrecorded inflows of funds but in the reverse case, there occurs flight of capital and the amount is normally negative. For example, when Iraq invaded Kuwait, the US balance of payments witnessed large flow of this kind on the credit side because there was a substantial flight of capital from the Middle East to the USA.

Statistical discrepancy, often known as errors and omissions, arises on account of disparity in the compilation of trade data or estimated unrecorded transfer of funds.

Balance of Payments

- Balance of trade = Export of goods–Import of goods
- Balance of current account = Balance of trade + net earnings on invisibles
- Balance of capital account = Foreign exchange inflow–Foreign exchange outflow, on account of foreign investment, foreign loans, banking transactions and other capital flows
- Overall balance of payments = Balance of current account + balance of capital account + statistical discrepancy

When the overall balance is found to be in deficit, the monetary authorities arrange for capital flows to cover up the deficit. Such inflows may take the form of official borrowings or purchases (drawings) from the International Monetary Fund. From this point of view, the capital inflows are bifurcated into autonomous and accommodating inflows. If the inflow of funds on the capital account is for meeting the overall balance of payments deficit, it is termed as *accommodating or compensatory capital flow*. In other words, accommodating capital inflows aim at putting the balance of payments in equilibrium. Autonomous capital flows, on the other hand, take place regardless of such considerations. A foreigner paying back the loan or the inflow of foreign direct investment is an apposite

While autonomous capital flow is found in normal course of business, accommodating capital flow occurs to meet the balance of payments deficit.

example of autonomous capital inflow. This is why autonomous capital inflow goes "above-the-line", while accommodating capital inflow goes "below-the-line".

Official Reserves Account

Components

The monetary authorities of a country, normally the central bank of the country, maintain the reserves of foreign exchange. The foreign exchange reserves or the official reserves have three components: the first is gold, the second is SDRs allocated by the IMF from time to time and the third is the foreign currency assets that are obtained through the current account and capital account transactions and the last one is reserve tranche funds that has been kept in IMF against the quota. The reserve tranche position has also been started in order to conform to the international practice from 2004. The amount deposited with the IMF under the reserve tranche is also treated as a component of official reserves held by a country.

The following exhibit shows the position of the official reserves account maintained by the RBI or the Indian central bank as of March 2024:

Component	*Amount in US $, billion*
Foreign currency assets	570.95
Gold	65.26
SDRs	17.84
Reserve tranche funds	5.04
Total	622.50

Source: RBI Bulletin.

Notes:

1. Gold includes the value of 822.1 metric tonnes of gold purchased from the IMF as of march 2024.
2. SDRs' value includes the value of SDR allocations also—general and special, by the IMF in March 2024.

Uses

The basic purpose of maintaining official reserves is to maintain the foreign exchange incomings and to meet the balance of payments deficits. If the overall balance of payments is deficit, there is a withdrawal from the official reserves account in order to meet the deficit. On the contrary, if the overall balance of payments is surplus, the surplus is transferred to the official reserves account.

Deployment of the official reserves

The Reserve Bank of India Act 1934 provides for the deployment of foreign exchange reserves in different ways. It may take the form of deposits with (a) central banks of other countries, (b) Bank for International Settlements, (c) top-rated foreign commercial banks, (d) sovereign bonds and the bonds of supra-national institutions, and (e) the instruments of any other institution approved by the central board of the RBI.

Looking against this provision, one finds that out of 822.1 metric tonnes of gold which has forex value contribution of US $ 65.26 billlion forming about 8.15 per cent of the total foreign exchange reserves in value terms as on 31st March, 2024, 408.31 tonnes were held domestically 387.26 tonnes are held abroad in deposits/ safe custody with the Bank of England and the Bank for International Settlements. Additionally, 26.53 tonnes were held in the form of gold deposits.

As far as foreign currency assets are concerned, on March 31, 2024, out of the total foreign currency assets of US $ 570.95 billion, about 82.14% or US $ 468.99 billion was invested in securities, about 10.89% or US $ 62.17 billion was deposited with other central banks, BIS and the IMF and 6.97% US $ 39.79 billion was placed with the External Asset Managers (EAMs). A small portion of the reserves has been assigned to the EAMs with the main objective of gaining access to and deriving benefits from their expertise and market research.

PROBLEM 2.3

Find out the amount of foreign exchange reserves on 31.3.2024, if:

Foreign exchange reserves on 31.3.2023:	$ 80,000
Balance of current account during 2023–24:	$ –6,500
Balance of capital account during 2023–24:	$ 3,000
Statistical discrepancy during 2023–24:	$ –450

Solution

$ 80,000 + $ (–6,500) + $ 3,000 + $ (–450) = $ 76,000.

EQUILIBRIUM, DISEQUILIBRIUM, AND ADJUSTMENT

Accounting Equilibrium

Since the balance of payments is constructed on the basis of double-entry book-keeping, credit is always equal to debit. If debit on current account is greater than the credit, funds flow into the country that are recorded on the credit side of the capital account and the excess of debit is wiped out. Thus the concept of balance of payments is based on the concept of accounting equilibrium, that is

$$\text{Current account} + \text{Capital account} = 0 \tag{2.1}$$

The accounting balance is an *expost* concept. It describes what has actually happened over a specific past period. Accounting disequilibrium occurs when the two sides of the autonomous flows differ in size but in such cases, accommodating flows bring the balance of payments back into equilibrium.

Disequilibrium and the Focus of Adjustment

In the economic sense, balance of payments equilibrium occurs when a surplus or deficit is eliminated from the balance of payments. But normally, such equilibrium is not found. Rather, it is the disequilibrium in the balance of payments that is a normal phenomenon.

Though several external economic variables influence the balance of payments and give rise to disequilibrium, domestic economic variables like national output and national spending, money supply, exchange rate, and interest rate are more significant causative factors.

If national income exceeds national spending, the excess amount (saving) will be invested abroad, resulting in capital account deficit. Conversely, excess of national spending over national income causes borrowings from abroad which would push the capital account into a surplus.

Disparity in national income and national spending influences the capital account via the current account also. If national output exceeds national spending, the difference manifests itself in export causing current account surplus. The surplus is invested abroad which means a capital account deficit. The excess of national spending over national output leads to import. Deficit appears on the current account. The country borrows to meet the current account deficit and the borrowing results in a capital account surplus.

Increase in money supply raises the price level, exports turn uncompetitive and fall in export earnings leads to a deficit in the current account. Similarly, the higher prices of domestic goods make the price of imported commodities competitive as a result of which imports rise and a deficit appears in the current account.

If the currency of a country depreciates, exports become competitive and export earning improves. On the other hand, imports become costlier. If, as a result, imports are restricted, the trade account balance will improve but if imports are not restrained, a deficit will appear on the trade account. In fact, the net effect depends upon how price-elastic is the demand for export and import.

Any increase in domestic interest rate causes capital inflow in search of higher returns and the capital account turns surplus. The reverse is the case when the interest rate falls. However, disequilibrium becomes a cause for concern when it is associated with the current account because it represents a shift in real income; and also because adjustments on this account are not very easy. In fact, it is the balance of trade account that is largely responsible for the disequilibrium. If the balance of trade is surplus, its correction is not difficult; the surplus amount is used either for meeting the deficit on invisible trade account or may be invested abroad but if the balance of trade is in the deficit zone and if the deficit is too large to be covered by the invisible trade surplus, a current account deficit will occur. Its correction is not easy, insofar as the autonomous and accommodating capital flows are not so smooth. Again, if deficit on current account continues to persist, the official reserves will be eroded. If the country borrows large amounts to meet the deficit, it may fall into a vicious debt-trap. This is why adjustment measures are primarily directed at correcting disequilibrium in the trade account.

DIFFERENT APPROACHES TO ADJUSTMENT

The Classical View

The issues of connection between domestic economic variables and the balance of payments responsible for disequilibrium in the latter and its adjustment have been investigated by a number of experts. The classical economists had thought of the balance of payments disequilibrium, but they held the view that it was self-adjusting. Their view, which was based on the price-specie-flow mechanism, stated that an increase in money supply raises domestic prices, exports become uncompetitive, export earnings drop, foreign goods become cheaper and imports rise. As a result, the current account balance goes deficit. Precious metal flows out of the country to finance imports, the quantity of money drops and that lowers the price level. Lower prices in the economy lead to increased exports resulting in the trade balance regaining equilibrium. This way, the classical version of the balance of payments adjustment was a refutation of the mercantilist belief that a country could achieve a lasting balance of trade surplus through trade protection and export promotion.

> Price-specie-flow mechanism shows the relationship between trade, movement of gold and the domestic price level.

Elasticity Approach

After the collapse of the gold standard, the classical view could not remain tenable. The adjustment in the balance of payments disequilibrium was thought of in terms of changes in the fixed exchange rate, that is, by devaluation or upward revaluation but its success was dependent upon the elasticity of demand for export and import. Marshall and Lerner explained this phenomenon through the "elasticity" approach (Marshall, 1924; Lerner, 1944).

The elasticity approach is based on partial equilibrium analysis where everything is held constant except the effects of exchange rate changes on export or import. It is also assumed that elasticity of supply of output is infinite so that the price of export in home currency does not rise as demand increases, nor does the price of import fall with a squeeze in demand for import. Again, the approach ignores the monetary effects of variation in exchange rates. Based on these assumptions, devaluation helps improve current account balance only if

> Elasticity approach explains that depreciation in the currency leads to greater export and diminished import and the resultant squeeze in trade deficit.

$$E_m + E_x > 1 \tag{2.2}$$

where E_m is the price-elasticity of demand for import and E_x is the price-elasticity of demand for export. If the elasticity of demand is greater than unity, devaluation will lead to contraction of import in the wake of escalated cost of import which is known as "pass-through effect" and increase in export as a result of lower prices of export in the international market (Froot and Klemperer, 1989). The trade deficit will improve. However, the problem is that the trade partner may also devalue its own currency as a retaliatory measure. Moreover, there may be a long lapse of time on account of a time lag either in consumer responses or due to producer responses before the quantities adjust sufficiently to the changes in price. Till then, trade balance would be even worse than that before devaluation. As shown in Figure 2.1, the trade balance moves deeper into the deficit zone immediately after devaluation but then gradually improves and crosses into the surplus zone. The curve resembles the letter J and so, is known as the *J-curve effect*.

> Pass-through effect refers to contraction in imports due to its rising cost on account of devaluation of the currency.

> J-curve effect explains that devaluation of the currency first raises trade deficit and then lowers it.

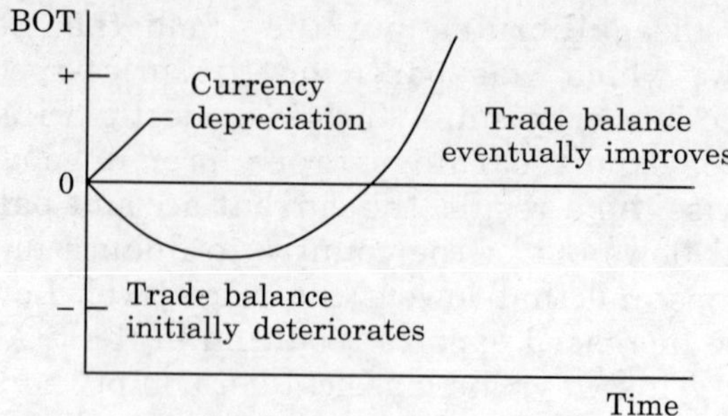

FIGURE 2.1 J-curve Effect.

The weakness of the elasticity approach is that it is a partial equilibrium analysis. It does not consider the supply and cost changes as a result of devaluation nor does it take into account the income and the expenditure effects of exchange rate changes. The narrow scope of the analysis has led to the formulation of other theories.

Stern (1973), however, incorporated the concept of supply elasticity in the elasticity approach. According to him, devaluation could improve balance of payments only when:

$$X\left(\frac{ED_x - 1}{1 + \frac{ED_x}{ES_x}}\right) + M\left\{\frac{ED_m \times \left(1 + \frac{1}{ES_m}\right)}{\left(\frac{ED_m}{ES_m} + 1\right)}\right\} > 0 \tag{2.3}$$

where

X and M are exports and imports,
ED_x is elasticity of demand for exports,
ES_x is elasticity of supply for exports,
ED_m is elasticity of demand for imports, and
ES_m is elasticity of supply for imports.

Based on the figures of British exports and imports, Stern has come to a conclusion that the balance of trade should improve if:

1. The elasticity of demand for exports and imports is high and is equal to one coupled with elasticity of supply both for imports and exports which is either high or low.
2. The elasticity of demand for imports and exports is low but the elasticity of supply for imports and exports is lower.

On the contrary, if the elasticity of demand is low matched with high elasticity of supply, the balance of trade should worsen.

The Keynesian View

The Keynesian view took into consideration the income effect. If there is exogenous increase in export, domestic income will rise which will lead to greater import. Greater import will match the increased export and bring back the trade balance into equilibrium. However, the achievement of equilibrium depends upon operation of the foreign trade multiplier that is in turn subject to marginal propensity to import. If the marginal propensity to consume or to import is very low, the foreign trade multiplier will be very small and income will not raise the imports as desired. Normally, in practice, owing to low marginal propensity to consume or to import, an exogenous rise in export does not bring about a comparable increase in import, and full balance of trade equilibrium is not restored (Metzler, 1968).

Absorption approach

The absorption approach is one of the earliest approaches representing the Keynesian view. Alexander (1959) treats balance of trade as a residual given by the difference between what the economy produces and what it takes for domestic use or what it absorbs. He begins with the contention that the total output, Y is equal to the sum of consumption, C, investment, I, government spending, G, and net export $(X - M)$. Mathematically, this can be expressed as

> Absorption means the sum of consumption, investment and governmental spending.

$$Y = C + I + G + (X - M)$$

Substituting $C + I + G$ by absorption, A, the above equation can be rewritten as

$$Y = A + X - M$$

or

$$Y - A = X - M \tag{2.4}$$

This means that the amount by which total output exceeds total spending or absorption, is represented by export over import or the net export which means a surplus balance of trade. This also means that if $A > Y$, a deficit balance of trade will occur because excess absorption in absence of desired output will cause imports. Thus in order to bring about equilibrium in the balance of trade, the government has to increase output or income. Increase in income without corresponding and equal increase in absorption will lead to improvement in balance of trade. This is called the *expenditure switching policy*.

In respect of full employment where resources are fully employed, output cannot be expanded and the balance of trade deficit can be remedied through decreasing absorption without a corresponding fall in output. This is known as the *expenditure-reducing policy*. On the contrary, where full employment is yet to be achieved, output can be increased and/or absorption can be reduced in order to bring about equilibrium in trade balance. It may be noted that the validity of the absorption approach depends upon the operation of the multiplier effect that is essential for accelerating output generation. It also depends on the marginal propensity to absorb that determines the rate of absorption.

Black (1959) explains the absorption in a slightly different way. He ignores the governmental expenditure, G and equates $X - M$ with $S - I$ (where S is saving and I is investment). He is of the opinion that when balance of trade is negative, the country has to increase saving on the one hand and reduce investment on the other. In case of full employment, he suggests the redistribution of national income in favour of profit earners who possess greater propensity to save.

The impact of devaluation on the absorption can be explained broadly in three ways. First is the real balance effect. Costly imports in the sequel of devaluation raise the general price index. Under the assumption that the money stock does not change, the economic agents cut down the direct absorption in order to maintain their money balances. Second is the income distribution effect. A rise in the general price index in the wake of devaluation forces redistribution of income away from the fixed-income segment to the variable-income segment. Since the poor have a high propensity to absorb, the redistribution helps reduce the direct absorption. Third is the Laursen-Metzler (1950) effect. Devaluation leads to deterioration in terms of trade which in turn: (1) lowers the national income and thereby the income-related absorption; and (2) raises the consumption of domestically produced goods. While the former is the income effect, the latter is the substitution effect. Absorption will be lower if the income effect is bigger than the substitution effect.

Mundell-Fleming approach

Mundell-Fleming (1962) approach, developed in the Keynesian framework, focuses through IS-LM curve on how the internal and external balance is influenced by fiscal and monetary policies. The IS curve for an open economy shows various combinations of output and interest rate. It shows:

$$S + M = I + G + X \tag{2.5}$$

The left side of the equation is known as the leakages and the right side is known as the injections. Savings include autonomous savings plus savings on account of risen income based on marginal propensity to save. Imports include autonomous imports plus imports on account of risen income based on marginal propensity to import. Investment is assumed to be an inverse function of rate of interest. Exports and governmental expenditure are autonomous with respect to interest rate and the level of national income. Considering all these, the IS curve slopes downward towards right.

The L-M schedule shows various combinations of level of income and rate of interest under the assumption that the supply of money is equal to demand for money meaning that the money market is in equilibrium. Money is demanded either for transaction purposes or for speculative purposes. Larger the income, bigger is the money held for transaction purposes meaning that transaction demand for money is a positive function of income. The demand for money for speculative purposes has an inverse relationship with the rate of interest. Taking together these two forms of demand, L-M schedule is upward sloping from left to right because the income levels require comparatively bigger transaction balances than the speculative balances.

The balance of payments (BP) schedule shows various combinations of rate of interest and income accruing in the balance of payments. As far as current account is concerned, export is assumed to be independent of the level of national income and then rate of interest. But import is assumed to be positively related to income which means higher income, higher the imports and deficit is the current account. Current account deficit, if any, is offset by surplus in the capital account. Net capital account flow is positively related to the rate of interest which means higher interest rate in the country attracts inflow of capital. Thus the current account and capital account schedules taken together slope upward from left to right.

The balance of payments is in equilibrium when IS and LM schedules intersect at a point on the BP schedule corresponding to a given interest rate and the level of income, as shown in Figure 2.2(a).

If income and imports increase and interest rate decreases following an expansionary monetary policy, the LM curve will shift downward toward right. The balance of payments will turn deficit [Figure 2.2(b)]. On the contrary, contractionary monetary policy will shift the LM curve upward toward left. Surplus will emerge on the balance of payments [Figure 2.2(c)].

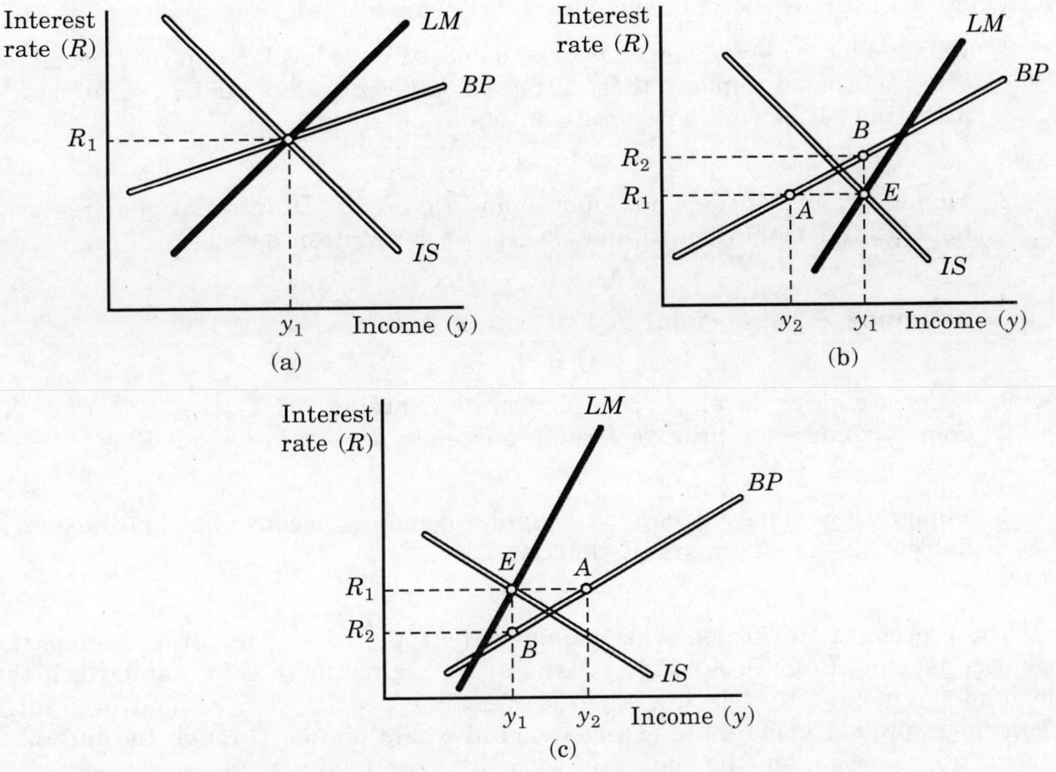

FIGURE 2.2 BOP equilibrium through IS-LM curve.

The new Cambridge school approach

This is a special case of absorption approach. It takes into account savings (S) and investment (I), taxes (T) and government spending (G), and their impact on the trade account. In the form of equation, it can be written as

$$S + T + M = G + X + I$$

or
$$(S - I) + (T - G) + (M - X) = 0$$

or
$$(X - M) = (S - I) + (T - G) \tag{2.6}$$

The theory assumes that $(S - I)$ and $(T - G)$ are determined independently of each other and of the trade gap. $(S - I)$ is normally fixed as the private sector has a fixed net level of saving. And so the balance of payments deficit or surplus is dependent upon $(T - G)$ and the constant $(S - I)$. In other words, with constant $(S - I)$, it is only the manipulation of $(T - G)$ which is a necessary and sufficient tool for balance of payments adjustment.

Monetary Approach

The monetarists believe that the balance of payments disequilibrium is a monetary and not structural phenomenon (Connolly, 1978). The adjustment is automatic unless the government is intentionally following an inflationary policy for quite a long period. Adjustment is brought about through making changes in monetary variables. To explain the phenomenon, it is assumed that:

1. Demand for money, L, depends upon domestic price level, P and real income, Y. The relationship among these three variables does not change significantly over time. It can be written as an equation thus:
$$L = kPY \tag{2.7}$$
2. Money supply, M, depends upon domestic credit, D, international reserves held, R and money multiplier, m. It can be written as
$$M = (R + D)m$$
Assuming m being equal to 1, it can be rewritten as
$$M = R + D \tag{2.8}$$
3. Domestic price level, P depends on the foreign price level, P^*, and the domestic currency price of foreign currency, E. We can write P as
$$P = EP^* \tag{2.9}$$
4. Demand for money equals the supply of money because an equilibrium is held in the money market, that is
$$L = M \tag{2.10}$$

The process of adjustment varies among the types of exchange rate regime the country has opted for. In a fixed exchange rate regime or in gold standard, if the demand for money, that is the amount of money people wish to hold is greater than the supply of money, the excess demand would be met through the inflow of money from abroad. On the contrary, with the supply of money being in excess of the demand for it, the excess supply is eliminated through the outflow of money to other countries. The inflow and the outflow influence the balance of payments. To explain it further, with constant prices and income and thus constant demand for money, any increase in domestic credit will lead to outflow of foreign exchange as the people will import more to lower the excessive cash balances. As a result, the balance of payments will turn deficit. Conversely, a decrease in domestic credit would lead to an excess demand for money. International reserves will flow in to meet the excess demand. Balance of payments will improve.

However, in a floating-rate regime, the demand for money is adjusted to the supply of money through changes in exchange rate. In a clean float, when the Central Bank makes no market intervention, the international reserves component of the monetary base remains unchanged. The balance of payments remains in equilibrium with neither surplus nor deficit. The spot exchange rate is determined by the quantity of money supplied and the quantity of money demanded. When the Central Bank increases domestic credit through open market operations, supply of money is greater than the demand for it. The households increase their imports. With increased demand for imports, the domestic currency will depreciate and it will continue depreciating until supply of money equals the demand for money. Conversely, with decrease in domestic credit, the households reduce their import. Domestic currency will appreciate and it will continue appreciating until supply of money equals demand for money.

In the case of managed floating, the Central Bank often intervenes to peg the rates at some desired level. And so this case is a mix of fixed and floating rate regimes. It means that changes in the monetary supply and demand influence not only the exchange rate but also the quantum of international reserves.

Different Approaches to BOP Adjustment

- Classical view: Self-adjusting process. Trade deficit → outflow of gold → decreased money supply → lower prices → higher exports → elimination of trade deficit
- Elasticity Approach (Marshall/Lerner's view): Trade deficit → devaluation → (demand for export and import being price-elastic) exports cheaper abroad and higher export earnings + costlier imports and squeezed import bill → elimination of trade deficit.
  Stern added the concept of supply elasticity meaning that supply elasticity for import and export must be favourable.
- Absorption Approach (Alexander's view): Trade deficit → decrease in absorption (consumption + investment + government expenditure) so that total output > absorption → elimination of trade deficit.
- Black suggests for increasing saving and reducing investment in order to eliminate trade deficit.
- Mundell-Fleming view based on Adjustment in real income and nominal interest rate: Rise in interest rate → lower income → lower import → elimination of trade deficit. Again, rise in interest rate → inflow of foreign investment → improvement in capital account to absorb trade deficit.
- New Cambridge School Approach: Greater taxes + lower governmental expenditure → lower income → lower import → elimination of trade deficit.
- Monetary Approach:
  - Fixed exchange rate: Reduction in credit creation → decreased supply of money → lower import → falling trade deficit
  - Floating exchange rate: Size of credit → size of money supply → exchange rate → balance of trade.

CAPITAL ACCOUNT CONVERTIBILITY

It is true that the focus of disequilibrium and its adjustment lies primarily on the trade account, but it never means that the capital account transactions have no relevance. Even if there is deficit on the current account but if the capital account shows sufficient inflow of funds, disequilibrium on the current account does not matter much at least for some time. However, the flow of funds on the capital account depends on how far the government follows a liberal policy in respect of capital account transactions. In this very context, we like to discuss the various aspects of capital account convertibility.

Meaning and Rationale

The term, *capital account convertibility* (CAC), means relaxing controls on capital account transactions. The control manifests in different ways. For example, it could be quantitative restriction on capital movement, a multiple exchange rate system meaning separate exchange rates for commercial and financial transactions or explicit/implicit tax on international financial transactions so as to discourage capital flow. If these are the different forms of control on capital account transactions, CAC means, as a natural corollary, either absence of quantitative control/taxes on capital account transactions or the presence of market-based exchange rate system.

CAC means relaxing controls on capital account transactions. Control manifests in quantitative restriction/tax on the outflow of funds and/ or adoption of multiple exchange rates.

In the process of external sector reforms that witness, inter alia, transition from a controlled regime to a market-determined regime, CAC is one of the concluding-phase steps. However, there is often a question whether the monetary authorities of a country should go for CAC. The advocates of capital control are of the view that control has three basic advantages (Mathieson and Rojas-Suarez, 1993):

1. It softens the balance of payments crisis and reduces instability in exchange rates consequent upon volatile flow of capital.
2. It ensures that domestic savings meet the investment requirements and helps avoid the foreign ownership of domestic factors of production.
3. It helps maintain the authorities' ability to tax domestic financial activities.

CAC is preferred because:
1. Control is often not effective,
2. Access to global financial market is easier,
3. Investment can be diversified leading to optimal allocation of resources.

In order to ensure CAC, the advocates arguing for the relaxation of control are, however, of the view that the arguments behind control are not flaw-free. It is not completely true that volatile capital flow essentially tends to design the exchange rate. The domestic savings do finance the investment, but they often fall short of the requirements. Moreover, foreign capital has many advantages that the domestic capital has not. Similarly, taxing of the domestic financial activities is not completely fool-proof (Mathieson and Rojas-Suarez, 1993).

More importantly, the experience of capital control measures in developed as well as developing countries shows that such measures have hardly been effective. If capital control has to be made effective, it requires a technically sophisticated bureaucracy, which developing countries do not possess. Moreover, firms are capable of transferring funds across borders through transfer-pricing techniques making controls ineffective. There is often diversion of export receipts from the commercial market to parallel foreign exchange market. Haque and Montiel (1990, 1991) have found that there was a high degree of capital mobility despite extensive capital control in many cases.

If capital control becomes less effective, there is created inefficiencies in the domestic financial system that inhibit risk diversification which in turn weakens the competitive position of export and brings in domestic financial shocks. If the control mechanism is tightened further to ensure its efficacy, further distortions are created in the economy. The licences granting capital account transactions are sold at a premium in the market.

In fact, it is the growing difficulties of enforcing capital control that have led Quirk and Evans (1995) and Cooper (1998) to argue for capital account liberalisation. In the process of capital account liberalisation, the capital account transactions are made independent of day-to-day approval of the monetary authorities. The entire process is left to the market forces. The result is that the process of economic growth gets stimulus. This is so because the financial market of the country gets integrated with the foreign financial markets, and the economy is able to avail of large amount of external resources.

Again, there is greater freedom for individual decision-making as to how to get necessary resources and how to use the excess reserves. The residents are able to hold internationally diversified portfolio of assets, which lessens the risks involved in investment and augments the risk-adjusted return on capital. Since the resources are allocated internationally on the basis of supply of, and demand for, funds, the allocation is optimal, maximising the welfare gains.

The increased competition from abroad forces domestic providers of financial services to turn more efficient. Apart from fostering efficiency in the domestic financial market, CAC permits an economy to access international financial market.

It gets the desired amount of external funds with minimal borrowing cost. However, CAC cannot work successfully in the presence of domestic distortions, such as lop-sided development of the domestic financial market. If information is asymmetric in the market, CAC may not lead to efficient allocation of resources. This is so because under these conditions, investment portfolio may not be optimum and there may appear 'herding' behaviour where the investors tend to follow the lead taken by successful investors. The market may face sudden movements causing crisis in the market (Stigliz and Weiss, 1981; Devenow and Welch, 1996). Dooley (1996) is of the view that even if information is symmetric, experiences from the industrialised countries are diverse.

Experiences and Pre-conditions

Experiences have shown that Canada, Switzerland and the USA maintained a liberal policy in respect of capital flows from the very beginning of 1950s, but in others, liberalisation set in quite late, in 1970s through 1990s, in the wake of some eye-catching developments in the international economy. There was a switch-over in general from the pegged exchange rate regime to a floating-rate regime of exchange rate. The international financial market turned broader and more viable. Subsequently, there was fast growth of multinational corporations causing huge capital flow across national borders. However, in some cases, CAC could not go a long way. Controls were readopted. For example, Ireland, Portugal and Spain imposed control on the movement of capital following the ERM crisis of 1992.

The experiences from the developing world too were diverse. For instance, Argentina presented a case where the balance of payments deficit improved following CAC. On the contrary, in Venezuela, malpractices in banks posed a hurdle to the success of CAC.

Thus, in view of the experiences from the developed as well as developing countries, Quirk and Evans (1995) talk about some preconditions for CAC. In their view, there should be proper sequencing. The CAC process should be gradual and a phased one, unlike in countries, such as Costa Rica, Hong Kong, Jamaica, Kyrgyz Republic, Mauritius, Singapore and Venezuela where it was less gradual.

It means that the current account convertibility should precede CAC in order to make the latter sustainable.

Again, there should be simultaneous reform in the financial sector so as to obtain support from this sector. In Malaysia, interest rate came to be market-oriented the moment CAC was introduced. Mauritius and Trinidad and Tobago switched over from pegged exchange rate to free float at the time of the commencement of CAC. There are many other such cases where the financial sector as well as the external sector was reformed simultaneously with CAC.

Yet again, since CAC may lead to increased risk as perceived by banks, there should be constant supervision by the monetary authorities. Internationally accepted accounting and disclosure norms should be followed.

Multilateral and Regional Frameworks

CAC is supported at the international as well as the regional level. The IMF supports move towards CAC, provided the country has experienced current account surpluses followed by large inflow of capital and also has attained development of a full-fledged financial market. It is a fact that the IMF has called for caution in moving to the CAC, but there are occasions when it has encouraged an accelerated transition to CAC. The IMF has also provided technical assistance in the area of foreign exchange management to a number of developing countries. Its technical assistance has supported the operational aspects, such as linkages with monetary management, development of instruments and markets for securities, inter-bank operations and reporting practices. The purpose has been to pave the way for the success of CAC.

Apart from the IMF, the OECD permits CAC, the details of which can be found in the Codes of Liberalisation of Capital Movements first adopted in 1961 and revised from time to time. The OECD codes do have legal status, but the obligation to move to CAC does not imply the need to harmonise the national laws or to deregulate according to some international standards. Article 7 of the Code permits a country to go for CAC, provided the economic and financial situation justifies it and the balance of payments position is considerably strong.

Similarly, the directives of the European Union passed in early 1960s permitted CAC, but only five countries, viz. Belgium, Germany, Luxembourg, Netherlands and UK had abolished control on capital movements by early 1980s. The Maastricht Treaty too incorporated the provisions for CAC but greater emphasis was placed on the convergence criterion to make it successful.

Last but not least, WTO supports CAC through the provisions related to the General Agreement on Trade in Services (GATS). The GATS provides for withdrawing restrictions from capital transactions related to the provision of services identified in such agreements.

SUMMARY

- The balance of payments is a statement showing a country's commercial transaction with the rest of the world. It shows inflow and outflow of foreign exchange. It is divided into current and capital accounts. The former records the transaction in goods and services, the latter incorporates the flow of financial assets.

- The major economic variables influencing the balance of current and capital accounts are national output, national spending, money supply, exchange rate and interest rate. The concept of disequilibrium is normally associated with the current account and that too with the trade account.
- There are various approaches to adjustments in the balance of payments disequilibria. The classical economists believed in automatic adjustment through the flow of precious metals. The neo-classical economists emphasised devaluation and upward revaluation. The focal point of the Keynesian approach was the income effect. The proponents of the absorption approach suggested a proper alignment between output and absorption while the monetarists argued for changes in the monetary variables for adjustment in the balance of payments.
- Relaxation of control from capital account transaction is known as *capital account convertibility*. It is advocated on many grounds. But the experiences vary widely among countries.

CASE STUDY 1

INDIA'S BALANCE OF PAYMENTS DURING LIBERAL ECONOMIC REGIME

In the very beginning of the liberal economic policy regime that was adopted in India in mid-1991, current account deficit was huge. The capital account was highly strained and the foreign exchange reserves were minimal. The aim was to reduce the trade deficit not through import restrictions but through export promotion for which import liberalisation was a prerequisite. Tariff rates were axed. Advance and special licenses were given. The scope of the open general licence was broadened. Exporters were given incentives. A number of items of export that had been restricted or banned were made open for export. The exchange rate policy was rationalised making the rupee convertible on current account and adopting a system of managed floating.

Invisible earnings were taken care of. A comprehensive plan was drawn up to boost income from travel and tourism. Indian firms were encouraged to operate abroad so as to boost investment income. Foreign loans on hard terms were discouraged so as to reduce interest payments.

On the capital account, the industrial policy was changed to open a larger area of the economy to foreign investment and provide greater equity participation to the foreign direct investors. Foreign portfolio investment in the form of investment by the foreign institutional investors in the Indian capital market and raising of funds by the Indian companies through Euro-equities and Euro-bonds was for the first time permitted.

With liberal trade policy, imports increased at higher rate than export. The result was the growing trade deficit that moved up from US $ 2.8 billion in FY 1991–92 to US $ 16.7 billion in FY 2003–04. Thereafter, with still greater increase in imports, trade deficit got far larger touching US $ 130 billion during FY 2010–11. Invisibles came to the rescue and the deficit on current account was smaller. To be precise, the current account balance was positive consecutively for three financial years from 2001–02 and for the year 2020–21. In other financial years, it was deficit in the range of US $ 1.2–88.16 billion, and likewise the upheaval of the deficit in the balance of current account is continued to be there and currently this is US $ 23.268 billion in the year 2023–24.

TABLE CS2.1 India's Balance of Payments—Current Account

(US $ million)

Year	*Import*	*Export*	*Trade balance*	*Invisibles (net)*			*Balance of current account*
				Total	*Investment income*	*Remit-tances*	
1991–1992	21,064	18,266	–2,798	1,620	–3,830	3,798	–1,178
1992–1993	24,316	18,869	–5,447	1,921	–3,423	3,865	–3,526
1993–1994	26,739	22,683	–4,056	2,898	–3,270	5,287	–1,158
1994–1995	35,904	26,855	–9,049	5,680	–3,431	8,112	–3,369
1995–1996	43,670	32,311	–11,359	5,460	–3,205	8,539	–5,899
1996–1997	48,063	33,764	–14,294	10,638	–3,250	11,139	–3,631
1997–1998	51,126	34,849	–16,277	9,804	–3,457	11,830	–6,473
1998–1999	47,544	34,298	–13,246	9,208	–3,544	10,587	–4,038
1999–2000	55,383	38,285	–17,098	12,935	–3,559	12,638	– 4,163
2000–2001	59,264	44,894	–14,370	12,106	–3,918	12,798	–2,264
2001–2002	57,618	44,915	–12,703	14,054	–2,654	12,125	1,351
2002–2003	65,474	53,000	–12,474	16,182	–4,882	14,448	3,708
2003–2004	79,658	62,952	–16,706	25,425	–4,703	19,444	8,719
2004–2005	1,18,961	80,831	–38,130	31,699	–2,848	21,048	–6,431
2005–2006	1,56,993	1,05,152	–51,841	42,655	–5,510	24,102	–9,186
2006–2007	1,91,995	1,27,090	–64,905	55,296	–4,846	27,195	–9,609
2007–2008	2,48,521	1,58,461	–90,060	72,657	–5,239	40,778	–17,409
2008–2009	3,08,521	1,89,001	–1,19,520	91,605	–6,626	44,567	–27,915
2009–2010	3,00,609	1,82,235	–1,18,374	79,991	–8,040	52,055	–38,383
2010–2011	3,80,935	2,50,468	–1,30,467	86,186	–14,863	53,368	–44,281
2011–2012	4,99,953	3,09,774	–1,89,759	16,609	64,069	64,214	–78,169
2012–2013	5,02,237	3,06,581	–1,95,656	1,07,493	1,16,551	2,24,044	–88,163
2013–1014	4,66,216	3,18,607	–1,47,609	1,15,313	2,33,569	1,18,256	–32,296
2014–2015	4,61,484	3,16,545	–1,44,940	1,18,081	2,41,645	1,23,564	–26,859
2015–2016	3,96,444	2,66,365	–1,30,079	1,07,929	2,35,044	1,27,116	–22,151
2016–1017	3,92,580	2,80,138	–1,12,442	98,025	2,42,051	1,44,025	–14,417
2017–1018	4,69,006	3,08,970	–1,60,036	1,11,319	2,83,406	1,72,087	–48,717
2018–2019	5,17,519	3,37,237	–1,80,283	1,23,027	3,06,483	1,83,457	–57,256
2019–2020	4,77,937	3,20,431	–1,57,506	1,32,850	3,21,712	1,88,862	–24,656
2020–2021	3,98,452	2,96,300	–1,02,152	1,26,064	3,07,253	1,81,188	23,912
2021–2022	6,18,623	4,29,164	–1,89,459	1,50,693	3,69,600	2,18,906	–38,766
2022–2023	7,21,364	4,56,073	–2,65,291	1,98,236	4,65,804	2,67,568	–67,055
2023–2024	6,83,549	4,41,484	–2,42,065	2,18,779	5,01,419	2,82,640	–23,286

Sources: 1. Ministry of Finance, Govt. of India (2023–24), *Economic Survey* 2023–24, New Delhi.
2. Reserve Bank of India (2023–24), *Reserve Bank of India Bulletin*, May 2024.
3. www.rbi.org.in

TABLE CS2.2 Capital Account Transactions during the Period of Reform

Year	*External assistance (net)*	*Commercial borrowings (net)*	*IMF funds (net)*	*Foreign investment (net)*	*Total capital account (net)*	*Foreign currency assets at year-end*
1991–1992	3,031	948	786	133	3,777	5,631
1992–1993	1,856	–1,445	1,288	567	2,936	6,434
1993–1994	1,896	–84	187	4,235	9,695	15,068
1994–1995	1,518	1,517	–1,143	4,807	9,156	20,809
1995–1996	867	1,334	–1,715	4,604	4,678	17,044
1996–1997	1,101	1,855	–975	5,834	10,454	22,367
1997–1998	877	4,010	–618	4,993	11,924	25,975
1998–1999	799	4,367	393	2,312	8,565	29,522
1999–2000	891	333	–260	5,117	10,242	35,058
2000–2001	410	4,016	–26	2,911	7,487	39,554
2001–2002	1,204	–1,147	n.a.	5,925	9,545	51,049
2002–2003	–2,460	–1,698	n.a.	4,555	12,638	71,890
2003–2004	–2,661	–1,853	–	14,472	22,122	1,12,959
2004–2005	1,922	5,947	–	11,944	32,175	1,35,571
2005–2006	1,682	2,723	–	17,724	23,400	1,45,108
2006–2007	1,770	16,084	–	15,499	44,944	1,91,924
2007–2008	2,114	22,165	–	44,806	1,08,031	2,99,230
2008–2009	2,441	7,862	–	5,785	6,768	2,41,426
2009–2010	2,893	2,808	–	51,167	53,397	2,54,685
2010–2011	4,941	11,927	–	37,434	59,747	2,74,300
2011–2012	2,212	10,370		51,615	67,763	12,819
2012–2013	982	30,142		19,819	91,989	3,826
2013–2014	1,032	67,733		21,564	47,804	15,508
2014–2015	1,725	1,459		31,251	88,265	61,406
2015–2016	1,505	–6,139		36,021	40,055	17,905
2016–2017	2,013	366		35,612	35,967	21,550
2017–2018	2,944	13,717		30,286	92,292	43,574
2018–2019	3,413	12,437		30,712	53,917	–3,339
2019–2020	3,751	21,935		43,013	84,154	59,498
2020–2021	11,167	–4,264		43,955	63,374	87,286
2021–2022	5,366	28,240		38,587	86,266	47,501
2022–2023	5,521	2,749		27,986	57,920	–9,135
2023–2024	7,460	–5,766		9,790	86,988	63,702

Sources: 1. Ministry of Finance, Govt. of India (2023–24), *Economic Survey 2023–24*, New Delhi.
2. Reserve Bank of India (2023–24), *Reserve Bank of India Bulletin*, May 2024.
3. www.rbi.org.in

The deficit on current account was met by inflow of funds, especially in the form of foreign investment. The role of external assistance was only marginal. The external commercial borrowing fluctuated in a wide range. However, the size of foreign investment was so large that it met the current account deficit and, over and above, led to an increase in the foreign currency assets. At the end of March the foreign currency assets were as huge as US $ 274 billion.

QUESTIONS

1. Is it true that the liberal economic policy has a positive impact on India's trade?
2. Explain the factors behind current account surplus in some of the years.
3. Show how have the foreign exchange reserves moved up fast over the years.

CASE STUDY 2

CAPITAL ACCOUNT CONVERTIBILITY: A TIGHT ROPE WALK FOR INDIA

In the year 1991, when India went through a major change in its economic policy especially towards international business and trade, the issue of capital account convertibility came into the limelight. Capital account convertibility is the freedom as well as restriction given by the central bank to convert any foreign currency into domestic currency and vice versa. This is one of the most important policies that significantly affects the valuation of foreign exchange reserves as well as the exchange rate of the country.

For a weak and growing economy like India in the year 1991, it was a tough situation to decide its capital account convertibility policy, but India had very prudently designed its CAC. India has restricted capital account convertibility based on certain sector and certain limit in its early 90s times and kept on increasing its capital account convertibility from then onwards.

The concept of impossible trinity or trilemma is one of the fundamental economic principles talked about, in macroeconomic policy in which it is impossible to maintain three policies simultaneously; viz 1. Independent monetary policy 2. Free capital movement (full capital account convertibility) 3. A stable foreign exchange rate. India has skillfully supported growth and stability through the flow of capital and selective capital account convertibility, whereas India has managed its exchange rate and monetary policy.

Despite serious concerns like the impact of global capital flight to India, the impact of volatility of the global market to Indian economy, unstable global financial market, and weak forex reserve which can lead to serious impact on the exchange rates of domestic currency to other currencies, India has taken significant steps to achieve capital account convertibility. Over the years India has liberalized its capital flows, the policymakers and regulators cautiously and skilfully devised a middle path to balance on tight rope of stable exchange rate and monetary policy along with liberalizing capital account convertibility. The recent incidents of the COVID-19 crisis and the Russia–Ukraine war along with tensions in the Middle East which shot up the oil prices and impacted the global economy negatively, India stands firm in all these economic downturns and supported its economy from serious recession along with promoting growth and stability in the economy.

During the twin crisis of Covid led to an economic slowdown and global economic instability and later the Russia–Ukraine war, India has shown its power of robust monetary policy and external trade skills, where India was one of the leading growing economies globally, India attracted a good amount of foreign capital as in the turbulent time India was a lucrative option for investors globally which boosted Indian capital markets and supported Indian economy in a turbulent time.

The journey of India to global leader in the economic scoreboard is not easy, there are serious challenges to it, 1. Maintaining exchange rate volatility: Unrestricted flow of capital may disrupt the exchange rate stability and impact the trade of India with other countries. 2. Global economic tensions: serious tensions between countries of the world may lead to positive or even adverse impacts on the Indian capital market and economy if there is an easy flow of money in India. 3. Robust regulatory framework: before going for full capital account convertibility India has to prepare a very robust capital markets regulatory framework. 4. Domestic shock absorption: India has to prepare its domestic market for shock absorption induced by domestic capital so that the market can be stabilized, in the recent few years we have witnessed the resilience of DII against the movement of FPI, earlier which used to destabilize the Indian financial markets.

QUESTIONS

1. What measures India can take to manage risks associated with capital account convertibility?
2. How can India balance the need for foreign investment with domestic economic stability?
3. Discuss the potential impact of global economic conditions on India's capital accounts.
4. How does the impossible trinity affect India's monetary policy decisions?

REVIEW QUESTIONS

Objective-Type Questions

1. State whether true (T) or false (F):

(a) Unilateral transfers are entered in capital account. ☐
(b) Any increase in revenue from tourism helps improve the balance of trade. ☐
(c) Direct and portfolio investments are entered in capital account. ☐
(d) Interest on loans is a part of capital account. ☐
(e) Overall BOP deficit adds to official reserves account. ☐
(f) Control on capital account transactions is often effective. ☐

2. Choose the correct answer:

(a) According to elasticity approach, trade balance should improve if

(i) demand for export and import is price-elastic
(ii) demand for export and import is price-inelastic
(iii) none of these

(b) According to the absorption approach, BOP adjustment in a situation of full employment can be brought about through:
   (i) increase in output
   (ii) decrease in absorption
   (iii) none of these

(c) Classical economists viewed that BOP adjustment:
   (i) was automatic
   (ii) was possible through devaluation
   (iii) none of these

(d) Accommodating capital flow goes:
   (i) above the line
   (ii) below the line
   (iii) none of these

(e) Invisibles influence:
   (i) trade balance
   (ii) balance of current account
   (iii) none of these

(f) CAC is supported by:
   (i) OECD
   (ii) WTO
   (iii) Both of them

Short-Answer Questions

1. Distinguish between:
   (a) Current account and capital account
   (b) Monetary and non-monetary movement of gold
   (c) Autonomous and accommodating capital flows
2. Explain:
   (a) Unilateral transfer
   (b) Statistical discrepancy
3. Is BOP in equilibrium from accounting point of view?
4. What do you mean by CAC? Is it preferable to exchange control?

Long-Answer Questions

1. Discuss the elasticity approach to the BOP adjustment. How does it differ from the classical approach?
2. Explain the different views concerning the Keynesian approach to BOP adjustment.
3. Explain the monetary approach to BOP adjustment.
4. How far are the recommendations for the Fuller Capital Account Convertibility different from the earlier ones?

Numerical Problem

1. Find the balance of trade, balance of current account and the overall balance of payments with the help of the following figures:

Item	*Debit (US $, million)*	*Credit (US $, million)*
Trade in goods	55,383	38,285
Services, such as travel, transport & others	11,865	15,720
Statistical discrepancy	–	323
Unilateral transfer	34	12,672
Foreign investment	7,123	12,240
External assistance	2,183	3,074
External commercial borrowings	2,874	3,207
Investment income	5,490	1,931
Banking capital	8,532	11,259
Rupee debt service	711	–
Other capital transactions	2,510	4,018

REFERENCES

Alexander, S.S. (1959), Effects of a devaluation: A simplified synthesis of elasticity and absorption approaches, *American Economic Review*, IL, 22–42.

Black, J. (1959), Saving and Investment Approach to Devaluation, *Economic Journal*, LXIX, 267–274.

Connolly, M. (1978), The monetary approach to an open economy: The fundamental theory, in Putnam, B.H. et al. (Eds.), *The Monetary Approach to International Adjustment*, New York, Praeger, pp. 46–59.

Cooper, R.N. (1998), Should Capital-Account Convertibility Be a World Objective?, in Kenen, P.B. (Ed.), *Should the IMF Pursue Capital-Account Convertibility*, Essays in International Finance no. 207, Princeton: Princeton University.

Devenow, A. and I. Welch (1996), Rational Herding in Financial Economics, *European Economic Review*, XL (3–5), 603–15.

Dooley, M. (1996), Capital Controls and Emerging Markets, *International Journal of Finance and Economics*, I (July), 197–205.

Fleming, J.A. (1962), "Domestic Financial Policies under Fixed and Floating Exchange Rates", *IMF Staff Papers*, 9 (3), 369–80.

Froot, K. and P. Klemperer (1989), Exchange Rate Pass-Through When Market Share Matters, *American Economic Review*, LXXIX, 3, 637–654.

Haque, N.U. and P.J. Montiel (1990), How Mobile is Capital in Developing Countries, *Economics Letters*, XXX (Aug.), 359–62.

Haque, N.U. and P.J. Montiel, (1991), Capital Mobility in Developing Countries: Some Empirical Tests, *World Development*, XIX(5), 1391–98.

Laursen, S. and L.A. Metzler (1950), "Flexible Exchange Rates and the Theory of Employment", *Review of Economics and Statistics.*

Lerner, A.P. (1944), The Economics of Control, New York, The Macmillan Co., Chaps. 28–29.

Marshall, A. (1924), *Money, Credit and Commerce,* Book III, London, Macmillan.

Mathieson, D.J. and L. Rojas-Suarez (1993), *Liberalization of the Capital Account: Experiences and Issues,* Washington, D.C.: IMF, Occasional Paper no. 103.

Metzler, L. (1968), The process of international adjustment under the conditions of full employment: A Keynesian view, in Caves, R. et al. (Eds.), *Readings in International Economics,* Homewood (Illinois), Richard D. Irwin, pp. 465–486.

Mundell, R.A. (1962), "The Appropriate use of Monetary and Fiscal Policy for Internal and External Stability", *IMF Staff Papers,* 9(1), 70–79.

Quirk, P. and O. Evans (1995), *Capital Account Convertibility: Review of Experience and Implications for IMF Policies,* IMF Occasional Paper no. 131, Washington D.C.: International Monetary Fund.

Reserve Bank of India (1997), *Report of the Committee on Capital Account Convertibility,* Bombay.

Stern, R.M. (1973), *The Balance of Payments,* London, Macmillan.

Stiglitz, J. and A. Weiss (1981), Credit Rationing in Markets with Imperfect Information, *American Economic Review,* LXXI (3), 393–410.

SUGGESTED FURTHER READING

Chacholiades, M. (1978), *International Monetary Theory and Policy,* New York, McGraw-Hill, Chap. 2.

Melvin, M. (1985), *International Money and Finance,* New York, Harper & Row, Chap. 6.

CHAPTER 3

Developments in International Monetary System

Learning Objectives

International monetary system manifests in the arrangements that facilitate international payments as well as international liquidity. The present chapter traces the developments in this regard and focuses on the IMF system. In particular, it attempts:

- To explain the earliest monetary system known as the Specie Commodity Standard.
- To delineate the functioning of Gold Standard and the reasons behind its abandonment during 1930s.
- To explain the IMF's exchange rate regime during 1945–73, known as the Bretton Woods Exchange Rate Regime and the reasons behind its collapse.
- To explain the present system of exchange rate regime characterised with varying options.
- To comment on the IMF's role in improving international liquidity.
- To describe the IMF's role in dealing with the financial crisis.
- To show the changing faces of the European Monetary Union.

Economic and financial transactions among different countries require some sort of arrangement that could facilitate settlement of payments. These arrangements form the subject matter of the international monetary system. The international monetary system we find today is the result of a century-long evolution going back to the days of the gold standard and even earlier when costly metals were used for making payments. This chapter discusses the various phases of development of the international monetary system, especially since 1940s when the IMF came into being.

SPECIE COMMODITY STANDARD

In early days, prior to the evolution of an international monetary system, trade payments were settled through barter, but there were many inconveniences; and so to overcome those difficulties, traders began using metal, especially gold or silver, for settling payments. Subsequently, metal took the form of coin which had the stamp of the sovereign on the basis of weight and fineness giving birth to the specie commodity standard. The coins were *full-bodied* coins meaning that their value was equal to the value of metal contained therein. However, with the lapse of time, the process of coin debasement started. Lower-value metal was mixed with the coin with the result that the value of metal came to be lower than the face value of the coin. *Debased* coins were largely used as medium of exchange. Full-bodied coins were mainly used for store of value and for melting and selling them as gold and silver. The process of coin debasement in England during 1542–1551 drove the full-bodied coins almost completely out of circulation by 1560 and Queen Elizabeth I had to replace debased coins by full-bodied coins.

> Full-bodied coins contain metal value equal to face value. Debased coins have less of the metal value.

The Coinage Act of 1792 in the USA accepted the dollar as the monetary unit of the country and fixed its value in terms of gold and silver. This led to the emergence of the *bimetallic standard*. France adopted the bimetallic standard in 1803 but the mint ratio between gold and silver was 1:15 in the USA as compared to 1:15.5 in France. This difference led to the US export of gold to France for the purchase of silver. The diminution of gold stock in the USA led that country to adopt a *mono-metallic silver standard*. But then with changes in gold-silver mint ratio to 1:16, the US Government was able to follow a *mono-metallic gold standard*. These currencies helped settlement of trade and other payments.

GOLD STANDARD

The gold standard possessed broader features than the specie commodity standard. It originated in England in the seventeenth century when the pound was minted of gold but it was officially announced in 1816 when gold became the official tender for payment of public and private debt. By the 1870s, the gold standard was widely adopted. Germany adopted it in 1871, and the United States followed suit in 1879. The last quarter of the nineteenth century and till the outbreak of the First World War, was the hey-day for the gold standard.

Different Forms

The form of gold standard was not the same in all the countries adopting it. In the UK and the USA, gold coins were minted and bank notes were also exchanged for gold on demand. The price of gold was fixed under law. It was the price at which gold could be bought and sold. It was the purest form of gold standard and was known as the *gold specie standard*.

A modified version of the gold standard was known as the *gold bullion standard*. It had all advantages of gold standard without any compulsion to maintain gold coinage. Individual bank notes were not convertible to gold directly and for conversion, gold bars were purchased at fixed rates.

> In gold standard, currency is pegged to a specific value of gold with 100% gold backing and with restrictions-free flow of gold.

The *gold exchange standard* was an even more economical form of gold standard where neither gold coinage was required, nor the convertibility via purchase of gold bars existed. A country on the gold exchange standard linked its currency to the currency of a country on the gold specie standard. If a country on the gold exchange standard held the pound as its reserves, its currency was convertible into pounds and the pound was convertible into gold. Thus, convertibility existed but not directly. The country reaped the advantages of the gold standard so long as its linked currency continued to be on the gold specie standard. Many countries maintained the gold exchange standard. The Scandinavian countries adopted it in 1885 and Russia followed suit in 1894. They all held huge reserves of British treasury bills.

The Broad Rules

The essential features of the gold standard were:

- The government adopting it fixed the value of currency in terms of specific weight and fineness of gold and guaranteed a two-way convertibility
- Export and import of gold were allowed so that it could flow freely among the gold-standard countries
- The central bank acting as the apex monetary institution, held gold reserves in direct relationship with the currency it had issued
- The government allowed unrestricted minting of gold and melting of gold coins at the option of the holder.

Gold standard possesses automatic mechanism for domestic price stability, fixed exchange rate and balance of payments adjustment.

Since fixed weight of gold had formed the basis for a unit of the currency and since free flow of gold was allowed among the countries, the gold standard possessed an automatic mechanism for domestic price stability, fixed exchange rates, and adjustment in balance of payments.

Let us first explain the mechanism of exchange rates. The rates depended upon the content of gold in different currencies. Suppose a pound sterling contained a half ounce of gold and one dollar contained a one-fourth ounce of gold, the exchange rate was fixed at £ 1 = $ 2. In practice, one ounce of gold was then valued at £ 4.24 and the same weight of gold with similar fineness was valued at $ 20.67. Naturally, one pound was exchanged for $ 20.67/4.24 or $ 4.87. This rate was known as the *mint parity* or the mint exchange rate.

The actual exchange rate remained close to mint parity because free flow of gold between two countries helped avoid any major deviation. Suppose the value of the dollar depreciated to $ 5.25 a pound. The arbitrageurs would buy one ounce of gold in the United States for $ 20.67 and sell it in the United Kingdom for £ 4.24 and then they could exchange the pound for the dollar in the foreign exchange market for $ 5.25 × 4.24 = $ 22.26. This brought them a profit of $ 22.26 – 20.67 = $ 1.59. The process of arbitrage continued till the original parity was re-established. It may be noted that this process involved a transaction cost or transportation cost of gold that might not help equate the actual exchange rate to mint parity. But the difference from the mint parity was limited to only that amount.

Turning to automatic adjustment in the balance of payments, one finds that any deficit was made up through the price-specie flow. Suppose that England faced a deficit on its trade account which could lead to outflow of gold for the settlement of trade thus reducing the money supply within the country. The emerging deflation in the wake of shrinkage of money supply would make the English exports competitive and the resultant rise in the export would wipe out any deficit on this account. There was one more explanation for automatic adjustment in the balance of payments. Reduced money supply raised the interest rate. The banking system restricted credit in view of the reduced money supply and to this end, the central bank raised the bank rate. Ultimately, lured by the higher interest rate, foreign investment moved into the economy meeting any deficit on the capital account.

The currency being backed fully by gold, money supply was constant in view of constant gold reserves and with constant money supply, prices were constant. Any deviation could occur only after discovery of new gold mines. That was the case in the USA when the Californian gold mines were discovered in 1847. Prices increased and this increase was transmitted to other countries through the flow of gold.

Suspension of Gold Standard

Constancy in money supply helped maintain price stability but it came in the way of the expansionary process. When the First World War broke out in 1914, the warring nations required expansion in money supply for financing the war activities. This was not easy under the gold standard. Moreover, the strained political relations impeded free flow of gold from one country to another, which considerably impaired automatic adjustment in external balance. The warring nations increased the money supply and had to suspend convertibility of currency into gold. The exchange rate parity was then greatly disturbed. All this was a deviation from the norms of the gold standard. Besides, there was a transfer-of-funds problem that shook the balance of payments. USA demanded repayment of war debt from France, and France demanded reparation from Germany to meet the war debt. USA joined the War in 1917. Prior to that, it supplied goods to Europe and this helped her to enjoy a trade surplus. The dollar turned stronger whereas the European currencies became weak. For these reasons, the gold standard was suspended during the First World War.

Inter-War Years

After the end of the First World War, the countries on the gold standard during pre-War years came back to it. The USA adopted it in 1919, the UK in 1925, and France in 1926. The other European countries followed soon after. However, in Germany and Austria, which were in the grip of hyper-inflation, in the early 1920s, parity between the currency and gold was set at higher than the pre-War level. On the contrary, the pre-War parity was conceived in the UK in the sequel of temporary deflation as well as of recommendations of the Cunliffe Committee. When deflation ended, the pre-War level parity created problems. The pound stood overvalued, especially after France devalued its currency and imbalances between internal and external values of the pound emerged. Consequently, the gold standard was not very successful after the War.

Another feature of the gold standard during the 1920s was that it was mainly a *gold exchange standard*. The reason was that the central banks of a number of European countries did not have sufficient gold as reserves. The production of gold during 1915–22 was lower as also there was a colossal outflow of gold to the USA. Had the gold standard in its purest form been re-established, there would have been a scramble for gold leading to an unmanageable upswing in gold prices. It was perhaps for this reason that the Genoa Conference in 1922 recommended the adoption of the gold exchange standard. What is more, it was primarily a managed gold standard. The monetary authorities did not leave the mechanism to remain as automatic as it was during the classical gold standard period. The purpose behind this control was to insulate the domestic economy from the inward movement of inflation. Unfortunately, the modified version of the gold standard too could not be carried on for long. When France insisted on accepting gold in settlement for the enormous surplus accruing to it during 1928, this decision put pressure on the deflated economies. The Bank of France refused to accept the sterling-denominated assets held by the French commercial banks. The Bank of England had to pay gold that it was not able to sustain. Moreover, England had to follow a policy of monetary expansion to reverse the adverse effects of the Great Depression and that did not set well with the gold standard. All this compelled that country to make a final return from the gold standard in September 1931.

England's return from the gold standard led to a *floating-exchange-rate* regime. Exchange rates were volatile. Investors preferred gold to foreign currency denominated securities and the scramble for gold increased. Nor did it leave US dollar untouched: the gold stock of the US monetary authorities too dwindled rapidly. This led the US Government to abandon the gold standard in 1933. Some other countries followed the lead. The collapse of the gold standard was evident in two stages: one when the UK and the USA left it and the other when France and other net creditor countries abandoned it in 1936.

Following the collapse of the gold standard, there came up various currency areas especially for the purpose of stabilising exchange rates. France and other net creditor countries, such as Belgium, Italy, the Netherlands, Sweden and Switzerland formed the *Gold Bloc*. England, along with all Commonwealth countries, except Canada, formed the *Sterling Area*. The currencies of the Commonwealth countries maintained a fixed relationship with the pound sterling. Later on, the Scandinavian countries, Iran and Latvia too came under the Sterling Area. The application of Imperial Preference in 1932 firmly bonded the Sterling Area countries.

> Currency area represented a group of countries maintaining fixed exchange rates among themselves.

The countries of North, Central and South America maintained a fixed parity of their currencies with the US dollar. This group was known as the *Dollar Area*. There were also some other countries that maintained their own exchange rate system. Germany and Austria maintained the external value of their currency through various methods of exchange control. The intra-bloc trade was conducted on a fixed exchange rate basis, but the inter-bloc trade was conducted on changing exchange rates. Efforts were made to stabilise inter-bloc exchange rates. The Exchange Equalisation Account was created in the UK and the USA that brought stability at least to some extent. Moreover, a tripartite discussion was held between the UK, the USA and France in 1936 that was an important step in this direction.

Economic prosperity began during the late 1930s but the Second World War broke out in 1939 that hit then prevailing exchange rate regime. Exchange control was applied on a large scale. The US economy was not hurt as the country joined the war much later. Rather, it enjoyed a large trade surplus on account of its supplying goods to the warring nations. Thus on the whole, from 1914 through to the Second World War years, the international monetary system was never in stable shape; the exchange rates were highly volatile, exchange control was rampant and retaliatory measures were common.

BRETTON WOODS SYSTEM OF EXCHANGE RATES

In view of the unstable exchange rates during the 1930s and early 1940s, various moves were afoot to create an orderly international monetary system. Finally, at the Bretton Woods Conference, it was resolved to create the International Monetary Fund. The IMF, that evolved a novel exchange rate system was established in 1945. Since the new system was the outcome of the Bretton Woods Conference, it is often termed as the *Bretton Woods System*.

Fixed Parity System

The IMF articles provided for an orderly exchange rate regime. Each member country was to set a fixed value—called the *par value*—of its currency in terms of gold or the US dollar. It was the par value that determined the rate of exchange between two currencies. Minor fluctuations in the exchange rate within a narrow band of one per cent above and below the established parities could not be ruled out and were to be corrected through active intervention of the monetary authorities of the concerned country.

> Fixed parity system linked the value of currencies with a fixed amount of gold/US dollar. Adjustable peg meant devaluation/ upward revaluation of a currency.

It may, however, be mentioned that the fixed parity under the Bretton Woods system was not like that of the gold standard of 1880–1914. It was a fixed parity with adjustable pegs meaning that any member country could alter the value of its currency or, in other words, could devalue its currency in case of "fundamental disequilibrium" in the balance of payments. Changes up to five per cent did not require prior approval of the IMF, but beyond it, IMF's approval was necessary. Fundamental disequilibrium was never formally defined; but in practice, it meant continued and chronic balance of payments problems and colossal loss of reserves. The purpose of the adjustable peg system was, therefore, to establish a balance between the objectives of stable exchange rates and the macroeconomic goals of the countries going for such adjustments as also to help avoid any use of exchange control and trade-restrictive measures. In other words, it brought flexibility in the fixed exchange rate system for the purpose of attaining equilibrium in the balance of payments. The provisions also contained cautions so that there might not be competitive devaluation. It was maintained through supervision and scrutiny over desired exchange rate changes.

Again, an important aspect of the Bretton Woods exchange rate system was that the US dollar was convertible into gold at a fixed rate of $ 35 per troy ounce of gold. The other currencies were convertible into gold via the US dollar. This currency was given the position of intervention currency in the system in view of the fact that in the immediate post-War period, it was the strongest currency. This system was, therefore, likened with the gold exchange standard where countries redeemed their currency into gold-convertible currency and not necessarily into gold directly. In the post-War system, the US dollar came to be the intervention currency replacing the British pound which had played this part during the early decades of the twentieth century.

US dollar was an intervention currency as it was directly convertible into gold. Other currencies were convertible into gold through US dollar.

Collapse of Fixed Parity System

The Bretton Woods system stabilised exchange rates but there were some inherent weaknesses. The adjustable peg system was highly rigid and by the time a fundamental disequilibrium could be manifest, colossal losses had occurred in member countries in the form of misallocation of resources. Moreover, the fixed parity system failed to consider the fast-growing activities of the MNCs which caused large flow of funds among different countries that necessitated changes in exchange rates. More importantly, the element of confidence lay at the root of the system. The moment confidence was shaken, the system was bound to collapse. During the first decade, there was no confidence problem. The member countries held large reserves in the form of dollar-denominated assets and the functioning of the exchange rate system was smooth but in the late 1950s, the US balance of payments swung into deficit because of its ambitious economic aid programme and other factors such as expansionary domestic policies, etc. Viewing this deficit, the European countries began to lose confidence in the US dollar and began converting their dollar-denominated assets into gold. The gold-holdings of the US Treasury plummeted by $ 8.0 billion by 1960. This eroded confidence again in the US dollar. A vicious circle emerged and was accelerated by the rapid deterioration in the US balance of payments during 1960s in the wake of the Vietnam war. Financing the war caused large budgetary deficit and monetary expansion and inflation followed. It led in turn to deficit on current account and the dollar stood overvalued which resulted in preference for gold, when the gold conversion ability of the US treasury was not beyond doubt. That US citizens were barred from buying gold further eroded confidence. Expectation of a record deficit in 1971 in the US balance of payments resulted in massive selling of the dollar in the international financial market. Gold price in the free market rose putting thereby an adverse influence on the fixed parity between the US dollar and gold. A speculative run on the dollar, which would have been impossible for the US Government to sustain, was expected. At the same time, Germany decided to float its currency against dollar, the Netherlands followed suit and Austria and Switzerland revalued their currency. By August 1971, a full-blown crisis had developed against dollar. During the first half of that month, the US Government's reserves fell by $ 1.1 billion. The Nixon Administration then suspended convertibility of the dollar into gold thus dealing a serious blow to the fixed parity system.

Smithsonian Arrangement

In December 1971, a conference was held at the Smithsonian Institute in Washington DC which decided to take the following actions to restore stability of the system:

Smithsonian arrangement realigned parity through devaluation of US dollar and widened the fluctuation band.

- Realignment of the par value of major currencies so as to better conform to their realistic values. For this purpose, the gold parity of the US dollar was changed from 35 to 38.02 per troy ounce entailing a devaluation of 8.57 per cent. On the other hand, the currencies of surplus countries were revalued upward by percentages ranging from 7.4 for the Canadian dollar to 16.9 for the Japanese yen.
- The band for the fluctuation from the par values was widened from +/–1.0 per cent to +/–2.25 per cent with a view to providing more leeway to member countries to manage their exchange rates and their monetary policies.

In short, the purpose of the Smithsonian arrangement was to inject greater flexibility into the par value system, although convertibility of the US dollar was never guaranteed. Unfortunately, the arrangement could not go far. There was a tide of speculation against the weak currencies, such as the dollar and the pound sterling, and of a massive flow of capital towards strong-currency countries, such as Germany, Switzerland, the Netherlands, France and Japan. The US Government was forced to devalue the dollar by 10.0 per cent raising the price of gold to $ 42.22 per troy ounce in February 1973. It could not check the currency flow in favour of European countries and Japan. At last the exchange markets were closed in March 1973 to avert a crisis. When they reopened, the major currencies came on to float thus delivering a death blow to the Bretton Woods exchange rate regime.

EXCHANGE RATE REGIME SINCE 1973

In view of the collapse of the Bretton Woods system of exchange rate, the Board of Governors of the IMF appointed Committee of 20 to suggest guidelines for evolving an exchange rate system that could be acceptable to the member countries. The report suggested various options that were discussed at Rambouillet in November 1975 and approved at the Jamaica meet in January 1976. They were formally incorporated into the text of the Second Amendment to the Articles of Agreement that came into force from April 1, 1978. The broad options under the new exchange rate regime were:

- Floating—Independent and Managed
- Pegging of currency
  - to a single currency
  - to a basket of currencies
  - to SDRs
  - crawling peg
  - currency board arrangement
- Target-zone arrangement

TABLE 3.1 Foreign Exchange Turnover Data: September 23–September 27, 2024

All Figures are in USD Millions

Position Date	*MERCHANT*						*INTER BANK*					
	FCY/INR			*FCY/FCY*			*FCY/INR*			*FCY/FCY*		
	Spot	*Forward*	*Forward Cancel*	*Spot*	*Forward*	*Forward Cancel*	*Spot*	*Swap*	*Forward*	*Spot*	*Swap*	*Forward*
Purchases												
23-09-2024	5,687	1,153	974	542	445	345	21,046	21,627	2,180	9,428	3,083	196
24-09-2024	5,840	2,937	713	463	801	402	23,492	16,678	1,703	12,345	3,253	391
25-09-2024	7,544	2,674	1,284	554	729	462	24,587	17,353	2,163	7,956	2,967	334
26-09-2024	8,855	4,528	2,387	963	963	1,220	26,639	20,561	1,939	11,693	5,588	639
27-09-2024	6,423	2,203	1,804	467	725	591	19,513	19,746	774	9,400	3,917	322
Sales												
23-09-2024	5,767	2,071	962	541	478	344	22,203	18,420	1,569	9,517	2,737	196
24-09-2024	6,738	1,825	608	462	567	405	27,271	14,400	1,016	11,858	2,996	392
25-09-2024	5,497	2,812	1,611	572	678	463	25,879	15,426	2,176	7,969	2,778	335
26-09-2024	6,820	4,271	3,296	974	961	1,226	25,285	19,311	1,943	11,655	5,393	639
27-09-2024	5,301	3,577	1,022	476	740	591	21,056	18,965	470	9,188	3,771	323

As per the data of the Reserve Bank of India, it is showing daily merchant and Inter-bank transactions in foreign exchnage for the period September 23–September 27, 2024.

Floating-rate Regime in General

In a floating-rate regime, the exchange rate is determined by the market forces—the forces of supply and demand in respect of a particular foreign currency. It is not fixed, nor administered, and it moves along with the changes in demand and supply positions. The readers may find the exchange rate determination in Chapter 4.

Now the question is whether the floating-rate regime is superior to fixed-rate regime. On the ground of economic efficiency, it is argued that a fixed-rate regime does not need hedging of exchange rate risk and so it does not entail expenditure of resources, not that it needs establishment of elaborate hedging mechanism. But this benefit is outweighed by other considerations. In a fixed-rate regime, the exchange rate is not fixed for ever. It is realigned in order to suit the changing economic scenario. If it is not realigned according to changes in macro-economic indicators, there arises a gap between nominal and real exchange rates which in turn hampers, among other things, the export performance. But if realignment is made, it is often costly and painful.

> Floating-rate regime involves market forces determining the exchange rate. Its merits are:
> 1. Exchange rates are automatically adjusted to changes in macro-economic variables.
> 2. Exchange rate is almost stable around the equilibrium in the long run.
> 3. Currency remains insulated from the shocks emanating abroad.
> 4. Trade and investment get stimulus.

Firstly, it may involve loss of foreign exchange to the monetary authorities and to other parties. In Mexico, after the 1994 devaluation of peso, many non-Mexican bondholders and share traders suffered huge losses. Thus it would be wrong to say that the fixed-rate regime does satisfy completely the economic efficiency norm. On the contrary, in a floating-rate regime, exchange rate tends to change automatically in line with the changes in macro-economic variables and so there does not appear any gap between the real and the nominal exchange rates (Friedman, 1953). For example, if inflation grows, the domestic currency depreciates automatically in a floating-rate regime. Naturally, there is no cost or pains of adjustment.

Secondly, as far as stability in the exchange rate is concerned, floating-rate regime scores quite high. The exchange rate does move but it tends to be closer to the equilibrium in the long run. If there is inflation, the currency depreciates, but depreciation in currency leads to greater volume of export and, ultimately, greater export leads to currency appreciation. The equilibrium is maintained.

Thirdly, the advocates of the floating-rate regime argue that this system has insulation properties and hence the currency remains isolated from the shocks emanating abroad. The government can adopt an independent economic policy (Friedman, 1953). This is quite in contrast with the fixed-rate regime where the insulation properties are absent. The experiences from Thailand reveal the situation. Thai currency, baht, was pegged to US dollar. During 1980s and early 1990s, when the US dollar had depreciated, Thailand experienced export boom. But in 1996, when the US dollar appreciated, Thai economy had to suffer heavy losses on trade account. Had baht been on float, it would have remained unaffected by dollar appreciation.

Fourthly, on the basis of experience, it is also said that the governments, under a floating exchange regime, are less likely to restrict trade and capital flows which leads to greater trade and investment and the associated welfare gains.

However, the empirical findings do not essentially support the arguments in favour of floating-rate regime. MacDonald (1988) finds that the exchange rate changes among the countries on floating rate during 1973–85 were much more volatile than warranted by changes in fundamental monetary variables. Dunn (1983) finds absence of insulation properties. During the early 1980s, when the USA was practising a tight monetary policy through raising of interest rates, the European countries raised interest rates so as to prevent large outflow of capital to the USA.

Again, since the nominal exchange rate tended to adjust more rapidly than the market prices of goods, nominal exchange rate turbulence was closely related to real exchange rate turbulence (Frenkel and Mussa, 1980). It is very difficult to confirm that greater uncertainty in real exchange rates has caused stagnation in international trade during the past two decades; but Cushman (1983) feels it has adversely affected trade among several industrialised countries. Dunn (1983) gives an example of Canadian firms borrowing long-term funds from the USA. They faced heavy losses due to 14 per cent real depreciation of Canadian dollar during 1976–79. He also finds that substantial appreciation in the real value of the pound during the late 1970s had led to insolvency of many UK firms as their products turned uncompetitive in the world market.

Developing countries in particular do not find floating rates suitable for them. Since their economy is not diversified and since their export is subject to frequent changes in demand and supply, they face frequent changes in exchange rates. This is more, especially when foreign demand for their products is price-inelastic. When the value of their currency depreciates, export earnings usually sag in view of inelastic demand abroad. Again, greater flexibility in exchange rates between a developed and a developing country generates greater exchange risk in the latter because of the low economic profile of developing countries and also because they have limited access to the forward market and to other risk-reducing mechanisms.

In short, it is difficult to say whether flexible exchange rate regime is better than the fixed rate one or vice versa. A government adopts a particular regime which is better suited to its macro-economic environment.

Managed Floating

Floating is generally managed in the sense that the system of managed floating involves direct or indirect intervention by the monetary authorities of the country to stabilise the exchange rate. It is different from independent floating which does not involve intervention. This is why independent floating is often termed as *clean floating*, whereas managed floating is known as *dirty floating*. However, the difference is only theoretical. In practice, intervention is found also in the case of independent floating. In independent floating, the purpose of intervention is simply to moderate the exchange rate and to prevent any undue fluctuation. In the case of managed floating, it is meant to establish a level for the exchange rate.

When the monetary authorities stabilise the exchange rate through changing the interest rates, it is indirect intervention. In the case of direct intervention, on the other hand, the monetary authorities purchase and sell foreign currency in the domestic market. When they sell foreign currency, its supply increases, and domestic currency appreciates against the foreign currency. When they purchase foreign currency, its demand increases and the domestic currency tends to depreciate vis-à-vis the foreign currency. The IMF permits such intervention. If intervention is aimed at preventing long-term changes in exchange rate away from equilibrium, it is known as *leaning-against-the-wind* intervention. But if the intervention supports the current trend in the exchange rate already moving towards equilibrium, it is known as *leaning-with-the-wind* intervention.

Intervention helps move the value of domestic currency up or down also through the expectations channel. When the monetary authorities begin supporting the foreign currency, speculators begin buying it forward in the expectation that it will appreciate. Its demand rises and in turn, its value appreciates vis-à-vis the domestic currency.

Intervention may be stabilising or destabilising. *Stabilising intervention* helps move the exchange rate towards equilibrium, while *destabilising intervention* is found in cases where rates are moving away from the equilibrium despite intervention. The former causes gain of foreign exchange, while the latter causes loss of foreign exchange. Suppose the rupee depreciates from 33 a dollar to 36 a dollar. The Reserve Bank sells US $ 1000 and the rupee improves to 33. The RBI will be able to replenish the lost reserves through buying the dollar at ₹ 33/US $. The gain will be US $ (36,000/33 – 1000) or US $ 91. But after intervention, if the rupee falls to 40 a dollar, the loss will be US $ (36,000/40 – 1000) or US $ 100. The monetary authorities do not normally resort to destabilising intervention, but it is very difficult to know in advance whether intervention would be really destabilising. The empirical studies show both the stabilising and destabilising intervention. Longworth's study (1980) finds stabilising intervention in case of the Canadian dollar, while Taylor (1982) finds destabilising intervention in the case of some European countries and Japan during the 1970s.

Indian Rupee Finally on Managed Float

Indian rupee went through varying experiences. India being a member of Sterling Area, rupee was linked to British pound. Under the fixed parity regime, the value of Sterling-linked rupee was fixed as equivalent to 0.268601 gram of fine gold. In 1949, its devaluation changed its gold content to 0.186621 gram of gold and again as a result of 1966 devaluation, its gold content dropped to 0.118489 gram. In August 1971, it was briefly pegged to US dollar at ₹ 7.50/$ for about five months till December. But then it was pegged again to British pound at ₹ 18.9677 per pound.

After the collapse of the fixed parity system, rupee was de-linked from Sterling in September 1975 and was pegged to a basket of five currencies, viz. US dollar, British pound, French franc, German mark and Japanese yen. In July 1991, during the external sector reforms, rupee was devalued by about 20 per cent to ₹ 25.80/$.

Finally, from March 1993, rupee came on to managed float with Reserve Bank of India making off and on intervention in order to stabilise the exchange rate.

Again, intervention may be sterilised or non-sterilised. When the monetary authorities purchase foreign currency with the help of created money, the money supply in the country increases. It leads to inflation. This is an example of *non-sterilised intervention.* But if simultaneously, securities are sold in the market to mop up the excess supply of money, intervention does not lead to inflation. It takes the form of *sterilised intervention.* The study of Obstfeld (1983) reveals that sterilised intervention has generally been ineffective; on the other hand, non-sterilised intervention is common. However, on the whole, Loopesko (1984) confirms the effect of intervention on exchange rate stabilisation.

Finally, the intervention may be a coordinated one where central banks of two or more countries are simultaneously involved in stabilising a particular currency. The G-5 governments attempted for making US dollar consistent with the then economic indicators under the Plaza Agreement of 1985. At Louvre Palace in Paris in 1987, they noted their success, although as Bordo and Schwartz (1991) feel, the coordinated intervention under the Plaza Agreement distorted the foreign exchange market and the central banks had to face excessive risk of loss.

Pegging of Currency

Normally, a developing country pegs its currency to a strong currency or to a currency with which it has a very large part of its trade. Pegging involves a fixed exchange rate with the result that the trade payments are stable, but in case of trading with other countries, stability cannot be guaranteed, and hence pegging to a single currency is not advised if the country's trade is diversified. In such cases, pegging to a basket of currency is advised; but if the basket is very large, multi-currency intervention may prove costly. Pegging to SDR is not different insofar as the value of SDR itself is pegged to a basket of four currencies. Ugo Sacchetti (1979) observes that many countries did not like to peg to SDR in view of its declining value. Statistics show that the number of currencies pegged to SDR fell from

Pegging of a currency means its fixed value in terms of:
1. a single currency,
2. a basket of currencies,
3. SDRs.

seven in 1989 to two during the third quarter of 1997 (IMF, 1998). Presently, there is no currency pegged to SDRs.

Again, a few countries had a system of a crawling peg. Under this system, a country pegs its currency to the currency of another country but allows the parity value to change gradually over time to catch up with the changes in the market-determined rates. It is a hybrid of fixed-rate and flexible-rate systems. So this system avoids too much of instability and too much of rigidity. Edwards (1983) confirms this advantage in case of a sample of some developing countries.

> Crawling peg involves periodic adjustment of fixed exchange rate to catch up with market-determined rates.

Last but not least, in a currency board arrangement, the country does not have a central bank, rather it has a currency board that links the domestic currency stock to the foreign exchange holding. In other words, the currency board pegs the domestic currency to the currency of another nation and buys and sells the foreign currency reserves in order to maintain the parity value. The purchase and sale of the foreign currency determines the amount of domestic money in circulation. However, the currency board has normally only limited functions and powers compared to a central bank and so it cannot frame a discretionary monetary policy as central banks do.

Dollarisation

Full or official dollarisation means the use a foreign currency, usually US dollar, as legal tender parallel to or instead of the local currency. The money supply is denominated in dollars and is supported by comfortable foreign currency reserves. Ecuador, El Salvador, Panama, Liberia, Monaco, Puerto Rico, Greenland, Micronesia, etc. have adopted dollarisation as their exchange rate regime.

On the contrary, unofficial or de facto dollarisation means that private economic agents use dollars with or without formal legal approval as means of payment or even as a store of value in addition to the local currency. Unofficial dollarisation is found in Argentina, Mexico, Bolivia, Peru, Georgia, Russia, Ukraine, Turkey, Romania, Vietnam, Zimbabwe, Mozambique, etc.

Besides, semi-official dollarisation refers to dollars existing legally or illegally parallel to the local currency. However, in most cases, dollarisation, although in existence for many years, has not been legally approved.

Whatever may be the form, dollarisation stems from a loss of confidence by businesses and consumers in the local currency due to high inflation, fears of confiscation and frequent serious depreciations in the exchange rate of the local currency.

The merits of dollarisation are: increased credibility, less exchange rate volatility, lower interest rates and lower inflation, lower transaction cost, improved information, and increased international integration. Dollarisation can also enhance the internationalisation of the financial system, whereas beneficial influences may flow from the diminished possibility of financial contagion and the increased predictability of economic policy and general economic developments.

On the contrary, the demerit manifests in the form of loss of seigniorage. It may be noted that seigniorage profit is the result of the power accorded to government to print fiat money. By creating base money, the central bank can buy real resources almost costless, except for the cost of printing the money and the interest on bank reserves. Another problem is related to dealing with asymmetric shocks and business cycles. With a floating exchange rate, a country can adjust differently, act counter-cyclically, and devaluate to adjust its economy. This is not possible under dollarisation. Last but not least, a country with dollarisation cannot have an independent monetary policy.

Target-zone Arrangement

Target-zone arrangement involves member countries having fixed exchange rate among their currencies. Alternatively, they may use a common currency.

In case of target-zone arrangement, a group of countries either maintain fixed exchange rate among their currency through a common currency or have a common currency instead of their own currency. A few European countries opted for a target-zone arrangement which came to be known as the European Monetary System (EMS) or later as the European Economic and Monetary Union (EMU). Each currency in the EMU had a central rate expressed in terms of a European Currency Unit (ECU) that has been substituted by the Euro since 1999. This led to a fixed exchange rate among the members' currencies, although fluctuation was allowed within the prescribed band. When the exchange rate fluctuations moved towards the prescribed limit and tried to cross it, the central banks intervened as in the case of managed floating and if intervention did not succeed, realignment of the parity grid took place.

This arrangement provided stability at least to some extent in the exchange rates within the Union, but since the performance of the different member countries was not uniform, the emergence of disparity between the value of different currencies could not be ruled out. Even intervention was helpless on many occasions as a result of which there occurred many realignments in the value of the members' currencies during the 1980s. However, with greater efforts towards convergence in the wake of the Delors Plan and with the Euro coming into being finally as the sole currency of the EMU, the earlier problems are over. Besides EMU, target-zone arrangement has been adopted also in other parts of the world. The details about the EMU are given in the study topic to this chapter for guidance of the readers.

INTERNATIONAL LIQUIDITY

The Three Bases

International liquidity refers to the size of internationally used money available in the international economy.

The other important aspect of the international monetary system is international liquidity. In the early IMF system, *stock of gold* lay at the very root of international liquidity. Again, since the US dollar was convertible into gold and since the US treasury had held around three-fourths of the world's gold holding, *stock of US dollar-denominated* assets provided sufficient liquidity. Yet again, there was a provision for an *international pool of reserves* with the IMF to which the members contributed according to their quota prescribed on the basis of their GNP and foreign trade etc. One quarter of the contribution was in form of gold and the rest in form of their own currency, usually non-interest-bearing notes. In return, a member country could draw from the pool up to a prescribed limit for meeting its balance of payments deficit. The drawings involved the purchase of other members' currencies, normally the US dollar or other scarce currencies, in exchange for the drawer's own currency. Thus, the size of international liquidity was dependent not only upon the size of gold holding and the elasticity and strength of the reserve currency, say, the US dollar, but also upon the size of the reserves pool with the IMF. Now the question is whether these three elements of international reserves were sufficient for meeting the demand for international liquidity since the supply of gold which was the principal component, was limited by the conditions of its production and the rise of production cost relative to its fixed price.

As regards the US dollar, which was the other important component of international reserves, there was no problem in the initial years of the IMF but since the late 1950s, when the US balance of payments faced deficit and when the ratio of reserves to import in the USA fell from 122 per cent in 1959 to 41 per cent in 1969, international liquidity faced constraints. The weakening of the US dollar and the consequent loss of confidence in it added fuel to the fire. The countries possessing large dollar-denominated assets began converting those assets into gold. By 1968, the US gold stock covered only two-thirds of US liabilities to all foreign official holders.

As a result, international liquidity was jeopardised. The size of the reserves pool with the IMF, though it was augmented with upward revisions of quotas of member countries, was limited in view of the growing need for it. At the end of 1968, the outstanding drawings (net) which amounted to US $ 6.7 billion were far from being adequate. The resources with the IMF were supplemented through borrowings from ten industrialised countries under the General Arrangements to Borrow (GAB) scheme from 1962. The size of contribution under GAB was enlarged subsequently to 17 billion SDRs, but fell short of the requirements. In early 1997 following the Mexican crisis, the IMF announced a New Arrangement to Borrow (NAB) scheme that could provide up to 34 billion SDRs or US $ 48 billion, the borrowing to be made from 25 potential participants when supplementary resources would be needed by the IMF to deal with some exceptional situations. This decision was in effect originally for five years but it was extended in 2002 for another term of five years. The NAB scheme was amended to admit new participants as well as to raise the amount of resources available to the IMF. The amendment came to be effective from March 11, 2011 and by November 15, 2011, the total size of contribution moved up to SDR 370 billion or around US $570 billion.

Creation of SDRs

With the persisting wide gap between the supply of, and demand for, international reserves, several ideas were floated during the 1960s for the creation of international fiat money, the stock of which could be controlled by the IMF so as to generate confidence in it. At the 1967 Rio de Janeiro annual meeting, it was decided to create such a reserves asset, called the Special Drawing Rights (SDRs) that could supplement the then existing reserves asset. This decision entered into force with the first amendment to the Articles of Agreement in July 1969. The reserves asset of the member countries was to be increased through the allocation of SDRs to them in proportion of their quota. The first allocation, based on the need for international liquidity, amounted to US $ 9.5 billion during 1970–72. The second allocation of SDRs 12.3 billion was

> Special drawing rights are international reserves asset created by the IMF.

made in 1979 for a three-year period. The third allocation approved by the IMF Board in September 1997 amounted to US $ 21.4 billion and was meant for those countries that had joined the IMF after the second allocation, namely the East European countries and a few others. Again, to help mitigate the effects of the financial crisis, an SDR allocation of SDR 161.2 billion was made on 28 August, 2009. Separately, the Fourth Amendment to the Articles of Agreement became effective from 10 August, 2009 and provided for a special one-time allocation of SDR 21.5 billion. The purpose of the Fourth Amendment was to enable all members of the IMF to participate in the SDR system on an equitable basis and correct for the fact that countries that had joined the IMF after 1981—more than one-fifth of the current IMF membership—never received an SDR allocation until 2009. The 2009 general and special SDR allocations together raised total cumulative SDR allocations to about SDR 204 billion. The SDRs possess members' confidence insofar as they are handled by a supra-national body.

Again, in order to make the system of international liquidity more viable, the IMF decided to reduce the role of gold in the international monetary system. It took a concrete shape with the second amendment to the Articles of Agreement that came into force from April 1978 which made SDRs the principal reserves asset of the world monetary system. The role of gold as a common denominator of the par value of currencies ended in favour of SDRs and the obligation to use gold in transaction with the IMF came to an end. SDRs replaced gold as a means of payment by the members to the IMF. This means that they were to pay 25 per cent of their quota to the reserves pool not in gold but in SDRs. The IMF sold 25 million ounces of gold and used the proceeds for the benefit of the poorer developing countries. A similar amount of gold was restituted to the members. The official price of gold was abolished. IMF's borrowings etc. were denominated in SDRs. A number of international organisations also adopted SDRs as the unit of account.

The value of SDR was fixed initially in terms of gold with the same gold content as the 1970 US dollar. Till November 1971, one unit of SDR was equal to one unit of US dollar, but with the devaluation of the US dollar, the value of SDR appreciated vis-à-vis US dollar. During February 1973–June 1974, SDR 1 was equal to US $ 1.20635. From July 1974, the value of SDR came to be determined in terms of a basket of 16 currencies whose share in the world trade was more than one per cent during 1968–72. Since the basis of valuation of SDRs' was broad, their value remained almost stable. From January 1981, the basket came to comprise five currencies that share the largest part of the world export. They were the US dollar, the British pound, the French franc, the German mark and the Japanese yen. Effective from January 1999, the German mark and the French franc were replaced by Euro for the valuation of SDR, based on fixed conversion rate announced by the European Council on the closing day of 1998. The weight remained changing from time to time. Beginning from 2001, the SDR valuation basket weights came to be: 45 per cent for US dollar, 29 per cent for Euro, 15 per cent for Japanese yen, and 11 per cent for British pound. The value is established daily on the basis of the representative market exchange rates. From January 2006, the weight for the four currencies in the basket changed as 44 per cent for US dollar, 34 per cent for euro and 11 per cent each for Japanese yen and British pound. The weight was altered again effective from January 2011. Now, it is 41.9 per cent for US dollar, 37.4 per cent for euro, 11.3 per cent for British pound and 9.4 per cent for Japanese yen.

The supply of SDRs depends upon their creation and allocation. Any allocation is effected by a minimum vote of 85 per cent. Cancellation requires similar percentage of votes. The SDR holding is subject to interest receipt and payments. If a member country holds SDRs in excess of its allocation, it earns interest on the difference. If the holding is below the allocated amount, it has to pay interest in line with the market rate of interest that is equal to those on primary domestic market instruments in the five countries whose currencies form the basket. The rate is calculated weekly.

Thus with the creation and allocation of SDRs, the position of international liquidity has eased considerably. Moreover, to ease it further, the IMF has created several facilities for drawing from the reserves pool. These facilities are discussed hereunder.

IMF's Funding Facilities

The funding facilities of IMF can be grouped under three heads. They are:

1. Permanent facilities for general balance of payments support such as
   (c) Stand-by arrangements
   (d) Flexible credit line
   (e) Extended fund facility
   (f) Precautionary credit line
2. Special facilities such as
   (a) Emergency assistance
      (i) Natural disaster
      (ii) Post-conflict
3. Facilities for low-income countries such as
   (a) Extended credit facility
   (b) Stand-by credit facility
   (c) Rapid credit facility

The Reserve tranche drawings indicate unconditional borrowings of a part, or full, of the quota held by a particular member. A few experts do not consider such drawings as the using of the IMF credit as it is the amount deposited by the borrower.

The credit tranche or the stand-by arrangement was created in 1952. It is the IMF's basic financing facility addressing the short-term balance of payments problem. Such credits are available normally in four equal instalments on the condition that the borrower would follow a policy to overcome the balance of payments difficulties within a reasonable time period. The instalments are released subject to performance criteria. The borrowing is repaid within three and a-quarter to five years.

> Conditionality denotes the policy that a country receiving balance of payments support from the IMF adopts in order to address the root causes behind the balance of payments problems. It is related, among other things, to: (1) achievement of a realistic exchange rate, (2) elimination of subsidies and control so as to ensure an efficient allocation of resources, (3) reduction of trade and investment barriers, and (4) squeeze in the government spending so as to eliminate excess demand.

The guidelines shaping conditionality evolved on a broader scale in 1979 that were further delineated and elaborated in 2002.

The argument for imposing conditionality on the borrower is that it helps proper utilisation of the IMF funds so that the economic conditions in the country should improve and the country would find itself in a position to repay the funds to the IMF.

The conditionality turned tougher in recent decades. In 1982, less than 5 per cent of the IMF's upper tranche arrangements contained 11 or more performance criteria. By 1999, 92 per cent of such arrangements contained these criteria. However, the compliance rate declined fast. Moreover, the balance of payments support helped improve the balance of payments but had negative impact on the growth and income distribution.

Based on:

1. Joyce, J.P. (2004), "The Adoption, Implementation and Impact of IMF Programme: A Review of the Evidence", *Comparative Economic Studies*, 46 (2).
2. Kapur, D. (2005), "Conditionality and Its Alternatives", in A. Buira (Ed.), *The IMF and the World Bank at Sixty*, London: Anthem Press.
3. Vasudevan, A. (2002), "IMF's New Guidelines on Conditionality", *Economic and Political Weekly*, Oct. 19.

The extended fund facility (EFF), set up in 1974, addresses the balance of payments difficulties caused by long-term structural problems. The support is provided when the credit tranches support is not just sufficient to meet the balance of payments problem. The annual limit is 100 per cent of the quota and the cumulative limit to the assistance is 300 per cent of the quota as in case of the credit tranche facilities. The borrower has to adopt a three-year programme for structural adjustment. The borrowing is repaid within 10 years.

Flexible credit line was created in 2009 meant for addressing the actual and potential balance of payments requirements, subject to a mid-term review after one year. Precautionary credit line created in 2010 is meant especially for those countries possessing sound macro-economic fundamentals and policies. It is subject to semi-annual review.

Emergency assistance for natural disaster was created in 1962, but that for post-conflict was created in 1995. The conflict relates to civil unrest, political turmoil and international armed conflict.

There are facilities for the low-income countries. The extended credit facility (ECF) was created in 2010 substituting poverty reduction and growth facility. It is primarily meant for structural adjustment that helps ultimately in reduction of poverty. The stand-by credit facility (SCF) was created in 2010 for short-term balance of payments support for twelve to twenty-four months. Lastly, rapid credit facility (RCF) was also created in 2010 to meet the balance of payments problem arising on account of exogenous shocks where other credit tranche facilities were not feasible. It involves a single purchase and does not require review.

An Appraisal of Liquidity Promotion Measures

It is a fact that IMF has tuned its financing facility in response to the needs of the members, especially among developing countries. But the issues that need evaluation are whether:

- the SDR allocations have a relevance in the changing world capital market scenario;
- the drawings from the IMF have helped improve the external balance of the member countries;
- conditionalities associated with the drawings have proved to be of benefit to the member countries;
- the developing countries have been able to make greater use of the IMF resources; and
- IMF resources have been able to meet the current account deficit in the member countries.

It is believed in some quarters, that in view of phenomenal growth in the international capital market where ample funds are available, SDR allocations do not have as much significance as in the earlier decades, but at the same time, it is observed that the supply of international liquidity has been erratic and unreliable owing to lack of coordination in policies among creditors, especially the private sector creditors. The terms of lending have also been harder. All this has renewed the significance of the SDR allocation. Moreover, there is also a provision in the Articles of Agreement for checking unwarranted liquidity creation through cancellations. In fact, SDR allocations are normally moderate and improve overall quality of international reserves. However, they are based on a quota and so do not take into account the liquidity need of individual member countries.

As regards the second question, a few studies can be referred to. Connors (1979) felt that the IMF's funding facilities were mostly ineffective. Reichmann and Stillson (1978) found that during 1963–72, only one-quarter of 79 standby agreements helped improve the balance of payments of the drawing countries. They felt that for the following three years, the IMF's contribution in this respect was less than satisfactory.

As far as conditionality, which is associated virtually with all the drawings except reserve tranche drawings, is concerned, it is justified on the ground that it helps in proper utilisation of funds, particularly in low income countries where the administrative machinery is too weak to do this. The economic, social and political structure in these countries, however, is such that they cannot abide by the conditionalities and they fail to get desired funds from the IMF for that reason.

Again, the quota of individual developing countries in relative terms has not increased over time despite increase in the overall quota because when the SDR scheme was established, it was the global liquidity, and not the liquidity needs of the individual member country, that was taken into consideration. The study of Granade (1972) reveals that a developing country drew far less than a developed country. At the end of 1971, the withdrawal of a developing country was on an average SDR 25 million as compared to SDR 441 million by an industrialised country. However, in September 1997, the IMF Board decided to distribute 75 per cent of the SDR allocation on the basis of the existing proportion of the holdings.

Fifteen per cent of the remainder were to be allocated on the basis of some selective criteria, such as economic strength of the member country and ten per cent on the basis of some *ad hoc* considerations. But, despite the policy changes, the low-income countries have been the lowest beneficiary of IMF funds.

Again, notably, the IMF resource flow has lagged behind the size of current account deficit of the net-oil importing countries. It is found that deficit on current account of these countries rose from US $ 11.5 billion in 1973 to US $ 97.5 billion in 1981 but the IMF resources available to them accounted for 4.0 to 11.5 per cent of the deficit (Sharan, 1985).

This state of affairs leaves these countries with two options: one, that they go in for non-official credits, in which case, their debt problem may become unmanageable; and two, that they resort to forced adjustments with the resources available with them which too would be a painful process in that the welfare cost associated with the decline in national income would be very high. The study of Dell and Lawrence (1980) confirms that the losses on account of diminution in economic growth and in the levels of living standard were considerable among developing countries as a sequel to forced adjustments during mid-1970s.

IMF SOLUTION FOR FINANCIAL CRISIS

Nature of Financial Crisis

Besides the design and management of the exchange rate regime and international liquidity in normal course of business, the IMF helps manage financial crisis faced occasionally by member countries. The financial crisis has been gripping both the developed countries and the developing countries, but its frequency and intensity has been greater in case of the developing countries.

Financial crisis manifests in different ways. One of the forms is *currency crisis.* In this case, speculative attacks on the exchange rate of the currency tend to push down the value of the currency. The situation does not improve much even after market intervention by the monetary authorities of the country. The second form of financial crisis is known as *banking crisis.* This involves potential or actual bank runs. The monetary authorities suspend the internal convertibility of banks' liabilities and provide financial assistance. But this action sometimes leads to the loss of confidence among the borrowers and depositors. Loss of confidence leads to bank runs. The third form, known as the *systemic financial crisis* brings disruption in the financial market causing large-scale disinvestments. If disinvestment pertains to the foreign institutional investors, it may lead to currency crisis. The fourth form is the *foreign debt crisis* where the country finds it difficult to service external debt either on account of very high interest rates or on account of mal-utilization of the borrowed funds.

> Financial crisis takes the form of:
> 1. Currency crisis,
> 2. Banking crisis,
> 3. Systemic financial crisis, and
> 4. Foreign debt crisis.

All these different forms of crisis have normally a common origin; which is, unsustainable economic imbalances and malalignment of asset prices or exchange rates often in the context of financial sector distortions and structural rigidities. There is sudden loss of confidence in currency or the banking system prompted by sudden correction of asset prices or by disruption of credit or external financial flows underlying economic and financial weaknesses. These different forms of crisis are inter-linked. The worst is when all the different forms of crisis occur simultaneously.

IMF Response

The IMF provides sizeable financial assistance either out of its own funds or in collaboration with some other agencies, such as the World Bank or any other agency. Moreover, it helps implement reforms in macroeconomic policies so that the financial assistance is put to the best possible use and the crisis is resolved.

Let us first take the case of the Mexican 1982 debt crisis. After the oil price rise in the 1970s, the huge earnings of the oil-exporting countries were recycled through international banks to developing countries, especially the Latin American countries. They faced a big volume of debt. Between 1973 and 1981, Mexico's external debt grew at an average annual rate of more than 30 per cent—from US $ 4 billion to US $ 43 billion. The inflation rate in the early 1980s was 25 per cent and the current account deficit/GDP ratio was as high as 4.5 per cent. The hike in interest rate in Europe and the USA added fuel to the fire. In August 1982, Mexico declared its inability to service debt. In the sequel, the international banks tightened their lending policy that befell further on the capacity to service debt. There was a huge current account deficit. Peso fell by over 40 per cent.

In such a situation, IMF supported Mexico's macroeconomic stabilisation and structural transformation through a US $ 50 billion assistance.

Firstly, the strategy aimed at attaining external viability and laying the foundations for the private-sector-led growth that included tight financial policies, use of the exchange rate as a nominal anchor, comprehensive structural reforms, including privatisation and trade and exchange liberalisation, and restructuring of external debt. All this yielded good results. Fiscal deficit dropped. Inflation was reduced from 160 per cent in 1987 to 8 per cent in 1993. Economic growth recovered from an average not much higher than zero in 1985–88 to 3 per cent in 1989–93. The restructuring of external debt paved the way for a resumption of access to international financial markets, and private capital inflows surged, contributing to a large increase in international reserves.

Secondly, it was the Russian rouble crisis of 1992–95 when the value of the rouble had fallen from 125 to 5130 per US dollar and when the economy was facing a four-digit inflation rate. In order to remedy the crisis, the IMF conferred membership on Russia as early as in June 1992. It disbursed one billion US dollar in August 1992 and in June 1993, a new facility was created for the transition economies through which US $ 1.5 billion was pumped into the economy. Again, in April 1995, US $ 6.5 billion was provided to the economy as stand-by assistance. Inflation was brought under control. The exchange rate system was changed through the introduction of managed floating. And finally, a three-year agreement was signed for structural adjustment with a focus on boosting up tax collection and controlling the budgetary deficit.

The Asian crisis of 1997 was more serious in the sense that all forms of the financial crisis occurred almost simultaneously. High growth rate and strong financial sector, loss of export competitiveness and deteriorating capital account balance, upsurge in the credit facilities to the private corporate sector and structural rigidities in the financial sector were at the root of the crisis. The crisis began in the first quarter of 1997 in Thailand with a sharp fall in the price bubble in the real estate sector and also a sharp fall in the equity prices, that in turn led to a fast depreciation of the baht. The Government announced to float baht, but because of the weak economy, it depreciated further. The spill-over effects spread to other neighbouring countries. The neighbouring governments, viz. Indonesia, Malaysia, Philippines, etc. took restrictive measures to revamp the economy in general and to stabilise the external value of the currency, but that did not serve anything. It was because such measures led to erosion of confidence in the economy. By October 1997, the cumulative decline of the currency of the above four countries against the US dollar exceeded 20–30 per cent. Mounting political uncertainty added fuel to the fire. In order to contain damages, the IMF provided $ 117 billion to these countries and helped implement the macro-economic policy reforms. The measures could be categorised in four groups.

First, there were financial and corporate sector reforms including closure of insolvent financial institutions with their assets transferred to restructuring agency, limited use of public funds for bank restructuring, strengthening of prudential norms for loan operation, liberalisation of foreign investment in domestic banks, restructuring of domestic and external corporate debt, etc.

Secondly, the measures were related to competition and governance policies. It included the liberalisation of restrictive marketing arrangements of some key commodities, privatisation of government assets, strengthening of bankruptcy laws and exit policies, and liberalisation of FDI in non-financial sector.

Thirdly, the social policy included labour-intensive public work programmes, price control of essential items meant for low-income persons, stress on health and education and the development of small-scale industry.

Fourthly, measures were related to trade reforms such as import liberalisation and export promotion.

The International Financial Crisis of 2008–09 was still a major crisis being greater in intensity and engulfing many more countries. The rising real estate prices in the USA almost for a decade and then a sudden downturn made the collateral subprime. There was a huge default on bank loan. The banks found themselves in acute jeopardy. The financial institutions having great stake in the banks too had to face the distress. The liquidity position ebbed below the sustainable level as a result of which the output, employment and income were badly hit.

The IMF took a note of it and made lending under stand-by arrangement to a number of crisis-affected countries, the cumulative value of which crossed US $ 48 billion mark by March 2009. The lending was fraught with rigorous conditionalities so as to help improve the situation. The USA, in turn, took a number of measures, such as narrowing the spread of primary credit rate over the target Federal funds rate, extension of the terms for which the banks could borrow from the discount windows, expansion of the liquidity programmes, and rescue packages designed to prevent collapse of the national banking system. The crisis-hit European countries too unveiled the economic recovery programme worth 200 billion euro, provided government guarantee for inter-bank loans and increased government deposit insurance to enhance confidence of the depositors.

Although the European government debt crisis appeared in 2009, it was distinctly visible in early 2010 in the Euro zone as a whole. In Euro area, the government debt/GDP ratio was very high at 86 per cent in 2010. But it was still more severe among Greece, Ireland and Portugal. Its spread-effect was to be found in Belgium, France, Italy and Spain. In fact, the debt burden turned severe in the wake of international financial crisis of 2008 and the accompanying recession among the developed market economies. It was also the faulty fiscal policy related to government revenue and expenses and to bailout of ailing banking industry and private bondholders. The international trade imbalances made this problem from bad to worse. Over and above, the case-specific reasons varied from one country to the other. Ireland's banks lent heavily for real estate development but when the real estate prices crashed, the Irish Government assumed the private debts. In Greece, the Government increased its commitments to the public workers with high salaries and perks.

The views of rating agencies aggravated the problem. S&P wrote that the credit condition in the Euro zone as a whole was very tight; risk premium on the euro zone sovereign was very high; the economic, financial and fiscal convergence among the euro zone members was utterly lacking; and the rising risk of recession was hanging on their head.

In such a situation, the euro zone ministers took many internal measures and also agreed to boost up IMF resources by Euro 150 billion to ward off the debt crisis. The IMF approved Euro 2.9 billion (US $ 3.78 billion) to Portugal under a Euro 78 billion IMF-EU financing package approved in May 2011.

SUMMARY

- The developments in the international monetary system date back to the specie commodity standard when metallic coins were used for international transactions.
- It was followed by the gold standard that was officially announced in England in the early nineteenth century and that had its heyday during the last quarter of that century and through the first one-and-a-half decades of the twentieth century. The gold standard which was adopted in different forms by different countries, such as gold specie standard, gold bullion standard and gold exchange standard, possessed automatic mechanism for domestic price stability, stability in exchange rate and for balance of payments adjustment.
- Gold Standard could not be sustained during the First World War and was suspended. After the war, it was readopted but failed to prove very successful in face of the changed environment. So it was finally abandoned in the 1930s.
- The following years till the outbreak of World War II witnessed unstable exchange rates, although efforts were made to bring in stability to some extent. Finally, the IMF was created to bring back stability to the system.
- The IMF adopted a fixed parity system with adjustable pegs. The US dollar was the intervention currency but with the weakening of the dollar from the late 1950s, this currency gradually stood overvalued and got 'mal-aligned' with the strong currencies. The Smithsonian arrangement brought about reforms for proper alignment of different currencies but with the fast weakening dollar, proved unsuccessful. The major currencies opted for floating in the early 1970s and the fixed parity system, which was commonly known as the Bretton Woods system, collapsed in 1973.

- Under the new system, there were many options ranging from floating—independent or managed—to the system of a crawling or fixed peg, or a target-zone arrangement. These different options have merits; but at the same time, suffer from limitations. Different member countries have adopted systems that suit their own convenience and their own macroeconomic fundamentals. However, on the whole, there is a marked, clear-cut dent in favour of floating over the years.
- This is not all. The IMF looks after international liquidity. Initially, it was dependent upon the size of the gold holding, the strength of the intervention currency, the US dollar and the size of reserves pool with the IMF. In the early years of the IMF, there was no problem of international liquidity but with the weakening dollar and with the growing need of the member countries to meet the current account deficit, it proved inadequate. Thus, SDRs were created to substitute gold in order to enhance the strength of the reserves in the subsequent period. The creation of SDRs and their allocation enhanced international liquidity. Moreover, the various facilities created by the IMF for the purpose of balance of payments support eased the problem of liquidity. But the question how far the balance of payments problem of the developing member countries has been really solved, still remains unresolved.
- Last but not least, the IMF also provides support to overcome financial crises in the member countries in different ways.

STUDY TOPIC

Changing Face of European Economic and Monetary Union (EMU)

EARLY PHASE: SNAKE IN THE TUNNEL

The European Monetary Union (EMU) is an important chain in the West European economic cooperation that began in late 1950s. The European Common Market was formed and it gained sizeable ground over the years. But the monetary cooperation did not get the desired attention. It was for the first time emphasised in the Werner Report during the early 1970s. When the Smithsonian arrangement did not prove successful, in early 1972, six of the West European countries, then members of the European Common Market, created "snake in the tunnel". As a result, the spot spread between the parities of any two member currencies (snake) was restricted to +/–1.125 per cent that was one-half of the fluctuation band prescribed under the Smithsonian arrangement (tunnel). There was provision for intervention for preventing the snake from leaving the tunnel. The purpose was to narrow the fluctuation margin among the European currencies while preserving the US dollar's central role in the system.

The move was successful to some extent. In May 1972, the pound sterling, the Irish pound and the Danish krone joined the snake but there was no stability. Since the sterling was rapidly swept away by the continuous wave of speculation against the dollar, it left the snake as well as the tunnel along with the Irish pound. The Danish krone left it the following October. The first oil shock of 1973 and the resulting balance of payments problem disrupted the functioning of the snake. A few currencies of Europe joined the snake, while a few others left it. In February 1973, the Italian lira too deported. Moreover, there was no unanimity on monetary issues among the member countries; some of the currencies were floated jointly, while some others were floated independently. Divergence in the economic performance of these countries was another factor coming in the way of smooth functioning of the snake. In other words, this new arrangement remained fragile in the increasingly volatile international economic environment. So, in April 1978, an idea was floated to form the European Monetary System (EMS) which was approved in December 1978. By March 1979, EMS, now known as EMU, began its functions. Most of the EU members, initially their number being ten, joined the EMS.

PRINCIPAL FEATURES OF EMS

European Currency Unit

Prior to the creation of the Euro in January 1999, the European Currency Unit (ECU) was the monetary unit of the EMS. ECUs were created and allocated among the EMS member countries. It was a composite monetary unit made up of a basket of specified amounts of the currencies of 12 EU member countries. Each specified amount was determined on the basis of the country's GDP and foreign trade. One ECU was equal to the sum of the fixed amount of such currencies.

The process of valuation of the ECU is shown in Table ST3.1 where the fixed amount of different currencies is translated into a common currency, say, the DM. The sum of the translated amount is equal to one ECU. In the table, one finds that one ECU is equal to DM 2.037483. In terms of the Italian lira, it is equal to 2.037483 × 744.6 = 1517.1098.

Exchange Rate Mechanism

The EMS had a unique mechanism for exchange rate stabilisation. This mechanism had two aspects. One related to bilateral parity, i.e., the ECU helped determine the parity grid or the grid of bilateral rates of exchange. It means that the exchange rate between two member countries' currency was fixed through their share in the ECU valuation. Any fluctuation in the bilateral parity grid was not unexpected in view of widely differing macroeconomic variables in different member countries. So a fluctuation band was prescribed that was initially +/–2.25 per cent except for the Italian lira where it was 6.00 per cent. Any fluctuation beyond the prescribed limit was restricted through intervention by the central banks. In practice, intervention was made much before the prescribed limit was reached. This type of optional intervention prevented any compulsory intervention having to be made when the prescribed limit was reached.

The other aspect of the exchange rate mechanism related to the rules governing the divergence indicator. A divergence limit was set at 75 per cent of 2.25 per cent, that is 1.6875 per cent. In case of a particular member currency, this depended upon its weight in the ECU basket. As per Table ST3.1, the DM had 30.6 per cent weight. Its divergence limit was 1.6875% × (100 – 30.6) or 1.171125 per cent. Thus, the moment the DM fluctuated to 1.17 per cent, it was subject to intervention under the provisions of the divergence indicator. It may be mentioned that since this type of intervention was in relation to the ECU and not any single currency, it was comparatively a diversified intervention. However, when intervention failed, the very central rates were realigned. Experience has shown that during the first eight years of the EMS, there were a number of realignments, although during 1988–91, there was stability in central rates (Frankel, 1993). Again, during the closing months of 1992 that spilled over to 1993, the parity grid suffered a serious crisis but this time, the Governing Council did not favour realignment. Rather, it widened the fluctuation band to +/–15.0 per cent. Germany and the Netherlands decided bilaterally to stick to the +/–2.25 per cent fluctuation band.

Monetary Support

The third principal feature related to the credit mechanism or monetary support. The monetary support originating from the EMCF or the EMI, (now European Central Bank), had varying maturity. The very short-term credit was to assist the central banks for intervention. Short-term credit met the balance of payments deficit. Medium-term credit was meant for a medium-term balance of payments support. Besides all these, there was also a provision for medium-term financial support for fostering convergence between the economically weak and the economically strong member countries. Such credits flowed from the European Investment Bank.

TOWARDS GREATER CONVERGENCE

Delors' Plan

Exchange rate stability is the first and foremost objective of the EMU, but this objective could not be achieved completely over the years owing to the disparate economic performance in different member countries. It is true that the inflation differential had narrowed from 16 percentage points in 1980 to around 4 percentage points in 1990, but it rose again. The architects of the EMS realised that unless and until disparity in macroeconomic performance was checked, exchange rate stability could not be ensured. Disparity in macroeconomic performance could be avoided through convergence of economic policies among the member countries. In order to bring about a greater degree of convergence, the Committee for the Study of Economic and Monetary Union, 1989 put forth a three-stage plan. This was commonly known as the Delors Plan that was approved at Maastricht in February 1992 and came into force from November 1993.

The first stage, which was formally to begin from July 1990, focused on currency convertibility through removal of exchange control and through encouraging free capital movement. At least something was achieved inasmuch as controls were removed and the use of the ECU was extended. The members pulled out 10 per cent of their foreign exchange reserves to create the European Reserves Fund that could help intervention in the foreign exchange market.

The second stage, focused on institutional development began in January 1994. The European System of Central Banks (ESCB) was to be set up for the purpose of envisaging a common monetary policy. The exchange rate mechanism (ERM) was to be hardened through narrowing the exchange rate fluctuation band.

The time table for the third stage was to begin from January 1999. In the first year, budgetary coordination was to be brought about. The EMI, now the ECB was responsible for fostering monetary coordination in the then proposed framework of the Euro, the new European currency, that was created in January 1999. In the following three years, the exchange rate of member currencies was to be irrevocably pegged to one another. It was the duty of the ECB to watch over the exchange rate mechanism (ERM). From July 2002, the national currencies of the member countries were to retire in favour of the Euro.

The Delors Plan suggested a full convergence of economic and monetary policies. The Maastricht Treaty, which had envisaged a leak-proof EMU, was very specific on this issue. Before becoming a full member of the EMU, each member had to meet the following convergence criteria:

1. Nominal inflation rate was to be within 1.5 per cent above the average of the three member countries having the lowest rates
2. Long-term interest rates were to be within 2.0 per cent above the average for the three member countries having the lowest interest rates
3. The fiscal deficit was to be confined within 3.0 per cent of GDP
4. Government debt was to be confined within 60 per cent of GDP.

Greece and Sweden were struggling hard to become full members at the time of launching of Euro. Greece improved its macroeconomic fundamentals and joined the EMU on 1st January 2001. And then, a few more countries joined the EMV. Presently, the members are: Austria, Belgium, Cyprus, Estonia, Finland, France, Germany, Greece Ireland, Italy, Luxembourg, Melta, Netherlands, Portugal, Slovakia, Slovenia, and Spain.

Towards a Single Currency

The first phase: Keeping in view Delors' Plan, Euro was created in January 1999 as the currency of the EMU. It replaced ECU on a one-for-one basis. It was divided into 100 Euro cents. In the first phase, there were no notes/coins, but payments could be made through cheques and electronic device. The currency of member countries too existed side by side. The exchange rate between Euro and member country currency was fixed. One Euro was equal to: DM 1.95583, French franc 6.55957, Italian lira 1936.27, Spanish peseta 166.386, Dutch guilder 2.20371, Belgian franc 40.3399, Austrian shilling 13.7603, Portuguese escudo 200.482, Finnish Markka 5.94573, Irish pound 0.787564 and Luxembourg franc 40.3399. The exchange rate between Euro and the non-member currency was to be determined by the market forces. Initially, one Euro was equal to US $ 1.1665.

The second phase: In January 2002, Euro bank notes and coins were issued and by the end of February 2002, Euro completely replaced the members' currency. Now, there is one currency throughout the EMU and that is the Euro. Euro bank notes are issued by both the ECB and the national central banks with full understanding between them. Out of the total size of the issue, 8.0 per cent are allocated to the ECB and the remaining 92 per cent are allocated to the national central banks. The coins are minted by the national authorities.

Prospects for Euro: The Euro has some benefits but at the same time, there may be costs too. First of all, the benefits shall manifest in eliminating transaction cost that occurs at present on account of exchange of one member currency for another. Secondly, goods produced in different member countries shall be priced in a single currency that will lead to price transparency and encourage market integration. Thirdly, there will be no exchange rate changes and thereby no foreign exchange exposure in intra-Union trade. With no exchange rate exposure, intra-Union trade will expand leading to increase in capital productivity and national income. Fourthly, the existence of a single currency is expected to minimise the market imperfections that will be apparent more in financial services. In a nearly perfect financial market, number of participants will increase. All this will help develop the financial market within the Union. Fifthly, there will be no problem in the consolidation of accounts by multinational corporations operating within the Union as translation of currency will not be required. But, on the other hand, in absence of multiple currency system, the number of transactions exchanging one currency for another will reduce significantly the bankers' income.

Again, as far as the use of Euro for invoicing of trade with a third country is concerned, its success depends upon the stability of its value in the foreign exchange market and on the demand for it in international transactions. In fact, this is the reason that US dollar is invariably the currency of invoice even where the USA is not involved in the trade. If one looks at the figures, it is found that 37 per cent of the world trade was invoiced in the EU member countries' currency as against 48 per cent of the world trade invoiced in US dollar. On this basis, one can be confident about the successful use of Euro in international transactions. Moreover, there was an indication from the Bank of Japan to hold Euro as reserves. If it is followed by the central bank of other countries, Euro has a good prospect. Again, the bonds denominated in EMU member currencies accounted for around one-half of dollar-denominated bonds. Now Euro-denominated bonds are common.

However, the experience of the Euro is not very impressive. It depreciated gradually against US dollar reaching US $ 0.8252 on 26th October 2000. The reasons for the decline are perhaps the larger current account deficit in the EMU than in the USA and falling rate of industrial production in the EMU as compared to that in the USA. Nevertheless, these trends are not permanent. It showed some improvements since the year 2001. The European crisis influenced euro adversely, yet the value of euro improved and reached 0.73 per US dollar on September 14, 2011. If the macro-economic fundamentals in EMU area improve, euro shall turn still stronger.

QUESTIONS

1. How did EMS function? What were the major problems?
2. Explain the three stages of Delors' Plan.
3. Do you think Euro has bright prospects?

Review Questions

Objective-Type Questions

1. State whether true (T) or false (F):
   (a) Gold coinage was essential under gold exchange standard. ☐
   (b) Gold standard was marked with high degree of domestic price instability. ☐
   (c) Canada came under the Sterling Area during 1930s. ☐
   (d) US balance of payments deficit was the main reason behind collapse of the Bretton Woods system of exchange rate. ☐
   (e) Wider discrepancy between real and nominal exchange rates is a key feature of the floating-rate regime. ☐
2. Choose the correct answer:
   (a) SDRs are:
      (i) International reserves assets
      (ii) US currency
      (iii) none of these
   (b) The currency of the EMU members is:
      (i) under target-zone arrangement
      (ii) on crawling peg
      (iii) pegged to SDRs
   (c) Conditionality is attached to:
      (i) borrowings under the reserve tranche
      (ii) borrowings under the first instalment of the credit tranche
      (iii) subsequent borrowings
   (d) Sterilised intervention by the monetary authorities is expected to:
      (i) increase the money supply in the country
      (ii) bear no ultimate effect on the money supply
      (iii) none of these
   (e) "Fundamental disequilibrium" in the Bretton Woods system meant:
      (i) consistent balance of payments deficit
      (ii) consistent devaluation
      (iii) rising inflation rate in the country

Short-Answer Questions

1. Distinguish between:
   (a) stabilised intervention and destabilised intervention
   (b) sterilised intervention and non-sterilised intervention
   (c) leaning-with-the-wind and leaning-against-the-wind intervention
   (d) full-bodied coins and debased coins
   (e) mono-metallic and bi-metallic standard
   (f) gold specie standard, gold bullion standard and gold exchange standard

2. What is mint parity found in gold standard?
3. "Crawling peg is a compromise between fixed exchange rates and floating exchange rates." Discuss.

Long-Answer Questions

1. "Gold Standard provided price stability besides automaticity in exchange rate and BOP adjustment." Discuss.
2. Mention the broad features of the fixed parity system of exchange rate initiated by the IMF during 1940s. What were the factors responsible for its collapse by early 1970s?
3. Do you agree that floating exchange rate regime is a better option than the fixed exchange rate regime?
4. What do you mean by SDRs? Has their creation and allocation been able to improve international liquidity?
5. What are the different funding facilities through which IMF provides balance of payments support to member countries?
6. Write a note on the developments in the European Monetary Union.

REFERENCES

Akin, C. and A. Kose (2007), "Changing Nature of North-South Linkages: Stylised Facts and Explanations", *IMF Working Paper*, Washington, D.C., no. 07/280.

Bordo, M. and A. Schwartz (1991), What has Foreign Exchange Market Intervention since the Plaza Agreement Accomplished, *Open Economies Review*, II, 1, 39–64.

Connors, T.A. (1979), The Apparent Effects of Recent IMF Stabilisation Programmes, Federal Reserve System International Finance Division, Paper No. 135.

Cushman, D. (1983), The Effects of Real Exchange Rate Risk on International Trade, *Journal of International Economics*, XV, 45–64.

Dell, S. and R. Lawrence (1980), *The Balance of Payments Adjustment Process in Developing Countries*, Oxford, Pergamon Press, Chaps. 2 and 4.

Dunn, R.M. (1983), The Many Disappointments of Flexible Exchange Rates in *Essays in International Finance*, Princeton, Princeton University Press, No. 154.

Edwards, S. (1983), The Demand for International Reserves and the Exchange Rate Adjustments: The Case of LDCs: 1964–72, *Economica*, L, 269–280.

Frankel, J.A. (1993), *On Exchange Rates*, Cambridge (Mass.): MIT Press, pp. 347–359.

Frenkel, J. and M. Mussa (1980), The Efficiency of Foreign Exchange Markets and Measures of Turbulence, *American Economic Review*, LXX, 374–381.

Friedman, M. (1953), The Case for Flexible Exchange Rates in *Essays in Positive Economics*, Chicago, University of Chicago Press, pp. 157–203.

Granade, H.R. (1972), The Use of International Monetary Fund Facilities by Different Groups of Countries: 1952–71, *Southern Economic Journal*, XXXIX, 257.

IMF (1998), *International Financial Statistics*, Washington, D.C., August.

———(2003), *International Financial Statistics*, Washington, D.C.

———(2005), *Annual Report: 2004*, Washington, D.C.

Longworth, D. (1980), Canadian Intervention in Foreign Exchange Market: A Note, *Review of Economics and Statistics*, LXII, 284–287.

Loopesko, B. (1984), Relationships among Exchange Rates, Intervention and Interest Rates: An Empirical Investigation, *Journal of International Money and Finance*, III, 257–277.

MacDonald, R. (1988), *Floating Exchange Rates*, London, Unwin Hyman, pp. 5–20.

Obstfeld, M. (1983), Exchange Rates, Inflation and the Sterilisation Problem: Germany 1975–81, *European Economic Review*, XXIII, 161–189.

Reichmann, T.M. and R.T. Stillson (1978), Experience with Programmes of Balance of Payments Adjustment: Standby Arrangements in the Higher Credit Tranches: 1963–72, *IMF Staff Papers*, XXV, 293–309.

Sacchetti, U. (1979), The SDR: Ten Years of Experience, *Banca Nazionale del Lavoro Quarterly Review*, 395–405.

Sharan, V. (1985), *The International Economic Order and the Less Developed Countries*, New Delhi, Sterling Publishers, pp. 40–44.

Taylor, D. (1982), Official Intervention in the Foreign Exchange Market or Bet against the Central Bank, *Journal of Political Economy*, XC, 356–368.

Winckler, G., et al. (1996), Deficits, Debt and European Monetary Union: Some unpleasant fiscal arithmetic, University of Vienna Working Paper, No. 9615.

SUGGESTED FURTHER READING

Eichengreen, B. Ed. (1986), *The Gold Standard in Theory and History*, New York: Methuen.

IMF, *International Financial Statistics*, Washington, D.C., Annual No., latest issue.

Scammel, W.M. (1975), *International Monetary Policy: Bretton Woods and After*, New York: Wiley.

Tew, B. (1995), *Evolution of International Monetary System*, New York: Wiley.

CHAPTER 4

Exchange Rate Mechanism

Learning Objectives

In a floating-rate regime, exchange rate is determined by market forces. The present chapter thus discusses the process of its determination, although in the beginning, it acquaints the readers with the basics of how exchange rates are quoted. In particular, the chapter attempts:

- To explain how exchange rates are quoted in spot and forward markets.
- To explain the distinction between nominal, real and effective exchange rates.
- To present how demand and supply forces determine the exchange rate in spot market.
- To show how some macroeconomic variables, such as inflation rate and interest rate influence the exchange rate.
- To show how the interest rate differential influence the forward exchange rate and to evaluate the interest rate parity theory in this context.
- To show how covered/uncovered interest arbitrage takes place when interest rate differential is not equal to forward rate differential.
- To examine different theories of the exchange rate behaviour.

In Chapter 3, we discussed different forms of the exchange rate regime ranging from the gold standard to the adjustable peg under the Bretton Woods system and to the independent and managed floating and target-zone arrangement in recent decades. Since major currencies dominating the international financial and foreign exchange market today are on float, their value is subject to variations depending upon changes in macroeconomic variables and market forces. The present chapter discusses the determination of exchange rate that is of utmost significance for a floating-rate regime and especially for those who deal in foreign exchange. However, in the beginning, let us understand the fundamentals of exchange rate quotation, so that we may better understand the exchange rate determination process.

EXCHANGE RATE QUOTATIONS

In a foreign exchange market where different currencies are bought and sold, it is essential to know the ratio between different currencies; or how many units of one currency will equal one unit of another currency. The ratio between two currencies is known as an *exchange rate.* The various exchange rates are regularly quoted in newspapers and periodicals.

Direct and Indirect Quote

The methods for quoting exchange rates are both direct and indirect. A *direct quote* gives the home-currency price of a certain amount of foreign currency, usually one or 100 units. If India quotes the exchange rate between the rupee and the US dollar in a direct way, the quotation will be written as ₹ 35/US $. On the other hand, in case of indirect quoting, the value of one unit of home currency is presented in terms of foreign currency. If India adopts indirect quotation, the banks in India will quote the exchange rate as US $ 0.02857/₹.

> Direct quote places domestic currency on the numerator of the quote. Indirect quote is just the opposite.

If the quotation is published in a third country to which neither of the two currencies belongs, the usual practice is to put the stronger currency on the numerator. For example, if the US dollar—Indian rupee rate is published in London, it will be quoted as US $ 0.02857/₹. In practice, the method of quotation varies from one market to another. Continental European dealers normally use the direct quote, while the indirect quote is used in London. Both methods are in use in the USA.

PROBLEM 4.1

If direct quote is ₹ 45/US $, how can this exchange rate be presented under indirect quote?

Solution

US $ 1/₹ 45 = US $ 0.0222/₹.

PROBLEM 4.2

If indirect quote is US $ 0.025/₹, how can this exchange rate be shown under direct quote?

Solution

₹ 1/US $ 0.025 = ₹ 40/US $.

Buying and Selling Rates

Normally, two rates are published—one being the buying rate and the other the selling rate. The buying rate is also known as the *bid rate.* The selling rate is known as the ask rate or offer rate. The bid rate is always given first, followed by the ask rate quote. If the rupee-US dollar rate is ₹ 40.00–40.30/US $, then the former is the buying rate and the latter the selling rate. In other words, the buying rate is the rate at which the banks purchase a foreign currency from the customer. Suppose, in India, a customer exchanges the US dollar for the rupee, the bank will buy the US dollar at the buying rate, which is at ₹ 40.00 a dollar. The selling rate, on the other hand, is the rate at which the banks sell foreign currency to their customers. For example, a bank in India selling one US dollar to a customer, will charge the selling rate, that is ₹ 40.30 per US dollar. Since the banks need to make a profit in these transactions, the selling quote is higher than the buying rate. The difference between these two quotes forms the banks' profit and is known as the *spread.* In the above example, the spread is ₹ 0.30 per US dollar. The bid-ask spread is often stated in percentage terms that can be computed as follows:

> Buying quote of a currency denotes the rate at which banks buy it; selling quote at which banks sell it.

$$\text{Spread} = (\text{Ask price} - \text{Bid price})/\text{Ask price} \times 100 \quad (4.1)$$

Thus in the above example,

$$\text{Spread} = (40.30 - 40.00)/40.30 \times 100 = 0.744\%$$

The size of spread in respect of a currency depends upon many factors, like its strength, the type of transaction, and its supply and demand position with the transacting bank. The spread is smaller in a widely traded currency because it is easy for the banks to transact in such a currency. In a scarcely traded currency, the banks have to face some difficulty, and hence the spread is large. Again, for individuals and firms, the spread is bigger than for banks. An individual and a firm buy a foreign currency at a higher rate and sell at a rate lower than that quoted in the newspapers, although in big transactions, they get some relief. Similarly, if the bank is temporarily short of a foreign currency, the spread will be larger particularly if the demand for that foreign currency is high. On the contrary, if the supply position of that foreign currency is comfortable, the spread will be lower.

PROBLEM 4.3

Consider the following bid-ask prices: ₹ 40–40.50/US $. Find the bid-ask spread.

Solution

$$(40.50 - 40.00)/40.50 = 0.0123 \text{ or } 1.23\%$$

PROBLEM 4.4

Find out the bid rate if ask rate is ₹ 40.50/US $ and the bid-ask spread is 1.23%.

Solution

$$(40.50 - x)/40.50 = 0.0123$$

or $$40.50 - x = 0.0123 \times 40.50$$

or $$40.50 - 0.50 = x$$

or $$x = 40.00.$$

Forward Market Quotation

The quotes for the forward market are also published in the newspapers and periodicals. The quoting rates may be expressed as outright quotes, or as swap quotes. The outright quote for the US dollar in terms of the rupee can be written for different periods of forward contract as follows:

Spot	*One month*	*Three months*
₹ 40.00–40.30	₹ 39.80–40.20	₹ 39.60–40.10

The swap quote, on the other hand, expresses only the difference between the spot quote and the forward quote. It can be written as follows:

Spot	*One month*	*Three months*
₹ 40.00–30	₹ (20)–(10)	₹ (40)–(20)

It may be noted that decimals are not written in swap quotes.

EXCHANGE RATE QUOTATION: The Value of Different Currencies in Terms of INR

Currency	To Rupees	From Rupees	%
Australian Dollar	55.558	0.01800	–0.33%
Bahraini Dinar	223.68	0.004471	0.02%
British Pound	109.00	0.009174	–0.17%
Canadian Dollar	60.542	0.01652	–0.29%
Euro	90.836	0.01101	–0.20%
Fijian Dollar	37.408	0.02673	–0.20%
Kuwaiti Dinar	274.67	0.003641	0.08%
Malaysian Ringgit	19.378	0.05160	0.02%
Mauritian Rupee	1.8239	0.5483	0.02%
Omani Rial	218.73	0.004572	0.02%
Philippine Peso	1.4406	0.6941	–0.05%
US Dollar	84.102	0.01189	0.02%
Sri Lankan Rupee	0.2858	3.4990	–0.38%

Source: www.rupeerates.in, October,2024

Forward Premium and Discount

In the above quotes, it is found that the longer the maturity, the greater is the change in the forward rates. Again, with longer maturity, the spread too gets wider. This is because of uncertainty in the future that increases with lengthening of maturity. The change in forward rates may be upwards or downwards. With such movements, disparity arises between spot and forward rates. This is known as the *swap* or *forward rate differential*.

Forward rate differential represents the difference of forward and spot rates divided by spot rate shown in terms of annualised percentage.

If the forward rate is lower than the spot rate, it will be a case of forward discount. On the contrary, if the forward rate is higher than the spot rate, it would be known as *forward premium*. Forward premium or discount is expressed as an annualised percentage deviation from the spot rate. It is computed as follows:

$$\text{Forward premium (discount)} = \frac{n\text{-day forward rate} - \text{spot rate}}{\text{spot rate}} \times \frac{360}{n} \qquad (4.2)$$

where n is the length of forward contract expressed in number of days.

Applying the above example of a one-month forward quotation, we get

$$\frac{39.80 - 40.00}{40.00} \times \frac{360}{30} = -0.06 \text{ or 6 per cent forward discount.}$$

PROBLEM 4.5

Find out the forward rate differential if spot rate of US $ is ₹ 45.00 and one- month forward rate is ₹ 45.80.

Solution

360/30 {(45.80 – 45.00)/45.00} × 100 = 21.33 per cent. It will be known as a forward premium as the value of US dollar has increased.

PROBLEM 4.6

Find the one-month forward rate of US dollar if spot rate is ₹ 45.00 and the forward premium is 12 per cent.

Solution

$$\frac{360}{30}\left\{\frac{x - 45.00}{45.00}\right\} = 0.12$$

or $$(x - 45) = 0.12 \times 45 \times \frac{30}{360}$$

or $$x = 45 + 0.45 \text{ or } x = 45.45$$

Cross Rates

Sometimes the value of a currency in terms of another one is not known directly. In such cases, one currency is sold for a common currency; and again, the common currency is exchanged for the desired currency. This is known as *cross rate trading* and the rate established between the two currencies is known as the *cross rate*. Suppose, a newspaper quotes ₹ 35.00–35.20/ US $; and at the same time, it quotes Canadian $ 0.76–0.78/US $ but does not quote the exchange rate between the rupee and the Canadian dollar. Thus the rate of exchange between the rupee and the Canadian dollar will be found through the common currency, the US dollar. The technique is similar for both spot and forward cross rates.

Cross exchange rate between two currencies is found out through their value in a common currency.

Spot cross rates

The selling rate of the Canadian dollar in India can be worked out by selling the rupee for the US dollar at ₹ 35.20/US $ and then buying Canadian dollars with the US dollar at C$ 0.76/US $. This means

₹ 35.20/US $ 1 × US $ 1/C$ 0.76 = ₹ 46.32/C$

The buying rate of the Canadian dollar in India can be found through buying the Indian rupee for the US dollar at ₹ 35.00/US $ and selling the Canadian dollar for US dollar at C$ 0.78/US $. This means that

₹ 35.00/US $ 1 × US $ 1/C$ 0.78 = ₹ 44.87/C$

Combining the two, we get

₹ 44.87–46.32/C$

Forward cross rate

In this case too, the selling rate of one currency is divided by the buying rate of another currency and vice versa. Suppose, one month forward rate in case of the two currencies is ₹ 34.50–34.80/US $ and C$ 0.79–0.83/US $. The forward rate of the Canadian dollar in terms of the rupee can be found as

₹ 34.80/C$ 0.79 = ₹ 44.05/C$
₹ 34.50/C$ 0.83 = ₹ 41.57

Combining the two, we get ₹ 41.57–44.05/C$.

PROBLEM 4.7

Find ₹/Euro exchange rate if: the two exchange rates are: ₹ 43.93–43.95/US $ and Euro 0.83–0.84/US $

Solution

Bid rate = ₹ 43.93/0.84 = ₹ 52.30
Ask rate = ₹ 43.95/0.83 = ₹ 52.95
= ₹ 52.30–52.95/Euro

NOMINAL, REAL AND EFFECTIVE EXCHANGE RATES

Nominal and Real Exchange Rates

The exchange rates mentioned in the preceding section are the nominal exchange rates/bilateral exchange rates. They represent the ratio between the value of two currencies at a particular point of time. The real exchange rate, on the other hand, is the price-adjusted nominal exchange rate. The relationship between nominal exchange rate, e and the real exchange rate, e_r can be written in the form:

Real exchange rate is the inflation-adjusted nominal exchange rate.

$$e_r = eP/P^* \quad (4.3)$$

where P and P^* are domestic and foreign price indices. If the price index in India and the USA rises from 100 in 2021 to 120 and 110, respectively in 2024 and if the nominal exchange rate between the two currencies between the two dates remains at ₹ 40/US $, the real exchange rate will move to:

40.00 × 120/110 = ₹ 43.64/US $

In a floating-rate regime, as discussed in Chapter 3, the nominal exchange rate moves automatically with a change in the price level. But in a fixed-rate regime, it does not happen so because the rate is administered. As a result, there arises a gap between the nominal exchange rate and the real exchange rate.

PROBLEM 4.8

The administered exchange rate in India was ₹ 7.91/US $ during 2015–24. The price index in India and the USA rose by 67 per cent and 26 per cent respectively. Find out whether there was any change in real exchange rate during this period.

Solution

There was no change in the nominal exchange rate as it was an administered one. But there was change in the real exchange rate depending on the price level differential. The change in real exchange rate = ₹ 7.91 × 167/126 = ₹ 10.48/US $.

PROBLEM 4.9

The spot exchange rate between Indian rupee and US dollar in 2020 was ₹ 30/US $ when the price index in both the countries was 100. By 2024, rupee was devalued to ₹ 45/US $ and at the same time, the price index moved up during this period in India and USA to 110 and 125 respectively. Find out the extent of change in nominal and real exchange rates.

Solution

Change in nominal exchange rate:

US dollar appreciated by (45 – 30)/30 = 50 per cent during the period.

Change in real exchange rate:

In 2020 there was no difference in the real and nominal exchange rate inasmuch as the price index was the same in both the countries. But in 2024, the real exchange rate moved to:

₹ 45 × (110/125) = ₹ 39.60/US $

The real exchange rate changed only by 32 per cent compared to 50 per cent change in the nominal exchange rate. This is because of disparate growth in the price level in the two countries.

If the domestic currency depreciates more than the rise in inflation rate differential, it simply means a rise in the real exchange rate. The movement in the real exchange rate this way indicates the country's competitive position in the international commodity market. At the macro-level, a rise in the real exchange rate tends to improve the country's balance of trade. In fact, it is based the elasticity approach explaining the adjustment in the balance of trade. At the micro-level, any rise in the real exchange rate helps improve the cash flows and thereby the value of the firm.

Effective Exchange Rates

It is possible that the Indian rupee tends to depreciate against US dollar, but it appreciates against Japanese Yen. It is also possible that rupee depreciates vis-à-vis different currencies at different rates. So it is essential to develop an index or a summary measure of how rupee fares, on an average, in the foreign exchange market. Such an index is called an *effective exchange rate*. In other words, effective exchange rate is the measure of the average value of a currency relative to two or more other currencies. The relationship between an effective exchange rate and the nominal exchange rate is similar to that between the general price index and the price of an individual commodity.

> Effective exchange rate is the measure of the average value of a currency relative to two or more other currencies, normally shown in form of an index.

For the construction of an effective exchange rate index, the first step is to select the currency for the basket, for it is not feasible to include all the currencies of the world. Only those currencies are included that matter significantly in the country's trade. The second step is to find out the weight of different currencies in the basket. This is because different currencies do not carry the same importance. If India' largest trading partner is USA, the US dollar should be assigned the largest weight. Suppose India has trade link with only two countries, viz. USA and Japan. India's exports to USA and Japan value, respectively, $ 6,000 and $ 4,000, and its imports from these two countries value, respectively, $ 7,000 and $ 3,000. The weight for these two countries will be:

$$\text{USA} = (6{,}000 + 7{,}000)/[(6{,}000 + 7{,}000) + (4{,}000 + 3{,}000)] = 0.65$$
$$\text{Japan} = (4{,}000 + 3{,}000)/[(4{,}000 + 3{,}000) + (6{,}000 + 7{,}000)] = 0.35$$

The third step in this process is to find out the exchange rate index. Suppose, in 1998, the exchange rate was ₹ 40/US $ and ₹ 50/Yen 100; in 2001, the exchange rate changed to ₹ 44/US $ and ₹ 60/Yen 100. If 1998 is the base, the exchange rate index in 2001 will be 110 for the US dollar and 120 for Yen.

If the effective exchange rate index for 1998 is

$$EER_{1998} = [(0.65 \times 100) + (0.35 \times 100)] = 100,$$

Then the effective exchange rate index for 2001 will be

$$EER_{2001} = [(0.65 \times 110) + (0.35 \times 120)] = 113.5$$

This means the rupee depreciated on an average by 13.5 per cent during the period.

So far we have discussed the nominal effective exchange rate. Sometimes the real effective exchange rate is also shown. In the calculation of real effective exchange rate, the same process is applied with the exception that the real exchange rate is taken into account. In other words, the real effective exchange rate is based on real bilateral exchange rates, while the nominal effective exchange rate is based on nominal bilateral exchange rates.

PROBLEM 4.10

The USA, EU and Japan are India's biggest trade partners sharing 40 per cent, 35 per cent and 25 per cent of its trade respectively. Assuming 2019–20 as the base year, when the exchange rates were ₹ 45.68/US $, ₹ 41.48/Euro and ₹ 0.414/Yen. These rates changed over the years and in 2023–24, they were as: ₹ 43.91/US $, ₹ 52.67/Euro and ₹ 0.408/Yen. Find out the effective exchange rate index during 2023–24.

Solution

Exchange rate index:

(i) ₹ appreciated against Dollar to 43.91/45.68 × 100 = 96.13
(ii) ₹ depreciated against Euro to 52.67/41.48 × 100 = 126.98
(iii) ₹ appreciated against Yen to 0.408/0.414 × 100 = 98.55

$$0.40 \times 96.13 + 0.35 \times 126.98 + 0.25 \times 98.55 = 107.53$$

The effective exchange rate index in 2023–24 will be 107.53 against 100 in 2019–20.

DETERMINATION OF EXCHANGE RATE IN THE SPOT MARKET

The exchange rate between two currencies in a floating-rate regime is determined by the interplay of demand and supply forces. The exchange rate between, say, the rupee and the US dollar depends upon the demand for the US dollar and its availability or supply in the Indian foreign exchange market. The demand for foreign currency comes from individuals and firms who have to make payments in foreign currency mostly on account of import of goods and services and purchase of securities. The supply of foreign exchange results from the receipt of foreign currency normally on account of export or sale of financial securities to foreign entities.

In Figure 4.1, the exchange rate designated by the price of the US dollar (foreign currency) in terms of the rupee, is shown on the vertical axis, and the supply of, and demand for, the US dollar is shown on the horizontal axis. The demand curve slopes downward to the right because the higher the value of the US dollar, the costlier are the Indian imports and the importers curtail the demand for imports and consequently the demand for foreign currency falls. Similarly, a higher value of the US dollar makes Indian export cheaper and thereby stimulates the demand for export. The supply of the US dollar increases in the form of export earnings and the supply curve of the US dollar moves upward to the right with a rise in its value. The equilibrium exchange rate is reached where the supply curve intersects the demand curve at Q_1. This rate as shown in the figure is ₹ 40/US $.

If demand for import rises owing to some factors at home, the demand for the US dollar will rise to *D*′ and intersect the supply at Q_2, the exchange rate will then be ₹ 42/US $. But if export rises as a result of decline in the value of the rupee and the supply of the dollar increases to *S*′, the exchange rate will again be ₹ 40/US $. Quite evidently, the frequent shifts in the demand and supply conditions cause the exchange rate to also adjust frequently to a new equilibrium.

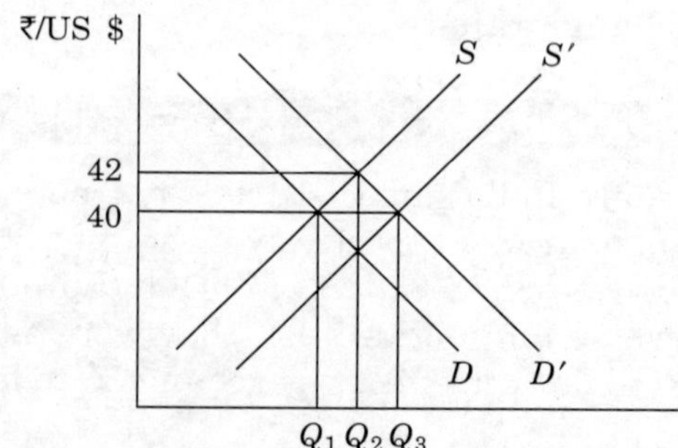

FIGURE 4.1 Exchange Rate Determination.

FACTORS INFLUENCING EXCHANGE RATE

Flow of Funds on the Current and Capital Accounts

A country with current account deficit experiences a depreciation of its currency. It is because there is demand for foreign currency to make payment for imports.

On the contrary, a current account surplus country possesses a large supply of foreign exchange with the result that the country experiences an appreciation of its currency. An apposite example of current account deficit country is the USA whose trade deficit was one of the important causes for depreciation in dollar during the post-2002 years. On the other hand, the currency of Japan and Switzerland appreciated in view of surplus current account. However, the current account alone is not responsible for this state of affairs. Capital account flows help change the situation. Larger inflow on the capital account leads to an appreciation of the currency. The Indian case is an apposite example. Rupee appreciated in 2007 because of large inflow of foreign investment and depreciated when FIIs' net disinvestment was large during 2008. There are countries, such as Australia, Britain, Iceland and New Zealand that experienced greater appreciation in their currency in the first half of 2008 even after having large deficits on their current account relatively to Japan and Switzerland that witnessed surpluses on their current account and, at the same time, smaller appreciation in their currency. In fact, this paradox is the result of carry trade that explains why trade flows are dwarfed by capital flows on account of interest rate differential.

Impact of Inflation

It is normally the inflation rate differential between the two countries that influences the exchange rate between the two currencies. The influence of inflation rate finds a nice explanation in the *Purchasing Power Parity* (*PPP*) *theory* (Cassel, 1921; Officer, 1976). This theory suggests that at any given time, the rate of exchange between two currencies is determined by their purchasing power. If e is the exchange rate and P_A and P_B are the purchasing power of two currencies, A and B, the equation can be written as

> PPP theory shows exchange rate determined by the purchasing power of the two currencies.

$$e = P_A / P_B \quad (4.4)$$

Prior to 1914, the purchasing power of a unit of a currency was reckoned in terms of gold. The principle applies even today, but now it is reckoned in terms of tradable commodities. As a corollary, a country experiencing higher inflation will experience a corresponding depreciation of its currency, while a country with a lower inflation rate will experience an appreciation in the value of its currency. In fact, this theory is based on the *theory of one price* in which domestic price of any good equals its foreign price quoted in the same currency. For instance, if the exchange rate is ₹ 2/US $, the price of a particular commodity, if it is ₹ 100 in India, must be US $ 50 in the USA. In other words,

> Theory of one price explains how domestic price of a product equates its foreign price quoted in the same currency.

US $ price of a commodity × price of US $ = ₹ price of the commodity (4.5)

If inflation in one country causes a temporary deviation from the equilibrium, arbitrageurs will begin operating and, as a result, equilibrium will be restored through changes in the exchange rate. Suppose the price of a commodity soars in India to ₹ 125, the arbitrageurs will buy that commodity in the USA and sell it in India to earn a profit of ₹ 25. This will go on till the exchange rate moves to ₹ 2.5/US $ and the profit potential of arbitrage is eliminated.

The exchange rate adjustment as a sequel to inflation may be further explained. Thus if the Indian commodity turns costlier, its export will fall. At the same time, the import price being cheaper, its import from the USA will expand. Higher import will raise the demand for the US dollar in turn raising its value vis-à-vis the rupee.

However, this version of the theory, which is known as the *absolute version*, holds good if the same commodities are included in the same proportion in the domestic market basket and the world market basket. If it is not, PPP theory will not hold good despite the law of one price holding good. Moreover, this theory does not cover the non-traded goods and services where transaction cost is significant.

PROBLEM 4.11

Explain on the basis of the following data: whether
(a) Absolute version of PPP theory holds good
(b) Law of one price holds good

USA			*India*		
Unit	Goods	US $ Price/Unit	Unit	Goods	₹, Price/Unit
4	Rice	1	20	Rice	40
20	Wheat	2	10	Wheat	80

Exchange rate ₹ 40/US $

Solution

The law of one price holds good because:

₹ 40/US $ = ₹ 80/US $ 2 = ₹ 40/US $ 1.

But the absolute version of PPP theory does not hold good as the weight of the two commodities in total consumption basket in the two countries is different. For PPP theory, one has to weight the price of each commodity by its share in the total consumption basket in the country. The dollar value of goods in USA is:

$$4 \times 1 + 20 \times 2 = 44$$

Now the share of rice in US consumption basket is: $(4 \times 1)/44 = 0.0909$ and the share of wheat in USA is $(20 \times 2)/44 = 0.9091$.

Thus the price level in USA is: $1 \times 0.0909 + 2 \times 0.9091 = \$\ 1.9091$

Similarly in India:

The share of rice is $(20 \times 40)/1600 = 0.5$ and the share of wheat is $(10 \times 80)/1600 = 0.5$. And on this basis, the price level in India will be:

$$40 \times 0.5 + 80 \times 0.5 = ₹\ 60.$$

As a result, the exchange rate will be ₹ 60/US $ 1.9091 = ₹ 31.43/US $ which is not equal to ₹ 40/US $. Hence the absolute version of PPP theory does not hold good.

In view of the above limitation, another version of this theory has evolved which is known as the *relative version* of the *PPP theory*. The *relative version* states that a change in exchange rate that would retain the original level of relative price of tradable to non-tradable goods in the economy, would establish an equilibrium exchange rate. It further states that the exchange rate between currencies of any two countries should be a constant multiple of the general price indices prevailing in them. In other words, percentage change in exchange rate should equal the percentage change in the ratio of price indices in the two countries. To put it as an equation,

$$e_t/e_0 = (1 + I_A)^t/(1 + I_B)^t \tag{4.6}$$

where I_A and I_B are the rates of inflation in country A and country B, e_0 is the value of A's currency in terms of one unit of B's currency in the beginning of the period, and e_t is the spot exchange rate in period t.

For example, inflation rate in India is 5 per cent and that in USA 3 per cent, and if the initial exchange rate is ₹ 40/US \$, the value of the rupee in a two-year period will be

$$e_2 = 40(1.05/1.03)^2$$

or

₹ 41.57/US \$

PROBLEM 4.12

If exchange rate at the end of 2004–05 is ₹ 43.91/US \$ and if the rate of inflation in India and USA during 2005–06 is respectively 7 per cent and 4 per cent. Find:

(i) inflation rate differential between the two countries, and
(ii) the exchange rate at the end of 2005–06.

Solution

Inflation rate differential between India and USA:

$$(1.07/1.04) - 1 = 0.0288 = 2.88 \text{ per cent}$$

Exchange rate at the end of 2005–06:

$$(1.07/1.04) \times 43.91 = 45.18$$

₹ 45.18/US \$.

Such an inflation-adjusted rate is known as the *real exchange rate*. This means that if the real exchange rate is constant, currency gains or losses from nominal exchange rate changes will be offset by the difference in relative rates of inflation. Sometimes when a government sticks to a particular exchange rate without caring for prevailing inflation, a gap emerges between the real and the nominal exchange rates which results in lowering of export competitiveness and in turn, the trade deficit. This is why, this theory suggests that a country with high rate of inflation should devalue its currency relative to the currency of the countries with lower inflation rates. Again, it is the real exchange rate, and not the nominal exchange rate, that has a bearing on the performance of the economy.

The theory holds good only if:

- Changes in the economy originate from the monetary sector,
- Relative price structure remains stable in different sectors; since changes in the relative prices of various goods and services may lead to differently constructed indices to deviate from each other, and
- There is no structural change in the economy, such as changes in tariff, in technology, and in autonomous capital flow.

Again, if the difference of inflation rate between the two countries is small, its effect on competitiveness may be offset by other factors, such as balance of payments performance, development in real income, and interest-rate differential, etc. As a result, comparison of inflation rates may not explain changes in exchange rates.

A number of studies have tested empirically the two versions of the PPP theory. The absolute version has been tested by Isard (1977) and McKinnon (1979). Both of them find violation of the theory in the short run, but in the long run, they find the theory holding good to some extent. As regards the relative version, the studies made till the early 1980s found normally relationship existing between rate of inflation and exchange rate, especially in the long run (Aliber and Stickney, 1975; Dornbusch, 1976; Mussa, 1982). But subsequent studies find clear-cut violation of the theory also in the long run (Adler and Lehmann, 1983; Edison, 1985). Taylor (1988) finds very little evidence for PPP to hold good. In a review of 14 cases, MacDonald (1988) finds that in 10 cases, the theory is not applicable even in the long run, but in four cases it holds good.

Primarily, there are three factors why the PPP theory does not hold good in real life. *Firstly*, the assumptions of this theory do not hold good in real life. *Secondly*, extraneous factors such as interest rates, governmental interference, etc. influence the exchange rate. In the early 1990s, for instance, some of the European countries experienced higher inflation rates than the USA, but their currencies did not depreciate against the dollar because their high interest rates attracted capital from the USA. *Thirdly*, when no domestic substitute to an import is available, the material is imported even after the prices go higher in the exporting countries.

Interest Rate

Experts differ on how changes in interest rate influence the exchange rate. The flexible price version of the monetary theory explains that any rise in domestic interest rate lowers the demand for money, and the lower demand for money in relation to the supply of money causes depreciation in the value of domestic currency. The sticky price version of the monetary theory has a different explanation which is that a rise in interest rate increases the supply of loanable funds which leads to greater supply of money and a depreciation in domestic currency. At the same time, however, it shares the views with the balance of payments approach where a higher interest rate at home than in a foreign country attracts capital from abroad in lure of higher return and the inflow of foreign currency results in increase of the supply of foreign currency and raises the value of domestic currency.

However, Fisher suggests, this proposition cannot be thought of in isolation of inflation, inasmuch as inflation negates the return on capital to be received. If the interest rate is 10 per cent and the rate of inflation is 10 per cent, the real return on capital would be zero. This is because the gain in the form of interest is cancelled out by the loss on account of inflation. In fact, since it was Irving Fisher who decomposed nominal interest into two parts—the real interest rate and the expected rate of inflation, the relationship between these two elements is known as the *Fisher Effect*.

Fisher Effect explains that nominal interest rate is the amalgam of real interest rate and inflation rate.

The Fisher effect states that whenever an investor thinks of an investment, he is interested in a particular nominal interest rate which covers both the expected inflation and the required real interest rate. Mathematically, it can be expressed as

$$1 + r = (1 + a)(1 + I) \tag{4.7}$$

where

r = nominal interest rate,
a = real interest rate, and
I = expected rate of inflation.

Suppose the required real interest rate is 4 per cent and the expected rate of inflation is 10 per cent, the required nominal interest rate will be:

$$1.04 \times 1.10 - 1 = 14.4\%$$

Suppose, the interest rate in the USA is 4 per cent and the inflation rate in India is 10 per cent higher than in the USA. A US investor will be tempted to invest in India only when the nominal interest in India is more than 14.4 per cent.

PROBLEM 4.13

If real interest rate is 5 per cent and the inflation rate is 8 per cent, what would be the nominal interest rate?

Solution

$$1.05 \times 1.08 - 1 = 0.134 = 13.4 \text{ per cent}$$

PROBLEM 4.14

Find the real interest rate if nominal interest rate is 10.0 per cent and rate of inflation is 4.0 per cent.

Solution

$$1.10/1.04 - 1 = 0.0577 = 5.77 \text{ per cent}$$

PROBLEM 4.15

Find the rate of inflation if nominal and real interest rates are respectively 15 per cent and 5 per cent.

Solution

$$1.15/1.05 - 1 = 0.0952 = 9.52 \text{ per cent}$$

The concept of real interest rate applies to all investment—domestic and foreign. An investor invests in a foreign country if the real interest rate differential is likely to be in his favour, but when such a differential exists, arbitrage begins in the form of international capital flow that ultimately equals the real interest rate across countries. For instance, if the real interest rate is 5 per cent in India and it is 4 per cent in the USA, capital will begin flowing from the USA to India. In the USA, the declining volume of capital will raise the real interest rate, while the increasing volume of capital in India will push down the interest rate. The capital flow will continue till the real interest rate in the two countries becomes equal. This means that the process of arbitrage helps equate the real interest rate across countries, and since the real interest rate is equal in different countries, the country with higher nominal interest rate must be facing a higher rate of inflation.

For this type of arbitrage, however, it is necessary that the capital market be homogeneous throughout the world so that the investors do not differentiate between the domestic capital market and the foreign capital markets. In real life, such homogeneous capital market is not found in view of government restrictions and varying economic policies in different countries. As a result, interest rates vary among countries. Mishkin (1984) confirms this view and finds that investors have a strong liking for the domestic capital market in order to insulate themselves from foreign exchange risk; and so, there will be no arbitrage even if real interest rate on foreign securities is higher. Again, the Fisher effect holds good normally in case of short-maturity government securities and very seldom in other cases (Abdullah, 1986).

The empirical tests present different results. Gibson (1970, 1972) and Fama and Schwert (1977) find the result in favour of the Fisher effect; while the studies of Mishkin (1984) and Cumby and Obstfeld (1984) do not support it.

Combined Effect of Interest Rate and Inflation

There is also Fisher's open proposition, known as the *International Fisher Effect* or generalised version of the Fisher effect. It is a combination of the conditions of the PPP theory and Fisher's closed proposition. It may be recalled that the PPP theory suggests that exchange rate is determined by the inflation rate differentials, while the latter states that the nominal interest rate is higher in a country with higher inflation rate. Combining these two propositions, the International Fisher effect states that the interest rate differential shall equal the inflation rate differential. It can be written as

> International Fisher Effect suggests that interest rate differential is equal to the inflation rate differential.

$$\left(\frac{1+r_A}{1+r_B}\right)=\left(\frac{1+I_A}{1+I_B}\right) \qquad (4.8)$$

The rationale behind this proposition is that an investor likes to hold assets denominated in currencies expected to depreciate only when the interest rate on those assets is high enough to compensate the loss on account of depreciating exchange rate. As a corollary, an investor holds assets denominated in currencies expected to appreciate even at a lower rate of interest because the expected capital gain on account of exchange rate appreciation will make up the loss on yield on account of low interest.

The equality between interest rate differential and inflation rate differential can be explained with the help of the following example. Suppose, India is expecting 8 per cent inflation rate during the next one year as compared to 3 per cent inflation rate in the USA. If the exchange rate in the beginning of the year is ₹ 40/US \$, the value of the rupee will fall vis-à-vis the US dollar at the end of the period to:

₹ 40(1.08/1.03) = ₹ 41.94/US \$

Suppose further that at the beginning of the period, interest rate in India is 7 per cent as against 4 per cent in the USA. At the end of the period, interest rate in India will rise to an extent that will equate approximately the inflation rate differential. In order to find out the change in interest rate, the following equation may be applied:

$$e_t/e_0 = 1 + r_{IND}/1 + r_{USA} \quad (4.9)$$

Basing on the above equation, we have

$$41.94/40 = (1 + r_{IND})/1.04$$

or $$1 + r_{IND} = 1.09$$

or $$r_{IND} = 0.09 \text{ or } 9\%$$

If the rate of interest in India rises to 9 per cent, the interest rate differential between the two countries will be: 1.09/1.04 or 4.81 per cent which will be approximately equal to the inflation rate differential which is 1.08/1.03 or 4.85 per cent.

PROBLEM 4.16

If the rate of inflation in India and the USA is 7 per cent and 4 per cent respectively and if interest rate in the USA is 6 per cent, find the interest rate in India.

Solution

$$1.07/1.04 = 1 + x/1.06$$

or $$1 + x = 1.07/1.04 \times 1.06$$

or $$x = 0.0906 = 9.06\%$$

PROBLEM 4.17

If interest rate in India and the USA is 9.06 per cent and 6 per cent and if spot exchange rate is ₹ 43.91/US $, find the exchange rate during the next year.

Solution

1.0906/1.06 × 43.91 = ₹ 45.18/US $.

Intervention by Monetary Authorities

When the market forces do not influence the exchange rate in the country's favour, then its monetary authorities intervene in the foreign exchange market through buying and selling of foreign currency and influence the exchange rate. The mechanism of intervention has been explained in Chapter 3 and readers are advised to refer to that portion of the discussion.

Participants' Psyche and Bandwagon Effect

Yet the other factor influencing the exchange rate is the psychology of the participants in the foreign exchange market. When a speculator being dominant in the foreign exchange market expects a drop in the value of a particular currency, he begins selling it forward. The other speculators follow the lead. Ultimately, the currency depreciates even if the inflation and interest rates are in a position to push up the value of the currency. In fact, this factor played a crucial role in the depreciation of British pound in 1992 and of rupee during the closing months of 1997.

EXCHANGE RATE DETERMINATION IN FORWARD MARKET

Forward exchange rate is normally not equal to the spot rate. The size of forward premium or discount depends mainly on the current expectation of future events. Such expectations determine the trend of the future spot rate towards appreciation or depreciation and thereby determine the forward rate that is equal to, or close to, the future spot rate. Suppose, the dollar is expected to depreciate, then holders of dollars will start selling forward. These actions will help depress the forward rate of the dollar. On the contrary, when the dollar is expected to appreciate, the holders will buy it forward and the forward rate will improve.

The determination of exchange rate in a forward market finds an important place in the theory of Interest Rate Parity (IRP). It is, therefore, relevant to explain this theory and how it helps in exchange rate determination in a forward market and how the arbitrageurs behave when the forward rate differential is not equal to the interest rate differential.

Interest Rate Parity Theory

The IRP theory states that equilibrium is achieved when the forward rate differential is approximately equal to the interest rate differential. In other words, forward rate differs from the spot rate by an amount that represents the interest rate differential. In this process, the currency of a country with lower interest rate should be at a forward premium in relation to the currency of a country with higher interest rate.

IRP theory suggests that forward rate differential is approximately equal to the interest rate differential. It thus helps determine forward exchange rate.

Equating forward rate differential as per Eq. (4.2) with interest rate differential as shown in Eq. (4.8), we find that

$$A \times (n\text{-day } F - S)/S = (1 + r_A)/(1 + r_B) - 1 \tag{4.10}$$

Determination of Forward Exchange Rate

On the basis of the IRP theory, the forward exchange rate can easily be determined. One has simply to find out the value of forward rate (F) in Eq. (4.10). The equation can be re-written as

$$F = \frac{S}{A}\left\{\frac{1+r_A}{1+r_B} - 1\right\} + S \tag{4.11}$$

Suppose interest rates in India and the USA are respectively 10 per cent and 7 per cent. The spot rate is ₹ 40/US \$. The 90-day forward rate can be calculated thus,

$$F = \frac{40}{4}\left\{\frac{1.10}{1.07} - 1\right\} + 40$$

or

$$F = ₹\ 40.28/\text{US } \$$$

This means that the higher interest rate in India will push down the forward value of the rupee from 40 to 40.28 a dollar.

PROBLEM 4.18

Calculate the 3-month forward rate, if spot rate is ₹ 46/US $; interest rate in India and the USA is respectively 6 per cent and 3 per cent.

Solution

Applying the interest rate parity theorem,

$$\text{3-month forward rate} = 46/360/90[(1.06/1.03) - 1] + 46$$
$$= ₹\ 46.34/\text{US}\ \$.$$

Covered Interest Arbitrage

If the forward rate differential is not equal to the interest rate differential, covered interest arbitrage will begin and it will continue till the two differentials become approximately equal. In other words, a positive interest rate differential in a country is offset by annualised forward discount. A negative interest rate differential is offset by an annualised forward premium. Finally, the two differentials will be equal. In fact, this is the point where the forward rate is determined.

> Covered interest arbitrage involves borrowing and lending in two markets and also buying spot and selling forward the respective currencies so as to attain parity conditions.

To explain the process of covered interest arbitrage, suppose the spot rate is ₹ 40/US $ and the three-month forward rate is ₹ 40.28/US $ involving a forward differential of 2.8 per cent. The interest rate is 18 per cent in India and 12 per cent in the USA involving interest rate differential of 5.37 per cent. Since the two differentials are not equal, covered interest arbitrage will begin. The successive steps shall be as follows:

- Borrowing in the USA, say, US $ 1,000 at 12 per cent interest
- Converting the US dollar into the rupee at spot rate to get ₹ 40,000/-
- Investing ₹ 40,000 in India at 18 per cent interest
- Selling the rupee 90-day forward at ₹ 40.28/$
- After three months, liquidating the ₹ 40,000 investment which would fetch ₹ 41,800
- Selling ₹ 41,800 for US dollars at the rate of ₹ 40.28/US $ to get US $ 1,038
- Repaying loan in the USA which amounts to US $ 1,030

Reaping profit: US $ 1,038 – 1,030 = US $ 8.

So long as inequality continues between the forward rate differential and the interest rate differential, arbitrageurs will profit and the process of arbitrage will go on. But with this process, the differential will be wiped out for the following reasons:

1. Borrowing in the USA will raise the interest rate there.
2. Investing in India would increase the invested funds and thereby lower the interest rate there.
3. Buying rupees at spot rate will increase spot rate of the rupee.
4. Selling rupees forward will depress the forward rate of the rupee.

The first two actions narrow the interest rate differential, while 3 and 4 widen the forward rate differential.

PROBLEM 4.19

Find out the amount of profit out of covered interest arbitrage if interest rate in India and the USA is respectively 9 per cent and 4.50 per cent and the 6-month forward and spot exchange rates are respectively ₹ 45.00 $ and ₹ 45.20 $.

Solution

There will be covered interest arbitrage insofar as the interest rate and forward rate differentials are not equal.

To start with, borrowing $ 1,000 in the USA, converting it into rupee for 45,000 and investing the rupee for six months will fetch ₹ 47,025. Selling ₹ 47,025 forward will fetch $ 1,045. After repaying dollar loan along with interest for 1,022.50, the arbitrageur profits $ 1,045 – 1,022.50 = $ 22.50.

However, the real life experience shows that the two differentials—interest rate and forward rate—are equal only approximately and not precisely. It is because the interest rate parity theorem assumes no transaction cost, no tax rate differences and political stability. But the assumptions do not hold in real life.

First of all, there is always transaction cost involved in selling a currency spot and buying it forward. The transaction cost, which is manifest in the bid-ask spread, forces forward rate differential to deviate from the expected one. The transaction cost, which is involved also in borrowing and investing, influences the effective interest rate and thereby the interest rate differential.

Secondly, there is disparity in the tax rate on interest income in different countries. Such a disparity allows the interest rate differential to deviate from the expected one.

Last but not least, if there is political unrest in the country where the funds are invested, the cost of investment will be greater and this will influence the interest rate differential.

Uncovered Interest Arbitrage

When one talks about interest arbitrage, it would be worthwhile to note that interest arbitrage may not be only covered, it may also be uncovered. However, in an uncovered interest arbitrage, the arbitrageur does not take advantage of the forward market and does not go for any forward contract for reaping profit. Rather the decision behind profit-making depends upon the expectation about the future spot rate, inasmuch as the interest rate differential between two countries leads to changes in future spot rate.

Uncovered interest arbitrage does not involve forward market transactions as interest-rate differential leads to changes in future spot rate.

If interest-rate differential is equal to changes in the future spot rate, uncovered interest parity will exist. This can be represented in the form of an equation:

$$(1 + R_A)/(1 + R_B) = (S_{e+1} - S)/S \qquad (4.12)$$

where S_{e+1} is the expected future spot rate, and R_A and R_B are the interest rates in Country *A* and Country *B*.

So long as equality is not reached, the arbitrageurs will go for uncovered interest arbitrage and reap profits. Suppose the interest rate on the Indian treasury bill is

7.0 per cent and that on the UK treasury bill is 4.0 per cent and so the interest rate differential is 2.88 per cent. If the investor expects a depreciation of 4.0 per cent in the future spot rate of Indian rupee he/she will invest in the UK treasury bill because a fixed amount of British pound will fetch greater amount of Indian rupee at a future date. This will go on till the two differentials are equal. This is uncovered interest arbitrage.

PROBLEM 4.20

Interest rate in India and the USA is respectively 6 per cent and 5 per cent. Spot exchange rate at present is ₹ 42.32/US $. Because of higher interest rate, arbitrageurs are tempted to make investment in rupee market. But by the time their investment matures, rupee is expected to depreciate to ₹ 45.20/US $. Find whether there would be uncovered interest arbitrage. If there will be arbitrage, what will be the process?

Solution

Interest rate differential = 1.06/1.05 – 1 = 0.95 per cent

Future spot rate differential = (45.20 – 42.32)/42.32 = 6.81 per cent

Since these two differentials are not equal, uncovered parity does not exist. As a result, there will be uncovered interest arbitrage.

Again, under this type of situation, arbitrageurs will take back their investment out of rupee market for fear of lower return in terms of US dollar. As a result of lower supply of money there, Indian interest rate will ascend to achieve uncovered parity.

Evaluating IRP Theorem

Does the IRP theory hold good in real life or do the arbitrageurs respond to the interest rate differential? The study of Marston (1976) shows that the IRP theorem held good with greater accuracy in the Euro-currency market in view of the complete freedom from controls and restrictions. Similar findings emerge from the work of Giddy and Duffey (1975). However, there are studies that identify deviation from the theorem (Officer and Willet, 1970; Aliber, 1973; Frenkel and Levich, 1975).

The reasons for derivations are:

(i) Since different rates prevail on bank deposits, loans, treasury bills, etc., short-term interest rate cannot be specific and the chosen rate can hardly be the definitive rate of the formula.

(ii) The marginal interest rate applicable to borrowers and lenders differs from the average interest rate because interest rate changes with successive amount of borrowing.

(iii) The investment in foreign assets is more risky than that in domestic assets. If greater diversification is applied to foreign investment in order to lower the risk element, the law of diminishing returns may apply; and as a result, the arbitrageurs may not respond to the interest rate differential as envisaged by the IRP theorem.

(iv) There are also cases when interest rate parity is disturbed owing to the play of extraordinary forces leading to speculation. It is basically the market expectation of future spot rates that influences the forward rate. If market expectations are strong enough, they can push forward rates beyond the point which interest rate parity would dictate.

(v) Even the covered interest arbitrage does hardly help achieve interest rate parity. The reasons are:

(a) There is transaction cost involved in the arbitrage process which the IRP theory does not take into account.

(b) Control on capital account transactions is found in many countries that hinders a smooth arbitrage process.

Modern Theory

The IRP theorem explains the forward rate differential in terms of interest rate differential between two countries and emphasises the role of arbitrageurs who help equalise the two differentials and help determine the no-profit forward exchange rate. The proponents of the modern theory feel that it is not only the role of the arbitrageurs but of all participants in the foreign exchange market, such as the traders and hedgers and speculators, that influences the forward exchange rate. If they are taken into account, the forward exchange rate may differ from the no-profit forward exchange rate as explained by the IRP theorem (Grubel, 1966; Stoll, 1968).

The proponents of this theory explain the role of all the different participants. We can present a simple illustration here. Suppose, the forward rate of the British pound in relation to the US dollar is expected to be higher than the no-profit forward rate, then the arbitrageurs will be selling the British pound forward for the US dollar. In the reverse case, they will buy the pound forward for US dollars. The larger the difference between the two rates, the greater will be the size of forward purchase or sale by the arbitrageurs.

The arbitrageurs are risk-averse, but the traders are fully risk-averse. They cover their transaction exposure either through forward market hedge or money market hedge or through both. So when the forward rate of the British pound is going to appreciate, the British exporter will sell the dollar forward if the export bill is invoiced in US dollars.

Speculators, however, are risk-takers. They have their own perception of exchange rate changes. If they expect that the future spot rate of the British pound in relation to the US dollar will be higher than the forward rate, they purchase the pound forward. On the maturity, they buy pounds and with the pound, they purchase dollars at the future spot rate thus making a profit. On the contrary, when future spot rate of the pound is expected to be lower than the forward rate, they will sell the pound forward. On the maturity, they sell the pound at the forward rate, get the US dollar, convert the US dollar into pounds at the future spot rate and make a profit. The greater the expected difference between the two rates, the larger will be the size of their forward purchase and sale. Thus, the activities of different participants will force the forward rate of exchange with different intensity. The equilibrium rate will be established where different forces will come to equilibrium. In other words, *the equilibrium forward rate is represented by a weighted average of the no-profit forward rate of exchange and the expected future spot rate.*

THEORIES OF EXCHANGE RATE BEHAVIOUR

The present section refers to a few major postulates that explain exchange rate behaviour and the ways in which some important macroeconomic variables influence the exchange rate movement. These different theories are compartmentalised into the balance-of-payments approach and the asset-market model. The latter is again compartmentalised into two approaches on the basis of substitutability between domestic financial assets and foreign financial assets. Perfect substitutability between the two led to the monetary approach, while the lack of perfect substitution has led to the portfolio balance approach. The monetary approach, which is an outgrowth of PPP theory and the quantity theory of money, has two versions: one being the flexible-price version and the other being the sticky-price version.

Exchange Rate Theories

- Balance of payments theory:
  1. Higher inflation rate differential at home → greater import and lower export → greater demand for foreign currency → depreciation of domestic currency.
  2. Greater real income at home → greater import → depreciation of domestic currency.
  3. Greater interest rate at home → inflow of foreign capital → greater supply of foreign currency → appreciation of domestic currency.
- Monetary Approach—Flexible Price Version:
  1. Increase in money supply → higher price level → depreciation of domestic currency.
  2. Money supply being less than real domestic output → excess demand for money balances → lower domestic prices → appreciation of domestic currency.
  3. Rise in interest rate → lower demand for money → domestic currency depreciates.
- Monetary Approach—Sticky Price Version:
  1. Increase in money supply → depreciation of domestic currency.
  2. Increase in money supply → price rise → lower real interest rate → lower inflow of capital → depreciation of domestic currency.
  3. Rise in interest rate → greater inflow of capital → appreciation of domestic currency.
  4. Rise in interest rate → increase in money supply (loanable funds) → depreciation of domestic currency.
- Portfolio Balance Approach
  1. Domestic income/wealth increase → greater demand for foreign financial assets → depreciation of domestic currency.
  2. Foreign financial assets being more risky → demand for them decreases → appreciation of domestic currency.

Balance of Payments Approach

Let us begin with the balance of payments approach (Allen and Kennen, 1978) that suggests that an increase in domestic price level over the foreign price level makes foreign goods cheaper. It lowers export earnings and boosts the import bill. Lower export reduces the supply of foreign exchange, and at the same time, greater import increases the demand for foreign exchange and domestic currency depreciates as a result. Similarly, growth in real national income causes larger imports if marginal propensity to import is positive. Larger import will cause greater demand for foreign currency and thereby depreciation in the value of domestic currency.

Increase in domestic interest rate, on the contrary, causes greater capital inflow that increases the supply of foreign exchange and thereby causes appreciation in the value of domestic currency. The first two factors influence the current account, while the third factor influences the capital account.

However, the empirical study of Pearce (1983) shows that none of the above-mentioned variables was very significant in the case of exchange rate between the Canadian dollar and the US dollar. On this ground, he has suggested for an alternative theory.

Monetary Approach

The **flexible-price version** of the monetary approach emphasises the role of demand and supply of money in determining the exchange rate (Frenkel, 1976). The exchange rate between two currencies, according to this approach, is the ratio of their values determined on the basis of the money supply and money demand positions of the two countries. The demand for money—either in domestic economy or in a foreign economy—is positively related with prices and real output and negatively related with the rate of interest. Any increase in money supply raises the domestic price level (based on the quantity theory of money) and the resultant increase in price level lowers the value of the domestic currency. But if the increase in money supply is lower than the increase in real domestic output, the excess of real domestic output over the money supply causes excess demand for money balances and leads to a lowering of domestic prices which causes an improvement in the value of domestic currency. This explanation thus runs contrary to the balance of payment approach where increase in real output causes depreciation in the value of domestic currency through greater imports. Again, the monetary approach is different from the balance of payments approach in the sense that the former explains that a rise in domestic interest rate lowers the demand for money in the domestic economy relative to its supply and thereby causes depreciation in the value of domestic currency. However, the critics of this theory argue that since the purchasing power parity theory is not applicable in the short run, this theory does not hold good in such cases.

Dornbusch (1976), the proponent of the **sticky price version**, feels that the simple assumption of the flexible price version that the PPP holds continuously and the real exchange rate never changes is unrealistic. In the real life, real exchange rate has changed at least in the short run, although the variability of nominal exchange rate has been greater. He assumes further that the pace of adjustment of asset prices is faster than the pace of adjustment of goods prices. Thus, when the goods prices are sticky, it is necessary for the asset prices to move more than in the flexible price case for attaining a temporary equilibrium.

The sticky price version has proved that gradual adjustment of goods prices following a monetary shock imparts a "dynamic adjustment path" to the exchange rate. The real exchange rate alters in the short run but returns to the original level in the long run on account of PPP deviations.

The sticky-price version makes a more detailed study of interest rate differential. The interest rate differential has three components. One denotes that when interest rate rises, the money balances held by the public come to the money market lured by the high interest. The increase in money supply leads to currency depreciation. The other denotes that if interest rate rises, financial institutions release more funds into the money market as a result, the value of domestic currency depreciates. The third is that a rise in interest rate stimulates the capital flow into the country that, similarly as in the balance of payments approach, causes appreciation in the value of domestic currency.

The sticky price version is based on at least three assumptions. The first is the perfect capital mobility which means that the interest rate parity conditions prevail. The second is the slow price adjustment. The third is the element of certainty which means that the traders are aware of the fact when shocks will be hitting the market and how to respond to them.

Portfolio Balance Approach

The portfolio balance approach (McKinnon, 1969) suggests that not only the monetary factor but also the holding of financial assets, such as domestic and foreign bonds influences the exchange rate. If foreign bonds and domestic bonds turn out to be perfect substitutes and if the conditions of interest arbitrage hold good, the portfolio balance approach will not be different from the monetary approach. But since these conditions do not hold good in real life, the portfolio balance approach maintains a distinction from the monetary approach.

The portfolio balance approach is based on two financial assets: money and bonds of both the domestic country and the foreign country. There is no restriction on the allocation of wealth among domestic money, domestic bonds and foreign bonds. Thus, for accounting purposes,

$$\text{Wealth} = \text{domestic money} + \text{domestic bonds} + \text{foreign bonds}$$

The exchange rate establishes an equilibrium or a balance in investor's portfolio which includes all these three forms of wealth. If there is any change in the three forms of portfolio on account of change in real income, interest-rate, risk and price level, the investor re-establishes a desired balance in its portfolio. This re-establishment needs some adjustments which, in turn, influence the demand for foreign assets. Any such change influences the exchange rate. For example, a rise in real domestic income or a rise in interest rate abroad leads to a greater demand for foreign bonds. Any rise of demand for foreign currency will result in depreciation of the domestic currency. Again, the legal, political and economic conditions in a foreign country may be different from those at home. If foreign bonds turn out to be more risky on these grounds, the demand for foreign currency will decrease, in turn appreciating the value of the domestic currency. Similarly, a rising inflation in the foreign country would make foreign bonds risky and the demand for foreign currency will drop and so domestic currency will appreciate. When the exchange rate changes, the above mentioned variables also change leading to a shift in the desired balance in the investment portfolio. Thus the two-way interaction continues until equilibrium is reached. The equilibrium is, however, short-lived.

Again, when a country's wealth increases, holding of foreign assets also increases, and demand for foreign currency goes up which causes depreciation in the value of domestic currency. In this context, the possibility of substitution effect cannot be completely negated; because it outweighs the impact of wealth effect. The portfolio balance approach is more comprehensive but as Bisignano and Hoover (1982) find, data do not support the hypothesis of this approach.

Wealth effect explains that increase in wealth leads to demand for foreign assets and thereby to depreciation in domestic currency.

SUMMARY

- Exchange rate denotes the ratio between the value of two currencies. It is quoted in newspapers either in a direct or in an indirect way. The quote shows buying and selling rates. The difference between the two, known as *spread* forms the banks' income. The quote also shows the spot quote and the forward quote. The difference between the two is either forward premium or forward discount. The cross rate between two currencies is established through a common currency.
- In a floating-rate regime, rate of exchange is determined by the forces of supply and demand. With higher demand for, or lower supply of, a foreign currency, its value appreciates vis-à-vis the domestic currency.
- Various different factors influence the demand and supply forces, important among them being the inflation rate and interest rate differentials. The PPP theory suggests that the higher the inflation rate, the lower is the value of currency. Again, the real interest rate tends to equalise, but it is the differing inflation rate that creates nominal interest rate differential. A higher interest rate encourages inflow of capital and the value of domestic currency rises. The monetary authorities try to stabilise the value of currency through intervention in the foreign exchange market.
- In a forward market, the rate of exchange is determined by the interest rate differential that finds a place in the Interest Rate Parity theory. This theory tells us that the interest rate differential equals the forward rate differential. If these two differentials are not equal, covered interest arbitrage begins and equalises the two. In case of uncovered interest arbitrage, the arbitrageur takes into account, the expected future spot rate and not the forward rate.
- These different variables as discussed above form the basis for the explanation of different theories that essentially concern exchange rate determination. The balance of payments approach links exchange rate behaviour with the changes in capital and current account of the balance of payments. The monetary theory lays emphasis upon the demand for, and supply of, money as a factor influencing the exchange rate. However, the sticky-price version of the monetary approach gives a more detailed explanation of interest rate differential. The portfolio balance approach includes also the holding of financial assets—domestic and foreign bonds—that influences the exchange rate.

CASE STUDY

INTRODUCTION OF MANAGED FLOATING EXCHANGE RATE REGIME IN INDIA

The High Level Committee on Balance of Payments, commonly known as the Rangarajan Committee (1992), suggested a dual exchange rate system or a mix of official and market rates at least for a year before finally stepping into a managed floating exchange rate system in March 1993. The managed float involves essentially RBI's intervention in the foreign exchange market either directly through the purchase and sale of US dollars or indirectly through making changes in the repo rate and the resultant size of liquidity in the monetary and financial system. It is true that the new system of exchange rate along with reforms in trade and investment policies helped boost up trade and investment (Sharan and Mukherji, 2001), but the oscillations in exchange rate at times could not completely be ruled out.

Ensuring Stability in the Exchange Rate

The issue of financial stability attained significance in the late 1990s in view of keeping at bay the spill-over effects of the turbulence in the South-East Asian financial markets and also the deepening of the financial crisis in Russia. The RBI announced a set of policy measures in June 1998. These measures emphasised on the RBI's role of meeting mismatches between the demand and supply of foreign currency through market intervention, allowing the foreign institutional investors (FIIs) to manage their exchange rate exposure through undertaking foreign exchange cover on their incremental investment, advising traders and banks to monitor their foreign currency position and allowing domestic financial institutions to buy back their debt from international financial market. Foreign Exchange Management Act (FEMA) replacing the Foreign Exchange Regulation Act (FERA) came into force from June 1, 2000. It aimed at promoting an orderly development and maintenance of the foreign exchange market in India. The Act provides transparent norms relating to the RBI's approval for acquiring and holding of foreign exchange and the limits to which foreign exchange is admissible to current/capital account transactions from the viewpoint of full current account convertibility and growing convertibility on capital account.

TABLE CS4.2 RBI's Foreign Exchange Reserve

(Rupees crore)

Year	*Absolute variation*	*Per cent*
2009–10	15,539.45	1.22
2010–11	1,27,023.99	9.88
2011–12	2,222.99	15.7
2012–13	571.47	3.5
2013–14	2,271.35	13.10
2014–15	3,517.86	18.38
2015–16	1,781.95	7.86
2017–18	2,792.12	11.16
2019–20	8,562.18	28.90
2021–22	3,79,865.92	9.00
2023–24	6,36,991.34	13.40

Sources: RBI, *Annual Report*, various issues.

QUESTIONS

1. What do you mean by managed floating exchange rate regime? Why was it adopted in India?
2. Comment on the trend of the exchange rate of rupee during the managed floating regime.
3. How was fluctuation in the rupee/dollar exchange rate controlled?

REVIEW QUESTIONS

Objective-Type Questions

1. State whether true (T) or false (F):

(a) Domestic currency is on the numerator in case of direct quote. ☐
(b) Bid rate and buying rate are synonyms. ☐
(c) Ask rate/offer rate and selling rate carry the same meaning. ☐
(d) Forward differential is greater in case of shorter maturity. ☐
(e) Cross rate is found out through a common currency. ☐

2. Choose the correct answer:

(a) Demand for foreign currency is influenced primarily by:
  (i) size of export
  (ii) size of import
  (iii) none of these

(b) Supply of foreign currency is influenced by:
  (i) size of export
  (ii) size of import
  (iii) none of these

(c) Domestic currency tends to depreciate owing to:
  (i) high inflation rate
  (ii) lowering of inflation rate
  (iii) constant inflation rate

(d) Nominal interest rate is the product of:
  (i) real interest rate and rate of inflation
  (ii) real interest rate and exchange rate
  (iii) none of these

(e) Covered interest arbitrage takes place when:
  (i) forward rate differential is equal to interest rate differential
  (ii) forward rate differential is not equal to interest rate differential
  (iii) none of these

Short-Answer Questions

1. Distinguish between:

(a) direct and indirect quote of exchange rate
(b) buying and selling rate
(c) outright forward quote and swap quote

2. How do you compute the forward rate differential?
3. What is bid-ask spread? How is it computed?
4. What is cross rate? How is it computed?

Long-Answer Questions

1. Explain the PPP theory. Is it applicable to both short term and long term?
2. What do you mean by Fisher effect? Is it true that interest rate differential equals inflation rate differential?
3. Explain the IRP theory. Is it sufficient to explain the forward exchange rate?
4. "The spot exchange rate in a floating-rate regime is determined by the supply and demand forces." Explain.
5. Examine different theories of exchange rate determination.
6. Explain covered interest arbitrage with suitable example. Is it different from uncovered interest arbitrage?

Numerical Problems

1. If direct quote is: ₹ 50/US $, how can this exchange rate be presented under indirect quote?
2. Consider the following bid-ask prices: ₹ 40.00–40.50/US $. Find out

   (a) the bid-ask price for rupee, and
   (b) the bid-ask spread.
3. Find the cross rate for Mex. Peso/Euro, if: Euro 4.25–4.28/US $ and Mex. Peso 65.20–65.30/US $.
4. Explain on the basis of the following data: whether

   (a) absolute version of PPP theory holds good
   (b) law of one price holds good

USA			*India*		
Unit	*Goods*	*US $ Price/Unit*	*Unit*	*Goods*	*₹, Price/Unit*
4	Rice	1	20	Rice	40
20	Wheat	2	10	Wheat	80

Exchange rate ₹ 40/US $

5. The exchange rate between rupee and US $ is ₹ 40/US $ at the end of Period 1. The rate of inflation in India and the USA is 6 per cent and 3 per cent, respectively. What is the likely exchange rate at the end of Period 2?
6. If the nominal rate of interest is 15 per cent and the rate of inflation is 6 per cent, what would be the real interest rate?
7. Calculate the forward differential if the spot rate is ₹ 40/US $ and the 3-month forward rate is 40.50/US $.
8. Calculate the 3-month forward rate, if the spot rate is ₹ 46/US $; the interest rate in India and the USA is, respectively, 6 per cent and 3 per cent.

9. The spot exchange rate between Indian rupee and US dollar in 1995 was ₹ 30/US $ when the price index in both the countries was 100. By 2000, rupee depreciated to 45/US dollar and at the same time, the price index moved up during this period in India and USA to 110 and 125, respectively. Find out the extent of change in nominal and real exchange rates.

REFERENCES

Abdullah, F.A. (1986), *Financial Management for the Multinational Firm*, Englewood Cliffs, Prentice Hall International, p. 59.

Adler, M. and B. Lehmann (1983), Deviations from Purchasing Power Parity in the Long Run, *Journal of Finance*, XXXVIII, 1471–1487.

Aliber, R.Z. (1973), The Interest Rate Parity Theorem: A reinterpretation, *Journal of Political Economy*, LXXXI, 1451–1459.

Aliber, R.Z. and C.P. Stickney (1975), Accounting Measures of Foreign Exchange Exposure: The long and short of it, *The Accounting Review*, L, 4–57.

Allen, P.R. and P.B. Kennen (1978), *The Balance of Payments, Exchange Rate and Economic Policy*, Athens (Georgia), Centre for Planning and Economic Research.

Baig, T. (2001), "Characterising Exchange Rate Regimes in Post-crisis East Asia", Technical Report, WP/01/152, IMF, Washington, DC.

Bisignano, J. and K. Hoover (1982), Some Suggested Improvements to a Simple Portfolio Balance Model of Exchange Rate Determination with Special Reference to US Dollar/Canadian Dollar Rate, *Archiv Weltwirtschaftliches*, CXVIII, 19–37.

Cassel, G. (1921), *The World's Monetary Problems*, London, Constable. Chakrabarti, R. (2006), *The Financial Sector in India: Emerging Issues*, New Delhi: Oxford University Press.

Cumby, R.E. and M. Obstfeld (1984), International Interest Rate and Price Level Linkages under Flexible Exchange Rates: A review of the evidence, in J.F.O. Bilson and R.C. Marston (Eds.), *Exchange Rate Theory and Practices*, Chicago, Univ. of Chicago Press, pp. 121–152.

Dornbusch, R. (1976), Expectations and Exchange Rate Dynamics, *Journal of Political Economy*, LXXXIV, 1161–1176.

Edison, H. (1985), The Rise and Fall of Sterling: Testing alternative models of exchange rate determination, *Applied Economics*, XVII, 1003–1021.

Edwards, S. (1982), "Exchange Rates and 'News': A Multicurrency Approach", *Journal of International Money and Finance*, 1, 211–24.

Fama, E.F. and G.W. Schwert (1977), Asset Returns and Inflation, *Journal of Financial Economics*, V, 115–146.

Frenkel, J.A. (1976), A Monetary Approach to Exchange Rate: Doctrinal aspects and empirical evidence, *Scandinavian Journal of Economics*, LXXXVIII, 200–224.

Frenkel, J.A. and R.M. Levich (1975), Transaction Costs and Interest Arbitrage: Tranquil and turbulent periods, *Journal of Political Economy*, LXXXIII, 325–338.

Gibson, W.E. (1970), Price Expectations Effects on Interest Rates, *Journal of Finance*, XXV, 19–34.

———(1972), Interest Rates and Inflationary Expectations, *American Economic Review*, LXII, 854–865.

Giddy, I.H. and G. Duffey (1975), The Random Behaviour of Flexible Exchange Rates, *Journal of International Business Studies*, VI, 1–32.

Grubel, H.G. (1966), Forward Exchange, *Speculation and the International Flow of Capital*, Palo Alto, Stanford University Press.

Hansen, L.P. and R.J. Hodrick (1983), "Risk-averse Speculation in the Forward Foreign Exchange Markets: An Econometric Analysis of Linear Models" in J.A. Frenkel (Ed.), *Exchange Rates and International Macroeconomics*, Chicago: University of Chicago Press.

Isard, P. (1977), How Far We Can Push the Law of One Price, *American Economic Review*, LXVII, 942–948.

Kohlhagen, S.W. (1975), "The Performance of Foreign Exchange Markets: 1971–74", *Journal of International Business Studies*", 6, 33–39.

MacDonald, R. (1988), *Floating Exchange Rates: Theories and evidence*, London, Unwin, pp. 201–219.

Marston, R.C. (1976), Interest Arbitrage in the Euro-currency Markets, *European Economic Review*, VII, 1–13.

McKinnon, R.I. (1969), Portfolio Balance and International Payments Adjustment, in R.A. Mundell and A.K. Swoboda (Eds.), *Monetary Problems in International Economy*, Chicago, Univ. of Chicago Press, pp. 199–235.

———(1979), *Money in International Exchange*, Oxford: Oxford University Press, pp. 117–137.

Mishkin, F. (1984), Are Real Interest Rates Equal Across Countries? An empirical investigation of international parity conditions, *Journal of Finance*, XXXIX, 1345–1358.

Mundell, R. (1961), "The International Disequilibrium System", *Kyklos*, 14, 154–72.

Mussa, M. (1982), A Model of Exchange Rate Dynamics, *Journal of Political Economy*, XC, 74–104.

Officer, L.H. (1976), The Purchasing Power Parity Theory of Exchange Rates: A review article, *IMF Staff Papers*, XXVII, 1–60.

Officer, L.H. and T.D. Willet (1970), The Covered Arbitrage Schedule: A Critical Survey of Recent Developments, *Journal of Money*, Credit and Banking, II, 247–257.

Patnaik, I. (2003): "The Consequences of Currency Intervention in India", Working Paper no. 114, *ICRIER*, New Delhi.

Patnaik, R.K. et al. (2003), "Exchange Rate Policy and Management: The Indian Experience", *Economic and Political Weekly*, May 31.

Pearce, D. (1983), Alternative Views of Exchange Rate Determination, *Economic Review*, 16–30.

RBI (2006), *Annual Report: 2005–06*, Mumbai.

Sharan, V. and I.N. Mukherji (2001), *India's External Sector Reforms*, New Delhi: Oxford University Press.

Sharma, A.K. and A. Mitra (2006), "What Drives Forward Premia in the Indian Foreign Exchange Market?", *RBI Occasional Paper*, no. 27 (1&2).

Stoll, H. (1968), An Empirical Study of the Forward Exchange Market under Fixed and Flexible Exchange Rate Systems, *Canadian Journal of Economics*, I, 56–78.

Taylor, M.P. (1988), An Empirical Examination of Long-run Purchasing Power Parity using Cointegration Techniques, *Applied Economics*, XX, 1369–1381.

Unnikrishnan, N.K. and R. Mohan (2003), "Exchange Rate Dynamics: An Indian Perspective", *RBI Occasional Papers*, June.

SUGGESTED FURTHER READING

Fama, E. (1988), Forward and Spot Exchange Rates, *Journal of Monetary Economics*, XIV, 319–338.

Isard, P. (1980), *Factors Determining Exchange Rates: The roles of relative price levels, balance of payments, interest rates and risk*, Washington, D.C.: Federal Reserve Board, International Finance Discussion Paper No. 171.

Krueger, A.O. (1983), *Exchange Rate Determination*, Cambridge: Cambridge University Press.

PART 2

Markets for Foreign Exchange and Derivatives

CHAPTER

5 Foreign Exchange Market

Learning Objectives

The present chapter deals with the foreign exchange market and the operations therein. In particular, it:

- Explains the distinctive characteristics of foreign exchange market.
- Delineates who actually participates in the foreign exchange market.
- Describes how various types of transactions take place in spot and forward markets.

One of the major international financial functions is the exchange of currencies. Currencies are exchanged or, in other words, bought and sold in foreign exchange market that is spread around the globe. The present chapter thus deals with the various aspects of the foreign exchange market and with the varieties of transactions taking place therein.

CHART 5.1 Daily Average of Global Foreign Exchange Turnover

DISTINCTIVE FEATURES

The foreign exchange market is a market where foreign currencies are bought and sold. If an Indian importer imports goods from the USA and has to make payments in US dollars, it will approach the foreign exchange market to buy US dollars for rupees. An exporter converts the export proceeds obtained in a foreign currency into its own currency. These two are the simplest examples of transactions in the foreign exchange market. There are many types of transactions that involve the purchase and sale of different currencies.

Foreign exchange market:
1. is over-the-counter market,
2. operates round-the-clock,
3. involves normally transaction of strong, stable and convertible currencies.

The foreign exchange market is an *over-the-counter* market. It does not denote a particular place or floor where dealers assemble and transact foreign currencies. Rather, it consists of trading desks at major agencies dealing in foreign exchange throughout the world that are connected by telephone, telex, etc. This is why transactions are based normally on oral followed by written communication. It may, however, be mentioned that although the market is global, the market features in each country are influenced by the local regulatory framework. In the UK or the USA, the market relies more on the communication network; while in Frankfurt, Paris and some other European countries, physical meeting of participants at bourses is also customary.

Since foreign exchange dealers are spread all over the globe, the time of transaction differs from one place to another depending upon the longitude of the place. If a dealer in India transacts at 10 A.M., it will just be 4.30 A.M. in London. In order to accommodate dealers from different countries, the foreign exchange market has to function round-the-clock.

Again, the currencies transacted in the foreign exchange markets are normally the strong, stable and convertible currencies which are in great demand because of their strength, stability and convertibility.

The market has two segments: one is the wholesale segment and the other is the retail segment. The wholesale segment is also known as the inter-bank market where the size of transaction is quite large and the operators are the commercial banks, investment banks, the central bank of the country, companies and high net-worth individuals. On the contrary, in the retail segment, the volume of transaction is small and the operators are normally the tourists, hotels, shops and individuals, etc.

From the viewpoint of the relative ranking of foreign exchange trading centre, banks located in the United Kingdom accounted for 36.7%, of all foreign exchange market turnover, followed by the United States (18%), Japan (6%), Singapore (5%), Switzerland (5%), Hong Kong SAR (5%) and Australia (4%).

Source: BIS website

MAJOR PARTICIPANTS

The participants in the foreign exchange market are individuals, firms, banks, governments, and occasionally the international agencies. Individuals are normally the tourists who exchange the currencies, as also migrants sending a part of their income to their family members living in their home countries. The firms are generally the importers and exporters. An exporter prefers to get the payments in its own currency or in a strong convertible currency. Importers need foreign exchange for making payments for their imports. When firms and individuals approach the local branch of a bank, the local branch in turn approaches the foreign exchange department in its regional office or head office. The latter deals actually in foreign exchange with other banks on behalf of the customers.

Participants are: individuals, firms, banks, central banks and international organisations. Functionally, they are hedgers, arbitrageurs and speculators.

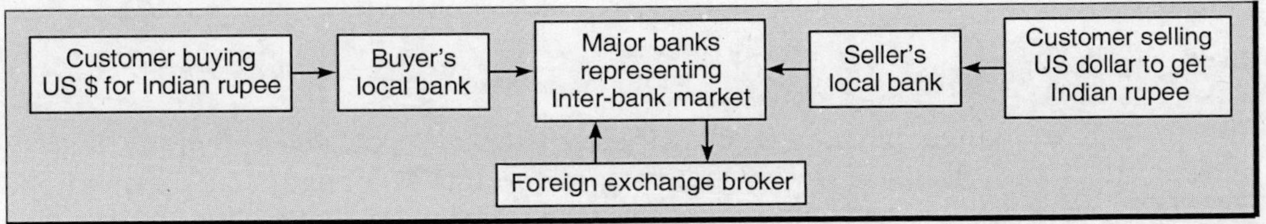

Thus there are two tiers in the foreign exchange market: one tier involves the transactions between ultimate customers and the banks while the other tier consists of the transactions between banks. Since the purpose of inter-bank transactions is not only to meet the foreign exchange demand of the ultimate customers but also to reap gains out of movement in foreign exchange rates, it is the second tier of the market that accounts for the largest segment of the total foreign exchange transactions in the market. In some cases, the inter-bank dealings take place directly without any help from an intermediary, but generally the banks operate through foreign exchange brokers.

It is either because of the length of transactions passing through two tiers of the market or because of the profit motive involved in the transactions that there is often a gap between the amount of purchase and the amount of sale of a currency by banks. If a bank buys less of a currency than it contracts to sell, the position is known as a *short position* in that currency. The reverse situation, where a bank buys more of a currency than it contracts to sell, is known as a *long position* in that currency. When the quantum of sale and purchase is equal, the equality denotes a *square position*.

Short position = supply of a currency < demand for currency
Long position = supply of a currency > demand for currency
Square position = supply of a currency = demand for currency

Though it is a fact that commercial banks dominate, the governments or monetary authorities too participate in the foreign exchange market but to help stabilise the value of domestic currency. The market intervention by the monetary authorities has been discussed in detail in Chapter 3. International agencies sometimes purchase and sell foreign currencies in the foreign exchange market, but that is not a routine affair.

Again, the participants may be grouped also according to their motive and behaviour in their foreign exchange transactions as follows:

- Non-banking entities which simply exchange currencies to honour their obligations or to get the desired currency.
- Non-banking entities such as traders that use the foreign exchange market for the purpose of hedging their foreign exchange exposure on account of changes in the exchange rate.

- Banks which exchange currencies on behalf of their customers. In such cases, their profit is limited to the amount of spread between the bid and the ask rates.
- Arbitrageurs who change currencies because of varying rates of exchange in different markets. The varying rates are the source of their profit.
- Speculators who buy or sell currencies when they expect movement in the exchange rate in a particular direction. They make their profit from movement of exchange rate in the desired direction.

SPOT MARKET

Features

Spot market transactions require immediate delivery of the traded currency. In forward market, currencies are delivered at a future date.

The foreign exchange market is classified either as spot market or as forward market. It is the timing of actual delivery of foreign exchange that distinguishes between spot market and forward market transactions. In the spot market, currencies are traded for immediate delivery at a rate existing on the day of transaction. For making book-keeping entries, delivery takes two working days after the transaction is complete although in the case of Canadian dollar the delivery of currencies takes place the very next working day. If a particular market is closed on Saturday and Sunday and if transaction takes place on Thursday, delivery of currency shall take place on Monday. Monday in this case is known as the *value date* or *settlement date*. Sometimes there are short-date contracts where the time zones permit the delivery of the currency even earlier. If the currency is delivered the same day, it is known as the *value-same-day contract*. If it is done the next day, the contract is known as the *value-next-day contract*.

In view of the huge amounts involved in the transactions, there is seldom any actual movement of currencies. Rather, debit and credit entries are made in the bank accounts of the seller and the purchaser. Most of the markets affect the transfer of funds electronically thus saving time and energy. The system existing in New York is known as the *Clearing House Inter-bank Payment System (CHIPS)*.

Currency Arbitrage in Spot Market

With fast development in the telecommunication system, rates are expected to be uniform in different foreign exchange markets. Nevertheless, inconsistency exists at times. The arbitrageurs take advantage of the inconsistency and garner profits by buying and selling of currencies. They buy a particular currency at cheaper rate in one market and sell it at a higher rate in the other. This process is known as *currency arbitrage*. The process influences the demand for, and supply of, the particular currency in the two markets which leads ultimately to removal of inconsistency in the value of currencies in two markets.

Suppose,

In New York : $ 1.9800 – 10/£; and
In London : $ 1.9700 – 10/£.

The arbitrageurs will sell pound in New York and buy pound in London making a profit of $ 1.9810 – 1.9700 = $ 0.0110 per pound sterling.

In the above example, two currencies are involved and two markets where the particular currency is bought or sold. This is why it is known as *two-point arbitrage*. There are also examples of *three-point arbitrage* or *triangular arbitrage* where three currencies and three markets are involved.

Suppose, bid rate in:

New York : $ 1.9810/£,
London : DM 3.1650/£, and
Frankfurt : $ 0.6250/DM

In this case, the arbitrageur will exchange the dollar, say $ 1,000 for DM in Frankfurt to get DM 1,600. He will convert DM 1,600 for pound sterling in London to get £ 505.63. Finally, he will sell £ 505.63 for dollars in New York to get $ 1,001.46. This means that he would gain $ 1.46 per $ 1,000 through triangular arbitrage.

The above example does not, of course, include transaction cost. In real world a transaction cost exists that lowers the amount of gain. Suppose, transaction cost is 0.5 per cent. When $ 1,000 is converted into DM in Frankfurt, the arbitrageur would receive DM 1,600 × (1 – 0.005) or DM 1,592 and the receipt of the exchanged currency will be similarly lower at the other two points. It follows, therefore, that arbitrage will take place only when the burden of transaction cost is lower than the gain from the exchange.

PROBLEM 5.1

If the rate of exchange is:

US $ 2.0000–2.0100/£ in New York
US $ 1.9800–1.9810/£ in London

Explain how the arbitrageurs will gain.

Solution

The arbitrageur will sell Pound in New York and with the same dollar, buy Pound in London. The profit per pound, assuming no transaction cost, will be:

$ 2.0100 – 1.9800 = 0.0300.

Note: It is the difference between the selling rate and the buying rates of Pound in the two markets.

Speculation in Spot Market

Speculation in the spot market occurs when the speculator anticipates a change in the value of a currency. Suppose the exchange rate today is ₹ 40/US $. The speculator anticipates this rate to become ₹ 41/US $ within the coming three months. Under these circumstances, he will buy US $ 1,000 for ₹ 40,000 and hold this amount for three months, although he is not committed to this particular time horizon. When the target exchange rate is reached, he will sell US $ 1,000 at the new exchange rate, that is at ₹ 41 per dollar and earn a profit of ₹ 41,000 – ₹ 40,000 = ₹ 1,000.

PROBLEM 5.2

Presently, the spot rate is ₹ 44.50/US $. A speculator feels that, after a week, US dollar should appreciate to ₹ 44.60. What should he do if he has ₹ 10,000 at his disposal?

Solution

The speculator should buy US dollar today to get 10,000/44.50 = US $ 224.72. After a week, he should sell those dollars to get 224.72 × 44.60 = ₹ 10,022.47. The profit from speculation will be: ₹ 10,022.47 – ₹ 10,000.00 = ₹ 22.47.

FORWARD MARKET

Features

In the forward market, contracts are made to buy and sell currencies for future delivery, say, after a fortnight, one month, two months and so on. The rate of exchange for the transaction is agreed upon on the very day the deal is finalised. The forward rates with varying maturity are quoted in the newspapers and those rates form the basis of the contract. Both parties have to abide by the contract at the exchange rate mentioned therein irrespective of whether the spot rate on the maturity date resembles the forward rate or not. In other words, no party can back out of the deal if changes in the future spot rate are not in his or her favour.

The value date in case of a forward contract lies definitely beyond the value date applicable to a spot contract. If it is a one-month forward contract, the value date will be the date in the next month corresponding to the spot value date. Suppose a currency is purchased on 1 August. If it is a spot transaction, the currency will be delivered on 3 August.

Value date/ settlement date is the day on which the traded currency is delivered.

But if it is a one-month forward contract, the value date will fall on 3 September. If the value date falls on a holiday, the subsequent date will be the value date. In this case, the maturity date will be different from the value date. Then the maturity date will be the 3rd of September and the value date will be the 4th of September. If the value date does not exist in the calendar, such as the 29 February (if it is not a leap year), the value date will fall on the 28 February.

PROBLEM 5.3

Three one-month forward deals were contracted respectively on the 28th and 29th January 2024. What would be the settlement date?

Solution

28th February

Sometimes the value date is structured to enable one of the parties to the transaction to have freedom to select a value date within the prescribed period. This happens when the party does not know in advance the precise date on which it would be able to deliver the currency, for instance, an exporter who sells a foreign currency forward without knowing in advance the precise date of shipment.

Again, the maturity period of forward contract is normally for one month, two months, three months and so on but sometimes it may not be for the whole month and a fraction of a month may also be involved. A forward contract with a maturity period of 35 days is an apposite example. Naturally, in this case, the value date falls on a date between two whole months. Such a contract is known as a *broken-date contract*.

Broken-date contract is a forward contract with a maturity of not a whole month.

PROBLEM 5.4

What will be the forward rate for 1 month and 10 days (broken date contract) if:

Spot	:	₹ 40.00–40.10/$
1-month forward	:	₹ 40.50–40.70/$
3-month forward	:	₹ 40.80–41.10/$

Solution

For one month and 10 days, swap points:

Buying rate: $50 + (80 - 50) \times 10/60 = 55$

Selling rate: $70 + (110 - 70) \times 10/60 = 77$

The forward rate for one month and 10 days = ₹ 40.55–40.77/$.

Arbitrage in Forward Market

In Chapter 4, we discussed that the forward rate differential is approximately equal to the interest rate differential. Sometimes there may be marked deviation between these two differentials. In such cases, covered interest arbitrage begins and continues till the two differentials become equal. This is arbitrage in a forward market. The explanation can be found in the preceding chapter. The readers are suggested to go through it.

Forward Market Hedging

The forward market is used not only by the arbitrageurs but by the hedgers too. Changes in the exchange rate are a usual phenomenon. Such changes entail some foreign exchange risk in terms of loss or gain to the traders and other participants in the foreign exchange market. The risk is reduced or hedged through forward market transactions. Under the process of hedging, currencies are bought and sold forward. Forward buying and selling depends upon whether the hedger finds himself in a long, or a short, position. An export billed in foreign currency creates a long position for the exporter. On the contrary, an import billed in foreign currency leads to a short position for the importer.

Export Position	*Import* Long Short Position
↓	↓
Sale of Foreign Currency	Purchase of Foreign Currency

Let us first take the long position. An Indian exporter enters into a contract for mica export to the USA for US $ 1,000. The export proceeds are to be received within three months. The exporter fears a drop in the value of the US dollar that may diminish the export earnings in terms of rupee. To avoid this diminution, the exporter opts for a three-month forward contract and sells forward one thousand US dollars. Suppose the spot as well as the forward rate is ₹ 40/US $. If the dollar depreciates to ₹ 39 after three months, the export earnings will diminish to ₹ 39 thousand, but since the exporter has already sold forward similar amount in dollars, the loss due to depreciation of the dollar will be met through the forward contract. By selling dollars, it would fetch ₹ 40 thousand that will be equal to the original export value.

However, the forward deal has disadvantages too. The advantage is that if the value of the dollar falls, the exporter will not have to suffer any loss of income while the disadvantage is that if the value of the dollar appreciates, the exporter will not benefit from the appreciation. Moreover, in case a part of the merchandise is not accepted by the importer, the exporter will have to arrange for the dollars to honour the forward contract.

In the event of a short position where the Indian importer buys goods from the USA for US $ 1,000, and where the importer fears an appreciation in the value of the US dollar, the forward deal will involve the buying of dollars. If the dollar appreciates to ₹ 41 after the three-month period, the importer will have to pay ₹ 1,000 more but if he has opted for a forward deal to buy a similar amount in dollars, he will purchase US $ 1,000 with ₹ 40,000 and pay US $ 1,000 to the exporter and so save himself from the ₹ 1,000 loss. Here again, if the dollar appreciates, the importer eliminates the loss, but if it depreciates, the importer does not benefit from the depreciation.

PROBLEM 5.5

An Indian importer expects appreciation of US dollar while importing goods for US $ 1,000. So he goes for buying $ 1,000 one-month forward coinciding the time of payment for the import. The spot rate and the forward rate is respectively ₹ 40 and ₹ 40.50. Surprisingly, the future spot rate (on the maturity) is only ₹ 40.30/$, will the forward deal be beneficial?

Solution

After entering into the contract, the importer has to abide by the contract. He will buy $ 1,000 for ₹ 40,500. Had he not gone for the contract, he would have bought US dollar only for ₹ 40,300. Thus forward contract causes a net loss of ₹ 200.

In these two examples of forward deals, we have assumed that the spot rate and the forward rate are equal but this is not always true. There may be either a forward premium or a forward discount. Suppose the spot rate is ₹ 40/US $, and the three-month forward rate is ₹ 39.50/US $. In this case, if the spot rate after the expiry of three months turns out to be ₹ 39/US $, and if the Indian exporter has a forward contract for selling the same amount in dollars, he will be able to diminish the loss by ₹ 500 because he will get ₹ 39,500 from the forward deal. Had there been no forward contract, the exporter would have received only ₹ 39,000 following the depreciation of the US dollar. If however, the US dollar depreciates only to ₹ 39.80, the forward deal will cause a loss for ₹ 300 because it would fetch only ₹ 39,500 instead of ₹ 39,800 that would have been received in the absence of a forward deal.

The advantage or disadvantage of the forward deal is reaped not only by the exporter but also by the importer. In case of a short position, a forward discount is favourable to the hedger because it enables the hedger to obtain foreign exchange at a rate lower than the current spot rate. On the contrary, a forward premium is unfavourable because it makes the forward foreign currency costlier. However, the exact magnitude of loss or gain to the importer depends upon the difference between the forward rate and the future spot rate that we have just discussed. If the forward rate is ₹ 39.50/US $ and if the future spot rate is ₹ 39.80/US $, the Indian importer will be able to save ₹ 300 because he will get US $ 1,000 only for ₹ 39,500 under the forward contract; whereas he would have had to pay ₹ 39,800 for one thousand dollars, had there been no forward contract. But if the future spot rate comes down to ₹ 39/US $, the importer will have to face a loss of ₹ 500 under the forward contract. Thus hedging in a forward market, whether it concerns a long position or a short position, is a double-edged sword and if the trend in the exchange rate movement is not according to expectations, it can result in a loss.

Limitations to forward and futures hedges

In view of the above discussion, a hedger's decision to go for a forward/futures hedge depends on two factors. They are:

(c) Difference between future spot rate and the forward rate
(d) Expected transaction costs

Hedging in a forward market will be beneficial for an importer only when the future spot rate of the currency in which he/she has to make the payments is higher than the forward rate. Alternatively, it will be beneficial for an exporter when the future spot rate of the currency in which it has to receive the export proceeds is lower than the forward rate. If these conditions are not met, the hedging in the forward market will not be helpful.

The above discussion of the forward market hedging is based on the assumption that there is no transaction cost. But in the real world, the transaction cost exists. Thus, the forward market hedge is lucrative only till the transaction cost is lower than the total gains from hedging.

Speculation in Forward Market

In addition to the arbitrageur or the hedger, speculators are also very active in forward market operations. Their purpose is not to reduce the risk but to reap profits from the changes in the exchange rates. The source of profit to them being the difference between the forward rate and the future spot rate, they are not very concerned with the direction of the exchange rate change.

Suppose a speculator sells US $ 1,000 three-month forward at the rate of ₹ 40.50/US $. If, on maturity, the US dollar depreciates to ₹ 40, the speculator will get ₹ 40,500 under the forward contract. At the same time, he will exchange ₹ 40,500 at the then future spot rate of 40/US $ and will get US $ 1,012.50. Both these activities—the selling and the purchasing of US dollars will be simultaneous. Thus without making any investment, the speculator will make a profit of US $ 12.50 through the forward market deal. This is an example of speculation in the forward market.

Forward market speculation cannot be extended beyond the maturity date of the forward contract. However, if the speculator wants to close out the speculation operation prior to the maturity, say by one month, he may buy an *offsetting contract*. In other words, if he has already entered into a three-month forward contract for selling US dollars, he would have to opt for a two-month forward contract for buying US dollars. The profit or loss would naturally depend upon the exchange rate involved in the two forward contracts.

> Offsetting contract is a reverse contract following the original contract.

The aforementioned is a very simple example. Many other examples can be cited about speculation in the forward market. In fact, the type of speculation depends upon the expected movement of the future spot rate.

PROBLEM 5.6

Spot rate is ₹ 44.50/$. Three-month forward rate is ₹ 44.30/$. Speculator's own estimate is that the future spot rate after three months should be ₹ 44.10/$. Will the speculator go for a forward contract if he has $ 10,000 at his disposal?

Solution

The speculator will sell dollar in the forward market to get ₹ 4,43,000. Immediately after getting rupee, he will convert rupee into dollars in the open market to get $ 10,045.35. Profit will be: $ 10,045.35 – 10,000 = $ 45.35.

Swapping of Forward Contracts

The purpose of swap in the forward market is to reap profits. There are two kinds of swap. One is known as an *option forward* while the other is known as a *forward-forward swap*. In the former, the basis of swap is the difference between the spot rate and the forward rate and in the latter, it is the difference between the two forward rates.

Contracts for option forward take place normally between a bank and its customers. Two delivery dates are mentioned between which delivery of currencies is made. One of the two dates is the date on which the deal is finalised. The other is a future date that may be the date of maturity. Similarly, two exchange rates are mentioned. One is the spot rate prevailing on the date when the deal is finalised and the other is the forward rate. The bank exchanges the currency with the customer on any date between the two dates at one of the two rates which is favourable for it. Suppose there is a contract for an exchange between rupees and dollars and the two dates are 1 January and 1 April. The spot rate on 1 January is ₹ 40/US $ and the three-month forward rate is ₹ 39.50/US $. This shows depreciation of the dollar and in this case, if the customer sells rupees to the bank, the latter will buy them at the spot rate. If the customer buys rupees, the bank will sell them at the forward rate.

In case of a *forward-forward swap*, two future dates are chosen and profit emerges from the difference between the two forward rates. Suppose the trend of the quote shows appreciation in the dollar for the next six months followed by depreciation during the following three months. The spot rate and the forward rates would be:

Forward-forward swap means buying and selling a currency forward depending upon differing exchange rates for differing maturities.

Spot rate	:	₹ 40–40.20/US $
6-month forward rate	:	₹ 41.50–41.80/US $
9-month forward rate	:	₹ 40.25–40.75/US $

In this case, it would be beneficial for the customer to sell the dollar 6-month forward and buy the dollar 9-month forward. If it involves US $ 1,000, the profit will amount to: (₹ 41.50 – 40.75) × 1,000 or ₹ 750.

PROBLEM 5.7

The following are the rates of forward market deals of different maturity. Explain what should be the process of forward-forward swap.

One-month forward rate	:	₹ 40.50/US $
Two-month forward rate	:	₹ 41.10/US $
Three-month forward rate	:	₹ 40.80/US $

Solution

(a) Buy US $ 1-month forward
(b) Sell US $ 2-month forward
(c) Buy US $ 3-month forward.

SUMMARY

- The foreign exchange market is a market where foreign currencies are bought and sold. It is an over-the-counter market. It operates round-the-clock.
- The participants are the real customers, such as the individuals and the firms who have to actually exchange one currency for another. The commercial banks are the most important participants, although the monetary authorities of the country also participate for the purpose of stabilising the exchange rates. The international agencies are also occasional participants whose aim is either hedging or arbitraging or speculation or restoration of exchange rate stability.
- The market may have spot as well as forward transactions. The former involves immediate delivery of currencies, while the latter involves delivery at a future date.
- Normally, the rates should not vary among different markets, but when they vary, arbitrage takes place conferring profits upon arbitrageurs and ultimately making the rates uniform among different markets.
- The forward market is normally used for hedging risk but sometimes it is used by arbitrageurs who take advantages of differences in interest rates among different markets. Speculators too use the forward market for making profits. Forward options and forward-forward swap are common tools for making profits in the foreign exchange market.

STUDY TOPIC

Indian Foreign Exchange Market

STRUCTURE OF THE MARKET

The Indian foreign exchange market, broadly concentrated in big cities, is a three-tier market. The first tier covers the transactions between the Reserve Bank and the authorised dealers (ADs). As per the Foreign Exchange Regulation Act, now FEMA, the responsibility and authority of foreign exchange administration is vested with the RBI. It is the apex body in this area and for its own convenience, has delegated its responsibility of foreign exchange transaction functions to ADs, primarily the scheduled commercial banks. They have formed the Foreign Exchange Dealers' Association of India which frames rules regarding the conduct of business, coordinates with the RBI in the proper administration of foreign exchange control and acts as a clearing house for information among ADs. Besides the commercial banks, there are the money-changers operating on the periphery. They are well-established firms and hotels doing this business under licence from the RBI. In the first tier of the market, the RBI buys and sells foreign currency from and to ADs according to the exchange control regulations in force from time to time. Prior to the introduction of the Liberalised Exchange Rate Management System, ADs had to sell foreign currency acquired by them from the primary market at rates administered by the RBI. The latter too sold pounds sterling or US dollars, spot as well as forward, to ADs to cover the latter's primary market requirements. But with the unified exchange rate system, the RBI now intervenes in the market to stabilise the value of the rupee.

The second tier of the market is the inter-bank market where ADs transact business among themselves. They normally do their business within the country, but they can transact business also with overseas banks in order to cover their own position. Though they can do it independently, they do it normally through a recognised broker. The brokers are not allowed to execute any deals on their own account or for the purpose of jobbing. Within the country, the inter-bank transactions can be both spot and forward. There may be swap transactions. Any permitted currency can be used. But while dealing with the overseas ADs, because the Indian market lacks depth in other currencies; the Indian banks can deal mainly in two currencies, viz. the US dollar and the pound sterling. Dealings with overseas banks or overseas branches must cover only genuine transactions relating to a customer in India or for the purpose of adjusting or squaring the bank's own position. Forward trading with overseas banks is also allowed if it is done for the above two purposes, that is for covering genuine transactions or for squaring the currency position, and does not exceed a period of six months. In case the import is made on deferred payment terms and the period exceeds six months, permission has to be obtained from the RBI.

Cancellation of forward contracts is allowed in India, although it has to be referred to the RBI. Previously, the banks used to get the forward transactions covered with the RBI, but since 1994–95 the RBI has stopped giving this cover and has permitted the banks to trade freely in the forward market. Cancellation of a forward contract involves entering into a reverse transaction at the going rate. Suppose, US $ 1,000 was bought forward on 1 February for three months at ₹ 40/US $. On 1 March, it is cancelled involving selling the US dollar at the rate prevalent on this day. If the exchange rate on 1 March is ₹ 39.50/US $, there will be a loss of ₹ 500 (the dollar sold for ₹ 39.5 minus dollar bought at ₹ 40.00). The loss is borne by the customer. If the value of the US dollar is greater on the cancellation day, the customer shall reap the profit. Recently, RBI has allowed ADs to re-book cancelled forward contract falling due within one year.

The third tier of the foreign exchange market is represented by the primary market where ADs transact in foreign currency with the customers. The very existence of this tier is the outcome of the legal provision that all foreign exchange transactions of the Indian residents must take place through ADs. The tourists exchange currency, exporters and importers exchange currency, and all these transactions come under the primary market.

TYPES OF TRANSACTION

There are cases where delivery of foreign exchange takes place the same day. Such transactions are known as *ready transactions*. When the actual delivery takes place the next day, the transactions are known as the *value next day transactions*. There are also spot transactions where the actual delivery takes place within two business days. Forward transactions, as per the regulations in India, cannot normally exceed six months. Truly speaking, the forward contracts between banks and the non-bank customers are of the option-forward type. The general rule for the quotation of option rate is to quote the worst of the rates prevailing at the beginning and at the end of the option period. If a currency is purchased when forward premium exists, the premium prevailing at the beginning of the option period will be used, and when a currency is sold forward, the premium prevailing at the end of the period will be taken into account.

Forward premium/discount is governed not entirely by interest rates because of the existence of exchange control, at least to some extent. Nevertheless, call money market rates influence largely the forward premia/discount. Moreover, they are influenced also by the supply of and demand for forward dollars on account of exporter' and importers' involvement. In the Indian foreign exchange market, third currency forward is also available where a firm may have forward deal between the currency of exposure and any other currency.

ADs are allowed to hedge their exchange risk either through cross-currency options or through foreign currency-rupee options for long-term exposure in foreign currency. Banks with minimum capital to risk-adjusted asset ratio of 9 per cent are allowed to offer foreign currency rupee options on a back-to-back basis since July 2003. ADs with adequate risk management systems are allowed to run an option book after obtaining one-time approval from RBI. Option writing by customers is not permitted.

The options market has been an over-the-counter market. It is only since October 2010 that the exchange-traded options have been started at the National Stock Exchange.

Besides options, the currency futures market was started at NSE, BSE and MCX during the second half of 2008. The readers may have a glimpse of options and futures market in India in the following two chapters.

Exchange Rates

In India, since August 1993 direct quote is used where the rupee value is shown per unit of foreign currency. Buying and selling rates are quoted separately. There are different rates prevailing in the Indian market. One is known as the *merchant rate* when ADs quote rates to their customers maintaining a cushion over and above the inter-bank rate in order to hedge the risk arising from changes in the exchange rate since whenever ADs quote rates to their customers, they are based on the previous day's London market quotation. There is always possibility for a variation between the closing rates of the previous day and the opening rates of today in London market. The cushion is, therefore, deducted from the buying rate and added to the selling rate in the direct method of the quote. The merchant rate is the rate that emerges out of such adjustments.

The other is the *telegraphic transfer (TT) rate*. This is normally applicable to inward remittances. Suppose, an exporter gets a bank draft issued by a bank based in New York on a bank based in Bombay. The Bombay-based bank, on the presentation of draft by the Indian exporter, will buy the US dollar at the TT buying rate which is fixed after deducting exchange margin on account of bank charges from the base rate or the inter-bank bid rate. If the inter-bank bid rate is ₹ 40/US $ and the exchange margin is 1.0 per cent, the TT buying rate would be ₹ 40 × (1 – 0.01) or ₹ 39.60.

The TT selling rate is applicable when the bank is selling a foreign currency draft. Suppose an Indian importer asks its banker in Bombay to issue a draft in favour of a bank in New York. The Bombay-based bank will charge rupees from the customer at the TT selling rate. This rate is equal to the inter-bank selling rate plus the exchange margin. If the inter-bank selling rate is ₹ 40.20/US $ and exchange margin is 1.0 per cent, TT selling rate will be ₹ 40.20 × (1 + 0.01) or ₹ 40.60. However, the spread between the spot merchant rate and the spot TT rate should not exceed 2.0 per cent in case of British pound, Euro and Japanese yen, and 1.0 per cent in case of the US dollar.

Yet again, there are *bill buying rates* and *bill selling rates*. Suppose an Indian exporter draws a bill on a New York-based importer. The AD in India will buy the bill and collect the amount from the US-based importer. This involves an additional margin; and so, this rate will be equal to the TT buying rate minus the additional margin. When an AD in India has to collect funds from an Indian importer and to transmit the funds to a US-based exporter, the rate charged by the AD would be known as the *bill selling rate* that would be equal to the sum of TT selling rate and the additional exchange margin. Besides the above, there are traveller's cheque rate and CCY rate, the computation of which is the same as TT rates, and bills buying and selling rates.

The normal practice is to quote the rates in inter-bank transactions up to 4 decimal points, but in case of transactions between a bank and the customer, the rate is quoted to 2 decimal points.

Foreign Exchange Clearing

Clearing and Settlement of Inter-Bank Dollar-Rupee Transactions by CCIL

The Clearing Corporation of India Limited (CCIL) facilitates the clearing and settlement of inter-bank dollar-rupee transactions through a multilateral netting mechanism. Acting as a central counterparty that guarantees trade settlements, CCIL employs a process called **novation**, whereby it interposes itself as a buyer to the seller and a seller to the buyer, creating two contracts from the original trade. This ensures efficient and secure settlements. CCIL initiated live operations in this area in **November 2002**.

For the US dollar leg of the transaction, settlement occurs through CCIL's account with its designated settlement agent in the USA, while the rupee leg is cleared via member banks' current accounts maintained with the Reserve Bank of India (RBI). This dual-leg arrangement provides banks with significant cost and time advantages, enhancing the efficiency of rupee-dollar transaction clearing and settlement.

To further streamline foreign exchange (forex) operations, CCIL introduced its forex trading platform, **FX-CLEAR**, on **August 7, 2003**. This platform facilitates smoother settlement of foreign exchange transactions. In addition, CCIL offers **FX-Direct**, a platform that enables real-time order matching and negotiation for forex trading. Complementary tools like **Refinitiv Matching (formerly Reuters D2)** and **Refinitiv Market Data System** ensure faster and more precise data operations.

In response to growing counterparty credit and settlement risks in foreign exchange forward trades, CCIL launched **clearing and settlement services for forex forward trades from the trade date in December 2009**. This development mitigated risks and enhanced transparency, further solidifying CCIL's role in the Indian financial markets.

QUESTIONS

1. Comment on the structure of Indian foreign exchange market.
2. Explain the different types of transactions.
3. What is a forward contract? Can it be cancelled?
4. In what way the merchant rate is different from the TT rate?
5. How are the transactions settled and cleared?

CASE STUDY

FOREIGN EXCHANGE TRANSACTIONS TURNOVER IN INDIAN MARKET

The Indian market involves transactions between Indian rupee and a foreign currency and between different foreign currencies. They are both merchant and inter-bank as well as both spot and forward. The following table shows the turnover for the whole of the month.

Turnover in the Indian Foreign Exchange Market during October 2024

(US $ million)

Position Date	Merchant						Inter-bank					
	FCY/INR			FCY/FCY			FCY/INR			FCY/FCY		
	Spot	Forward	Forward Cancellation	Spot	Forward	Forward Cancellation	Spot	Swap	Forward	Spot	Swap	Forward
	1	2	3	4	5	6	7	8	9	10	11	12
Purchases												
October 1, 2024	4,753	1,162	1,041	681	520	447	16,089	21,263	1,941	10,726	3,344	286
October 3, 2024	5,845	1,766	406	709	706	479	17,465	19,609	2,452	12,030	2,704	308
October 4, 2024	5,585	1,144	682	755	267	592	15,665	24,170	2,000	8,602	1,940	162
October 7, 2024	4,908	992	1,423	563	457	382	14,945	21,846	2,244	6,605	1,983	185
October 8, 2024	4,461	1,168	289	505	294	316	13,438	22,345	1,987	7,782	2,544	221
October 9, 2024	5,656	1,204	1,141	411	226	227	11,740	23,266	1,743	6,438	2,497	220
October 10, 2024	3,741	1,065	538	660	462	322	8,356	19,893	1,731	7,202	3,177	338
October 11, 2024	4,777	1,379	980	303	355	360	22,394	18,561	1,351	5,351	2,609	196
October 14, 2024	2,536	1,534	640	317	187	235	7,222	6,809	2,067	4,528	1,468	142
October 15, 2024	5,175	1,378	1,120	502	397	410	14,247	19,420	3,323	10,502	3,027	201
October 16, 2024	6,185	908	1,322	598	442	472	15,267	22,585	2,900	8,430	2,726	201
October 17, 2024	7,030	1,744	1,315	661	540	383	12,743	20,248	2,707	8,331	2,333	340
October 18, 2024	4,035	770	2,336	453	577	497	14,700	21,268	3,347	8,291	3,117	222
October 21, 2024	4,994	1,027	834	387	263	300	15.232	23,076	3,370	5,473	2,100	159
October 22, 2024	6,265	1,003	1,292	554	359	274	13,614	21,971	2,096	6,997	2,562	238
October 23, 2024	11,919	1,006	1,038	582	452	354	13,472	24,132	2,134	7,924	3,683	254
October 24, 2024	4,642	867	907	594	505	562	11,008	22,546	2,896	8,805	2,911	283
October 25, 2024	3,704	991	817	371	364	417	13,721	14,752	2,221	6,865	2,212	122
October 28, 2024	6,050	2,059	1,460	492	513	290	9,665	18,248	2,201	6,935	2,517	343
October 29, 2024	6,469	2,529	1,933	936	634	833	11,614	20,589	3,864	7,103	3,874	367
October 30, 2024	5,331	2,797	1,558	538	548	477	10,995	17,168	2,769	6,682	4,689	326
October 31, 2024	3,853	1,125	431	407	373	513	9,836	14,770	565	4,781	3,337	275
Sales												
October 1, 2024	6,687	1,674	464	676	534	447	16,404	20,676	1,640	10,699	3,104	357
October 3, 2024	6,331	1,809	635	714	695	478	16,525	17,258	1,845	12,148	2,461	286
October 4, 2024	5,868	1,753	659	774	275	592	15,496	18,178	2,145	8,523	1,782	307
October 7, 2024	6,634	2,634	990	586	479	382	13,960	17,827	1,580	6,484	1,790	185
October 8, 2024	6,510	791	585	523	321	316	13,353	18,653	785	7,669	2,268	221
October 9, 2024	6,001	2,273	744	414	245	227	10,924	19,342	1,118	6,438	2,320	220
October 10, 2024	5,581	951	882	675	487	322	7,947	17,675	696	7,097	2,945	338
October 11, 2024	5,150	2,139	886	315	345	360	19,015	14,975	2,655	5,346	2,477	196
October 14, 2024	1,941	2,521	354	335	193	235	6,828	7,911	1,610	4,528	1,466	142
October 15, 2024	7,074	1,802	416	541	397	410	14,811	17,552	1,989	10,512	2,672	201
October 16, 2024	5,802	2,248	563	605	443	472	14,366	20,891	2,246	8,375	2,536	201
October 17, 2024	6,175	2,580	1,063	679	436	383	12,656	15,702	2,676	8,540	2,063	343
October 18, 2024	7,631	2,058	552	456	591	498	14,143	15,525	2,249	8,201	2,928	220
October 21, 2024	7,732	1,612	397	405	289	301	14,675	20,063	1,720	5,439	1,909	158
October 22, 2024	6,531	2,363	734	547	370	274	12,784	19,158	1,419	7,227	2,344	237
October 23, 2024	11,192	2,860	488	594	435	354	13,159	21,236	1,712	8,011	3,477	254
October 24, 2024	5,082	2,473	375	607	530	563	9,584	19,828	1,313	8,786	2,640	284
October 25, 2024	4,544	1,761	430	386	359	417	12,248	15,124	1,115	6,803	1,985	122
October 28, 2024	6,395	2,846	733	528	540	290	9,621	17,781	1,293	6,912	2,220	343
October 29, 2024	5,778	3,104	1,540	945	617	833	11,080	18,460	2,110	7,071	3,630	367
October 30, 2024	5,992	2,661	2,006	553	540	478	9,741	15,079	950	6,703	4,463	326
October 31, 2024	2,932	1,102	723	403	373	513	8,019	12,477	1,028	4,683	3,111	276

INR: Indian Rupee FCY: Foreign Currency

Note: Data relate to sales and purchases of foreign exchange on account of merchant and inter-bank transactions. Data are provisional.

QUESTIONS

1. Do spot contracts dominate the scene? Give possible reasons for that.
2. Does cancellation of the forward contracts figure large? If so, why?
3. Why do contracts between two foreign currencies figure large in case of inter-bank dealings?
4. Analyse the figures presented in the table.

REVIEW QUESTIONS

Objective-Type Questions

1. State whether true (T) or false (F):
   (a) The purpose of arbitrage is to minimise/eliminate exchange rate risk. ☐
   (b) Value date/settlement date is the date on which currency is actually delivered. ☐
   (c) In practice, exchange rate differs among markets. ☐
   (d) Settlement date in spot market transaction falls after a week. ☐
   (e) Exporters are in short position in respect of the currency they are to receive. ☐
2. Choose the correct answer:
   (a) Swap quote in forward market:
      (i) makes use of decimal
      (ii) does not make use of decimals
      (iii) none of these
   (b) Currency arbitrage between two markets is encouraged because
      (i) the exchange rates in two markets are different
      (ii) the exchange rates in two markets are the same
      (iii) none of these
   (c) Speculators will buy a foreign currency through a forward market deal if:
      (i) future spot rate of that currency is expected to be lower than the forward rate
      (ii) future spot rate of that currency is expected to be higher than the forward rate
      (iii) future spot rate is expected to be equal to the forward rate

Short-Answer Questions

1. Distinguish between:
   (a) option forward swap and forward-forward swap
   (b) long and short positions in respect of a currency
   (c) two-point arbitrage and triangular arbitrage
2. What do you mean by over-the-counter market?
3. What is broken-date contract in a forward market?

Long-Answer Questions

1. Who are the participants in foreign exchange market?
2. Explain with suitable examples hedging in a forward market.
3. How is speculation done in forward market?

Numerical Problems

1. Three one-month forward deals were contracted respectively on the 27th, 28th and 29th January 2001. What would be the settlement date?
2. The followings are the rates of forward market deals of different maturity. Explain what should be the process of forward-forward swap.
   One-month forward rate: ₹ 40.50/US $
   Two-month forward rate: ₹ 41.10/US $
   Three-month forward rate: ₹ 40.80/US $
3. If the rate of exchange is:
   US $ 2.0000–2.0100/£ in New York
   US $ 1.9800–1.9810/£ in London
   Explain how the arbitrageurs will gain.
4. An Indian importer expects appreciation of US dollar while importing goods for US $ 1,000. So he goes for buying $ 1,000 one-month forward coinciding the time of payment for the import. The spot rate and the forward rate are, respectively, ₹ 40 and ₹ 40.50 per US dollar. Surprisingly, the future spot rate (on maturity) is only ₹ 40.30/$. Will the forward deal be beneficial?

SUGGESTED FURTHER READING

Bhardwaj, H.P. (1994), *Foreign Exchange Handbook*, New Delhi, Wheeler Publishing Co.

Walmsley, J. (1983), *Foreign Exchange Handbook: A user's guide*, New York, John Wiley.

CHAPTER

6 Market for Currency Futures

Learning Objectives

Currencies are bought and sold also in the market for derivatives. One such market is known as the market for currency futures. The present chapter discusses how this market operates. In particular, it:

- Delineates the characteristics of currency futures market as distinct from a currency forward market.
- Discusses hedging in currency futures market.
- Explains how speculators go for futures deal.
- Examines the relationship between futures prices, forward prices and the expected spot prices on delivery.

Besides spot and forward markets, foreign currencies are traded in the market for currency futures and the market for currency options. The market for currency futures and options is known as the *market for derivatives* because the prices in these markets are driven by the spot market price. Their discussion is an essential part of any discussion on the foreign exchange market as they are an integral part of the foreign exchange market. The present chapter deals with the market for currency futures, while the following chapter will deal with the currency options.

UPSURGE IN CURRENCY FUTURES CONTRACTS

The foreign exchange market involving forward contracts has a long history but the market for currency futures has a comparatively recent origin. It came into being in 1972 when the Chicago Mercantile Exchange had set up its international monetary market division for trading of currency futures. Other exchanges were established for this purpose in the subsequent period. Notable among them are the Philadelphia Board of Trade, London International Financial Futures Exchange, Singapore International Monetary Exchange and Sydney Futures Exchange. The volume of transactions in the currency futures market is very low compared to that in the spot and forward markets in general. As per an estimate, the volume of currency futures turnover during 2000 came to around 8–13 per cent of the turnover in the global spot and forward market (BIS, 2004). This percentage stands well maintained. However, in absolute terms, the average daily volume of transactions swelled from $ 20 billion in early 2002 to $ 104 billion in 2010 to more than $ 170 billion in 2023. (BIS website).

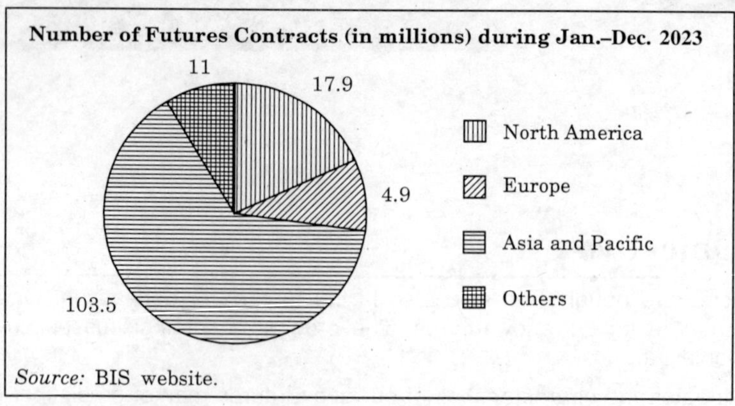

CHART 6.1 Number of Future Contracts.

FEATURES OF CURRENCY FUTURES CONTRACTS

Size and Maturity of the Contract

Despite the fact that a currency futures contract, like a forward contract, involves trading of an underlying currency at a specified exchange rate and for a fixed maturity, there are primary differences between the two. Currency futures are traded only in a limited number of currencies. The size of contract is standardised involving a fixed amount of different currencies. At the Chicago Mercantile Exchange, it is £ 62,500, Can. $ 1,00,000, Australian $ 1,00,000, Euro 1,25,000, Swiss fr. 1,25,000, and Japanese ¥ 1,25,00,000. The date of delivery is also fixed normally on the third Wednesday of January, March, April, June, July, September, October and December. On the contrary, in case of forward contract, many currencies are available for the contract; delivery date is not fixed; nor is the size of the contract.

> Currency futures market is an organised market, and not over-the-counter, for the sale and purchase of specified amount of currencies.

Use of Pits

A forward contract is finalised on telephone, etc. meaning that it represents an over-the-counter market. But in case of currency futures, brokers strike the deals sitting face to face under a trading roof, known as *pits*. The brokers can trade for themselves as well as on behalf of their customers. When they trade for themselves, they are called *locals* or *floor traders*. The locals are sometimes called *scalpers* who hold their position—long or short—for not more than a few minutes. They make profit out of volume trading and at the same time provide liquidity to the market. Some locals are also known as *day traders* who hold their position for a comparatively long period that is less than a full trading session. They make profit out of movement in price but avoid the risk of holding a position for a longer period. Again, some locals are *position traders* who hold a position for a period ranging from overnight to a week or a month. On the other hand, when the brokers trade on behalf of their customers, they are known as *commission brokers or floor brokers*. They charge commission from their clients. This is why there are no bid and ask rates and the commission serves the purpose of spread. Traders acting for themselves as well as on behalf of their customers are known as *dual traders*. One of the demerits of the dual traders is that they act more for their own benefit and not so much for their clients. Such favourable treatment for their own account at the expense of their clients is known as *front-running*.

> Pit is a place where the currencies are traded.

> Brokers are the persons trading currencies either for themselves or for the customers.

> Front running occurs when brokers try to gain at the expense of the clients.

Transactions through a Clearing House

In every deal, the exchange or the clearing house is necessarily involved as a party. Suppose A and B are traders. A strikes a deal with the clearing house. B too strikes a deal with the clearing house. A, if it is a buyer of the currency, shall acquire a long position with the clearing house while B being the seller of the currency shall acquire a short position with the clearing house. In fact, the obligation of the buyer and the seller does not lie with each other but with the clearing house. After a transaction is recorded, the clearing house substitutes itself for the other party, meaning that it becomes the seller to every buyer and buyer from every seller. This way it guarantees the performance of every transaction done on the floor of the exchange. If a buyer of a currency futures contract likes to close out its position before the settlement date, it sells an identical futures contract. The difference between the price of purchasing futures and the price of selling futures will determine the loss/gain to the party. Similarly, a seller of a futures contract closes out its position by purchasing a currency futures contract.

> Clearing house is a part of the system with which traders strike the deal.

Margin Money

Trading in currency futures is subject to specific margin and maintenance requirements. A margin is justified on the ground that the traders represent a source of credit risk to the exchange or the clearing house as long futures traders may not have sufficient funds to buy the underlying foreign currency. In order to cover the risk, they are required to deposit margin money with the clearing house. This is normally in the form of cash deposits, although liquid securities are also used. The initial margin amount varies from one exchange to the other. It is returned

> Margin money represents traders' deposit with the clearing house for the adjustment of gain/loss.

on the completion of the contract. If it is in the form of securities, the interest earned thereon is also paid to the traders. In case of forward contracts, there is no question of margin and maintenance requirements.

The margin money has two components. One is the initial margin which is the amount of money that must be deposited at the time of signing of the contract. The other is the maintenance margin. It denotes the minimum level to which the margin is allowed to fall in the sequel of loss. If the balance drops below the maintenance level, additional amount known as variation margin is deposited to restore the minimum balance.

The variation margin depends on the probability of exhaustion. The probability of exhaustion,

$$P = 2[1 - N(\omega)]$$

where

$$\omega = D/(V \times K \times \sqrt{T}) \tag{6.1}$$

Here, D is the cash deposit for each futures contract, V is the standard deviation of daily change in the price of futures contract, K is the value of 1 futures contract, T is the number of trading days over which calculation is based and $N(\omega)$ is the cumulative distribution function for a standardised normal variant.

Suppose a finance manager goes for a pound futures contract in the US futures market at an assumed spot rate of US $ /£. V is 0.0040. Exhaustion takes not more than 10 per cent of the time. And T is 9 days. In this case,

$$\omega = D/(0.0040 \times 62{,}500 \times \sqrt{9}) = D/750$$

If exhaustion occurs not more than 10 per cent of the time, $P = 1 - 0.90 = 0.10$. So ω must be determined so that

$$0.10 = 2[1 - N(\omega)] \text{ or } N(\omega) = 0.95$$

From a normal distribution table, we find that

$$\omega = 1.90$$

Hence,

$$D/750 = 1.90 \quad \text{or} \quad D = 750 \times 1.90 = 1{,}425$$

This means that the finance manager should keep $ 1,425 deposited for each pound futures contract for the purpose of meeting variation margin calls in addition to the maintenance margin.

PROBLEM 6.1

Find out the size of variation margin call of a Euro futures contract with the help of the following data:

(a) 1 Euro futures contract
(b) Spot price is US $ 1.50/Euro
(c) 0.0040 is standard deviation of daily changes in the price of futures price
(d) Probability of exhaustion is 0.05
(e) Number of days is 9 for which calculation is to be made

Solution

One Euro futures contract involves Euro 1,25,000. Converting this amount in terms of US $, it comes to US $ 1,87,500. Applying Eq. (6.1), we get

$$\omega = D/(0.0040 \times 1{,}87{,}500 \times \sqrt{9}) = D/\$\ 2{,}250$$

Since $P = 0.05$, $N(\omega) = 0.975$, from the normal distribution table, it is found that

$$\omega = 1.96 = D/2,250$$

or

$$D = 2,250 \times 1.96 = \$\ 4,410$$

In other words, US $ 4,410 is the size of variation margin call.

Marking to the Market

In case of forward contracts, the deal is settled on the maturity but in case of currency futures, the rates are matched every day with the movements in spot rates; and on this basis, gains and losses are settled every day. This process is called *marking to the market.*

> Marking to market involves daily comparison of spot rate with yesterday's rate up to the maturity for the assessment of loss/gain.

The process of marking to market can be explained with the help of an example. Suppose an investor buys Can. dollar futures (Can. $ 1,00,000) at US $ 0.75 on a Monday morning which is to mature within two days. At the close of Tuesday, if the price moves up to US $ 0.755, the investor shall profit 1,00,000 × (US $ 0.755 – 0.750) or US $ 500, and if the price falls to US $ 0.749, the investor will have to bear the loss. The amount of loss will be deducted from the margin money. If the loss is big and as a result, the margin money falls below a certain level, which is known as the *maintenance margin*, the investor receives a margin call for depositing the margin money within a specified period. Again, on Wednesday, the prevailing price on that particular day will be compared with the price prevailing on Tuesday and the gain or loss will be determined. On the maturity day, the investor receives the amount of the contract after the adjustment of the profit/loss. However, it may be mentioned that in very few cases, the amount of the contract flows to the investor. In majority of the cases, there is a matching contract in the opposite direction. The investor gets only the difference.

PROBLEM 6.2

An importer buys Pound 62,500 in the futures market at $1.750/£ for the purpose of hedge on 20th September. The maturity falls on 27th September. The spot exchange rate of US dollar per pound is as follows:
21/9: $ 1.752, 22/9: 1.755, 23/9: 1.753, 24/9: 1.753, 25/9: 1.754, 26/9: 1.755 and on 27/9: 1.758. Find out how much will be added to/subtracted from the margin money.

Solution

21/9: $1.752 – 1.750 = 0.002
22.9: $1.755 – 1.752 = 0.003
23/9: $1.753 – 1.755 = –0.002
24/9: $1.753 – 1.753 = 0
25/9: $1.754 – 1.753 = 0.001
26/9: $1.755 – 1.754 = 0.001
27/9: $1.758 – 1.755 = 0.003

Net gain = $ 0.008. Total gain = $ 0.008 × 62,500 = $ 500 that will be added to the margin money.

Methods of Transaction

When a trader has to enter a currency futures contract, he informs his agent who in turn informs the commission broker at the stock exchange. The commission broker executes the deal in the pit for a commission/fee. After the deal is executed, the commission broker confirms the trade with the agent of the trader (client or principal). The agent furnishes details to the principal about the transaction and the futures price. The principal deposits the margin money with the clearing house at the very start of the next day. Settlement, known as marking to the market takes place every working day. The final settlement is made on the maturity date.

Final settlement, as already mentioned, is done either through the delivery of the underlying foreign currency on full settlement or through an offsetting contract. Offsetting contract means taking an equal but opposite position. It means that if a person has gone for buying dollars in the futures market with a delivery date of 29 August 2024, he can have a dollar selling contract maturing on 28th of September 2024. The gain or loss will be transferred to him. Alternatively, he can go for selling any other currency for the same value date in order to offset his original contract. But the currency chosen for this purpose is that one which has a positive correlation with the underlying currency in the earlier contract.

Types of Order

There are different types of order that may be placed by the principal.

- A *limit order* that stipulates a particular price at which a deal is to be made.
- A *fill-or-kill order* in which the commission broker is instructed to fill an order immediately at a specific price. The order is cancelled if it is not transacted quickly.
- The *all-or-none order* in which the commission broker transacts different parts of the deal at different prices.
- An *on-the-open order* involves transaction within a few minutes of opening of the stock exchange.
- An *on-the-close order* which means transacting during the closure of the stock exchange.
- A *stop order* which involves a reversing trade when the price hits a prescribed limit. Its purpose is to protect against losses on existing position.

Costs in Futures Deal

There are different costs associated with the transactions in the market for currency futures. The first is the *brokerage commission* that is charged by the commission brokers and covers both the opening and the reversing trade. The second is the *floor trading* and *clearing fee* charged by the stock exchange and its associated clearing house. Normally, this fee is included in the brokerage commission but when the locals trade for themselves, the fee is quite exclusively found. The third is the *delivery cost* that is related to the delivery of the currencies but since actual delivery of the currencies seldom takes place, such cost is not common.

Costs involved in futures deal are:
1. brokerage commission
2. floor trading and clearing fee
3. delivery cost.

Limits

In order to prevent sudden and violent changes in the price of the underlying currency, daily price limits have been prescribed. The floor and the ceiling is fixed on the previous day's closing price along with some adjustments made in sync with the current market trends. However, the futures exchange can change the price limits if it is artificially created and undermines the normal trading.

Futures Contract Compared to Forward Contract

The discussion of the features of currency futures contracts reveals that they are different from forward contracts at least on a few counts. For example, the daily settlement procedure in futures market enables the less credit-worthy investors to participate. Forward contracts, on the other hand, witness cash flow only on the date of maturity that makes the contract more risky. Nevertheless, forward contracts are widely used because they are available at many financial centres, their amount can be tailored to individual needs as they have no standard size and maturity. The size and the maturity of thousands of transactions taking place daily are not necessarily compatible with those of the futures. The distinction between forward and futures contracts is shown in Table 6.1.

TABLE 6.1 Distinction between Forward and Futures Contracts

Characteristics	*Forward contract*	*Futures contract*
Size of contract	Tailored to individual needs	Standardised
Maturity	Tailored to individual needs	Standardised
Method of transaction	Over-the-counter deal	Dealing on the floor of the exchange
Volume of transactions	Very large	Very low, say around 1 per cent of forex market
Bid-offer spread	Tighter	Greater than in forex market
Commission	Spread between the banks' buying and selling price	Brokerage fee
Security deposit	Not required except compensating bank balances	Margin money to be deposited with the clearing house
Clearing operation	No clearing house	Clearing house for daily settlement
Access	Limited to very large customers who deal in foreign trade	Open to any one who needs hedging or speculation
Regulation	Self-regulating	Regulated by the rules of the stock exchange
Liquidation	Mostly settled by actual delivery; a few by offsetting contract	Mostly by offsetting contract and a few by actual delivery

HEDGING IN CURRENCY FUTURES MARKET

Traders make use of the market for currency futures in order to hedge their foreign exchange risk. For instance, suppose a French importer importing goods from USA for $ 1.0 million needs this amount for making payments to the exporter. It will purchase US dollar futures contract which would lock in the price to be paid to the exporter in terms of US dollar at a future settlement date. By holding a futures contract, the importer does not have to worry about any change in the spot rate of the US dollar over time. On the other hand, if the French exporter exports goods to a US firm and has to receive US dollar for the exports, the exporter would sell a US dollar futures contract. This way the exporter will be locking in the price of the export to be received in terms of US dollar. It will protect itself from the loss that may occur in case of depreciation of the US dollar over time.

Hedge Ratio

Hedge ratio is found out through dividing the value of the futures contract by the amount of money exposed to currency risk. A zero hedge ratio means perfect hedge where the entire risk is eliminated through the hedge. But in futures market, there is no perfect hedge because of the dissimilar size of transaction from the futures size or dissimilar maturity date from the delivery date or both.

However, the question is whether futures hedge can be a perfect hedge. It is particularly in view of the fact that while forward deal can be tailored to any size of the currency transaction and to any maturity, the futures cannot be, insofar as both the size of the contract and the maturity of the futures deal are fixed. Suppose a German importer decides to import on 1st of September from Canada for which C$ 62,500 has to be paid on December 1. If the maturity in the futures market falls on December 26, the maturity does not match with that of the actual cash transaction. Again, since the size of the Canadian dollar futures is C$ 1,00,000, it does not match with the size of cash transaction. On this ground, futures hedge cannot normally be a perfect hedge.

If the maturity of futures contract mismatches, futures hedging is known as a *delta hedge.* If maturity matches but the size of the futures contract does not match, one can go for a cross hedge. If both the size and maturity do not match, the hedger can go for a delta-cross hedge.

Delta Hedge

Delta hedge exists when the maturity does not coincide with the hedger's need for the currency.

Suppose for a moment that the value of import made on September 1 is C$ 1,00,000. The amount is to be paid on December 1. If the German importer goes for a forward contract, he will buy Canadian dollar three-month forward. In case of forward contract, forward rate on the date of maturity can easily be calculated on the basis of the interest rate parity theory. As per the above example, if spot rate on September 1 is Euro 0.90/C$ and the interest rate is 5 per cent and 4 per cent respectively in Germany and Canada, the forward rate on December 1 will be Euro [(1.05/1.04) – 1]0.90/4 + 0.90/C$ or Euro 0.9092/C$. But in a futures hedge, where maturity falls on December 26, 25 days are still left for the maturity during which the interest rate differential may change. So a futures hedge cannot be a perfect hedge and there will be some variations in the hedged pay-offs. It can, however, be very nearly a perfect hedge if there is no change in the interest rate differential. It is because there is virtually no basis risk if interest rate differential does not change. It may be noted here that basis risk arises on account of unexpected change in the relationship between spot rate and futures rate.

Cross Hedge

Let us take another example where the value of import is C$ 62,500 and the payment has to be made on December 26. Here the maturity matches, but the size of the contract does not. In this case, the size of payment matches with that of the British pound futures. Importer can go for buying pound in the futures market if there is a high degree of correlation between British pound and the Canadian dollar. The futures hedge can be made a perfect hedge this way.

> Cross hedge exists when the amount of the futures contract does not tally with the actual amount to be hedged.

Delta Cross Hedge

It is a case when there is both maturity and size mismatch. In such cases, it is difficult to eliminate the basis risk. As a result, the futures hedge is normally not a perfect hedge. The hedger can, however, go simultaneously for a cross hedge and a delta hedge in order to make the hedge a perfect one as far as possible.

> Delta cross hedge is a combination of delta hedge and the cross hedge.

SPECULATION WITH CURRENCY FUTURES

Speculators make use of the currency futures for reaping profits. When they expect that the spot rate of a particular currency will move up beyond those mentioned in the currency futures contract, they buy currency futures denominated in that particular currency. On the other hand, if the spot rate of a particular currency is expected to depreciate below the rate mentioned in the currency futures contract, the speculators will sell currency futures in that currency. It may be noted here that these transactions involve cost that is to be deducted from the gain. The transaction cost is very nominal for the locals, but is significant for the speculators.

Intra-currency Spread

Speculators can buy or sell futures of the same currency for two delivery dates if the rates for those two dates differ. This is known as *intra-currency spread.* To make the example simple, we ignore here any marking to market. Suppose pound is expected to appreciate till June and then it is expected to depreciate at least by September at a faster rate than the futures rate. In this case, a speculator will buy a pound futures contract for June delivery and sell another one for the September delivery. Suppose pound futures are available at $ 0.650/£ for June delivery and at

> Intra-currency spread exists when a speculator buys/ sells the same currency for two delivery dates.

$ 0.640/£ for September delivery. The spot rate of pound rises to $ 0.655 on the June maturity but, contrary to the speculator's expectations, falls only to 0.642/£ by September maturity date. The speculator will gain $ 0.005 per pound on the June-delivery contract but will lose $ 0.002 on the September contract. The net gain will be equal to $ (0.005 – 0.002) × 62,500 = $ 187.5.

PROBLEM 6.3

Suppose spot rate on April 1 is 1.785/£. Pound futures contract is sold at $ 1.790 for June delivery and at $ 1.785 for September delivery. Expecting that pound will depreciate fast after June, a speculator buys the former and sells the latter. Later he finds that pound may appreciate by June but may not depreciate subsequently. So he reverses the two contracts respectively at $ 1.78 and $ 1.76. Suppose the exchange rate on both the maturity dates is $ 1.795/£. Find how much the speculator gains/loses.

Solution

Buying pound futures contract:

Gain per pound from the original contract = $ 1.795 – 1.790 = $ 0.005 and gain from the reverse contract = 1.795 – 1.760 = $ 0.035. Total gain $ 0.040 per pound.

Selling pound futures contract:

Loss per pound from the original contract = $ 1.795 – 1.785 = $ 0.010 and from the reverse contract = $ 1.795 – 1.780 = $ 0.015. Total loss = $ 0.025 per pound

Net gain = $ 0.040 – 0.025 = $ 0.015 per pound = $ 0.015 × 62,500 = $ 937.50.

Had there been no reversal of the contracts, the speculator would have lost to an extent of $ 0.005 – 0.010 = $ 0.005 per pound or in all $ 0.005 × 62,500 = $ 312.50.

Note: It ignores marking to market.

Inter-currency Spread

Besides the intra-currency spread, inter-currency spread is also used by the speculators. Such spread occurs when the deal involves purchase and sale of future contracts with the same delivery date but with two different underlying currencies. Suppose the speculator expects an appreciation of Canadian dollar relative to the British pound. He will buy Canadian dollar futures and sell pound futures. Before maturity, he will reverse the two contracts. If the price difference of the two reverse contracts is less than the price difference of the original contracts, the speculator will make a profit.

Inter-currency spread exists when a speculator buys/sells two or more currencies for the same delivery date.

PROBLEM 6.4

If pound futures contract is available at $ 1.690 and Euro futures contract is available at $ 1.250. Pound is expected to appreciate and Euro is expected to depreciate. In such a situation, a speculator will buy a pound futures contract and sell Euro futures contract for the same maturity. If, contrary to the expectations, pound depreciates to $ 1.680 and Euro depreciates to $ 1.235, find out the gain to the speculator from the inter-currency spread.

Solution

Loss on pound futures contract = $ 1.690 – 1.680 = $ 0.010 per pound or total loss = $ 0.010 × 62,500 = $ 625.
Gain on the Euro futures contract = $ 1.250 – 1.235 = $ 0.015 per pound or total gain = $ 0.015 × 1,25,000 = $ 1,875.
Net gain = $ 1,875 – 625 = $ 1,250.
Note: It ignores marking to market.

FUTURES PRICES, FORWARD PRICES AND EXPECTED SPOT PRICES ON DELIVERY

Conditions of Risk-neutrality

Whether or not there is equality among the forward prices, futures prices and the expected spot prices at delivery is an important question. The general view is that if investors are risk-neutral, forward prices are equal to the expected spot prices at delivery because investors' marginal rate of substitution between different outlets of investment is constant, as a result of which their utility function is linear and the co-variance between their marginal rate of substitution and the exchange rate of the contract at delivery is zero. As far as equality between forward prices and futures prices is concerned, the interest rate parity theory suggests that the two are equal if investors are risk-neutral and the interest rate is constant. As a natural corollary, the three—*forward prices, futures prices and the expected spot prices at delivery*—are equal under the conditions of risk-neutrality.

If investors are risk-neutral, forward prices are equal to the expected spot prices at delivery

Conditions of Risk-aversion

In real life, however, the investors are risk-averse; and the interest rate is not constant either. As a result, the futures prices are not equal to forward prices and so, it follows that the futures prices are not equal to the expected spot prices at delivery. Even if we assume risk-neutrality, the prices of currency futures and those of forward contracts differ. *Firstly*, the settlement procedure of futures is different from that of the forward contract. In the latter, cash flow occurs only on maturity, but in case of currency futures, settlement takes place daily; and the daily margin, if it represents a gain, is reinvested. *Secondly*, interest rates are normally not constant. If interest rate is ascending, the reinvestment will earn a greater amount and this will stimulate the price of futures to a level that is higher than the price of the forward contract. If interest rate is descending, the futures price will turn lower than the forward price.

When investors are risk-averse and when interest rate is not constant, one finds that currency forward prices equal expected spot prices at delivery plus the hedging or risk premium; currency futures prices equal to sum of expected spot prices at delivery, plus the hedging premium, term premium and the reinvestment rate premium.

When investors are risk-averse and when interest rate is not constant, one finds that currency forward prices equal expected spot prices at delivery plus the hedging or risk premium; currency futures prices equal to sum of expected spot prices at delivery, plus the hedging premium, term premium and the reinvestment rate premium.

Therefore, currency futures prices are the sum of currency forward prices, term premium and reinvestment premium.

Here different types of premium need an explanation. *Firstly*, the term premium arises from the existence of liquidity premium involved in the term structure of the contract. The shorter the maturity, the greater is the liquidity. The premium is normally constant across currencies. *Secondly*, the reinvestment rate premium is associated with the margin earned on the daily settlement of the futures contract. The higher the interest rate, the greater is the premium. This is generally varying among different currencies as the interest rate varies among different countries. *Thirdly*, the hedging premium depends upon the co-variance between the exchange rate at delivery and the investor's marginal rate of substitution. The co-variance may be positive with the result that the forward rate will be greater than the expected spot rate at delivery. This position is known as *contango*. On the other hand, the co-variance may be negative meaning a situation of *normal backwardation* where forward rates are lower than the expected spot rate at delivery. In fact, co-variance depends upon the investor's overall portfolio from which wealth is drawn for consumption (Cox, et al., 1981).

Contango means forward rate being greater than expected spot rate at delivery. Normal backwardation is just the opposite.

Nevertheless, as is sometimes argued, disparity between the price of currency futures and the price of forward contract exists only in the short run. In the long run, it tends to evaporate because of active participation of the arbitrageurs in the foreign exchange market. Suppose, rate of sterling futures is US $ 1.75 and the forward rate of the same currency and with the same maturity is US $ 1.77. In such a case, the arbitrageurs will buy sterling futures and sell sterling forward with similar maturity and for the same amount. On the maturity, the profit will be reaped at US $ (1.77 – 1.75) × 62,500 or US $ 1,250. The process of arbitrage will continue till the disparity between the two rates is wiped out. Selling forward will depress the forward rates, while buying futures will raise the futures rate. The two will be equal somewhere between US $ 1.75 and US $ 1.77.

Moreover, Empirical findings reveal that the different types of premium do not matter much, as a result of which the different prices are almost equal. Edwards (1982), Kohlhagen (1979), and Longworth (1981) find that hedging premium is non-existent. The studies by Hodrick and Srivastawa (1984) and Fama (1984) suggest that hedging premium does exist but is negligible. Thus in essence, the two prices—forward rate and expected spot rate at delivery—are almost the same. Similarly, Cornell and Reinganum (1981) find that the other two premiums hardly exist. They are of the view that the forward prices and the futures prices are nearly the same.

Empirical findings reveal that the different types of premium do not matter much, as a result of which the different prices are almost equal.

SUMMARY

- Currency futures are known as derivatives. Their market evolved in the early 1970s. They involve delivery of currencies on a future date and so, are similar to forward contracts. But in many ways, the two are different. To mention some of the more important differences, the size of the futures contract is fixed. The maturity date is fixed. The deals are transacted on the pits by locals or brokers for which they charge commission from the principal traders or clients. On the other hand, the size of the contract and the maturity date in a forward contract are tailored to the needs of the traders. The forward market is an over-the-counter market. It does not involve any brokerage fee; rather the difference between the buying and the selling rates forms the profit of the bank. In the futures market, margin money is deposited to compensate the loss on daily settlements. In forward contracts, settlement is done only on maturity. Forward deals are contracted directly between two parties, but in case of futures, deals are contracted with the clearing house.

- When a client has to make a futures deal, it contacts the commission brokers through its own agent. After the deal is transacted, the client deposits the margin money with the clearing house. Daily settlement begins and continues till final settlement on maturity. In the majority of contracts, delivery of currencies is not made but is offset by a reversing deal. The client gets only the difference between the two deals. There are many types of orders that the commission brokers receive from their clients. Such a deal involves costs, such as brokerage commission, clearing house charges and the delivery fee.
- The market for currency futures is used by both the hedgers and the speculators. The former use it for reducing their risk appearing on account of changes in exchange rate. The latter use it for reaping profits. Apart from simple speculation, they involve themselves in intra-currency and inter-currency spreads. The former takes place when the rate of the same currency varies on two maturity dates. The latter involves two currencies with the same maturity.
- Under the conditions of risk-neutrality and constant interest rates, forward prices, futures prices, and the expected spot prices at delivery, are equal. But under conditions of varying interest rates, the futures prices and forward prices differ inasmuch as the former involve daily settlement and the gain from settlement is reinvested at varying interest rates. Nevertheless, this difference is only short-lived. In the long run, the process of arbitrage helps wipe out such differences. Moreover, empirical studies show that the difference is not significant.

STUDY TOPIC

Currency Futures Market in India

Rupee currency futures were started in Dubai in 2007 at the Dubai Gold and Commodity Exchange. In India, after a green signal from the Raghuram Rajan Committee and the Expert Group at the RBI, three Indian exchanges, viz. BSE, NSE and MCX, applied for dealing in currency futures. RBI and SEBI released the guidelines in this respect on the 6th of August 2008. Finally, NSE started operating on the 29th of August 2008. MCX and BSE followed the suit.

The guidelines allowed only US dollar-rupee contracts with a size of $ 1,000 for a maturity not exceeding 12 months. The trading is done on Monday through Friday excluding public holidays between 9.00 AM and 5 PM and the settlement is done on the last working day of the month, and not earlier. Thus, the standardised size is smaller than those at the international exchanges. The contracts are quoted and settled in rupee.

The membership of the currency futures market would be separate from the membership of derivatives/cash segment. Again, only a resident Indian, including banks, can participate in the deal. This means that the foreign institutional investors/non-resident Indians are not entitled to participate in the deal. A bank being a member must have reserves worth ₹ 5 billion, 10 per cent CRAR, an NPA of 3 per cent at the maximum and a profit record for at least three years. The trading limit for an individual client is $ 5 million or 6.0 per cent of the total open interest, whichever is higher. For a trading member—bank or broker, it is $ 25 million or 15.0 per cent of the total open interest, whichever is higher.

The hedger or the client is first registered with the trading member who buys or sells the currency futures contract on behalf of the client. The marking to market is based on the daily settlement price which is arrived at after taking the weighted average of last half an hour's transactions. The loss or gain arising out of this process is settled on the t + 1 basis. At the end of the day, net positions are reset with respect to the current day's daily settlement price and are carried forward to the next day. Finally, on the settlement day, the settlement is done in cash payable in rupee.

In the entire process, the clearing member has a crucial role to play. At the NSE, its wholly-owned subsidiary, National Securities Clearing Corporation Ltd. (NSCCL) carries out the entire clearing and settlement process. It acts as counter-party to all transactions and guarantees the final settlement. It carries out also novation which means that it helps replacement of one obligation with another with the mutual consent of both the parties. The clearing banks help NDCCL in carrying out clearing and settlement.

The NSCCL monitors the members' operation on-line and asks for immediate halt of any transaction if the open position or the margin money requirements are violated. Here it may be mentioned that the margin requirements are enforced by the NSCCL. It calculates the initial margin money requirements on the client's level using the Standard Portfolio Analysis of Risk methodology and informs the trading members daily about the clients' margin liability. The trading members submit the compliance report. The extreme loss margin in case of the trading members is 1.0 per cent of the value of their gross open position.

Now the question is whether the currency futures are better than the forwards transacted in India. First of all, while in the case of OTC forward contracts, the banks quote different bid-ask rates for different customers, the futures rates are shown on the screen of the exchange. Thus, the price discovery is more transparent in the case of futures.

Secondly, participants such as exporters and importers can go for a forward contract only for their underlying transactions. Their purpose cannot be speculation. But in the case of currency futures, no underlying securities are required.

It may be stressed that the quantum of operation in the Indian currency futures market has increased over the years but decreased in the recent years. At the NSE, the number of contracts increased from 32.8 million in FY 2008–09 to 378.6 million in FY 2009–10 and to 712.2 million in FY 2010–11. As a natural corollary, the turnover in this market rose from ₹ 1.626 trillion to ₹ 17.826 trillion and to

₹ 32.79 trillion during the respective fiscal years. But at the NSE, the number of contracts decreased from 1241.42 million in FY 2022–23 to 851.90 million in FY 2023–24 and to 107.46 million in FY 2024–25. As a natural corollary, the turnover in this market got down from ₹ 1.0116 trillion to ₹ 0.7202 trillion and to ₹ 0.0905 trillion during the respective fiscal years. At the MCX_SX, the respective figures of turnover were ₹ 8.58 trillion, ₹ 7.16 trillion and ₹ 39.74 turnover trillion. Currency futures transactions have also been started long ago at the USE. The amount of turnover was low, being ₹ 396.29 billion during the first four months of FY 2023–24.

QUESTIONS

1. Explain the essential features of currency futures trading in India.
2. Comment on the role of NSCCL in clearing and settlement.
3. What are the different types of margin money?
4. Explain how hedging is done at the currency futures market.

REVIEW QUESTIONS

Objective-Type Questions

1. State whether true (T) or false (F):

(a) Normal backwardation means a situation where forward rates are lower than the expected spot rate at delivery. ☐

(b) *Contango* means a situation where forward market rate is lower than the expected spot rate at delivery. ☐

(c) Inter-currency spread occurs where the deals involve purchase and sale of futures contracts with the same delivery date but with two underlying currencies. ☐

(d) Intra-currency spreads involve two currencies for the same delivery date. ☐

(e) The size of futures contract can be tailored according to the needs of the client. ☐

2. Choose the correct answer:

(a) Marking to the market is done:
   (i) only on the date of maturity
   (ii) everyday
   (iii) on the day contract is signed

(b) A limit order:
   (i) stipulates a particular price at which a deal is to be made
   (ii) is an order in which the commission broker transacts the different parts of a deal at different prices
   (iii) none of these

(c) A stop order:
   (i) involves a reversing trade with a view to protecting against losses against the existing contract

(ii) means transacting during the closure of the stock exchange
(iii) none of these

(d) Pits are:
(i) the place where deals are made
(ii) a type of broker
(iii) a form of margin money

(e) The size of futures contract is:
(i) fixed in terms of the value of the currency
(ii) not fixed
(iii) none of these

Short-Answer Questions

1. What are the different types of brokers operating in the market for currency futures?
2. Explain the role of clearing house in the market for currency futures.
3. What is marking to the market? Explain it with suitable example.
4. What are the different types of orders?
5. Distinguish between contango and normal backwardation.

Long-Answer Questions

1. Distinguish between a forward contract and a futures contract. Is the value of a futures contract equal to the value of a forward contract?
2. How are transactions finalised in the market for currency futures?
3. Explain delta hedge, cross hedge and delta-cross hedge in the market for currency futures.

Numerical Problems

1. A US importer negotiates to buy goods valuing Euro 1,25,000, the payment of which coincides with the maturity date in the currency futures market. Expecting appreciation of Euro, he buys for a Euro future in order to hedge the exposure. The spot rate is US $ 0.60/Euro, the futures rate is US $ 0.63/Euro and the spot rate on the maturity is US $ 0.65/Euro. Explain whether futures contract is able to hedge the risk.
2. Find out the basis as well as the futures price of a Euro futures contract based on the following data:
   Spot: US $ 0.60/Euro
   Days to maturity: 90 days
   Three-month interest rate in Germany and the USA is 6 per cent and 5 per cent, respectively.
3. Find out the size of variation margin call of a Euro futures contract with the help of the following data:

   (a) One Euro futures contract
   (b) Spot price is US $ 1.50/Euro

(c) 0.0040 is standard deviation of daily changes in the price of futures price
(d) Probability of exhaustion is 0.05
(e) Number of days is 9 for which calculation is to be made

REFERENCES

BIS (2004), *Triennial Central Bank Survey*, Geneva.

Cornell, B. and M. Reinganum (1981), Forward and Futures Prices: Evidence from the Foreign Exchange Markets, *Journal of Finance*, XXXVI, 1035–1045.

Cox, J., et al. (1981), The Relation between Forward and Futures Prices, *Journal of Financial Economics*, IX, 321–346.

Edwards, S. (1982), Exchange Rates and News: A Multi-currency Approach, *Journal of International Money and Finance*, I, 11–14.

Fama, E. (1984), Forward and Spot Exchange Rates, *Journal of Monetary Economics*, XIV, 319–338.

Hodrick, R. and S. Srivastawa (1984), An Investigation of Risk and Return in Forward Foreign Exchange, *Journal of International Money and Finance*, III, 5–29.

Kohlhagen, S. (1979), The Forward Rate as an Unbiased Predictor of the Future Spot Rate, *Columbia Journal of World Business*, XIV, 77–85.

Longworth, D. (1981), Testing the Efficiency of Canadian-US Exchange Market under the Assumption of No Risk Premium, *Journal of Finance*, XXXVI, 43–49.

SUGGESTED FURTHER READING

Carlton, D. (1984), Futures Markets: Their Purpose, Their History, Their Growth, Their Success and Failures, *Journal of Futures Markets*, IV, 237–271.

CHAPTER 7

Market for Currency Options

Learning Objectives

The market for currency options is the other form of the market for derivatives where currencies are traded. The present chapter acquaints the readers with specific characteristics of this form of market and also with how it works. In particular, it:

- Delineates the broad features and types of a currency options contract.
- Describes different forms of the currency options market.
- Explains commonly used terminologies in this respect.
- Evaluates the gains and losses of the options traders.
- Discusses options pricing and the factors influencing it.
- Examines how hedgers and speculators operate in this market.

The market for currency options is the other form of the derivatives market representing large-scale sale and purchase of currencies. This form of market possesses some distinguishing features and also the methods of operation are different. The present chapter thus acquaints the readers with the functioning of the market for currency options.

BROAD FEATURES

Privilege of Non-execution of Contract

Foreign currencies are traded in the market for currency options as well. The purpose is either the hedging of foreign exchange exposure or making of profits

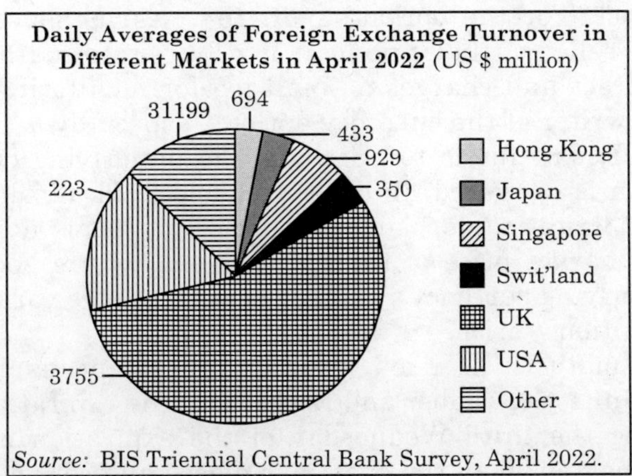

CHART 7.1 Daily Averages of Foreign Exchange Turnover in Different Markets in April 2022.

through speculation. As in currency forward and futures contracts, the buyer of currency options possesses the right to buy or sell foreign currency after the lapse of a specified period at a rate determined on the day the contract is made, but the currency options contract has a distinctive feature that is not found in a forward or futures contract. It is that the buyer of currency options has the freedom to exercise the option if the agreed-upon rate turns in his favour. If the rate does not turn in his favour, he can let the options expire. Thus the exercising of options is the buyer's right but not his obligation. For this privilege, the buyer has to pay a premium to the option-seller. Suppose a person decides to acquire call options to buy Swiss francs at a price of US $ 0.70 along with a premium for US $ 0.02. On the maturity date, if spot rate of the Swiss franc is lower than the agreed upon rate, he will let the option expire because he will be able to buy it in the spot market at a cheaper rate. But if the spot rate is US $ 0.75, he will exercise the option because his cost of buying Swiss francs under the options contract (inclusive of premium) will be US $ 0.72, whereas he can sell this currency in the spot market at a higher rate and can thereby earn a profit.

> Currency options contract confers on options-buyer privilege of not exercising the contract when exchange rate is not in his favour.

Some features of currency options contracts are common irrespective of their type or the market in which these contracts are formalised. But some of the features vary from one type of market or of options contract to another. The three different types of currency options market are explained here so as to reveal the distinctive features of these contracts.

Types of Options Market

Listed currency options market

The first such market was set up at the Philadelphia Stock Exchange in December 1982. Initially, trading was done in British pounds, but subsequently, some other currencies such as the Australian dollar, Canadian dollar, Deutsche mark, French franc, Japanese yen and Swiss franc were added to the list. Listed currency options are standardised contracts. In such contracts, the clearinghouse is essentially a party to the contract. For the option-buyer, the clearinghouse is a seller of the options and for the seller of the options, it is a buyer. It guarantees both sides of the contract and charges a small fee for facilitating such contracts.

Options market may be:
1. listed one being located at stock exchange
2. over-the-counter market where banks dominate
3. futures options market being a listed one with marking to market facilities.

The writer of the currency options, especially a 'put' option, may not have sufficient funds to purchase the underlying currency when such an option is exercised. In order to avoid such a risk, the clearinghouse asks the writer to deposit margin money that is normally equal to the current market price of the option along with a specific percentage of the underlying currency's value. This percentage varies with the changes in the option's price.

The maturity is fixed in this market and expiration months are March, June, September and December. The expiration day is the Friday preceding the third Wednesday of the expiration month. The trading process begins when the customer places an order with a broker who is a member of the exchange. The broker relays the order to the broker's booth located on the exchange trading floor. The broker's floor trader shouts out his bid that is answered by offers to sell from other traders. The offers are made either by specialists, or market makers or by floor brokers acting as agents for other customers. Specialists are normally the firms employed by the exchange to manage the limit orders for each currency. The market maker is a member firm that transacts on its own account. When a transaction is finalised, it is recorded by the exchange's reporting system. The floor trader communicates the deal to the broker who passes on this information to the customer.

Currency futures options market

In this market, which is basically a listed currency options market, the contracts present a mixture of currency futures and currency options. They are basically currency options because the buyer of the contract possesses the privilege of either exercising the option or letting it expire. The buyer and the seller of options have, however, to deposit margin money with the exchange that is equal to a small fraction of the contract price. The options are marked to market meaning that they undergo daily settlement as in the case of a futures contract.

Comparison between Listed Currency Options Market and the Over-the-counter Options Market

	LCOM	*OTCOM*
Contract specifications	Standardised and Customised contract	Only customised contract
Regulation	Regulated by regulatory authorities	Self-regulated
Types of market	Open outcry, auction market	Dealers' market
Counter-party to each transaction	High-rated options clearing house	Bank on the contra side
Transparency	Yes	No
Margin required for short position	Yes	No

(Contd.)

Orders anonymously represented in the market	Yes	No
Required to mark positions daily	Yes	No
Audit trail	Yes (for each transaction)	No
Participants	Individuals, institutions/corporate	Institutions/corporate

Over-the-counter options market

The second type of market for currency options is known as the *inter-bank currency options market* or the *over-the-counter options market*. Such a market is centred in New York and London and the size of transactions is many times that of the market in the organised exchanges. The amount involved in a particular contract is also larger. It is usually US $ 1.0 million or more of foreign currency. Again, European options are usually found in over-the-counter market, while American options are prevalent in the organised exchanges. The number of currencies exchanged in the over-the-counter market is larger and the options are tailored to the clients' needs. The size of contract is standardised, but the banks repackage sizes according to the clients' needs. The organised clearinghouse is not in evidence, rather the commercial banks or investment banks write the options for the clients. In order to offset their exposure, these banks transact currency options on the listed stock exchanges.

The over-the-counter market is a two-tier market. The retail market embracing non-bank customers dealing with the banks forms one tier while the other is the wholesale market representing transactions among the banks.

Types of Options

Broadly speaking, there are two types of options. In a call option, the buyer of the option agrees to buy the underlying currency, while in a put option contract, the buyer of the option agrees to sell the underlying currency.

> In a call option, options-buyer buys the underlying currency. In a put, he sells it.

The call and put options are also of two types. One, known as the *European option*, is exercised only on maturity. The other, the *American option*, may be exercised even before maturity. It is normally in the buyer's interest to exercise the option before maturity and so American options command higher prices than European options.

> European options cannot be exercised before maturity. American options can be.

In recent years, some more variants of options often known as *exotic options* have become available. The first is, for example, known as a *forward reversing option*. In this case, a call option premium is paid only when the spot rate is below a specified level. The premium is quoted by the seller who charges the premium only when the options are not exercised. This way the buyer gets liberal terms. Secondly, there are *preference options* in which the buyer gets an additional privilege to designate the option either as a call option or as a put option. Though this privilege is exercised only after the lapse of a specified period. In the case of *average rate options*, it is the arithmetic average of the spot rate during the life of the option that is taken into account at maturity instead of the spot rate. This type of option enables the buyer to hedge a series of daily cash inflows over a given period in one single contract. If the average rate on maturity is lower than the strike price, the buyer gets the difference between the two. If the average rate is higher than the strike rate, the buyer lets the option expire.

A *look-back option* gives the holder the right to purchase or sell foreign currency at the most favourable exchange rate realised over the life of the option. For example, the buyer of a call has the right to buy the underlying currency at the lowest exchange rate realised between the creation of the call and the expiry date. The buyer of a put option has the right to sell the underlying currency at the highest exchange rate during the life of the option. All this means that the strike rate in a look-back option is not known until the expiry date. Naturally, because of this speciality, the premium of a look-back option is normally higher than the premium of a traditional option.

Exotic options contracts are:
1. forward reversing options,
2. preference options,
3. average rate options,
4. look-back options,
5. cylinder/tunnel options,
6. down and out options,
7. down and in options,
8. basket options.

In a *cylinder* or *tunnel option*, two strike rates exist. When the spot rate is lower than the lower strike rate, the buyer has to pay the lower strike rate. He pays the higher strike rate if the spot rate is higher than the higher strike rate. If the spot rate is between the two strike rates, the buyer pays the spot rate.

There are also barrier options. In the case of *down-and-out option*, the option expires automatically if the spot rate reaches a level mentioned in the contract. In a *down-and-in option*, option is activated only when the spot rate reaches a specified barrier within the expiry date.

The *basket option* caters to buyers who are confronted with foreign exchange risk in respect of many currencies.

OPTIONS TERMINOLOGY

For a clear understanding of currency options, the readers must acquaint themselves with some terms that are used in this context.

Option buyer: A person or a firm who gets the right to buy options, is also known as the *option-holder*.

Option seller: The party having obligation to perform if option is exercised or the party who charges the premium for granting such privilege to the buyer, is also known as the *option-writer*.

Call option: An option bought by an option buyer for buying a particular currency.

Put option: An option bought by an option buyer to sell a particular currency.

Exercise price: The price at which options are exercised, is also known as the *strike price*.

At-the-money: The situation is known as at-the-money when the strike price is equal to the spot price on the maturity date.

In-the-money: The situation is known as *in-the-money* if in case of a call option, the strike price is lower than the spot rate. In case of a put option, an in-the-money situation warrants that the spot rate should be lower than the strike price. In that situation when the option-buyer exercises the option, he is in the money because then only he can gain.

Out-of-the-money: This is the exact opposite situation of the in-the-money situation. This entails that the spot rate should be lower than the strike rate in case of a call option; and higher than the strike rate in case of a put option.

Premium: Also known as the option value or option price, premium is the value or price of the option that the option-buyer pays to the option-seller at the time of signing the contract. It is not refundable even when the option is not exercised. The amount of premium is the sum of the option's *intrinsic value* and its *time value* which are explained hereunder.

Intrinsic value: Intrinsic value denotes the extent to which an option would currently be profitable to exercise. In other words, it represents the gains accruing to the holder on the exercise of the option. In case of a call option, it is the excess of the current spot rate over the strike price. If S is the current spot rate and X the strike price, the intrinsic value of a call option,

$$I_{call} = S - X \tag{7.1}$$

The intrinsic value of a put option will naturally be represented by an excess of strike price over the current spot rate. In other words, the intrinsic value of a put option is

$$I_{put} = X - S \tag{7.2}$$

Thus, it can be said that when the option is in-the-money, it has some intrinsic value. The intrinsic value of an option—put or call—may be positive. It may be zero. But it cannot be negative because the option-buyer will not exercise the option if the option is out-of-the-money.

Time value: Time value of an option represents the sum of money that a buyer is willing to pay over and above the intrinsic value. Time value of an option exists because the spot rate of the underlying currency is expected to move towards an in-the-money position between the signing of the contract and the maturity date. On the maturity date, the time value of the option is zero and the premium is entirely represented by the intrinsic value. Again, if there is an at-the-money position that means that there is no intrinsic value, and option premium is represented entirely by the time value. Between these two positions, the premium is represented partly by the intrinsic value and partly by the time value. Suppose the strike price of a call option is ₹ 83.00/£. The premium is ₹ 0.05 per British pound. The spot rate is ₹ 83.02/£.

The amount of premium = ₹ 0.05 × 62,500 = ₹ 3,125
Intrinsic value = ₹ (83.02 – 83.00) × 62,500 = ₹ 1,250
Time value = ₹ 3,125 – 1,250 = ₹ 1,875

(*Note:* The standard size of a pound options contract is £ 62,500)

GAINS OR LOSSES OF THE OPTION TRADERS

The gains accruing to the option-buyers are unlimited, while the loss borne by them is limited to the amount of premium paid by them. On the other hand, the option-seller's risk of loss is unlimited and its gain is limited to the amount of premium it receives. This is why the market for currency options carries an asymmetry between income and risk of loss. Let us examine this phenomenon separately for call option and put option.

Call Options

The buyer will gain if spot price is greater than the strike price along with the premium, C. This means:

> Gain to options buyer in a call $= S - X - C$. In a put, it is $X - S - C$. The loss is limited to premium. Gain/loss to the options seller is just the mirror image of that of the buyer.

$$\text{Buyer's gain} = S - X - C \tag{7.3}$$

Suppose a firm buys a call option at a strike price of ₹ 83.50/£ along with a premium for ₹ 0.05 per pound sterling. If the spot rate at maturity is ₹ 83.60, the gain to the option-buyer will be:

$$₹\ (83.60 - 83.50 - 0.05) \times 62{,}500 = ₹\ 3{,}125$$

If the spot rate at maturity is ₹ 83.55, gain to the option buyer will be zero. Any spot rate between ₹ 83.50 and ₹ 83.55 will make up partially any loss on account of the premium. If the spot rate is below ₹ 83.50, the buyer will let the option expire. The maximum loss will then be the amount of premium, that is ₹ 3,125.

For the seller of the call option, a profit profile is simply the mirror image of the loss profile of the option-buyer. If the buyer does not exercise the option, the gain accruing to the seller will be equal to the amount of the premium, but if the buyer exercises the option, the seller will have to face a loss equal to the excess of the spot price over the strike price.

PROBLEM 7.1

A pound options call contract has strike rate of \$ 1.820/£ and a premium of \$ 0.08. Spot rate on maturity is \$ 1.920/£. Find gain/loss to options buyer/options seller.

Solution

Since $S > (X + P)$, options buyer will gain. If options buyer gains, options seller has to lose.

Gain to the options buyer = \$ 1.920 – 1.820 – 0.08 = \$ 0.02/£.

Total gain = \$ 0.02 × 62,500 = \$ 1,250.

The seller of pound gets \$ 0.10 less than the rate in the open market but he gets a premium for \$ 0.08. Thus his loss per pound is \$ 0.02. Total loss is \$ 0.02 × 62,500 = \$ 1,250.

PROBLEM 7.2

A pound options call contract has strike rate of \$ 1.820/£ and a premium of \$ 0.08. Spot rate on maturity is \$ 1.812/£. Find gain/loss to options buyer/ options seller.

Solution

Here $S < X$ and so contract is out-of-money. The buyer will not exercise the contract. His loss will be \$ 0.08/£ as he has to pay the premium. The seller has nothing to pay, rather he will get the premium. Premium is the seller's gain.

Put Options

In the case of put option, the buyer will let the option expire if the spot rate is greater than the strike rate. The buyer will be put to a loss equivalent to the amount of premium, and profit will accrue to the buyer only if the spot price is lower than the strike price by more than the amount of the premium. That is,

$$\text{Buyer's Gain} = X - S - C \tag{7.4}$$

Suppose the put option price of a deal is ₹ 83.50/£ along with a premium of ₹ 0.02 per pound. If the spot price at maturity falls to ₹ 83.45, the profit to the buyer will be:

₹ (83.50 – 83.45 – 0.02) × 62,500 = ₹ 1,875

As far as the seller is concerned, the profit will be equal to the amount of premium when the buyer does not exercise the option. It occurs when the spot price is greater than the strike rate. On the other hand, the seller will face a loss if the option is exercised. The amount of loss will vary depending upon how much lower the spot price is.

PROBLEM 7.3

A pound options put contract has strike rate of \$ 1.820/£ and a premium of \$ 0.08. Spot rate on maturity is \$ 1.830/£. Find gain/loss to options buyer/ options seller.

Solution

The contract is out-of-money. The options buyer will not exercise the put. His loss will be equal to the amount of premium that he will pay to the seller. On the other hand, the premium received will be the seller's gain. The amount of gain/ loss will be \$ 0.08 × 62,500 = \$ 5,000.

PROBLEM 7.4

A pound options put contract has strike rate of \$ 1.910/£ and a premium of \$ 0.05. Spot rate on maturity is \$ 1.810/£. Find gain/loss to options buyer/options seller.

Solution

The buyer will exercise the contract. The gain will be: \$ 1.910 – 1.810 – 0.05 = \$ 0.05. The seller will have to pay \$ 0.10 more than the market rate, but he will get \$ 0.05 premium. So his loss will be \$ 0.10 – 0.05 = \$ 0.05.

OPTIONS PRICING

Numerous models of pricing of options have been developed, important among which are the ones developed by Garman and Kohlhagen (1983), Grabbe (1983), and Bizer and Hull (1983). Explanation of these models lies outside the scope of the present work. However, the readers will be acquainted with the concept of option pricing. The value of an option, which is known as the premium, is equal to the sum of its intrinsic value and time value. The meaning of intrinsic value and time value has already been explained in this chapter. Here the discussion will be confined to the factors that influence the value of an option. Knowledge about the factors to which the value of an option is sensitive is very important for the hedgers and speculators who trade in the options. These factors or sensitivities are:

- Changes in forward rates
- Changes in spot rates
- Time to maturity
- The degree of volatility in exchange rate
- Interest rate differential
- Alternative strike price

Changes in Forward Rates

The current spot rate and the interest rate differential form the basis of option pricing as well as the forward rate. This is why option rates are close to the forward rates. In other words, forward rates are central to option pricing and so, changes in the forward rates influence the pricing of an option.

Changes in Spot Rates

Changes in the spot rates influence the option prices. At an at-the-money position, the intrinsic value is zero and the entire premium is represented by the time value. At the out-of-the-money position, the intrinsic value is zero but it cannot be negative because in that case, the option will not be exercised. But as the spot rate moves to in-the-money position, intrinsic value will emerge and the premium will be made up partly of the intrinsic value and partly of the time value. Again, with the spot rate moving into the in-the-money position, both the intrinsic value and the time value will change and as a result, and so will the premium. The extent of change in the premium due to change in the spot rate is represented by *delta*. This means:

$$\text{Delta } (\delta) = \text{Change in premium/Change in spot rate} \qquad (7.5)$$

If we know the value of delta, the impact of the spot rate changes on the value of option value can easily be determined. Suppose spot rate moves from ₹ 83.00/£ to ₹ 83.15/£ and delta is 0.5, the premium of a call option will increase by ₹ (83.15 – 83.00) × 0.5 = 0.075. If the initial premium is ₹ 0.02, it will move up to ₹ 0.095. Delta varies between +1 and 0 for a call option and between –1 and 0 for a put option.

Time to Maturity

The longer the time to maturity, the greater is the option's value. The impact of change in time to maturity on the option value is represented by *theta*. In other words,

$$\textit{Theta}\ (\theta) = \text{Change in premium/Change in time} \tag{7.6}$$

If theta is 0.5 and if time to maturity diminishes from 30 days to 29 days, the value of the option will diminish by 0.5 × (30 – 29) = 0.5.

Theta represents an exponential, and not a linear, relationship between time to maturity and the value of an option. The option price shrinks fast as maturity approaches. A trader buying options for shorter maturity has to pay proportionately less. A six-month option's value is approximately 2.5 times more expensive than that of a one-month option, but a 12-month option is only 3.5 times costlier than a one-month option.

Volatility in Exchange Rate

Volatility is expressed as the standard deviation of daily percentage changes in the spot rate of the underlying currency. It is stated as per annum percentage. If the annual volatility is 10.0 per cent, a single day volatility can be found as:

$$10.0\%/\sqrt{365} = 10.0\%/19.105 = 0.523\%$$

The larger the volatility, the larger is the chance for the spot rate moving into the in-the-money zone and greater is the value of the option.

The impact of volatility on the option's value is expressed by *vega*. In other words,

$$\textit{Vega} = \text{Change in premium/Change in volatility} \tag{7.7}$$

If *vega* is 0.5 and the annual volatility changes from 10 per cent to 12 per cent, the option's value will increase by 0.5 × (0.12 – 0.10) = 0.01. This is normally a linear relationship meaning that the doubling of volatility will double the option's value. However, the problem is that it is difficult to know the extent of volatility in advance. The traders base their forecast on historical data but that is not always correct because the changes in the spot rate are influenced by a number of economic and non-economic factors that may or may not happen to exist in the future.

Sensitivity to Varying Interest Rate Differential

It is evident from the theory of option pricing that an option value is either equal to the difference between the strike price and the forward rate, or it may be higher. It has already been explained in the earlier chapters that the changes in interest rate differentials lead to a change in the forward rate, and the changes in the interest rate differential will also cause changes in the value of an option. The impact of changes in domestic interest rate on the option's value is expressed by *rho* and the impact of change in the foreign interest rate on the option's value is expressed by *phi*. If foreign interest rate increases, forward rate of the foreign currency will be at a discount and the value of the option denominated in this currency will fall. But if the domestic interest rate rises, the value of this option will improve.

Changing Strike Price

Any change in the strike price leads to a change in the intrinsic value and thereby in the value of an option. In a call option, if the strike price falls with the spot rate being constant, the intrinsic value will be larger and the option's price will be higher. But in a put option, the lowering of strike price with the spot price being constant will lower the intrinsic value. The value of the option will fall.

European Options versus American Options

The different factors explained above may work in the same direction or in different directions and the value of an option would change accordingly. However, it should be noted here that the value of an American option is different from that of a European option. We have just discussed about sensitivity in the context of a European option. The value of an American option will be somewhat different insofar as it is exercised even before the expiry date. In a call option, if the spot rate, although higher than the strike price, is tending towards depreciation, the buyer of the American option will like to exercise the option earlier. In case of a European option, which cannot be exercised before maturity, the spot price may have depreciated more by the expiration date, as a result of which the profit reaped by the buyer would have been eroded. In a put option, when spot rate is tending towards appreciation, the buyer would like to exercise the option earlier in order to avoid erosion of profit. He can do it in case of the American option but not in the case of a European option. *American options command a greater value* for the reason.

HEDGING WITH CURRENCY OPTIONS

Hedging through Purchase of Options

In order to hedge their foreign exchange risks, if it is a direct quote, the importers buy a call option and the exporters buy a put option. Take first the case of an *importer*. Suppose an Indian firm is importing goods for £ 62,500 and the amount is to be paid after two months. If an appreciation in the pound is expected, the importer will buy a call option on it with maturity coinciding with the date of payment. If the strike price is ₹ 83.00/£, the premium is ₹ 0.05 per pound and the spot price at maturity is ₹ 83.20, the importer will exercise the option. It will have to pay ₹ 83.00 × 62,500 + 3,125 = 51,90,625. If the importer had not opted for an option, it would have had to pay ₹ 62,500 × 83.20 = 52,00,000. Buying of the call option reduces the importer's obligation by ₹ 52,00,000 – 51,90,625 = 9,375. If, on the other hand, the pound falls to ₹ 82.80, the importer will not exercise the option since his obligation will be lower even after paying the premium.

> Hedgers in short position buy a call or sell a put or go for both simultaneously.

However, one question that arises is whether hedging through buying of an option is preferable to forward market hedging. Buying of currency options is preferred only when strong volatility in the exchange rate is expected and if volatility is only marginal, forward market hedging is preferred. Suppose, in the earlier example, the pound appreciates to only ₹ 83.04 or depreciates to only ₹ 82.97, the amount of premium paid by the importer will be more than the benefit from hedging through purchase of options. There will then be net positive cost of hedging through buying of option.

The *exporter* buys a put option. Suppose an Indian exporter exports goods for £ 62,500. It fears a depreciation of pound within two months when payments are to be received. In order to avoid the risk, it will buy a put option for selling the pound for a two-month maturity. Suppose the strike rate is ₹ 83.00, the premium is ₹ 0.05 and the spot rate at maturity is ₹ 82.80. In case of the hedge, it will receive ₹ 62,500 × 83.00 – 3,125 = 51,84,375. In the absence of a hedge, it will receive only ₹ 51,75,000. This means, buying of a put option helps increase the exporter's earnings, or reduces its exposure, by ₹ 51,84,375 – 51,75,000 = ₹ 9,375.

Hedgers in long position buy put and sell a call or go for both simultaneously.

Hedging through Selling of Options

Hedging through selling of options is advised when volatility in exchange rate is expected to be only marginal. The importer sells a put option and the exporter sells a call option. Let us first take the case of *importers*. Suppose an Indian importer imports for £ 62,500. It fears an appreciation in the pound and so it sells a put option on the pound at a strike price of ₹ 83.00/£ and at a premium of ₹ 0.15 per pound. If the spot price at maturity goes up to ₹ 83.05, the buyer of the option will not exercise the option. The importer as a seller of the put option will receive the premium of ₹ 9,375 which it would not have received if it had not sold the option. If the spot price at maturity falls to ₹ 82.95, the buyer of the option will exercise the option. But in that case, the importer received premium of ₹ 9,375. The net gain to the importer will be ₹ 9,375 – 3,125 = ₹ 6,250.

The *exporters* sell the call option. If an Indian exporter exports for £ 62,500 and fears that the pound will depreciate and sells a call option on the pound at a strike price of ₹ 83.00 at a premium of ₹ 0.15 per pound. If the spot rate at maturity really falls to ₹ 82.95, the buyer of the call option will not exercise the option. The exporter being the seller of the call option will get ₹ 9,375 as the premium.

Tunnels: Simultaneous Purchase and Sale of Options

Foreign exchange exposure can be hedged also through the use of tunnels or, through simultaneous sale and purchase of options. An importer buys a call and sells a put option. The exporter buys a put and sells a call option.

Tunnel means combining call and put.

The importer buys an out-of-the-money call and sells an out-of-the-money put option. As a result, neither the call, nor the put option is exercised if the exchange rate moves within a narrow margin. Here the premium to be received on the sale of the put must be enough to cover the premium to be paid on the purchase of the call option.

The exporter buys a put and sells a call—both out-of-the-money. If the exchange rate moves within a narrow margin, the premium received covers the premium paid. But if the currency depreciates sharply, the put option is there to guarantee a minimum price.

PROBLEM 7.5

An American importer importing goods from UK fears an appreciation in pound. Pound options are available at a strike price of $ 1.830/£ with a premium of $ 0.03/£. The spot rate on the maturity rises to $ 1.930/£. How will he compensate his loss?

Solution

The importer will buy a call and sell a put. Call gives him a gain of $ 1.930 – 1.830 – 0.03 = $ 0.07/£. Selling put will bring him premium as put will not be exercised. The extent to which risk would be reduced is $ 0.03/£. The total amount of risk reduced will be $ 0.10/£ = $ 0.10 × 62,500 = $ 6,250.

PROBLEM 7.6

An American exporter exporting goods to UK fears a depreciation of pound. Pound options are available at a strike price of $ 1.884/£ with a premium of $ 0.03/£. The spot rate on the maturity falls to $ 1.824/£. How will he compensate his loss?

Solution

The exporter will buy a put and sell a call. Put gives him a gain of $ 1.884 – 1.824 – 0.03 = $ 0.03/£. Call will not be exercised by the buyer and so, as a seller of the call, the exporter will receive the premium of $ 0.03/£. Consequently, risk will be reduced to the extent of $ 0.06/£ or in all $ 0.06 × 62,500 = $ 3,750.

SPECULATING WITH OPTIONS

Purchase of Options

Speculators make profit out of purchase of currency options. *They normally buy call options when they expect upward movement in the value of the underlying currency.* On the expiry date, they buy the currency at the agreed-upon rate and sell it in the open market at a higher rate and thereby reap profits. On the contrary, *they buy put options when they expect depreciation of the underlying currency.* They sell the underlying currency at an agreed-upon rate that is higher than the spot rate. This way they get more of the other currency than they could get in the open market. Besides these simple operations, they often go in for complicated deals mixing either two calls or two puts or one call and the other put. Here we explain some of the common modes of options transactions.

> Speculators buy a call when the underlying currency is to appreciate. They buy a put if the currency is to depreciate.

PROBLEM 7.7

Pound is expected to appreciate to $ 1.930. Pound options are available at a strike price of $ 1.830/£ with a premium of $ 0.03/£. How do speculators react to the appreciation of pound?

Solution

Speculator will buy a call. On the maturity, he will get £ 62,500 at $ 1.830/£. Immediately after getting pound, he will sell those pounds in the open market to get dollar back and this way, he will gain $ (1.930 – 1.830 – 0.03) × 62,500 = $ 4,375.

PROBLEM 7.8

Pound is expected to depreciate to \$ 1.730. Pound options are available at a strike price of \$ 1.830/£ with a premium of \$ 0.03/£. How do speculators react to the depreciation of pound?

Solution

Speculator will buy a put. On the maturity, he will get \$ 1,14,375 through selling £ 62,500 at \$ 1.830/£. Immediately after getting dollar, he will sell those dollars in the open market at \$ 1.730/£ to get pound back and this way, he will gain \$ (1.830 – 1.730 – 0.03) × 62,500 = \$ 4,375.

Spreads

In a spread, speculators combine either two calls or two puts. In case of two calls or puts, one is sold and the other is purchased. If the expiry of the two is the same but the strike prices differ, it is known as a *vertical spread*. When the strike price is the same but the expiry differs, it is known as a *horizontal spread*. When the strike price and the expiry date both differ between the two calls, it is known as a *diagonal spread*. Similar features are marked with two puts.

> Spread means combining either two or more calls or two or more puts.

Vertical spread on call combinations

Vertical spread may be either bullish or bearish. The former generates profit when exchange rate moves upward. The latter is profitable when the exchange rate moves downward.

> Vertical spread involves differing strike rates of two or more calls/puts.
>
> Horizontal spread involves differing maturities of calls/ puts.
>
> Diagonal spread involves differing strike price and differing maturities, both.

In a bullish vertical spread, different strategies can be applied. One involves purchase of in-the-money call and sale of out-of-the-money call. Suppose a speculator purchases a call on the British pound with a strike price of ₹ 83.00 with a premium of ₹ 0.05 and sells a call with strike price of ₹ 83.90 and with the same premium. If the spot rate at expiry moves up to ₹ 83.20, he will exercise the option and make a profit of ₹ 0.20 × 62,500 – 3,125 = 9,375. Since the other call will not be exercised, the speculator will receive the premium amounting to ₹ 3,125. His total income will be ₹ 12,500 through this kind of bullish spread.

The other strategy in a bullish spread is to buy an in-the-money call and to sell another in-the-money call with a higher strike price. If the spot price moves up and crosses the strike price of the second call only marginally, and possibly if the premium to be received on the second call is greater than its intrinsic value, the exercise of the second call will add to the gain accruing from the first call.

In a *bearish vertical spread* too, there are different strategies. One is to purchase a call with a strike price below the spot exchange rate and to sell another call with a lower strike price. If the spot rate at expiry falls to a level below the two strike rates, neither of the options will be exercised, but if the amount of premium varies and the premium received is greater than the premium paid, there will be net gain to the speculator.

Horizontal spread on call combinations

The strike price of the two calls may be the same, but the spot rate may vary between two expiry dates and so the sale and purchase of two calls may give different profitability to the speculator. Suppose the speculator buys a call option for the pound with 31 July as expiry date and at a strike price of ₹ 83.00 and at a premium of ₹ 0.03. He sells another call expiring on 31 August at the same strike price and a premium of ₹ 0.05. If the pound is depreciating from a current rate of ₹ 83.20 to ₹ 83.10 on the 31 July and to ₹ 82.95 on the 31 August, this combination will give the speculators a profit. As a buyer of the call option, he will exercise it and gain ₹ 0.10 × 62,500 – 1,875 = 4,375. But on 31 August, the option will not be exercised and the speculator will receive premium to the tune of ₹ 3,125. In all, his profit will be ₹ 4,375 + 3,125 = 7,500. If the spot rate falls below ₹ 83.00 on the two expiry dates, the speculator's earning will be equal to the difference in the amount of premium.

Diagonal spread on call combinations

Diagonal spread is a combination of vertical and horizontal spreads. The speculator buys a call with a relatively long maturity and sells another call with a shorter maturity and a higher strike price. If the spot rate of the underlying currency moves up and is greater than the strike rate of the first call, the first call option will be exercised and the speculator as an option-buyer will reap profits. At the same time, with a higher strike rate of the second call option, there is every possibility of its not being exercised and the speculator as a seller of the option will get the premium. Thus his total profit will be equal to the sum of profit in the first case and the premium in the second case. He reaps the advantages of both vertical and horizontal spreads, but at the same time, his cost is equal to the sum of the cost of the two spreads.

Spread on combination of puts

In a *bullish vertical spread*, the speculator buys one put and sells another put with the same maturity but a lower strike price. There may be different variants. In one case, both strike prices are higher than the spot rate. In the other, price of the bought put is higher than the spot rate but the price of the sold put is lower. Suppose the speculator buys a put option for the pound at ₹ 83 and sells another put at ₹ 82.90 with a premium of ₹ 0.03. The spot rate at maturity is ₹ 82.95. In the first, his gain as buyer will be ₹ 62,500 × (83.00 – 82.95 – 0.03) = 1,250. As a seller, he will get the premium amounting to ₹ 1,875 as it will not be exercised.

In a *bearish vertical spread*, the speculator buys one put and sells another put with two different strike prices. In one case, the put is exercised, while in the other case, it is not. The speculator's gain depends upon this possibility.

In a *horizontal spread*, the speculator buys a put with a longer maturity and sells another put with a shorter maturity. Since the premium varies with the maturity, the difference in premium may result in gain to the speculator.

Combination of Calls and Puts

As a practice, different from spreads, the speculators combine calls with puts and such combinations are of two types. One is known as *straddles* where the two options have the same strike price and the same expiry date. The other, called *strangles* is when the strike price and maturity differ in case of the two options of the combination.

Straddles and strangles involve a combination of one call and the other put. The former involves the same strike price and maturity. In the latter, strike price and expiry differ in the combination.

Straddles

The technique of straddles is used when the exchange rate is expected to change suddenly and in a big way. When the speculators buy straddles and the currency appreciates, the bought call gives profit, while the bought put is not exercised. The gain is equal to the profit earned on the bought call minus the premium paid on the bought put. When the currency depreciates, the put generates profit and the call is not exercised. The gain in this case is equal to the profit on the bought put minus the premium paid on the bought call. It may be noted that if the change in the exchange rate is not big, there is every possibility of loss and this is biggest when the spot rate is equal to the strike price on the expiry date. When the speculators sell straddles, they sell one call and one put. In such cases, the risk is normally high and so it is practised only by well-qualified speculators.

Strangles

A speculator can buy strangles or it can sell strangles. In the former, the speculator buys one call and one put with different strike rates and with different maturity. In the latter, it sells one call and one put but with different strike rates and different maturity. The difference in strike rates and the difference in the premium depending upon the difference in the maturity result in gain to the speculators.

Various Combinations of Options

Tunnel for importers	Buying call and selling put
Tunnel for exporters	Buying put and selling call
Vertical spread: call	Buying one call and selling another call with same expiration but different strike prices
Vertical spread: put	Buying one put and selling another put with same expiration but differing strike prices
Horizontal spread: call	Buying one call and selling another call with same strike price but different expiry dates
Horizontal spread: put	Buying one put and selling another put with same strike price but different expiry dates
Diagonal spread: call	Buying one call and selling another call with varying expiry and strike prices
Diagonal spread: put	Buying one put and selling another put with varying expiry and strike prices
Buying of Straddles	Buying a call and buying a put with same expiry and strike price
Selling of Straddles	Selling a call and selling a put with same expiry and strike price
Buying of Strangles	Buying a call and buying a put with different expiry and strike prices
Selling of Strangles	Selling a call and selling a put with differing expiry and strike prices

PROBLEM 7.9

Two pound options are available at two different rates. One is available at a strike rate of \$ 1.830/£ with a premium of \$ 0.003/£. The other is available at strike rate of \$ 1.815/£ with a premium of \$ 0.007/£. The spot rate on maturity is \$ 1.825/£. How will speculators react?

Alternative 1

A speculator may go for spread treating both these options as call. If he has bought both these calls, his profit/loss will be:

Profit \$ (1.825 – 1.815 – 0.007) = \$ 0.003 per pound on the second call minus payment of premium on the first call @ \$ 0.003 as it will not be exercised = zero profit/loss.

Alternative 2

If the speculator sells the first call and buys the second call, the profit on the second call @ \$ 0.003 plus the receipt of premium on the first call will mean a combined profit of \$ 0.006 per pound. Total profit = \$ 0.006 × 62,500 = \$ 375.

Alternative 3

If the speculator sells both the calls, there will be receipt of premium at \$ 0.003 per pound on the first call but loss on the second call at \$ 0.003 meaning combined profit/loss being zero.

Alternative 4

If the speculator buys the first call and sells the second call, the combined loss will be \$ 0.006 per pound.

Alternative 5

The speculator treats both the options as put. Buying both the puts means a profit of \$ 0.002 from the first put and loss of \$ 0.007 from the second put meaning a combined loss of \$ 0.005 per pound.

Alternative 6

The speculator buys the first put and sells the second put. Profit from the first put at \$ 0.002 and receipt of premium from the second put mean a combined profit of \$ 0.009 per pound.

Alternative 7

The speculator buys the second put and sells the first put. There will be a loss of \$ 0.009 per pound – loss of \$ 0.002 from the first put and loss of \$ 0.007 from the second put.

Alternative 8

The speculator sells both puts. There will be loss of \$ 0.002 from the first and gain of \$ 0.007 from the second put meaning a combined gain of \$ 0.005 per pound.

Alternative 9

The speculator designates the first as a call and the second as a put. If he buys the call and sells the put, there will be a combined loss of \$ 0.006 per pound.

Alternative 10

The speculator designates the first as a call and the second as a put. If he sells the call and buys the put, there will be a combined gain of $ 0.006 per pound.

Alternative 11

The speculator designates the first as a put and the second as a call. If he buys the call and sells the put, there will be a combined gain of $ 0.001 per pound.

Alternative 12

The speculator designates the first as a put and the second as a call. If he sells the call and buys the put, there will be a combined loss of $ 0.001 per pound.

Note: There are 12 possibilities. The speculator will choose that option where the gain is the maximum.

SUMMARY

- Currency options are derivatives like currency futures. They involve trading of currencies normally for hedging of exchange risk or for speculative purposes. However, they differ from the futures and also from forward contracts insofar as the buyer of currency options possesses the freedom of exercising the options or letting them expire. For this privilege, the buyer pays a small premium to the option seller.
- The currency options market exists normally at the organised exchanges, although there is also an over-the-counter market for them. The futures-type options are traded in the currency futures option market. The features of the options traded in these markets are broadly the same, though the details vary among them.
- Options are either call options or put options. In the former, the option buyer agrees to buy the underlying currency. In the latter, it agrees to sell the underlying currency. European options cannot be exercised before expiry, but the American options can be. Over the years, a few other variants of the options have emerged. These are known as the *second-generation options*.
- The gain of the buyer of call option is represented by the excess of the spot rate over the sum of the strike rate and the premium. In case of the put option, it is represented by how far the spot rate is lower than the sum of the strike rate and the premium. The loss to the option-buyer is limited to the amount of premium. On the other hand, the loss to the option-seller is unlimited while the gain is limited to the amount of premium.
- The value of the options, which is equal to the sum of intrinsic value and time value, depends, *inter alia*, upon changes in the forward rate and spot rate, time to expiration, degree of volatility of the exchange rate, the interest rate differentials and the strike rate. American options that may be exercised earlier command greater value than the European options.
- Currency options are used by traders and speculators. The importers buy call and sell put and the exporters buy the put and sell the call options. The speculators buy calls when they expect appreciation of the underlying currency. When they expect a depreciation, they buy puts. But more often, they blend two call options or two puts or calls and puts—commonly known as *spreads, straddles and strangles*.

STUDY TOPIC

Currency Options Trading at Philadelphia Stock Exchange (PHLX)

The United Currency Options Market of the Philadelphia Stock Exchange, the pioneering Exchange for options, offers both customised and standardised currency options. It involves individual as well as institutional traders, although the purpose of these two groups of trader is different. While individuals try to make profits from foreign investment and the directional change in the underlying currency, the institutional investors/corporate treasurers use options to limit risk against adverse currency fluctuations, lock in maximum cost/minimum revenues on a foreign exchange transaction with an uncertain completion date.

Standardised Options

Currency options are quoted in two ways: first, American terms in which a currency is quoted in terms of US dollar per unit of foreign currency; second, European terms where dollar is quoted in terms of a foreign currency. The exchange lists six dollar-based standardised currency option contracts which settle upon exercise in the actual physical currency. The size of the contract is:

Currency	*Units*
US $/Australian	$ 50,000 AUD
US $/British pound	31,250 GBP
US $/Canadian $	50,000 CAD
US $/Euro	62,500 Euro
US $/Japanese yen	62,50,000 Japanese yen
US $/Swiss franc	62,500 CHF

Both European and American options are transacted. Maturity falls in March, June, September and December with two additional near-term months—on Friday preceding the third Wednesday of the month. Exercise price, expressed in terms of US cents per unit of foreign currency, relates to prevailing currency values.

Customised Options

Customised options are traded on any combination of currencies currently available for trading. Foreign currency is matched with US dollar only. Premium is denominated in US dollar. Maturity falls on any business day up to two years from the date of trade. Expiry time is 10 A.M. as against the standardised options that expire at 2.30 P.M. Unlike in the standardised options, exercise notice must be received by 10 A.M. Again, only European options are traded.

Since the customised options are meant for the institutional investors, there is the minimum operating transaction size that equates/exceeds 50 contracts. Trading is done in an open outcry auctions market. The floor member presents a request for quotes to an Exchange staff member for dissemination. Subsequently, competing market makers generate responsive quotes.

Again, unlike in standardised options where market makers give the price to specialists who look after proper execution of orders, no specialist exists in case of customised options. It is the market maker who is responsible for the job.

Both the standardised and customised options are marked to market daily. The US Securities and Exchange Commission regulates the transactions. There is physical settlement of the transaction.

Source: Philadelphia Stock Exchange.

QUESTIONS

1. Differentiate between standardised options market and customised options market.
2. Why is there a minimum operating transaction size in customised options?
3. How do you distinguish between American terms and European terms?
4. When does the maturity fall?

CASE STUDY

CURRENCY OPTIONS TRADING IN INDIA

There are two types of options market. While one is the cross-currency options, the other is the rupee-foreign currency (INR-FC) options. It was January 1994 when the RBI permitted the ADs to write cross-currency options to residents to cover their exposure. These options are OTC options and so they are initiated by those who foresee exchange rate exposure. The banks can purchase call or put options to hedge their cross-currency proprietary trading positions. But they have to fulfil the condition that "no stand-alone" transactions are initiated. This type of options was not widely used in the 1990s because the small exporters and importers could not use them in view of large standard size. Initially, such options were found in US dollars but these days they are found in many currencies, such as British pound, Japanese yen and euro.

The introduction of INR-FC options enables the foreign exchange market participants to hedge dollar-rupee risk. If an Indian company is bidding for an international assignment where the bid quote is in dollar and the costs are in rupees, then the company runs a risk till the contract is awarded. In such cases, currency options create the reverse positions if the company is not allotted the contract. The options contract will freeze the liability only to the options premium paid up-front.

The underlying currency is US dollar. The contract size is US $ 1000. Option premium is expressed in rupee terms. It is paid in cash on t + 1 day. Margin money requirements depend on the exchange norms. The options in the Indian market are European options but they can be squared up early through taking off-setting positions in the market. The maturity falls on two working days prior to the last working day of the expiry month. The settlement takes place in rupee terms.

Besides the OTC market, currency options were introduced at the National Stock Exchange (NSE) and the United Stock Exchange on 29 October, 2010. For a small company, it is easier to hedge the currency risk on an exchange, as banks have become strict and ask for letter of credit, supplier consignment or some other form of guarantee which has to be shown in the full amount. But on an exchange, companies can trade by paying only the margin.

The volume of exchange traded currency options rose sharply after the Reserve Bank of India banned small companies, with net worth less than ₹ 2.00 billion and export-import turnover of less than ₹ 10.00 billion, from using the OTC market. The average daily turnaround in currency futures at NSE in FY 2023–24 was ₹ 72,017.41 billion. The precise volume of exchange traded options at the NSE can be shown in the following table.

FY	*Currency Futures*		*Currency Options*	
	No. of contracts	*Turnover ₹ in billion*	*No. of contracts*	*Turnover ₹ in billion*
2023–24	851,902,719	72,017.41	3,370,318,509	304.04
2024–25 (Apr.–Nov.)	109,991,838	9,259.79	20,619,830	3.71

QUESTIONS

1. Explain the different types of currency options market in India.
2. Why has the options dealing at the NSE/USE been more popular?

REVIEW QUESTIONS

Objective-Type Questions

1. State whether true (T) or false (F):
   (a) Straddles are a combination of two calls. ☐
   (b) Strangles are the combination of two puts. ☐
   (c) Diagonal spread is a combination of vertical and horizontal spread. ☐
   (d) Options are exercised when they are in-the-money. ☐
   (e) In a call option, the option buyer buys the underlying currency. ☐
   (f) The intrinsic value cannot be negative. ☐

2. Choose the correct answer:
   (a) Tunnels are:
      (i) a combination of one call and the other put
      (ii) a combination of two calls
      (iii) none of these
   (b) In strangles:
      (i) the strike price and maturity differ between two deals
      (ii) strike price and maturity do not differ
      (iii) none of these
   (c) In a cylinder option:
      (i) two strike rates exist
      (ii) two strike rates do not exist
      (iii) none of these

(d) Options are exercised when they are:
   (i) in-the-money
   (ii) out-of-the-money
   (iii) at-the-money

(e) The time value of options on the date of maturity is:
   (i) zero
   (ii) negative
   (iii) more than the intrinsic value

Short-Answer Questions

1. What are the types of the currency options market?
2. Distinguish between:
   (a) Call option and put option
   (b) American option and European option
   (c) Exercise rate and spot rate
   (d) Vertical and horizontal spread
   (e) Straddles and strangles
3. Explain that premium is the sum of the intrinsic value and time value of an option contract.

Long-Answer Questions

1. How do you arrive at the gain from the options contract accruing both to the options buyers and sellers?
2. What are the factors on which the value of an options contract depends?
3. How do the exporters and importers hedge in the market for currency options?
4. How do the speculators operate in the market for currency options?

Numerical Problems

1. On the basis of the following figures, find out:
   (a) The intrinsic value of the British Pound options contract assuming it (i) call option, and (ii) put option
   (b) Gain/loss to the option buyer assuming it (i) call option, and (ii) put option
   (c) Gain/loss to the option seller assuming it (i) call option, and (ii) put option
      (i) Spot rate on maturity: US \$ 1.68/£
      (ii) Strike rate: US \$ 1.60/£
      (iii) Premium: US \$ 0.05/£
2. A US importer importing goods for Pound 62,500 fears an appreciation of Pound. He likes to hedge the risk through options. Options are available to him at two different strike rates. One is US \$ 1.60/£, and the other is US \$ 1.70/£. The premium in both the cases is US \$ 0.03/£. If the spot rate on the maturity goes up to US 1.65/£, what will be his course of action?

REFERENCES

Bizer, N. and J. Hull (1983), The Valuation of Currency Options, *Financial Management*, XII, 24–28.

Garman, M. and S. Kohlhagen (1983), Foreign Currency Option Values, *Journal of International Money and Finance*, II, 231–237.

Grabbe, J.O. (1983), The Pricing of Call and Put Options on Foreign Exchange, *Journal of International Money and Finance*, V, 239–253.

SUGGESTED FURTHER READING

Hull, J. (1989), *Options, Futures and Other Derivative Securities*, Englewood Cliffs, New Jersey, Prentice Hall.

Ritchken, P. (1987), *Options: Theory, Strategy and Applications*, Illinois, Scott Foresman.

PART

3

Foreign Exchange Exposure Management

CHAPTER

8 Forecasting Exchange Rates

Learning Objectives

In a floating-rate regime, when the exchange rate changes with changes in the market forces, it is significant to make a forecast of the exchange rate and to design the financial activities accordingly. With this purpose, the present chapter explains the techniques of exchange rate forecast. In particular, it:

- Examines how far exchange rate forecast is relevant in a floating-rate regime.
- Explains the different techniques of forecast.
- Discusses the forecast in a controlled exchange rate regime.

A reliable forecast of future spot rates provides essentially an informational input for the management of foreign exchange exposure. It is for this reason that this section of the book dealing with management of foreign exchange risk begins with a chapter on exchange rate forecast. The chapter opens with discussion of the need for exchange rate forecasts and is followed by that of different techniques of forecasting. The entire discussion of forecasting relates to a floating exchange rate regime, though a large number of currencies represent a controlled exchange rate regime. In this case, the currency is pegged either to another currency, a basket of currencies or to SDRs. The exchange rate though administered, is adjustable. This chapter concludes with a brief discussion of the forecasting procedure in such a regime.

NEED FOR EXCHANGE RATE FORECASTS

Forecast Irrelevance Approach

Efficient market exists when the exchange rate reflects all available public and private information.

The *market efficiency hypothesis* suggests that the foreign exchange market is efficient meaning that the exchange rate reflects all available information. If it is so, there is no need for forecast. The exact need, however, depends upon the degree of market efficiency. Basing on Fama's classification of efficiency, in the security market, the efficiency in the foreign exchange market is classified as weak, semi-strong and strong (Fama, 1970). In a market with weak efficiency, the series of historical exchange rates contain no information that can be used for forecast of future spot exchange rates. This means that in a weak-efficient market, forecasts can be generated. On the other hand, if efficiency is semi-strong, it is believed that there is a large and competitive group of market participants who have access to publicly available information for the purpose of forming an expectation about future spot rates. In this case, the above hypothesis suggests, forecast is not required. Again, if efficiency is strong, not only public but also private information is available which can tell about the future spot rates and which rules out any need for forecast.

The empirical findings differ on the issue of weak efficiency. Dooley and Shafer (1976) cover a two-and-a-half year period from March 1973 and find no support for the concept of weak efficiency. On the other hand, Logue and Sweeney (1977) find significant evidence for the weak efficiency hypothesis in the context of changes in the French franc-US dollar rates.

Forecast Relevance Approach

There are reasons to believe that the content of "efficiency" is found in the foreign exchange market. But even then, this does not deny the need for exchange rate forecast. Forecasts of exchange rates are worthwhile for various reasons, and more so in case of multinational corporations that have to shape their policy decision on the basis of expected exchange rate changes. Let us discuss some of the situations that necessitate exchange rate forecasting.

Hedging decision

Forecast is required in order to decide whether to go in for hedging or not. Suppose an importer has to pay in foreign currency. If the forecast value of foreign currency is higher than the forward rate, it will be in the interest of the importer to take a forward market hedge but if the forecast shows lower rate of foreign currency than the forward rate, there will be no need for this. The forecasting of the exchange rate is thus a major tool of the traders.

Investment of short-term funds

An international company, when having surplus cash, makes short-term investments in different currencies. It naturally prefers currencies whose future spot rate is expected to rise more than the forward rate, because such investment would bring it profits. Thus forecasting is a necessity for those who make short-term investments of cash.

Long-term investment of funds

When an international company wishes to set up offices in foreign countries, among other things, it compares, the behaviour of their currencies because such behaviour will influence cash flows. The greater the accuracy with which the future cash flows are determined, the more correct would be the decision to make long-term investment in a particular country, and exchange rates are forecast with this aspect in mind.

Financing decision

A borrower prefers to borrow a currency whose value is expected to fall in the near future or over a period as this will lead to a reduced burden of repayment.

Assessment of earnings

The earnings of subsidiaries are normally reported to the parent company. Moreover, the financial statements of the different units of a firm operating in different countries are consolidated. All this is done with a view to judge the viability of the international operation and for this process, forecasting of the rates of different currencies is quite essential.

Problems in Exchange Rate Forecast

Exchange rate forecasting faces several significant obstacles. One primary challenge is that most forecasting methodologies rely on the assumption that historical economic data can accurately predict future trends. This premise, however, may prove unreliable, particularly in economies subject to frequent structural disruptions. In such scenarios, it becomes crucial to identify these structural shifts and adjust the forecast models accordingly. Another issue arises from the fact that forecasts typically focus on nominal exchange rate movements. For countries experiencing persistently high inflation rates, the real exchange rate can deviate substantially from its nominal counterpart, potentially rendering predictions based on the latter inaccurate. Additionally, the common practice of providing exposure management guidance on an individual currency basis often fails to offer a comprehensive assessment of overall risk.

TECHNIQUES OF FORECASTING

The forecasting techniques can be categorised as technical, fundamental, market-based and mixed forecasting. A discussion of these techniques follows:

Technical Forecasting

In this technique, historical rates are used for estimating future rates because in a majority of the cases, past movements give an indication about movements in future.

Technical forecasting is based on the movement of historical rates.

The technical analysis includes:

1. Classical charting techniques embracing line chart, bar chart, candlestick chart, and point-and-figure chart.
2. Statistical techniques embracing, among other things, moving average systems—simple and weighted moving averages.
3. Mathematical techniques seeking trends through linear regression and cycles through spectral and Fourier analysis and Box-Jenkins autoregressive integrated moving average model forecasts.

Short-term predictions typically employ technical forecasting methods, which generally have a limited scope. When a currency's value increases, forecasters assume its demand has risen and make future value predictions without delving into specifics. Speculators commonly use these technical forecasts, though a model that proves profitable at one time may not be effective later. Relying on technical forecasts often leads to losses for speculators, who also face substantial transaction costs due to frequent trading activities.

The companies do not benefit much from technical forecasts as these forecasts focus on the near future and not on the distant future. Moreover, companies do not rely on this technique since the technical forecasts fail to estimate future exchange rates in precise terms.

PROBLEM 8.1

The value of rupee vis-à-vis US dollar for the first nine days of January 2005 is respectively as follows: ₹ 45.11, 45.10, 45.15, 45.15, 45.10, 45.30, 45.39, 45.50, and 45.41. Find a forecast of the exchange rate for the 10th day.

Solution

The average for the first four days is ₹ 45.13 and the average for the last four days is ₹ 45.40. On this basis, the actual value from the middle of 2nd and 3rd January to the middle of 7th and 8th January is ₹ 45.40 – 45.13 = ₹ 0.27. It means a daily increment in the value of dollar being ₹ 0.27/5. If the average trend value for the middle of 7th and 8th is ₹ 45.40, the exchange rate on the 10th of January will be:

$$₹\ 45.40 + 5/2 \times 0.27/5 = 45.40 + 0.1350 = ₹\ 45.5350.$$

Fundamental Forecasting

In this technique, various sets of macroeconomic variables and not historical rates are the guide for future rates. Future rates are estimated on the basis of changes in the economic variables. If inflation differential is the cause for exchange rate changes and if the rate of inflation in country A is higher than in country B by 5.0 per cent, the value of country A's currency vis-à-vis country B's currency will decline by this percentage. Suppose the inflation rate in India is 8.0 per cent and 5.0 per cent in the USA. The value of the rupee, which is presently ₹ 40 a dollar, will fall within a two-year period to:

> Fundamental forecast is based on the macro-economic variables and not on historical rates.

$$₹\ 40.00 \times (1.08/1.05)^2 = ₹\ 42.32$$

In this example, we have taken into consideration only one variable, namely the inflation rate. But in practice, many variables are taken into account and forecast is made with the help of regression analysis. It may be that while one variable is forcing down the value of a currency, another one is forcing it to move up.

Suppose, for estimating the Re/US $ rate, the forecaster takes into consideration the income growth rate and the rate of inflation in India as compared to that prevailing in the USA. He fits the quarterly percentage change in these two differentials, inflation (I) and income (Y) into a regression equation. The value of rupee will be defined as:

$$\text{Re} = b_0 + b_1 I + b_2 Y + \mu \qquad (8.1)$$

where b_0 is constant, b_1 and b_2 represent the sensitivity of the rupee to changes in I and Y respectively and μ represents an error term.

After the value of the *bs* is generated, the movement in the value of the rupee will be indicated. Suppose the value of b_0, b_1 and b_2 is respectively 0.002, 0.6 and 0.8 and inflation differential and income differential during the preceding quarter are respectively 4.0 per cent and 2.0 per cent, (India with lower inflation rate and lower income growth rate) the value of the rupee will tend to appreciate in the following quarter by

$$0.002 + 0.6(4\%) + 0.8(2\%) = 0.2\% + 2.4\% + 1.6\% = 4.2\%.$$

Some of the variables have immediate impact while in other cases, there may be a lag. In order to meet this problem, the forecaster uses sensitivity analysis. The more rigourous the technique, the greater is the accuracy. In this age of computers, a host of factors can be taken into account. However, the scope of subjectivity cannot be completely ruled out. Though this technique is simple and more reliable, it possesses a few limitations. *Firstly*, the precise timing of impact of a particular variable is not known. There are factors that have a delayed impact and in those cases, forecast will be erroneous. *Secondly*, there are some factors whose impact is instantaneous, though those factors may not always be obvious and if they are not included, the forecast may not be correct. *Thirdly*, the coefficient derived from the regression model may be changing over the period. If the US Government in our example imposes fresh trade barriers, the impact on the value of the rupee will be different. So, there is always a margin of error which the forecaster should take into consideration.

PROBLEM 8.2

If the average exchange rate in the first quarter of 2005 is ₹ 45.10/US $ with India having a positive interest rate differential of 2.30 per cent and a positive inflation rate differential of 3.10 per cent over that in the USA, and if sensitivity of rupee to interest rate and inflation rate differential is 50 per cent, find a forecast of the exchange rate during the second quarter assuming a constant term as 0.02.

Solution

Fitting these figures into a regression equation,

$$0.02 + 0.5 \times 0.023 + 0.5 \times 0.031 = 0.0470 = 4.70 \text{ per cent}$$

Rupee will depreciate by 4.70 per cent. The exchange rate forecast in the second quarter will be ₹ 47.22/US $.

Market-based Forecasting

In this technique, the estimation of future rates depends on the spot and forward rates prevailing in the market and on the expectations about the future. Suppose one US dollar is presently sold for ₹ 40, but due to some pressures—economic or non-economic—the dollar is expected to appreciate to ₹ 40.50 in the near future. If the speculators have this kind of expectation, they will begin buying the dollar at the present point of time, so that in the near future, when the dollar becomes costlier, they can sell and thereby make profits equal to ₹ 40.50 – 40.00 or ₹ 0.50 per dollar. The moment the buying pressure starts, the value of the dollar will rise as a result of greater demand and there is every possibility for reaping of profits of this kind.

Market-based forecast is based on the expected trend in the market.

This is not the case only with the spot rate. If the value of a currency is expected to be higher than its forward rate of a given maturity, speculators begin buying that currency at the forward rate, so that they will get the currency at maturity at a lower rate and immediately thereafter, sell it at a higher rate and thereby reap a profit. Pressure of buying forward will raise the forward prices of the dollar. Thus in both these cases, expectation about the future influences the future rate, and for this reason, when future value of a currency is estimated, expectation and the present rates form the basis of the forecast.

When the forecast concerns a long-run period where the forward rate for such a long period is not available, the interest rate is taken into account. Consideration of the interest rate is based on the interest rate parity theory where a country with a higher rate of interest faces a reduction in the value of its currency. Suppose, interest rate in India is 12.0 per cent, while that in the USA is 10.0 per cent. After a three-year period, the present value of the US dollar (₹ 40/US $) will appreciate by:

$$\text{Premium (Discount)} = \{(1 + I_{Ind})^3/(1 + I_{US})^3\} - 1$$
$$= (1.404928/1.331) - 1 = 0.0555 = 5.55\%$$

PROBLEM 8.3

The average spot rate during the first quarter of 2005 is ₹ 45.10/US $. But if there is pressure on dollars and its demand is expected to move up by 10 per cent, find out the forecast for the second quarter.

Solution

Assuming the supply of dollars being constant, the exchange rate in the second quarter should be:

₹ 45.10 × 1.10 = ₹ 49.61/US $.

Mixed Forecasting

Mixed forecast is a weighted average of technical, fundamental and market-based forecasts.

The techniques of forecasting explained above suffer from one limitation or the other because they are based on different types of information and relying on a particular technique may produce biased results. In order to avoid this problem, the forecaster uses a blend of different techniques. This is known as *mixed forecasting*. Each of the techniques is assigned a particular weight, the total weight being 1. The result of each technique is multiplied by the weight and they are then summed up to reach the final forecast. Thus the actual forecast of the currency would be a weighted average of the various forecasts developed. Suppose, for instance that the value of the rupee after a three-month period is forecast by different techniques as ₹ 40, ₹ 40.6 and ₹ 40.2. If the forecaster assigns weight respectively at 20 per cent, 40 per cent and 40 per cent, the weighted average will be:

$$₹\ 40.0 \times 0.2 + 40.6 \times 0.4 + 40.2 \times 0.4 = ₹\ 40.32.$$

PROBLEM 8.4

The technical forecast, fundamental forecast and the market-based forecast of rupee vis-à-vis US dollar for the second quarter of 2005 are respectively as follows: ₹ 45.54, ₹ 47.22 and ₹ 49.61. If the forecaster assigns 30 per cent, 30 per cent and 40 per cent weight respectively to above forecast, what would the weighted average of the forecasts, often known as *mixed forecast*?

Solution

Mixed forecast will be:

$$0.3 \times 45.54 + 0.3 \times 47.22 + 0.4 \times 49.61 = ₹\ 47.67/\text{US }\$.$$

Forecast Error

In the context of forecasting of exchange rate, the making of forecast is important, but monitoring of the forecast is also very important. For this purpose, the forecaster compares the forecast with the actual value or the realised value and comes to know the extent of difference between the two. The more accurate the forecast, the smaller will be the difference.

Forecast error is the difference between forecast value and the realised value divided by the realised value.

The difference between the actual value and the forecast value is known as the *forecast error*. In percentage terms, the forecast error is equal to:

(Value forecasted – realised value)/realised value (8.2)

If forecast value is ₹ 40.32/US $ and the realised value is ₹ 40.60, the forecast error will be:

$$(40.32 - 40.60)/40.60 = -0.69\%$$

Error is normally computed in terms of its absolute value in order to avoid a possible offsetting effect at the time of the determination of mean forecast error. However, when the forecast error of different currencies is compared, it is important that their relative size is taken into consideration and the relative error factor is considered. For example, if the value of one US dollar is forecast as rupees 40.32 and taka 60.00 after a three-month period. When the period matures, it is found that the actual value of the US dollar comes to rupees 40.00 and taka 60.40. In absolute terms, the forecast error is greater in case of the taka, but it may be different if the relative size of the two currencies is taken into account. The relative forecast error for the two currencies will be as follows:

For rupee: (40.32 – 40.00)/40.00 = 0.8%
For taka: (60.00 – 60.40)/60.40 = –0.66%

PROBLEM 8.5

If forecast of exchange rate is ₹ 47.67, but the actual spot rate is ₹ 47.50, what would be size of forecast error?

Solution

Forecast error = ₹ (47.67 – 47.50)/47.50 = 0.00358 = 0.358%

FORECAST IN A CONTROLLED EXCHANGE RATE REGIME

By a controlled exchange rate regime, we mean a pegged, yet adjustable, exchange rate. The exchange rate is fixed and administered, yet the monetary authorities change the value of the currency when fundamental disequilibrium in the balance of payments occurs or when corrective fiscal or monetary policies prove economically ineffective and politically unacceptable.

> Forecast in a controlled regime is subject to the macroeconomic changes for the purpose of resorting to devaluation/ upward revaluation.

The first step in an attempt to forecast is to review the economic indicators in order to ascertain whether fundamental disequilibrium has really occurred. In this context, the forecaster reviews the information regarding price level, money supply, foreign trade, international reserves, etc. Higher rate of inflation, shrinkage of international reserves, decreasing coverage of imports by export earnings, a high foreign debt-service ratio, etc. are the indicators for the emergence of fundamental disequilibrium in the balance of payments.

If the balance of payments is under serious strain, the forecaster measures the pressure of the market forces on the prevailing exchange rates as also the ability of the central bank to hold on the prevailing exchange rate. He will assess the extent of the change in the exchange rate necessary to bring the balance of payments back on to the rails. The process can be executed within two frameworks: the Purchasing Power Parity (PPP) theory, which relies on inflation differentials, or the forward market anticipation of future spot exchange rates. However, in controlled exchange rate regimes where forward markets are absent, the black market rate serves as the basis for analysis. This rate is influenced by the discrepancy between official and equilibrium exchange rates, as well as the expected penalties for illicit transactions. Forecasters also strive to determine the government's intended corrective policies. When faced with a structural balance of payments deficit, authorities may implement deflationary measures or a combination of restrictive monetary and fiscal policies. If these approaches prove politically untenable, devaluation becomes the recourse. In such instances, forecasters attempt to estimate the extent of the impending devaluation.

SUMMARY

- Exchange rate forecasting plays a crucial role in managing foreign exchange risks. While the efficient market hypothesis suggests that forecasting is unnecessary since exchange rates already reflect all available information, companies still rely on forecasts. These forecasts are essential for making informed decisions about hedging receivables and payables, as well as planning short-term and long-term financing and investment strategies.

- Forecasting techniques can be categorized into four groups: technical, fundamental, market-based, and mixed. Each method has its own limitations, prompting forecasters to combine all these techniques. By calculating a weighted average of the results from different methods, forecasters aim to arrive at values closer to the actual outcomes. However, even this approach is not flawless, as forecast errors persist, which are typically expressed in either absolute terms or as relative percentages.
- The discussion above pertains to a floating exchange rate regime. In the case of a pegged but adjustable exchange rate regime, the forecaster begins by assessing the likelihood of a fundamental disequilibrium in the balance of payments using the available economic variables. If such a disequilibrium is identified, the forecaster determines the potential extent of adjustment needed in the exchange rate and makes a final decision based on the corrective policies the government intends to implement.

REVIEW QUESTIONS

Objective-Type Questions

1. State whether true (T) or false (F):
   (a) Technical forecasting is usually applied to short-term forecast. ☐
   (b) In fundamental forecasting, important macroeconomic variables are taken into account. ☐
   (c) Mixed forecasting is the combination of different types of forecast. ☐
   (d) Forecast error is the product of actual and forecasted values. ☐
   (e) Market-based forecast depends on spot and forward rates prevailing in the market and on the expectation about the future. ☐

2. Choose the correct answer:
   (a) Charting is used in:
      (i) fundamental analysis
      (ii) technical analysis
      (iii) market-based analysis
   (b) The forecast error is
      (i) the difference between the forecast value and the realised value
      (ii) the use of an inappropriate method of forecasting
      (iii) none of these
   (c) Technical analysis of forecast is based on:
      (i) past trend
      (ii) macroeconomic variables
      (iii) behaviour of the speculators

Short-Answer Questions

1. What do you mean by efficient foreign exchange market?
2. What are the problems while forecasting exchange rates?
3. What is forecast error?

Long-Answer Questions

1. Is forecasting of exchange rate relevant? Discuss.
2. What are the different techniques of forecasting exchange rate?

Numerical Problem

1. Find out the forecast error if the forecast value is ₹ 40.00/$, and the realised value is ₹ 41.00/$.

REFERENCES

Dooley, M.P. and J.R. Shafer (1976), Analysis of Short-run Exchange Rate Behaviour: March 1973 to September 1975, International Finance Discussion Paper No. 76, Federal Reserve System, Washington, D.C.

Fama, E. (1970), Efficient Capital Markets: A review of theory and empirical work, *Journal of Finance*, XXV, 383–417.

Hansen, L.P. and R.J. Hodrick (1980), Forward Exchange Rates as Optimal Predictors of Future Spot Rates: An econometric analysis, *Journal of Political Economy*, LXXXVIII, 829–853.

Levich, R.M. (1983), Exchange Rate Forecasting Techniques, in A.M. George and I.H. Giddy (Eds.), *International Finance Handbook*, New York, Wiley, pp. 8.1.1–8.1.29.

Logue, D.E. and R.J. Sweeney (1977), White Noise in Imperfect Markets: The case of the franc/dollar exchange rate, *Journal of Finance*, XXXII, 761–778.

SUGGESTED FURTHER READING

Goodman, Stephen H. (1979), Foreign Exchange Rate Forecasting Techniques: Implications for business and policy, *Journal of Finance*, XXXIV, 415–427.

CHAPTER 9

Nature and Measurement of Foreign Exchange Exposure

Learning Objectives

Fluctuation in exchange rate influences a firm's cash flow as well as the assets/liabilities position which means the firms have to face more often the exchange rate exposure. From the viewpoint of managing exposure, it is important to know the type and extent of exposure. This is why the present chapter:

- Explains the very concept of exposure.
- Discusses its different types.
- Shows how the size of the different types of exposure can be assessed.

Changes in exchange rate lead to gain in some cases but loss in other cases. Gain and loss, both represent exchange rate risk that needs to be assessed. It is thus the present chapter discusses the various types of exchange rate risk/exposure and also how they are assessed.

THE CONCEPT

Meaning

In a floating exchange-rate regime, the value of a currency changes frequently. Such changes influence the value of those firms that are involved in international transactions. The value of their assets and liabilities changes as does their very cash flow—present and future. In other words, they face foreign exchange exposure.

When one talks about foreign exchange exposure, it may be noted that such exposure occurs because of *unanticipated change in the exchange rate*. Suppose the spot rate is ₹ 40/US $ and the one-month forward rate is ₹ 40.30/US $. This means that the market has already anticipated a depreciation in the value of the rupee vis-à-vis the US dollar by ₹ 0.30. If the value of the rupee depreciates to 40.30 per US dollar, there would be no foreign exchange exposure inasmuch as this depreciation is anticipated by the market, but if the rupee value depreciates to 40.50, foreign exchange exposure would be said to exist because it is beyond expectation.

Types of Exposure

The literature on the subject divides foreign exchange exposure into two classes. One is known as *accounting* or *translation exposure*, while the other is known as *economic exposure*. The basic difference between the two is that the accounting exposure is derived from the consolidated financial statements of the parent company and it does not influence the cash flow. Economic exposure on the contrary, is the result of the altered cash flow of a company.

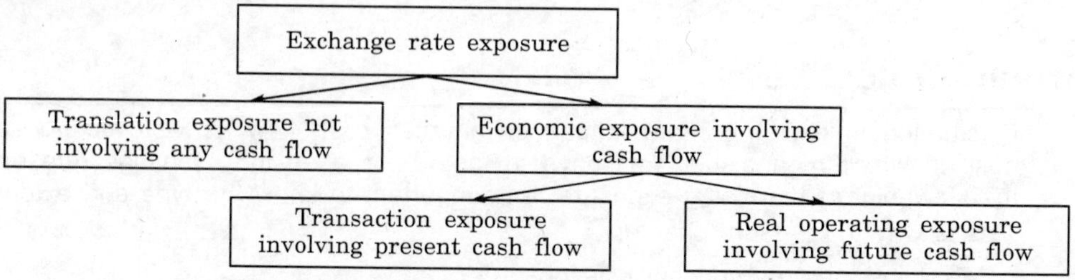

FIGURE 9.1 Types of Exchange Rate Exposure.

The economic exposure is further divided into transaction exposure and real operating exposure. Transaction exposure refers to the foreign exchange loss or gain on transactions already entered into and denominated in a foreign currency, as a result of changes in the exchange rate. In other words, transaction exposure is concerned with the changes in the present cash flows. Real operating exposure on the other hand, is related to changes in future cash flows. It is concerned with the impact of exchange rate changes along with the changes in inflation rate on the cost and revenue structure of a firm. In the present chapter, we discuss the nature and measurement of these three types of exchange rate exposure. Let us first consider how relevant such exposure is.

Relevance of Exposure

One perspective dismisses the significance of exchange rate exposure, citing the Purchasing Power Parity (PPP) theory. This theory suggests that exchange rate fluctuations are offset by price adjustments, leaving a firm's financial performance unaffected. For example, if India experiences higher inflation than the USA, the rupee's value would decline against the dollar. This would increase the cost of imported components for Indian firms, affecting their competitiveness against domestic producers. However, the PPP theory argues that the overall impact on the firm's financial health would be neutral due to the balancing effect of exchange rates and prices.

There will, therefore, be no change in the competitive position between the importing firm and the domestic firms even after the changes in the exchange rate. In other words, the exchange rate exposure is irrelevant.

The other view suggests that the exchange rate exposure is very relevant because the PPP theory is not applicable in the short run. Even in the long run, there are so many factors, and not only the inflation rate differential, that influence the exchange rate. Suppose the exchange rate changes on account of some other factors, the resulting exposure will then not be matched by changes in the inflation rate differential, and the exchange rate exposure could really matter.

> Exposure needs consideration as PPP theory often does not work.

Moreover, unstable exchange rates lead to instability in a firm's growth and may lead to bankruptcy. This is why firms are very vigilant as far as changes in exchange rate are concerned and on the application of various hedging tools in order to protect themselves from foreign exchange exposure.

TRANSACTION EXPOSURE

Let us begin with the transaction exposure that is concerned with the impact of changes in exchange rate on present cash flows. Transaction exposure emerges mainly on account of export and import of commodities on open account, borrowing and lending in a foreign currency and intra- firm flows in an international company.

> Transaction exposure means changes in the present cash flow of a firm consequent upon the exchange rate changes.

Export and Import on Open Account

Suppose an Indian firm exports goods to the USA and the bill is invoiced in US dollars. It has to receive payments within two months, but within this period, the US dollar depreciates. This will cause a reduction in earnings in rupee terms. If the US dollar appreciates, it will make the export earning bigger in rupee terms. Change in cash flow occurs in both the cases. In one case, there is loss; in the other, there is gain. Similarly, when an Indian importer imports goods from the USA and if the US dollar appreciates before payment is made in US dollars, it will have to pay more rupees. If the US dollar depreciates, on the other hand, less rupees will have to be paid. In this case too, the cash flow changes. This type of change in cash flow is known as *transaction exposure.* In other words,

> Transaction exposure appears primarily on account of trade, borrowing/lending and intra-firm cash flow.

Transaction exposure (gains or loss) = rupee worth of accounts receivable (payable) when actual settlement is made *minus* rupee worth of accounts receivable (payable) when the trade transaction was initiated.

The transaction exposure on account of trade is divided into three parts. The first part, known as *quotation exposure* is created when the exporter quotes a price in foreign currency and exists till the importer places an order with the exporter at that price. The second part is *backlog exposure* that exists between the placement of order by the importer and the shipping and billing by the seller. The third part is the *billing exposure* and exists between the billing of the shipment and the settlement of the trade payments (Eiteman, et al., 1995).

Borrowing and Lending in a Foreign Currency

Transaction exposure occurs when financial obligations, such as borrowing or lending, are denominated in a foreign currency. If the foreign currency appreciates, the domestic currency equivalent of the obligation increases, resulting in a higher cost for borrowers. Conversely, depreciation of the foreign currency lowers the domestic currency cost. Similarly, lenders receive higher domestic currency returns if the foreign currency appreciates and lower returns if it depreciates. Fluctuations in exchange rates impact both the principal amount and interest payments associated with the transaction.

Intra-firm Flow in an International Company

In the case of international companies, when funds flow among the different units that are located in different countries, any change in the exchange rate alters the value of cash flow. Suppose, the Indian subsidiary of an American firm has declared a dividend and it has to repatriate it to the parent company. If in the meantime, the rupee depreciates, the amount of dividend to be received by the parent company in dollar terms will be lower and this will amount to a loss to the parent company. If the exchange rate moves the other way, there will be gain to the parent company.

Mahindra & Mahindra reported a decline of 17 per cent in its net profit during the first quarter of FY 2008–09 – from ₹ 1,912 million during the previous year's first quarter to ₹ 1,593 million. The net profit of Tata Motors too fell by over 30 per cent from ₹ 4,668 to ₹ 3,261 million during the same period. The most important reason behind it is the oscillation in the exchange rate. The decline of rupee by 6.8 per cent during April–June 2008 led to higher import cost in both the firms. Tata Motors had additionally greater debt obligations (interest payment on loans) related to the purchase of Land Rover and Jaguar. In fact, such losses are recorded as a notional loss on foreign currency debt obligations translated into rupee.

Source: Based on Reports published in Mint, 31.7.2008.

Consolidated Net Exposure

When we talk about the transaction exposure of a multinational corporation, we should consider it in terms of consolidated net exposure. The word, "net" comprises both the inflow and outflow of funds and it is the net amount that determines the size of transaction exposure. If the Indian subsidiary of a US company is repatriating dividends to the parent company, any depreciation of the rupee will lower the value of dividend to be received by the parent company in dollar terms, but if the Indian subsidiary exports goods to its parent company invoiced in rupees, the parent company will have to pay a smaller amount in terms of dollars for this transaction in the event of rupee depreciation. So loss on account of dividend has to be adjusted with the gain on account of trade transaction and it is only the net amount that will determine the size of transaction exposure.

Consolidated net exposure means changes in net cash flows from all sources.

Again, international parent company thinks in terms of its overall financial performance. Since subsidiaries are located in different countries, changes in the value of different currencies may push its transaction exposure in different directions. This means that change in the value of one currency may cause gain, while change in the value of another currency may cause loss to the parent company. Consequently, it is the consolidated net figure of cash flow with which the parent company is concerned. The severity of exposure thus depends upon the correlation between the changes in the value of different currencies. If it is a positive correlation, the magnitude of transaction exposure will be large, but if it is a negative correlation, the loss in one case is compensated by gain in the other and the size of transaction exposure will be small. Table 9.1 gives a picture of consolidated net exposure in case of a US company that has subsidiaries in Canada, Germany, and Switzerland. There is inflow and outflow of funds between the subsidiaries and the parent company and so it is the net flow that determines the magnitude of transaction exposure. The value of currency in all the three host countries changes as a result of which transaction exposure comes to exist in all the three cases. But since the loss in two cases is compensated by gain in the third, the consolidated net exposure amounts to only US $ 45,000.

TABLE 9.1 Transaction Exposure of a US Parent Company

(Million units of different currencies)

Location of subsidiaries	*Inflow*	*Outflow*	*Net flow*	*Pre-change rate US $*	*Post-change rate US $*	*Pre-change value US $*	*Post-change value US $*	*Size of exposure US $*
Canada	C$ 5.0	– 3.0	2.0	0.80	0.78	1.6	1.560	– 0.040
Germany	Euro 3.0	– 4.0	–1.0	0.50	0.53	– 0.5	–0.530	–0.030
Switzerland	Sf 4.0	– 3.5	0.5	0.60	0.65	0.3	0.325	0.025

Again, if the transaction exposure manifests in terms of gain, it has to be considered for tax. It is because the gain adds to the profitability but it is the net profit (after taxes) that really matters. Table 9.1 does not show any gain but, suppose there had been gain and the tax rate been 50 per cent, then transaction exposure would have been:

$$\text{US \$ } 45{,}000 \times (1 - 0.50) = \text{US \$ } 22{,}500$$

PROBLEM 9.1

Find out the transaction gain/loss on the basis of the following data pertaining to India's foreign trade:

	US $, million	*Japanese Yen, million*	*British Pound, million*
Import	1,250	650	800
Export	1,150	625	850
Pre-change rate	₹ 45/$	₹ 0.40/Yen	₹ 70/Pound
Post-change rate	₹ 47/$	₹ 0.41/Yen	₹ 68/Pound

Solution

Net inflow	*Pre-change value (₹, million)*	*Post-change value (₹, million)*	*Size of exposure (₹, million)*
$ –100	–4,500.00	–4,700.00	–200.00
Yen –25	–10.00	–10.25	–00.25
Pound 50	+3,500.00	+3,400.00	–100.00

Net transaction exposure: ₹ 300.25 million.

REAL OPERATING EXPOSURE

Real operating exposure manifests in changes in inflation-adjusted future cash flow of a firm following exchange rate changes.

Real operating exposure arises when changes in exchange rate, together with rates of inflation, alter the amount and risk element of a company's future revenue and cost stream. The word, "real" denotes the concept of real exchange rate which means nominal exchange rate adjusted for inflation. The word, "operating" is used because we are concerned with the operating cash flow a change in which causes change in the value of the firm.

The measurement of real operating exposure is not very easy, insofar as the measurement of inflation rate differential in the years to come is not easy, especially when the countries are experiencing a highly volatile rate of inflation. However, if inflation rate differential is forecast correctly, real operating exposure can be estimated. Let us take a simple example. If the rupee depreciates by 10 per cent, Indian exports will turn competitive and imports will become costlier, and this will impact the cash flows. If, however, the inflation differential in India also goes up by 10 per cent, the ultimate result may manifest in zero real operating exposure.

Again, the impact of inflation and changes in exchange rate on the future cash flow may vary under different market conditions. As far as revenue is concerned, the impact may vary if the firm produces:

1. for the export market,
2. for the domestic market but competition from import is present, and
3. for the domestic market and there is no competition from abroad.

Similarly, the impact of inflation and exchange rate changes on the cost structure shall be different if the firm:

1. imports inputs,
2. procures inputs from domestic sources, but competition from foreign supplier is present, and
3. gets inputs from domestic sources and there is no competition from foreign suppliers.

Impact of Inflation on Revenue

When a firm engages in export production, it may have the capacity to transfer the effects of inflation to consumers if the demand for the product exhibits price inelasticity, the product is significantly differentiated, and the exporter holds a monopoly position. If the impact of inflation is successfully transferred to consumers abroad, the firm's revenue will experience an increase relative to the pre-inflation period. However, if these conditions are not met, inflation cannot be transmitted to consumers, resulting in a decrease in revenue.

Furthermore, when a firm produces for the domestic market and faces competition from foreign entities, imports will fulfill domestic demand if it demonstrates high price elasticity. In such cases, inflation will manifest as a substantial reduction in revenue. Conversely, when foreign competition is absent, domestic demand will exhibit minimal sensitivity to price increases, leading to a larger revenue stream in the post-inflation period.

Impact of Inflation on Cost

When a firm imports the inputs, the foreign supplier, if it is in a monopoly position, can raise the price of its supply to the extent of the inflation. In that case, the cost will rise in the post-inflation period. But if the foreign supplier is operating below full capacity, it may not raise the price in which case, cost will remain unchanged. When a firm gets locally available inputs, the supplier will not raise the price if imports are competing with the local supply, and the cost will not rise in the post-inflation period, but if there is no competition from the foreign supplier, the local supplier may raise the price thus increasing the cost.

Impact of Depreciation on Revenue

Exchange rate fluctuations can lead to currency appreciation or depreciation. The effects of currency appreciation are the inverse of those of depreciation, so this discussion will focus solely on depreciation.

Currency depreciation typically increases exports for price-elastic products, assuming the firm has the capacity to meet increased demand. This results in expanded revenue streams. For products intended for the domestic market facing import competition, sales will likely increase as imports become more expensive due to the exchange rate change. This also leads to increased revenue. Additionally, when there is no foreign competition and demand is price-inelastic, the firm can raise prices to increase revenue.

Depreciation and the Cost Stream

Currency depreciation naturally increases import costs, impacting the cost structure of firms reliant on foreign inputs. The extent of this impact is directly proportional to the proportion of imports in the total input. However, if domestic substitutes are available, the adverse effect on the cost structure can be mitigated by sourcing inputs from local suppliers.

It is important to note that even if imports are invoiced in domestic currency, domestic currency depreciation indirectly exposes importing firms to economic risks. While the importing firm's costs may not immediately rise, the supplier faces reduced export earnings in their domestic currency, potentially leading to price increases for the supplied goods. This ultimately results in higher input costs for the importing firm.

Measuring the Impact on Cash Flow

For a precise estimate of the real operating exposure, one has to take into consideration the expected inflation rate differential, the expected change in the exchange rate, the price-elasticity of demand for the output, the differentiated feature of the product, the ratio of imported input in the total input, possibility of substitution of the imported input by domestically available input, etc. There will be many combinations of these factors and in each combination, the amount of cash flow will be different. What the foreign exchange analyst does is that he estimates the cash flow—revenue and cost stream—considering all these combinations or possibilities. When cash flow of different combinations over the years is estimated, it is converted to present value and this is compared with the present value of the cash flow that is expected to occur in the case of a stable real exchange rate. The difference between the two is the real operating exposure.

Suppose for the present that there are only two scenarios in case of currency depreciation, namely that the firm produces entirely for the foreign market and the demand for the product in the foreign market is price-inelastic in which case sale will not move up and since the imported inputs will be costlier, the net cash inflow would turn negative. The other scenario is that the sale expands both in the local market as well as the foreign market, substitutes for imported inputs are available in domestic market and so the cost does not rise.

Period	*First scenario*	*Second scenario*
Year 1	₹ –4,500	₹ 8,000
Year 2	–5,000	7,000
Year 3	–6,000	6,500

If discount rate is 10%,

Scenario 1: $-4{,}500/1.10 + -5{,}000/(1.10)^2 + -6{,}000/(1.10)^3 =$ ₹ –12,731.

Scenario 2: $8{,}000/1.10 + 7{,}000/(1.10)^2 + 6{,}500/(1.10)^3 =$ ₹ 17,942.

If we suppose there is no change in the real exchange rate, the cash flow over the three-year period is ₹ 10,000. The size of real operating exposure will be ₹ 22,731 in one case and ₹ 7,942 in the other.

For estimating the real operating exposure, Adler and Dumas (1984) have suggested regressing actual cash flows from past periods converted into domestic currency, on the average exchange rate during the corresponding period. The regression coefficient will be computed thus:

$$PCF_t = a_0 + a_1 e_t + \mu_t \tag{9.1}$$

where

PCF_t = percentage change in inflation-adjusted cash flows
e_t = percentage change in the exchange rate of the currency over period t
a_0 = intercept
a_1 = slope coefficient
μ_t = random error term

In this regression analysis, if additional currencies are to be assessed, they can be included as additional independent variables. The regression coefficient will be different for different currencies.

PROBLEM 9.2

A company expects cash flow from its new project to the extent of $ 5,000; $ 6,500 and $ 6,000 respectively during the first three years of its operation. However, due to changes in exchange rate/inflation rate, the cash flow is affected and it will change to $ 4,000, $ 5,800 and $ 5,200. Find the magnitude of the possible real operating exposure during the initial year of operation assuming a discount rate of 10 per cent.

Solution

Original expectation of cash flow = $ 5,000/1.10 + 6,500/1.21 + 6,000/1.331 = $ 14,425.23

Cash flow expectation after inflation rate/exchange rate changes = 4,000/1.10 + 5,800/1.21 + 5,200/1.331 = $ 12,336.59

Size of real operating exposure = $ 14,425.23 – 12,336.59 = $ 2,088.64.

Exposure in Case of MNCs

The discussion of the measurement of real operating exposure becomes significant in case of MNCs as compared to that in a domestic firm because the operating cash flow is governed not only by inter-firm transactions but also by intra-firm transactions. Moreover, a larger number of currencies are involved there than in the case of a domestic firm. Some currencies may appreciate, while the others may depreciate. So it is only the net effect that determines the size of real operating exposure. The measurement of net effect is a bit more complex.

TRANSLATION EXPOSURE

Translation exposure, which is also known as accounting exposure, emerges on account of consolidation of financial statements of different units of a multinational firm. The parent company is normally interested in maximising its overall profitability and to make it possible to ascertain overall profitability, it consolidates the financial statements of its subsidiaries with its own. The other objective of consolidation of financial statements is to evaluate the comparative performance of different subsidiaries.

Translation exposure is mismatch between the translated value of assets and liabilities following exchange rate change.

Parent unit consolidates the accounts of subsidiaries to assess global profit or overall financial position of the firm.

Whatever may be the objective of consolidation, it is done through translating the items of the financial statements of subsidiaries denominated in different currencies into the domestic currency of the parent company. When the currency of any of the host countries changes its value, its translated value in the domestic currency of the parent company changes as does the picture of the consolidated statement. The extent of this change represents the magnitude of translation exposure. If the subsidiary maintains its account in the reporting currency, i.e. the domestic currency of the parent company as is sometimes done by the extended departments of a firm abroad, the translation exposure does not emerge. Normally though, the subsidiaries maintain their accounts in a functional currency that is normally the currency of the host country, and there is every possibility for the translation exposure to emerge in the wake of exchange rate changes.

It is sometimes argued that the translation exposure is irrelevant, because it does not influence the cash flow, nor is the subsidiary's earning actually converted into the parent's currency. But since the change in the value of the currency of the host countries has an impact on the net worth of the firm as a whole, measurement of the accounting exposure is highly relevant.

The size of accounting exposure depends no doubt on the extent of change in the value of related currencies, but it depends also upon the extent of involvement of subsidiaries in the parent's business, on the location of the subsidiaries in countries with stable or unstable currency and on the methods that are used in the translation of currencies. The larger the involvement of subsidiaries in the parent's business, the greater will be the exposure. Again, if the subsidiaries are located in countries where the currency is highly unstable, the accounting exposure will be large. Similarly, as methods vary in their approach, it is natural for different methods to yield different results. The methods are thus really relevant to this context and so they need to be discussed.

Methods of Translation

The different methods of translation vary among themselves insofar as they are not unanimous on the items of the financial statement which are exposed to changes in the exchange rate. Every method has its merits and demerits. A particular method is used depending upon the circumstances and the legal and accounting procedures adopted in a particular country. The methods are:

1. Current rate method
2. Current/non-current method
3. Monetary/non-monetary method
4. Temporal method

Current rate method

The current rate method is also known as the *closing rate method*. In this method, all items of the income statement and the balance sheet are translated at current rate or the post-change rate. This method is preferred in case of those host countries where the local currency accounts are periodically adjusted for inflation. The translation exposure in this case is simply the net worth of the affiliate as stated in local currency.

The merit of this method is that the relative proportion of individual balance-sheet accounts remains the same and the process of translation does not distort the various balance sheet ratios. But the demerit is that the fixed assets are also translated at current rate and that goes against the principles of accounting.

Current/non-current method

Under this method, current assets and current liabilities of the subsidiary are translated at current rate or the post-change rate. The fixed assets and long-term liabilities are translated at the historical or pre-change rate or at a rate at which they were acquired. In fact, this approach is based on traditional accounting that makes a clear-cut distinction between current and long-term items. The magnitude of the exposure is measured by the difference between current assets and current liabilities, that is, the subsidiary's working capital. The critics of this approach opine that the long-term debt which is also exposed to exchange rate change is ignored by this method. This is perhaps the reason that this method is not frequently used.

As far as the income statement items are concerned, they are translated at the average rate of exchange—the average of the pre-change and the post-change rates. However, there are a few income statement items which by virtue of being closely related to the non-current assets and long-term liabilities are translated at the pre-change rate.

Monetary/non-monetary method

Under the monetary/non-monetary method, the assets and liabilities are classified as monetary and non-monetary. Items that represent a claim to receive, or an obligation to pay, a fixed amount of foreign currency such as cash, accounts receivable, accounts payable, etc. come under the monetary group, while the physical assets and liabilities such as fixed assets, inventory and long-term investment are treated as non-monetary items. The monetary assets and liabilities are translated at current rate, while the non-monetary items are translated at historical rate. The translation exposure under this method is measured by the net monetary assets or by the difference between the monetary assets and the monetary liabilities.

As far as the income statement items are concerned, they are translated at average rate and those closely related to non-monetary assets and liabilities are translated at historical rate.

Temporal method

The temporal method uses historical rate for the items that are stated at historical cost. For example, fixed assets are translated at historical rate but items that are stated at replacement cost, realisable value, market value or expected future value, are translated at current rate. This is done in order to preserve the value of assets and liabilities as shown in the original financial statement. As regards income statement items, the same norm is applied as in the monetary/non-monetary method.

The temporal method to a great extent resembles the monetary/non-monetary method. The main difference is that under the temporal method, inventory is translated at current rate if it is shown at market value. In the monetary/non-monetary method, it is translated at historical rate in all probabilities.

Table 9.2 presents a summary of all the different methods, followed by Table 9.3 that presents a numerical example.

TABLE 9.2 Summary of Translation Methods

Exchange rate	*Current rate method*	*Current/non-current method*	*Monetary/non-monetary method*	*Temporal method*
Current rate	All items	Current assets and current liabilities	All liabilities and current assets except inventory	All liabilities and all current assets if inventory shown at market price
Historical rate		Fixed assets and long-term liabilities	Inventory and fixed assets	Fixed assets and inventory if not shown at market price
Average rate		Income statement items except those related to fixed assets	Income statement items except those related to fixed assets	Income statement items except those related to fixed assets

TABLE 9.3 Results of Different Methods of Currency Translation

(Reporting currency = US $)

Balance-sheet items	*Rupee: Local currency*	*Historical rate = ₹ 30/US $*	*Current rate = ₹ 35/US $*			
			Current rate	*Current/ non-current*	*Monetary/ non-monetary*	*Temporal*
Current assets—inventory	2,000	67	57	57	57	57
Inventory (market value)	4,000	133	114	114	133	114
Fixed assets (net of depreciation)	4,000	133	114	133	133	133
Goodwill	1,000	33	29	33	33	33
Total assets	11,000	366	314	337	356	337
Current liabilities	4,000	133	114	114	114	114
Long-term debt	3,000	100	86	100	86	86
Share capital	2,000	67	57	67	57	57
Retained earnings (assets–liabilities)	2,000	67	57	56	100	80
Total liabilities	11,000	366	314	337	356	337
Translation gains (Loss)			(10)	(11)	33	13

Table 9.3 presents an example of translation based on different methods and how the results of different methods differ. This is related to items of an imaginary balance-sheet of an Indian subsidiary being consolidated by its US-based parent company. It is evident that there is translation loss if the current or current/non-current method is used. The loss differs even in these two cases, although the difference is only marginal. On the contrary, there is translation gain in case of the other two methods. The gain too differs in these two cases. All this has happened because of different assumptions of the different methods regarding the items that get exposed as a result of exchange rate changes. This is why different countries adopt different methods according to what suits them. A discussion of methods used in international accounting and consolidation of financial statements forms Part VII of this book.

PROBLEM 9.3

Find out the translation loss/gain on the basis of the following data supplied by the Indian subsidiary to its parent unit in the USA:
(Amount, ₹, million)

Liabilities		*Assets*	
Current liabilities	400	Cash	100
Share capital	1,000	Marketable securities	100
Bonds	600	Debtor	200
Retained earnings	400	Inventory	300
		Land & Building	600
		Plant & Machinery	800
		Furniture & Fixtures	300

Historical rate = ₹ 40/US $. Current rate = ₹ 46/US $

Solution

(Amount US $, million)

Items	*Historical rate*	*Current-rate method*	*Current/ Non-current*	*Monetary/ Non-monetary method*	*Temporal method*
Cash	2.5	2.17	2.17	2.17	2.17
Marketable securities	2.5	2.17	2.17	2.17	2.17
Debtors	5.0	4.34	4.34	4.34	4.34
Inventory	7.5	6.51	6.51	7.50	6.51
Land & Building	15.0	13.02	15.00	15.00	15.00
Plant & Machinery	20.0	17.36	20.00	20.00	20.00
Furniture & Fixtures	7.5	6.51	7.50	7.50	7.50
Total assets	60.0	52.08	57.69	58.68	57.59
Current liabilities	10.0	8.68	8.68	8.68	8.68

Share capital	25.0	21.70	25.00	21.70	21.70
Bond	15.0	13.02	15.00	13.02	13.02
Retained earning	10.0	8.68	9.01	15.28	14.19
Total liabilities	60.0	52.08	57.69	58.68	57.59
Gain/(Loss)		(1.32)	(0.99)	5.28	4.19

It is found that the current and current/non-current methods yield translation loss, while the other two methods yield translation gain on account of rupee depreciation.

Real balance sheet exposure indicates mismatch between assets and liabilities in terms of their respective market value.

The literature on the subject often explains the accounting exposure not only in terms of the impact of exchange rate changes on the book value of assets and liabilities, but also in terms of real balance sheet exposure that arises when a firm's real net asset position is affected by the exchange rate changes (Click and Coval, 2002). What is real net asset position? It is the market value of total assets net of the market value of liabilities. It shows the real value of the balance sheet as it is based on the market value and not on the book value. For measuring the net worth exposure, one needs to distinguish between the monetary assets and non-monetary assets. Monetary assets earn nominal returns manifest in the interest rates. The Interest Rate Parity theory suggests, among other things, that the depreciation in currency is matched by a rise in interest rate. So if the value of a monetary asset of the subsidiary falls in terms of the parent country currency in the wake of the currency depreciation in the host country, that monetary asset will be earning higher interest to compensate the loss in the value. If the loss in the value is exactly matched by the gain in terms of interest, there will be no net worth exposure insofar as it does not represent a deviation from the interest rate parity theory. Net worth exposure will arise only when there is unanticipated deviation from the interest rate parity meaning that the loss/gain on account of exchange rate changes is not exactly matched by changes in interest rates. Suppose the exchange rate is ₹ 40/$. In India, the annual rate of interest is higher by 3 per cent over that in the USA. Based on the interest rate parity theory, rupee will depreciate after one year to ₹ 41.20/$. The fall in the value of the monetary asset of the US subsidiary in India on account of depreciation of rupee will be compensated by the gain on account of higher interest rate earned by the monetary asset and there is no net worth exposure. But if the exchange rate changes to ₹ 41.30/$, there will be net worth exposure to the extent of ₹ 41.30 – 41.20 = ₹ 0.10 per dollar of the value of the asset.

Similarly, in case of non-monetary assets, net worth exposure will arise only when there is deviation from the PPP theory. If inflation is higher in India than in the USA, rupee will depreciate vis-à-vis US dollar. If depreciation is matched by a rise in the market price of the asset, there is no net worth exposure. The net worth exposure will arise only when the rise in the asset price is not matched by the depreciation in rupee.

SUMMARY

- Changes in exchange rate beyond anticipation cause foreign exchange exposure and firms involved in international transactions or operation have to face foreign exchange gains or losses. Foreign exchange exposure is of two types, namely accounting exposure, and economic exposure. The former does not affect the cash flows, while the latter influences the cash flow. Economic exposure too is bifurcated into transaction exposure and real operating exposure. The former is concerned with present cash flows, while the latter is concerned with future cash flows.
- Transaction exposure, that is, the difference between expected cash flow and actual cash flow on account of exchange rate changes, emerges owing to either foreign trade on open account or borrowing and lending in foreign currency or intra-firm cash flows. In case of MNCs, it is the consolidated net figure of cash flows that determines the size of transaction exposure.
- Real operating exposure, which is concerned with real exchange rate changes influencing the future operating cash flows, varies if the cost and revenue streams differ under different market conditions. In order to measure the size of this exposure, cost and revenue streams under different market conditions are estimated. They are brought to the present value and that is compared with the expected cash flow in absence of any change in exchange rate. It can be estimated also with the help of regression analysis.
- Translation exposure emerges on account of consolidation of financial statements of foreign subsidiaries by the parent company. With changes in the exchange rate between the host countries and the home country, the picture of the consolidated statement changes. This change represents the size of translation exposure. However, there are different methods of translation of the financial statement items, each of them having different views regarding the exposed assets and liabilities. This causes disparity in the results of the different methods. Each country adopts a particular method according to its individual requirements. Accounting exposure is explained also in terms of net worth exposure where the changes in exchange rate affect the market value of assets and liabilities.

STUDY TOPIC

A Note on Accounting Standard 11 of India

In India, AS 11 deals with the effects of the changes in the foreign exchange rates. It means that AS 11 is to be followed in case of the transactions in foreign currencies as also in case of the translation of foreign currencies for the consolidation of financial statements of overseas operations. Here foreign operation is a subsidiary, associate, joint-venture or branch of the reporting enterprise, the activities of which are based in a country other than the country of the reporting enterprise.

Foreign Currency Transactions

A foreign currency transaction is either denominated in a foreign currency or is settled in a foreign currency including the transactions involving sale or purchase of goods and services in a foreign currency, borrowing and lending in a foreign currency, forward contract, and acquisition and disposal of assets/settlement of liabilities in a foreign currency. A foreign currency transaction needs to be recorded in the reporting currency after translation at the exchange rate applicable to the date of transaction.

When the transactions are reported at subsequent balance sheet dates, a clear-cut distinction is made between monetary items and non-monetary items. Cash, receivables, and payables are the examples of monetary items. Fixed assets, inventories and investment in equity shares are examples of non-monetary items. As per the rule, foreign currency monetary items should be reported using the closing date. When the closing date is not realistic, particularly when there are restrictions on remittances, the relevant monetary item should be reported in the reporting currency at the amount which is likely to be realised from, or required to disburse, such item at the balance sheet date.

Non-monetary items, which are carried in terms of historical cost denominated in a foreign currency, should be reported using the exchange rate at the date of the transaction. Again, non-monetary items, which are carried at fair value or other similar valuation denominated in a foreign currency should be reported using the exchange rates that existed when the values were determined.

Exchange differences arising on the settlement of monetary items or on reporting an enterprise's monetary items at rates different from the originally recorded ones should be treated as income/expense in the period when they arise. If exchange difference arising in respect of monetary items forms a part of the net investment of an enterprise in a non-integral foreign operation, it should be accumulated in a foreign currency translation reserve until the disposal of the net investment. Thereafter it should be treated as income/expense.

Financial Statements of Foreign Operations

For the purpose of the financial statement items, a distinction is made between an integral and a non-integral foreign operation. An integral foreign operation is simply an extension of the reporting enterprise's operation, e.g. a unit selling products of the parent unit and remitting proceeds thereof to the parent unit. If the exchange rate changes, it involves immediate cash flow and it is simply a monetary item. In an integral operation, the cost and depreciation of tangible fixed assets is translated at the exchange rate applicable to the date of purchase of the asset. The cost of inventories is translated at a rate existing when those costs were incurred. The realisable value of an asset is translated using the exchange rate at the date at which realisable value was determined. Here it may be noted that for the reporting enterprise, the realisable value of an asset, and not the carrying value, is relevant.

On the contrary, a non-integral operation is that where such operation is carried out with a significant degree of autonomy; where the transaction with the reporting enterprise is not significant; where the foreign operation is financed mainly out of local funds; and where the sale occurs mainly in a foreign currency. When such an operation accumulates cash and other monetary items primarily in a local currency, there is no direct impact on the present and future cash flows from operations. The change in the exchange rate influences the reporting enterprise's net investment rather than the monetary/non-monetary items.

While translating the financial statements of a non-integral foreign operation for incorporation in its financial statement, the reporting enterprise:

(a) Translates the assets and liabilities, both monetary and non-monetary, at the closing rate.
(b) Translates income and expense items at exchange rates applicable to the date of transaction.
(c) Accumulates exchange differences in a foreign currency translation reserve until the disposal of the net investment.
(d) Translates a contingent liability at the closing rate for its disclosure in the financial statement of the reporting enterprise.

On the disposal of a non-integral foreign operation, the cumulative exchange differences are treated as income/expense in the same period in which the gain/loss on disposal is recognised.

Forward Exchange Contracts

The premium/discount arising at the inception of a forward contract should be amortized as expense/income over the life of the contract. Exchange differences are to be included in the profit and loss account in the reporting period in which the exchange rate changes. Any profit/loss arising out of cancellation/renewal of the forward contract is recognised as income/expense for the period.

Source: Based on the original text of ASI-11.

QUESTIONS

1. Mention the scope of ASI-11.
2. How are the monetary and non-monetary items translated in respect of a foreign currency transaction?
3. How are the exchange differences treated?
4. How do you distinguish between an integral foreign operation and a non-integral foreign operation?
5. How are the financial statement items translated in respect of an integral and a non-integral foreign operation?

REVIEW QUESTIONS

Objective-Type Questions

1. State whether true (T) or false (F):

   (a) Translation exposure involves cash flow. ☐
   (b) Transaction exposure involves present cash flow. ☐

(c) Real operating exposure involves present cash flow. ☐
(d) Real operating exposure does not consider changes in price level. ☐
(e) Functional currency is the currency in which subsidiaries convert their financial statement figures for the purpose of reporting to the parent unit. ☐

2. Choose the correct answer:

(a) Real operating exposure takes into account
   (i) only changes in cash flow
   (ii) only changes in price level
   (iii) both the changes in price level and exchange rate

(b) Real operating exposure includes
   (i) only the present cash flows
   (ii) future cash flows
   (iii) both the present and future cash flows

(c) Translation exposure takes into account
   (i) present cash flows
   (ii) future cash flows
   (iii) none of these

(d) Transaction exposure arises on account of
   (i) borrowing and lending
   (ii) consolidation of financial statements by the parent unit
   (iii) none of these

(e) Translation exposure arises
   (i) when reporting and functional currencies are the same
   (ii) when reporting and functional currencies are not the same
   (iii) none of these

Short-Answer Questions

1. Distinguish between:
   (a) translation exposure and transaction exposure
   (b) transaction exposure and real operating exposure
   (c) monetary/non-monetary method of translation and temporal method of translation
2. What do you mean by consolidated net transaction exposure?

Long-Answer Questions

1. How do you arrive at the amount of real operating exposure?
2. Do the different methods of translation arrive at different sizes of translation exposure? Explain.

Numerical Problems

1. Find out the translation loss/gain on the basis of the following data supplied by the Indian subsidiary to its parent unit in the USA:

(Amount ₹ million)

Liabilities		*Assets*	
Current liabilities	400	Cash	100
Share capital	1,000	Marketable securities	100
Bonds	600	Debtor	200
Retained earnings	400	Inventory	300
		Land & Building	600
		Plant & Machinery	800
		Furniture & Fixtures	300

Historical rate = ₹ 40/US \$, Current rate = ₹ 46/US \$.

2. Find out the transaction gain/loss on the basis of the following data pertaining to India's foreign trade:

	US \$, million	*Japanese Yen, million*	*British £, million*
Import	1,250	650	800
Export	1,150	625	850
Pre-change rate	₹ 45/\$	₹ 0.40/Yen	₹ 70/£
Post-change rate	₹ 47/\$	₹ 0.41/Yen	₹ 68/£

REFERENCES

Adler, M. and B. Dumas (1984), Exposure to Currency Risk: Definition and Measurement, *Financial Management*, XIII, 41–50.

Click, R.W. and J.D. Coval (2002), *The Theory and Practice of International Financial Management*, New Delhi: PHI.

Eiteman, D.K., et al. (1995), *Multinational Business Finance*, Reading (Mass.), Addison- Wesley, pp. 186–187.

SUGGESTED FURTHER READING

Aliber, Robert Z. (1979), *Exchange Risk and Corporate International Finance*, New York, Wiley.

Jacque, Laurent L. (1983), *Management of Foreign Exchange Risk*, Lexington, D.C. Heath & Co.

Shapiro, Alan C. (1975), Exchange Rate Changes, Inflation and the Value of the Multinational Corporation, *Journal of Finance*, XXX, 485–502.

CHAPTER

10 Management of Foreign Exchange Exposure

Learning Objectives

Exchange rate exposure often causes loss to firms involved in international transactions. So they need to be managed. The present chapter includes the discussion on how different kinds of exposure are managed. In particular, it:

- Presents a comparative view of the contractual hedging techniques and also the natural hedging techniques of managing transaction exposure.
- Deals with the strategies adopted for managing real operating exposure.
- Discusses how translation exposure is managed.

How changes in exchange rate lead to foreign exchange exposure has been discussed in the previous chapter. If such an exposure results in loss to a firm, it needs to be hedged; that is, it needs to be eliminated or reduced. The process of hedging is, in fact, the management of exchange rate exposure. In some quarters, hedging is not favoured as it is not very relevant, but in others, the need for hedging is emphasised and various hedging techniques are resorted to. We now discuss need for, and techniques of, hedging.

NEED FOR HEDGING

Whether firms should hedge their foreign exchange risk has been the subject of long debate (Stulz, 1984; Smith and Stulz, 1985; Levi and Sercu, 1991; Froot, et al., 1993). One school of thought believes that exposure in the wake of exchange rate changes is not an issue because, as the PPP theory suggests, movement in exchange rate offsets the changes in price level. Suppose inflation rate in India is higher than that in the USA by 5.0 per cent, the rupee will depreciate by an appropriate percentage vis-à-vis the US dollar, and hence, *firstly*, there will be no price risk and the cost of the Indian goods in the USA will remain the same. *Secondly*, the changes in the exchange rate do cause both gain and loss to firms involved in foreign transactions but the gains and losses tend to average out over a period. *Thirdly*, the shareholders are competent enough to minimise the currency risk through diversification of their investment portfolio. *Fourthly*, hedging does not add to the value of the firm and instead uses up, scarce resources of the firm and may thus lower the value of the firm. It is also argued that when the market is in equilibrium in respect of parity conditions, the expected net present value of hedging is zero.

On the other hand, those who support hedging argue that the PPP theory is generally not applicable in the short run; and what more is, there is a lag between changes in the price level and changes in the exchange rate. They also argue that hedging not only prevents the cash flow from falling below the desired level but also leads to increase in future inflow of cash that may increase the value of the firm. They believe that the management can hedge the risk in a better and more efficient way than the shareholders. They also believe that the market is normally in disequilibrium due to institutional and structural imperfections and so the expected net present value of hedging is often positive.

> Exposure needs to be hedged because:
> 1. PPP theory often does not work.
> 2. Hedging helps-maintain cash flow.
> 3. NPV of hedging is often positive.

The debate is basically academic. In practice, firms are found greatly involved in various kinds of hedging. Had hedging not conferred benefits upon them, they would not have resorted to it on any large scale. The fact that they do, shows that it is significant.

HEDGING OF TRANSACTION EXPOSURE

The techniques for hedging transaction exposure are sometimes grouped as *internal* and *external techniques*. The former form a part of the firm's regulatory financial management and do not involve any contractual relationship with any party outside the firm. The latter involve contractual relationship with the parties outside the firm for insuring against potential foreign exchange loss (Buckley, 1996). However, we group the hedging techniques as:

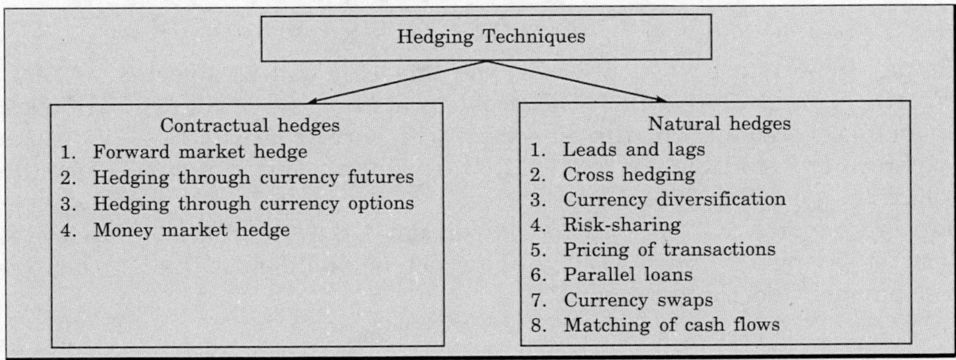

Contractual Hedges

Contractual hedges include forward market hedge, money market hedge, futures market hedge and options market hedge. In the *forward market hedge*, the exporter sells forward and the importer buys forward, the foreign currency in which the trade is invoiced. In the futures contract too, similar transactions are found. In the process of hedging in the currency options market, the importer buys a call option or sells a put option or performs both the functions at the same time. The exporter buys a put option and sells a call option or performs both the functions simultaneously. The forward market hedge and hedging through the use of derivatives have already been discussed in the earlier chapters. The discussion in this chapter will be limited to the money market hedge and to a comparative analysis of the different types of contractual hedges.

Money market hedge

This hedge involves a money market position to cover a future payables or receivables position. An importer, who has to cover future payables, first borrows local currency; then, converts the borrowed local currency into the currency of payables; and finally, invests the converted amount for a period matching the payments to be made for the import. An exporter, on the other hand, who has to hedge the receivables, first borrows the currency in which the receivables are denominated, then converts the borrowed currency into local currency; and finally invests the converted amount for a maturity coinciding with the receipt of export proceeds.

> Money market hedge involves a money market position in order to cover a future payables/receivables position.

The money market hedge may be *covered* or it may be *uncovered*. If the firm has sufficient cash out of business operations to buy the foreign currency or to repay the foreign currency loan, it is called a *covered hedge* but if it purchases foreign currency with borrowed funds or repays the foreign currency loan by purchasing foreign currency in the spot market, it is known as an *uncovered money market hedge*.

Let us first take the case of the money market hedge in case of *accounts payable*. Suppose the Indian importer has to make payments for import worth US $ 1,000 after 90 days. If it is a covered hedge, it creates 90-day investment in foreign currency in which the import is invoiced. The amount of initial investment will be such that the principal plus interest after 90 days equals the payments for import. Thus, if the rate of interest on investment is 12 per cent per annum and if the amount of import is US $ 1,000, the sum of initial investment will be:

US $ 1,000/1.03 = US $ 970.87

On the day imports are to be paid for, the importer will receive US $ 1,000 from the investment and there will be no problem even if the exchange rate changes.

In an uncovered hedge, the importer will borrow ₹ 970.87 × 40 (assuming the spot rate of ₹ 40/US $) = ₹ 38,834.80. It will convert the rupee amount into US dollars to get US $ 970.87 and invest it at 12 per cent p.a. interest rate. On the day the imports will be paid for, it will get US $ 1,000 and there will be no problem in paying for imports. The only cost it would have had to bear is the interest payment on the borrowing.

In case of 90-day *receivables*, if the export amounts to US \$ 1,000, the exporter will borrow US \$ 970.87, convert this amount into ₹ 38,834.80 and invest this amount at 12 per cent p.a. interest. On the day the export proceeds are received, the investment (principal + interest) will amount to ₹ 40,000. The exporter will not be exposed to exchange rate changes, if any. The cost of hedging it would have to bear is the payment of interest on the borrowing.

Let us first consider *whether the money market hedge yields the same result as the forward market hedge.* If the interest rate parity conditions prevail and if transaction cost does not exist, the two shall yield similar results but since the transaction cost is always present, the results tend to differ. A *break-even investment rate* can be computed at which the hedger will be indifferent between a money market hedge and the forward market hedge. Assuming r as the 90-day investment rate that would equate the proceeds from the two streams—money market hedge and the forward market hedge, we get

$$\text{Borrowing amount} \times (1 + r) = \text{forward proceeds} \tag{10.1}$$

If the 90-day forward rate is ₹ 40.40/US \$, the forward proceeds based on the above example will be ₹ 40,400. Basing again on the above example,

$$38{,}834.80 \times (1 + r) = 40{,}400$$

or $$1 + r = 40{,}400/38{,}834.80$$

or $$r = 0.0403$$

or $$\text{the annualised } r = 0.0403 \times 360/90 = 0.1612 = 16.12 \text{ per cent}$$

Here, r is more than the rate of interest on investment, 12 per cent p.a. under money market hedge, which means that the money market hedge is not so beneficial as the forward market hedge and so the importer should go for the forward market hedge. But if the forward rate is ₹ 39.80 per US \$, the value of annualised r will be 9.94 per cent which is lower than the interest rate on investment. The money market hedge will be the preferred option in this case.

PROBLEM 10.1

The rate of interest on investment in the money market is 9 per cent p.a. Spot rate is ₹ 45.10/\$ and a 90-day forward rate is ₹ 45.15. Which of the two hedge should be preferred by an importer of \$ 1,000 import?

Solution

$$\$\ 1{,}000/1.0225 = \$\ 978 \times 45.10 = ₹\ 44{,}107.58$$

Break-even investment rate, $r = 44{,}107.58 \times 1 + r = 45{,}150$

$$= 45{,}150/44{,}107.58 - 1 = 0.0236$$

The annualised rate = 0.0236 × 360/90 = 0.0944 or 9.44 per cent
Here forward market should be preferred as it has a greater investment rate than what is estimated in the money market.

Comparison between Alternatives of Contractual Hedge

When different alternatives of contractual hedge are available, the hedger has to choose an alternative that gives him the largest amount in terms of local currency. Again, if the funds available under different alternatives of hedging are lower than in the no-hedge alternative, the hedger should not go in for hedging and should opt for accepting the transaction exposure. Let us now discuss four alternatives as applied to an importer and an exporter:

1. No hedge
2. Hedging in the forward market
3. Hedging in the money market
4. Hedging in the currency options market

Suppose:

(a) Spot rate is ₹ 40/US $
(b) 90-day forward rate is ₹ 39.50/US $
(c) Interest rate on borrowing in India and the USA is 6 per cent p.a.
(d) Interest rate on deposit/investment is 5 per cent p.a.
(e) A 90-day call option is having a strike price of ₹ 39.60 and a premium of ₹ 0.05 per dollar
(f) A 90-day put option is having exercise price of ₹ 39.80 and a premium of ₹ 0.05 per dollar
(g) Spot rate on the 90th day is ₹ 39.80/US $.

For the importer

Suppose the Indian importer imports goods worth US $ 1,000 from the USA and it has to make payments after 90 days. The importing firm is expecting changes in the exchange rate, and so it thinks about selecting a particular alternative.

(i) No hedge: The importer will have to pay ₹ 39,800 for the import and will reap a gain for ₹ 200 on account of the exchange rate changes.

(ii) Forward contract: The importer will have to pay only ₹ 39,500 for US $ 1,000 required for the payment for the import. It saves further ₹ 300 because of the forward contract.

(iii) Money market hedging: As shown below, under the money market hedge, the importer will have to pay ₹ 40,098.77 for covering the import for US $ 1,000. Had there been no hedge, it would have had to pay only ₹ 39,800.

Amount of US dollar invested = US $ 1,000/(1 + 0.0125) = US $ 987.65

Amount of investment in rupee at the spot rate = ₹ 40.0 × 987.65
= ₹ 39,506.17

Repayment of borrowing (principal + interest) = ₹ 39,506.17 × (1 + 0.015)
= ₹ 40,098.77

(iv) Hedging in options: The importer will profit if it buys a call option and exercises it.

₹ (39.80 – 39.60 – 0.05) × 1,000 = ₹ 150

If the importer performs both the functions, that is, buys a call and sells a put simultaneously, the total profit will be equal to ₹ 200 because the put option will not be exercised and so the profit to be reaped by the importer as a seller of put will be equal to the amount of the premium, that is ₹ 50.

A comparative picture shows that the benefit in case of a forward market hedge is the greatest. The importer will naturally go in for it.

For the exporter

In case of hedging of receivables, where the Indian exporter has to get US $ 1,000 as export proceeds after 90 days and where the future spot rate is expected to fall, the exporter will naturally think about hedging. Basing on the above figures; the outcomes would be as follows:

(i) No hedge: The exporter will receive only ₹ 39,800. The loss will amount to ₹ 200 on account of exchange rate changes.

(ii) Hedging in forward contract: The exporter will receive only ₹ 39,500. The loss will be of the order of ₹ 500 on account of exchange rate changes.

(iii) Hedging money market: The loss on account of exchange rate changes amounts to ₹ 98.02 as shown below:

$$\text{Borrowing} = \text{US \$ } 1{,}000/(1 + 0.015) = 985.22$$

The converted amount in Rupees at ₹ 40.0 per dollar = ₹ 39,408.87
The investment after 90 days (principal + interest) fetching:

$$₹\ 39{,}408.87 \times (1 + 0.0125) = ₹\ 39{,}901.98$$

(iv) Hedging in options: The exporter will buy a put and sell a call. If it buys only a put, the put will not be exercised and the exporter will have to pay the premium amounting to ₹ 50. This means, the loss on account of exchange rate changes will be ₹ 200 + 50 = ₹ 250. If the exporter sells the call only, the call will be exercised and the loss to the exporter will be ₹ 200 – 50 = ₹ 150. If it buys the put and sells the call simultaneously, the loss will amount to ₹ 400 on account of exchange rate changes.

Thus in this case, the money market hedge is preferable as it involves the minimum loss on account of exchange rate changes.

PROBLEM 10.2

An Indian importer imports goods worth $ 62,500. He expects an appreciation of pound. So he goes for hedging the risk. The currency market has the following data:

(a) Spot rate on the date of the contract ₹ 68.00/£
(b) Three-month forward rate ₹ 68.50/£
(c) Strike rate in a three-month call option ₹ 68.60/£ with 5% premium
(d) Strike rate in a three-month put option ₹ 68.80/£ with 5% premium
(e) Spot rate on the date of payment/maturity ₹ 68.90/£

Will he go for a hedge? If so, which of the options he will select?

Solution

Option 1: He does not go for hedge:
The size of exposure (loss) = 62,500 × (68.90 – 68.00) = ₹ 56,250
Option 2: He goes for a forward market hedge:
He will have to pay only ₹ 31,250 extra on account of appreciation of pound. The size of exposure will reduce to ₹ 31,250.
Option 3: He goes for a tunnel in the currency options market:
On call, he will gain ₹ 15,625. On put, he will get premium for ₹ 3,125 as put is out-of-money. Total gain will be ₹ 18,750. The size of exposure will reduce to ₹ 37,500.

The importer will go for forward market hedge as the size of exposure is the minimum in this case.

Natural Hedges

Natural hedge is applied when the contractual hedge fails to give good results. It may be mentioned that the contractual hedge provides only temporary protection against exchange rate movement. Sometimes the currency to which the firm is exposed cannot be hedged in view of the absence of a forward market or of a market for derivatives. So when a perfect contractual hedge is not available or is not of much use, the firm adopts the natural hedge. Let us now discuss the different techniques adopted in case of the natural hedge.

Leads and lags

Lead means accelerating or advancing the timing of receipt or of payment of foreign currency. *Lag* is just the reverse and means decelerating or postponing the timing of receipt or payment of foreign currency. Suppose a firm is located in a country with weak currency and it has to pay debts denominated in a hard currency. There is every possibility of the hard currency appreciating against the weak currency. In such a situation, the debtor firm would like to lead the payments. On the contrary, if a firm located in a hard currency country has to pay debts denominated in weak currency, it would like to lag the payment. The purpose in both the cases, is to lower the debt burden.

Lead means advancing the timing of receipt/ payment. Lag means postponing it.

Leading and lagging are practised between two independent firms. They may also be found in intra-firm transactions. In case of inter-firm transactions, practising of this technique is normally opposed because if one firm gains, it will cause the other firm to lose. If the former uses this technique, the latter will naturally oppose it but may agree if the former offers some discount. Normally, the discount is equal to the interest rate differential between the two countries for the period of pre-payment or post-payment.

In the case of intra-firm leading or lagging, there would be no opposition from any of the units as it is a part of the firm's overall strategy. For the success of this strategy, however, it is necessary that the parent company possesses majority of the equity holding in the subsidiaries. Otherwise, the local shareholders may oppose this move.

It is found that some governments have limited the time involved in leading and lagging in order to regulate the inflow and outflow of funds. The international companies must be aware of the governmental regulations before they can venture to practise this technique.

Cross-hedging

It is adopted when the desired currency cannot be hedged. In this case, the firm has first to identify a foreign currency that can be hedged, and at the same time, volatility of which is highly correlated with that of the desired currency. The hedging of the identified currency in the forward market will be a substitute for the forward market hedging of the desired currency.

Cross-hedging occurs in some other currency having positive correlation with the desired currency.

Currency diversification

The smaller the number of currencies in which a firm transacts, the greater will be the magnitude of risk. If the number is quite large, there is every possibility that if one currency depreciates, some other currency will appreciate and, the magnitude of net exposure may be lower in the end. The risk will be much lower if volatility of different currencies in which a firm transacts is negatively correlated to a high degree. So, to lower the size of exposure, a firm is advised to diversify its operation in a larger number of currencies as a hedging tool.

> Currency diversification means transacting in as many currencies as possible. It reduces risk if they are negatively correlated.

Risk-sharing

Risk-sharing is a contractual arrangement through which the buyer and the seller agree to share the exposure. Both the parties normally agree to such a proposal if their business relationship is a long-term one. Under this arrangement, a base rate is fixed with mutual consent that is generally the current spot rate. A neutral zone is also agreed upon which is a few points minus and plus the base rate. When the exchange rate changes within the neutral zone, the transaction takes place at the base rate, but if the exchange rate crosses the neutral zone, the risk is shared equally by the two parties. Suppose the base rate is ₹ 40/US $ and the neutral zone is +1.0/–1.0 per cent. If the rupee depreciates to 42 a US dollar and if the value of the transaction is US $ 1,000, the size of exposure will be ₹ (42.0 – 40.0) × 1,000 = ₹ 2,000. One-half of the exposed amount, that is ₹ 1,000 will be borne by one party and the other half will be borne by the other party. In other words, the Indian party is able to hedge ₹ 2,000-exposure by 50.0 per cent through the use of this technique.

> Risk-sharing means the loss/gain being shared by both of the transacting parties if exchange rate moves beyond the neutral zone.

Pricing of transactions

In exposure management, the pricing policy adopted is of two kinds, namely price variation, and the currency of invoicing. Price variation involves marking up or marking down of the sale price to counter the adverse effects of exchange rate changes. The normal rule is to charge the price in foreign currency on the basis of forward rate and not the spot rate. In case of sequential payments to be made or received at different times, a weighted average of forward rates of different dates is computed. Charging of a different price from the arm's-length price is a usual practice in case of intra-firm transactions. But for the purpose of exposure management, this practice is adopted also in inter-firm transactions.

> Pricing of transaction involves marking up/down of prices as also billing in a desired currency.

In invoicing of transactions, the exporter may be willing to invoice the bill in its own currency or in the currency in which it incurs the cost so that the transaction exposure is avoided but if the importer is dominant, the bill is normally invoiced in the importer's currency. In other cases, the exporter follows the market leader or its major competitors, although it avoids currencies in which the forward market is limited or the convertibility of which is limited. It also avoids highly volatile currency.

The experts believe that with the US dollar depreciating against the Indian rupee by more than 12% during 2007 and with the USA accounting for over a quarter of India's export of apparel and textiles, Indian textile industry faced shrinkage in these exports to the USA. To remedy the situation, Madura Garment Exports Ltd., which supplies to well-known international brands such as Marks & Spencer, Ralph Lauren, Polo, Next, Tommy Hilfiger and Menswear House reduced invoicing of its trade in US dollars, apart from other measures. Earlier, 57% of its exports were invoiced in US dollars, but after dollar depreciation, this percentage reduced to 43%.

Source: *Mint*, 14.4.2008.

In nations where exchange control measures restrict taking positions in foreign currencies, exports and imports are typically invoiced in the domestic currency, regardless of its strength or weakness. This approach represents a defensive strategy. However, an aggressive policy may also be adopted, wherein exports are invoiced in a strong currency and imports are invoiced in a weak currency.

It is important to note that this technique is not as prominent in intra-firm transactions, as the gain realized by one unit is often offset by the loss incurred by another unit within the firm. Nonetheless, the advantages arising from tax differentials between two countries can incentivize intra-firm transactions to be invoiced in either an appreciating or depreciating currency. For instance, consider two subsidiaries of a firm located in country A and country B, where the marginal tax rate in country A is higher than in country B. In such a scenario, assuming all other factors remain constant, the subsidiary in country A may invoice transactions with B in the weaker currency, while the subsidiary in country B may invoice transactions in the stronger currency. This approach allows the before-tax profit of the subsidiary in country A to be transferred to the subsidiary in country B if the currency depreciates further, ultimately reducing the overall tax burden for both subsidiaries.

Parallel loans

A parallel loan is often known as a *back-to-back loan* or *credit swap loan*. Under this arrangement, the amount of the loan moves within the country but it serves the purpose of a cross-border loan. At the same time, such loans are not exposed to the changes in exchange rate because the funds do not move across the national border. Suppose a US parent company has a subsidiary in India. At the same time, an Indian parent company has a subsidiary in the USA. Suppose further that the US parent company has to lend US $ 1,000 to its subsidiary in India for a specific period. The Indian parent company too has to lend to its subsidiary in the USA a similar amount for the same maturity. If the funds move between the two countries and if the exchange rate changes, transaction exposure will result. To avoid this exposure, the Indian parent company will lend the above amount converted into rupees at the spot exchange rate to the US subsidiary. Simultaneously, the US parent company will lend similar amount in terms of US dollars to the Indian subsidiary. At the expiry of the specified period, the two loans will be repaid to the respective lenders. Chart 10.1 shows how the transactions take place under the back-to-back loan arrangement.

Parallel loan is a loan actually moving within the country but serving the purpose of a cross-border loan.

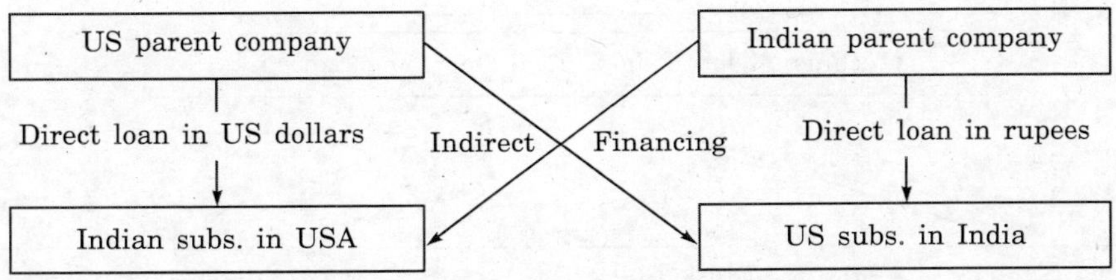

CHART 10.1 Creation of Back-to-Back Loan.

This is no doubt an efficacious technique of hedging the transaction exposure, but it is difficult to find a firm that has to lend a similar amount for a similar maturity. If such a firm, known as a *counter-party*, is located, it cannot be guaranteed that the counter-party would repay the loan within the specified period. If it fails to make repayments, counter-party risk would emerge. It is this particular limitation with the parallel loan that has made the currency swap popular.

Currency swaps

Under this arrangement, two borrowers exchange the currency of borrowing with each other through a swap dealer. This technique is discussed at length in Part V, Ch. 19, under the head, Financial Swaps.

Currency swap means exchanging of currencies through a swap dealer.

Matching of cash flows

Under this mechanism, a firm matches its foreign currency inflow with the outflow in that currency not only in respect of size but also in respect of timing. But for this purpose, the firm must have both inflows and outflows in the same currency.

HEDGING OF REAL OPERATING EXPOSURE

Given that the scope of real operating exposure encompasses future cost and revenue streams, the measures implemented to manage such exposure must incorporate the management of future cost and revenue. Consequently, this responsibility falls not only within the purview of the finance manager but also extends to the production and marketing managers. In essence, the management of real operating exposure encompasses strategies related to finance, production, and marketing. The selection of a specific strategy considers, among other factors, whether the exchange rate fluctuations are trending towards equilibrium, that is, whether the nominal exchange rate is converging with the real exchange rate. In such scenarios, the nominal exchange rate remains stable at a particular level for a prolonged duration. Conversely, if it is diverging from the real exchange rate, the duration of stability at a specific point is very brief. Let us elucidate the various strategies.

Financial Strategy

The hedging techniques used for the transaction exposure, especially those that are used for long-term transaction exposure, are also used for managing real operating exposure, such as long-term forward contract, currency swaps and parallel loans.

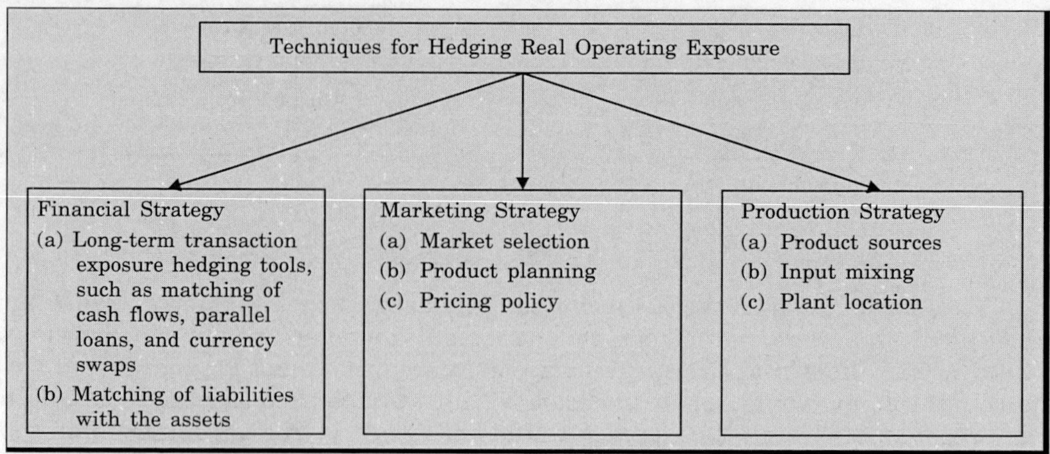

However, they are of little use in this case because the effects of currency changes on the expected cash flows are hard to predict. It is, therefore, better to use sophisticated computerised tools for this purpose. Nevertheless, while developing a financial strategy, the finance manager has to see that the firm's liabilities during the application of marketing and production strategies are so structured that they can be matched to a reduction in assets' earnings during that period. This means that if assets' earnings drop, the servicing burden of liabilities too should be lower and assets and liabilities are restructured to this end.

Financial strategy includes contractual and natural hedges used for long-term transaction exposure.

Marketing Strategy

The marketing strategy includes, among other things, selection of market, product planning and pricing policy. The policy in this respect is influenced by the geography of the market, dominance of the firm in the international market and the elasticity of demand for the product. The policy is redesigned when there is change in the value of domestic currency, or importers' currency or that of competing countries.

Market selection

If the firm is an exporter and if the domestic currency appreciates or if the currency of the importing country or competing country depreciates, the firm's export would turn uncompetitive on account of price. The strategy in this case should be to pull out of the existing market and to develop new markets and market segmentation within a particular importing country may be adopted. If the product is demanded more by the affluent class of consumers, the appreciation of domestic currency may not matter much. The strategy should, therefore, be to concentrate on this class of consumers. Again, if the firm is a dominant supplier of the product or if the price-elasticity of demand for the product is low, the firm can stick to the existing market without making changes in price.

Marketing strategy includes:
1. Market selection.
2. Product planning.
3. Pricing policy.

Product planning

The firm can respond to changes in exchange rate through modifying its product strategy. It can innovate and introduce a new product, or bring modification in the features of the existing product meaning that it can introduce a new variety of the existing product. The greatest advantage of an innovated product is that it generates demand among consumers. If appreciation of the home currency leads to a drop in export of the existing product, an innovated product may fill this gap.

Pricing policy

Pricing policy encompasses the adjustment of product prices in response to exchange rate fluctuations. Consider a scenario where the dollar appreciates from ₹ 35 to ₹ 42. An American company selling its product in India with a price denominated in rupees at ₹ 70 will experience a reduction in its profit when measured in dollar terms. To maintain its profit margin, the company would need to increase the price to ₹ 84. However, such a price increase may lead to a decrease in demand, particularly in the presence of competition from local suppliers. In this situation, the firm may need to accept a lower profit margin.

Conversely, if the dollar depreciates from ₹ 40 to ₹ 35, the selling price of the American product at ₹ 80 could be reduced to ₹ 70 without diminishing the profit margin in dollar terms. Moreover, lowering the denominated price may stimulate demand and consequently increase sales volume. If the denominated price remains unchanged, the profit margin will increase. Thus, a critical decision arises between increasing profit per unit and expanding market share and total revenue. This decision is influenced by factors such as price elasticity of demand, economies of scale, cost structure associated with output expansion, and the likelihood of competition. For instance, in the presence of evident economies of scale, maintaining lower prices may be a more advantageous strategy. Additionally, in the absence of competition, there may be less pressure to reduce prices. Price increases may be feasible when the product is differentiated.

Nevertheless, a crucial consideration is whether the firm should adopt a policy of frequent price list adjustments, particularly in the context of volatile exchange rates. While price list volatility may serve the seller's interests, it creates uncertainty among consumers, potentially affecting sales prospects. Therefore, the firm must evaluate the extent to which price list changes contribute to its profitability.

Production Strategy

The production strategy concentrates primarily on product sources, input mixing and plant location.

Product sources

If the currency of the country supplying inputs appreciates, the input-buying firm has to find some other sources of supply that may be cheaper. If the home currency appreciates, it would be in the interest of the input-buying firm not to change the source of supply, and preferably to buy input from the countries to which it exports its final product because then its terms of trade will improve. This step would be highly beneficial if the imported inputs account for a large part of the total inputs.

> Production strategy involves:
> 1. Product sourcing.
> 2. Input mixing.
> 3. Plant location.

Again, it is not only the cost of material that counts but also the cost of labour. It is for this reason that MNCs headquartered in the developed countries procure their labour-intensive inputs from developing countries where labour is cheap, and set up their labour-intensive assembly units in the developing countries.

Sometimes the strategy begins with establishing multiple sources of inputs. This is to save the foreign exchange to be spent on importing inputs from an appreciating-currency country.

Input mixing

If a firm is unable to buy cheaper inputs from any source, it can arrest rise in the cost of production through mixing local inputs which may be cheaper. This requires expenditure on research and development so that a new technology using cheaper inputs in a greater proportion can be evolved. To arrive at the correct course of action the benefit of input-mixing must be weighed against the cost of research and development.

Plant location

Alternatively, the firm can locate its plant in a country whose currency has depreciated provided that the inputs are available there. In a case where inputs are available only in one particular country, the firm will have to import them even if the currency of the input-supplying country appreciates.

There are thus different options open for improving the future cost-revenue streams. A firm chooses any one of them or a combination of more than one options depending upon the requirements of each case.

MANAGING TRANSLATION EXPOSURE

There is a view that hedging of translation exposure is not necessary as it does not affect the cash flow but that firms try to hedge it in view of its potential impact on the reported consolidated earnings. The emphasis on hedging of this type of exposure, of course, vary from one set of multinationals to the other set and from one country to the other. Belk and Glaum (1990) have found that companies in the UK stress more on managing translation exposure than their counterparts in the USA.

The most common technique in this case is the balance-sheet hedge that is often supplemented by contractual and natural hedges, especially when balance-sheet hedge gives rise to transaction exposure.

Balance-sheet Hedge

Translation exposure emerges out of mismatch between the net assets and the net liabilities. Balance-sheet hedge attempts at eliminating such mismatches. Table 9.3 in the preceding chapter shows the extent of translation exposure arising on account of lower amount of liabilities than the assets and its impact on the net worth. If fresh borrowings are made to eliminate this mismatch, it would be called a *balance-sheet hedge*. However, it is to be considered that borrowing should be made in weaker currency. If, on the other hand, the situation is reverse meaning that the amount of

> Balance-sheet hedge removes mismatch between liabilities and assets through creating liabilities/assets.

asset is lower than that of liabilities, assets need to be matched with the liabilities through making investment. But the investment should be made in stronger currency. It is because the whole mechanism of balance-sheet hedge rests on the belief that strong currencies normally tend to appreciate vis-à-vis weak currencies that are prone to depreciation. So the exposure can be hedged if strong-currency assets substitute the weak-currency assets and if strong-currency liabilities are substituted by weak-currency liabilities. For this purpose, weak-currency assets are converted into hard-currency assets and hard-currency liabilities are converted into weak-currency liabilities.

Limits of Contractual Hedges

When borrowings/investments are made under the process of balance-sheet hedge, there is every possibility for the emergence of transaction exposure in face of changing exchange rate. If this is the case, contractual and natural hedges, discussed in the preceding pages, may be adopted.

However, the contractual hedges have some limitations as far as translation exposure is concerned. *First*, exchange rate forecasts are usually inaccurate. *Second*, forward, futures and options contracts are not available for many currencies. *Third*, forward market gain or loss emerges depending upon the difference between the forward rate and the future spot rate, while the translation gain or loss reflects the average exchange rate over the period of concern. *Last*, sometimes, contractual hedging of translation exposure serves to increase the transaction exposure.

PROBLEM 10.3

A US company, while consolidating the financial statement of its Indian subsidiary, finds that after translating the assets and liabilities of the subsidiary, the magnitude of assets is greater by $ 566 than the translated value of the liabilities. Do you think to apply the balance-sheet hedge?

Solution

The balance sheet hedge will apply in this case insofar as there is mismatch between assets and liabilities. The process would be to create a liability for $ 566. Care should be taken to create this liability in weak currency.

SUMMARY

- When foreign exchange exposure appears, efforts are made by firms to hedge it although there is a long debate on whether hedging is really required. Those who argue for no hedging believe in the applicability of the PPP theory, in efficiency of the foreign exchange market and in the shareholders' ability for diversifying risk. Hedging, according to them, does not add to the value of the firm. On the other hand, those who argue for hedging believe in the imperfectness of the market and in the firms' greater ability to hedge the risk. They believe that hedging raises the value of the firm.
- Transaction exposure is managed by both contractual hedges and natural hedges. There are different techniques of contractual hedges, such as hedging

in forward, futures and options markets, and the money market hedge. A firm adopts a particular technique where the cost is smallest or the gain is largest. Under the natural hedge, the usually adopted techniques are leads and lags, price variation and currency of invoicing, matching of currency flows, currency swaps, currency diversification, risk sharing, cross hedging, parallel loans, etc.

- While managing real operating exposure, some of the natural hedging techniques are applied that are especially meant for hedging long-term transaction exposure but in this case, the firm applies a combination of financial, marketing and production strategies so that the future net cash inflow should improve significantly to offset the adverse effects of exchange rate changes.
- In the case of translation and real balance-sheet exposure management, some of the financial hedging techniques are adopted, but the balance-sheet hedge is the most common. In fact, the adoption of any particular technique depends upon its suitability in a particular case and its efficacy in dealing with the exposure.

CASE STUDY

MANAGING EXCHANGE RATE RISK

Mahendra International (India) imports engine spares annually from the USA and the UK to mitigate risks associated with supply disruptions. The company imported 2,000 pieces of spares from the USA in 2022 at a price of $2.5 per piece, with an average exchange rate of ₹ 75/$, making the cost ₹ 187.50 per piece. Simultaneously, the company sourced spares from a British manufacturer at ₹ 188 per piece, slightly costlier than the American option.

In 2023, the US dollar appreciated to ₹ 82/$, causing the cost of American spares to rise to ₹ 205 per piece, surpassing the cost of British spares. As a result, Mahendra International reduced its order from the USA to 500 pieces, redirecting the majority of its imports to the UK. This led to significant losses for the US exporter while increasing procurement challenges and costs for the Indian company. The case highlights the implications of exchange rate fluctuations on international trade.

QUESTIONS

1. Calculate the total cost in INR for the American spares in 2022 and 2023. How did the exchange rate appreciation impact the cost difference between American and British spares?
2. Suggest two alternative strategies Mahendra International could adopt to better manage exchange rate risks and maintain stable supply chain costs.
3. Analyze how exchange rate fluctuations influenced the procurement decisions of Mahendra International and discuss their broader impact on the company's relationship with suppliers in the USA and UK.

REVIEW QUESTIONS

Objective-Type Questions

1. State whether true (T) or false (F):
   (a) Money market hedge is a natural hedge technique. ☐
   (b) Options market hedge is a natural hedge technique. ☐
   (c) Leads and lags are a natural hedge technique. ☐
   (d) Balance-sheet hedge is adopted for hedging real operating exposure. ☐
   (e) Currency diversification normally increases the exchange rate risk. ☐

2. Choose the correct answer:
   (a) Money market hedge involves:
      (i) a position to cover a future payables/receivables position
      (ii) going for a forward contract
      (iii) going for a futures contract
   (b) Lag means:
      (i) postponing the payment of foreign currency
      (ii) accelerating the payment of foreign currency
      (iii) none of these
   (c) Lead:
      (i) is the same as lag
      (ii) is opposite to lag
      (iii) none of these
   (d) Matching of cash flows means:
      (i) matching of cash inflows and outflows
      (ii) matching of cash inflow from two different sources
      (iii) none of these

Short-Answer Questions

1. Explain:
   (a) money market hedge
   (b) parallel loans
   (c) leads and lags
2. What is balance-sheet hedge?
3. Name the major techniques of contractual hedge.

Long-Answer Questions

1. What are the techniques adopted for the natural hedge?
2. How do you hedge real operating exposure?

Numerical Problem

1. An Indian importer imports goods worth $ 62,500. He expects an appreciation of pound. So he goes for hedging the risk. The currency market has the following data:

   (a) Spot rate on the date of the contract ₹ 68.00/£
   (b) Three-month forward rate ₹ 68.50/£
   (c) Strike rate in a three-month call option ₹ 68.60/£ with 5% premium
   (d) Strike rate in a three-month put option ₹ 68.80/£ with 5% premium
   (e) Spot rate on the date of payment/maturity ₹ 68.90/£

   Will he go for a hedge? If so, which of the options—forward market hedge or options market hedge—he will select?

REFERENCES

Belk, P.A. and M. Glaum (1990), The Management of Foreign Exchange Risk in UK Multinationals: An Empirical Investigation, *Accounting and Business Research,* XXI (Winter), 52–66.

Buckley, A. (1996), *Multinational Finance,* 3rd ed., New Delhi, Prentice-Hall of India, Chaps. 12 and 13.

Froot, K.A., et al. (1993), Risk Management: Coordinating corporate investment and financing policies, *Journal of Finance,* IIL, 1629–1658.

Levi, M.D. and P. Sercu (1991), Erroneous and Valid Reasons for Hedging Foreign Exchange Rate Exposure, *Journal of Multinational Financial Management,* I, 25–37.

Smith, C.W. and R.M. Stulz (1985), The Determinants of Firms' Hedging Policies, *Journal of Financial and Quantitative Analysis,* XX, 391–405.

Stulz, R.M. (1984), Optimal Hedging Policies, *Journal of Financial and Quantitative Analysis,* XIX, 127.

SUGGESTED FURTHER READING

DeRosa, David F. (1991), *Managing Foreign Exchange Risk,* Chicago, Probus.
Moffett, Michael H. and Jan Karl Karlsen (1994), Managing Foreign Exchange Rate Economic Exposure, *Journal of International Financial Management and Accounting,* V, 157–175.

Ruland, Robert G. and T.S. Doupnik (1988), Foreign Currency Translation and the Behaviour of Exchange Rates, *Journal of International Business Studies,* XIX, 461–476.

PART 4

International Investment Decision

11. Foreign Direct Investment
12. International Capital Budgeting
13. Evaluation and Management of Political Risk
14. International Portfolio Investment

CHAPTER

11 Foreign Direct Investment

Learning Objectives

MNCs operate primarily through foreign direct investment (FDI). The present chapter acquaints the readers with the fundamental issues concerning FDI. In particular, it:

- Explains the motivations behind making FDI.
- Evaluates the costs and benefits of FDI from the viewpoint of both home and host countries.
- Describes the various FDI strategies.
- Focuses on controlling MNCs' operations so as to minimise the cost and maximise the benefits.

There is a long list of companies that have expanded their operation beyond their national boundaries. Figuring large among them are the multinational corporations (MNCs). The MNCs' operation grew phenomenally with the result that the international investment, especially foreign direct investment (FDI) comprising investment for establishment of a new enterprise in foreign country either as a branch or as a subsidiary, and acquisition of an overseas business enterprise increased manifold during past few decades.

Whenever an MNC decides to make foreign direct investment, it confronts a host of questions. A few being more important among them are:

1. What are the motivating factors behind such a move?
2. What should be the mode of investment?
3. Which country should it move to?
4. Is the project viable in terms of cash flow?
5. How much is the risk involved in the operation?

The present chapter is confined to explaining the motivations behind foreign direct investment that manifest in various theories, the benefits and costs of FDI, the strategies followed in this context and something about the control of the MNCs.

THEORIES OF FDI

MacDougall–Kemp Hypothesis

The literature explaining why a firm seeks to make FDI is ample. One of the earliest theories was developed by MacDougall (1958), subsequently elaborated by Kemp (1964). Assuming a two-country model—one being the investing country and the other the host country, and the price of capital being equal to its marginal productivity, they explain that when capital moves freely from one country to another, its marginal productivity tends to equalise between the two countries. This leads to improvement in efficiency in the use of resources which leads ultimately to an increase in welfare. Despite the fact that the output in the investing country decreases in the wake of foreign investment, national income does not fall because the country receives returns on capital invested abroad which is equivalent to marginal productivity of capital times the amount of foreign investment. So long as the income from foreign investment is greater than the loss of output, the investing country continues to invest abroad because it enjoys greater national income than that prior to foreign investment. The host country too witnesses increase in national income as a sequel to the greater magnitude of investment that is not possible in the absence of foreign investment inflow.

FDI moves from a capital-abundant economy to a capital-scarce one till the marginal productivity of capital is equal in both the countries.

Industrial Organisation Theory

Most of the theories explaining FDI assume an oligopolistic or imperfect market in which the investing firm operates. Market imperfections arise in many cases, such as product differentiation, marketing skills, proprietary technology, managerial skills, better access to capital, economies of scale and government-imposed market distortions, etc. Such advantages confer on the MNCs an edge over their competitors in foreign locations and thus help compensate the additional cost of operating in an unfamiliar environment.

One of the earliest theories based on the assumptions of the imperfect market was propounded by Hymer (1976). To Hymer, a multinational firm is a typical oligopolistic firm that possesses some sort of superiority and that looks for control in an imperfect market with a view to maximising profits. Despite the fact that the international firm is posted disadvantageously in a foreign host country where it does not have intimate knowledge of language, culture, legal system and consumers' preference, it possesses certain specific advantages that outweigh the disadvantages. The firm-specific advantages in Hymer's view are mainly the technological advantages that help the firm to produce a new product different from the existing one. It is in fact related to the possession of knowledge that helps in developing special marketing skills, superior organisational and management set-up and improved processing. What is significant in this theory is that these

An MNC with superior technology moves to different countries to supply innovated product making in turn ample gains.

advantages are transmitted more effectively from one unit to another irrespective of their geographical distance. Since the market is imperfect, rival firms do not avail of the technological advantage and so the international firm harvests huge profits. Graham and Krugman (1989) find empirically that it was the technological advantage possessed by the European firms that had led them to invest in the USA. Caves (1971) feels that the firm- specific advantages are transmitted more effectively if the firm participates effectively in the production in the host country, than through other ways such as export or licencing agreements.

Location-specific Theory

Hood and Young (1979) stress the locational factors. They argue that since real wage cost varies among countries, firms with low-cost technology move to low-wage countries. Again, in some countries, trade barriers are created to restrict import. The MNCs invest in such countries to start manufacturing there and so evade the trade barriers. Sometimes the availability of cheap and abundant raw material encourages the MNCs to invest in a particular country.

> FDI moves to a country with abundant raw material and cheap labour force.

Product Cycle Theory

Hymer explained "why" foreign investment takes place, Hood and Young explained "where" foreign investment takes place, but it was Vernon (1966) who added "when" to the "why" and "where" based on data obtained from US corporate activities. Raymond Vernon's theory is known as the *product cycle theory*.

> FDI takes place only when the product in question achieves a specific stage in its life cycle.

Vernon feels that most of the products follow a life cycle that is divided into three stages. The first stage is known as the "innovation" stage. In order to compete with the other firms and to have a lead in the market, the firm innovates a product through research and development. The product is manufactured in the home country primarily to meet the domestic demand, but a portion of the output is also exported to other developed countries. The quality of the product, and not the price, forms the basis of demand because the demand is price-inelastic at this stage.

> Innovation stage is characterised with quite newness of product having price-inelastic demand.

The second stage is known as "maturing product" stage. At this stage, demand for the new product in other developed countries grows substantially and so it turns price-elastic. Rival firms in the host country itself begin to appear at this stage to supply similar products at a lower price owing to lower distribution cost, whereas the product of the innovator involves the transportation cost and tariff which are imposed by the importing government. Thus in order to compete with the rival firms, the innovator decides to set up a production unit in the host country itself that would eliminate the transportation cost and tariff. This leads to internationalisation of production. The imposition of tariff in the host country encouraging foreign direct investment is confirmed by Uzawa and Hamada, but they feel that entry of foreign capital in protected industry reduces welfare in the host country (Kojima, 1978).

> Maturing product stage appears when the product turns price-elastic along with similar products in the market.

At the final or "standardised product" stage, when the product is standardised and the production techniques are no longer the exclusive possession of the innovating firm, rival firms from the home country itself or from some other developed country present stiff competition. This is not unusual because the follow-the-leader theory developed by Knickerbocker (1973) suggests that there is a tendency among the followers to snatch the benefits of international production from the innovator. At this stage, price competitiveness becomes even more important; and in view of this fact, the innovator shifts the production to a low-cost location, preferably a developing country where labour is cheap. The product manufactured in a low-cost location is exported back to the home country or to other developed countries.

Standardised product stage with greater price competitiveness motivates firm to start production in a low-cost location.

The literature on the subject finds one more stage in the product's life cycle. It is known as the "dematuring" stage when development in technology or in the consumers' preference breaks down product standardisation. Sophisticated models of the product are manufactured again in the technology-advanced, high-income countries so that the firm could have a close linkage with the consumers' taste and with the basic infrastructure required for production. Cheap labour does not matter much at this stage as sophisticated models involve a capital-intensive mode of production. Globerman (1986) has explained the four stages with a simple example of the television set which was first produced in the United States and then in other advanced countries. Technology became standardised, the production got concentrated in Japan owing to the cheaper labour cost, and the dematuring stage appeared when sophisticated models were developed and produced in the USA itself.

Dematuring stage breaks down product standardisation with sophisticated models of the product being manufactured in high-income countries.

The product cycle theory explains very clearly the early post-Second World War expansion of US firms in other countries but with changes in international environment, different stages of the product life cycle did not follow necessarily in the same way. Vernon (1979) himself has pointed out this limitation in his later writing that in the second stage itself, the firms are found moving to the developing world to reap the advantages of cheap labour. This has been possible with narrowing of the information gap.

Again, the assumptions of the theory that the "export threat" causes a firm to set up subsidiaries in the country are not always true. Had this been so, all US firms should have set up subsidiaries abroad where they had been exporting (Bhagwati, 1972). Yet again, development in the second stage and in the third stage is contradictory in the sense that the former is anti-trade-oriented vis-à-vis the latter which is trade-oriented. In fact, it is this difference that characterises US firms as quite different from the Japanese ones (Kojima, 1985).

Internalisation Approach

Buckley and Casson (1976) too assume market imperfection, but imperfection, in their view, is related to the transaction cost that is involved in the intra-firm transfer of intermediate products such as knowledge or expertise. In an international firm, technology developed at one unit is passed on to other units normally free of charge. This means that the transaction cost in respect of intra-firm transfer of technology is almost zero, whereas such costs in respect of technology transfer to other firms are usually exorbitantly high putting those firms in a disadvantageous position. Coase (1937) too believes that the MNCs bypass the regular market and use internal prices to overcome the excessive transaction cost of an outside market. Thus it is the internalisation benefit manifesting in the cost-free intra-firm flow of technology or any other knowledge that motivates a firm to go international. It can be said that the views of Buckley and Casson are more or less in consonance with the contents of the appropriability approach of Magee (1979) that emphasises the potential returns from technology creation as a prime mover behind the internationalisation of firms.

Internalisation is a process when an MNC passes on improved technology to its foreign subsidiary at zero/low cost in order to grab the market.

There are, of course, critics who argue that intra-firm transaction cost may not necessarily be low. If subsidiaries are located in an unfamiliar or uncongenial environment, the transaction cost is generally high. Kogut and Parkinson (1993) are of the view that if the transfer of intermediate goods involves substantial modification of well-established practice, transaction cost is very large. Franke, Hofstede and Bond (1991) opine that if the cultural differences between the home country and the host country are wide, the internalisation process will be a costly affair.

The internalisation theory, says Rugman (1986), is a general theory explaining FDI and so lacks empirical content. However, in a subsequent study, he feels that with a precise specification of some additional conditions, successful testing is possible. Buckley (1988) himself is suspicious of the very limitation, but he is hopeful of getting satisfactory results from a rigorous and precise test.

The Eclectic Paradigm

Dunning's eclectic paradigm is a combination of the major imperfect market-based theories of FDI, viz. industrial organisation theory, internalisation theory and location-specific theory. It postulates that at any given time, the stock of foreign assets owned by a multinational firm is determined by a combination of firm-specificity or ownership advantage (O), the extent of location-bound endowments (L), and the extent to which these advantages are marketed within the various units of the firm (I). Dunning is conscious that configuration of the O-L-I advantages varies from one country to another and from one activity to another and that foreign investment will be greater where the configuration is more pronounced.

It is the combination of three advantages–ownership, location and internalisation–that motivates a firm to make FDI.

He also introduces a "dynamised add-on" variable to his theory. This is nothing but a variable of strategic change which may be either autonomous or strategy-induced. International production during a particular period would be the sum of the strategic responses of the firm to the past configuration of O-L-I and to changes in such configuration as a sequel to exogenous and endogenous changes in environment. The example of autonomous change in strategy may be that a firm makes foreign investment more in innovatory activities because of greater O-advantage, or it invests more in a particular country because of L-advantage or it adopts a different marketing strategy depending upon the greater amount of I-advantage. Similarly, the strategy-induced change may be evident from the fact that a market-seeking investment has a different O-L-I configuration from that of a resource-based investment. And ultimately, it is the varying configuration that shapes the direction and the pattern of FDI (Dunning, 1980, 1993). The eclectic approach has thus a wider coverage. It has also been empirically tested by Dunning himself with satisfactory results.

Currency-based Approaches

The currency-based theories are normally based on the imperfect foreign exchange and capital market. One such theory developed by Aliber (1971) postulates that internationalisation of firms can best be explained in terms of the relative strength of different currencies. Firms from strong-currency countries move out to weak-currency countries. In a weak-currency country, the income stream is fraught with greater exchange risk. As a result, the income of a strong-currency country firm is capitalised at a higher rate. In other words, such a firm is able to acquire a large segment of income generation in the weak-currency country's corporate sector. The merit of Aliber's hypothesis lies in the fact that it has stood up to empirical testing. FDI in the United States, Canada and the United Kingdom has been found in consistency with the hypothesis. However, the theory fails to explain why there is FDI in the same currency area.

A firm moves from a strong-currency country to a weak-currency country.

Another theory based on the strength of currency has been developed by Froot and Stein (1989). Their view is that depreciation in the real value of currency of a country lowers the wealth of domestic residents vis-à-vis the wealth of the foreign residents. As a result, it is cheaper for the foreign firms to acquire assets of domestic firms. The authors have found that this factor has been one of the determinants of foreign investment in the United States.

Yet another theory in this context has been propounded by Caves (1988) in one of his later writings. Caves mentions a couple of channels through which exchange rate influences FDI. *First*, changes in exchange rate influence the cost and revenue stream of a firm. If the domestic currency depreciates, the import bill will expand diminishing in turn the net income, but if export expands in the wake of currency depreciation, income will rise. *Second*, exchange rate changes influence FDI through giving rise to capital gains. Depreciation in the value of currency, that is expected to be reversed in the near future, will lead to capital gains following appreciation and in lure of capital gains, foreign capital will flow in. This theory has been tested empirically by Caves himself who finds a negative correlation between the level of exchange rate and the level of FDI in the USA.

Politico-economic Theories

The politico-economic theories concentrate on political risk. Political stability in the host countries leads to foreign investment therein (Fatehi-Sedah and Safizedah, 1989). Similarly, political instability in the home country encourages investment in foreign countries (Tallman, 1988). However, Schneider and Frey (1985) believe that the theory underlying the political determinants of FDI is less well-developed than those involving economic determinants. The political factors are only additive ones influencing foreign investment.

A firm moves from a politically unstable country to a politically stable country.

Modified Theories for Third World Firms

The theories discussed above apply also to the international firms headquartered in the developing countries, but they need some modifications. These firms have long been importing technology from the industrialised countries but since the imported technology is mainly designed to cope with a large market, the firms export a part of their output after meeting the domestic demand. The products become gradually mature and then the firms set up units in the product-importing countries. This is, however, different from the product cycle theory insofar as the firms do not necessarily innovate the product; rather, they modify it to suit the consumers' needs in different countries. The modification is of the scaling-up kind when it concerns the consumers in the developed countries; on the contrary, a scaling-down modification is done for low-income customers. However, it cannot be denied that modifications of these types confer upon the firms a sort of firm-specific advantage (Sharan, 1985). Ting (1982) cites an example of a Taiwanese firm manufacturing pressure cookers and table fans. The firm modified the technology and set up units not only in the developing countries but also in the country from where it had originally imported the technology.

> Developing country firms too possess firm-specific advantages on account of modification of technology.

Again, the firms in the developing countries possess a pool of cheap labour that accompanies the investment. On the other hand, the host country possesses in some cases, an abundance of natural resources which is very much in keeping with the location theory. Thus the theories discussed so far apply also to the MNCs of the developing world.

COSTS AND BENEFITS OF FDI

When direct investment flows from one country to another, it creates benefits both for the home country and the host country. At the same time, it involves some costs too. Thus, when a firm decides to make FDI, it takes into account the benefits and costs to be accrued to not only its home country but also to the host country. The host country perspective is no less significant because cooperation from the host government depends upon the benefits derived by the host country. In the present section, the benefits and costs of FDI are mentioned from the point of view of the home country as well as the host country. Since the host country perspective is more sensitive, it will be discussed first.

Benefits and Costs of FDI

Benefits to the Host Country:	Cost to the Host Country:
• Availability of scarce factors of production • Improvement in the balance of payments • Building of economic and social infrastructure • Fostering of economic linkages • Strengthening of the government budget	• Strained balance of payments following reverse flow • Dependence on the import of • technology • Employment of expatriates • Inappropriate technology • Unhealthy competition Cultural and political interference

(Contd.)

Benefits and Costs of FDI

Benefits to the Host Country:	Cost to the Host Country:
• Availability of raw material • Improvement in balance of payments • Employment generation • Revenue to the government • Improved political relations	• Undesired outflow of factors of • production Possibility of conflict with the host-country government

Benefits to the Host Country

Availability of scarce factors of production

FDI brings in scarce foreign exchange, skilled labour force, specific raw material and improved technology.

FDI helps attain a proper balance among different factors of production through the supply of scarce factors and fosters the pace of economic development. FDI brings in capital and supplements the domestic capital. This is a significant contribution where the domestic savings rate is too low to match the warranted rate of investment. It brings in scarce foreign exchange that activates the domestic savings that would not have been put into investment in absence of the availability of foreign exchange. It happens when the investment outlay possesses foreign exchange component, and in absence of foreign exchange, domestic savings remain idle. It also happens when the local investors are afraid of the large risk involved in the investment project. In case of FDI, foreign investors share the risk and the investment project is implemented.

Sometimes FDI is accompanied by labour force that performs those jobs that the local labour force is either not willing to do or is incapable of doing on account of lack of skill. Besides, the foreign labour force infuses non-traditional mental attitudes among the local labour force. Also, foreign investors make available raw material and improved technology. Raw material is normally not a very important consideration for the host country, but this factor becomes significant in a situation where some vital raw material is concerned. At the same time, the host countries often encourage FDI inflow because they get improved technology; and more importantly, an ongoing access to continued research and development programmes of the investing country.

Improvement in the balance of payments

FDI improves balance of payments through greater export and import substitution.

FDI helps improve the balance of payments of the host country. The inflow of investment is credited to the capital account. At the same time, the current account improves because FDI helps either import substitution or export promotion. The host country is able to produce those items that were being imported earlier. It is also able to augment export because the foreign investors bring in knowledge of exporting mechanics and of foreign markets. They bring in improved technology to produce goods of international standard at lower cost. They possess a world-reputed brand name that is helpful in promoting export. They are also more capable of availing of export credits from the cheapest source in the international financial market.

Building of economic and social infrastructure

When the foreign investors invest in sectors such as the basic economic infrastructure, social infrastructure, financial markets and the marketing system, the host country is able to develop a support system that is necessary for rapid industrialisation. Even if there is no investment in these sectors, the very presence of foreign investors in the host country creates a multiplier effect and the support system develops automatically.

Fostering of economic linkages

Foreign firms have forward and backward linkages. They make demand for various inputs that in turn helps develop the input-supplying industries which is known as *crowding-in effect*. They employ labour force and so help raise the income of the employed people that in turn raises the demand and industrial production in the country. They make available quality goods of a large variety normally at a competitive price and thus help improve the living standard of the consumers. They train the labour force that creates a pool of trained personnel in the country.

> Crowding-in effect means buying input from local sources and thereby fostering development in the local economy.

Strengthening of government budget

The foreign firms are a source of tax income for the government. They pay not only income tax, but tariff on their import as well. At the same time, they help reduce the governmental expenditure requirements through supplementing the government's investment activities. All this eases the burden on the national budget.

Benefits for the Home Country

FDI benefits the home country too. The country gets a supply of necessary raw material if the investor makes investment in the exploration for a particular raw material. The balance of payments improves insofar as the parent company gets dividend, royalty, technical service fees and other payments, and from the rising export of the parent company to the subsidiary. If FDI takes place in order to develop a vertical set-up abroad, the export is quite significant. When personnel accompany the investment, it results in greater employment of the nationals. The parent company makes an entry into new financial markets through investment abroad. What is more, the government of the home country generates revenue through taxing the dividend and other earnings of the parent company. There is revenue also from imposing tariff on the import of the parent company from its subsidiary abroad. Again, since FDI is a complement to foreign aid, it helps develop closer political ties between the home country and the host country which is beneficial for both the countries.

Cost to the Host Country

It is a fact that the inflow of foreign investment helps improve the balance of payments, but the outflow on account of imports and the payments of dividend, technical service fees, royalty, etc. deteriorate the balance of payments. There are

Backward linkages and other relationships between foreign affiliates and local enterprises and organisations

Form	*Relationship of foreign affiliate to local enterprise*			*Relationship of foreign affiliate to non-business institution*
	Backward (sourcing)	*Forward (distribution)*	*Horizontal (co-operation in production)*	
"Pure" market transaction	• "Off-the-shelf" purchases	• "Off-the-shelf" sales		
Short-term linkage	• Once-for-all or intermittent purchases (on contract)	• Once-for-all or intermittent sales (on contract)		
Longer-term linkage	• Longer-term (contractual) arrangement for the procurement of inputs for further processing • Subcontracting of the production of final or intermediate products	• Longer-term (contractual) relationship with local distributor or end-customer • Outsourcing from domestic firms to foreign affiliates	• Joint projects with competing domestic firm	• R&D contracts with local institutions such as universities and research centres • Training programmers for firms by universities • Traineeships for students in firms
Equity relationship	• Joint venture with supplier • Establishment of new supplier-affiliate (by existing foreign affiliate)	• Joint venture with distributor or end-customer • Establishment of new distribution affiliate (by existing foreign affiliate)	• Horizontal joint venture • Establishment of new affiliate (by existing foreign affiliate) for the production of same goods and services as it produces	• Joint public-private R&D centres/training centres/universities
"Spillover"	• Demonstration effects in unrelated firms – Spillover on processes (incl. technology) – Spillover on product design – Spillover on formal and on tacit skills (shopfloor and managerial) • Effects due to mobility of trained human resources • Enterprise spin-offs • Competition effects			

Source: UNCTAD, *World Investment Report*, 2001.

evidences to prove that such outflows have exceeded the investment inflows in some years in India (Sharan, 1978). This is not only the case of balance of payments. Raw materials are exploited keeping in view the interest of the home country that is sometimes detrimental to the interest of the host country. Again, the parent company supplies technology to the subsidiary, but normally does not disseminate it to the host market. The result is that the host country remains dependent on the home country for the technology that is often received at an exorbitant price. Sometimes the technology is inappropriate for the local environment and in that case, the loss to the host country is substantial.

As far as employment of locals is concerned, the MNCs normally show reluctance to train the local people. Technology being normally capital-intensive does not assure larger employment. Sometimes, the manufacturing processes followed by the foreign investors do not abide by the pollution norms or by the norms regarding optimal use of the natural resources or the norms regarding location of industries. All this is not in the host country's interest.

The foreign investors are generally more powerful and the domestic industrialists do not compete with them with the result that the domestic industry fails to grow. The foreign companies charge higher prices for their products in view of their oligopolistic position in the market. The higher prices hamper the interest of the consumers as well as lead to inflationary pressure. The foreign companies infuse foreign culture into the industrial set-up and also into the society. Sometimes they are so powerful that they are even able to subvert the government.

Cost to the Home Country

The cost accruing to the home country is only little. However, it cannot be denied that making of investment abroad takes away capital, skilled manpower and managerial professionals from the country. Sometimes the outflow of these factors of production is so large that it hampers the home country's interest. This is not all. The MNCs operate in different countries in order to maximise their overall profit. To this end, they adopt various techniques that may not be in the interest of the host country. This leads to a tussle between the host government and the home government which may have a deleterious effect on bilateral relations.

FDI does possess bright features, but at the same time, it has dark spots too and is not an unmixed blessing. Global benefit can be achieved only if it is carefully handled.

STRATEGY FOR FDI

When a firm decides to operate in a foreign land, it needs to follow a specific strategy in order to make its operation a viable one. The strategy must be designed so as to enable it to have an edge over competing firms. To this end, the firm may concentrate either on product innovation, product differentiation, on the cartels and collusion, or on some other strategies. In fact, the strategy depends to a great extent on how mature the product is or how designed its cost structure is. The existence of competing firms and the opening up of the sectors to foreign investors in the host country are some of the factors which would influence the strategy to be employed.

Firm-specific Strategy

When a firm has already spent a huge sum of money on research and development, it normally stresses on serving the consumers abroad with an innovated product and this gives it a definite edge over competing firms. Such products are generally price-inelastic which helps the firm earn greater profits but the life span of this strategy is limited. After some time, the technology does not remain the exclusive monopoly of the firm and the competing firms too begin to produce similar goods.

Firm-specific strategy means offering new kind of product or differentiated product.

When the product-innovation strategy fails to work, a firm may adopt a product-differentiation strategy. This is done through putting a trademark on the product, or in other words, through branding the product. Branding substitutes to a great extent the product-innovation strategy insofar as the branded product enjoys an exclusive status, quite different from similar products in the market. It gives specific identity and identification mark to the product and guarantees a certain level of quality and satisfaction. This is perhaps the reason that differentiated products remain normally price-inelastic and help the firms to reap large gains.

Sometimes the firm adopts different brands for different markets to make them more suitable for a local market on different grounds or to reap market segmentation benefits. For instance, Unilever's low-lather fabric washing product is marketed under five different brands in Western Europe. Wrigley had trouble with its Spearmint in Germany as it was difficult to pronounce; so it changed the spelling to Speermint there. On the other hand, there are cases when the firm uses a single trademark all over the world. Bata's operation in 92 countries under the same trademark is an apposite example. A single brand gives a better marketing impact, eliminates confusion and reduces advertising cost.

Cost-economising Strategy

When a firm's product becomes standardised and it faces competition from similar products of other firms, the firm tries to locate its subsidiary in a country where either raw material or labour is cheap. Cheapness of these factors of production provides the firm an opportunity to reduce the cost of production and to maintain an edge over other firms. For instance, if an MNC invests abroad in the raw material sector, it would be able to get that particular raw material at a lower cost and to export it either to the parent unit or to any other subsidiary. The unit getting cheap raw material will be at a competitive advantage. Again, it is the availability of cheap labour force in developing countries that has led the US and other multinationals to go for off-shore operations there. Such operations are normally vertical operations where the capital-intensive part of production is located in industrialised countries and labour-intensive part of production is located in the developing world.

Cost can be lowered through moving firm to a raw material-abundant/labour-abundant location.

Strategy of Entering in New Areas

Since the two strategies mentioned above have limited life span, the firm tries to enter a new area where competition is yet to begin. Shapiro (1995) has cited an example of Crown Cork and Seal which is headquartered in Philadelphia and has gone for operation in Thailand, Malaysia, Zambia and Peru making bottle tops and cans. The very reason for its foreign operation was that the field was uncultivated and there was no competition.

Cross-investment Strategy

In some cases, a firm begins its foreign operation not primarily for capturing the foreign market or for reducing the cost of production, but to avoid price cuts by competing firms. If a country A firm sets up a manufacturing or trading unit in country B, there is probability for a country B firm to operate in country A. In such cases, if the former goes for a cut in the price, the latter too will adopt the same strategy as a retaliatory measure. Thus for the fear of retaliation, there will be no such competition.

Joint-venture with a Rival Firm

Sometimes, when a rival firm in the host country is so powerful that it is not easy for the MNC to compete, the latter prefers to join hands with the host country firm for a joint-venture agreement and the MNC thus is able to penetrate the host-country market. Shapiro (1995) refers to the case of Armco, USA Lightweight Plastic Composites for which the Japanese market was almost impenetrable. The company then joined hands with Mitsubishi of Japan under a foreign collaboration agreement, and as a result, Armco's products were well marketed in Japan.

Whatever strategy is adopted by the MNCs abroad, there are certain necessary pre-conditions. *First*, they should have an idea of the profitable investment opportunities and the ways to tap those opportunities. *Secondly*, each and every strategy must be carefully evaluated since a particular project may not be competitive on all fronts. If one strategy is not useful, the firm should go in for another strategy. *Thirdly*, the firm must evaluate the life span of each strategy. It must possess the flexibility of switching over from one strategy to another, especially when the life span of a particular strategy comes to an end.

Investment Mode Strategy: Merger versus GI

The mode of investment abroad is one of the most crucial strategies. If the mode is not suitable, the investment cannot be a viable venture. However, it may be noted that selection of a particular mode does not depend solely on the wishes of the investing company, but also upon the economic and political environment in the host country. If the host government does not allow a particular mode, the investing company cannot adopt it even if it is the most suitable for it.

The mode of FDI has already been explained in Chapter 1. However, a comparison between greenfield investment and M&As is presented here to show when a particular mode should be preferred. It is often said that GI and M&As are the substitutes of each other. It may be correct if the level of economic development, institutional framework and the FDI policy in the two countries—home country and the host country—are similar. Moreover, in the developed world where financial markets are quite developed, M&As may serve as an alternative to the GI. But in a developing country, M&As should not be treated so. The reason is that:

1. The level of technology and management expertise is different from that in a developed country.
2. There are still governmental restrictions on the M&A despite liberalisation of economic policies.
3. Asset market is underdeveloped as also accounting standard is poor with the result that the assets of the target companies are often undervalued causing loss to the target company.

First, from the viewpoint of the inflow of the financial resources into the host economy, it can be said that the financial resources provided under M&As do not necessarily add to the capital stock required for production. It is because they involve transfer of the ownership of the local assets to foreign hands normally in return for some amount of disposable shares. However, in case of distress sale when the target company is on the verge of bankruptcy and is not able to get financial resources from any of the sources, M&A adds to the foreign exchange resources of the host country. There are cases to show that during the Asian Crisis, many firms could be saved in the crisis-hit countries through cross-border M&As. Moreover, M&As often lead to currency appreciation of the host country insofar as the investment inflow is often lump-sum and immediate. GI does not lead to such effects because the investment inflow spreads over time and in most cases, it is in kind. Similarly, outflow of resources in form of dividend repatriation in case of M&As is sooner than in case of GI. Again, the GI represents necessarily an investment in the plant; on the contrary, the M&As' consideration value is fungible and can be used also for non-productive purposes.

Investment under M&A does not normally add to capital stock in the host country.

Secondly, from the viewpoint of the transfer, upgrading, diffusion and generation of technology, the two modes differ to some extent. Since M&As involve working with an existing facility and the GI is concerned with setting up a new one, the latter is more likely to involve newer equipment from the very beginning. However, this is not always the case. Caves (1998) finds that since technology gap between a developed and a developing country is large, M&As too are found injecting new technology in the target firm and additionally, they help preserve the technology developed by the acquired firm.

M&A involves existing technology, but its diffusion is greater.

As far as technological upgrading is concerned, it depends more upon the market orientation of the investment, local skills and capabilities in the host country and the corporate strategy and not much on the entry mode. However, the empirical studies have shown that FDI through M&As has led to considerable technological upgrading (United Nations, 2000).

Apart from transfer and upgrading of technology, diffusion of technology is greater in case of M&As insofar as the acquired firms enjoy greater linkages with the local economy, whereas it takes time to develop such linkages in case of the GI. However, in the context of innovation or generation of technology, the views are different. It is true that if the R&D in the acquired firm is uneconomic, the acquiring firm's sword falls on it. But there is nothing wrong if uneconomic R&D is substituted by an economic one. If the existing R&D in the acquired firm is economic, there is no reason for its substitution. Rather, in case of efficiency-seeking or created-asset-seeking foreign direct investment, the acquired company avails of the R&D capabilities within no time. In case of GI, it takes long time to develop R&D activities.

Thirdly, from the viewpoint of quantity and quality of employment, the two modes—M&As and GI differ substantially. GI generates new employment, while M&As transfer responsibility for existing employees who may be laid off by the new owner on the ground of efficiency or over-staffing. In fact, the impact of M&A on employment generation depends on the motivation behind it as also on the characteristics of the acquired firm. First, if M&A is a market-seeking one, the impact on the employment generation is expected to be neutral or, to some extent, positive in the short run and medium term as the existing employees are retained to work for the new market. Second, if M&A is strategic-asset-seeking, employment in the acquired firm is expected to expand as the employees possess valuable skills and capabilities. Third, if M&A is efficiency-seeking, employment in the acquired firm may decrease if it has substantial excess capacity or has duplicate functions. Cross-border M&As in automotive, financial and service industries during 1980s and 1990s led to cut in employment despite increase in output (United Nations, 2000). Fourth, if the motive is financial, employment may decrease owing to restructuring or asset-stripping. Fifth, if the motive is to privatise a public-sector unit, employment may decrease as a result of restructuring. Evidences from cross-border M&As in seven countries of Central and Eastern Europe support this phenomenon (United Nations, 1999). But if the acquired firm had been liquidated in absence of M&A, M&A would have been employment-conserving, even if there was lay-off to some extent.

> Market-seeking M&A is neutral to employment generation; strategic asset-seeking one generates employment; and efficiency-seeking M&A reduces employment in the target firm.

This is all about the impact of M&As on direct employment generation. There may be positive impact on indirect employment generation following forward and backward linkages of the acquired firm with other enterprises in the economy.

Turning to the qualitative aspects of employment, it is often found that both greenfield investment and M&As provide better-quality employment. But in specific circumstances, wages may be lowered and facilities may be cut on the ground of cost reduction.

Fourthly, greenfield investment is more useful for building export competitiveness when the host-country firm does not possess large export potential. However, the experience varies from one case to the other. In Hungary, M&As were less export-oriented than greenfield investment. In Czech Republic, export potential of M&As was the same as that of greenfield investment (United Nations, 2000). Again, when greenfield projects have weak linkages with local firms and depend more on imported inputs, imports tend to rise.

Fifthly, it is normally believed that GI adds to the number of enterprises and reduces market concentration. But this is not always true. If the investing firm were present earlier in the market through other modes, there will be no creation of new firms. Again, if the new foreign affiliate offsets the dominant market positions of incumbent firms or takes a dominant market position itself, market will be more concentrated.

On the contrary, cross-border M&As may have a positive impact on the market structure if an ailing firm is acquired that would have otherwise been forced out of the market. But if it is a monopolising or quasi-monopolising M&A, the market structure will turn more concentrated. In India, when Hindustan Lever Ltd., the Indian subsidiary of Unilever acquired its main rival, Tata Oil Mills Co., market for toilet soap and detergent got concentrated. However, when market is open to imports and to foreign investment, the domestic concentration level may not necessarily make a difference to effective competition.

Acquiring ailing firm has a positive impact on the market structure, but the monopolising M&A does not have.

CONTROL OF MNCS

Since a lion's share of FDI is accounted for by the MNCs, controlling FDI means controlling the operations of the MNCs with a view to minimising the cost and maximising the gains.

Conflicts with Home Country and Measures of Control

It is found that a large number of multinational corporations shift their profits to a tax haven country and from there only they make further investment in different host countries. Again, they hide their actual profit through transfer pricing technique in order to evade taxes. It is true that they do it in order to minimise their tax burden but it is a loss of foreign exchange and income to the State Exchequer.

Sometimes the R&D activities are spread over a number of subsidiaries. It is true that the requirements of the host countries are taken into consideration but the home country remains deprived of such facilities. It puts a negative impact on the employment of scientific and technical personnel.

Again, MNCs enjoy economies of scale on account of large production with the result that they charge low price for a product for which the price in the domestic market is high. Consequently, the domestic manufacturers are thrown out of the market in the very home country.

More often, under competitive pressures, the MNCs locate a part of their operation in resource-rich/labour-cheap countries under a vertical set-up. It helps cut the cost and confer on the company to enjoy competitive advantage but causes loss of employment generation and full use of the locally available resources in the home country.

These are the major sources of conflict of interest between the home-country government and the MNCs. In the sequel, the home country takes up a number of measures. It is easier for the domestic government to take up restrictive measures insofar as the home country executives as well as the home country shareholders may support the government's move.

The home-country government can:

1. Prohibit any investment in a particular host country.
2. Design fiscal and monetary disincentives, and strict approval rules.
3. Introduce extra-territoriality provisions to interfere with foreign subsidiaries.

First, the home government can prohibit any investment in, or any technical collaboration with, a particular host country. For example, the US Government had not allowed the transfer of the latest computer technology to East European countries during 1980s. *Secondly*, it can design fiscal and monetary disincentives to deter any outflow of investment. Discriminatory tax can be levied. Exchange control mechanism can be implemented. When the US balance of payments was sailing on rough weather during late 1950s and early sixties, the Government had restricted the outflow of its currency for overseas investment. *Thirdly*, the home government can tighten the approval rules and regulations ultimately restricting FDI outflow. In India, during 1970s and 1980s, the Government had permitted foreign joint ventures and also the capital investment but the policy was restrictive. *Fourthly*, the government can introduce extra-territoriality provisions and can interfere with the activities of its MNC's foreign subsidiary, although this is a very rare exercise. Last but not least, the home government can design the anti-trust law that can trim its MNCs wings to operate in foreign markets.

Conflict with the Host Government and the Measures of Control

The conflict between MNCs and the home government is not very severe as it is with the host government. There is often a feeling in the host country that the MNCs are taking advantage of cheap resources available there and share the largest share of the profits emerged. The result is that the government imposes high tax on the profits of the MNCs. The MNCs do not like it because they feel that they are utilising the unused resources, catering to the demand of the local population and giving employment to the locals.

The trade unions oppose the multinationals because they do not find themselves in a bargaining position in view of manoeuvrability power of the firm during strikes. Again, when senior positions are filled up by expatriates, it causes loss of employment which is detrimental for the host country interest.

The local firms competing with the MNCs do not like them. The cost structure in local industries is often high in view of poor technology and lower size of production. They cannot market the goods at lower price as the MNCs are able to do. The result is that they are easily driven out of the market.

Sometimes consumers resent the existence of the MNCs. It is often found that after the MNCs are able to drive out the local manufacturers from the market on account of cheaper product, they enjoy the monopolistic position. They raise the price abnormally and exploit the consumers.

The MNCs charge abnormally large price for the transfer of technology. They use their own inputs imported from the home country or a sister unit in some other country at a high price. They use transfer pricing on a large scale. All this entails upon the balance of payments of the host country. In the Indian case, for example, it was found that the balance of payments was severally affected by the operation of the MNCs during 1970s (Sharan, 1978).

Last but not least, MNCs adopt in many cases unethical practices, such as bribing the officials, encouraging cross-border transfer of funds circumventing the exchange control regulations in the host country, etc. In few cases, through bribing the politicians, they cause threat to the very political set-up in the host country (Boatright, 1993).

Thus with a view to limit the malpractices of the MNCs, the host government tries to implement some measures. *First*, the government insists on appointing government representatives on the management board and on manning the senior positions with

> The government in the host country insists normally on:
> 1. appointing government representatives on the management board and on manning the senior positions with local personnel.
> 2. domestic participation in the equity share capital.
> 3. purchase of inputs from local sources.
> 4. checking unwarranted activities.

the local personnel who are expected to work in the interest of the host country. Recruitment for low-grade job with locals may lead to employment generation.

Secondly, the government insists on the domestic participation in the equity share capital. The profits are distributed among the local shareholders minimising the outflow of scarce foreign exchange. Moreover, in such cases, there is every possibility of policy design keeping intact the interest of the host country.

Thirdly, the government insists on the purchase of inputs from the local sources. The practice provides stimulus to local industries supplying input, helps conserve the scarce foreign exchange and also curbs the possibility of transfer pricing.

Fourthly, the host government puts in restrictive clauses in the import rules and encourage strict surveillance in order to check unwarranted activities.

Last but not least, the host government expropriates the assets of the MNCs lying in its own country. Sometimes it pays the compensation, but sometimes it does not do. Even if compensation is paid, the amount is normally inadequate and that too takes a long time. However, it is the last resort, especially when the MNC do not at all abides by the host country rules and regulations.

Code for Control at the International Level

For the first time in 1971, the Group of 77 resolved to have surveillance on the activities of the MNCs so that the balance of payments of the low-income countries is not strained on account of greater outflow. Again, it was reiterated at the Non-aligned Conference of 1972 that foreign investment should be in conformity with the national development objectives in the host country. During 1970s, the UN Commission on Transnational Corporations prepared a code of conduct for the MNCs. The code requires an MNC to abide by the rules and regulations of the host country, adhere to its economic policy and socio-cultural objectives, share information with the host government and not to engage in unethical activities.

Again, in 1977, the International Labour Organisation adopted a code that was concerned with employment, training, working conditions and industrial relations. The code stressed the need for consultation between the MNCs' management and the employees for a meaningful negotiation on a particular issue of discord.

The UNCTAD too issued two codes with respect to the operation of the MNCs. The first code issued in 1980 was concerned with the prevention of restrictive business practices. The second code issued in 1983 related to the transfer of technology. The emphasis was given on a reasonable payment for the technology received, especially by the developing countries and on the building up of technological capabilities in the technology receiving developing countries.

> The codes drafted at the international level are only suggestive and not binding on MNCs, with the result that they are not very effective.

There are thus a number of mechanisms for control of the MNCs' operation—at the national and the international levels. The mechanisms at the national level are better implemented. But those at the international level are only suggestive and not binding on the MNCs with the result that they are not very effective. The need of the day is to make the international codes binding by law.

SUMMARY

- Foreign direct investment (FDI) represents investment for setting up, or expansion, of a branch or subsidiary abroad, or for acquiring a going firm abroad. A number of theories have been developed to explain why a firm makes FDI despite being unfamiliar with the host country environment. One of the earliest theories explains that foreign investment helps equalise marginal productivity of capital in the home and the host countries and thereby helps generate positive welfare effects in both. Some other theories assume imperfect market conditions. It is said that an MNC possesses ownership or firm-specific advantage in view of superior technology or managerial and marketing skills that give it an edge over the host country firms. It is also said that intrafirm transfer of intermediate goods takes place at a very low cost and this advantage possessed by an MNC provides it an edge over the host country firms. It is also stated that the availability of cheap labour and raw material in the host country that attracts foreign investment. The eclectic paradigm combines all these three advantages and explains that it is the relative intensity of a particular advantage that shapes the character and direction of FDI. The product cycle theory is a combination of organisational theory and the locational advantage theory.
- A few theories are based on the assumption of an imperfect capital market. Firms from strong-currency countries move to weak-currency countries because of either higher capitalisation rate or rise in wealth and capital gains of the strong-currency-country firms. Again, the politico-economic theories believe that it is political stability in the host country or political instability in the home country that facilitates FDI.
- The above-mentioned theories were developed primarily in the context of the MNCs of the industrialised world, but with minor modifications they are applicable also to the third world MNCs.
- FDI is beneficial for both the home country and the host country but it involves costs too. The host country gets scarce factors of production. Its balance of payments improves with inflow of foreign investment but it gets strained when imports of these firms exceed the export generated or when dividend and other payments are quite substantial. The host economy develops through the building of economic and social infrastructure by foreign firms and through backward and forward linkages with the foreign enterprise. The home country is assured of regular supply of raw material or finished goods from the host country. Its income increases through the receipt of various types of fund transfers from the host country. The political relations between the host country and the home country become amicable. However, when the MNCs operate in disregard of the interest of the host country, bilateral relations may be affected which would be detrimental for both the countries.
- There should be perfect strategy for FDI so that the venture should be viable. This means that the MNC should maintain an edge over the host country firms. To this end, the firm should introduce an innovated or differentiated product. It should adopt a cost-economising strategy or it should enter a new unexploited area. The selection of mode is also an important strategy.

Besides start-from-scratch modes like branches and foreign collaborations, the firm may go in for M&A as it has some additional benefits. Whatever the strategy may be, it should be flexible and should accommodate the interest of the home country as well as of the host country.

- FDI needs to be controlled in view of the fact the MNCs often do not operate essentially in the interest of the home/host country. So the home/host country take some measures to control them. There is also international code of conduct in this respect.

Least Developed Countries Report 2023

The cost of debt is highly uneven among least developed countries

Public and publicly guaranteed debt servicing costs, millions of dollars, 2020 and 2021

Name	*2020*	*2021*	*Change*
Least developed countries	19.903	27.328	37.30%
Afghanistan	28.7	19.2	–33.00%
Angola	6962.6	8881.1	27.60%
Bangladesh	2014	2772.1	37.60%
Benin	210.5	726.8	245.20%
Bhutan	46.8	116.2	148.50%
Burkina Faso	135.9	142.6	4.90%
Burundi	14.1	18.7	32.00%
Cambodia	359.1	395.9	10.20%
Central African Republic	5.2	6.6	27.10%
Chad	111.3	150	34.80%
Comoros	3.4	3.2	–4.80%
Democratic Republic of Congo	255.6	347.8	36.10%
Djibouti	53.3	42.5	–20.20%
Eritrea	21.5	21.9	1.50%
Ethiopia	1970.1	1989.1	1.00%
Gambia	27.2	31	13.80%
Guinea	74.1	108.9	46.90%
Guinea-Bissau	23.3	43.5	86.20%
Haiti	9.7	14.9	53.00%
Lao People's Dem. Rep.	639.7	664.7	3.90%
Lesotho	59.8	298.3	398.60%
Liberia	24.2	17.6	–27.00%
Madagascar	104	128.8	23.90%
Malawi	72.6	81.5	12.20%
Mali	229	269.8	17.80%
Mauritania	270	397.3	47.10%
Mozambique	606.6	583.7	–3.80%
Myanmar	508.4	2227.1	338.10%

(Contd.)

Name	*2020*	*2021*	*Change*
Nepal	255.5	263	2.90%
Niger	172.6	192.4	11.50%
Rwanda	113.3	647.4	471.20%
Sao Tome and Principe	1.7	2	13.70%
Senegal	1575.8	1441.8	–8.50%
Sierra Leone	51.2	55.1	7.50%
Solomon Islands	6.3	6.5	3.10%
Somalia	480.9	16.6	–96.50%
Sudan	143.7	1621.1	1028.40%
Timor-Leste	8.1	9.6	19.20%
Togo	86	105.5	22.60%
Uganda	311.9	589.5	89.00%
United Republic of Tanzania	1199.3	1543.7	28.70%
Yemen	86.1	91.4	6.20%
Zambia	569.5	241.4	–57.60%

Note: Data for Kiribati, South Sudan and Tuvalu are not available.

Source: UNCTAD secretariat calculations based on World Bank, International Debt Statistics database (accessed May 2023).

CASE STUDY

FDI AND DEVELOPMENT IN LEAST DEVELOPED COUNTRIES (LDCs)

FDI inflow to the 48 LDCs has been on the decline. The inflow, as shown in the table below, fell by a further 0.6 per cent in 2010 to $ 26 billion, following the 20 per cent fall a year earlier that had interrupted the upward trend of the previous decade. Almost two-fifths of the LDCs, particularly Yemen, Mauritania, Burkina Faso, Djibouti, Rwanda, Equatorial Guinea and Sudan—saw their FDI inflows reduced. This unprecedented two-year retreat in FDI inflows to LDCs has taken place against a backdrop of rising commodity prices, a modest recovery in global FDI flows, and a 10 per cent increase in inflows to developing and transition economies.

Foreign Direct Investment: Inward and Outflow flows and stock, annual (US$ at current prices in millions)

YEAR	*2021*	*2022*	*2023*
ECONOMY			
LDCs (Least Developed Countries)	–393	1377	1160
LDCs: Africa	–587	1205	992
LDCs: Asia	215	203	181
LDCs: Islands and Haiti	–20	–31	–13

The data indicates a variable trend in foreign direct investment (FDI) directed towards Least Developed Countries (LDCs). In 2021, least developed countries (LDCs) had a net investment outflow. In 2022, there was a notable increase in

FDI inflows, presumably influenced by post-pandemic recovery and advantageous investment conditions. Although foreign direct investment (FDI) remained positive in 2023, it decreased relative to the prior year, possibly indicating a worldwide investment slowdown or changes in investor preferences.

The research also underscores geographical differences. Africa witnessed significant volatility, marked by a steep rise in 2022, succeeded by a downturn in 2023. The Asia and Islands & Haiti group exhibited more stable, though diminishing, trends.

Global economic conditions, national policies, resource endowments, and infrastructure quality likely impact these FDI trends. Analysing sector-specific FDI, sources of investment, and economic indicators will provide significant information.

Foreign Direct Investment: Inward and Outflow flows and stock, annual (US$ at current prices in millions)

YEAR	*2021*	*2022*	*2023*
ECONOMY			
WORLD	1881922	1574724	1550584
Africa	5144	9232	61
America	424691	518550	543998
Asia	746231	707903	667118
Europe	702435	217675	329688
Oceania	3421	121364	9718
BRICS	280733	223510	217409
G20	1289214	1384691	1166072
G-77	390090	410983	347352
OECD	1300547	1019716	1027352

The worldwide foreign direct investment (FDI) landscape had a varied trend from 2021 to 2023. Although 2021 experienced a zenith in FDI inflows, the following years observed a downturn. This variation can be ascribed to multiple variables, including global economic conditions, geopolitical conflicts, and alterations in investment policies across nations.

Africa experienced an increase in foreign direct investment in 2022, but this trend diminished in 2023. Conversely, America demonstrated a consistent rise in foreign direct investment over the three-year span. Asia and Europe witnessed a reduction in foreign direct investment, with Europe exhibiting a more pronounced decrease in 2022, subsequently followed by a modest rebound in 2023. Oceania's foreign direct investment exhibited volatility, marked by a substantial rise in 2022 followed by a decline in 2023.

BRICS and G20 experienced a reduction in foreign direct investment, whilst G-77 and OECD exhibited varied trends. These fluctuations highlight the intricate interaction of factors affecting FDI flows.

Further analysis is required to attain a comprehensive knowledge of these trends, considering specific national statistics and economic factors. This analysis would elucidate the fundamental factors influencing FDI fluctuations and their consequences for various regions and economic blocs.

Source: UNCTADstat Data centre

QUESTIONS

1. Comment on the trend of FDI in LDCs.
2. Do you feel that the sectoral flow of FDI is conducive to the economic development of these countries?
3. Comment on the factors responsible for investment from the developing world flowing to LDCs.

REVIEW QUESTIONS

Objective-Type Questions

1. State whether true (T) or false (F):

(a) FDI flows from a capital-abundant to a capital-deficit country. ☐
(b) MNCs tend to move to low-wage, raw material-abundant country. ☐
(c) Demand is price-inelastic at the innovation stage of the product cycle. ☐
(d) Demand is price-inelastic during the maturing product stage. ☐
(e) Appropriability approach emphasises the potential returns from technology creation as a prime mover behind the internationalisation of firms. ☐

2. Choose the correct answer:

(a) FDI helps improve the balance of payments of the host country through:
  (i) making available foreign exchange.
  (ii) transfer of technology.
  (iii) managing the host unit.

(b) M&As' investment often leads to currency appreciation in the host country because:
  (i) the investment is huge, lump sum and at a single point of time.
  (ii) supply of foreign currency increases.
  (iii) both of the two.

(c) When M&A is strategic asset-seeking:
  (i) employment in the acquired firm increases.
  (ii) employment in the acquired firm decreases.
  (iii) none of the two.

(d) UNCTAD's code issued in 1983 for the control of MNCs related to:
  (i) transfer of technology.
  (ii) prevention of restrictive practices.
  (iii) both of the above.

(e) Host government expropriating the assets of the MNCs:
  (i) never pays compensation.
  (ii) always pays compensation.
  (iii) sometimes pays compensation.

Short-Answer Questions

1. When are M&As beneficial?
2. What are the factors influencing the consideration value in M&As?
3. How does home/host country control the operations of an MNC.
4. Comment on the international code relating to MNCs' conduct.

Long-Answer Questions

1. Explain the major theories of FDI.
2. Discuss FDI strategies.
3. Explain the benefits from FDI to the host and the home countries.

REFERENCES

Aliber, R.Z. (1971), The Multinational Enterprise in a Multiple Currency World in J.H. Dunning (Ed.), *The Multinational Enterprise*, London, George Allen & Unwin, pp. 49–56.

Bhagwati, J. (1972), Book Review—Raymond Vernon, Sovereignty at Bay: The multinational spread of US enterprises, 1971, *Journal of International Economics*, XIV, 456–457.

Boatright, J.R. (1993), *Ethics in the Conduct of Business*, Englewood Cliffs: Prentice-Hall.

Buckley, P.J. (1988), The Limits of Explanation: Testing of internalisation theory of the multinational enterprise, *Journal of International Business Studies*, XIX, 181–193.

Buckley, P.J. and Mark Casson (1976), *The Future of the Multinational Enterprise*, New York, Holmes and Meier, pp. 32–84.

Caves, R.E. (1971), International Corporations: The industrial economics of foreign investment, *Economica*, XXXVIII, 5–6.

———(1988), Exchange Rate Movements and Foreign Direct Investment in the United States, Harvard Institute of Economic Research, Discussion Paper No. 1383.

Coase, R.H. (1937), The Nature of the Firm, *Economica*, IV, 386–405.

Dunning, J.F. (1980), Towards an Eclectic Theory of International Production, *Journal of International Business Studies*, XI, 9–31.

———(1993), *The Globalisation of Business*, London, Routledge, Chap. 4.

Fatehi-Sedah, K. and M.H. Safizedah (1989), Association between Political Instability and the Flow of Foreign Direct Investment, *Management International Review*, XXIX, 23–36.

Franke, R.H., G. Hoptede and M.H. Bond (1991), Cultural Roots of Economic Performance: A research note, *Strategic Management Journal*, XII, 165–173.

Froot, K.A. and J.C. Stein (1989), Exchange Rates and Foreign Direct Investment: An imperfect capital market approach, Cambridge (Mass.): NBER, Working Paper No. 2914.

Globerman, S. (1986), *Fundamentals of International Business Management*, Singapore, Prentice-Hall, pp. 40–42.

Graham, E.M. and P.R. Krugman (1989), *Foreign Direct Investment in the United States*, Washington D.C., Institute of International Economics.

Hood, N. and S. Young (1979), *The Economics of Multinational Enterprise*, London, Longman, pp. 44–86.

Hymer, S.H. (1976), *The International Operations of National Firms: A study of direct investment*, Cambridge (Mass.), MIT Press.

Kemp, M.C. (1964), *The Theory of International Trade*, Ithaca, Prentice-Hall, pp. 13–14.

Knickerbocker, T. (1973), *Oligopolistic Reaction and the Multinational Enterprise*, Boston, Harvard Graduate School of Business Administration.

Kogut, B. and D. Parkinson (1993), The Diffusion of American Organising Principles to Europe in B. Kogut (Ed.), *Country Competitiveness and the Organisation of Work*, Oxford, Oxford University Press, pp. 17–28.

Kojima, K. (1978), *Direct Foreign Investment: A Japanese model of multinational business operations*, London, Croom Helm, pp. 73–76.

———(1985), Japanese and American Direct Investment in Asia: A comparative analysis, *Hitotsubashi Journal of Economics*, XXVI, 1–36.

MacDougall, G.D.A. (1958), The Benefits and Costs of Private Foreign Investment Abroad: A theoretical approach, *Economic Record*, XXXVI, 13–35.

Magee, S.P. (1979), Information and the Multinational Corporation: An appropriability theory of direct foreign investment in D.R. Lessard (Ed.), *International Financial Management*, Boston, Warren Gorham & Lamont, p. 57.

Rugman, A.M. (1986), New Theories of Multinational Enterprise: An assessment of internalisation theory, *Bulletin of Economic Research*, XXXVIII, 101–118.

Schneider, F. and B.S. Frey (1985), Economic and Political Determinants of Foreign Direct Investments, *World Development*, XIII, 161–175.

Shapiro, A.C. (1995), *Multinational Financial Management* , New Delhi, Prentice-Hall of India, Chap. 17.

Sharan, V. (1978), Multinational Corporations and Balance of Payments Problems in a Developing Host Country: An Indian experience, *Indian Economic Journal*, XXVI, 199–215.

———(1985), Internationalisation of Third World Firms: An Indian case study, *International Marketing Review*, II, 63–71.

Tallman, S.B. (1988), Home Country Political Risk and Foreign Direct Investment in the United States, *Journal of International Business Studies*, XIX, 219–234.

Ting, W. (1982), The Product Development Process in NIC Multinationals, *Columbia Journal of World Business*, XVII, 76–81.

Vernon, R. (1966), International Investment and International Trade in the Product Cycle, *Quarterly Journal of Economics*, LXXX, 190–207.

———(1979), The Product Cycle Hypothesis in a New International Environment, *Oxford Bulletin of Economics and Statistics*, LXI, 255–267.

SUGGESTED FURTHER READING

Earl, P. and F.G. Fisher, (1986), *International Mergers and Acquisitions*, London, Euromoney Publications.

Reuber, G.L. (1973), *Private Foreign Investment in Development*, Oxford, Clarendon Press.

Sharan, V. (1995), Theories of International Business: A Review of Literature, *Foreign Trade Review*, XXX, 315–331.

CHAPTER 12

International Capital Budgeting

Learning Objectives

After reaching a decision to invest abroad, the firm evaluates proposals/projects and selects one or more of them that ranks high from the viewpoint of adding to the corporate wealth. The process, known as international capital budgeting, is discussed in the present chapter. The purpose is:

- To acquaint the readers with different evaluation criteria.
- To show how cash flow relating to proposal/project is computed from the viewpoint of both parent and subsidiary.
- To discuss the cost of capital that acts as a cut-off rate.
- To explain adjusted present value approach that is an alternative approach to evaluation of projects.
- To discuss real options that demand a fresh look at the project appraisal.
- To discuss evaluation of an M&A proposal.
- To examine the relevance of non-financial factors in international capital budgeting.

The decision to invest abroad takes a concrete shape when a future project is evaluated in order to ascertain whether the implementation of the project is going to add to the value of the investing company. The evaluation of the long-term investment project is known as *capital budgeting*. The technique of capital budgeting is almost similar between a domestic company and an international company. The only difference is that some additional complexities appear in the case of international capital budgeting. These complexities influence the computation of the cash flow and the required rate of return. In the present chapter we discuss the complexities that arise in international capital budgeting, but in the beginning, we look at the fundamentals of capital budgeting techniques. For a detailed idea of domestic capital budgeting process, reference may be made to any textbook on corporate finance.

EVALUATION CRITERIA

Non-discounting Methods

The methods for evaluating investment proposals are grouped as discounting and non-discounting methods. The non-discounting methods are simple. One such method involves the *average accounting rate of return* earned by the project. It represents the mean profit on account of investment prior to interest and tax payment. The mean profit is compared with the hurdle rate or required rate of return. A project is acceptable if the mean profit is higher than the hurdle rate. Despite being a simple method, it has some shortcomings, namely, it is based on the accounting income and not on the cash flow; it considers profit before tax, rather than post-tax profit. And finally, it ignores the time value.

PROBLEM 12.1

Find out the accounting rate of return based on the following data:

Year	Gross Profit	Depreciation	Net Profit	Investment
1	$ 2,000	5,332	–3,332	13,334
2	6,000	5,332	668	8,000
3	10,000	5,332	4,668	2,666
Average			668	8,000

Solution

Accounting rate of return = 668/8,000 = 8.35%

The other non-discounting method is known as the *pay-back period*, that is the number of years required to recover the initial investment. If the investment is not recovered within the pay-back period, the project should not be accepted. Thus this method stresses on early recovery of funds, but fails to consider the cash flow after the pay-back period and so does not consider profitability over the life of the project. It also fails to consider the time value of money. Nevertheless, non-discounting methods are widely used. Buckley (1996) finds that 10 to 20 per cent of large US multinationals are reported as using the accounting rate of return method as their primary evaluation technique, while 28 per cent are found to have opted for the pay-back period method.

PROBLEM 12.2

Considering target pay-back period as two years, the cash flow of two proposals is as follows:

		Proposal A	Proposal B
Initial investment ($)		–2,000	–2,000
Net cash benefits:	Year 1	1,200	1,200
	Year 2	800	400
	Year 3	–	300
	Year 4	–	300

Find which project can be accepted.

Solution

Proposal A will be accepted because initial investment is recovered within the target pay-back period despite the fact that Proposal B gives a greater return.

Discounting Methods

Discounting methods take normally three forms:

1. Net present value (NPV) method
2. Profitability index (PI), method
3. Internal rate of return (IRR) method

Net present value is the residue after deducting the initial investment from the present value of future cash flows relating to a project. Positive NPV means additions to the corporate wealth.

Net present value (NPV) rule

In this case, projects are accepted where the present value of net cash inflow during the life span of the project is greater than the initial investment. The difference adds to the corporate wealth. The equation is:

$$\text{NPV} = \sum_{t=1}^{n}\left[\frac{CF_t}{(1+k)^n}\right] - I_0 \tag{12.1}$$

where

CF_t = expected after-tax cash flow from t_1 to t_n, including both the operating cash flow and the terminal cash flow,

I_0 = initial investment,

k = risk-adjusted discount rate, and

n = life span of the project.

PROBLEM 12.3

A project involves initial investment for $ 50,00,000. The net cash inflow during the first, second and the third year is expected respectively $ 30,00,000, $ 35,00,000 and $ 20,00,000. At the end of the third year, the scrap value is indicated at $ 10,00,000. The risk-adjusted discount rate is 10 per cent. Calculate NPV.

Solution

$$t_1 + t_2 + t_3 - I_0 = \frac{30,00,000}{1.10} + \frac{35,00,000}{(1.10)^2} + \frac{20,00,000 + 10,00,000}{(1.10)^3} - 50,00,000$$

$$= \$\ 28,73,778.$$

Project would be accepted because NPV is positive.

Profitability index (PI)

Profitability index is the ratio between the present value of future cash flows and the initial investment.

This shows the relationship between net cash inflows and initial investment. It shows the relative gains and would be expressed as the following equation:

$$\text{PI} = \sum_{t=1}^{n}\left[\frac{(CF_t / (1+k)^n}{I_0}\right] \qquad (12.2)$$

Basing on the above example, the profitability index (PI) is calculated as

PI = 78,73,778/50,00,000 = 1.57

The project may be accepted because PI is more than 1.

Internal rate of return (IRR) rule

Internal rate of return is the discount rate equating the present value of future cash flows and the initial investment. For accepting a project, IRR > hurdle rate.

IRR is that discount rate which must bring down the value of cash inflows (net) during the life of the project to equate the value of initial investment. Expressed as an equation,

$$\sum_{t=1}^{n}\left[\frac{CF_t}{(1+\text{IRR})^n}\right] - I_0 = 0 \qquad (12.3)$$

The project shall be acceptable if IRR is greater than the required rate of return.

Based on the above example, IRR is 40 per cent. Since the required rate of return is 10 per cent, the project would be accepted.

PROBLEM 12.4

A proposal involves \$ 20,00,000. The annual cash flow is \$ 10,00,000 for three years. Find out the IRR.

Solution

Since the initial investment divided by the annuity is 2/1, one has to find out 2 in the annuity table. The annuity factor closest to 2 for three years is 1.9520 at 25 per cent discount rate and 2.1065 at 20 per cent discount rate. The annual cash flow will be multiplied by these two annuity factors and then a difference of the product from the initial outlay is found out. It is as follows:

(a) At 20% discount rate: 10,00,000 × 2.1065 – 20,00,000 = 106.50
(b) At 25% discount rate: 10,00,000 × 1.9520 – 20,00,000 = –48.00

Since NPV is greater than 0 at 20 per cent discount rate, one needs a higher discount rate to equate NPV to initial investment.

IRR = 20 + (106.50/154.50) × 5 = 23.45%

Ranking of Proposals

If there are two or more mutually exclusive proposals, they need to be ranked in order of preference. Under the NPV rule, first preference is given to a proposal with the highest NPV but judged by the IRR method and if initial outlay differs, the decision could be erroneous. In such cases, the incremental approach is considered. Suppose there are two proposals. Proposal A involves an initial investment of $ 2,000 with an annual net cash inflow of $ 610 for five years while proposal B having an initial outlay of $ 3,000, has a net cash inflow of $ 900 annually for five years. In the former IRR is 16 per cent, while it is 15.2 per cent in the latter and both the proposals will be accepted if the required rate of return is 10 per cent. If only one proposal has to be taken up, proposal A will be accepted on the basis of higher IRR. If incremental approach is taken into account, it is found that the incremental outlay is $ 1,000 and the incremental net cash inflow is $ 290 per annum for five years. The incremental IRR would be 13.8 per cent. In this case, proposal B would be accepted as it ranks first. The only condition is that IRR should be higher than the cost of capital.

Choice between Net Present Value and Internal Rate of Return

Sometimes the result of the two methods (NPV and IRR) differs because they rest on different assumptions concerning the reinvestment of funds released from the project. The NPV rule implies reinvestment at a rate equivalent to the required rate of return used as a discount rate, while the IRR rule assumes that the funds are reinvested at IRR. However, in such cases, the NPV rule is preferred in view of some limitations inherent in IRR. *First*, where projects of different lives are considered, the IRR rule will possibly inflate desirability of a short-life project as IRR is a function of both the time involved and the size of capital investment. *Secondly*, IRR tends to be lower on projects with a longer gestation period, even when NPV remains larger. This is because IRR ranks high in those projects where several benefits accrue in early part of their economic life. *Thirdly*, while computing IRR, there is possibility of more than one solution rate, inasmuch as IRR is calculated by a polynomial equation. If the polynomial is of degree n, there will be n roots and n solution rates and in a changing cost-of-capital framework, the computation of IRR would not make an easy comparison, whereas the NPV rule incorporates such changes into the calculation of the cost of capital.

Profitability Index versus Net Present Value

If the initial investment differs, the same amount of cash inflow may yield different results under the two methods. It is possible that PI may be higher in case of lower NPV and so the decision would be different in case of these two different methods. However, since NPV represents an absolute value, it should be relied upon even if the PI is higher.

COMPUTATION OF THE CASH FLOW

Basics of Cash Flow

The taking up of a new project demands a part of a firm's current wealth, but in return, brings in funds and adds to the firm's stock of wealth in future. The former results in cash flow from the firm, while the latter is represented by cash flows into the firm. Cash outflow occurs on account of capital expenditure, other expenses (excluding depreciation), and the payment of taxes. Cash inflow includes revenue on account of additional sale or cash from eventually selling of an asset which is known as *salvage value.*

Cash flows are grouped under three heads:

1. Initial investment during the period, t_0;
2. Operating cash flow during the period, t_1 to t_n;
3. Terminal cash flow or the salvage value that emerges at the end of the period, t_n.

To compute the operating cash flow, the following facts should be taken into account.

Depreciation is a non-cash expense having no direct bearing on cash flow pattern, although it has a bearing on tax liability. Since it influences the amount of tax to be paid, the depreciation amount is deducted from the revenue in order to arrive at the pre-tax profit. But since it does not represent cash outflow, it is added again to the amount of net profit. The procedure can be illustrated as follows:

Suppose a project generates $ 20,000 annually. The operating expenses amount to $ 10,000 and depreciation amounts to $ 5,000. The tax rate is 50 per cent. The net cash inflow will be:

Cash receipt	$ 20,000
Less operating expenses	$ 10,000
Balance	$ 10,000
Less depreciation	$ 5,000
Taxable income	$ 5,000
Less taxes	$ 2,500
Net profit	$ 2,500
Add depreciation	$ 5,000
After-tax cash inflow	$ 7,500

The following factors should be noted:

(a) The cash flow is considered only on an after-tax basis.

(b) Financing cost is not included despite the fact that capital has a cost because such costs are considered elsewhere while determining the project's required rate of return.

(c) Cash flow is computed on an incremental basis and represents the difference between cash flow after the investment and cash flow in the absence of investment.
(d) There are certain costs that do not involve cash flow but necessarily involve the opportunity cost. If there is such cost, that is included in the decision process.

Parent Unit's Perspective and the Cash Flow

At the very beginning of multinational capital budgeting, the question arises whether the cash flow should be computed from the viewpoint of the parent company or from the viewpoint of the subsidiary. This question arises because the cash flow accruing to the subsidiary may not be represented entirely by the cash flow accruing to the parent company. In some cases, the cash outflow of the subsidiary is treated as the cash inflow of the parent company. It is also possible that the cash inflow accruing to the subsidiary may be large enough to justify the investment proposal, but its size accruing to the parent company may be too small. In such cases, it seems difficult to take a decision regarding acceptance or rejection of the investment proposal. In fact, there may be many situations when the disparity in the cash flow between the parent and its subsidiary occurs. For if example, tax rates in the home country and the host country are different, disparity in cash flow shall arise. It is possible that on account of lower tax rates in the host country, after-tax cash inflow is large enough to justify the investment proposal. On the other hand, owing to high tax rates in the home country, the investment proposal may not be feasible from the viewpoint of the parent company. The parent company may not accept the investment proposal due to low inflow of cash on account of exchange control applied by the host government, despite the fact that the cash flow of the project in question is sufficient for implementation. In a situation where the parent company charges an exorbitant price for the technology and management, the cash inflow accruing to the parent company will be larger justifying the investment proposal, but such exorbitant payments may lower the cash flow of the subsidiary and the subsidiary may not like the investment proposal. Lastly, changes in exchange rate may change the cash flow of the parent company. When the currency of the host country appreciates, the parent company gets a larger flow of cash in terms of its own currency. This may change its accept-reject decision.

The ethics of the corporate financial management are very clear on this issue; that the value of the project is determined by the net present value of the future cash flows available to the investor. Since the parent company is the investor, it is the cash flow of the parent company that is taken into account in the context of international capital budgeting. This is why cash flowing from subsidiary company to parent company either in the form of royalty and technical service fees, or in any other mode is treated as cash inflow. On the contrary, any cash flowing from the parent company to the subsidiary, is treated as cash outflow. The parent company will agree to investment in a foreign project only if the net present value of the cash flow is positive from its own point of view.

The cash flow, as mentioned earlier, is broadly compartmentalised into three heads. These are:

1. Initial investment
2. Operating cash flow
3. Terminal cash flow

Here the parent's perspective will be explained in case of these three heads of cash flow.

Initial investment

Let us first take the case of initial investment. If the entire project cost is met by the parent company, the entire amount of initial investment is treated as the cash outflow. In some cases, the project is partly financed by the subsidiary itself through local borrowing but such borrowings of the subsidiary do not form a part of the initial cash outflow.

In some cases, the subsidiary makes additional investment for expansion out of retained earnings. At the first instance, there is apparently no flow of cash from the parent company to the subsidiary but it should be treated as an opportunity cost because in the absence of retention of earnings, these funds could have been remitted to the parent company rather than invested in the project in question. Thus, the investment out of retained earnings should be treated as cash outflow from the parent company's perspective. The issue of blocked funds is also very pertinent in this respect. Sometimes the host government imposes exchange control and does not allow any cash to flow to the parent company. These funds are known as *blocked funds.* For this reason, that part of the cash inflow of the subsidiary which is represented by blocked funds is not treated as cash inflow from the parent's perspective. Suppose the incremental cash inflow of a project is $ 20 million, out of which only $ 15 million is allowed by the host government to flow to the parent company. In this case, only the sum of $ 15 million will be treated as the cash inflow. If, however, the blocked funds are invested in some new project, that amount is treated as the investment by the parent company and is recorded as cash outflow. In the event of the host government providing subsidised initial establishment for the subsidiary, the amount does not form a part of the initial investment of the parent company.

Example: A project of the subsidiary costs $ 15.5 million. The parent company makes an initial investment of $ 10 million, a sum of $ 2 million is invested out of blocked funds, another sum of $ 2 million is taken out of retained earnings, and $ 1 million is met by the subsidiary out of local borrowing. At the same time, the host government provides some subsidised establishment for the project that brings in a gain for $ 0.5 million. Thus in this case, the cash outflow recorded for initial investment from the parent's perspective will be: $ 10 + 2 + 2 = $ 14.0 million. It may be mentioned here that the initial investment outflow out of blocked funds and retained earnings is shown at the spot exchange rate.

PROBLEM 12.5

The cost of the subsidiary's project is $ 20 million. It is financed through different modes of funds. The parent unit makes an investment for $ 12 million. A sum of $ 3 million is drawn out of retained earnings and another sum of $ 2 million is drawn out of the blocked funds. The subsidiary borrows $ 2 million from the host country market. The remaining $ 1 million is in the form of free land and building supplied by the host country government. Find out the amount of initial investment from the viewpoint of the parent unit.

Solution

Initial investment from parent's viewpoint = $ 12 + 3 + 2 = 17 million.

Operating cash flow

Besides the initial investment, the operating cash flow too needs some adjustment. As a normal practice, the revenue generated through the sale of a subsidiary's product in the local market as well as in other countries, is shown as the operating cash inflow from the parent's perspective but it is subject to downward adjustment by the lost income on sales previously realised through the parent company's export to these markets. On the contrary, if the operation in the subsidiary leads to import of components and raw material from the parent company, the value of such import will be added to the revenue.

Example: A subsidiary is fetching $ 15 million through sale of the product in the local market and a sum of $ 3 million through export to a third country, but this sale replaces the parent company's export to these markets by $ 7 million. Again, the subsidiary imports components from the parent company worth $ 2 million. The total operating cash inflow on account of sales in this case will be: $ 15 + 3 + 2 – 7 = 13 million.

The operating cash flow is influenced by some other factors also. Let us assume the subsidiary pays royalty to the parent company worth $ 3 million, the operating cash inflow in the above example will rise to $ 16 million, but if the parent company faces loss on account of diseconomies of scale due to shifting of production to the host country to the extent of $ 1 million, the operating revenue will come down to $ 15 million.

The transfer pricing, when the parent company or any other unit of the firm charges arbitrary prices for intrafirm movement of intermediate goods, also influences the operating cash flow. It may be noted here that transfer pricing is adopted either for better working capital management or for reducing the overall burden of taxes on the company through shifting of the before-tax profit to a country with lower tax rates. If transfer pricing lowers the overall tax burden of the company and thereby increases the revenue of the parent company, the additional revenue or saving should be treated as cash inflow. It may, however, be noted that such inflows are discounted at a higher rate because they involve greater risk.

If a host government offers incentives, they should be included in the capital budgeting decision. For example, if the host government offers tax incentives or provides loan at a subsidised rate, the amount of gain on this account should be added to the operating cash inflow. When the subsidiary makes local borrowings to meet a part of the initial investment and pays interest on such borrowings, the amount of interest payment is deducted from the operating cash inflow. Had it been a case of domestic capital budgeting, the interest payment on such borrowings would not have formed a part of cash flow since financing cost is included in the discount rate; but in case of international capital budgeting, the cash remitted to the parent company will stand overstated if interest payments are not treated as cash outflow. The present value of cash flow received by the parent company should take into consideration the interest paid by the subsidiary on the local borrowing and then only it should be compared with the initial investment made by the parent company.

Inflation influences both the cost and revenue streams of the project and hence the inflation rate differential also needs to be taken into account. If the inflation rate is higher in the host country and if the import from the parent company constitutes a significant portion of the input of the subsidiary, the cost will not move up very high but if the inputs are obtained locally, the cost increase may be substantial. Again, as far as revenue is concerned, it will move up if there is no competition from foreign suppliers and if the demand for the product is price-inelastic. So the computation of cash flow relies on the inflation forecast in the host country and its possible effects. If, however, the inflation is quite volatile from year to year, as is found in many developing countries, an accurate forecast is not easy to make.

> Inflation rate differential needs consideration as it influences the cash flow.

The exchange rate fluctuation influences the size of cash flow. Changes in the exchange rate are themselves tagged with the changes in the rate of inflation but there are other factors too that shape the exchange rate fluctuations. It is difficult to predict the behaviour of all those factors. Nevertheless, the cash flow computation process incorporates different scenarios of exchange rate movements. From the parent company's point of view, appreciation in the currency of the host country will be favourable and will increase the size of the cash inflow in terms of the currency of the home country. This gain may partially be offset by higher inflation rate for the moment, but if the rate of inflation is expected to be lower in future thus helping appreciate the value of the host country's currency, the subsidiary may invest locally the amount of its payments to the parent company till the strengthening of the currency. The accumulated earning of the parent company will be larger after the appreciation of the host country's currency.

> Exchange rate changes influence the cash flow and also the discount rate.

PROBLEM 12.6

Calculate the operating cash flow on the basis of the following data:

(a) Sales in the domestic market = \$ 10 million
(b) Export = \$ 4 million
(c) Replacement of parent's export = \$ 2 million
(d) Parent's export of components to subsidiary = \$ 3 million
(e) Royalty payment by subsidiary = \$ 0.5 million
(f) Dividend flow to the parent = \$ 0.5 million

Solution

$$\$\ 10 + 4 + 3 + 0.5 + 0.5 - 2 = \$\ 16 \text{ million.}$$

Terminal cash flow

Besides adjustments in the initial investment and in the operating cash flow, some adjustments have to be made for the salvage value that influences the terminal cash flow. If there is provision in the foreign collaboration agreement for reversion of the project to the host government after a certain period of time on the payment of a specific amount, that specific amount is treated as the terminal cash inflow. Also, if the first condition is not present, the net cash flow generated in the terminal year is multiplied by a specific number of years and the product is treated as the terminal cash inflow. In case the project is dismantled in the terminal year, the scrap value is treated as the terminal cash inflow.

When the salvage value is uncertain, the parent company makes various estimates of the salvage value or terminal cash flow and computes the NPV based on each possible outcome of the terminal cash flow. Alternatively, it computes the break-even salvage value which is the terminal cash flow necessary to achieve zero NPV for the project. The break-even salvage value or the break-even terminal cash flow is then compared with the estimated terminal cash flow. If the estimated terminal cash flow is less than the break-even salvage value, the investment proposal will be rejected because it means, the NPV will be negative. On the contrary, if the parent company assesses that the subsidiary would sell for more than the break-even salvage value, it will incorporate this assessment into its accept-reject decision.

Break-even salvage value exists at zero NPV.

Here the break-even salvage value needs some further explanation. Rearranging Eq. (12.1) and segregating the cash flow beginning from the first year to the nth year into the operating cash flow, OCF_t and the terminal cash flow, TCF_n, break-even salvage value can be derived:

$$\begin{aligned}
\text{NPV} &= \sum_{t=1}^{n}\left[\frac{\text{OCF}_t}{(1+k)^t}\right] + \left[\frac{\text{TCF}_n}{(1+k)^n}\right] - I_0 \\
0 &= \sum_{t=1}^{n}\left[\frac{\text{OCF}_t}{(1+k)^t}\right] + \left[\frac{\text{TCF}_n}{(1+k)^n}\right] - I_0 \\
I_0 &= -\sum_{t=1}^{n}\left[\frac{\text{OCF}_t}{(1+k)^t}\right] = \frac{\text{TCF}_n}{(1+k)^n} \\
\text{TCF}_n &= \left[I_0 - \sum_{t=1}^{n}\frac{\text{OCF}_t}{(1+k)^t}\right] \times (1+k)^n
\end{aligned} \qquad (12.4)$$

Thus it is clear from Eq. (12.4) that for the computation of the break-even terminal cash flow, there is need to estimate the present value of operating cash flows or the future cash flows without the salvage value. When computed, it is deducted from the initial investment and the difference is then multiplied by $(1 + k)^n$.

Suppose the net cash inflow in a three-year period, which is the life span of the project is respectively, \$ 10,000, \$ 12,000 and \$ 13,000. If the initial investment is \$ 20,000 and the discount rate is 10 per cent, the break-even salvage value will be: \$ [20,000 – {10,000/1.10 + 12,000/1.10^2 + 13,000/1.10^3}] × $(1.10)^3$ = \$ –11,680

PROBLEM 12.7

Find the break-even salvage value if:

(a) Initial investment = $ 30 million

(b) The net cash inflow during the first and the second year respectively = $ 20 million and $ 15 million

(c) Discount rate = 10%

Solution

Applying Eq. (12.4), we get

$$[30 - (20/1.10 + 15/1.21)] \times 1.21 = \$\ 0.70 \text{ million.}$$

Computation of Blocked Funds

In many cases, the host government imposes restrictions on the outflow of funds from the country in view of strained balance of payments. Such funds, as mentioned earlier, are known as *blocked funds*. Suppose if the host government says that the net revenue will be transferred to the parent only after the completion of the project and not every year, this provision will certainly influence the cash flow.

> Blocked funds occur when the host government restricts outflow of funds from the country.

Let us take an example where a US subsidiary in India takes up a project that has a life of three years with the expected net operating cash flow of $ 20,000, $ 40,000 and $ 42,000 respectively in the first, second and the third years. Discount rate is 10 per cent. One can think of three possible scenarios in this case. *First*, the Indian Government allows the outflow of cash to the home country every year. *Secondly*, the Indian Government allows the outflow of cash only after the life of the project and not every year. The blocked fund thus created is not invested by the subsidiary. *Thirdly*, the subsidiary invests the blocked funds that earn 10 per cent interest. The amount of cash flow will be different in each of these three scenarios.

If there is no such exchange control and the cash flows to the parent every year, the total cash flow will be:

$$\$\ 20{,}000/1.10 + 40{,}000/(1.10)^2 + 42{,}000/(1.10)^3 = \$\ 82{,}795$$

Again, if there is exchange control and the subsidiary does not invest the blocked funds, the amount of cash flow to the parent unit after the third year will be:

$$\$\ (20{,}000 + 40{,}000 + 42{,}000)/1.10^3 = \$\ 76{,}634.$$

Yet again, if there is exchange control, but the subsidiary invests the blocked funds, the cash flowing to the parent unit inclusive of interest earned after the third year may be calculated as:

$$\$\ 20{,}000\ (1.10)^2 + 40{,}000\ (1.10) + 42{,}000 = \$\ 1{,}10{,}200$$

$$\$\ 1{,}10{,}200/(1.10)^3 = \$\ 82{,}795$$

PROBLEM 12.8

A project of the subsidiary with an initial investment of $ 10 million has a net operating cash flow of $ 10 million each for three years during the life time of the project and a salvage value of $ 4 million. The host government permits the cash flow to the home country only after the life time of the project. But the subsidiary invests the funds at a rate of 12 per cent till the actual outflow takes place. Find the NPV assuming a discount rate of 10 per cent. What will be the NPV if (a) the funds are not invested, and (b) there is no restriction on the outflow of funds.

Solution

The total invested value = \$ 10 $(1.12)^2$ + 10(1.12) + 10 = 12.544 + 11.2 + 10
= \$ 33.744 million

NPV = –10.0 + (33.744 + 4.0)/1.103 = \$ 18.357 million.

If the funds are not invested,

NPV = –10.0 + (10.0 + 10.0 + 10.0 + 4.0)/1.331 = \$ 15.545 million

If there is no restriction, the funds will flow annually to the home country without any investment.

NPV = –10.0 + 10/1.10 + 10.0/1.21 + 14.0/1.331 = \$ 17.873 million.

Parent-Subsidiary Perspective: An Alternative Approach

The analysis of project appraisal in the earlier pages of this chapter takes into account the parent unit's perspective, of course, on valid reasons. Even in this case, the parent unit takes into account the subsidiary's perspective at least to some extent and makes adjustments in the cash flow and the discount rate under the NPV framework. But it is often argued that for a more transparent appraisal of the investment project, project appraisal needs to be made in greater details—both from the parent's point of view and from the viewpoint of the subsidiary. It is for this reason that in a survey of 121 US MNCs operating in early 1980s, 48 per cent of the decisions were made on the basis of the project's cash flow, 36 per cent were taken on the basis of the parent's cash flow while 16 per cent of the decisions considered both the viewpoints (Stanley and Block, 1983).

The very rationale of this argument is that if project's NPV is positive, it is bound to add to the corporate wealth of the firm as a whole. Under this approach, two NPVs are computed. One is the NPV from the parent's perspective (NPV_P) and the other is the NPV from the viewpoint of the project itself that is known as the subsidiary's perspective (NPV_S). Finally, acceptance/rejection decision of the project is based on the NPV of both of them.

In order to find out the NPV_P, the following successive steps are taken:

1. Estimate the cash flow in the host-country currency
2. Estimate the future spot exchange rate on the basis of available forward rates
3. Convert the host-currency cash flow into the home-country currency
4. Find NPV in home-country currency using the home-country discount rate.

Here the cash inflow represents all cash flowing towards the parent unit in a manner similar to what has been explained earlier. Cash outflow will represent cash flowing out of the parent unit.

Similarly, to find out the NPV_S, the following steps are taken:

1. Estimate the cash flow in host-country currency
2. Identify the host-country discount rate
3. Discount the host-currency cash flow at the host-country discount rate
4. Convert the resultant NPV into the home-country currency at the spot exchange rate.

In this case, the cash inflow represents the earnings of the project in the host-country currency irrespective of the fact whether cash moves towards, or away from, the parent unit.

These two methods assume all-equity capital structure and so, if the parity conditions existed in the real world, the result of the two approaches would have been the same. But in the real world, debt is normally included in the capital structure in order to lower the cost of capital; and moreover, the parity conditions do not exist. Naturally, the result of the two approaches will differ. The possible results will be:

1. NPV_P and NPV_S both being negative. In such case, project cannot be accepted.
2. NPV_P and NPV_S both being positive. In such case, project shall be accepted.
3. $NPV_P > 0 > NPV_S$. The project is attractive from the viewpoint of the parent unit but not attractive from the subsidiary's viewpoint. In such case, project may be accepted but there will be chances for loss in the value in terms of the host-country currency.
4. $NPV_P < 0 < NPV_S$. The project being attractive from the subsidiary's perspective shall be unattractive from the parent's perspective. The project may be accepted but it is doubtful how far it will be useful for the parent unit.

COST OF CAPITAL

In the preceding section, the discussion was limited to the numerator of the NPV-rule equation. The denominator of the equation, which is known as the *discount rate* or the *hurdle rate* and which is based on the risk-adjusted cost of capital, is also very significant for the computation of cash flow. We now discuss the concept of the cost of capital, and the adjustments in it that are required for international capital budgeting decision.

Average Cost of Capital

Average cost of capital represents the weighted average of the cost of equity and the cost of debt. As an equation, the average cost of capital,

$$k = k_d(1 - t)W_d + k_e W_e \tag{12.5}$$

where k_d is the cost of debt, k_e is the cost of equity, W is the relative weight of different forms of capital in the capital structure and t is the tax rate.

Cost of Debt

Interest is the cost of debt adjusted for taxes because interest is tax-deductible and is debited in the income statement before tax is calculated. Tax-adjusted cost of debt,

$$k_d = \text{interest/principal} \times (1 - t) \tag{12.6}$$

The cost of new debt differs from the cost of existing debt as the former includes the floatation cost. The cost of new debt is

$$k_d\,(\text{new}) = [I + \{(P - \text{NP})/n\}/\{(P + \text{NP})/2\}] \times (1 - t) \tag{12.7}$$

where I is the interest, P is the principal, NP is the net proceeds after floatation cost and n is the maturity.

Example: If annual interest charges amount to \$ 5,000, the cost of \$ 1,00,000 ten-year debt with a tax rate of 50 per cent will be:

$$5{,}000/1{,}00{,}000 \times (1 - 0.50) = 2.5\%$$

If it is a new debt and the floatation cost is \$ 2,000, the cost of debt will be: [5,000 + {(1,00,000 – 98,000)/10}/{(1,00,000 + 98,000)/2}] × (1 – 0.50) = 2.63%.

When a debt instrument is issued at a premium or discount, the net proceeds differ from the face value and the same procedure is used that is used in case of new debt. Suppose a ten-year bond having a face value of \$ 100 is sold at \$ 90 with a coupon of 5 per cent. The cost of debt with a 50 per cent tax rate will be:

$$[5 + \{(100 - 90)/10\}/\{(100 + 90)/2\}] \times (1 - 0.50) = 3.15\%$$

Again, if the company raises debt from another country's financial market, the cost of debt will be inclusive of the changes in the exchange rate. For example, suppose an Indian company raises debt from the US dollar market at an interest rate of 6.0 per cent. But if dollar appreciates by 3.0 per cent, the cost of debt in terms of rupee will be higher than 6.0 per cent. It will be:

$$(1 + 0.06)\ (1 + 0.03) - 1 = 0.0918 = 9.18\%$$

The readers are suggested to go through Chapter 15 for a detailed discussion.

Cost of Equity Shares

Dividend is the cost of equity shares. The computation of the cost of equity shares is not so easy as there is no fixed contractual obligation for the payment of dividend to equity shareholders. Sometimes the cost is based on the historical rate of return, but the problem with this method is that it does not embrace the expectations about future performance of the firm. The usual practice is to rely on the current value of shares. The price of equity share P, is equal to the present value of expected dividend D given the risk-adjusted rate k_e required by the investors. To arrive at the cost of equity shares, the normal practice is to divide the expected amount of dividend at the year-end by the current value of shares. In equation form,

$$k_e = D/P_0 \qquad (12.8)$$

But since the investors expect growing rate of dividend per share, growth factor g is added to Eq. (12.8). Then

$$k_e = (D/P_0) + g \qquad (12.9)$$

Example: If dividend in the past has grown at 5 per cent per annum and the firm expects to pay dividend at \$ 4 per share at the year end, the cost of equity share with a current price of \$ 50 will be:

$$(4/50) + 0.05 = 13\%$$

As far as the cost of new share is concerned, it is computed after adjustment of floatation cost. This means that the floatation cost is deducted from the market price of the share. Suppose, the floatation cost is \$ 5 per share, then the cost of equity share will be:

$$4/(50 - 5) + 0.05 = 13.89\%$$

There is one more method for computing the cost of equity shares. It is based on the security market line where *Beta* is used as a measure of risk (Friend and Blume, 1970). Under this method, the cost of equity share,

$$k_e = k_r + (k_m - k_r)\beta_e \tag{12.10}$$

where

k_r is the riskless rate of interest,

k_m is the expected rate of return (average) on the portfolio of all securities in the market, and

β_e is the product of the standard deviation of the return on the equity share in question SD_e, and their correlation with the market, $corr_{em}$ divided by the standard deviation of the rate of return on the market portfolio, SD_m.

The estimate of β is made from the past rates of return since historical β is often close to real or true β. If β is equal to 1, it means that the risk contained in the equity shares is equal to that found in the total portfolio in the market. A higher β shows share risk higher than in the market. Similarly, riskless rate is equal to the rates found in class-one securities. The average market rate is close to the historical average rate of return in a large sample of securities.

Example: If k_r is 10%, k_m is 15%, and β is 0.8, then

$$k_e = 0.10 + (0.15 - 0.10) \times 0.8 = 0.14 = 14\%$$

Cost of Retained Earnings

Funds for investment come normally from the retained earnings. In case of domestic investment, the cost of such funds is not calculated separately because the market price of shares, which determines the cost of equity, embodies also the influence of retained earnings. But in case of international investment, cost of retained earning is calculated separately because the earnings repatriated by the subsidiary to the parent company are subject to tax. Thus, the normal practice is to make tax adjustments in the cost of retained earnings. The after-tax cost of retained earnings

$$k_s = k_e(1 - t) \tag{12.11}$$

If the retained earnings involve transfer cost when they move from the parent to subsidiary, Eq. 12.11 will be written as

$$k_s = k_e (1 - t) (1 - c) \tag{12.12}$$

where c = transfer cost

Example: An American subsidiary operating in India has 15.0 per cent as cost of equity. The repatriation of retained earnings causes an incremental tax of 20.0 per cent. The transfer cost in remittance is expected to be 2.0 per cent. The cost of retained earnings will be:

$$0.15 (1 - .20) (1 - 0.02) = 0.1176 = 11.76\%$$

PROBLEM 12.9

Calculate the weighted average cost of capital when the capital structure shows:

(a) Existing debt of \$ 5.0 million at 10 per cent for 6 years (tax rate is 30 per cent),

(b) New debt of \$ 3.0 million at 8 per cent for 10 years with a floating cost of \$ 2,00,000,

(c) Existing equity shares of \$ 7.0 million (\$ 15 per share), EPS \$ 4, growth rate of 5 per cent and dividend pay-out ratio of 50 per cent, and
(d) Proposed equity share (1,00,000 shares) to be sold at \$ 15 with \$ 2,00,000 floatation cost.

Solution

Cost:
Existing debt: 0.10 (1 – 0.30) = 0.07
New debt: [2,40,000 + {(30,00,000 – 28,00,000)/10}]/(30,00,000 + 28,00,000)/2
= 0.08965 (1 – 0.3) = 0.062755
Existing equity: 2/15 + 0.05 = 0.1833
New equity share: 2/13 + 0.05 = 0.2038
Proportions:
Existing debt: \$ 50,00,000/1,65,00,000 = 0.31
New debt: 30,00,000/1,65,00,000 = 0.18
Existing equity: 70,00,000/1,65,00,000 = 0.42
New equity: 15,00,000/1,65,00,000 = 0.09
Weighted average cost:
Existing debt: 0.31 × 0.07 = 0.0217
New debt: 0.18 × 0.0628 = 0.0113
Existing equity: 0.42 × 0.1833 = 0.0770
New equity: 0.09 × 0.2038 = 0.0183
Weighted average: 0.1283 = 12.83%

Significance of Weight

We have seen Eq. (12.5) where the cost of equity and the cost of debt are added up along with their relative weight. The weight is significant in the sense that the cost of debt, as it is tax-deductible, is often lower than the cost of equity; and so, if the capital structure consists more of debt or the lower-cost capital, the weighted average cost of capital will be lower and for this reason the introduction of debt in the capital structure called *financial leverage* lowers the average cost of capital and thereby raises the return on investment. However, there is difference in views as to what extent the use of debt reduces the weighted average cost of capital.

The net income approach suggests that with growing proportion of debt, the average cost of capital declines and is the minimum where the entire capital is composed of debt. One of the shortcomings of this approach is that it does not take into account the risk borne by the equity shareholders as a result of increasing share of debt in the capital structure. The net operating income approach on the other hand, takes this very fact into account and suggests that the risk borne by the equity shareholders rises at the rate at which the cost of capital falls after the introduction of debt. The ultimate result is that the average cost of capital remains constant irrespective of the changing ratios between debt and the equity capital. However, there is a compromising view which suggests that up to a certain point, an increase in debt-equity ratio does not lead to a rise in the risk borne by equity shareholders with the result that the average cost of capital begins to fall but if the company goes on increasing the debt-equity ratio beyond this point, the increase in such risk outweighs the benefit of increasing debt and the average cost of capital begins to rise. This means that the average cost of capital curve is U-shaped.

Solomon (1963) agrees with the compromise approach but suggests that the average cost of capital curve in actual practice is not exactly a U but a saucer-shaped one. It is because both the cost of equity and the cost of debt rise with a continual rise in the debt-equity ratio. Increasing debt raises risk not only of the equity shareholders but also of the bondholders because increasing debt raises the risk of default. The optimal debt-equity ratio represents the point where the average cost of capital is lowest.

Average and Marginal Cost of Capital

When a firm sets up a subsidiary and makes additional investment for this purpose and if the relative weight of different forms of capital and their cost remain constant even in respect of additional capital raised, the average and the marginal cost of capital are the same. But since these two variables change with raising of additional capital, marginal cost of capital is different from average cost of capital. Thus, while setting up a subsidiary, this factor needs to be considered, especially when the sources and the cost of capital change.

International Investment and Cost of Capital

Let us first consider why the cost of capital in case of an MNC's operation is not necessarily the same as in case of a domestic company. The size of an MNC is quite large, so it gets preferential treatment from the creditors and the size of its issue being large, the floatation cost per share or bond also works out lower.

MNCs' easy access to international capital market lowers the cost of capital, but the existence of exchange rate and political risks raises it.

It has easy access to the international capital market and so it gets funds from the least-cost source. The subsidiary too borrows from the domestic capital market if it finds the cost of capital low there. Importantly, an MNC can internationally diversify its sources of funds and so ensure a stable inflow of funds which reduces the probability of bankruptcy and lowers the cost of capital. But at the same time, as the flow of funds in multinational operation is highly exposed to exchange rate changes, it raises the bankruptcy cost and compels the creditors and shareholders to require a higher rate of return on the capital. Again, the international operation is subject to political risk which also requires a higher rate of return on capital. Thus these facts need to be incorporated into the computation of the cost of capital in the context of multinational investment.

Parent's Perspective and Adjustment to Cost of Capital

Those who believe in efficient capital market suggest that the cost of capital in different countries is analogous and hence the parent company's cost of capital may be used for discounting the cash flow from foreign operations without any adjustment. But in practice, the international capital market is segmented which requires adjustments to the parent unit's cost of capital. If the cash flow is discounted at the subsidiary level, the cost of capital obtained in the host country is used for this purpose. But in cases where the parent unit uses the home-country cost of capital, it makes some adjustments to it.

First, the cost of capital should be adjusted for the variation in capital structure norms that is very evident in international investment. Normally, the MNCs whose operation is well diversified across countries have a comparatively stable cash flow and can handle more debt. They have large share of debt also because they have easy access to credit, and are exposed to lower credit risk. On the other hand, the MNCs which have relatively large profits, use more of their retained earnings and not debt.

Determinants of Capital Structure

The debt-equity ratio in a multinational firm depends on the company's own characteristics as well as on the economic environment in the host country. Higher debt-equity ratio is found if there is:

1. Stable cash flow
2. Easier access to the sources of debt
3. Low interest rate and low credit risk
4. Low level of retained earnings
5. Restrictions in the host country on the participation in equity shares
6. Restrictions in the host country on dividend repatriation
7. High degree of exchange rate risk and political risk in the host country

The capital structure norms depend also on the rules and regulations in the host country. In host countries where foreign equity participation is restricted to lower limits, the debt-equity ratio is generally high. Again, when the subsidiary is more exposed to exchange rate risk, a higher debt-equity ratio is desirable. Yet again, when political risk is very high in the host country, the MNCs rely more on loan from host-country creditors because the creditors will then put pressure on the local government to maintain good relations with the MNC. If however, the interest rate is high in the host country as it is in many developing countries, the MNC uses more of equity capital. Capital structure norms thus vary from one host country to another and from one MNC to another. If the same MNC invests in different countries, its target capital structure in each host country will differ from its global target capital structure. In order to minimise this difference, the MNCs adopt different norms in different host countries. If they rely more on debt in one host country, they try to rely more on equity in another host country. If the debt-equity mix in all the subsidiaries taken together does not match its (parent unit's) own capital structure norms, it tries to adjust its norms to the global target capital structure norms through adding a premium to, or making a discount from, the parent unit's cost of capital.

If debt-equity norms in host countries differ greatly from those of the parent company, the MNC makes adjustment in its global target capital structure norms.

Secondly, the parent unit's cost of capital is adjusted in keeping with the extent to which the subsidiary is able to get funds at lower cost either from the domestic financial market or from the international financial market. If the cost is lower than the cost of capital of the parent unit, the discount rate needs to be reduced.

Thirdly, the discount rate also needs adjustment for inflation. If the cash flow is adjusted for inflation, it should be discounted by the real discount rate or the inflation-adjusted discount rate, but if the cash flow is not adjusted for inflation, it should be discounted by the nominal discount rate.

Fourthly, the discount rate is adjusted for various types of risks, political, economic, or both prevalent in the host country. If these risks are expected to be present in the host country, the discount rate needs an upward revision. The extent of upward revision depends upon the severity of the risks.

ADJUSTED PRESENT VALUE APPROACH

Lessard (1979) has developed a technique for international capital budgeting that is known as the *adjusted present value (APV) technique*. It incorporates most of the complexities emerging in the computation of cash flow and in the determination of the discount rates already explained in the preceding sections.

Under the APV technique, the *initial cash flow* consists of the capital cost of the project minus blocked funds, if any, in the host country activated by the project. This amount is converted into the home-country currency at the spot exchange rate.

Similarly, the *operating cash flow* under the APV technique consists of:

- Present value of after-tax cash flow from subsidiary to parent converted into the home-country currency at the expected spot rate minus the profits on the lost sales of the parent company,
- Present value of tax-adjusted depreciation allowances in terms of the home-country currency,
- Present value of the contribution of the project to borrowing capacity in terms of home-country currency subject to adjustment for taxes,
- Face value of loan in the host-country currency minus the present value of repayments converted into the home-country currency,
- Present value of the expected savings on account of tax deferrals and transfer pricing, and
- Present value of expected illegal repatriation of income.

Terminal cash flow consists of the present value of residual plant and equipment. It may be noted that for tax adjustment, the APV technique takes into account the higher of the home-country and host-country tax rates. This technique is unique in that it uses different discount rates for different types of cash flows. The cash flow on account of sales and other such revenue is discounted at the all-equity cost of capital; depreciation allowances are discounted at the nominal rate; the contribution of the project to borrowing capacity is discounted at the riskless rate, and the repayment of loans in host-country currency is discounted at nominal interest rate prevalent in the host country. Again, the rate used for discounting the savings on account of taxes and of transfer pricing and illegal repatriation includes the risk premium.

Despite uniqueness of the APV technique, it has been found that if the complexities are incorporated in the cash flow and if the risk-adjusted weighted average cost of capital is taken as the discount rate, the adjusted present value approach is not different from the NPV approach (Booth, 1982).

PROBLEM 12.10

An Indian company is making appraisal of its project to be set up with its subsidiary in the USA. The initial project cost amounts to US \$ 1,25,000 which, as expected, will add ₹ 30 lakh to the Indian company's borrowing capacity over a period of three years. A sum of ₹ 40 lakh of the initial investment is met by the Indian parent and the remaining \$ 25,000 is borrowed at 10 per cent interest rate in the USA. The project has a life of three years. The net operating cash inflow is \$ 50,000, \$ 60,000 and \$ 72,000 respectively in the first, second and third year. The salvage value is expected to be \$ 10,000.

The spot exchange rate is ₹ 40/\$. It is assumed that PPP holds with no lag and that real prices remain constant in both absolute and relative terms. Hence the sequence of exchange rate reflects anticipated annual rates of inflation equating 8 per cent in ₹ and 5 per cent in dollar. Depreciation allowances amount to ₹ 15 lakh a year for three years. Tax rate is 30 per cent in India and 25 per cent in the USA. Expected tax saving from intra-firm transfer pricing is ₹ 50,000 a year in all the three years. Discount rate for cash flows assuming all equity financing is 20 per cent. Discount rate for depreciation/tax saving on interest deductions from contribution to borrowing capacity is 12 per cent. Discount rate relating to loan repayment is 20 per cent and on tax saving on account of transfer pricing is 25 per cent. Find the APV.

Solution

Spot exchange rate = ₹ 40/\$
Year 1 = ₹ 40 × (1.08/1.05) = ₹ 41.14/\$
Year 2 = ₹ 41.14 × (1.08/1.05) = ₹ 42.32/\$
Year 3 = ₹ 42.32 × (1.08/1.05) = ₹ 43.53/\$

Operating cash flow (including salvage value):
Year 1 = 50,000 × 41.14 = 20,57,000/1.20 = ₹ 17,14,167
Year 2 = 60,000 × 42.32 = 25,39,000/1.20^2 = ₹ 17,63,333
Year 3 = (72,000 + 10,000) × 43.53 = 35,69,460/1.20^3 = ₹ 20,65,660
Total = ₹ 55,43,160

Depreciation allowance × tax @ 0.30:
Year 1 = ₹ 15,00,000 × 0.3 = 4,50,000/1.12 = ₹ 4,01,785
Year 2 = ₹ 15,00,000 × 0.3 = 4,50,000/1.12^2 = ₹ 3,58,737
Year 3 = ₹ 15,00,000 × 0.3 = 4,50,000/1.12^3 = ₹ 3,20,307
Total = ₹ 10,80,829

Borrowing capacity:
Year 1 = ₹ 10,00,000 × 0.10 × 0.3 = 30,000/1.12 = ₹ 26,786
Year 2 = ₹ 10,00,000 × 0.10 × 0.3 = 30,000/1.12^2 = ₹ 23,916
Year 3 = ₹ 10,00,000 × 0.10 × 0.3 = 30,000/1.12^3 = ₹ 21,354
Total = ₹ 72,056

Tax saving on account of transfer pricing:
Year 1 = ₹ 50,000 × 0.3 = 15,000/1.25 = ₹ 12,000
Year 2 = ₹ 50,000 × 0.3 = 15,000/1.25^2 = ₹ 9,600
Year 3 = ₹ 50,000 × 0.3 = 15,000/1.25^3 = ₹ 7,680
Total = ₹ 29,280

Loan repayment (interest + amortisation):
Year 1 = 10,833/1.20 = $ 9,028
Year 2 = 10,000/1.20^2 = $ 6,944
Year 3 = 9,167/1.20^3 = $ 5,305
Total = $ 21,277
APV = ₹ −(1,25,000 × 40) + 55,43,160 + 10,80,829 + 72,056 + 29,280 + [(25,000 − 21,277) × 40] = ₹ 18,74,145

SENSITIVITY ANALYSIS

The focus of the foregoing discussion was on how adjustments are made in the cash flow and the discount rate in the case of international capital budgeting. It is true that the estimated cash flow is fitted into the evaluation rules, such as NPV and IRR. But the question arises as to how the estimates of cash flow vary under different scenarios. For example, if the host country experiences boom conditions, the cash flow will be different from that in case of a normal period or in case of a depression. Again, the subsidiary may substitute the parent company's export partially, or fully, depending upon varying conditions existing in the host country and if the host government agencies are strictly monitoring the international transactions, it will be difficult for the company to employ transfer-pricing techniques and the saving on this account will be minimum. Obviously, it is difficult to foresee the future possibilities and so equally difficult to estimate the future cash flows with complete certainty. Similarly, the cost of capital will vary widely under varying degrees of business, financial and political risk. The varying cash flows and the varying discount rates under different scenarios will have a bearing on the accept-reject decision. The sensitivity analysis considers the varying scenarios or "what-if" scenarios. The purpose is to determine how sensitive the NPV is to alternative values of the input variables.

It may be noted here that when the cash flow is not known with complete certainty, probabilistic techniques are used for this purpose. The magnitude of uncertainty is measured in terms of dispersion from the expected value and then it is included either in the cash flow or in the discount rate. The former is known as the *certainty equivalent approach*, while the latter is known as the *risk-adjusted discount rate approach*. In cases of sequential investment, a decision-tree approach is followed. The readers are advised to consult any book on corporate finance for the analysis of risk.

REAL OPTIONS AND PROJECT APPRAISAL

Real options start when there is expected a change in cash flow from that originally anticipated. They are concerning postponement/ abandonment/ expansion/ contraction of the operation.

International investment is more risky than domestic investment insofar as the foreign investor does not know much about the economic, political, and other conditions prevailing in the host country. There is every possibility for changes in the cash flow from the originally anticipated one. If demand falls suddenly, the operation would have to be suspended for some time. If situation does not improve, it may be abandoned. If, on the contrary, demand rises suddenly, operation may be expanded. In the cases where the investor needs more information, the operation may be postponed for some time. These are the options facing the international finance manager. These options are known as the *real options* as they influence the real assets. They influence the international cash flow and therefore form a part of international capital budgeting. At the present juncture, we shall take up only one or two options so that the readers are acquainted with how real options influence the cash flow.

Postponement

In case of postponement, option value is decomposed into the value of options if exercised today and the value if waiting is involved. Investing today is the intrinsic value and waiting for a specific period represents time value. Let us take an example to explain its impact on the cash flow. Suppose a petroleum exploration company has to undertake a project abroad. If it invests today, considering that perpetual cash flow begins in the first year, the NPV of investing today,

$$NPV_0 = [\{(P - V)Q\}/r] - I_0 \qquad (12.13)$$

If it waits for one year before making any investment, the NPV at time $t = 0$,

$$NPV_0 = [\{(P - V)Q\}/r]/(1 + r) - I_0 \qquad (12.14)$$

If initial investment is $ 5 million, risk-free interest rate is 10 per cent, the expected price level of oil is $ 10 per barrel, the variable cost is $ 4 per barrel, and the expected production is 1,00,000 barrels a year, the NPV of investing today will be:

$$[\{(10 - 4)1{,}00{,}000\}/0.10] - 50{,}00{,}000 = \$\ 10{,}00{,}000$$

If, on the contrary, the company waits for a year because price of oil is expected to go up to $ 15 per barrel, the NPV after one-year wait will be:

$$[\{(15 - 4)1{,}00{,}000\}/0.10]/1.10 - 50{,}00{,}000 = \$\ 50{,}00{,}000$$

Here NPV for wait is higher. So the company should postpone the investment for one year. The value of the option to postpone the investment can be viewed as managerial flexibility. It is because of this flexibility that the company gains more. However, if the price of oil per barrel shrinks unexpectedly to a lower value, the company will not make an investment after one year. It can be analogised with the out-of-money option when the option buyer does not exercise the option.

Abandonment

The project may be abandoned if the cost structure does not justify it. If the extraction and refining cost rises unexpectedly to $ 8 per barrel (with price per barrel being $ 10), the NPV of abandonment today will be:

$$[\{(10 - 8)\ 1{,}00{,}000\}/0.10] - 50{,}00{,}000 = \$(-)\ 30{,}00{,}000$$

The company will abandon the project in view of the negative NPV. But if price of oil is expected to rise by 100 per cent after one year, the project will not be abandoned. Rather, the company shall wait and watch for the price rise. If it rises as per expectations, it will continue to operate. If the price does not rise after one year, the project will be abandoned finally.

In fact, in case of MNCs, it is not easy to abandon a project and restart the same project. It is because they have to incur high entry and exit cost. If they once invest, they prefer to operate at loss for some time unless and until the loss attains abnormally a high level. Normally, they watch for some time in the expectation that favourable conditions will prevail. Such a situation is known as *hysteresis* that usually arises following changes in real exchange rates when the MNCs have to face loss for sometime and then gain if the exchange rates move in their favour.

Hysteresis denotes MNCs' behaviour when they prefer to operate at loss for some time in the expectation of favourable conditions to reappear.

Expansion and Contraction

If demand goes up suddenly and the company raises its production level, it will find out the option value of expansion. It will expand the level of operation if the NPV is greater than for the case when there is no expansion.

Again, if demand falls suddenly, the company will find out the NPV of contracted level of production. If it is greater than for the case with no contraction, it will go for contraction in the level of operation. The readers should try to compute the NPV in different scenarios and then conclude what should be the real option before the firm.

PROBLEM 12.11

A Japanese automobile company has decided to manufacture 10,000 motor cars per year in India with an initial investment of ₹ 500 crores. The price is ₹ 2 lakh and the variable cost including also the import cost of the spares is ₹ 1.30 lakh. The risk-free interest is 10 per cent. The car is the lowest-price car in the market and so the demand is expected to rise from 10,000 cars in the first year to 12,000 cars in the second year and even more in the following years. On the other hand, the rupee is expected to depreciate vis-à-vis yen and the variable cost is expected to rise fast from ₹ 1.30 lakh to ₹ 1.80 lakh. Find out what are the options available to the manufacturer.

Solution

At the current level of production,

$$NPV = [\{(2.00 - 1.30) \times 10{,}000\}/0.10 - 5{,}00{,}00{,}00{,}000 = ₹\ 2{,}00{,}00{,}00{,}000.$$

If demand moves up to 12,000 units,

$$NPV = [\{(2.00 - 1.30) \times 12{,}000\}/0.10 - 5{,}00{,}00{,}00{,}000 = ₹\ 3{,}40{,}00{,}00{,}000.$$

But if variable cost rises to ₹ 1.80 lakh due to exchange rate changes,

$$NPV = [\{(2.00 - 1.80) \times 10{,}000\}/0.10 - 5{,}00{,}00{,}00{,}000 = ₹\ -3{,}00{,}00{,}00{,}000.$$

The manufacturer will bear the loss within a reasonable period of time till any clear-cut indication is not visible for a favourable movement in the exchange rate. If favourable move is visible, production will be continued; otherwise, the project will be abandoned.

EVALUATING M&AS

Value of the Merged Firm and Gains from M&As

M&A is a gainful strategy only when the value of the combined firm is greater than the sum of the values of the two firms computed individually in the absence of the merger. In the form of an equation,

$$\text{Gain} = V_{AB} - (V_A + V_B) \tag{12.15}$$

However, the gain so derived has to be compared with the cost of M&A that is arrived at after deducting the value of the target firm from the price that the acquiring firm pays to the target company. This means that the net gain from M&A accruing to the acquiring firm exists only when

$$[V_{AB} - (V_A + V_B)] > (\text{Price} - V_B) \tag{12.16}$$

Thus, in this context, it is very significant to know what price the acquiring firm should pay to the target firm for acquisition and what the impact of the changes in price on the post-merger value of the firm would be. The price is known as the *consideration* value that is fixed within the two extremes. One is the *floor price* for the package, any price below which is not acceptable by the target company. It is basically the market value of the shares of the target company. For example, if Firm A acquires Firm B and if the market value of Firm B's share is $ 15, the consideration value must be at least $ 15. In practice, it is more than $ 15 as Firm B will attract a premium for the acquisition.

Consideration value is the price the acquiring company gives to the target company for acquisition.

However, this does not mean that the amount of premium will swell infinitely. If it moves up beyond a certain limit, the value of the acquiring firm will reduce and the very objective of the acquiring firm behind the merger will be marred. This limit is known as the *ceiling price* where the EPS of the acquiring firm in the post-merger period is equal to that in the pre-merger period. In other words, the ceiling price would be equal to the product of the EPS of the target firm and the P/E ratio of the acquiring firm.

Suppose the financial data of the two firms are as follows:

	Firm A	*Firm B*
Present earnings ($)	20,000.00	8,000.00
Shares (No.)	5,000.00	3,000.00
EPS ($)	4.00	2.67
Market value of shares	32.00	16.00
Price-earning ratio	8.00	6.00

At the floor price, the value of Firm B in the post-merger period will be the same as during the pre-merger period. The owners of Firm B will get 16/32 or 0.5 share in Firm A for their one share in Firm B. Thus, the wealth of Firm B in the post-merger period will be $ 32 × 1,500 shares or $ 48,000 which is equal to $ 16 × 3,000 shares during the pre-merger period.

At this floor price paid, the EPS of Firm A after the merger will increase to $ (20,000 + 8,000)/(5,000 + 1,500 shares) or to $ 4.31. Assuming a price-earning ratio of 8.0, the value of one share of Firm A after the merger will be $ 4.31 × 8.0

or \$ 34.48 and the value of the merged firm will be \$ 34.48 × 6,500 shares = \$ 2,24,120 which is higher than the sum of the value of the two firms in the pre-merger period. Using Eq. (12.16), the net gain from the merger will be:

$$\$ \{2,24,120 - (1,60,000 + 48,000)\} - (48,000 - 48,000) = \$ 16,120$$

The higher the price than the floor price, the lower will be the gain to the acquiring firm and higher the gain to the target company. However, Firm A may pay a large premium to Firm B in order to lure the latter for acquisition. The ceiling will reach where the price will be equal to the product of EPS of the target company and the price-earning ratio of the acquiring firm. In the above example, it is \$ 2.67 × 8 = \$ 21.36. At this price, Firm B will receive 0.6675 shares in Firm A in lieu of its one share or in all 2,003 shares in Firm A meaning that there will be in all 7,003 shares in the merged firm. The EPS will then be \$ 28,000/7,003 shares ≈ \$ 4.0 which is equal to the pre-merger EPS of Firm A. Assuming the price-earning ratio of 8, the value of the merged firm will be \$ 32 × 7,003 shares or \$ 2,24,096. Thus at both the ceiling price and the floor price, the value of the merged firm is almost the same, but at the ceiling price, the net gain to the acquiring firm would be zero because the gain from the merger will be reaped entirely by the target company.

In practice, the actual price is determined between these two limits depending upon the bargaining power of the acquiring firm and the target firm; and accordingly, the net gain is shared by the acquiring firm and the target firm. Suppose, the consideration value is \$ 20 per share of Firm B. In this case, Firm A will issue 0.625 share for one share in Firm B which would amount to 1,875 shares. The value of owners' wealth in Firm B would now be \$ 32 × 1,875 shares or \$ 60,000 as compared to \$ 48,000 in the pre-merger period. The EPS of the merged firm would be \$ 28,000/6,875 shares or \$ 4.07. Assuming a price-earning ratio of 8, the value of the merged firm will be \$ 32.56 × 6,875 shares or \$ 2,23,850 which is higher than the sum of the pre-merger value of the two firms. The net gain to the acquiring firm as per Eq. (12.16) will be:

$$\$ \{2,23,850 - (1,60,000 + 48,000)\} - (60,000 - 48,000) = \$ 3,850$$

Thus, at a price agreed upon between the floor and the ceiling, both the acquiring firm and the target firm will reap benefits and as a result, both will agree to the merger. However, there are cases when the acquiring firm opts for acquisition even when its net gain is zero. This is, however, done if some other significant benefits are going to accrue to the acquiring firm.

PROBLEM 12.12

Firm A absorbs Firm B on the basis of the following data:

(a) Present earnings: Firm A—\$ 40,000, Firm B—\$ 18,000
(b) No. of shares: Firm A—5,000, Firm B—3,000
(c) EPS: Firm A—\$ 8.0, Firm B—\$ 6.0
(d) Market price of shares: Firm A—\$ 40.0, Firm B—\$ 21.0
(e) Price-earning ratio: Firm A—5.0, Firm B—3.50

Find out the gain to Firm A if the consideration price is \$ 24.0 per share.

Solution

At a price of \$ 24.0, a share in B = 0.6 share in A. This means that 1,800 shares will be added to A's already existing 5,000 shares in the merged firm. The EPS in the merged firm will be: 58,000/6,800 = \$ 8.53. Assuming a P/E ratio of 5, the value of one share in the merged firm is \$ 42.65 and the value of total 6,800 shares at the rate of \$ 42.65 a share in the merged firm will be \$ 42.65 × 6,800 = \$ 2,90,020.

Applying Eq. (12.16), the gain will be

$$\$\ [2{,}90{,}020 - (2{,}00{,}000 + 63{,}000) - (72{,}000 - 63{,}000)] = \$\ 18{,}020.]$$

Factors Influencing the Consideration Value

The consideration value has so far been discussed in absence of any changes in the international environment, but in international M&A, such changes cannot be overlooked. One such change is the change in exchange rate. The lower the existing spot rate of the currency of the target-company country, the lower is the price to be paid by the acquiring firm. If it is higher, the salvage value will be higher from the viewpoint of the acquiring firm. If the future spot rate is expected to be higher, the acquiring firm will receive a greater cash flow.

The second is the required rate of return that influences the value of the acquisition because the cost of capital varies from one country to another. This is why acquisition of a particular country's firm may be more beneficial than that in another country.

Thirdly, the value of acquisition differs in case of different countries because of variation of the ability to use financial leverage among countries. Since acquisition is financed mostly through borrowings, acquisition of firms in a country where flexibility to borrow is large is more common. For example, in the United States, a high debt ratio is not preferred, and the acquiring firm does not get much incentives on this count.

Last but not least, the important factors in this respect are the legal formalities regarding tax and accounting. If they are favourable, they create competitive advantages for acquiring firms in some countries. This means that when these rules are more favourable and liberal, the acquiring firm may bid a higher price for acquisition.

NON-FINANCIAL FACTORS IN CAPITAL BUDGETING

In the international capital budgeting process, financial factors do dominate explaining how much cash flow the project is going to generate and what the discount rate should be but it does not mean that the non-financial factors are negated. Rodriguez and Carter (1984) group these factors as, the behavioural characteristics of the organisation, and the business strategy.

> Non-financial factors influencing capital budgeting decision are:
> 1. behavioural characteristics of the organisation, and
> 2. business strategy.

A firm has various levels of management depending upon its organisational structure. In an international set-up, the structure is more complex, based normally on the line-and-staff or functional pattern. Any decision passing through the different levels of management is influenced by the attitude of the managers. The view of one manager is normally different from that of another and consequently, the final decision is the result of bargaining among the different levels of management.

Divergence in the views of managers is more apparent in an international firm where the managers come from varying cultural and social backgrounds and are trained in diverse conditions. England and Lee (1971) have found that behavioural emphasis varies widely between Japanese and American managers; American managers emphasise organisational efficiency and profit maximisation, while Japanese managers lay greater stress on organisational growth and productivity. Thus the projects fulfilling the financial norms pass in the final selection only when they meet the expectations of the more powerful managers. It sometimes happens that the organisational factors considerably mar the impact of financial evaluation based on the cash flow analysis, although they do not negate it.

Apart from the organisational behaviour that influences the capital budgeting decision, proposals meeting the financial norms must fit into the corporate strategy. The management frames the combinations of strategies depending upon its preferences and capabilities and then fits the financially viable projects into its strategy framework. For shaping the strategy framework, the management develops a set of criteria including the product's life-cycle stage, market characteristics, possibilities for replacement or expansion, etc. Keeping in mind the product's life-cycle stage, the management groups various host countries on the basis of market size, investment climate, availability of local resources and access to market. An index is prepared for the products to be launched in each market and finally that product-country combination is chosen of which the index number is the highest.

As far as market characteristics are concerned, products are classified according to potential market growth and the present state of market penetration. In this context, the price of the product and the elasticity of demand are also taken into consideration. As regards the replacement-expansion decision, it is estimated as to which of the two options is more beneficial for the firm, preferably in a subjective way. Depending upon these considerations, a composite index is built and only those projects which are financially viable and have the highest score in terms of the index.

SUMMARY

- The evaluation criteria of domestic investment projects, such as accounting rate of return, pay-back period, NPV, IRR, and PI are followed also in case of international investment projects but since the parent's perspective and the subsidiary's perspective differ on a number of issues, some adjustments need to be made and care has to be exercised while computing the cash flows. The parent is the investor and so it is the parent's point of view that shapes the cash flows either as inflow or as outflow. Any cash flow from subsidiary to parent is treated as cash inflow and the reverse flow is treated as cash outflow. In fact, this is the principle on the basis of which the initial cash flow, the operating cash flow, and the terminal cash flow are entered into the evaluation formula. However, to make the appraisal more transparent, cash flow from the subsidiary's point of view is also calculated. Accept/reject decision is based on the two NPVs.

- The cash flow during period t_1 to t_n is discounted to the present value at a rate equal to the risk-adjusted cost of capital. The average cost of capital—the sum of the cost of debt, and the cost of equity along with their respective weight—is taken into account but the marginal cost of capital forms the basis of the discount rate, if it is different from the average cost of capital. Again, though MNCs are often able to raise finance at lower cost, there are some additional risks inherent in international business and the cost of capital is adjusted for these facts.
- Lessard has developed a technique for international capital budgeting that is known as the APV technique. This technique takes into account the various adjustments necessary in international capital budgeting and uses different discount rates for different types of cash flows. Again, the sensitivity analysis helps improve the quality of the capital budgeting process, for the finance manager gets a detailed idea of the quantum and pattern of cash flows under varying scenarios. The accept-reject decision will thus be more realistic. There are also real options facing international finance managers that influence the capital budgeting decisions.
- Evaluating M&As considers whether they bring in additional wealth to the acquiring company. In fact, the gain depends on the consideration value that needs to be determined with much care.
- Besides, the non-financial factors, such as the behavioural characteristics of the organisation and the corporate strategy are often crucial. They influence the final decision about taking up of the project.

CASE STUDY

KPMG COST OF CAPITAL STUDY

The global economy and stock markets exhibit rising uncertainty. The 18th edition of our Cost of Capital Study provides insights into how this change impacts company strategies and return expectations. Over 320 companies provide information and share their expertise.

The research titled "Unpredictability on the Rise! – Are Interest Rates Included?" What are the determinants and what are the repercussions? assesses the effects of heightened uncertainty and related interest rate and inflation trends on business models, corporate growth, and long-term return expectations (cost of capital), grounded in sector-specific analysis.

Substantial rise in the weighted average cost of capital

A modest rise in the weighted average cost of capital (WACC) from 6.6 per cent to 6.8 per cent occurred in the prior year, followed by a substantial increase to 7.9 per cent in the current survey period (30 September 2022 to 30 June 2023). This augmentation is likewise evident in the respective businesses.

Consistent with the prior year, the greatest weighted cost of capital in the current survey period was recorded in the Technology (9.2 per cent), Automotive (8.3 per cent), and Industrial Manufacturing (8.1 per cent) sectors. Consequently, it remains a worry for companies where political mandates and technological alterations to business models exert a fundamental influence.

Relative to the prior year, the most notable escalation in WACC was recorded in the Real Estate sector (+1.7 percentage points), Media & Telecommunications sector (+1.3 percentage points), and Consumer Markets sector (+1.3 percentage points). Nonetheless, no sector exhibits a reduction in WACC.

Inflation continues to be above the European Central Bank's mid-term consumer-oriented inflation target

The primary factors contributing to this situation include elevated energy costs, limited availability of raw resources, and geopolitical conflicts, notably the Russian invasion of Ukraine. Short-term inflation expectations have decreased; but, long-term inflation expectations, benchmarked against the central banks' target of 2.0 per cent, have stabilised at a considerably elevated level.

Assessments from more than 320 companies

A total of 322 companies engaged in this year's Cost of Capital research. Among the participating companies, 240 are located in Germany, including 65 per cent of the DAX-40 companies and 46 per cent of the MDAX companies. The response rate of corporations highlights the practical significance of our annual Cost of Capital Study.

REVIEW QUESTIONS

Objective-Type Questions

1. State whether true (T) or false (F):
   (a) Depreciation is included in the cash flow. ☐
   (b) Cash flow is considered only on after-tax basis. ☐
   (c) Average cost of capital is the weighted sum of cost of equity, cost of debt and cost of retained earnings. ☐
   (d) Cost of retained earnings is included in the cost of equity. ☐
2. Choose the correct answer:
   (a) International capital budgeting incorporates:
      (i) only financial factors
      (ii) financial and non-financial factors
      (iii) only the non-financial factors
   (b) Cost of new debt:
      (i) includes floatation cost
      (ii) does not include floatation cost
      (iii) does not include taxes
   (c) Free land and building given by the host-country government is
      (i) not included in the initial cash flow
      (ii) included in the initial cash flow
      (iii) added to the initial cash flow

(d) Higher exchange rate risk/political risk
  (i) adds to the cost of capital
  (ii) lessens the cost of capital
  (iii) bears no influence on the cost of capital

(e) Investment proposal is accepted if:
  (i) break-even salvage value is greater than the actual salvage value
  (ii) break-even salvage value is lower than the actual salvage value
  (iii) none of these

(f) The maximum amount of consideration value in M&As is equal to:
  (i) the product of EPS of the target company and the price-earning ratio of the acquiring firm
  (ii) the wealth of the merged firm during the pre-merger period
  (iii) none of these

Short-Answer Questions

1. Do you agree that the NPV rule is better than the IRR rule for international capital budgeting?
2. "Parent's interest dominates while making capital budgeting analysis." Explain.
3. How do you treat the use of blocked funds for calculating the initial cash flow?
4. How do you calculate the cost of debt and cost of equity?
5. Is it correct to say that cost of capital varies between domestic and international capital budgeting?

Long-Answer Questions

1. How do you compute the cash flow in international capital budgeting?
2. Explain the various methods of estimating terminal cash flow.
3. Explain the Adjusted Present Value approach.
4. How do you evaluate M&As? Explain the role of consideration value in this respect.

Numerical Problems

1. The cost of the subsidiary project is US $ 20 million. It is financed through different modes of funds. The parent unit makes an investment for $ 12 million. A sum of $ 3 million is drawn out of retained earnings and another sum of $ 2 million is drawn out of the blocked funds. The subsidiary borrows $ 2 million from the host country market. The remaining $ 1 million is in the form of free land and building supplied by the host country government. Find out the amount of initial investment from the viewpoint of the parent unit.
2. Calculate the operating cash flow (US $) on the basis of the following data:

   (a) Sales in the domestic market = US $ 14 million
   (b) Export = US $ 4 million

(c) Replacement of parent's export = US $ 2 million
(d) Parent's export of components to subsidiary = US $ 3 million
(e) Royalty payment by subsidiary = US $ 0.5 million
(f) Dividend flow to the parent = US $ 0.5 million

3. Find the break-even salvage value if:

(a) Initial investment = $ 30 million
(b) The net cash inflow during the first and the second year respectively = $ 20 million and $ 15 million
(c) Discount rate = 10%

4. A project of the foreign subsidiary has a beta of 1.10, the risk-free return of 15%, and the required return on the market being estimated at 20 per cent. Find out the project's cost of capital.

5. A firm with an overall debt-equity ratio of 1:2, an after-tax cost of debt at 7 per cent, and cost of equity capital at 15 per cent is taking up a project abroad. The debt-equity norm of the foreign project is not different but the systematic risk pulls down the cost of equity to 12 per cent. Again, there is no change in the expected after-tax cost of debt. Calculate the weighted average cost of capital.

6. Firm A absorbs Firm B on the basis of the following data:

(a) Present earnings: Firm A—$ 40,000, Firm B—$ 18,000
(b) No. of shares: Firm A—5,000, Firm B—3,000
(c) EPS: Firm A—$ 8.0, Firm B—$ 6.0
(d) Market price of shares: Firm A—$ 40.0, Firm B—$ 21.0
(e) Price-earning ratio: Firm A—5.0, Firm B—3.50

Find out the gain to Firm A if the consideration price is $ 24.0 per share.

REFERENCES

Booth, L.D. (1982), Capital Budgeting Frameworks for the Multinational Corporation, *Journal of International Business Studies*, XIII, 113–123.

Buckley, A. (1996), *Multinational Finance*, 3rd ed., New Delhi, Prentice-Hall of India, p. 345.

England, G.W. and R. Lee (1971), Organisational Goals and Expected Behaviour among American, Japanese and Korean Managers—A comparative study, *Academy of Management Journal*, III, 425–438.

Friend, I. and M. Blume (1970), Measurement of Portfolio Performance under Uncertainty, *American Economic Review*, LX, 561–575.

Lessard, D.R. (1979), Evaluating International Projects: An adjusted present value approach, in D.R. Lessard (Ed.), *International Financial Management: Theory and Application*, Boston, Mass., Warren Gorham & Lamont, 577–592.

Rodriguez, R.M. and E.E. Carter (1984), *International Financial Management*, Englewood Cliffs, Prentice Hall, Chap. 17.

Solomon, E. (1963), *The Theory of Financial Management*, New York, Columbia University Press, pp. 91–106.

Stanley, M.T. and S.B. Block (1983), An Empirical Study of Management and Financial Variables Influencing Capital Budgeting Decisions for Multinational Companies in the 1980s, *Management International Review*, XXIII, 61–72.

SUGGESTED FURTHER READING

Bugnion, J.R. (1965), Capital Budgeting and International Corporations, *Quarterly Journal of AIESEC International*, I, 30–54.

Shapiro, A.C. (1978), Capital Budgeting for the Multinational Corporation, *Financial Management*, VII, 7–16.

Solnik, B. (1988), *International Investments*, Reading (Mass.), Addison Wesley.

Stonehill, A.I. and L. Nathanson (1968), Capital Budgeting and the Multinational Corporation, *California Management Review*, XI, 39–54.

CHAPTER 13

Evaluation and Management of Political Risk

Learning Objectives

Desire to invest abroad does depend on the cash flow. However, the political environment prevailing in the host country figures very significant in this respect. The present chapter, therefore, discusses some of the important aspects of political risk. In particular, it:

- Delineates the meaning and forms of political risk.
- Explains how political risk is assessed/evaluated.
- Shows how political risk is managed at different levels of operation.

MNCs' long-term investment involves essentially, among other things, the assessment of political risk in the host country. If such risk is unusually large, an MNC may not go for investment in the host country despite large cash benefits. However, if it is within reasonable limits, efforts are made to manage it in order to make the investment a successful venture. The present chapter thus acquaints the readers with the nature of political risk, its assessment and with its management.

MEANING AND FORMS OF POLITICAL RISK

Political risk is a sudden and unanticipated change in the political set-up.

There is no precise definition of political risk. However, according to Thunell (1977), political risk is said to exist when sudden and unanticipated changes in political set-up in the host country lead to unexpected discontinuities that bring about changes in the very business environment and corporate performance. For example, if a rightist party wins election in the host country and the policy towards foreign investment turns liberal, it would create a positive impact on the operation of the MNCs. On the other hand, if a leftist party comes to power, it will have a negative impact on the operation of the MNCs. It is the negative impact that is normally the focus of attention of the transnational investors.

For a long period, political risk was narrowly interpreted in terms of expropriation of assets but for the past few decades, political risk has come to have a wider coverage of including also risk from ethnic, racial, religious or civil strife, political corruption and blackmail, etc. Stephen Kobrin (1982) classifies political risk as macro or country-specific risk, and micro or firm-specific risk. The macro political risk affecting all foreign firms in a country emerges on account of expropriation, ethnic and other strife, currency inconvertibility, and refusal of debt, etc. The micro-political risk affecting a particular industry or firm emerges on account of conflict between bona fide objectives of the host government and the operation of the MNC or on account of corruption which has become a way of life in many countries. Some of these forms need some explanation and are discussed in the sections which follow.

Expropriation

Expropriation means seizure of private property by the government. Confiscation is similar as expropriation. But the difference between the two is that expropriation involves payment of compensation, while confiscation does not involve such payments. International law provides protection to foreigners' property. It provides also for compensation in case of unavoidable seizure but the process of compensation is often lengthy and cumbersome. A firm usually requires going-concern value tied to the present value of lost future cash flows. On the other hand, the expropriating government prefers the depreciated historical book value which is lower in the eyes of the firm. The reason behind expropriation has been mainly political turmoil or specific political ideology. In the post-War period, foreign and domestic firms were nationalised in China and Eastern Europe after the imposition of the communist regime. The same factor was responsible for nationalisation of private sector firms in Cuba in 1960. However, sometimes it is economic compulsion which motivates expropriation. The Swedish government nationalised the ship-building industry at a time when this industry was hit hard by world-wide recession (Walters and Monsen, 1981). An estimate reveals that around 12 per cent of all foreign investment made in 1967 was nationalised within less than a decade (Jodice, 1980). There are still subtler forms of expropriation. For example, when Colonel Qadaffi headed Libya in 1969, wages as well as taxes were revised upward. Bank accounts of ESSO were seized, and the government acquired majority interest in foreign enterprises (Schnitzer, et al., 1985). They are the instances of domestication which is a subtler form of expropriation.

> Expropriation means seizure of property by the government after paying compensation. Confiscation does not involve compensation.

Currency Inconvertibility

Sometimes the host government enacts a law prohibiting foreign companies from taking their money out of the country or exchanging the host-country currency for any other currency. This could more appropriately be called a financial form of

Currency inconvertibility means prohibiting exchange of currency for other currency.

political risk as the reasons are both economic and political. Economic factors are concerned with the balance of payments problem while the political factor manifests itself in drastic changes in the internal politics of the country. The government of Nigeria imposed such restrictions in order to serve its economic and political objectives.

Credit Risk

Credit risk involves refusal to repay debt.

Refusal to honour a financial contract with a foreign company or to honour a foreign debt comes under this form of political risk. The reason is sometimes economic as when Mexico expressed its inability to repay its debt in the early 1980s but sometimes the political reasons are more prominent. When Khomeini came to power in Iran, the government refused to pay its debt on the ground that the loans were signed during Shah's regime (Micallef, 1981).

Risk from Ethnic, Religious or Civil Strife

Macro-political risk arises also on account of war and violence and racial, ethnic, religious, or civil strife within a country. Some recent examples of such risks are the slaughter in Bosnia and Herzegovina, the break-down of local authority in Somalia and Rwanda, and the upsurge of Islamic fundamentalism in Algeria and Egypt. Such developments become a major political risk for the MNCs operating in these countries.

Conflict of Interest

The interest of the MNCs is normally different from the interest of the host government. The former manifests in the maximisation of corporate wealth, while the latter is evident in the welfare of the economy in general and of the citizens in particular. It is the conflicting interest that gives rise to the micro political risk. To elaborate the nature of conflict it may be said that the government of the host country desires to have a sustainable growth rate, price stability, comfortable balance of payments, etc. but the policy of the MNCs operating there is sometimes found to be interfering with the smooth implementation of this policy. For example, transfer of funds by MNCs may influence the money supply and may cause inflation or deflation in the country. The MNCs may adopt transfer-pricing techniques that may cause loss of tax revenue. Similarly, the payment of an exorbitant amount of royalty, etc. by the subsidiary may worsen the balance of payments.

It is not simply the economic issues but also non-economic issues, such as national security, etc. that are the source of conflict. The US government did not permit the Japanese to purchase Fairchild Industries on grounds of national security.

Corruption

Corruption is endemic in many host countries, as a result of which MNCs have to face serious problems. McNulty (1994) gives an example of Cambodia where greedy bureaucrats created problems for the foreign firms. The foreign firms in Kenya had to sell a part of the equity to powerful politicians there (Eiteman, et al., 1995). Transparency International has surveyed 85 countries and has brought out the Corruption Perception Index. Many countries rank high on this index. This is perhaps the reason that in February 1999, 34 countries including the OECD members and five others signed a convention to ban bribery of foreign public officials in international business transactions (*The Economic Times*, 1999).

> Transparency International is a non-governmental organisation dedicated to increasing governmental accountability and curbing national and international corruption. Founded in 1993, it defines corruption as the abuse of public office for private gain. It works to ensure that the agendas of international corporations give high priority in their programmes to curbing corruption and strives to develop coherent international norms to fight and prevent corruption, especially in the field of auditing and international finance. Presently, the OECD too is taking up this issue after the Convention on Combating Bribery of Foreign Public Officials in International Business Transactions.
>
> *Source:* World Investment Report: 1999, p. 142.

EVALUATION OF POLITICAL RISK

Assessment of political risk is an important step before a firm undertakes to do business abroad because if such risks in a country are very high, the firm would not like to operate in that country. If the risk is moderate or low, the firm will operate in that country but with a suitable political-risk management strategy, but no such strategy can be formulated until one assesses the magnitude of the political risk. The assessment may be either qualitative or quantitative.

Qualitative Approach

> Qualitative assessment of risk involves gathering of information and analysing it.

Qualitative approaches involve interpersonal contact. People are often available who are well-acquainted with the political structure of a particular country or region. They may be persons within the enterprise, particularly those who are posted in that area or academics, or journalist or employees of foreign offices of the government of the host country. This approach has become common despite the fact that different persons may present different versions of the same fact. Kraar (1980) has mentioned the experience of Gulf Oil that hired persons from government and universities to know whether investment in Angola would be safe. The experts said "yes" and the investment turned out to be a successful venture even in the Angolan Marxist regime.

Sometimes a company sends a team of experts for on-the-spot study of the political situation in a particular country. This step is taken only after a preparatory study yields a favourable result. This method gives a more reliable picture but is always subject to availability of correct information from the local people in the host country.

The qualitative approach involves also the examination and interpretation of diverse secondary facts and figures. On the past trends of events, future trends are assessed (Kramer, 1981). For this purpose, companies maintain exclusively a risk-analysis division. Exxon has been found doing this job in terms of specific influence groups, such as politicians, labour unions and the military that influence the political stability of the country (Schnitzer, et al., 1985).

Quantitative Models

Quantitative approach uses quantitative techniques.

Quantitative tools are also used to estimate political risk. American Can uses a computer programme, known as 'primary risk investment screening matrix' involving about 200 variables and reducing them to two numbers. It represents an index of economic viability as also an index of political stability. The variables include, in general, frequency of changes in government, level of violence in the country, number of armed insurrections, conflicts with other nations, and economic factors such as inflation rate, external balance deficit, growth rate of the economy, etc.

Stobaugh (1969) uses a decision-tree approach to find out the probability of nationalisation. He begins his analysis from the very contention whether there will be a change in the government. If there is change, the new government may or may not go in for nationalisation. If it goes in for nationalisation, the question that arises is whether it will pay adequate compensation. Thus in each possible event, there are many possible sub-events. Probabilities of the occurring of events are indicated along the tree branches. Probabilities are multiplied along the branches and then they are summed up.

Example: There is 50 per cent probability of change in government and 50 per cent probability for no change in government. If the government changes, there is 40 per cent probability for nationalisation and 60 per cent probability for no nationalisation. Again, if there is nationalisation, there is 60 per cent probability for adequate compensation and 40 per cent probability for inadequate compensation. With these figures, the probability of nationalisation without adequate compensation would be:

$$0.5 \times 0.4 \times 0.4 = 0.08$$

Knudsen (1974) uses comparatively measurable variables and not very subjective ones. Notable among his variables are: degree of urbanisation, literacy rate, degree of labour unionism, national resource endowment, infant survival rate, calorie intake, access to civic amenities, per capita GNP, etc. Basing on these variables, he measures the national propensity to expropriate. It is found that Knudsen's measure identified successfully the nationalisation in some Latin American countries.

Haner (1979) uses a scale from zero to seven in order to rate political risk. He groups the factors leading to political risk into two parts—internal and external. The internal factors are fractionalisation of political spectrum, fractionalisation of social spectrum, restrictive measures required to retain power, xenophobia, socio-economic conditions, and strength of radical left government. The external factors on the other hand, are dependence on a hostile major power, and negative influence of regional political forces.

After adding up the rating points, if the total is 19 or below, he is of the view that the political risk is minimal. If the total lies between 20 and 34, the risk may be acceptable but if the total lies between 35 and 44, the risk is supposed to be very high. Lastly, if the total exceeds 44 rating points, it is not advisable to make any investment in that country.

Again, Euromoney (1993) takes into account three types of indicators for rating. The first is the economic indicator which comprises debt service ratio, current account deficit/GNP ratio and external debt/GNP ratio. This indicator has 40 per cent weight. The second indicator known as the credit indicator embraces debt service record and ease of rescheduling. It has 20 per cent weight. The third is the market indicator which has 40 per cent weight. It includes access to the bond market, sell-down of short-term papers and access to the forfaiting market. The Euromoney formula ranks countries from the highest to the lowest risk. For ranking, the highest figure in each category receives full marks for weighting while the lowest receives zero. The scores for other figures are calculated proportionately according to the following formula:

$$\text{Final score} = [\text{weighting}/(\text{maximum figure} - \text{minimum figure})] \times (\text{intermediate figure} - \text{minimum figure})$$

Simon (1982) provides a predictive analysis which he calls an early warning system. The technique involves the selection of lead indicators that would presage the emergence of a particular political risk. For example, continued demonstrations and riots may lead to internal disorder and to overthrow of the government. The early warning may be country-specific or industry-specific. In both cases, the lead indicators are monitored and the results are communicated to the management for evolving adequate strategy. Though there are some other rating methods, MNCs should not rely heavily on the ratings because they do not include an in-depth analysis which is necessary for investment decision. Individual countries must be assessed in detail.

MANAGEMENT OF POLITICAL RISK

The political risk management strategy depends upon the type of risk and the degree of risk the investment carries as also upon the timing of the steps taken. For example, the strategy adopted prior to the investment will be different from that adopted during the life of the project. Again, it will be different if it is adopted after expropriation of assets.

Management Prior to Investment

Investment will prove viable if political risk is managed from the very beginning, even before the investment is made in a foreign land. There are four ways to manage it at this stage.

Integration of risk in capital budgeting

The factor of political risk is included in the very process of capital budgeting. *Firstly*, the discount rate is increased but the problem is that it penalises the flows

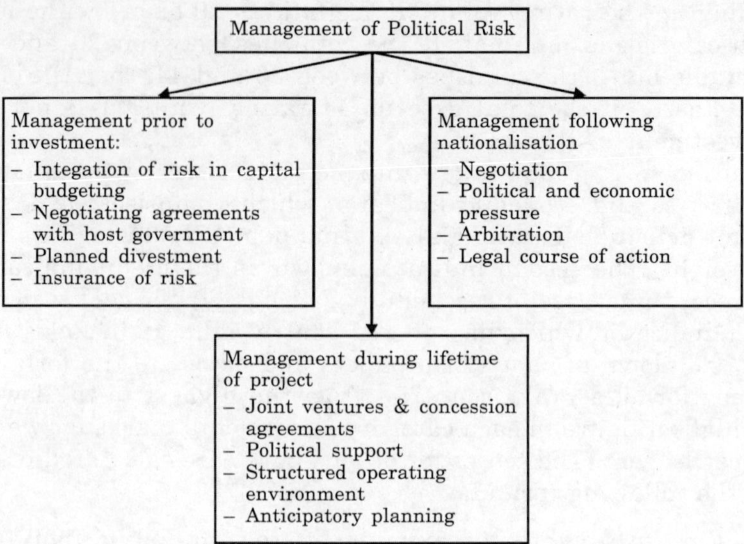

FIGURE 13.1 Management of Political Risk.

in the earlier years of operation, whereas the risk is more pronounced in the later years. *Secondly*, the risk can be reduced through reducing the investment flow from the parent to the subsidiary and filling the gap through local borrowing in the host country. In this strategy, it is possible that the firm may not get the cheapest funds, but the risk will be reduced. The firm will have to make a trade-off between higher financing cost and lower political risk.

Negotiating agreements with the host government

If the investing company enters into an agreement with the host government over different issues prior to making any investment, the latter shall be bound by that agreement and will not back out so the risk will be lower.

Planned divestment

> Planned divestment means gradual shift of control of business to local shareholders.

If the company plans an orderly shifting of ownership and control of business to the local shareholders and it implements the plan, the risk of expropriation will be minimal. In fact, the plan of divestment is negotiated with the host government at the very beginning of investment.

Insurance of risk

The investing firm can take out insurance against political risk. It can be purchased either from governmental agencies or from private financial service organisations, or from private property-centred insurers. The programmes for insurance are either multilateral or bilateral in character. Foreign Credit Insurance Association and Overseas Private Insurance Corporation are the bilateral agencies located in the USA. Besides, there are private property-centred insurance agencies, such as American International Group (AIG), Insurance Company of North America (INA), etc. They offer different types of coverage, although their range is not so wide as that of MIGA.

On the multilateral level, it is the Multilateral Investment Guarantee Agency (MIGA), set up in 1988 as a sister unit of the World Bank, that covers the non-commercial risk. MIGA insures eligible projects against losses relating to currency transfer restrictions, expropriation, war and civil disturbance, and breach of contract. It resolves potential investment disputes before they reach claim status. Its guarantees help investors obtain project finance from banks.

TABLE 13.1 Financial Highlights of MIGA

Financial Results

By fiscal year (US$, millions)	*2020*	*2021*	*2022*	*2023*	*2024*
Gross premium income	232.3	239.3	229.4	245	272.3
Net premium income*	117.1	121.3	116.3	123.9	130.5
Administrative expenses**	61.1	58.7	65	69.6	73.7
Operating income***	56	62.6	51.2	54.3	56.9
Net income	57.2	81.5	27.7	139.4	179.5
Administrative expenses	52%	48%	56%	56%	57%

*Net premium income equals gross premium income and ceding commissions less premium ceded to reinsurers and brokerage costs.

**Administrative expenses include expenses from pension and other post-retirement benefit plans.

***Operating income equals net premium income minus administrative expenses, including pension costs.

TABLE 13.2 Capital Measures

By fiscal year (US$, millions)	*2020*	*2021*	*2022*	*2023*	*2024*
Total economic capital*	756	768	759	773	811
Shareholders' equity	1,335	1,474	1,539	1,706	1,892
Operating capital**	1,591	1,724	1,777	1,923	2,103
Administrative expenses to net premium income ratio	47.50%	44.50%	42.70%	40.20%	38.60%
Risk capital***	1,001	1,054	1,083	1,092	1,140
Risk capital/operating capital	62.90%	61.10%	61.00%	56.80%	54.20%

*Amount of capital used in support of the guarantee portfolio as well as the investment portfolio and operational risk.

**Comprising paid-in capital, retained earnings/accumulated other comprehensive income/(loss) and insurance portfolio reserve, net.

***Risk metric and defined as the sum of total economic capital and buffer capital, with the latter computed using a stress testing tool developed around multiple macroeconomic and country-specific scenarios.

Source: www.miga.org, Annual Report 2024

Risk Management During Lifetime of the Project

Management of risk during the pre-investment phase lessens the intensity of risk but does not eliminate it. So the risk management process continues even when the project is in operation. There are a few ways to handle the risk in this phase.

Joint-ventures and concession agreements

In a joint-venture agreement, local shareholders participate who have a political lobby to pressurise the government to take a decision in their favour or in favour of the enterprise. In case of concession agreements that are found mainly in mineral exploration, the government of the host country retains ownership of the property and grants lease to the producer. The government is interested in earning from the venture and so it does not cancel the agreement. However, this is not a permanent solution. When the technology becomes standardised, the host government often cancels the agreement. Again, if a new government is formed, there is every possibility for the cancellation of the agreement concluded by the previous regime.

Concession agreements, often found in mineral exploration, involve leasing assets to foreign producers.

Political support

International companies sometimes act as a medium through which the host government fulfils its political needs. As long as political support is provided by the home-country government, the assets of the investing company are safe. However, such a relationship may change and the political alliance may be disturbed when a new government is formed. So the maintenance of political support is the key to managing political risk.

Structured operating environment

Political risk can be reduced through creating a linkage of dependency between the operation of the firm in a high-risk country and the operation of other units of the same firm in other countries. If the unit in a high-risk country is dependent on sister units in other countries for the supply of technology or raw material or for marketing of its products, or in other words, so long dependency is maintained, the former is normally not nationalised because the high-risk unit will not be in a position to operate without the imported technology or raw material. In fact, this was an important reason that the international oil companies operated in the Middle East without fear for a long time but when the host governments in the Middle East came to possess the necessary skill, many of those companies were nationalised.

Structured operating environment means creating a linkage of dependency between different units of a firm located in different countries.

Anticipatory planning

It is a fact that the investing company takes the necessary precautions against political risk prior to or after the investment but it is of utmost importance that the measures to be taken should be set in place well in advance. Gonzalez and Villanueva (1992) call it crisis planning. They give an example of the Philippines during the Marcos regime. Years before the 1986 revolution, the foreign companies began to foresee the fall of Marcos. They began assessing every move of the opposition and took the necessary measures well in advance.

Risk Management Following Nationalisation

Despite care taken by the international firms to minimise the impact of political risk, there are occasions when nationalisation takes place. In such cases, the investing company tries to minimise the effects of such a drastic measure, through many courses of action.

Negotiation

The investing company negotiates with the host government on various issues and shows its willingness to support the policy and programmes of the latter. Sometimes the investing company foregoes the majority control in order to placate the host government (Hoskins, 1970).

Political and economic pressure

After failure of negotiation with the host government, the investing company tries to put political and economic pressure. Embargo on trade is one of the examples but there are occasions when such pressures deepen the rift. Thus the firm should be cautious before resorting to such measures.

Arbitration

If nationalisation is not reversed through negotiation and politico-economic pressure, a firm may go in for arbitration. It involves the help of a neutral third party who mediates and asks for the payment of compensation. There are, of course, cases where the host government does not honour the verdict of the arbitrator.

Legal course of action

When arbitration fails, the only way out is to approach the court of law. International law suggests that the company has, first of all, to seek justice in the host country itself. If it is not satisfied with the judgement of the court, the company can go to the international court of justice for fixation of adequate compensation. However, there are occasions when the host government does not honour the verdict of the court. For example, the Cuban Government failed to pay compensation to US companies it had expropriated during 1959–1961 (Globerman, 1986).

SUMMARY

- Political risk arises when unanticipated changes in the political set-up influence the very performance of a firm. It may be a macro risk affecting all firms in the country or it may be a micro risk affecting a particular industry or firm. Expropriation of assets, currency inconvertibility, credit risks, risks on account of ethnic, religious or civil strife, corruption and conflict of interest are some of the major forms of political risk.
- It is necessary to evaluate risk before making a foreign investment. The evaluation involves a qualitative as well as a quantitative approach. The qualitative approach involves interpersonal contact, on-the-spot study or interpretation of secondary facts and figures. The quantitative models on the other hand, try to make a precise estimate.

- The strategy of political risk management depends upon the type, degree, and phase of the risk. The steps taken prior to investment consist of integration of risk factor in the very process of capital budgeting, negotiation with the host government, planned divestment, insurance coverage of risk, etc. During the operation of the project, the MNCs manage risk through joint-venture and concession agreement, political support from the home government and through creating intrafirm dependency linkages. Anticipatory planning is significant in this respect.
- If the firm is nationalised, it goes in for negotiation or for economic and political pressure. When these do not work, the firm opts for arbitration and when this too fails, law courts are the only alternative. But unfortunately, the verdict of the court also sometimes remains ineffective.

CASE STUDY 1

POLITICAL TURMOIL AND FDI IN PAKISTAN DURING LATE 2000s

Musharraf, coming to power through the 1999-coup, was re-elected as President of Pakistan for a second quinquennium in October 2007 in a controversial parliamentary ballot. Nevertheless, popular discontent with Musharraf was there that grew over time. Tensions culminated in November 2007 after he declared a state of emergency. The Supreme Court announced that it had to rule on cases lodged against his candidacy. He retained his dual position of President and Chief of Army at the time of the election, which was viewed as a constitutional breach. Again, the dismissal of Supreme Court judges and appointment of his own supporters was another event in the chain. Musharraf was able to ensure that the final ruling on the presidential polls went in his favour. Parliamentary elections took place in February 2008, and the opposition parties PPP and PML-N secured the most seats. These secular parties pledged to form an alliance in the new parliament. Musharraf stated that he would work with the newly elected parliament. The two opposition parties, however, lacked the two-thirds majority required to carry out their campaign pledges, such as reinstating the judges and impeaching Musharraf, although they could strengthen the alliance by adding additional parties. Nevertheless, there was also a long history of animosity between the PPP and the PML-N, which made the alliance extremely fragile. The process of political infighting could cause ongoing instability and high levels of violence. In the longer run, however, the elections could lead to real political improvements.

Pakistan's support for the US "war on terror", while unpopular domestically, brought valuable economic and military assistance. The opposition parties seemed willing to support continued cooperation with the United States. Nevertheless, the US would like to see progress in its war on terror, especially considering the upcoming presidential elections in the US. This is why it interfered in the coalition talks. This could cause tensions in the US-Pakistan relationship and also between the coalition parties.

The intensity of the conflict with India over Kashmir had substantially reduced after the signing of the cease-fire in 2003. Both India and Pakistan regularly voiced their commitment to lasting peace. Nevertheless, the Kashmir conflict remained unresolved and there was a latent risk that it could lead to war between the two nuclear-armed neighbours.

Capital inflows, both foreign direct investment and portfolio investment, did offset partly the shortfall on the current account, yet they were badly affected by the political turmoil during the elections. In addition, risk appetite could be harmed as a result of the turmoil on the financial markets and the government of Pakistan made little progress with regard to its privatisation programme.

To be precise, foreign direct investment ebbed from US $ 4,163 million in 2006 to US $ 3,839 million in 2007 and US $ 3,454 million in 2008. Similarly, foreign portfolio investment sagged from US $ 2,075 million in 2007 to US $ 1,333 million in 2008.

Source: Based on Rabobank (Netherlands) report.

QUESTIONS

1. Comment on the nature of political turmoil in Pakistan during 2007.
2. How do you correlate the political turmoil and the inflow of foreign investment in Pakistan?

CASE STUDY 2

POLITICAL RISKS IN MINERALS-RICH HOST COUNTRIES

1. Panama: The Cobre Mine Dispute: In December 2023, the Panamanian government ordered the Canadian firm First Quantum Minerals to halt operations at the Cobre Panama copper mine, citing breaches in environmental and financial commitments. This decision disrupted global copper supplies and highlighted Panama's growing resource nationalism. The government sought to renegotiate terms to ensure more revenue and environmental compliance. This move underscored the risks of sudden regulatory changes in host countries, impacting not only investors but also global supply chains reliant on copper (1).

2. Indonesia: Nickel Export Restrictions: Indonesia has cemented its position as a dominant global nickel supplier, essential for electric vehicle (EV) batteries. The government imposed export restrictions on raw nickel ore to boost domestic processing and value addition. Such policies, rooted in resource nationalism, aim to attract foreign investment and spur economic growth. However, they create market inefficiencies and heighten price volatility, impacting EV manufacturers globally. In 2024, the government considered extending similar restrictions to copper, further complicating global mineral supply chains (2).

3. Democratic Republic of Congo (DRC): Instability in Cobalt Mining The DRC produces over 70% of the world's cobalt, critical for battery production. However, political instability, corruption, and human rights violations have marred mining operations. Frequent changes in mining laws, demands for higher royalties, and socio-political unrest jeopardize investments. Multinational companies face reputational risks while navigating compliance with stringent environmental, social, and governance (ESG) criteria (2).

4. Chile: Lithium Reforms and Resource Nationalism: Chile, a leading lithium producer, enacted reforms mandating the use of Direct Lithium Extraction (DLE) technology to minimize water usage in the Atacama Desert. While these measures aim to balance environmental concerns with economic goals, they pose technical and financial challenges. Investors face uncertainties due to the high costs and nascent stage of DLE technology. Additionally, the government's push for greater state involvement in lithium mining has created tensions with private firms (1) (2).

5. China's Strategic Moves in Rare Earths: China dominates the global supply of rare earth elements, processing 60–90% of these critical minerals. To maintain its strategic edge, Beijing has implemented export restrictions on gallium, germanium, and graphite. These policies, aimed at countering Western technological advancements, exacerbate supply chain vulnerabilities for industries reliant on these materials. China's dominance highlights how geopolitical motives can amplify risks for importing nations dependent on a single supplier (2).

Source:

1. White & Case LLP: Geopolitics in Mining and Metals 2024.
2. Eurasia Group: The Fight for Critical Minerals: Top Risks of 2024.

Implications and Challenges
Political risks in minerals-rich countries have far-reaching consequences:

Economic Volatility: Sudden regulatory changes and export restrictions disrupt global markets, driving up prices for critical minerals.

Environmental Concerns: Stricter ESG requirements add layers of complexity for mining firms, which must balance profitability with sustainability.

Geopolitical Tensions: The race to secure critical minerals has intensified competition between nations, particularly the U.S., EU, and China, each pursuing industrial policies to reduce dependency on rivals.

Investment Risks: Unpredictable policy shifts deter foreign investments, especially in regions where legal and political frameworks are unstable.

Questions for Discussion

1. How can multinational corporations mitigate risks associated with resource nationalism in minerals-rich host countries?
2. What role do ESG criteria play in shaping investment decisions in the mining sector?
3. How do export restrictions by countries like China impact global supply chains and international relations?
4. What strategies should importing nations adopt to diversify their sources of critical minerals?

REVIEW QUESTIONS

Objective-Type Questions

1. State whether true (T) or false (F):

   (a) Expropriation, confiscation and domestication carry the same meaning. ☐

   (b) Confiscation involves payment of compensation. ☐

(c) Domestication is subtler form of expropriation. ☐
(d) Political risk can be managed even prior to making investment. ☐
(e) Planned divestment is an orderly shifting of ownership and control of business. ☐

2. Choose the correct answer:

(a) MIGA covers:
  (i) political risk
  (ii) commercial risk
  (iii) none of these

(b) Structured operating environment means:
  (i) creation of linkages of dependency between the operation of the unit in question and the sister units
  (ii) structuring of cash inflows and outflows
  (iii) creating congenial political environment

(c) Arbitration is adopted:
  (i) prior to any negotiation
  (ii) after negotiation fails
  (iii) after legal course of action fails

Short-Answer Questions

1. Distinguish between micro- and macro-political risk.
2. How is risk integrated in capital budgeting?
3. What do you mean by creation of structured operating environment?
4. Distinguish between expropriation, confiscation and domestication.

Long-Answer Questions

1. What are the different forms of political risk?
2. How is political risk managed?
3. Explain the qualitative and quantitative techniques for evaluating political risk.

REFERENCES

Eiteman, D.K., et al. (1995), *Multinational Business Finance*, Reading (Mass.), Addison-Wesley, Chap. 18.

Euromoney (1993), *The Euromoney Country Risk Method*, London, September.

Globerman, S. (1986), *Fundamentals of International Business Management*, Singapore, Prentice-Hall, p. 131.

Gonzalez, M.V. and E. Villanueva (1992), Steering a Subsidiary through a Political Crisis, *Risk Management*, October, 16–27.

Haner, F.T. (1979), Rating Investment Risks Abroad, *Business Horizons*, XXII, 18–23.

Hoskins, W.R. (1970), How to Counter Expropriation, *Harvard Business Review*, Sept./Oct., 110–112.

Jodice, D.A. (1980), Sources of Change in Third World Regimes for Foreign Direct Investment: 1968–76, *International Organisation*, XXXIV, 177–206.

Knudsen, H. (1974), Explaining the National Propensity to Expropriate: An ecological approach, *Journal of International Business Studies*, V, 54.

Kobrin, S.J. (1982), *Managing Political Risk Assessment: Strategic response to environmental change*, Berkeley, University of California Press, p. 35.

Kraar, L. (1980), The Multinationals Get Smarter about Political Risks, *Fortune*, March 24, 86–100.

Kramer, R.D. (1981), Political Risk Assessment: A brief review of the state of the art, *New International Realities*, VI, 23.

McNulty, S. (1994), Welcome to Cambodia's Business Wilderness, *Asian Wall Street Journal*, Jan. 13, p. 6.

Micallef, J.V. (1981), Political Risk Assessment, *Columbia Journal of World Business*, XVI, 47–52.

Schnitzer, M.C., et al. (1985), *International Business*, Ohio, South Western Publishing Co., Chap. 13.

Simon, J.D. (1982), Political Risk Assessment: Past trends and future prospects, *Columbia Journal of World Business*, XVII, 62–70.

Stobaugh, R. (1969), How to Analyse Foreign Investment Climates, *Harvard Business Review*, Sept./Oct., 100–108.

The Economic Times, Feb. 16, 1999.

Thunell, L. (1977), *Political Risks in International Business*, New York, Praeger, Chap. 1.

Walters, K.D. and R.J. Monsen (1981), The Spreading Nationalisation of European Industry, *Columbia Journal of World Business*, XVI, 64–72.

SUGGESTED FURTHER READING

Brewer, T.L. (1985), *Political Risks in International Business*, New York, Praeger. Ghadar, F., et al. (1983), *Managing International Political Risk: Strategies and techniques*, Washington D.C., Ghadar and Associates.

Sethi, S.P. and K.A.N. Luther (1986), Political Risk Analysis and Direct Foreign Investment: Some problems of definition and measurement, *California Management Review*, Winter, 57–68.

CHAPTER 14

International Portfolio Investment

Learning Objectives

It is not only FDI but also the international portfolio investment or the investment in international securities that is significant from the viewpoint of IFM. The present chapter discusses, first, the fundamental concept of portfolio investment and then its application for international portfolio investment. In particular, the purpose is:

- To discuss the basics of the concept of return and risk.
- To explain the role of systematic and unsystematic risk in this context.
- To show how portfolio of investment is optimised.
- To narrate the benefits and problems of international portfolio investment.
- To identify an optimal international investment portfolio.

The focus of Chapters 11–13 was on foreign direct investment (FDI). This chapter deals with foreign portfolio investment. The two are different in the sense that the former involves the control of foreign enterprise, while the latter is simply interested in the return the investor gets from foreign investment.

The very objective of portfolio investment management is to select an optimal portfolio where the risk-return trade-off is optimal. This denotes a position where return is maximum with a given level of risk or where the risk is minimum with a given level of return. In this context, a very important question is whether international investment helps in achieving an optimal portfolio of assets. If it does, it is also significant to know how international portfolio investment can be optimised. The discussion of these issues forms the subject matter of the present chapter.

CONCEPT OF OPTIMAL PORTFOLIO

There is voluminous literature on the portfolio theory of how to select an optimal portfolio. The readers are advised especially to refer to Markowitz's (1959) model, for its detailed analysis lies beyond the scope of this book. Nevertheless, this chapter provides some basic information regarding the selection of an optimal portfolio by striking a balance between risk and return.

Measurement of Returns

The concept of probability

No finance manager knows in advance what would be the actual returns from an investment. He or she may base his/her decision of the actual outcomes on the basis of probabilities. Probabilities are merely numbers that represent the likelihood of chance of occurrence of various outcomes. For example, if an oil drilling operation has 60 per cent chance for getting oil and 40 per cent chance for not getting oil, one can say that getting oil has a 60 per cent probability and not getting oil has 40 per cent probability. This means that the total probability equals 100 per cent or 1. Thus the probability distribution describes the outcomes and their associated probabilities.

The probability distribution may be either discrete or continuous. The former has only a finite number of outcomes, whereas in case of a continuous distribution, the outcome is not finite. If we say that there is 40 per cent probability for \$ 400 earning and 60 per cent probability for \$ 600 earning, it will be a case of discrete distribution as the outcome is finite. But if we say that there is 40 per cent probability for an earning between \$ 300 and \$ 500 and 60 per cent probability for an earning between \$ 600 and \$ 800, it will be a continuous probability distribution. This is because the outcome is not finite.

Discrete probability distribution has only a finite number of outcomes. Continuous probability distribution does not have it.

In fact, continuous distributions are more realistic descriptions of outcomes, but discrete distributions are normally used for practical applications. This is so since, *first*, it is simpler to use, and *secondly*, probability distributions are estimated on the basis of actual historical data that are usually finite numbers.

Expected return from a single investment

The expected return is the mean of probability distribution.

The expected return is the mean of probability distribution. It is the probability-weighted average of outcomes. In the form of an equation, the expected return is

$$\overline{A} = P_1A_1 + P_2A_2 + P_3A_3 + \ldots + P_nA_n$$

Summing up, we get

$$\overline{A} = \sum_{x=1}^{n} P_x A_x \qquad (14.1)$$

Example: If there is 20 per cent probability for an outcome of \$ 400, 60 per cent probability for an outcome of \$ 600, and 20 per cent probability for an outcome of \$ 900, then the expected value will be:

$$\overline{A} = (0.2 \times 400) + (0.6 \times 600) + (0.2 \times 900) = \$\ 620$$

Expected returns from international investment

In the case of international investment, the estimation of expected returns takes into account also the changes in the exchange rate. And so, the return from a security abroad in terms of home-country currency (HC) is calculated as

$$1 + R_{HC} = [1 + (S_1 - S_0 + I)/S_0] \times (1 + e) \qquad (14.2)$$

where S_0 = host-country currency value of security during t_0; S_1 = host-country currency value of security during t_1; I = income from dividend/interest; and e = the exchange rate changes.

Example: The present value of security in terms of host-country currency is \$ 100 and it goes up to \$ 102 after one year. The interest during the year is \$ 8. Dollar appreciates by 3 per cent, the return in terms of home-country currency

$$R_{HC} = [\{1 + (102 - 100 + 8)/100\} \times 1.03] - 1 = 0.133 = 13.3\%$$

Portfolio return

Portfolio return is the weighted average of the expected return from different securities existing in the portfolio. In a two-security portfolio model, the portfolio return,

$$R_p = R_A W_A + R_B W_B \qquad (14.3)$$

where R is the return, W is the relative share of investment and A and B are the two securities.

PROBLEM 14.1

An Indian investor invests in US bonds with a face value of \$ 10,000. The bonds have a market price of \$ 10,500 by the year-end and fetch \$ 700 as interest during the year. Dollar appreciates by 3 per cent during this period. Simultaneously, the investor invests in German bonds with a face value of 30,000 fetching 3,000 as interest and the market price of the bonds going up to 30,500 during the year. Euro depreciates by 2 per cent during this period. Calculate portfolio return.

Solution

$$[\{1 + (10,500 - 10,000 + 700)/10,000\} \times (1 + 0.03) - 1] \times 0.25 = 0.03840$$
$$[\{1 + (30,500 - 30,000 + 3,000)/30,000\} \times (1 - 0.02) - 1] \times 0.75 = 0.07075$$
$$0.03840 + 0.07075 = 0.10915 = 10.92\%$$

Concept and Measurement of Risk

Risk for a single investment

Risk represents the variance between the actual returns or the *ex post* returns and the expected returns or the *ex ante* returns. After the computation of the expected value or the mean, it is necessary to measure the variance or the deviation of outcomes from the mean. The deviation is known as *dispersion* or the *spread of probability distribution.* There are various dispersion measures; yet, in finance, it is traditionally measured by variance and standard deviation.

Risk represents variance between the actual outcome and the expected return.

Variance is a measure of dispersion of all possible outcomes around the mean. It is typically denoted by the Greek letters σ, as σ^2. In the form of an equation,

$$\sigma^2 = P_1(A_1 - \bar{A})^2 + P_2(A_2 - \bar{A})^2 + \ldots + P_n(A_n - \bar{A})^2$$

Summing up, we get

$$\sigma^2 = \sum_{x=1}^{n} P_x(A_x - \bar{A})^2 \qquad (14.4)$$

Again, standard deviation is the square root of variance. The standard deviation,

$$\sigma = (\text{Var})^{1/2} \qquad (14.5)$$

Example: There is 20 per cent probability for boom when the returns may be \$ 800. There is 20 per cent probability for depression when returns may fall to \$ 400. But there is 60 per cent probability for normal trend when the returns are expected to be \$ 600. Find out the expected value, variance and standard deviation.

Expected value

$$(0.2 \times 400) + (0.6 \times 600) + (0.2 \times 800) = \$\ 600$$

Variance

$$(0.2)\ (400 - 600)^2 + (0.6)\ (600 - 600)^2 + (0.2)\ (800 - 600)^2 = 16{,}000$$

Standard deviation

$$(16{,}000)^{1/2} = 126.49$$

Portfolio risk

The foregoing discussion shows how the return and the risk of a particular investment are computed. The investor tries to reduce the risk involved in the existing portfolio through diversification. Diversification means simultaneous investment in other securities: may be within the country or may be outside the country. But diversification will help reduce risk only when the covariance/correlation between the existing portfolio and the new portfolio is negative, which means that if returns in one set are increasing, they are falling in the other set. If it is positive, meaning that if returns in one set are increasing, they are increasing in the other set too, then diversification will raise the risk and it will be futile to attempt any diversification. Again, if covariance is zero or the returns from the two sets of investment are uncorrelated, it does not establish any linear relationship between the two sets of investment. Here it is very much relevant to know what is covariance and correlation.

Covariance is a statistical concept that relates movement in one set of variables to the movement in the other set of variables. The covariance between two sets of returns, A_1 and A_2 can be shown as:

Covariance represents relationship between the movements of two variables.

$$\text{Cov}(A_1, A_2) = \sum_{t=1}^{N} P_t(A_{1t} - \bar{A}_1)(A_{2t} - \bar{A}_2) \qquad (14.6)$$

Similarly, correlation, which is denoted by small Greek letter rho (ρ), serves the same purpose. The difference between covariance and correlation is that while the former is sensitive to the particular units of measurement, the latter removes this sensitivity. Covariance can take on any value, whereas the correlation coefficient can exist only between minus 1 and plus 1. The correlation coefficient

$$\rho_{1,2} = \text{Cov } A_1, A_2/\sigma_1\sigma_2 \tag{14.7}$$

After covariance/correlation is established between the existing portfolio and the new investment, it is easy to measure the risk of the entire portfolio that includes both the existing portfolio and the new portfolio. Different sets of portfolio have their weight, w, meaning how much of the total investment they represent. Portfolio risk, in terms of standard deviation, is

$$\sigma_p = \left[w_{A_1}^2 \text{ Var. } A_1 + w_{A_2}^2 \text{ Var. } A_2 + 2(w_{A_1})(w_{A_2})(\text{Cov. } A_1, A_2)\right]^{1/2} \tag{14.8}$$

Example: Calculate the portfolio return and risk using the following data:

Probability of occurrence of returns	*Existing portfolio (%)*	*New portfolio (%)*
0.30	10	8
0.30	7	12
0.40	13	7

Expected return

Existing portfolio = 0.3 × 10.0 + 0.3 × 7.0 + 0.4 × 13.0 = 10.3%

New portfolio = 0.3 × 8.0 + 0.3 × 12.0 + 0.4 × 7 = 8.8%

Portfolio return (assuming 70% investment on the existing portfolio and 30% on the new portfolio)

$$0.7 \times 10.3 + 0.3 \times 8.8 = 9.85\%$$

Variance and standard deviation

Existing portfolio: $\text{Var} = 0.3(10.0 - 10.3)^2 + 0.3(7.0 - 10.3)^2 + 0.4(13.0 - 10.3)^2$

$= 6.21$

$\text{SD} = 2.492$

New portfolio: $\text{Var} = 0.3(8.0 - 8.8)^2 + 0.3(12.0 - 8.8)^2 + 0.4(7.0 - 8.8)^2$

$= 4.56$

$\text{SD} = 2.14$

Covariance A_1, A_2

$$0.3(-0.3)(-0.8) + 0.3(-3.3)(3.2) + 0.4(2.7)(-1.8) = -5.040$$

Correlation coefficient A_1, A_2 = – 0.945

Portfolio risk in terms of variance

$$(0.7)^2\ (6.21) + (0.3)^2\ (4.56) + 2(0.7)\ (0.3)\ (-5.040) = 1.3365$$

Thus the above example shows that since the covariance/correlation coefficient between the existing portfolio and the new portfolio is negative, diversification through investment in the new portfolio reduces the risk (in terms of variance) from 6.21 to 1.3365. In terms of SD, it reduces from 2.49 to 1.16.

PROBLEM 14.2

An Indian investor invests in American and British securities in proportion of 75 per cent and 25 per cent. The expected return is 15 per cent from the former and 12 per cent from the latter. The risk manifesting in variance is 15 in US securities and 18 in British securities and their covariance is –2.25. Find out (a) portfolio return and (b) portfolio risk.

Solution

Portfolio Return:
Using Eq. (14.3), we obtain:

$$0.75 \times 0.15 + 0.25 \times 0.12 = 0.1425 = 14.25\%$$

Portfolio risk in terms of standard deviation:
Applying Eq. (14.8), we have

$$[(0.75)^2(15) + (0.25)^2 (18) + 2(0.75)(0.25)(-2.25)]^{1/2}$$

$$= \sqrt{8.71875} = 2.95.$$

Limitation to Diversification: Systematic Risk vs. Unsystematic Risk

We have just seen how portfolio risk could be reduced through diversification. However, diversification reduces only a particular type of risk. From this point of view, a particular asset or a portfolio of asset possesses two types of risk: one being the unsystematic risk that can be diversified away, and the other being the systematic risk that cannot be diversified away through investment in domestic securities.

The unsystematic risk is firm-specific and so simultaneous investment in other securities may lower it. On the other hand, systematic risk is a macro-economic risk. It is inherent in the performance of the economy as a whole. So it is similar for all the securities in the market. This is why it is also known as the *market risk*. It cannot be reduced through diversification in the domestic market although systematic risk too can be reduced through international investment as the macro-economic fundamentals vary in different countries.

> Systematic risk can be reduced through investment in international securities because the macro-economic variables are different in different countries.

When one talks about the systematic risk, it is worth knowing how it is measured. One way to measure the systematic risk of an individual asset or a portfolio of assets is to compare its returns over time with those of the market portfolio. The comparison reflects the asset exposure to the systematic risk factors. However, an asset's systematic risk is denoted by a capital Greek letter, beta (β). It shows how an asset's returns vary with the market portfolio's returns, as compared to the total risk of the market portfolio. In the form of an equation,

$$\beta = \text{Cov}(A_1, \overline{A}_M)/\sigma_M^2 \tag{14.9}$$

where $\overline{A}_M$ is the market portfolio return and σ_M^2 is the total risk of the market portfolio.

The discussion of *beta* involves three situations. *First*, a beta being more than 1 means that the assets adding to the portfolio systematic risk have high covariance with the market returns. *Secondly*, assets reducing portfolio systematic risk will have a low covariance and a beta of less than 1. *Thirdly*, in cases of assets neither increasing nor reducing the portfolio systematic risk, beta is equal to 1. Thus beta is a measure of relative risk as compared to portfolio variance that measures absolute risk. Beta indicates the variability of an asset's returns relative to the market portfolio.

Systematic risk can be avoided to a large extent through investment in risk-free securities. Literally speaking, there is no risk-free security. Even the government securities possess some amount of risk. But for all practical purposes, government securities are known as *risk-free securities*. In such a situation, if an investor invests in the market portfolio, he is prone to the systematic risk. Thus, he will like to invest in the market portfolio only when he gets a higher return than that from a risk-free investment. How much higher the return is required or how much should be the risk premium, it all depends upon the size of beta. Higher the beta, larger will be risk premium and larger will be the required rate of return. The Capital Asset Pricing Model (CAPM) suggests that the total expected return of a security should be the sum of the riskless return and its risk premium. In form of an equation,

$$A_1 = A_f + \beta_1 (\overline{A}_M - A_f) \tag{14.10}$$

When capital market is in equilibrium, Eq. (14.10) is called the security market line (SML).

Example: If risk-free rate of return is 8 per cent, the rate of return on the market portfolio is 12 per cent, the variance of the market portfolio is 200, and covariance between the particular asset and the market portfolio is 300, find out the required rate of return.

Applying Eq. (14.9), we find the systematic risk as

$$\beta = 300/200 = 1.5$$

Again, applying Eq. (14.10), we find the required rate of return,

$$A_1 = 8\% + 1.5(12\% - 8\%) = 14\%$$

PROBLEM 14.3

An Indian investor invests in a particular security that fetches 12 per cent return. The rate of return on the market portfolio is 11 per cent – 3 per cent higher than the risk-free rate. The variance of market portfolio is 150 and the covariance between the security in question and the market portfolio is 300. Find whether the return on the security is lower than the required rate of return?

Solution

$$\beta = 300/150 = 2.0$$

Required rate of return = 8% + 2.0(11% – 8%) = 14.0%

Thus the return on the security in question is lower than the required rate of return.

Optimisation of Portfolio

Optimisation of portfolio means selection of a particular portfolio that involves minimum risk with a given return or maximum return with a given risk. Suppose there are four portfolios—A, B, C and D involving similar amount of investment. Portfolios A, B and C have similar return of 10 per cent, while the risk in respect of them differs—from 1.0 per cent in A, to 1.50 per cent in B, and to 2.0 per cent in C. In the case of portfolio D, the risk is 2.0 per cent as in C, but the rate of return is higher at 13 per cent (see Figure 14.1).

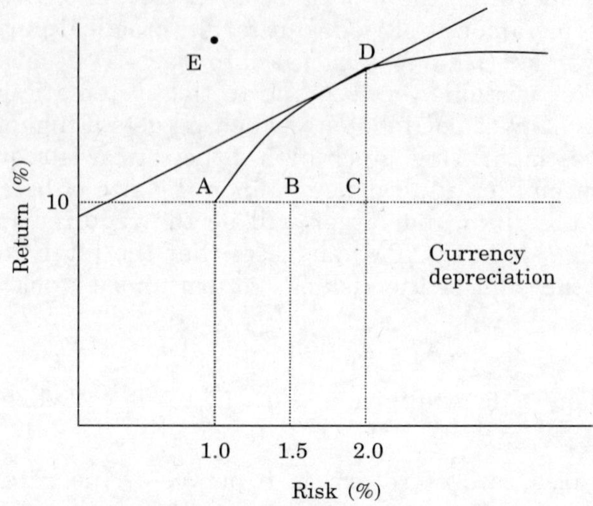

FIGURE 14.1 An Optimal Portfolio.

Thus, among the first three portfolios, A, B and C, portfolio A is the efficient portfolio because it carries the least risk with similar rate of return. Portfolio D is also an efficient portfolio because with the same amount of risk as portfolio C, it has a higher amount of return. The line connecting points A and D, is known as a *line of efficient frontier* which is the locus of efficient portfolios. Portfolio E has a greater return than all other portfolios and also carries lower risk than all other portfolios, but is unobtainable for the amount of investment available with the investor. The other portfolios are not efficient portfolios because either their risk is larger or their return is lower (Figure 14.1).

When the efficient portfolios are identified, how does the investor choose one of them? Given an efficient frontier, the investor chooses one (the optimal portfolio) among them on the basis of the security market line which constitutes various portfolios combining a riskless security and a portfolio of risky securities. The optimal portfolio lies at the tangency point between the security market line and the line of efficient frontier. Portfolio D is the optimal portfolio as shown in Figure 14.1. It represents the largest of expected return to risk ratio.

BENEFITS OF INTERNATIONAL PORTFOLIO INVESTMENT

An investor opts for international portfolio investment because international diversification of portfolio of assets helps achieve a higher risk-adjusted return. This means that an investor is able to reduce risk and raise return through international investment.

Reduction in Risk

International investment is superior to domestic investment insofar as the former helps reduce also the systematic risk. The empirical findings of Hunter and Coggin (1990) show that the intercountry correlation of stock market returns is normally lower than the intracountry correlation. Their study covers ten countries and reveals that the intracountry correlation of stock market returns was 1.0 compared to intercountry correlation ranging between 0.01 and 0.69. The study of Patrick Odier and Bruno Solnik (1993) provides more or less similar results. With the diversification of risk through the inclusion of an international portfolio, the magnitude of risk turns lower.

The reason for such a state of affairs is that the different sectors in an individual economy are in one way or the other interrelated; and as a result, are collectively subject to the same impact of the overall domestic policy. The returns from investment in different sectors of an individual economy respond jointly to prospects for domestic activity and to uncertainty about these prospects. All this manifests in limited independence of behaviour of an individual country's security. The gains from intracountry diversification are thus quite limited.

On the other hand, the macroeconomic fundamentals of different countries differ widely and do not witness exactly the same stage of business cycles. Moreover, different countries have securities of different industries in their stock market transactions. Correlation may be higher in case of intraindustry investment, but it is lower in case of interindustry investment. Thus the correlation of expected returns from investment in different countries is lower than that in case of a single country. All this means that foreign investment generates diversification benefits that cannot be reaped by investing in the domestic country alone.

Better Risk-return Trade-off

The international investment helps raise the return with a given risk and/or helps lower the risk with a given rate of return. This happens because more profitable investment avenues exist in an enlarged universe; and at the same time, the intercountry dissimilarities, as discussed above, reduce the risk. The empirical findings of Eaker and Grant (1990) based on a comparison between domestic investment entirely in the USA on the one hand, and the foreign-mixed investment on the other, reveal that with a gradual increase in foreign portfolio, returns from the investment increased. The process continued till the ratio of the foreign portfolio reached 60 per cent of the total portfolio.

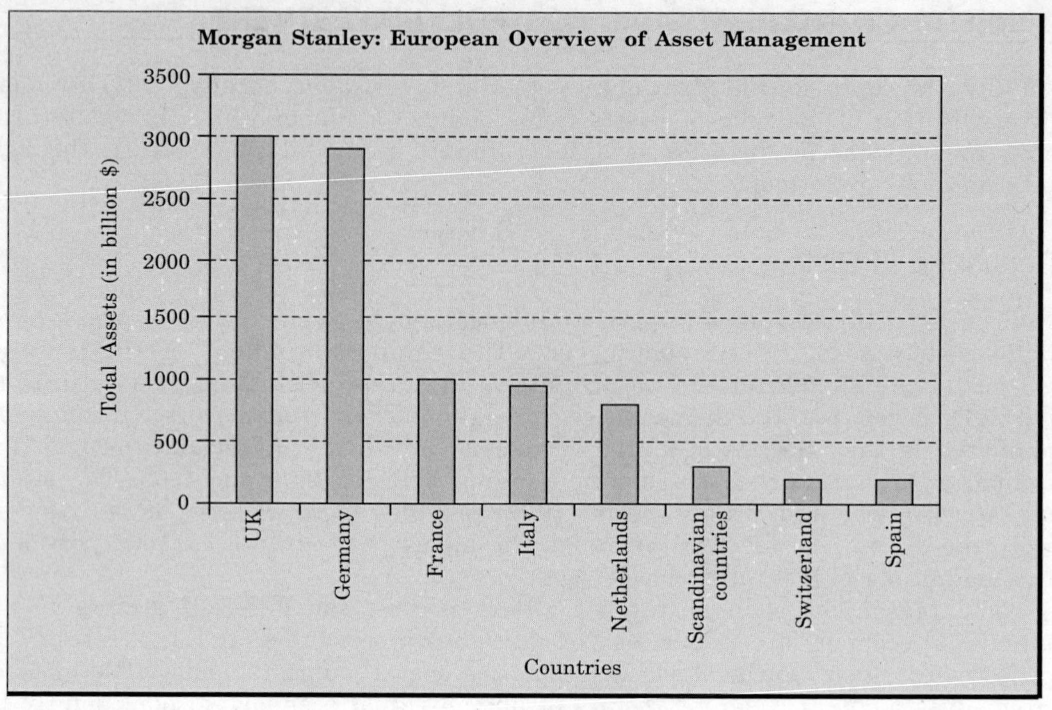

PROBLEMS OF INTERNATIONAL INVESTMENT

It is an established fact that the international diversification of portfolio is gainful. But there are also some problems that mar an optimal international diversification of portfolio. These problems are broadly:

1. Unfavourable exchange rate movement
2. Frictions in international financial market
3. Manipulation of security prices
4. Unequal access to information

Unfavourable Exchange Rate Movement

Exchange rate fluctuations are a critical factor for investors, especially in a floating-rate regime where such changes are common. These variations can directly and indirectly impact the value and returns of foreign investments. For instance, an American investor who purchases Indian securities may find the value of their holdings reduced if the Indian rupee depreciates against the US dollar. This depreciation also leads to a decrease in the returns when converted into US dollars. This represents the direct effect of exchange rate changes on investment. Moreover, exchange rate shifts can also indirectly affect international portfolios. Since the foreign exchange and securities markets are closely connected, a decline in the domestic currency, such as the rupee, can depress the overall stock market. This, in turn, lowers the value of the securities the investor holds, even when assessed in local currency terms.

It is normally expected that if the investor has invested in the securities of many countries, the loss in respect of one country's securities may be averaged out by gain in respect of the securities of other countries, but the study of Eun and Resnick (1984) finds that the diversification of investment among currencies does not substantially reduce the quantum of risk attributable to changes in exchange rate. In short, unfavourable exchange rate changes do have an adverse effect on the value of international portfolio of assets. If this is true, the adverse effects may wipe out the benefits from international diversification of assets. On this issue, Solnik (1988) is of the view that there are many techniques for managing exchange rate exposure that can help maintain the diversification benefits. Moreover, he has found empirically that even without hedging exchange rate exposure, the diversification benefits did exist.

Frictions in International Financial Market

There are market frictions manifesting in governmental controls, varying tax laws and explicit and implicit transaction costs. Governments often try to administer international financial flows through different forms of control mechanisms, such as multiple exchange rates, taxes on international flows and restrictions on the outflow of funds. If such controls persist, foreign investment inflow is hampered despite ample returns/low risk.

Again, varying tax laws and varying tax rates come in the way of international investment. In many countries, capital gains, dividend and interest income are taxed and there is tax also on financial transactions. If the rates are high, post-tax returns are obviously low. There are, of course, treaties to help avoid double taxation, even then taxes limit the scope of international portfolio investment.

Yet again, there are varieties of implicit and explicit transaction costs, such as trading commission/fees and bid-ask spreads, etc. In developed countries, transaction costs are often less cumbersome. But in emerging market economies, they figure large. Moreover, transaction cost per unit falls with growing size of transaction, but the small investors do not get this advantage.

Manipulation of Security Prices

It is true that in a perfectly competitive financial market, no investor can influence the market price of securities. But in the real world, it is the government and also the big brokers that influence the security prices. The government influences them through its monetary and fiscal policies. It can change interest rates, tax rates, etc. It can change the regulatory provisions. The manipulation is often large when the public sector financial institutions and banks hold big chunk of the securities traded on the stock exchange. In such cases, the asset portfolio lacks the desired liquidity with the result that the foreign portfolio investment becomes a costly and difficult proposition.

Unequal Access to Information

It is the wide cross-cultural differences that inhibit international portfolio investment. Accounting practices and the disclosure system vary among countries. The language varies from one country to the other. As a result, it is difficult for the international investors to collect information. In absence of desired information, it is difficult for them to act rationally.

MODES OF INTERNATIONAL PORTFOLIO INVESTMENT

There are different modes of international portfolio investment. An investor has to find out which one of them is more suitable. Some of the common modes are:

1. Buying foreign securities or depository receipts directly from the domestic stock exchange if such securities are listed there.
2. Approaching international mutual funds.
3. Approaching closed-end country funds.
4. Buying directly the securities of domestic companies having global operation.

In many countries, foreign securities are traded at the stock exchange. There are many companies that prefer to get their securities listed on the stock exchange of different countries in order to diversify risk. There are also global depositories or American depositories from whom an investor can buy global/American depository receipt. Sometimes when the investor finds the foreign company shares more liquid than the depository receipts, it maintains an open account with the local broker and buys the shares through it.

Alternatively, an investor buys the shares of an internationally diversified mutual fund. There are many open-end mutual funds that trade in international securities on behalf of the individual investor. They prefer liquidity and try to allocate portfolio in proportion to the market capitalisation of the more important stock exchanges. The mutual funds are normally no-load funds, but some of them charge up-front fees.

The closed-end funds are different from the open-end funds in that the former make investment initially in international securities and issue shares against the portfolio. They try to avoid any change in their investment portfolio depending upon the changes in the response of the investors. Such closed-end funds experienced a hey-day in 1980s with the setting-up of Korea Fund. Now they are popular.

Last but not least, an investor buys shares of domestic company that operates internationally. It is in fact indirect way of participating in the global economy. In this case, the investor does not have ample scope for reaping diversification benefits insofar as the systematic risk cannot be reduced to that extent.

IDENTIFICATION OF OPTIMAL INTERNATIONAL INVESTMENT PORTFOLIO

Greatest Excess Return to Risk Ratio

It has already been mentioned that the optimal investment portfolio is one that promises the greatest excess return to risk ratio. Thus, when an investor diversifies its portfolio of assets internationally, it tries to maximise this ratio. Eiteman, Stonehill and Moffett (1995) are of the view that such a position can be achieved if the ratio of excess return to risk in case of international portfolio is higher than in the case of the domestic portfolio by the greatest margin. For calculating this ratio, these authors base their decision on the capital asset pricing model. They divide the difference of the expected value of returns on the portfolio and the risk- free interest rate by standard deviation of returns on the portfolio. If R_p is the expected return on the portfolio, R_f the riskless rate of interest and σ the risk in terms of the standard deviation of the returns on the portfolio, the ratio of excess return to risk will be:

$$(R_p - R_f)/\sigma \tag{14.11}$$

This ratio is calculated separately for domestic investment and for international investment, and the difference between these two ratios is determined. The investor chooses the international portfolio where such difference is the largest.

PROBLEM 14.4

The risk-free interest rate is 8 per cent. The rate of return and the risk in terms of standard deviation in India and some foreign countries are respectively as follows:

India: 11% and 3.16
Australia: 10% and 4.05
UK: 9% and 1.80
USA: 14% and 5.40

Find the country/countries where an Indian investor should diversify its investment.

Solution

The ratio of excess return to risk will be: India: (0.11 – 0.08)/3.16 = 0.00949

Australia: (0.10 – 0.08)/4.05 = 0.00493
UK: (0.09 – 0.08)/1.80 = 0.00555
USA: (0.14 – 0.08)/5.40 = 0.01111

Here we find that in UK, risk is low but return is also low, the ratio of excess return to risk is lower than that in India. Similar is the case with Australia where return is higher than in the UK but the risk is also higher. But in case of USA, where the risk is high but return is also high, the above ratio is higher than in India. So the investor should choose USA for diversifying its investment portfolio internationally.

Mix of Equity Shares and Bonds

The context of identifying optimal international investment portfolio, one significant question is whether the international portfolio of assets should consist only of bonds or only of equity shares or of both. According to the study of Levy and Lerman (1988), the standard deviation of returns from bonds was lower than the standard deviation of returns from equity shares meaning that the investment in bonds was less risky than the investment in equity shares but the rate of return in case of bonds was found to be lower than in the case of equity shares. This is the reason why internationally diversified bond-cum-equity share portfolios were found better than the internationally diversified stock portfolio alone or the internationally diversified bond portfolio alone (Jorion, 1989).

Now the question is what should be the optimal portfolio combination. Solnik and Noetzlin (1982) identify three possible asset allocation methods. The first is the extrapolative approach. It bases the portfolio on the historical covariance matrix of bond and stock returns. The matrix can be used to develop minimum risk portfolios. It is true that the historical matrix may not be a guide for the future, but it can be useful to a great extent.

The second approach is known as simplified approach which suggests allocating equal amount of investment to all securities. This method implies that correlations are similar among all security pairs which is not always true. The third approach is known as passive approach. It allocates funds based on the degree of market concentration. It means that the securities of bigger countries would get more funds at the expense of smaller countries.

On the basis of the experience, it is found that the extrapolative approach is better than the other two. Despite covariance matrix being not fairly stable over time, it helps indicate pairs of securities exhibiting comparatively high or low correlations.

SUMMARY

- International portfolio investment does not involve the control of foreign enterprise. Rather, the purpose of the investor is to maximise risk-adjusted return. To this end, it selects an optimal portfolio that gives the maximum return with a given level of risk or carries minimum of risk with a given level of return.
- Inclusion of international portfolio gives an added advantage in that it helps to reduce risk as well as to raise return. There are, of course, risks associated with changes in the exchange rate, unfamiliarity with the environment in foreign countries and various measures of exchange control adopted by the governments concerned but the benefits from international diversification outweigh the costs or risks.
- There are different modes of international portfolio investment. Care should be taken while choosing a particular mode.
- The optimal international asset portfolio represents a situation where the risk-adjusted return on the international portfolio is greater than the risk-adjusted return on the domestic portfolio alone by the greatest amount. In this context, the portfolio combining equity shares and bonds is preferable to investment in equity alone or in bonds alone because the combination of equity and bonds raises the risk-adjusted return.

STUDY TOPIC

Trends in FIIs' Investment in India

The foreign institutional investors (FIIs) are none but the mutual funds, pension funds, asset management companies and other similar funds investing in the secondary market securities overseas. Their investment is known as portfolio investment insofar as they are interested in returns and not in the management of the companies whose securities they invest in. When they buy the securities, there is inflow of funds in the country where they invest. The funds flow out of the country when they sell the securities.

Policy Incentives

In the wake of liberal external sector/financial sector policies, the Indian Government allowed FIIs to invest in the secondary market of the country. It liberalised the rules from time to time. To mention a few liberalisation measures, the Securities and Exchange Board of India (SEBI) made the registration of FIIs mandatory, but at the same time, eased the process and cost of registration. It broadened the list of the types of FIIs, such as university funds, endowments, charitable trusts and proprietary funds, and, of late, the foreign central banks that could be registered as FIIs in India and the entities on behalf of whom that could invest. It also broadened the types of securities such as debentures and then government securities in which they could invest. It raised the caps for investment in different sectors and companies from initially 24 per cent to 30 per cent and then to 40 per cent and, in very special cases, to 49 per cent. Introduction of transparent disclosure norms, etc. was the other incentive. The Indian Government raised the cumulative investment ceiling for FIIs in debt funds from US $ 1.0 billion to US $ 1.75 billion. Against this background, the SEBI raised gradually the overall investment limit in case of government securities from US $ 100 million to US $ 3.2 billion. For the corporate bonds, the cumulative ceiling was raised to US $ 1.5 billion. FIIs' position limits for investment in stock-based derivatives were revised upwardly. Commodity exchanges were permitted to have FIIs' investment up to 23 per cent along with FDI up to 26 per cent, subject to specific terms and conditions. The FIIs and their sub-accounts were allowed to short sell, lend and borrow equity shares of Indian companies, subject to specific conditions. The registration fee for the FIIs was halved from ₹ 10,000 to ₹ 5,000. The investment limit was raised again to US $ 3.2 billion in government bonds, to US $ 3.0 billion in the case of private corporate bonds and to US $ 25.0 billion in the case of infra-structural bonds.

TABLE ST14.1 Portfolio investment, Net (BoP, current US$ million)

Country Name	*Years*	*Values*
India	1990	0
	2000	–234.52
	2014	–3774.03
	2015	–948.66
	2016	472.52
	2017	–3063.78
	2018	959.79
	2019	–2458.41
	2020	–1511.17
	2021	–571.82
	2022	1870.28
	2023	–3102.53

Source: https://data.worldbank.org/indicator/BN.KLT.PTXL.CD

Size of Net Investment

The size of FIIs' net investment or the gross purchase minus gross sales of securities rose consistently, except for the period of Asian Crisis during late 1990s and a few other years depending upon the changes in the international economic scenario and the Indian economic fundamentals. Table 14.1 gives a rough idea of their net investment on an annual basis.

The data supplied delineates a sequence of annual figures for India from 1990 to 2023. These values probably denote financial metrics, possibly associated with trade balances, foreign direct investment, or other critical economic indicators.

A prominent feature of the data is its considerable volatility, with values oscillating between positive and negative figures. This volatility indicates significant variability in the fundamental economic drivers. Numerous years display significant negative numbers, signifying instances of economic distress or deficits. Conversely, the years 2016 and 2018 are notable for their substantial positive numbers, indicating phases of economic expansion or surplus. The recent trend, evidenced by the negative figure for 2023, suggests a possible fall in the pertinent economic indicator for that year. Definitive interpretation is tough without detailed context regarding the nature of the values. Nonetheless, other plausible explanations for the observed patterns may be contemplated. The statistics may signify variations in India's trade balance, where negative numbers denote trade deficits and positive values denote trade surpluses. Alternatively, the values may represent fluctuations in foreign direct investment (FDI) flows, where negative values signify net outflow and positive values denote net influx. The data may also reflect fluctuations in other economic indicators, such the current account balance, capital account balance, or fiscal balance. A comprehensive examination is required to attain a deeper knowledge of the fundamental economic patterns. Analysing global economic conditions, India's domestic economic policies, and sector-specific factors can yield significant insights into the determinants of the observed patterns. Analysing these characteristics yields a more lucid understanding of the economic dynamics behind the data.

Investment in Equity and Debt Securities

As far as choice between debt and equity is concerned, the net investment in equity dominated the scene. In two financial years, viz. 2000–01 and 2005–06, due to net disinvestment in the case of debt securities, the entire net investment was accounted for by equities. In other financial years, the share of equity in total net investment varied between 73 per cent and 96 per cent.

TABLE ST 14.2 FPI/FII Net Investment in Equity and Debt Securities

Financial Year	*Equity*	*Debt*	*Debt-Vrr*	*Hybrid*	*INR Crores Total*
1998–1999	29973.2	–147.4	0	0	29825.8
1999–2000	9669.5	452.6	0	0	10122.1
2000–2001	10206.7	–273.3	0	0	9933.4
2001–2002	8072.2	690.4	0	0	8762.6
2002–2003	2527	162	0	0	2689

(Contd.)

Financial Year	*Equity*	*Debt*	*Debt-Vrr*	*Hybrid*	*INR Crores Total*
2003–2004	39959.7	5805	0	0	45764.7
2004–2005	44122.7	1758.6	0	0	45881.3
2005–2006	48800.5	–7333.8	0	0	41466.7
2006–2007	25235.7	5604.7	0	0	30840.4
2007–2008	53403.8	12775.3	0	0	66179.1
2008–2009	–47706.2	1895.2	0	0	–45811
2009–2010	110220.6	32437.7	0	0	142658.3
2010–2011	110121.1	36317	0	0	146438.1
2011–2012	43737.6	49987.9	0	0	93725.5
2012–2013	140032.6	28334.4	0	0	168367
2013–2014	79708.68	–28059.89	0	0	51648.79
2014–2015	111332.59	166127.09	0	0	277459.68
2015–2016	–14171.57	–4003.76	0	0	–18175.33
2016–2017	55702.67	–7291.64	0	0	48411.03
2017–2018	25634.19	119035.74	0	10.29	144680.22
2018–2019	–87.73	–42355.97	0	3514.24	–38929.46
2019–2020	6152.26	–48710.23	7331.17	7697.63	–27529.17
2020–2021	274031.96	–50443.62	33264.56	10247.09	267099.99
2021–2022	–140009.6	1628.53	12642.83	3498.41	–122239.83

Source: www.cdslindia.com, Annual Report, 2024

The supplied data indicates a significant change in net borrowing over the years. Periods of substantial net borrowing (shown by positive figures) are interspersed by intervals of net repayment (denoted by negative values).Debt has been the primary factor influencing the current scenario for both the volume and frequency of net borrowing. Although debt has been the primary catalyst, there is a recent inclination towards more dependence on debt-VRR as a funding source. Conversely, equity has consistently exhibited negative values, signifying a net repayment. Given that hybrid instruments remain relatively novel, their impact on net borrowing has been quite minimal.

Significant variations in net borrowing occur annually, indicating the data's high volatility. This unpredictability, coupled with the business's dependence on debt, can render the firm susceptible to significant financial risk, especially during economic downturns or periods of rising interest rates. Effective management of the loan maturity profile and the preservation of a sustainable debt level are crucial for guaranteeing long-term financial stability. Moreover, the ability of the enterprise to equilibrate debt and equity financing can influence investor confidence and the cost of capital. Moreover, modifications in legal frameworks may influence the accessibility and pricing of diverse financial tools.

It is essential to evaluate factors such as economic conditions, fluctuations in interest rates, alterations in regulatory regulations, and business-specific characteristics to gain a deeper understanding. Conducting an examination of the data with these factors allows for a more comprehensive understanding of the underlying trends and ramifications.

QUESTIONS

1. What do you mean by FIIs' investment? Does it provide liquidity to the financial market?
2. Comment on the trend of FIIs' investment in India.
3. What are the reasons for growing FIIs' investment in India?

REVIEW QUESTIONS

Objective-Type Questions

1. State whether true (T) or false (F):

(a) The objective of foreign portfolio investment is to acquire voting rights in the management of the company. ☐

(b) Risk is measured by dispersion of alternative returns around the expected value. ☐

(c) The total risk in respect of a security is the difference between systematic and unsystematic risk. ☐

(d) The weighted average of expected return from different securities in a portfolio of investment is known as the portfolio return. ☐

(e) Optimisation of portfolio means highest return with a given level of risk or lowest risk with a given return. ☐

2. Choose the correct answer:

(a) Optimal portfolio of investment means:
  (i) highest return with a given risk.
  (ii) lowest return with a given risk.
  (iii) lowest return with the highest risk.

(b) Inclusion of international investment normally:
  (i) helps reduce risk.
  (ii) helps increase the risk.
  (iii) none of these.

(c) A blend of equity shares and bonds:
  (i) is better from the viewpoint of maximising returns.
  (ii) is worse from the viewpoint of maximising returns.
  (iii) none of these.

Short-Answer Questions

1. What do you mean by expected value?
2. Distinguish between systematic and unsystematic risk.
3. What is portfolio return?

Long-Answer Questions

1. How is portfolio of investment optimised?
2. What are the benefits of international investment from the viewpoint of optimisation of investment portfolio?
3. Enumerate a few basic problems in the optimisation of international investment portfolio.

Numerical Problems

1. An Indian investor invests in American and British securities in proportion of 75% and 25%. The expected return being 15% from the former and 12% from the latter. The risk manifesting in standard deviation is 15% in US securities, and 18% in British securities, and 0.6 is their correlation. Find out (a) portfolio return and (b) portfolio risk.
2. India: Portfolio return: 10%, portfolio risk: 20%
   USA: Portfolio return: 8%, portfolio risk: 12%
   UK: Portfolio return: 10%, portfolio risk: 16%
   Riskless rate of interest: 6%
   Find out whether Indian investors should make investment abroad in the above two countries.

REFERENCES

Chakrabarti, R. (2001), "FII Flows to India: Nature and Causes", *ICRA Bulletin of Money and Finance*, 2 (Oct.–Dec.), 61–79.

Eaker, M.R. and D.M. Grant (1990), Currency Hedging Strategies for Internationally Diversified Equity Portfolios, *Journal of Portfolio Management*, XVII, 30–32.

Eiteman, D.K., A.I. Stonehill and M.H. Moffett (1995), *Multinational Business Finance*, Reading (Mass.), Addison-Wesley, Chap. 20.

Eun, C.S. and B.G. Resnick (1984), Estimating the Correlation Structure of International Share Prices, *Journal of Finance*, XXXIX, 1311–1324.

Gordon J. and P. Gupta (2003), "Portfolio Flows into India: Do Domestic Fundamentals Matter?", *IMF Working Paper*, no. 03/20.

Hunter, J.E. and T.D. Coggin (1990), An Analysis of the Diversification Benefit from International Equity Investment, *Journal of Portfolio Management*, XVII, 33–36.

Jorion, P. (1989), Asset Allocation with Hedged and Unhedged Foreign Stocks and Bonds, *Journal of Portfolio Management*, XV (Summer), 36–51.

Levy, H. and Z. Lerman (1988), The Benefits of International Diversification in Bonds, *Financial Analysts Journal*, II, 56–64.

Markowitz, H.M. (1959), *Portfolio Selection*, New York, John Wiley & Sons.

Narsimhan, M.S. and V. Ubaidullah (2007), "Does Daily FIIs Data Add Value or Volatility?", *Indian Journal of Capital Market*, 1(1), 14–19.

Odier, P. and B. Solnik (1993), Lessons for International Asset Allocation, *Financial Analysts Journal*, VII, 63–77.

Sharan, V. (forthcoming), *India's Financial Sector Reforms.*

Sharma, L. (2004), "Determinants of FIIs' Investment", *nse.india.com*

Solnik, B. (1988), *International Investments*, Reading (Mass.), Addison-Wesley, Chap. 2.

Solnik, B., and B. Noetzlin (1982), "Optimal International Asset Location", *Journal of Portfolio Management*, VIII (Fall), 11–21.

SUGGESTED FURTHER READING

Adler, M. and B. Dumas (1983), International Portfolio Choice and Corporation Finance, *Journal of Finance*, XXXVIII, 925–984.

Levy, H. and M. Sarnat (1970), International Diversification of Investment Portfolios, *American Economic Review*, LXXX, 668–675.

PART 5

International Financing Decisions

CHAPTER

15 Overview of the International Financial Market

Learning Objectives

After investment decision is final, an MNC raises funds from the international financial market to finance the assets. The present chapter, therefore, attempts:

- To present a bird's eye view of the sources of funds.
- To evaluate the changes in the structure of international financial market since 1950s.
- To explain the factors taken into account while selecting a particular source/form of funds.

When a multinational enterprise finalises its foreign investment project, it needs to select a particular source, or a mix of sources of funds to finance the investment project. Here it may be noted that a multinational enterprise positions itself on a better footing than a domestic firm as far as the procurement of funds is concerned. A domestic firm gets funds normally from domestic sources. It does get funds from the international financial market too but it is not as easy as in case of a multinational enterprise. The latter can use the parent company's funds for its foreign investment project. It can also get funds from the host country financial market, but more importantly, it tries to get funds from the international financial market. It selects a particular source, a mix of sources, a particular type, or types of funds that suit its corporate objectives.

When one discusses the sources of funds in the international financial market, the discussion takes into account both, the supply aspect and the demand aspect. It embraces, on one hand, the official and non-official sources of funds and the changing profile of the international financial market over past few decades; and on the other, the selection of the sources of funds by the multinational firms depending on the fulfilment of the corporate objectives. In this chapter, therefore, let us discuss the channels for the flow of funds, the structural changes that have taken place in the international financial market over the past few decades, and the criteria for the selection of a particular source or type of funds.

CHANNELS FOR INTERNATIONAL FLOW OF FUNDS

The international financial market can be compartmentalised into two segments. One is the international money market which is represented by the flow of short-term funds. International banks or the short-term securities come under this segment. On the other hand, the international capital market forms the other segment where medium and long-term funds flow.

> International money market is concerned with short-term funds. The international capital market deals with long-term funds.

Irrespective of such a distinction between the two segments, there are a number of agencies and instruments through which funds move to the resource-needy institutions or firms. The resource-providing agencies may be official or non-official. Among the official agencies, are the multilateral institutions, such as international development banks and regional development banks, and the bilateral agencies, such as the different governmental agencies. Multilateral or bilateral funds can be concessional or non-concessional. The highly concessional funds or funds having a large grant element, are known as *official development assistance*.

> Official development assistance involves concessional funds with a very large grant element.

International Financial Market

- Official sources
  - — Multilateral agencies
    - International development banks, such as the World Bank, IFC, etc.
    - Regional development banks, such as Asian Development Bank, NDB etc.
  - — Bilateral agencies or the different governmental agencies
- Non-governmental agencies
  - — Euro-currency market/International banks
  - — International securities market
    - Debt securities
    - Equities

The non-official channel comprises the borrowing and the lending streams such as the international banks on the one hand, and on the other, the securities market in which the Euro-equities and the debt instruments, such as international bonds, medium-term Euro-notes, short-term Euro-notes, and Euro-commercial papers are sold and purchased. It may be noted that the operation of the international financial market spreads beyond the lending and borrowing of funds or the sale and purchase of securities. Swap is also very common and it forms an integral part of international financial market. If a borrower needs fixed-rate funds but has access to the floating- rate loan market, he can go in for an interest-rate swap in order to exchange the floating-rate loan for the fixed-rate loan. Similarly, if a borrower does not get loan in a particular currency, the loan can be swapped for obtaining the desired currency.

CHANGING STRUCTURE OF THE INTERNATIONAL FINANCIAL MARKET

Multilateral Agencies

When one studies the development of the international financial market over the past half-century, many structural changes are manifest over the years. This has been in fact the result of the changing supply position of, and demand position for, international funds consequent upon the large-scale adoption of economic development programmes, growth of international trade, and a rapid advancement of technology are profoundly transforming the dynamics of trade and financial relations among multilateral agencies. The increasing implementation of data analytics, digital platforms, and initiatives aimed at financial inclusion has become prominent in this context. These agencies are adopting data-driven methodologies to enhance their decision-making processes and inform the development of effective policies. Such practices signify a move toward greater efficiency and responsiveness in addressing the complexities of global economic relations. On scrutinizing the official channels, it is found that up to the mid-1940s, there was no multilateral agency to provide funds and only in 1945 was the International Bank for Reconstruction and Development (IBRD) established that provided in the beginning loans for reconstruction of the war-ravaged economies of Western Europe and then from 1948 began providing development loans. The IBRD's function was limited to lending and so the provision of equity finance lay beyond its scope. Moreover, it lent only after the guarantee by the borrowing government. To overcome these problems, the International Finance Corporation (IFC) was established in 1956 which provided loans even without government guarantee and provided equity finance as well. However, one problem remained unsolved. It was that the poorer countries of the developing world were not in a position to utilise the costly resources of the IBRD because those funds carried the market rate of interest (Sharan, 1991). For their benefit, another sister institution was created in 1960 named as International Development Association (IDA). The two institutions—IBRD and IDA—together came to be known as the World Bank.

IBRD-IDA combine is known as the World Bank. Putting together also the IFC, ICSID and MIGA, the combine is known as the World Bank Group.

When IBRD was established, its main objective was not to make direct loans but to encourage private investment. It began lending on a large scale only when the desired amount of private investment failed to come up. Lending then became its major function but the issue of encouragement to international investment remained to exist. And to this end, the International Centre for Settlement of Investment Disputes (ICSID) was also set up in 1966 to encourage international investment. Again the Multilateral Investment Guarantee Agency (MIGA) was established in 1988 to cover the non-commercial risks of the foreign investors. All these five institutions—IBRD, IDA, IFC, ICSID, and MIGA—together are now known as the World Bank Group.

When the World Bank and the IFC emerged as a major funding agency, it was felt that its lending norms did not equally suit different member countries because the economic and political conditions as well as the requirements of the different regions of the globe were different. Thus, for tuning of the funding in line with varying requirements of the different regions, it was decided to set up regional development banks on the pattern of the international development banks. The decade of the 1960s marked the establishment of regional development banks in Latin America, Africa and Asia. The Asian Development Bank began operation from December 1966.

Bilateral Agencies

The history of bilateral lending is not older than that of multilateral lending. During the first half of the twentieth century, funds flowed from the empire to its colonies to meet a part of the budgetary deficit of the colonial government but it was not a normal practice, nor was it ever considered as the external assistance that we mean in the present-day context. Bilateral economic assistance was for the first time announced by the US President Truman in January 1951. The motivation behind the announcement was primarily political and economic. The cold war between the USA and the then USSR was at its peak in those days, and the US government tried to befriend the developing countries to bring them into its own camp to make itself politically more powerful. It could help the US economy to come closer to the developing economies and also to get the desired raw material and foodstuffs therefrom. The economic assistance could help build the infrastructural facilities in the developing countries that could in turn help increase the US private investment in those countries.

In the second half of the 1950s, the USSR bloc too announced its external assistance programme in order to counter the US move. By the late 1950s, many other governments of the Organisation of Economic Cooperation and Development (OECD) announced external assistance programmes and bilateral lending came into full bloom from the 1960s. In some cases, governments joined hands with private agencies and the export credits came to form a sizeable part of the bilateral assistance programme. In contemporary discourse, bilateral development agencies, exemplified by the United States Agency for International Development (USAID) and the Department for International Development (DFID), are progressively integrating technology into their operational frameworks. These agencies leverage digital payment solutions, mobile payment systems, and blockchain technology to foster enhanced accountability and mitigate corruption in development initiatives.

International Banks

Among the non-official funding agencies, international banks occupy the top position. If one looks at their development since the 1950s, distinct structural changes are evident. In the first half of the twentieth century and till the late 1950s, international banks were primarily domestic banks performing the functions of international banks. This means that they operated in foreign countries accepting deposits from, and making loans to, the residents of the host countries. They dealt in the currency of the host countries, and at the same time, dealt in foreign currency while making finance available for foreign trade transactions.

> Euro banks are international banks with the minimum of host government interference and dealing in any convertible currency other than the currency of the host country.

However, in the late 1950s and especially in the early 1960s, banks with purely international character emerged on the global financial scene. This new variety of banks came to be known as Euro banks. The Euro banks emerged on a footing quite different from the traditionally known international banks.

The Euro banks deal with both the residents and the non-residents, but they deal essentially in any currency other than the currency of the host country. For example, if Euro bank is located in London, it will deal in any currency other than the British pound. The deposits and loans of the Euro bank are remunerated at the interest rate set by the market forces operating in the Euro-currency market and not by the interest rate prevailing among the domestic banks in the host country. Again, the other difference between the traditional international bank and the Euro bank is that the former is subjected to rules and regulations of the host country, but the Euro banks are free from those rules and regulations.

The rationale behind the deregulation is that the activities of the Euro banks do not touch the domestic economy because they are concerned normally with the placement of the funds (foreign currency) from one foreign market to another foreign market and so they are neutral from the viewpoint of any direct impact on the balance of payments of the host country. International banks are now increasingly integrating advanced, technology-driven payment systems for cross-border transactions, exemplified by the emergence of digital banking. These institutions employ a variety of methods, including online banking platforms, mobile banking applications, artificial intelligence, and big data analytics. Such advancements have transformed the landscape of international banking by facilitating predictive analytics for credit risk assessment, enhancing fraud detection mechanisms, and personalizing banking services. As a result, banks are better equipped to evaluate market risks and optimize their lending strategies effectively and it also helps in enhancing greater accessibility, efficiency, and convenience.

Factors Behind Emergence of Euro Banks

It may be mentioned that after Stalin's death, the then USSR moved away from the closed economic policy and its trade with the West and the South began to expand since the late 1950s or the early 1960s. Those days the US dollar was the most desired currency in international transactions, so the USSR earned US dollars through trade and tried to earn more of this currency in view of its great strength in international transactions. Since the cold war between the two super powers was then at its peak, it preferred to keep its earned dollars in a bank outside the USA. London and a few other European financial centres were the best choice as they possessed the requisite infrastructure and a stable political climate. Those dollar deposits in London and other European country-based banks came to be known as *Euro dollars* and the banks accepting such deposits came to be known as *Euro banks*.

In the wake of the foreign exchange crisis of 1955–57, the British Government placed restrictions on the use of pound sterling for external transactions and the dollar was in great demand in the UK for external transactions, in view of the readily available supply of dollars. Moreover, the emerging convertibility of some European currencies by late 1950s led to the emergence of an active foreign exchange market in Europe linking the US dollar with those European currencies. These links enhanced in turn, the use of the US dollar by the banks located in Europe.

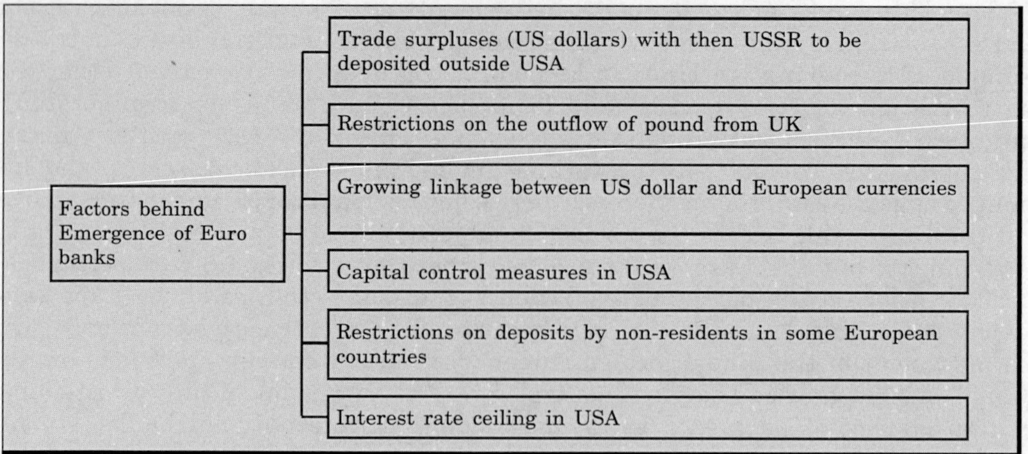

The emergence of Euro banking got support from some capital control measures by the US Government in the wake of the balance of payments crisis in the 1960s. In early 1965, the introduction of Voluntary Foreign Credit Restraint Programme limited the ability of US-based banks to lend directly to the non-residents, whereas this provision did not apply to foreign branches of the US banks. As a result, the foreign operation of the US banks shifted from those located in the USA to those located in other countries, mainly in Europe. Statistics show that the number of US banks having foreign branches rose from 11 in 1964 to 125 in 1973, the number of foreign branches of those banks moved up from 181 to 699 during this period and the assets of those branches went up from US $ 7.0 billion to US $ 118 billion during the same period (Johnston, 1982).

Some of the European governments imposed restrictions on holding of deposits by non-residents in domestic currency and on paying of interest on non-resident deposits. This encouraged the non-residents to hold deposits in Euro banks that were not subject to such regulations. The US Government too imposed an interest rate ceiling when credit was tight and the market interest rate had risen. The US banks could not raise the interest rate. On the contrary, the Euro banks that were not under the purview of such ceilings, raised interest rate on deposits and attracted depositors away from the US-based banks.

Again, when domestic credit was restricted, companies borrowed from Euro banks normally at lower rates of interest, and the increased lending and deposits contributed to the growth of the Euro banks. It was not only that the US banks came to be based in Europe; the European banks too spread their branches overseas perhaps as a defensive measure. Statistics reveal that the number of overseas branches increased from 1,860 in 1961 to 3,764 in 1973. The number of foreign branches of UK-based banks alone rose from 1105 to 1973 during the same period (Bhatt, 1991).

Off-shore Banking Centres

By late 1960s, a full-fledged eurocurrency market had been established as a global money market where Eurobanks accepted deposits, and lent funds, in Eurocurrency in a big way. The Eurocurrency market got further stimulus in the 1970s, when a new type of international banks emerged that were different from the traditional banks or from the Euro banks and that came to be known as *off-shore banking centres* (OBCs). The distinctive feature of the OBCs was that they dealt with non-residents only; although like the Euro banks, they did not deal in the currency of the host country. In fact, they channelled funds from one country to another without influencing the domestic financial market.

> The off-shore banking centres deal only with the non-residents and in any convertible currency other than the currency of the host country.

OBCs proliferated in those places and in those countries where: the governmental control and regulations were the least interfering, tax rates were very low, necessary infrastructure for their smooth operation, such as good systems of communication, a supportive climate and an experienced financial community, etc. existed, and which were politically and economically stable.

Looking at the specific cases, one finds that it was the non-flexibility of governmental restrictions that discouraged the growth of OBCs in Germany, France and Japan. On the other hand, it was this flexibility that helped London, Luxembourg, Singapore, Hong Kong and many others to attract OBCs. OBCs grew in the Bahamas, Luxembourg, Cayman Islands and in Panama in view of low rates of taxes. Better communication facilities and availability of experienced personnel were the additional factors for London-based OBCs. Presence of exchange control measures came in way of the growth of OBCs in the Latin American countries. On the contrary, Kuwait and Bahrain attracted OBCs on account of least governmental interference.

Whatever might the reasons for their growth have been, the OBCs attracted a large number of borrowers and lenders. The foreign currency liabilities of OBCs in European reporting countries rose from US $ 79.3 billion in 1970 to US $ 801 billion in 1979 and the total liabilities of US banks' branches in the Bahamas and Cayman Islands alone grew from US $ 4.8 billion to US $ 121.8 billion during the same period (Johnston, 1982). If we see the current OBC landscape that provides financial services to non-residents, has been benefiting from the various technological advancements, such as

1. It utilizes advanced encryption technology that helps in maintaining anonymity of transactions. Further Blockchain has also been there to bolster secure cross-border transfers.
2. As the increasing technological advancement also provides OBC to operate remotely, that increases convenience and attract international client base.
3. Tax envision and money laundering has always been a struggle for the OBCs, and with the technologies regulatory bodies have improved themselves in keeping eyes on it.

With this discussion we can say that technology has significantly made a transformation in off-shore banking centres, especially with the enhancement of security, and accessibility of its operations.

Euro-currency Market

Euro-currency market involves euro-banks and off-shore banking centres accepting deposits and making loans in a currency other than the currency of a country where the bank is located. The transactions do not involve necessarily foreign exchange but involve a transaction in a foreign currency. Nevertheless, the transfer of a euro-deposit is often accompanied by foreign exchange transaction in which the proceeds are switched into another currency. It has also been significantly influenced with the technological progress: as the global liquidity and competitiveness has increased with the adoption of Real-time Transactions that is technology enabled high-volume transactions. And it also fosters the global banking integration that enhances global connectivity as well as easy and quick movement of Eurocurrency with a huge size efficiently.

The market is not confined to a specific country, rather it represents a worldwide network, although it exists mainly in Canada, Japan, the Bahamas, the Cayman islands, Panama, Hong Kong, Singapore and Bahrain. The suppliers of the funds are the commercial and central banks, governments, international monetary institutions, non-financial institutions and individual investors. The borrowers, on the other hand, are banks, exporters and importers, security dealers, companies and government agencies. However, the inter-bank transactions figure large facilitating banks in adjusting their liquidity position, in foreign exchange hedging and arbitrage, and in the recycling of intermediate funds through loans and bond issue.

This market runs parallel to the domestic money market. But compared to the domestic money market, it enjoys absence of tight monetary control and also the economies of scale. This is an important reason that it operates on a narrower margin. There is tremendous possibility for credit creation simply on the lines the domestic commercial banks create credit.

The deposit and lending or, in other words, the financial intermediation, credit creation, short-term funds management, etc. in the euro-currency market are discussed at length in Chapter 17.

Syndication of Lending

Another structural change that took place during the 1970s was evident in the form of syndicated lending. In the wake of the international oil price rise, a number of oil-importing countries experienced huge deficits in their current account. Consequently, they had to resort to bigger loans that were normally not within the capacity of a single bank to provide. The banks joined hands to provide these large loans. They did so also to reduce the individual risk of lending. Besides, from the borrower's point of view, the cost of the syndicated loans were smaller than the sum of the cost of individual loans borrowed from many banks. Whatever the reasons for the coming together of the banks, such lending came to be known as *syndicated lending*. Such loans served the interest of both lenders and borrowers and so they took a great leap forward. Taking birth in the early 1970s, they crossed the US $ 88 billion mark by 1980 and reached US $ 320 billion by 1995 (IMF, 1997).

Syndicated lending involves two or more banks for lending.

Syndicated loans are different from general loans in that one of the lending banks is the lead manager who originates the transaction, structures it, selects the lending members, supervises the documentation, and in many cases, services the loan after the agreement is complete. It serves as a link between the borrower and the other banks of the syndicate. It collects interest and principal from the borrower and disburses the collected amount among the co-lenders. For its functions, the lead bank charges an additional fee. Large-scale projects are increasingly financed by a consortium of lenders, facilitated by advanced technologies. Syndication process is supported by advance platforms such as blockchain technology that helps in managing loan documents and automating compliance checks. The evaluation of borrower risk and structured loan syndications can be assessed effectively among participating banks with the adoption of the technology.

Move Towards Securitisation

There was a big leap in bank lending during the 1960s and more particularly during the 1970s after the international banks had acquired the surplus of oil exporting countries. During the 1980s, however, several factors emerged on the international economic scene, which led to a shift from bank lending to growing securitisation in the international financial market. With the stagnant oil prices, the international banks could not sustain any sizeable increase in loans, and external indebtedness in some of the borrowing countries turned unmanageable. The borrowers found themselves unable to repay loans. Mexico's refusal to repay loans added fuel to the fire. The risk of repayment got so considerable that the banks hesitated in lending. A drop in long-term interest rates during the 1980s, with the reappearance of positive real interest rates, and more importantly, a rising trend in the yield from the long-term bonds, led investors to invest in international bonds. The rising intermediation cost associated with bank lending also pushed the borrowers away from bank borrowing to borrowing through the use of securities (Honeygold, 1989). Moreover, the securities proved highly liquid as the investors could sell them in the secondary market which had also developed along with the growth in securitisation.

The more commonly used securities were international bonds for long-term funds, medium-term Euro notes that were meant for medium-term funds, and Euro notes and Euro commercial papers that were meant for short-term funds. The Euro bonds had taken birth in the earlier decade, but the other instruments emerged in the 1980s. The Euro equities were also issued through the global depository. Known as portfolio equity investment they became an important vehicle for transfer of resources in the international financial market during the late 1980s and 1990s.

Banks' Off-balance Sheet Activities

The slump in the banks' lending activities during the 1980s resulted not only in greater use of international securities but also in a shift in favour of the off-balance sheet activities of the international banks. It was because the banks had to maintain their earnings and the capital adequacy norms in the wake of the eroded lending business. These activities were nothing but the participation of the banks in the foreign exchange market. The banks involved themselves greatly in the swap deals, in the forward currency market, and in the market for currency options. The revolution in the telecommunication system and the greater use of computers eased their job considerably.

> Off-the-balance-sheet activities mean non-traditional activities, such as participation in foreign exchange market, etc.

Apart from the fallen lending business, the other factor responsible for the growing off-balance sheet activities was the fierce competition with the non-banking financial companies. The banks were compelled to adopt additional functions in order to prove their superiority over the non-banking companies. The loan commitments, derivatives, guarantees has now expanded with the technology, like in risk management artificial intelligence and advanced algorithms helps banks in managing the risks associated with Off-balance sheet transactions. The digitization in the trading platforms and markets enables the banking system in engaging more efficiently in electronic trading and derivative transactions.

Impact of Structural Change

Whatever the reasons for the structural change, there has definitely been product innovation and improvement in financial technology in the international financial market that has helped the borrowers as well as the lenders and investors, the technology adoption such as alternative trading venues, for example, the dark pools and peer-to-peer(P2P) lending platforms has now been putting a greater impact in the trading platforms and international financial market. The Dark Pools often involve institutional investors to execute a large block of securities for trade that are privately exchanged and these trades occur anonymously. Although dark pools often facilitate in increasing liquidity as these trades are done anonymously but that comes with a transparency concern, many large institutions and hedge funds uses this to bypass public exchanges and minimize trading costs.

The peer-to-peer (P2P) lending connect an individual lender directly with the borrowers, hence bypasses the previously established system of banking. This platform provide global access to investment and credit opportunities. All this has led to a considerable cut in transaction cost and to greater efficiency in the allocation of capital that might have a positive bearing on the world output. This is not all; with international diversification of the investment portfolio, the risk of investment has been reduced. The financial market now has greater liquidity as a result of which the volume of credit has increased. However, it cannot be denied that this has had an adverse effect on the traditional activities of the international banks. Since different segments of the international financial market are closely interwoven as a result of improvement in communication facilities, the shock in one part of the market is transmitted easily to other markets. Again, sometimes, the international financial market experiences an excess of liquidity which is not a healthy sign. But the benefits from the structural change seem to outweigh the costs. While online platforms boost global investment, they also increase risks in credit, investor protection, and cross-border lending due to regulatory gaps. This lack of standardization can heighten systemic risks and financial instability, requiring stronger global regulatory coordination.

SELECTION OF SOURCES AND FORMS OF FUNDS

When a firm selects a particular source or form of funds, it does so in order to suit its corporate objectives. Some of the major objectives are the minimisation of the effective cost of funds, matching the raised funds with target debt-equity and the target current-liability-long-term-liability ratio, and avoidance of lengthy legal and procedural formalities.

Minimisation of Cost of Funds

Effective cost of borrowing depends on both the interest rate and the exchange rate changes.

Minimisation of the cost of capital is the very motive behind selection of the sources of funds. The effective cost of the funds depends *inter alia* on the rate of interest and the changes in the exchange rate or in the value of the borrowed currency. The effective cost of borrowing in a foreign market is obtained as

$$k_{bf} = (1 + r_f)(1 + E_f) - 1 \qquad (15.1)$$

where r_f is the rate of interest in the foreign market and E_f is the change in the exchange rate.

For example, if interest rate in the London money market is 12 per cent compared to 14 per cent in New York, and the pound sterling is expected to appreciate by 4 per cent, the effective cost of borrowing in pounds would be

$$(1.12 \times 1.04) - 1 = 16.48\%$$

In this case, the multinational enterprise will borrow from the New York money market despite the fact that the rate of interest is lower in the London money market because the effective cost of borrowing in pounds is greater than that in dollars.

The expectation of change in exchange rate is based on the concept of probability. Suppose, there is 60.0 per cent probability for 4.0 appreciation and 40.0 per cent probability for 2.0 per cent appreciation in the pound, the effective cost of borrowing in pounds at 12 per cent interest rate is

$$(0.6) \times \{(1.12 \times 1.04) - 1\} + (0.4) \times \{(1.12 \times 1.02) - 1)\}$$
$$= 0.15584 = 15.58\%$$

In cases where the firm borrows from more than one financial market, the weighted average of effective cost of borrowing in different currencies is computed. Suppose the firm borrows not only in pounds but also in Japanese yen. Because there is 60.0 probability for 3.0 depreciation and 40.0 per cent probability for 1.0 per cent depreciation in the yen, the effective cost of the yen with 13.0 per cent interest rate is

$$(0.6) \times [(1.13) \times \{1 + (-0.03)\} - 1] + (0.4) \times [(1.13)$$
$$\times \{1 + (-0.01)\} - 1] = 0.10514 = 10.51\%$$

If the firm borrows in the two currencies in equal proportion, the weighted average of effective cost of the total borrowing is

$$(15.58\% + 10.51\%)/2 = 13.05\%$$

In this case, the firm would like to borrow from the Japanese financial market in greater proportion so that the effective cost of total borrowing becomes lower.

Carry Trades in Foreign Exchange Market

Carry trades are a simple and common form of leveraged investment strategy. Funds are borrowed in a low-yielding currency and immediately thereafter, they are invested in a high-yielding currency. In fact, it is a systematic roll-over to exploit the differences in interest rates. The investment horizon is typically short so that the exposure to currency risk is the minimum. In theory, high interest rates should be offset by depreciation of high-yielding currency. But, in practice, high-yielding currencies normally tend to appreciate. The appreciation helps increase the returns. Carry trades get the stimulus. When the expected volatility is low, the carry trades get additional boost. It is because the exchange rate risk is low enough to axe the gains reaped from the interest rate disparity.

Source: European Central Bank, *Financial Stability Review*, June 2007.

Again, the effective cost of total borrowing will be lower if there is negative correlation in the movement of the value of different currencies. The cost may move up if the correlation coefficient is positive. So the firm takes into account not only the expected change in the value of the currencies but also the correlation coefficient of the expected change in the value of different currencies so as to lower the effective cost of total borrowing.

PROBLEM 15.1

A firm borrows from the pound market. The rate of interest is 8 per cent. But there is 30 per cent chance for 2 per cent appreciation in pound and 70 per cent chance for 3 per cent appreciation in pound. Find the effective cost of capital.

Solution

$$0.3 \times [(1.08 \times 1.02) - 1] + 0.7[(1.08 \times 1.03) - 1] = 0.1092 = 10.92\%$$

PROBLEM 15.2

Borrowing in pound market involves 8 per cent interest rate with pound appreciating by 4 per cent. Borrowing in dollar market involves 9 per cent interest rate with dollar depreciating by 3 per cent. Should borrowing in pound market be combined with borrowing in dollar market? What will be the ultimate effective cost of borrowing if the same amount is borrowed in dollar market?

Solution

Borrowing in dollar market will pull down the effective cost insofar as there is negative correlation in the changes in the value of the two currencies.

The effective cost will be:

Pound market = $1.08 \times 1.04 - 1 = 0.1232$

Dollar market = $1.09 \times (1 - 0.03) = 0.0573$

Combined borrowing = $0.1232 + 0.0573 = 0.1805/2 = 0.09025 = 9.025\%$

Borrowing to Conform Capital Structure Norms

In a multinational firm, the design of the capital structure is a complex process. It is because the firm has to consider the capital structure of not only the parent unit but also of the subsidiaries that are operating in heterogeneous environment. The subsidiaries abroad may design the capital structure in conformity with the parent unit or they may have independent capital structure in view of taking advantages of the local economy and also the host country norms. The study of Sekely and Collins (1988) examines the capital structure norms among 677 firms in 9 industries of 23 countries and finds that the debt ratio may be large or small depending upon the economic, social, cultural and political factors. Since these factors tend to vary among countries, the capital structure norms too vary widely among them. On the whole, debt ratio is large in Scandinavian, Mediterranean and some of the Asian countries. It is low in some of the South Asian, Latin American and Anglo-American countries.

If the capital structure norms of the subsidiaries are in sync with the host country norms, they are well in line with the monetary and financial policy of the host government. They help evaluate and compare the return on equity with those of the local competitors. If the host country interest rates are lower, the debt ratio will be larger. But if the host country interest rates are higher, the target debt ratio will be smaller. On the contrary, if the capital structure norms of the subsidiaries are in line with the parent company's global target debt ratio, they are most suited for maximising the global profit. However, the parent firm designs the capital structure of its different subsidiaries in such a way that minimises the overall cost of capital. Nevertheless, there are a host of factors that influence the design of the capital structure of a multinational firm. Designing of the capital structure should consider the following issues:

(a) Capital structure should ensure *stability of cash flow* in order to service the debt. MNCs having a wider network can easily bring in stability of cash flows and thus can have a high debt equity ratio.
(b) Capital structure should aim at minimisation of the global tax burden of the firm. From this viewpoint, MNCs have a higher debt-equity ratio in a particular host country where the tax rate is higher and at the same time low debt-equity ratio where the tax rate is low. It rests on the basic principle that the interest is tax-deductible.
(c) An MNC has a high-debt equity ratio in those host countries whose currency is weak. It is because large borrowing in the host market will not raise the effective cost of borrowing for the parent. This means that in a host country with strong currency, the debt-equity ratio should be lower.
(d) An MNC can have a high debt-equity ratio in a host country where the financial market has enough of liquidity. It is because the loan will be available at lower interest rate and the average cost of capital will be lower. On the other hand, in a country with tight liquidity position, larger share of equity in the capital structure is preferred.
(e) Firms with low operating leverage may have high debt-equity ratio. It is because with a high operating leverage, business and financial risk is high and there may be cases of high default on repayment of the loans.

Selection of an Optimal Maturity

While raising funds from the international financial market, a multinational firm likes to maintain a proper balance between the short-term liabilities and the long-term liabilities. There is no confusion about financing of fixed assets because they are financed with long-term capital but as far as financing of current assets is concerned, determining the best ratio between the long-term capital and the short-term capital is an important issue. The normal view is that the permanent current assets should be financed with long-term capital and the fluctuating part of the current assets should be financed with short-term capital. This is but a trade-off between liquidity and profitability. Long-term capital is more liquid but lowers profitability. Short-term capital, on the other hand, does not push down profitability so much but is less liquid. However, if the finance manager is conservative, he uses more of long-term capital. If he is aggressive, short-term capital is greatly used. Thus whenever a multinational enterprise raises funds, it has in mind a perfect trade-off between short-term capital and long-term capital.

Avoidance of Legal and Procedural Formalities

Any firm raising funds does not like to undergo too many procedural formalities. From this viewpoint, the issue of international bonds is too complex, much more complex than the Euro notes. Again, the borrowing programme can be designed only in the framework of local laws. If the government prohibits the issue of a particular instrument, the borrower cannot issue it despite its cost efficiency. For example, prior to 1992, the Indian Government had not allowed the Indian companies to issue Euro equities or Euro convertible bonds. Sometimes these considerations become really significant.

Challenges of Regulating Global Financial Markets in a Digital Era

The International financial markets have been reshaped due to the technological advancements, that influences everything from multilateral or bilateral agencies to banks, eurocurrency markets, and offshore banking centers (OBCs), these changes have positively impacted global finance but they also come up with many regulatory challenges and difficulties in risk management to ensure stability. Since the era of technology is there the financial markets will continue to evolve, the technology will remain the central cause for this transformation in the field of global finance. But the regulatory body require a perfect coordinated global regulations and policy guidelines to manage risks and ensure stability.

To regulate the global financial market in the digital era there is a series of challenges emerges driven by fast technological advances, evolving financial products, and cross-border activities. The various challenges are as follows:

1. **Cross-border Regulatory Gaps:** Innovations such as blockchain technology and cryptocurrencies have surpassed national boundaries, resulting in the emergence of decentralized markets that function on a global scale. This phenomenon incentivizes financial institutions to establish operations in jurisdictions characterized by weaker regulatory frameworks, rather than

upholding stringent compliance measures. The variability in cross-border regulatory standards creates discrepancies that may be exploited, thereby posing risks to the integrity of the global financial system.

2. **Shadow Banking and off-Balance sheet Activities:** Shadow banking and off-balance sheet transactions, promoted by financial technological advancements, have made regulation more complicated. Entities like P2P lending and alternative investment funds often operate in less regulated areas (i.e., grey areas), which in turn raises potential contagion throughout the global financial system. Day by day, it becomes challenging for regulators to track them.
3. **Cybersecurity Threats:** Global financial systems are now more reliant on digital platforms and for that reason they are exposed to substantial risks from large-scale cyber threats. The cross border transactions and international financial networks are particularly vulnerable to cyberattacks that have widespread ripple effect on global markets, which regulators struggling to enforce uniform security standards across countries and institutions.
4. **Technology-Driven Market Fragmentation:** The rise of dark pools, alternative trading systems, and high-frequency trading contributes to market fragmentation. These platforms out sided the way of traditional operation and adopted to operate in different levels of oversight and transparency. The lack of transparency in these alternative venues makes it difficult for the global regulators to maintain market stability and ensure fair trading practices across borders.

As we have had a look on how the international financial system works and what are the challenges emerging in the digital era, the regulation of global financial markets in the digital age necessitates enhanced international collaboration, the real-time monitoring of emerging technologies, and the formulation of flexible regulatory frameworks. These frameworks must be capable of adapting to rapid innovations while effectively mitigating risks in an increasingly interconnected global landscape.

SUMMARY

- There are different channels for the international flow of funds. One channel is represented by the official agencies. These are either multilateral institutions like the international and regional development banks or bilateral, that is the different governmental agencies. Among the non-official agencies, the most important sources are the international banks. However, funds are raised also through the sale of international equity and short-term, medium-term and long-term debt securities.
- There has been a distinct structural change in the international financial market over the decades. The establishment of the international and regional development banks and the participation of different governments in the international lending business changed the very shape of the international financial market. More importantly, the character of the international bank changed—from its traditional form to a more unregulated form. The banks did not remain confined to the lending business but they widened their

functions to cover the off-balance sheet activities. Of late, the international securities market has become significant for raising funds.

- A firm that has to raise funds for investment selects a particular channel or a mix of channels and a particular currency or a mix of currencies with a view to minimising the cost of capital, and so it takes into account not only the interest rate but also the changes in the exchange rate that influence the effective cost of capital.
- Apart from the interest rate and the exchange rate, the raising of funds takes into account also the capital structure norms as well as a proper balance between the short-term funds and the long-term funds. They also influence the cost of capital but in a different way. Moreover, the fund-raising firms have to abide by the rules and regulations and the necessary formalities. They too influence the fund-raising decisions.

REVIEW QUESTIONS

Objective-Type Questions

1. State whether true (T) or false (F):
   (a) The Asian Development Bank is a bilateral financing agency. ☐
   (b) The World Bank is a combine of IBRD, IDA and IFC. ☐
   (c) Euro banks deal only with the non-residents. ☐
   (d) Off-shore banking centres deal both with residents and non-residents. ☐
   (e) Off-shore banking centres and Euro banks both deal in the currency of the country where they are located. ☐
2. Choose the correct answer:
   (a) International banks emphasised the off-balance sheet activities during:
      (i) 1960s
      (ii) 1970s
      (iii) 1980s
   (b) MIGA:
      (i) is a sister institution of the World Bank
      (ii) is an insurance agency of the US Government
      (iii) none of these
   (c) Selection of sources and forms of finance depends upon:
      (i) capital structure norms
      (ii) dividend policy of the firm
      (iii) none of these

Short-Answer Questions

1. Distinguish between traditional international banks, Euro banks and off-shore banking centres.
2. Discuss the factors behind the emergence of Euro banks.

3. What do you mean by syndication of lending?
4. What is off-balance-sheet activity of international banks?

Long-Answer Questions

1. Explain the various sources of international finance.
2. Give a brief account of the changing scenario of international financial market during the past four or five decades.
3. Explain the criteria followed while raising funds from international financial market.

Numerical Problems

1. A firm borrows from the pound market. The rate of interest in pound market is 10 per cent, but this currency is to appreciate by 3 per cent. On the other hand, the interest rate in dollar market is 11 per cent, but dollar is expected to depreciate by 3 per cent. From which market, should a firm borrow in order to lower the effective cost of funds?
2. What will be the effective cost of capital in the pound market if interest rate is 10 per cent and if the pound is to depreciate by 3 per cent?

REFERENCES

Bhatt, P.R. (1991), *International Banking*, New Delhi, Commonwealth Publishers, Chaps. 2 and 3.

Honeygold, D. (1989), *International Financial Markets*, New York, Woodhead-Faulkner, Chap. 2.

IMF (1997), *International Capital Markets*, Washington, D.C.

Johnston, R.B. (1982), *The Economics of the Euro Market: History, theory and policy*, New York, St. Martin's Press, p. 13.

Sekely, W.S. and J.M. Collins (1988), Cultural Influences on International Capital Structure, *Journal of International Business Studies*, XIX, 87–100.

Sharan, V. (1991), *The World Bank Group and the SAARC Nations*, New Delhi, Anmol Publishers, Chaps. 2 and 3.

———(1991), *Financial Management*, New Delhi, Anmol Publishers, Chap. 7.

SUGGESTED FURTHER READING

Fabozzi, F. J., Modigliani, F., Jones, F. J., and Ferri, M. G. (2021), Foundations of financial markets and institutions (5th ed.), Pearson.

Joshi, P.R. (1996), *Global Capital Markets*, New Delhi, Tata-McGraw Hill.

Madura, J. (2023), Financial markets and institutions (13th ed.), Cengage Learning.

Mishkin, F. S., and Eakins, S. G. (2021), Financial markets and institutions (9th ed.), Pearson.

Pilbeam, K. (2018), Finance and financial markets (4th ed.), Red Globe Press.

CHAPTER

16 Multilateral Development Banks

Learning Objectives

The present chapter takes a look at the international and regional development banks that form an important pillar of the official segment of the international financial market. It proposes:

- To discuss the organisational set-up and resource base of the World Bank and the nature, terms, magnitude and sectoral allocation of the funds flowing from the World Bank.
- To discuss the functions and financing activities of the IFC.
- To acquaint the readers with the Asian Development Bank and with its functions and financing activities.

The present chapter gives an idea about the international agencies and also the regional agencies providing funds both at the macro and the micro levels for an overall economic development in the borrowing country. The discussion is, however, limited to the financing activities of the World Bank, International Finance Corporation and the Asian Development Bank.

THE WORLD BANK

Organisational Set-up

In Chapter 15, we briefly mentioned about the working of the World Bank. Before discussing its working in detail, let us first discuss its organisational structure. The Board of Governors, which consists of one governor from each member country, is the apex body vested with all powers. It normally meets once a year, though it can meet even more often. The decisions taken by it are implemented by the Board of Executive Directors consisting of 22 members. The most important person on the Board of Executive Directors is the Chairman who is also the President of the World Bank.

The President is assisted by Vice-Presidents and a considerable number of personnel, both professional and non-professional. The organisational hierarchy is based on the classic line-and-staff pattern. The President is always an American but the other staff members come from different member countries. The present president is Ajay Banga.

The Resource Base

The resource base of IBRD is essentially a mix of equity capital and borrowings. The authorised capital, originally set at US $ 10 billion, was revised upwardly from time to time rising to the present level of over US $ 318 billion. The subscribed capital and the paid-up capital at the end of FY 2024 were US $ 296 billion and US $ 22 billion, respectively. The paid-up share capital is supplemented by reserves. Moreover, this institution borrows from the international capital market through the sale of securities.

In case of IDA, the share capital of US $ 1 billion is supplemented by replenishments from Part I member countries at every three-year period since 1962. The twenty first replenishment covering a period up to December 2024 and amounting to US $ 93 billion was finalized in December 2021. Moreover, contributions from IBRD and from different governments, of course very rarely, form the resource base of IDA.

Recipients of World Bank Funds

The earliest loans, known as *reconstruction loans* were directed to the war-ravaged countries of Western Europe. Another instalment of the reconstruction loans was extended to Bosnia and Herzegovina in 1996. *Development loans* began flowing from 1948. Prior to 1968, funds were directed to both, developed and developing countries but since then, the developing countries are the sole recipient. These developing borrowers are grouped as:

1. IBRD-only borrowers
2. IDA-only borrowers
3. Countries that borrow from both the IDA and the IBRD

The grouping is based usually on the per capita income level. The well-off among the developing countries can get loans only from the IBRD while the poorest developing countries get credits only from the IDA in view of the fact that the IDA credits are a much softer form of resources. Between the two extremes, there are the blend countries that receive loans from the IBRD and credits from the IDA.

Table 16.1 shows a high degree of geographic concentration in World Bank lending. The five largest borrowers including India accounted for over one-third; and if the other five borrowers were added to this list, the percentage went up to

52. This means that only ten countries accounted for over one-half of the World Bank lending. Three of them, viz. Argentina, Brazil and Mexico, are IBRD-only countries and the others are the blend countries.

TABLE 16.1 Major Borrowers of the IBRD (as on 31.11.2024)

Country	*Amount (US $ billion)*	*Percentage of Total*
India	24.25	9.09
Indonesia	21.64	8.11
Columbia	16.34	6.12
Brazil	15.23	5.71
China	14.64	5.48
Mexico	14.63	5.48
Ukraine	14.06	5.27
Philippines	13.89	5.21
Türkiye	12.05	4.51
Egypt	12.006	4.50
All countries	787.818	100.00

Source: IBRD disclosures of loans and disbursements

One of the reasons for geographic concentration was that many countries did not assure the viability of the project. Up to the mid-1960s, financial benefits and costs were the basis of a project's viability and on this ground, a few countries like Nepal and Upper Volta were once refused loans (Mason and Asher, 1973). However, since mid-1960s, the social benefit and cost have begun forming the basis of a project's appraisal (Little and Mirrlees, 1974; Dasgupta, Marglin and Sen, 1972).

Nature and Terms of the Funds

Except for the reconstruction loans that were non-project loans, project loans have dominated the lending business. For the first time, a non-project development loan was extended to Iran in 1957. It was only during the mid-1960s that President Woods advocated non-project assistance on the ground of utilisation of idle capacities in the industrial sector in a number of developing countries but such loans flowed from the World Bank's soft-lending window. Again, since the early 1980s, the structural adjustment loans have been mainly in the form of non-project loans though project loans have dominated the scene.

The World Bank loans have been untied loans, which means that the borrowers can use the amount of the loan for purchase of goods and services in any country they like on the basis of international bidding. This way, the suppliers under the aid programme do not get the chance to inflate the price of the supply as is the case with tied loans. The contribution of World Bank loans is thus greater than the tied loans flowing normally from bilateral donors.

It is a fact that the loans invariably possess a technical assistance component yet technical assistance is also exclusively extended by the World Bank. Prior to the mid-1960s, technical assistance was of a broad-based nature involving general survey of the economy of the borrower, but since then, such assistance has come to be mainly focussed on the merit of a particular project. In 1955, the Economic Development Institute was set up to train senior government officials of the borrowing countries. In 1975 a Project Preparation Facility was introduced to assist the borrowers in project preparation and carrying out projects. In 1985 another such facility was created for the IDA-only countries. Yet, technical assistance still forms a very small segment of World Bank lending.

> World Bank loans/credits are grouped as investment loans, adjustment loans and enclave loans.

Besides the general type of financial loans, there are some new forms of financial loans that have come up in recent decades. They are either investment loans, adjustment loans, or enclave loans. The purpose of investment lending is to support investment programme activities. Such loans are extended to support financial institutions in borrowing countries. The adjustment loans are designed to support the introduction of basic changes in economic and other policies for energising the process of economic development in the member countries. Such loans are of four types:

> Adjustment loans are meant for macro-economic policy reforms.

1. Structural adjustment loans that support specific policy changes and institutional reforms
2. Sectoral adjustment loans that are confined to reform in a particular sector
3. Rehabilitation loans that support government policy programmes meant for the private sector
4. Debt and debt-service reduction loans that support highly indebted countries in managing external debt.

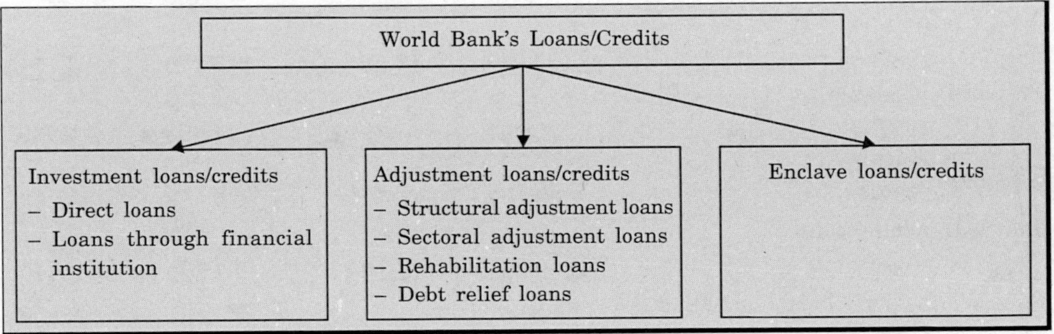

The enclave lending includes, on the other hand, IBRD's involvement in IDA-only countries although such lending is rare. Moreover, the World Bank participates in co-financing with private and public donors. Its co-financing activities became apparent during the mid-1960s and have achieved sizeable proportions since mid-1970s in view of the fact the other lenders find a lower lending risk and at the same time the borrowers get large amount of loans.

> Enclave loans being rare involve IBRD in IDA-only countries.

The IBRD loans carry the market rate of interest. The rate of interest is normally 50 basis points over the average cost of borrowing. In addition, a commitment fee is charged on the undisbursed portion of the loans at the rate of 75 basis points. The loans carry a three to five-year grace period and a maturity of 12 to 20 years. IDA, on the other hand, does not charge interest, but a service charge of 0.75 per cent. The loans are spread over 50 years with a ten-year grace period.

Magnitude of Loans/Credits

Table 16.2 shows the magnitude of loans/credits flowing from the World Bank. It is evident that the size of the flows from IBRD as well as IDA has been increasing over the years. The annual average of the IBRD flows that was barely a half-billion US dollars during President Black's regime, expanded to $ 15.8 billion during

TABLE 16.2 Magnitude of World Bank Loans/Credits

Authorisations (US $ million)

Presidency/FYs	*IBRD*		*IDA*	
	Total Amount	*Annual Average*	*Total Amount*	*Annual Average*
Eugene R. Black				
Up to 1955	2,274	253	–	–
1956–63	4,710	589	495	165
George D. Woods				
1964–68	4,264	853	1,294	265
Robert S. McNamara				
1969–73	9,089	1,818	3,975	795
1974–78	24,373	4,875	7,947	1,590
1979–81	23,442	7,814	10,341	3,447
A.W. Clausen				
1982–86	57,948	11,590	15,770	3,154
Barber B. Conable				
1987–91	76,955	15,391	24,693	4,939
Lewis T. Preston				
1992–95	63,197	15,799	25,563	6,391
James D. Wolfensohn				
1996–2005	1,12,094	11,209	67,699	6,770
Paul Wolfowitz/Robert B. Zoellick				
2005–2012	1,44,277	24,046	77,222	12,870
Jim Yong Kim 2012–2019	1,31,767	21,961	95,356	15,892
David R Malpas 2019–2023	97,601	24,400	93,032	23,258

Note: Since President Wolfowitz was associated with the World Bank for a very short period, the figures are combined with those of President Zoellick's regime.
Source: *The World Bank, Annual Report*, Washington, D.C., various issues.

President Preston's regime during FYs 1992–1995, although it fell marginally to $ 11.5 billion during FYs 1995–2005. Again, during Wolfowitz/Zoellick's regime, the annual average was higher at $ 12.8 billion. Similarly, the annual average of IDA credits rose from $ 165 million during the early 1960s to over $ 6.4 billion during FYs 1992–1995 and to $ 6.8 billion in the following ten-year period. During FYs 2006–2011, it was as high as $ 12.9 billion. The sizeable expansion in the quantum of flow is perhaps the aftermath of broadening and strengthening of the resource base of the World Bank. The share capital of the IBRD as well as its borrowing from the capital market increased over the years. At the same time, the replenishments made to the IDA's resource base expanded over the years. After that during the presidentship of Jim Yong Kim (2012–2019) the IBRD and IDA disbursed $1,31,767 and $95,356 million dollars respectively. While it went down in the years during COVID–19, the IBRD distributed $97,601 as the loan and IDA $93,032 respectively during the presidentship of David R Malpas from the year 2019–2023.

One important question remains however. Has the World Bank extended loans/credits commensurate to its ability? The ability is defined in terms of statutory lending limit that is equal to the sum of subscribed capital, reserves and surpluses. It is evident from the statistics that the outstanding loans as a percentage of statutory lending limit has come down from 84 in FY 1987 to 60 in FY 1992, 55 during FY 1996 and 53 in FY 1998, although revived to 57 during FY 2000. (The World Bank, 2000). All this means that despite the expansion in World Bank's lending in absolute terms, it cannot be said to be increasing relative to its capacity.

Sectoral Allocation

The sectoral allocation of the World Bank funds depended on the prevailing philosophy towards economic development, on the views of the president, and on the needs of the borrowing countries. The first one-and-a-half decades witnessed emphasis on infrastructure projects because the then economic thinking was in favour of huge investment in such projects. It was believed that the benefits of such investments would automatically spread to other sectors of the economy. President Black was influenced by such thinking. As a consequence, over two-thirds of the funds during his regime were meant for power, transport and communication (see Table 16.3).

President Black emphasised on infrastructure sector loans.

TABLE 16.3 Sectoral Allocation (per cent) of World Bank Loan/Credits

Sector/Purpose	*Up to FY 1963*		*FYs 1964–68*		*FYs 1969–73*		*FYs 1974–81*	
	IBRD	*IDA*	*IBRD*	*IDA*	*IBRD*	*IDA*	*IBRD*	*IDA*
Agriculture and rural development	7.5	23.6	9.7	15.0	12.3	32.8	25.8	40.7
Development finance companies	3.2	–	10.3	3.1	12.5	2.6	10.9	1.9
Education	–	1.0	0.9	9.4	5.2	6.4	4.1	5.7
Energy	–	–	–	–	–	–	3.0	1.3
Power	33.5	11.6	35.0	5.0	21.2	9.0	15.4	11.2
Environment	–	–	–	–	–	–	–	–
Financial sector	–	–	–	–	–	–	–	–
Industry including mining	12.9	2.0	5.1	–	3.8	2.9	7.7	5.1
Multisector	–	–	–	–	–	–	–	–
Non-project	10.8	–	2.4	34.4	7.2	13.9	3.8	9.1

(Contd.)

Sector/Purpose	Up to FY 1963		FYs 1964–68		FYs 1969–73		FYs 1974–81	
	IBRD	IDA	IBRD	IDA	IBRD	IDA	IBRD	IDA
Population, health, and nutrition	–	–	–	–	0.3	1.0	0.4	1.3
Public sector management	–	–	–	–	–	–	–	–
Small-scale enterprises	–	1.3	–	–	–	0.2	1.7	1.1
Social sector	–	–	–	–	–	–	–	–
Telecommunication	0.4	8.5	2.7	2.4	4.7	6.2	1.4	3.3
Technical assistance	–	–	Neg.	Neg.	–	0.3	0.2	1.0
Tourism	–	–	–	–	0.7	0.4	0.6	0.4
Transport	32.4	50.0	32.3	28.6	26.5	20.4	15.9	11.0
Urban development	–	–	–	–	0.2	0.7	3.3	2.2
Water supply and sewerage	Neg.	2.0	1.7	1.9	5.3	3.2	5.6	4.7

Source: The World Bank, *Annual Report*, Washington, D.C., various issues.

President Woods placed emphasis also upon the social sector with the result that the funds flowed for the first time in large measure for financing education projects. He was the greatest advocate for non-project assistance and so over one-third of the IDA credits were in this form during FYs 1964–69. The emphasis on the social sector including agriculture was more evident during the first five-year term of President McNamara but such flows were largely through the IDA window. Around one-third of the IDA's credit flowed to the agricultural sector, and another 11.3 per cent of such credits flowed for education, urban development, water supply and sewerage, and population, health and nutrition projects.

President Woods favoured loans also for social sectors.

During the early 1970s, it was found that despite large World Bank lending and high growth rate, poverty remained as the biggest threat in some borrowing countries. This means that the trickle-down strategy of earlier decades had failed to be efficacious. Consequently, the World Bank's emphasis from 1973 shifted to favour poverty alleviation programmes and projects. Such projects included integrated rural development projects and those covering the basic minimum needs of the target group. The share of rural development lending in the total agricultural sector loan rose to 61 per cent in 1977 compared to only 22 per cent during FYs 1969–73 (Hurni, 1980). Such lending covered not only rural poverty but also urban poverty. In 1976, specific loans for reducing urban poverty were extended.

President McNamara put greater emphasis on social sectors especially poverty alleviation and energy sector.

The other area that received emphasis during this period was the development of petroleum sector and the non-conventional energy sector such as solar, bio-mass and geo-thermal energy, etc. This was primarily in view of the first oil shock during 1973–74. The World Bank carried out a survey in around 70 countries for oil exploration, yet the bulk of assistance was meant for risk-free operation where the development of commercial discoveries had already been made (Zakariya, 1983). The statistics in Table 16.3 reveal that the non-conventional energy sector got World Bank funds for the first time during this period. The emphasis of the World Bank lending during 1980's, however, shifted in favour of structural adjustment loans. The features of such

Structural adjustment loans got support during President Clausen's regime.

loans have already been mentioned but it may be noted that the purpose of such loans was to speed up the process of development that was slow on account of defective macroeconomic policy. Since such loans were mainly in the form of non-project loans, President Clausen's regime witnessed a larger share of non-project loans than the preceding regime.

President Conable's policy was to blend the poverty-alleviation loans with the structural adjustment loans. The rationale behind it was that poverty could not be eradicated without making changes in the macroeconomic policies. At the same time, a ceiling was fixed for structural adjustment lending in view of large social costs associated with it. Loans flowed for ensuring food security and for human resource development including education, population control, health and nutrition, and women's role in development. For the first time in FY 1990 lending for education crossed the US $ 1.0 billion mark. The content of integrating women in development in the World Bank loans increased from 11 per cent in FY 1988 to 40 per cent in FY 1991 (The World Bank, 1991).

President Conable's policy combined structural adjustment with poverty alleviation.

President Conable interpreted environment in the context of improving the quality of life. The emphasis was on both the green environment and the brown environment and systematic environmental screening for projects was introduced in FY 1990. In FY 1991, 14 projects involving loans of US $ 1.5 billion had environmental content. In structural adjustment lending, debt-relief measures were especially stressed upon. It was for this reason that during this regime, the absolute size of non-project credit from the IDA window was the largest since the IDA came into being. Conable's policy focussed also upon the public sector restructuring and private sector development. In this context, the development of the financial sector was stressed upon for the first time and good number of loan agreements were signed in this area.

There was no perceptible change in lending policy during President Preston's regime. Nevertheless, Preston increased the poverty-reduction content in structural adjustment lending and created separate vice- presidencies for human resource development, for the environment, and for private sector development. Again, Preston interpreted the lending for housing in a broader perspective and there was a shift from low-cost housing in the 1970s and housing finance in the 1980s to a market-oriented system of property rights during his regime. Statistics reveal that during FY 1992–95, over one-tenth of IBRD loans, and approximately one-quarter of IDA credits were meant for human resource development. Environment shared around 2.0 per cent of lending and public sector restructuring and financial sector reforms attracted 13.3 per cent of IBRD loans and 9.1 per cent of IDA credits. This was a clear-cut tilt away from trends in the earlier regimes (Table 16.4).

President Preston tried to make the existing policy more effective.

President Wolfensohn laid greater stress on human resource development. He relied greatly on the non-government organisations (NGOs) for taking steps in this direction. Loans for this purpose including education, population, health and nutrition, urban sector development, water supply and other social sectors accounted for over one quarter of the World Bank lending during FY 2000. Private sector development was another focal point during this period. The World Bank extended loans also to those private sector enterprises that could provide infrastructural facilities. During FY 1996 alone, 23 loan agreements were signed for private sector infrastructural

President Wolfensohn stressed on human resource development and on improving the quality of the operation.

projects. Loans were provided in sizeable measure also to the financial sector. Statistics reveal that loans meant for financial sector reform constituted 12 per cent of the total assistance during FY 2000 (Table 16.4).

TABLE 16.4 Sectoral Allocation (per cent) of World Bank Loans/Credits

Sector/Purpose	*FYs 1982–1986*		*FYs 1987–1991*		*FYs 1992–1995*		*FYs 2000*	
	IBRD	*IDA*	*IBRD*	*IDA*	*IBRD*	*IDA*	*IBRD*	*IDA*
Agriculture and rural development	22.1	38.0	14.1	30.1	12.4	23.1	7.04	8.18
Development finance companies	8.2	3.4	11.5	5.1	–	–	–	–
Education	4.0	7.7	4.3	10.6	7.8	12.1	1.97	10.76
Energy	7.4	2.6	4.1	1.2	5.6	1.9	4.20	3.80
Power	17.0	11.2	15.0	4.3	12.7	4.7	6.84	5.68
Environment	–	–	–	–	1.9	0.4	4.16	1.38
Financial sector	–	–	–	–	8.3	5.0	15.21	3.84
Industry including mining	5.2	1.6	9.5	3.1	2.0	2.6	0.49	–
Multi-sector	–	–	–	–	12.4	14.7	Neg.	4.96
Non-project	7.8	9.4	12.0	11.2	–	–	–	–
Population, health, and nutrition	0.8	3.4	2.1	7.2	2.9	11.7	3.73	13.30
Public sector management	–	–	2.0	1.2	5.0	4.1	16.54	10.46
Small-scale enterprises	3.7	1.1	2.2	1.0	–	–	–	–
Social sector	–	–	–	–	1.2	0.3	6.56	8.82
Telecommunication	1.0	1.2	2.1	0.9	2.2	0.6	0.76	0.59
Technical assistance	0.3	2.2	0.6	1.8	–	–	–	–
Tourism	–	–	–	–	0.2	–	–	–
Transport	14.1	10.3	9.7	11.4	14.4	9.8	10.58	12.28
Urban development	3.9	4.3	6.6	6.1	6.5	4.4	5.38	0.79
Water supply and sewerage	4.7	3.6	4.2	4.8	4.6	4.6	7.27	2.52

Note: The classification was rearranged in FY 1994. The loans/credits for rural development and small-scale enterprises were regrouped as social sector loans/credits. The non-project loans/credits were shifted to the multi-sector allocation. The loans/credits available to development finance companies were allocated among different sectors. Similar was the case with the technical assistance.

Source: The World Bank, Annual Report, Washington, D.C., various issues.

President Wolfensohn emphasised the need for improving the quality and impact of the World Bank's operation so that the requirements of the member countries could be met more effectively. A new generation of country-assistance strategy (CAS) was introduced. Care was taken to efficiently manage the entire portfolio. To this end, the organisational structure was strengthened and professional standards were raised. The policy emphasis during Wolfowitz/Zoellick regime was on making the structural adjustment lending even more effective; giving strength to environmentally and socially sustainable development and the infrastructure network; on consolidating in a better way the financial and private sectors; and on improving the debt-relief process, especially among the low-income countries. In March 2006, the

World Bank agreed to financing package for the Multilateral Debt Relief Initiative (MDRI) cancelling $ 37 billion debt of the IDA-only countries. In the context of the middle-income countries, the strategy was to facilitate risk management and risk-enhancement products at lower transaction cost. The break of the cumulative assistance (since 1990) at the end of 2011 compared with that at the end of FY 2005, however, shows no major sectoral changes during Wolfowitz/Zoellick regime.

TABLE 16.5 Sectoral Allocation of World Bank Assistance at the end of FY 2005 and FY 2008 (Cumulative since 1990)

Sector end	*FY 2005-end*		*FY 2011-end*		*FY 2024-end*	
	Amount ($ million)	*% share*	*Amount US ($ million)*	*% share*	*Amount ($ million)*	*% share*
Law, justice & public administration	68,218	20	75,743	21	12,387	20
Transportation	48,143	14	60,390	17	5,509	9
Education	26,773	8	22,239	6	4,380	7
Financial sector	36,270	11	27,042	8	4,872	7
Agriculture	27,114	8	20,735	6	4,498	7
Water management, health & sanitation	58,772	17	59,350	17	10,830	17
Energy & mining	42,083	12	55,762	16	11,925	19
Industry & trade	31,493	9	29,704	8	3,680	6
Information & communication	4,319	1	3,967	1	2,894	4
Total	3,43,183	100	3,54,932	100	60,975	100

Source: The World Bank, Annual Report, various issues.

INTERNATIONAL FINANCE CORPORATION (IFC)

Since IFC is an institution of the World Bank Group, its organisational set-up is similar to that of the World Bank. This means that the Board of Governors is the apex body. The Board of Directors implements the policies framed by the Board of Governors. The President of the World Bank is the ex-officio President of the IFC. The President is assisted by the Executive Vice-President who is in turn assisted by a large number of professional and non-professional staff.

Resource Base

The resource base of the IFC is similar to that of the IBRD. It presents a mix of equity capital and borrowed funds. This institution was established with an authorised capital of US $ 100 million which was revised upwardly from time to time to cross US $ 2,450 million as of now. The share capital is supplemented by reserves created out of earnings and also by borrowings. The IBRD began lending to IFC in 1965. The borrowings from the market started from 1984.

Functions

The IFC supplements the financing activities of the World Bank. It seeks to achieve the objectives through providing and bringing together finance, technical assistance and management. This means that it extends not only financial and technical assistance, but also provides equity capital. The focus is definitely on the private sector. As far as financial assistance is concerned, IFC provides loans and makes equity and quasi-equity investment. Unlike IBRD loans, these loans do not require government guarantee. Long-term loans are made either on project-cost basis or on corporate-finance basis. Those loans that are written against IFC's own account, are known as *A-loans*. Maturity ranges normally between 7 and 12 years, although it can be extended to 20 and the grace period can go up to 4 years. The loans are mostly direct loans, but are provided also through financial intermediaries like banks, leasing companies or financial institutions. IFC Intermediary Services extends credit lines that are often aimed at a specific sector or small- and medium-size enterprises. However, since the mid-1980s, direct loans are also made to the small- and medium-size enterprises. In cases where IFC's own funds do not permit making big loans, it seeks out commercial banks and other financial institutions to join in loan syndication and parallel financing. Such loans are known as *B-loans*.

IFC provides loans even without government guarantee and makes equity and quasi-equity investment.

The African and South Pacific countries are beneficiaries of loans under a special scheme known respectively as the "Africa Project Development Facility" set up in 1986 and the "South Pacific Project Facility" set up in 1990. The Corporation has also introduced a multi-currency loan facility for mobilising medium-term foreign exchange loans from international banks for small-scale projects not suitable normally for direct financing by it. The sub-Saharan countries get such loans under the provisions of the Africa Enterprise Fund set up in FY 1989.

As regards equity investment, IFC began such investments in FY 1962. It can take up to 35 per cent stake of the equity, although its stake varies normally between 5 and 15 per cent. It can participate either in the equity of the project or of the financial intermediary. Equity is held for a period ranging between 8 and 15 years and is then listed. This helps the exit mechanism. Quasi-equity investment includes subordinated loans, convertible debt instruments, preferred stock and income notes. The *guaranteed recovery of investment principal* is one of the latest financial techniques that offers the investors guaranteed protection of principal in equity investment made through the IFC.

The IFC underwrites securities and helps firms in making swaps depending upon the need of the project and their ability to raise funds from other sources on reasonable terms. IFC's Risk Management Services enables firms to access the derivatives markets to hedge their exchange-rate exposure or interest-rate exposure. Guarantees are also available from the IFC for major-currency and local-currency bonds and loans.

As far as technical assistance is concerned, IFC finances identification and promotion of projects at the micro level. It covers feasibility studies, detailed engineering, market investigation and preparation of financial plan. At the macro level, it assists governments to formulate policies regarding industrial development. The Foreign Investment Advisory Service (FIAS) is being operated in collaboration with Multilateral Investment Guarantee Agency (MIGA) to provide technical advice to member countries on how to formulate policies and programmes so as to attract foreign investment. The Corporation collaborates also with the United Nations Development Programme for technical assistance. In recent years, IFC has been concentrating more on identification of suitable technology and innovative products, and on adapting them for entrepreneurs in developing countries. Under the Technical Assistance Trust Funds, donor countries make grants for technical studies. The Corporate Finance Services Department provides privatisation advice. Project Development Facilities in Africa, Asia and the Pacific help prepare business plans and share management skills.

Financing Activities

The financing activities of the Corporation have been expanding over the years. A brief view of these activities is presented in Table 16.6. In FY 1966 the first fiscal year of the second decade of its existence. IFC had approved an investment for $ 36 million involving 17 projects in 13 countries. The figures rose to $ 236 million involving 33 projects in 32 countries during FY 1976, $ 1,156 million involving 85 projects in 39 countries during FY 1986, $ 8,118 million involving 264 projects in FY 1996, $ 8,275 million involving 284 projects in FY 2006, $ 12,186 million for 518 projects in FY 2011 and to $ 43,700 million for 325 projects in FY 2023. The cumulative approval thus rose from $ 177 million in the beginning of the second decade of the IFC's operation to $ 1,505 million in the beginning of the third decade, $ 8,309 million in the beginning of the fourth decade, $ 30,381 million in the beginning of the fifth decade, $ 79.682 billion in the beginning of the sixth decade and to $ 70.100 billion at the end of FY 2023.

TABLE 16.6 IFC's Financing Activities

	FY 1966	*FY 1976*	*FY 1986*	*FY 1996*	*FY 2006*	*FY 2011*	*FY 2023*
1. Approved investment							
No. of projects	17	33	85	264	284	518	325
Amount ($ million)	36	236	1,156	8,118	8,275	12,186	43,700
2. Cumulative approval							
No. of projects	120	354	933	1,707	3,727	5,891	1,928
Amount ($ million)	177	1,505	8,309	30,381	79,682	1,39,713	70,100

Source: IFC, Annual Report, various issues.

ASIAN DEVELOPMENT BANK

Evolution and Structure

The norms of international development banks could not be applied equally to different regions because of their heterogeneous identity and varying economic needs. The needs of some of the regions remained unmet and this led to creation of the regional development banks that took into account the economic and political identities of different regions. Asian Development Bank (ADB) was created in this context. Efforts to create ADB had started in August 1963, but they gained momentum only after the USA and Japan offered to subscribe US $ 200 million each during April 1965. The formalities were completed by mid-1966 and ADB came into being from the 22nd of August of that year. It started functioning in December 1966. Its membership was open to the regional countries and the non-regional developed countries from where resources were to be obtained. Presently, it has 67 members—48 from the region and 19 from outside.

The apex policymaking body is the Board of Governors which is composed of representatives from member countries. In all there are 63 governors. The policies are implemented by the Board of Directors. The Chairman of the Board of Directors is the President of the ADB. He is assisted by managing director-general and four vice-presidents and professional and non-professional staff members. In practice, decisions are taken by consensus, although there is provision for voting. Every member country has one basic vote plus proportional votes depending upon the number of shares held in the capital structure. The regional members carry over two-thirds of the votes.

Financial Resources

The financial resource base is divided into two compartments. One is the ordinary capital resources (OCRs) comprising equity and borrowings. The other is the special funds made up largely of contributions from member countries and specially meant for concessional lending and technical assistance.

ADB is a replica of the World Bank for the Asian region providing market-rate loans out of its OCRs and soft loans/technical assistance out of special funds.

The authorised share capital is subject to upward revisions and has been revised to the present level of US $ 163.843 billion of which the subscribed capital is US $ 143.950 billion. The regional members subscribe to the capital stock according to their per capita GNP, tax revenue and export but there is no such norm for the non-regional members. Their subscription depends upon negotiation. Japan's share is around one-fifth of the subscribed capital, one-third is represented by Australia, China, India, Indonesia, Korea and Pakistan while the rest is accounted for by other members. The share capital is supplemented by reserves created out of various revenues.

As far as borrowing is concerned, the ADB had started borrowing from the international capital market in 1969. Since the early 1980s the borrowings have begun to figure prominently and at the end of December 2010 they stood at US $ 108.655 billion.

Apart from OCRs, there are three special funds namely the Asian Development Fund (ADF), the Technical Assistance Development Special Fund (TASF), and the Japan Special Fund.

ADF is replenished by member countries to finance the concessional lending to poorer members and the replenishment is authorised from time to time by a resolution of the board of governors.

TASF is meant for financing the technical assistance operations. It is created out of income from the ordinary lending operation, replenishments from member countries, direct voluntary contributions, and income from investment.

The Japan Special Fund was established in 1988 by way of contribution from Japan for financing or co-financing on a grant basis the technical assistance projects and the private sector projects through equity investment.

The Japan Special Fund was broadened subsequently to include additional objectives. First of all, Asian Currency Crisis Support Facility was created in 1999. Again, Asian Tsunami Fund and Pakistan Earthquake Fund were created. Last but not least, Regional Cooperation and Integration Fund was also created. All these funds were financed out of contributions.

Functions

Being a regional development bank, ADB provides the following financial and technical assistance for economic development of developing member countries (DMCs). The ADB:

- makes loan and equity investments;
- provides technical assistance for preparing and carrying out development projects and programmes and advisory services;
- helps mobilise additional resources within the region and helps attract investment from outside it; and
- assists regional and sub-regional schemes for the sake of promotion of regional economic cooperation.

Lending operation

As per the Articles, any developing member country of the region can borrow from ADB for any public or private sector enterprise. Funds are channelled from OCRs if the borrowing country possesses the necessary debt service capacity. If not, concessional loans are provided from the special funds. While lending, ADB takes into account the general economic conditions of the borrower, its access to other sources of funds, its actual need for the funds and its development plans and priorities. It aids only those projects that are economically and socially viable. Economic viability includes among other things, technical feasibility, financial soundness of the project, removal of economic bottlenecks, and raising of productivity, etc. The social aspect covers poverty reduction in general and amelioration of vulnerable groups in particular, development of human resources, especially the role of women, and reduction in regional disparity, etc. There are some less developed countries that do not possess the necessary infrastructure for preparing effective project reports. They are provided technical assistance for this purpose. Since July 1992, the OCR loans are provided either as dollar loan or as multi-currency loans. The interest rate depends upon London Inter-Bank Offer Rate (LIBOR). The maturity varies between 10 and 30 years including a grace period of 2 to 7 years. Concessional loans, on the contrary, do not carry interest but a service charge of one per cent per annum. Maturity is longer, between 35 and 40 years. The grace period extends to 10 years. The OCR and ADF loans are often supplemented by supplementary loans to meet the cost over-runs on the project.

The loans cover normally the foreign exchange cost, but sometimes they cover the local expenditure as well. They are normally tied to projects but not to purchases in a particular country. Traditionally, ADB has been financing the infrastructural projects, but more recently, it has been also financing social sector projects in the areas of poverty reduction, human resource development, education, population control, health, etc. In case of environmental projects, the emphasis has been on pollution-preventing schemes.

Co-financing

ADB lends not only on its own account, but also participates in co-financing activities, particularly when the project cost is large. It also arranges for the participation of other public and private finance-lending institutions so that the borrowers get large resources and the lending risk of individual lenders is reduced.

Technical assistance

Technical assistance is channelled for identifying, implementing and operating of projects or for strengthening the capability for formulating of development strategies in DMCs. Technology transfer is often a part of technical assistance. It is normally provided out of TASF either as a loan or as a grant.

Equity investment

Equity investment is available to private-sector enterprises and to financial institutions. The practice was started in 1983. Now it is common. This way ADB also provides risk capital.

Regional cooperation

Besides the traditional role of financing projects and programmes, ADB helps the process of regional cooperation among DMCs. Since different member countries are at different stages of development, regional cooperation benefits them all. A phased approach is being followed since 1992. In the first phase, ADB tries to create awareness through locating the potential areas for cooperation and through quantifying the potential benefit. In the second phase, it identifies the particular projects and programmes. In the third phase, funds are extended for identified projects and programmes that enhance regional cooperation.

Size and Structure of the Flows

Table 16.7 shows the amount of the flows during different time periods. It is evident from the figures that till 1980, the size of the flow was not large. The annual average of the loans was barely $ 578.0 million. But thereafter, it increased and was as large as $ 4,604 billion during 1981–2006. In 2007–2010, it was still higher at $ 10.980 billion. The OCR loans were always larger than the ADF loans.

TABLE 16.7 Flow of Funds from Asian Development Bank

(US $ million)

Types of Funds	*Approval/ Disbursements*	*1966–1980*	*1981–2006*	*2007–2010*	*1966–2010*	*2023*
Loan	Approval	8,093	1,15,100	43,923	1,67,116	20,200
	Disbursements	3,042	81,210	32,987	1,17,233	16,850
Out of which:						
OCR loans	Approval	5,653	84,870	35,844	1,26,367	18,800
	Disbursements	2,305	58,492	25,548	86,345	15,630
ADF loans	Approval	2,441	30,229	8,079	40,749	4,200
	Disbursements	738	22,718	7,432	30,888	2,650

(Contd.)

Types of Funds	*Approval/ Disbursements*	*1966–1980*	*1981–2006*	*2007–2010*	*1966–2010*	*2023*
Govt. & Govt.	Approval	8,093	1,12,356	40,949	1,61,398	–
guaranteed	Disbursements	3,042	79,405	30,934	1,13,381	–
Private	Approval	–	2,744	2,974	5,718	1,440
	Disbursements	–	1,804	2,048	3,852	1,230
Grants		–	2,600	1,759	4,359	770
Equity investment		–	1,301	636	1,937	105
Technical assistance		75	2,946	127	3,147	235
Co-financing		–	13,338	6,428	19,766	11,550

Source: ADB, Annual Report, different issues.

At the end of 2010, they accounted for 75.61 per cent of the total loans. The disbursements stood at 68.33 per cent of the approved amount. Again, a greater part of the loans was government and government-guaranteed loans. At the end of 2010, such loans stood at 96.58 per cent of the total approved loans. It means that the private sector loans were only meagre.

ADB provided also outright grant, but the grants accounted for only 2.61 per cent of the loans. Besides grant, ADB made equity investments and equity underwriting. It provided technical assistance but the amount was not large. Co-financing was also there that accounted for over 11.83 per cent of the loans.

In FY 2023, ADB approved $20.2 billion and disbursed $16.85 billion in loans, including OCR ($18.8 billion) and non-sovereign ($1.44 billion). Grants totaled $770 million, equity investments $105 million, and technical assistance $235 million. Co-financing mobilized $11.55 billion. ADB's diversified portfolio supported economic growth, climate resilience, and private sector development across member countries.

By 2024, the number of countries receiving funds from the Asian Development Bank (ADB) has increased significantly. A total of **68 countries** are now eligible for ADB financing, up from 40 countries by 2010. These include countries receiving funding through different ADB sources: OCR loans (market-based), ADF loans (concessional loans), or a combination of both. Notably, in the most recent years, ADB has expanded its geographical and sectoral focus to address a wider array of developmental challenges across Asia and the Pacific. As for sectoral funding, transport and communication, energy, finance, and economic management continue to be major beneficiaries, though climate resilience and infrastructure development are now prioritized as well.

SUMMARY

- The World Bank is a combine of IBRD and IDA. Since the latter is a soft-lending window, its resource base does not include borrowing. Rather, it comprises replenishments and other contributions, apart from the equity. There are three types of borrowers, such as IBRD-only countries, IDA-only countries and those that receive funds from both the agencies. The projects receiving funds meet the objectives of economic growth and social development. Loans are mainly project loans. They are untied to purchases in a particular country. Financial loans are accompanied by technical assistance. Co-financing activities are also found. By June 2005, the World Bank approved loans and credits of over US $ 525 billion. In the initial years, emphasis was laid on development of infrastructure but subsequently, significant amounts of social sector loans were made. During the 1970s poverty alleviation and energy-sector loans dominated. In the 1980s, the emphasis shifted to structural adjustment lending. Poverty alleviation and structural adjustment were brought together and emphasis was given to human resource development, environment and private sector development.

- IFC supplemented the World Bank financing activities by giving equity finance, and also loans without government guarantee. Being a sister institution of IBRD, its capital base is similar. Its cumulative approvals have crossed the US $ 64 billion-mark. Its financial assistance is spread over different sectors and different countries, although the private sector has remained the focal point.
- ADB is a regional development bank of the Asian region. Its capital base consists of OCRs and special funds. The former is used for hard-term loans, and the latter for technical assistance and soft lending. This institution makes equity investment and also provides technical assistance in addition to involving itself in co-financing.

CASE STUDY

AN EVALUATION OF IFC'S FRONTIER COUNTRY STRATEGY

IFC's Operations Evaluation Group independently evaluates IFC's investment and technical assistance and advisory operations and reports its findings to IFC's management and Board of Directors. OEG is a resource for helping staff understand what IFC has learned about getting better investment and development results.

IFC's frontier country strategy, which was adopted in 1998, has been successful in steering IFC's resources toward high-risk and, or, low-income countries where IFC's additionality is greatest. Historically, the best IFC project development and investment results have been achieved in countries that have improved their business climates and graduated into medium- or low-risk environments for investors. As a result of this graduation, the frontier country group is notably smaller than it was in 1998 in terms of number, absorptive capacity, and shares of private capital flows and poor people, raising the issue of whether expanding the group would enhance IFC's realized value-added at the margin.

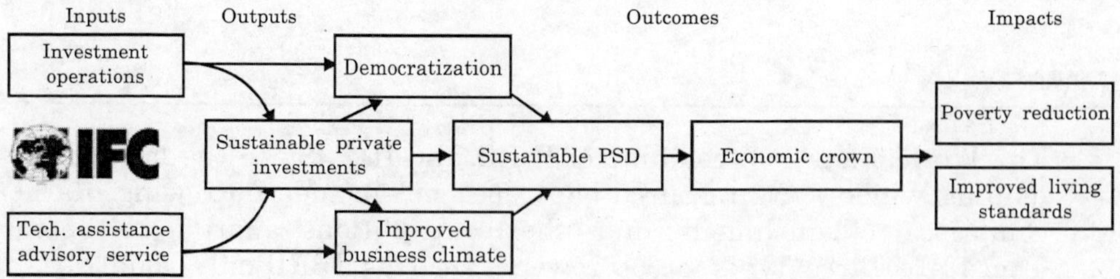

CHART CS16.1 IFC's activities helping catalyse, accelerate, and deepen the development process.

In the years before IFC first articulated its frontier focus in 1998, its approvals were concentrated in the frontier country group approximately to the same extent as gross domestic product (GDP), a proxy for their relative absorptive capacity. Foreign direct investment (FDI) was similarly concentrated. In contrast, in the 1999–2003 period, by pursuing its frontier country strategy, IFC concentrated its approvals at the frontier to an extent nearly twice that of FDI, and was also relatively more concentrated there than GDP. The graduation of large countries such as China and Russia from the frontier group accounts for much of the reduction in FDI and GDP shares after 1999.

As a result of its frontier country emphasis, applied with other screening criteria, IFC has concentrated its investment operations in poorer countries to a greater extent than FDI when account is taken of China as an outlier special case. In countries poorer than China, IFC is substantially more concentrated but has a relatively low concentration in China itself. In contrast, both FDI and GDP are heavily concentrated in China and higher-income developing countries.
Similarly, IFC has maintained a concentration in high-risk countries that is high relative to their share of GDP, and which is considerably higher than that of FDI (which is itself severely under-represented relative to GDP). At the other end of the risk scale, IFC has limited its operations in low-risk countries to investments in pioneering sectors, or where it has had a demonstrable role. Consequently, the concentration of IFC approvals in low-risk countries has remained consistently below—at about half—their share of GDP and FDI.

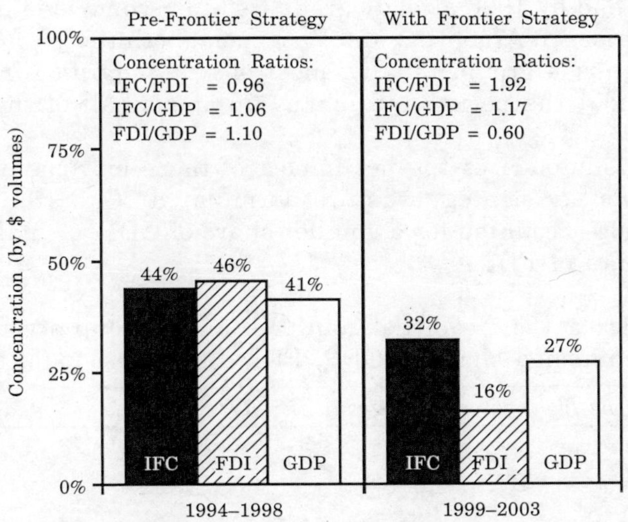

CHART CS16.2 Concentrations in Frontier Countries

Some countries are unable to support significant private sector investment in which IFC can participate. Typically these are countries that are war-torn or suffering from severe political crises, and feature among the World Bank-designated Low Income Countries Under Stress (LICUS). LICUS countries account for 18 per cent by number of the frontier country group in 2004. Even with the frontier focus, since 1998, IFC has managed to find less than 1 per cent of its investment opportunities in the current LICUS group, reflecting the lack of basic infrastructure for supporting private business. Their current share of developing country GDP is similarly low at 0.7 per cent, and only 1.6 per cent of FDI has found its way into these countries, mainly for extractive industries.

In addition to direct investments, IFC is providing TAAS to help create conditions conducive to sustainable private capital investment. This non-investment work has proliferated since the mid-1990s, with 80 per cent of the funds coming from donors and the remainder from IFC and IBRD. While the absolute concentration of IFC's investment approvals in high-risk countries has declined, IFC has increasingly focused its TAAS operations in these countries. In line with its frontier strategy, IFC is now applying more than half of these funds in high-risk countries, to address shortcomings in the local business climate and catalyse a pipeline of viable investment opportunities for the future. IFC has also used technical assistance to support the development of small and medium enterprises (SMEs).

Some Large Countries Have Graduated from the Frontier Group

Since 1998, the frontier strategy has been refined in successive IFC strategy papers but retains a fundamental focus on high-risk countries. In the intervening period, a number of countries have improved their risk ratings and have therefore graduated from the high-risk group, while others have deteriorated from economic or political crises, war, or insurgency. Russia and parts of Eastern and Southern Europe have improved from high-risk to medium- or low-risk. The large economies of Latin America had by 1996 already graduated to become medium-risk. However, following recent crises in Argentina and Venezuela, both these countries have fallen back into the high-risk group. Finally, most of sub-Saharan Africa has remained high-risk throughout the period and makes up about half of the current frontier group.

Table CS16.1 summarizes the net impact of these movements since 1997 (the year before the frontier strategy was first formulated). Overall, the frontier group of countries in 2004 accounted for a smaller share of GDP, a smaller average GDP, and a smaller share of FDI.

TABLE CS16.1 The evolved frontier country group accounting for a diminished share of GDP, FDI, and poor population

Characteristics of the frontier country group in 1997		*Excl. China & India*
Number (%) of countries	90 (20%)	88 (68%)
Share of GDP	38%	18%
Average GDP	\$ 28 bn	\$ 14 bn
Share of FDI	41%	13%
IFC approvals (share %)	\$ 1.1 bn (37%)	\$ 0.9 bn (28%)
Average country GNI per capita	\$ 975	\$ 984
Share of total population	76%	31%
Share of poor population	93%	31%

(Contd.)

Characteristics of the frontier country group in 2004:		*Excl. India*
Number (%) of countries	79 (61%)	78 (60%)
Share of GDP	21%	13%
Average GDP	$ 20 bn	$ 12 bn
Share of FDI	15%	13%
IFC approvals (share %)	$ 1.2 bn (24%)	$ 0.9 bn (19%)
Average country GNI per capita	$ 947	$ 952
Share of total population	30%	29%
Share of poor population	71%	34%

Among the frontier country group, the best project development impacts were achieved in countries with high-risk and middle-income status at the time of approval. This sub-set of frontier countries also yielded the highest aggregate equity returns. The reason for the better performance is that many of these countries subsequently graduated from the high-risk group to become medium- or low-risk by the time of evaluation. In fact, the quality of the investment climate at the time projects were approved has been less of a determinant of their performance than subsequent changes in the investment climate that have occurred during a project's life.

Table CS16.2 shows that among the 217 IFC investment operations evaluated in 2001–2003, development and investment outcomes (and also aggregate equity returns) were significantly better in countries that improved their risk rating and had graduated from the high-risk group by the time of evaluation. Conversely, projects in countries that deteriorated to become high-risk had much lower outcome success rates. In fact, successful projects are associated with improvements in a country's business climate generally, irrespective of the actual country risk group at approval and evaluation. Projects are less successful where country risk ratings deteriorate. These findings, and the growth in income levels shown in Chart CS16.3, highlight the importance of countries taking steps to improve and sustain macro stability and environment for private sector investment.

TABLE CS16.2 Improvements in investment climates and Development/ Investment outcome

A: Movement in country risk group: (based on IICC ratings at project approval and evaluation)	*No.*	*%*	*Development Outcome Success Rate*	*Investment Outcome Success Rate*
Improved from high-risk to medium/low-risk	21	10%	81%	67%
Stayed medium/low-risk	117	54%	62%	54%
Stayed high-risk	57	26%	54%	54%
Deteriorated from medium/low-risk to high-risk	22	10%	41%	32%
Total:	**217**	**100%**	**59%**	**53%**

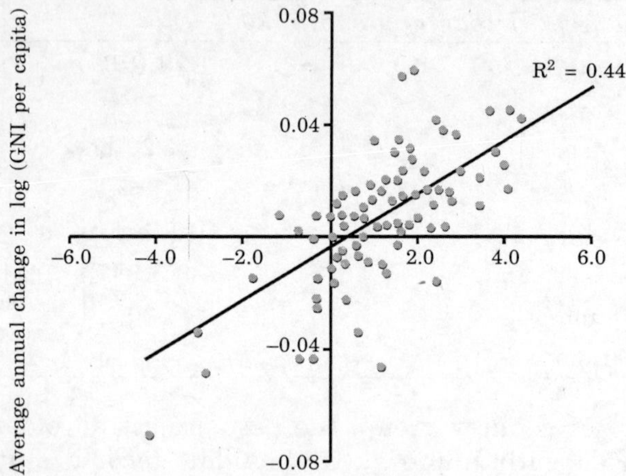

CHART CS16.3 Countries' investment climate and their income per capita.

These results support IFC's frontier strategy since there is considerable upside—for IFC, and the economies and populations of client countries—in helping high-risk countries improve their investment climates. Past performance in the poorest countries (that is, those of low-income status) has been more mixed, with low project business success and less-than-satisfactory environmental and social impacts. This suggests that an alternative frontier country strategy emphasizing poverty intensity alone would almost certainly have yielded worse outcomes—and, therefore, a lower development and investment return on scarce IFC resources—mainly because of insufficient absorptive capacity in the form of good sponsors with viable projects. Defining IFC's frontier strategy in terms of country risk reflects the fact that the quality of a country's business climate is the most appropriate indicator of IFC's potential additionality. IFC's presence on the ground, knowledge of frontier countries, and ability to diversify its risks across many project, sector, and country markets, allow it to address a market failure in supporting viable projects that cannot otherwise attract private capital.

The substantial shrinkage of the frontier country group in terms of its share of GDP and FDI could imply a relative scarcity of bankable projects. There is a risk, therefore, that IFC might direct its resources toward lower quality investments at the margin, relative both to the opportunities that were available in the 1997 frontier group and going forward, in countries that have IICC ratings just above 30. For example, the development outcome success rate for projects approved in Africa during 1996–1998 was significantly below average, a possible result of IFC's high concentration of investment in that period relative to the region's absorptive capacity.

Taking into account these findings, OEG recommended that IFC consider broadening the definition of the frontier country group to include countries with IICC ratings above 30 but that nevertheless qualify on grounds of relatively poor investment climates and, consequently, low private sector activity. Directing IFC resources toward these countries as a strategic priority would help catalyze improvements in their business climates and enable IFC to support more viable companies to grow and prosper, in line with its mission. In its 2005 strategy update.

IFC is considering this and other refinements to the frontier strategy including: expanding the frontier definition to included poor regions in some of the large, middle-income countries; integrating the work of the technical assistance facilities with IFC regional strategies; closer collaboration between IFC and IDA for the provision of infrastructure, micro, and SME finance and investment climate work; and expanding business development efforts in Africa to help build the investment portfolio in the region.

QUESTIONS

1. Explain the basic purpose of IFC's frontier country strategy.
2. Do you think that IFC's involvement has increased in frontier countries?
3. Comment on the impact of graduation of some countries from the frontier group.
4. Is risk related to economic performance? Discuss.

REVIEW QUESTIONS

Objective-Type Questions

1. State whether true (T) or false (F):
   (a) OCR and special funds of ADB are similar in nature. ☐
   (b) IFC provides also equity finance. ☐
   (c) The World Bank gives loans only after guarantee by the host government. ☐
   (d) IFC gives loans only after guarantee by the host government. ☐
   (e) Structural adjustment lending began during early 1960s. ☐
2. Choose the correct answer:
   (a) Least developed countries get funds:
      (i) only from IDA
      (ii) only from the IBRD
      (iii) both from IBRD and IDA
   (b) OCR funds from ADB flows:
      (i) only to poorer member countries
      (ii) only to well-off countries
      (iii) both to poorer and the well-off countries
   (c) Foreign Investment Advisory Services (FIAS) is meant for:
      (i) providing technical advice to member countries
      (ii) providing equity finance
      (iii) none of these

Short-Answer Questions

1. Are the lending terms of IBRD and IDA different?
2. Is the resource base of IBRD and IDA differently structured?
3. What do you mean by structural adjustment lending?

Long-Answer Questions

1. Comment on the World Bank's lending policy.
2. Describe the functions of IFC and comment on its performance.
3. What are the functions of ADB? How has it performed its functions?

REFERENCES

Asian Development Bank (2002), *Annual Report 1998*, Manila, ADB.

Dasgupta, P. et al. (1972), *Guidelines for Project Appraisal*, New York, UNIDO.

Hurni, B.S. (1980), *The Lending Policy of the World Bank in the 1970s: An analysis and evaluation*, Colorado, West View Press.

IFC (2003), *Annual Report*, Washington, D.C.

Little, I.M.D. and J.A. Mirrlees (1974), *A Project Appraisal and Planning for Developing Countries*, London, Heinemann.

Mason, E.S. and R.E. Asher (1973), *The World Bank since Bretton Woods*, Washington, D.C., Brookings Institute, p. 346.

The World Bank (1991), *Annual Report*, Washington, D.C.

——— (2005), *Annual Report*, Washington, D.C.

Zakariya, H.S. (1983), The Petroleum Lending Programme of the World Bank, *Journal of World Trade Law*, XVII, 471–495.

SUGGESTED FURTHER READING

Asian Development Bank, *Annual Reports*, Manila, ADB. IFC, *Annual Reports*, Washington, D.C.

Sharan, V. (1991), *The World Bank Group and SAARC Nations*, New Delhi, Anmol Publishers.

——— (1997), Three Decades of Asian Development Bank: A survey of performance, *Indian Journal of Commerce*, L, June, 28–37.

The World Bank, *Annual Reports*, Washington, D.C.

CHAPTER

17

International Banking

Learning Objectives

The present chapter acquaints the readers with the international banks/eurocurrency market meant primarily for short-term funds. The purpose of the discussion is:

- To explain the motives behind internationalisation of bank and the different modes of internationalisation.
- To present the nature of their financial intermediation function.
- To show the broad direction of their lending.
- To explain the lending risk.
- To describe their eurocurrency creation function, especially the process and the extent thereof.
- To explain the international cash management function.
- To explain banks' intermediation in the foreign exchange market.
- To focus on "Why" and "How" of Control of International banks.

In Chapter 15 we analysed the changing structure of international banking in different forms. Let us now explain the very process of internationalisation of banks, their functions—financial intermediation, credit creation, global cash management and off-the balance-sheet activities, and also their control. Here it may be mentioned that for all practical purposes, the functions of different forms of international banks differ only in minor details.

PROCESS OF INTERNATIONALISATION

Motivating Factors

Why banks go international is a very important question. In this context, Grubel's pioneering study (1977, 1989) explains that it was the spread of multinational enterprises that motivated the banks to follow them. This is natural because a particular bank serving a particular multinational corporation prefers to accompany it. When a multinational enterprise moves abroad and sets up its subsidiaries in different countries, the bank too moves there to provide banking services to its client. Since that bank is close to the parent company, it can provide necessary services to the client in a better way. Viewed from this angle, the bank enjoys an edge over other banks and this edge provides the stimulus for going international. Grubel argues also that the international banks operate on a narrow spread as compared to domestic banks. This means that the interest rate on deposits accepted by the international banks is normally higher than that in case of domestic banks and the interest rate on lending of the international banks is lower than that of domestic banks. This attracts borrowers and depositors from other countries as well which in turn further motivates such banks to go international.

Aliber (1984) feels that it is the difference in the cost of capital among different countries that is responsible for internationalisation of banks. In industrialised countries, capital is abundant and cost of capital is low whereas in developing countries, capital is costly. Naturally, a bank moves its operation from an industrialised country to a developing country to reap the advantages of such a difference.

According to Rugman (1981), it is the process of diversification that brings in stability in profits of the banks and also reduces their systematic risk. The more a bank is spread over countries, the greater the benefits of diversification it derives.

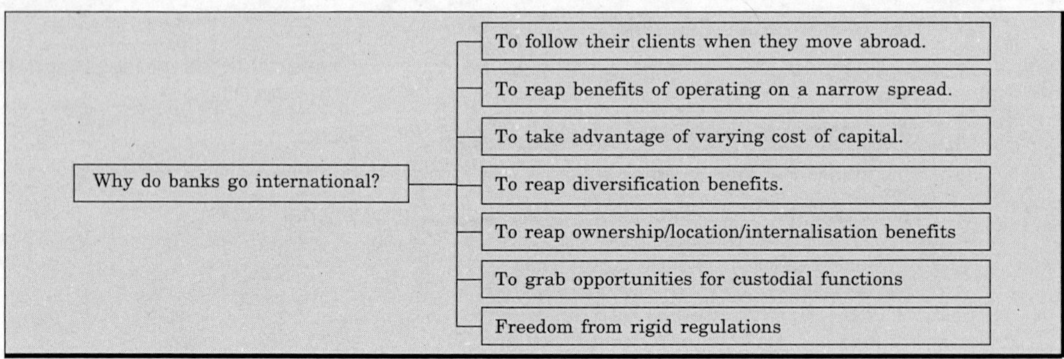

Dunning (1993) has extended his theory of eclectic paradigm (discussed in Chapter 11) to internationalisation of banks. In his view, the ownership advantages manifest in access to transnational clients, professional expertise, access to the international financial market, economies of scale, higher intrinsic value of reserve currencies, and control over the transborder communication network. The internalisation advantages reaped by international banks are normally quality control, economies of coordinating capital flows and the importance of international arbitraging.

Similarly, the location advantages are the absence of governmental regulation, low cost of foreign operation and psychic distance.

Levi (1996) refers to a couple of factors, such as the increasing custodial function of the banks and the avoidance of regulations. Custodial services are granted to Levi (1996) refers to a couple of factors, such as the increasing custodial function of the banks and the avoidance of regulations. Custodial services are granted to clients who make investment in overseas securities. The banks have to collect the securities, collect dividend and offer other related services. With the fast growth in such services that require banks to have overseas offices, banks have moved abroad. The other point Levi stresses is that banks move abroad to avoid reserve requirements, cumbersome reporting requirements, corporate taxes, and such other regulations that are found in the domestic jurisdiction.

Most of the arguments have been empirically tested. From a survey conducted by Khoury (1980), it is clear that the fast growth of international trade and investment has motivated banks to operate abroad. The study of Fielhke (1977) confirms that US foreign investment has a positive bearing on the assets of the US bank branches abroad. Again, from a regression model developed for the 1961–78 period by Goldberg and Saunders (1980), we find that it was the growth of external trade and government control on capital movement in the USA in view of the weakening dollar then that motivated the US banks to go international.

Foreign Banks Branches in India as of November 2024

Sl. No.	*Name of Bank*	*Country of Incorporation*	*No. of Branches in India*
1	AB Bank Ltd.	Bangladesh	1
2	Australia and New Zeland Banking Group ltd.	Australia	1
4	American Express Banking Corporation	USA	1
5	Antwerp Diamond Bank N.V.	Belgium	1
6	Bank Internasional Indonesia	Indonesia	1
7	Bank of America	USA	5
8	Bank of Bahrain & Kuwait BSC	Bahrain	4
9	Bank of Ceylon	Sri Lanka	1
10	Bank of China Ltd.	Bejing, China	1
11	Bank of Nova Scotia	Canada	5
12	Barclays Bank Plc.	United Kingdom	10
13	BNP Paribas	France	8
14	Credit Agricole Corporate & Investment Bank	France	1
15	CTBC Bank Co. Ltd.	Taiwan	2
16	Citibank N.A.	USA	42
17	DBS Bank Ltd.	Singapore	12
18	Deutsche Bank	Germany	17
19	Doha Bank	Qatar	1
20	Emirates NBS Bank P.J.S.C	UAE	3
21	FirstRand Bank Limited	South Africa	1
22	First Abu Dhabi Bank PJSC	UAE	1

(Contd.)

Foreign Banks Branches in India as of November 2024

Sl. No.	*Name of Bank*	*Country of Incorporation*	*No. of Branches in India*
23	HSBC Ltd.	Hong Kong	50
24	Industrial and commercial Bank of China	China	1
25	Industrial Bank of Korea	South Korea	1
26	J.P. Morgan Chase Bank N.A.	USA	1
27	JSC VTB Bank	Russia	1
28	KEB Hana Bank	South Korea	3
29	Kookmin Bank	South Korea	3
30	Mashreq Bank PSC.	UAE	1
31	Mizuho Corporate Bank Ltd.	Japan	6
32	MUFG Bank, Ltd.	Japan	6
33	Nong Hyup Bank	South Korea	1
34	NatWest Markets Plc	Scotland	5
35	PT Bank Maybank Indonesia TBK	Malaysian	1
36	Shinhan Bank	South Korea	5
37	Societe Generale	France	2
38	Sonali Bank Ltd.	Bangladesh	1
39	Standard Chartered Bank	United Kingdom	100
40	Sumitomo Mitsui Banking	Japan	1
41	United	Japan	3
42	UBS AG	Switzerland	1
43	United Overseas Bank Ltd.	Singapore	1
44	Woori Bank	South Korea	2

Source: www.rbi.org

Modes of Internationalisation

The process of internationalisation is a complex process and there are different phases and ways in which a bank can go international. In the first phase, the parent office of a bank creates only a separate department for handling international business transactions. With expansion in the volume of business, the department is further subdivided on functional basis. When the business swells further, the department of international business along with its various wings finds itself unable to manage its affairs. The parent office begins moving abroad in different ways depending upon its volume of business and the rules and regulations in the host country. The different forms and ways in which a bank goes international are as follows:

1. Setting up of representative offices abroad on a selective basis
2. Establishing network of correspondent banking system
3. Setting up of foreign branches
4. Interest acquisition in a foreign bank
5. Participation in the equity of foreign banks
6. Setting up of bank consortia

Setting up of a *representative office* abroad may be treated as an interim arrangement which is followed by setting up of a branch. It is a medium of internationalisation in those cases where the host government does not permit any branch of a foreign banking company or provides only a limited entry for the foreign banks. In a representative office, only a few home country officials who perform the work of liaison between the bank and foreign customers are employed. They do negotiate the transactions on behalf of the bank, but their function is limited. For example, they are not authorised to accept and transfer deposits, nor are they authorised to provide on-site operating services. The greatest advantage of this is that the cost of operation is minimum. But its disadvantage is that it cannot penetrate deep into the foreign market. Moreover, it is difficult to get qualified personnel for the representative office since they are usually reluctant to work for such an office.

In a *correspondent banking system*, the international bank comes in touch with a host-country bank. The latter performs all the transactions on behalf of the former. In other words, the host-country bank acts as an agent of the international bank. Correspondent banking system is better than the representative offices insofar as the latter's functions are limited. Moreover, this system does not involve additional establishment cost. The host-country bank is frequently in touch with the local customers, the benefit of which is reaped by the international bank. However, the disadvantage of the correspondent banking system is that the host-country bank does not prove always sincere for the international bank as it is concerned more about its own business. Sometimes it competes with the latter for a new business. All this prevents growth of the international bank.

The *branches* overcome the demerits of the above two modes. However, the branches are not separate entities from their parent unit. The parent unit has a full control over the functioning of the branches. From this point of view, the branches are a successful mode for implementing the parent company's policies and programmes. The branches perform all types of functions. This is another advantage. However, the governments in many host countries do not permit entry of branches. The officials of the parent company posted in branches take quite a long time to get acquainted with the host country's economic and social environment.

Acquisitions, when an international bank buys a retail bank of the host country, are alternative to the opening of branches. Through acquisition, the bank gets immediately an access to the local market business. However, the problem of this mode is that too much of energy and time is spent on looking for a bank for the purpose of acquisition.

Opening up of *subsidiaries* or *affiliates* is another way of going international. Since the branches face opposition from the host governments and since many banks are not agreeable to acquisition, subsidiaries are a common medium for the expansion of international banks. Under this process, the parent bank participates in the equity capital of the host-country bank. The advantage of this mode is that the parent company has control over the functioning of the subsidiary and is able to implement its policy. Because of the existence of the host-country bank, it comes easily in contact with the local customers. However, there is often conflict between the parent company and the subsidiary on the issue of implementing a particular policy.

When the volume of business is very large, beyond the means of a particular bank, a few international banks come together to set up a *consortium bank* in a host country. It represents a separate establishment. The different parent units represent on the board of control according to their investment in the capital stock of the consortium bank. Such banks were set up originally in the USA, but then they spread over many other countries in order to meet the huge demand for funds. The consortium bank suffers from at least one disadvantage: sometimes conflict arises among the parent units, which impairs their very functioning.

THE FINANCIAL INTERMEDIATION FUNCTION

Financial intermediation, which is a primary function, has two aspects. One is the procurement of funds. The other is the uses of funds. Short-term funds are procured by way of short-term borrowing/deposit from other banks, non-bank deposits, borrowing/deposit through negotiable certificates of deposit, and borrowing from parent unit or other units of the same firm. Experience shows that a major portion of the incoming of short-term funds is represented by inter-bank and intra-bank transfers. Long-term funds are obtained from the sale of equity shares and bonds.

Financial intermediation function is related to deposits, borrowings and lending.

The uses of funds are represented by intra-bank and inter-bank lending, foreign trade financing, loans to domestic and foreign companies and their subsidiaries, and loans to foreign governments.

Deposits

The international banks obtain deposits from:

1. Corporate sector
2. Governments
3. Other banks, known as inter-bank and intra-bank deposits

It is true that the deposits obtained from the government and the corporate sector is large, but inter-bank and intra-bank deposits are very significant from the viewpoint of liquidity. The reason is that a bank deposits frequently its short-period excess cash balance with other banks (Chart 17.1).

The objectives of the deposit management are to:

1. ensure continuity of the flow of funds at the minimal cost,
2. bring in stability in deposit base,
3. match the maturity of deposits with that of lending, and
4. gain from mismatching of interest rates and maturity, if possible.

The deposits of the Euro banks and off-shore banking centres are not subjected to any regulations. They are not required to make cash reserves ratio deposit with the central bank of the host government. However, like the domestic banks, international banks do maintain a precautionary reserve balance. They deposit such balances with the domestic banks or with the parent bank. The balances are very small and they come in the form of non-interest bearing demand deposits. Since the precautionary balance is very small, the international banks do not attach importance to demand deposits or checking account facilities. But they do accept time deposits with maturity varying between one day and several years, usually between seven days and six months. If demanded earlier, deposits are broken earlier with some cut in the interest rate. Because of the absence of large demand deposits, international banks are said to have no captive deposit base. This feature is quite different from that of a domestic bank.

Like domestic banks, international banks too rely on negotiable certificates of deposits as a means of accepting deposit/borrowing, although the nature of certificate of deposit in this case is different. In order to attract bigger amount of funds, the Euro banks issued certificates for the first time in 1960s. The usual form of certificates is known as *tap certificates of deposit.* They are issued in fixed multiples, irrespective of the amount of funds required by the bank at a particular point of time. The other variety is known as *tranche certificate of deposit* which is issued in successive instalments in smaller denomination. It is more common with the smaller banks with limited need for funds. Again, there are *forward certificates of deposit* also that represent a contract to issue such certificates at a fixed rate of interest and at a given future date.

Chart 17.1 shows the cross-border claims of international banks outstanding at the end of September 2024.

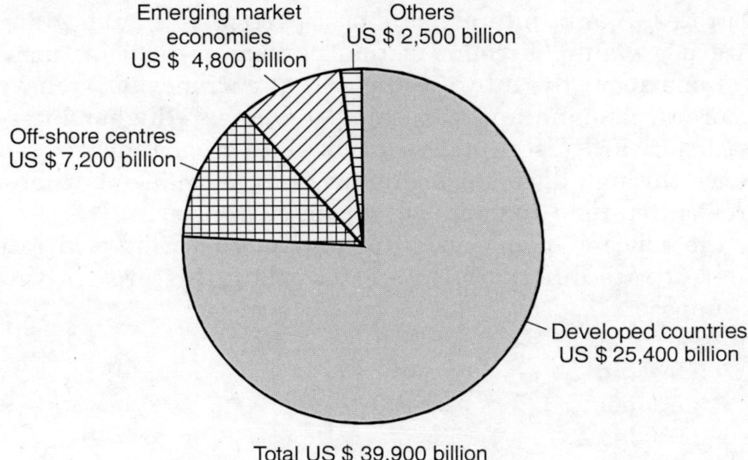

CHART 17.1 International bank cross-border claims outstanding as of September, 2024.

Source: *BIS Quarterly Review*, September 2024.

Lending

Unlike lending by a domestic bank, the loan agreements of international banks do not embrace normally restrictive covenants, such as ratio limits, dividend restrictions, and interest coverage. The reason is that there is greater amount of competition among international banks in view of absence of bar on the entry of banks in the Euro currency market or the international money market. Many banks, may be of different origins, compete for the same customer. It is a fact they apply preferably those clauses in the loan agreement that conform to the policy and practices of their parent organisation. But at the same time, they ignore applying restrictive clauses in order to allure the customers. The customers prefer to approach a bank which originates from their own country. For example, a Japanese firm prefers to approach a Japanese bank. These banks attract other customers through offering convenient terms.

A loan from an international bank available to an affiliate of a company should not be looked at in isolation of the company's entire network. For example, if a branch of an American bank gives loan to an American affiliate located in India, the loan is governed at least to some extent by the relations between the two parent companies. Any default may impair their relationship in the USA.

International bank loans are both short-term and long-term. Medium-term loans are also available for a period of one to five years.

Rate of Interest

The deposit rates in international banking are usually comparable with the rates of negotiable certificates of deposit. However, the rate varies from one case to another, depending on the tiering of the bank, maturity structure of deposits, liquidity of deposits, and the currency in which the deposits are made. A creditworthy bank is often able to get deposits at lower rates. Similarly, deposit with a longer maturity carries higher rates. Again, interest rate of a particular currency deposit depends upon the forward premium/discount of that currency which in turn is influenced by the expectations about the future value of that currency. Currency with forward premium is more in demand and naturally, it carries a higher interest rate than a currency with forward discount does. But since a currency is convertible into another currency through different techniques in the financial or foreign exchange market, interest rates tend to equalise among currencies.

Based on the concept of interest rate parity where forward rate differential equals the interest rate differential, we can explain this process with the help of an example. Suppose:

90-day interest rate:

SF: 5.0% bid
5.5% ask

Dollar: 6.0% bid
6.5% ask

Exchange rate: US $/SF 1: Spot: 0.38–0.382
Forward: 0.385–0.387

If dollar is borrowed and deposited in the SF market, the bank will earn, while covering them forward, 3.81 per cent which is shown as follows:

$$\text{Forward differential} = (0.387 - 0.382)/0.382 \times 365/90 = 5.31\%$$

The rate of SF deposit = 5.0 + 5.31 = 10.31% p.a.
Less dollar borrowing rate 6.50%
Net advantage gained by the bank 3.81%

(*Note:* When one borrows a currency, one has to pay to the bank the offer interest rate. When one sells a currency to the bank, one has to sell it at the bid rate.)

If such activities continue, the SF deposit rate will fall. The spot value of SF will improve and the forward value of SF will fall. A point will come where dollar interest rate will be equal to the sum of SF interest rate and the forward premium in the exchange market.

The inter-bank short-term lending rate, on the other hand, is greater than the deposit rate, usually by one-eighth of one per cent, so that the financial intermediation proves profitable for the banks. In fact, it is the lending rate that influences the deposit rate. The lending rate is determined by the arithmetic average of the rates at which six major banks in London are willing to deposit dollars or lend to each other in the forenoon on a particular day. This average is known as *LIBOR* or the *London Inter-bank Offer Rate*. In practice, lending rate is the sum of LIBOR and a contractually determined spread which generally ranges between 0.75 per cent and 3.0 per cent, depending on the market conditions, creditworthiness of the borrowers and the maturity structure. Spread is lower if the borrower is creditworthy or if credit market is not tight or if loans carry shorter maturity. Otherwise, spread will be large.

LIBOR is London Inter-bank Offer Rate determined by the average of the rates at which major banks in London make deposits/lending in the forenoon of a particular day.

What is LIBOR? How is it calculated?

London Inter-bank Offer Rate (LIBOR) represents the average of the rates at which 16 major banks of London borrow in the forenoon of a particular day. The rates are reported between 11 AM and 11.10 AM GMT. When 16 different rates are available, the two central quartiles are averaged to find out the day's LIBOR. LIBOR for that day is published at 11.30 AM GMT.

An example of LIBOR on 15.4.2024: The banks' rates in percentage terms are as follows:
HBOS: 5.35000; Credit Suisse: 5.34000; Bank of America: 5.33000; JP Morgan Chase: 5.32000; HSBC: 5.31000; Bank of Tokyo-Mitsubishi: 5.72000; Barclays:5.25000; Norinchukin Bank: 5.72000; Royal Bank of Canada 5.71750; Lloyds: 5.71000; Westdeutsche Landesbank: 5.71000; Rabobank: 5.71000; UBS AG: 5.71000; Royal Bank of Scotland: 5.70500; Deutsche Bank: 5.70000; and Citigroup: 5.70000.

After averaging the two centre quartiles, LIBOR comes out to be: 5.17765%.

Source: Mint: 17.4.2024.

In this context, a relevant question arises: Are international banks' lending/deposit rates influenced by these rates in the domestic banking sector? The answer does not seem to be negative. In fact, the rates in the domestic credit market fix up a floor and a ceiling for the international banks' rates. A customer approaches an international bank for making deposits only when the rate on deposit is higher than in the domestic banks. It borrows from an international bank only when the rates are lower than in the case of domestic bank. However, it is assumed in this case that the domestic banking sector is well developed to compete with the international banks.

The factors responsible for lower lending rates in an international bank may be that the activities of the bank are well developed and spread over a number of countries that lessen the lending risk. Similarly, deposit rate is higher because these banks need not abide by the statutory reserve requirements; nor do they come under the domestic regulations where deposit rates are administered. They are free to operate on a narrow margin between the lending and the deposit rates.

Again, interest rate in one market influences the interest rate in the other market. For example, if domestic interest rate in the US banking market rises, it will raise the interest rate in the Euro dollar market. Since there is possibility for arbitrage, the interest in Euro market, for example, will be influenced in the same way. However, the control on the movement on capital insulates one market from the other. This is because arbitrage does not work in this case. When Germany imposed control on the inflow of capital during 1970s, the Euro market deposit rate fell below the domestic deposit rate.

Interest rate on medium-term loan is higher than the interest rate on the short-term loans. It is not only because of longer maturity but also because of commitment fee charged on the undisbursed amount of the loan. In the case of syndicated medium-term loan, management fee and the agency fee are charged by the lead manager. Fee is different from the spread. Fee is paid at the front-end; on the other hand, spread is charged over the life of the loan.

DIRECTION AND PURPOSES OF LENDING

The loans of international banks, as it has been mentioned in the earlier section, move into different directions. They move to sister units of the same firm or to the parent unit, mainly from the viewpoint of working capital management. They move to other banks; this is, known as *inter-bank transaction*. The banks' loans move to exporters and importers for financing of foreign trade. They move to non-trading companies for meeting their short-term, medium-term and long-term financial requirements. They move also to different governments for easing of balance of payments problem. When the borrower's requirements are large, the loans flow in the form of syndicated loan, which has already been discussed in Chapter 15. Therefore, in this section, we like to explain inter-bank transactions, loans to the companies and loans to governments.

Inter-bank Transactions

Inter-bank transactions occupy a significant place in financial intermediation. As such, transactions account for between two-thirds and three-quarters of the banks' total external liabilities and claims. Inter-bank transactions may be within one financial centre or may cover many financial centres. Inter-bank borrowing, deposits and loans involve short-term funds and so they are very important from the viewpoint of smoothening of liquidity, transfer of liquidity and equitable allocation of international liquidity. If a bank is short of deposits required for maintaining liquidity, it can borrow immediately from other banks. On the contrary, if deposits are more than the required amount, the bank lends or deposits immediately the excess funds to/with other banks. This way inter-bank transactions are highly liquidity-smoothening.

> Inter-bank transactions relate to short-term borrowing, deposit and lending among different banks.

The question of liquidity is very crucial for small and less creditworthy banks, for they fail to attract the required amount of non-bank deposits. But in this case, they get inter-bank funds. The creditworthy banks, on the other hand, get large non-bank deposits and they lend/deposit the excess funds with the liquidity-short banks. Sometimes the banks go for inter-bank transactions just for the sake of continuing as an active participant in the inter-bank market. This adds to their prestige and financial position.

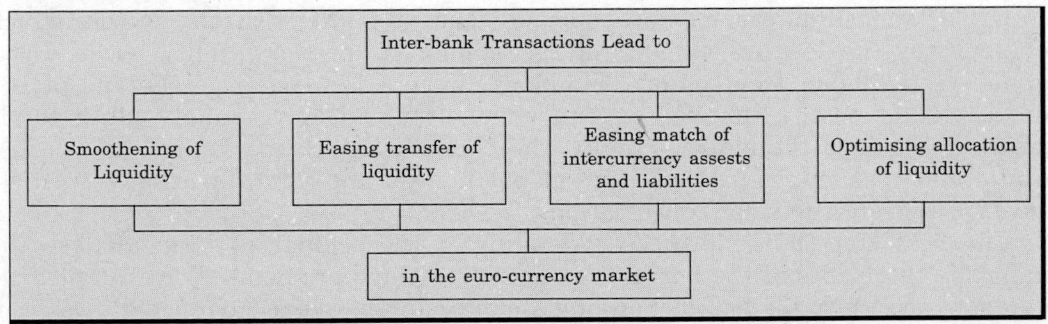

The inter-bank transactions help a bank in matching the currency composition of its assets and liabilities. A long position in a particular currency can easily be matched with the short-term position of another bank in that currency. The long and short positions in a particular currency are adjusted also through transactions in the foreign exchange market, but the adjustment through inter-bank transactions is easier.

As far as optimal allocation of liquidity is concerned, the inter-bank transactions are an effective tool. The banks borrow and lend in different currencies in different markets that influence the stock of a particular currency in a particular market. In other words, the market forces determine the stock of a particular currency in a particular market. This way, the allocation of liquidity in a particular market tends to move towards optimisation.

Inter-bank transfers are normally transacted on telephones, telex, etc. Each bank places a limit on the other bank in relation to the size of lending or deposit. The limit is prescribed on the basis of financial conditions of the bank. Sometimes approaching a fellow bank is costly and time-taking. In such cases, brokers are approached, who immediately quote the bid and ask rates of different banks. On getting confirmation from the transacting bank, they assist in the transactions.

Loans to Corporate Sector

Corporate sector loans are short-term, medium-term and long-term. Short-term loans finance carrying of receivables and inventory, tax and dividend payments, and purchase of short-term securities, etc. The medium-term loans finance plant expansion, equipment purchase, debt consolidation, joint-venture funding, and so on. Long-term loans to the corporate sector are not common. They are available for building of infrastructure and other facilities. The banks provide also bridge finance which is required during the period preceding start-up of operations. They provide foreign buyer's finance which includes purchase or discounting of notes and bills of exchange.

Besides, the banks provide different types of services that do involve finance in many cases. They arrange for equity placements and non-traditional debt financing. All this resembles merchant banking facilities. The banks arrange for leasing of capital equipment. They render bid bond facilities where the suppliers are to deposit some percentage of the contract value with the buyer so that the amount may compensate the loss if the award-winning firm withdraws subsequently.

Often, the suppliers have to deposit some amount with the buyer, which compensates the loss on account of the supply of inferior quality goods. Such funds are available from banks. Similarly, buyers pay some percentage of the contract value to the supplier well in advance for ensuring supply. Such funds are available from the banks. Finally, the banks assist companies in the working capital management, in underwriting money market and capital market securities, and in corporate financial consultations.

The first step in the process of lending to the companies is to analyse the financial statements of the borrowers. There are some problems. For example, the system of accounting is found changing among countries. The currency differs from one country to another. Again, the banks examine the quality of management, quality of operation, and the prospective mode of the uses of funds. If required, the bank officials visit the site.

When the bank is satisfied with the performance of the borrowing companies, it considers about the currency in which it has to lend. The loans may be secured. Or they may be unsecured, depending on the creditworthiness of the borrower. In the case of short-term loans, current assets may be used as security. In medium-term loans, fixed assets too can be pledged.

Recycling of Petro-dollars

In the wake of hike in international oil prices in 1973–1974, the oil-exporting countries experienced huge surpluses on current account. On the contrary, net-oil-importing countries—developed and developing—faced huge deficit on the current account. The surpluses were deposited with the international banks that lent to the deficit governments to solve their balance of payments problem. This type of financial intermediation came to be known as *recycling of petro-dollars*.

Recycling of petro-dollars means deposit of oil export proceeds with an international bank that is used subsequently for lending to oil-importing countries.

Statistics reveal that the current account surplus of the oil-exporting countries jumped up from US $ 6.0 billion in 1973 to US $ 67.0 billion in 1974. The second oil shock in 1979 inflated it to US $ 110.0 billion by 1980. On the other hand, the top ten industrial countries and Switzerland experienced a sudden shift in their current account—from a surplus of US $ 12.0 billion in 1973 to a deficit of US $ 13 billion in 1974 and to US $ 53.0 billion by 1980. The smaller developed countries too witnessed a deficit that moved on from US $ 16.0 billion in 1974 to US $ 24.0 billion in 1980. The oil-importing developing countries faced a deficit that mounted up from US $ 6.0 billion in 1973 to US $ 66.0 billion in 1980. The international banks came to their rescue and met about one-half of the deficit during these years (Johnston, 1982). The role of international banks was really significant, especially when the official donors were aid-weary.

However, there were some problems. The amount of bank loans did not correlate positively with the amount of deficit. In some years, when deficit was large, bank loans were small. In other years, when deficit was small, loans were large. All this was because the loans were guided by creditworthiness of the borrowers and not by their need. In this process, low-income countries got less loans. Moreover, higher interest on the loans led to the problem of servicing and indebtedness among the borrowers. Yet again, the banks attached importance to short-term economic indicators which resulted often in discontinuity in the flow of loans. These were the minus points of the recycling of petro-dollars.

CONCERNS OF THE LENDERS, BORROWERS AND DEPOSITORS

Lenders

Lenders have normally to face two kinds of risk. They are:

1. Country risk
2. Exchange rate risk

Country risk is classified as sovereign risk and transfer risk. Sovereign risk arises when a national government is unwilling or unable to repay loan. On the other hand, transfer risk emerges when a private borrower is unable to repay debt owing to political or economic conditions prevailing in the country. Walter (1983) explains the factors influencing the country risk. Important among them are supply-side elements, demand-side and monetary elements, external economic and political developments, quality of national economic management team, and domestic capital constraints. The supply-side elements include the country's ability to produce for export and for domestic consumption, qualitative and quantitative dimension of labour force, capital stock, natural resource base, level of technology, entrepreneurship, etc. On the demand side, banks should be interested in assessing the factors that influence taxes, government spending, transfer payments, and the fiscal soundness of public and private sector units.

Country risk arises when the borrowing government/private borrower fails to repay loan.

Similarly, the indicators of the monetary aspect are the domestic monetary base, money supply, net domestic credit, price index, net foreign capital assets and net foreign debt, the external reserves, etc. On the external economic front, volume and geographic pattern of foreign trade and the stability of export earnings may be considered.

Political factors are both external and internal. Internal political factors are often responsible for expropriation of foreign assets. So the government policy in this respect should be taken into account. The possibility of strikes, terrorism or sabotage, etc. may also be assessed. External political factors may take the form of invasion, foreign-inspired insurgency, and so on. Considering all the above-mentioned factors, the borrowing country should be rated. The lending policy should be redesigned accordingly.

Foreign exchange risk is related to the process of financial intermediation. The banks hold foreign currency positions for varying periods. The intra-firm and inter-firm payments move through banks for which foreign currencies lie with the banks for varying periods. This is why any change in the exchange rate influences the banks' earnings. The detailed nature and management of foreign exchange risk are discussed in Chapters 9 and 10. The readers are advised to go through the relevant pages, if needed.

Borrowers

Price of the loan is the prime factor for the borrowers. The international banks normally charge low rate of interest. But, as Levich (2001) explains, this is not enough. When one takes into account the upfront fee paid by the borrower in a lump-sum way, the reset in long-term floating rate loans and the collateral of any form, it is difficult to say how much lower is the interest rate charged by the international banks.

Again, there is interest rate risk always associated with the euro-currency loans. LIBOR changes lead, in turn, to the interest rate risk. The borrower may gain from a floating-rate loan when the interest rate is tending to fall. But what will happen if LIBOR tends to rise. However, the risk can be reduced through interest rate futures or other interest rate risk management techniques.

Depositors

The depositors are the worst-hit. If a euro-bank accepts deposits from a non-resident, the currency involved will not belong to the country where the bank is located. Nor will the currency belong to the depositor's country because the deposits involve normally a foreign currency. In such cases, if any dispute arises, it is difficult to know in advance which country will claim jurisdiction.

Again, the international banks provide access usually to big depositors. Small depositors avail this facility only indirectly through money market mutual funds. This means that all the depositors do not avail the facilities given by the international banks.

THE CREDIT CREATION FUNCTION

The essential features of international banks, as opposed to the non-banking financial intermediaries, are that they create credit, as a result of which they are able to lend more than what they receive as deposit. A bank lends more because it does not lend in cash but it gives the borrower the power to issue cheques for the loan amount, and all the cheques issued by the borrower are not presented for cash payment; rather, the cheques are deposited with the banks. Naturally, the bank does not need cash for honouring all the cheques issued. The amount by which the total deposit including redeposit exceeds the original cash deposit represents the amount of credit creation. The ratio between the total deposit and the original cash deposit is the *credit creation multiplier*.

Credit creation is the amount representing the difference between total deposit including redeposit and the original cash deposit.

The Process of Eurocurrency Creation

It would be relevant to explain here, the process of eurocurrency creation or the credit creation in the eurocurrency market. Let us take a simple example. A firm in the USA pays $ 1,000 for its import from a French exporter through a cheque drawn on a bank in the USA. The cheque is not encashed by the exporter but is deposited in the US bank. Both the accounts—the account on which the cheque is drawn and the account to which it is deposited represent demand deposit accounts. Thus there is no transaction of cash but the ownership of $ 1,000 stands transferred from domestic to foreign control.

The French exporter, being interested in earning interest, transfers the amount from the demand deposit account to a time deposit account in a bank based in London. The London-based bank deposits the same amount with its correspondent US bank as a demand deposit. Consequently, the amount moving out from the USA to the London-based eurobank reaches back the US bank. Moreover, the time deposit of the French exporter in the London-based euro bank represents creation of eurodollars without any movement of funds from the USA.

Again, the London-based eurobank cannot hold the demand deposit with the US bank for long because it has to pay interest to the French exporter on the time deposit. So it will lend this amount to a Swiss party who wishes to import from the USA. Now the Swiss importer, after obtaining loan, issues a cheque on its demand deposit in order to pay for the import to the US exporter. The US exporter will deposit the cheque with the US bank.

The above example shows that there is a chain of ownership between the original dollar depositor and the US bank. There is also a changing control over deposit and the use for which the money is put. Finally, the same amount of cash finances many transactions only through accounting entries.

The Extent of Credit Creation

There is of course one question. When the international banks do not normally accept demand deposits except for small non-interest bearing demand deposit under precautionary motive, the credit creation multiplier in their case should be lower than in the case of domestic banks. However, as Hewson and Sakakibara (1974) argue, since the international banks operate on a lower margin (higher deposit rates and lower lending rates), their ability to create credit is quite large as compared to that of domestic banks. Again, Lee (1973), Bell (1973), and Klopstock (1988) believe that, since the international banks need not abide by the regulatory norms of the host governments, such as cash reserves ratio, their ability to create credit is larger than that of domestic banks.

This does not mean that they are not aware of the leakage. An important leakage manifests in the form of re-deposits with non-banking financial institutions, especially when they offer better terms for attracting deposits. The greater the magnitude of leakage, the lower will be the credit creation multiplier. Various estimates have been made about the credit creation multiplier. Johnston (1982) estimates that if leakage coefficient is 1.0, there will be naturally no credit creation. But if it comes down to 0.2 and if there is no reserves provision, the multiplier will be 5.0. If there is no leakage and no reserves provision, the multiplier will attain infinity. The estimate by Lee (1973) set multiplier at 1.27 during March 1963 and at 1.92 during December 1969. Fratianni and Savons (1971) estimated the multiplier between 3.0 and 7.0. The estimate of Makin (1972) was quite liberal—between 10.31 and 18.45.

GLOBAL CASH MANAGEMENT

The international banks help their global customers, especially the MNCs in their cash management through an integrated payments and collection clearing mechanism. MNCs are found frequently transferring cash from one unit to the other or from/to the centralised cash pool as a part of their international cash management strategy. International banks ease such transfers. Moreover, there are millions of trade payments across countries. Such payments, if not collected in time, lead to huge cost on account of float. The international banks ease such payments and help reduce the float. It is because:

1. They have membership in all major clearing systems around the globe, viz. CHIPS and EUROCHAPS in the UK, EAF–2 and ELS in Germany, CHIPS in the USA and many others.
2. They do have outsourcing solutions for payments and collection.
3. They possess a range of liquidity management tools and structure multilateral netting arrangements.
4. They maintain electronic delivery system to expedite payments and collection.
5. They offer innovative business-to-business e-commerce solutions promoting cost-effective global transactions.

This way the global cash management function of the international banks is really significant.

INTERMEDIATION IN THE FOREIGN EXCHANGE MARKET

Besides financial intermediation, credit creation and global cash management, the other major function of international banks is the intermediation in the foreign exchange market, which is often known as *off-the balance sheet activities*. This function, as discussed in Chapter 15, emerged in 1980s with a sudden downtrend in the lending activities.

In the foreign exchange market, banks play the role of a middleman between the buyer and the seller of foreign currency. Suppose a person having a British pound likes to exchange it with the US dollar. There is another person who likes to buy the British pound for his US dollar. The bank helps in this exchange. The spread between the buying and the selling rate is the income to the bank.

The role of international banks goes even further. Banks are the market-maker. They take a position in a particular foreign currency for a specified period so that they may sell it when its price goes higher in future. This way they influence the supply of and demand for a particular currency and thereby determine the shape of the foreign exchange market.

The foreign exchange market is spread globally. But the banks bring remote locations to proximity. They transact business on telephones and encourage spot transactions between distantly located customers. They have both the forward and backward linkages—with the customers as well as with other banks.

The arbitrage operation of the international banks in the foreign exchange market is one of the most important functions. They buy cheap and sell dear. The process brings in equality in foreign exchange rates.

The forward transactions are done through banks. The banks play a vital role in the market for currency options. For the purchaser of options, they act as a seller of options. For the seller of options, they act as a purchaser of options. It is because of the increasing role of the international banks that over-the-counter options market accounts for a large segment of the currency options transactions.

CONTROL OF INTERNATIONAL BANKS

Control of the activities of international banks involves two fundamental questions. One is *why* they should be controlled. The other is *how* they should be controlled. These two issues are the subject-matter of this section.

The "Why" of Control

There are four main reasons often put forth for the control over the activities of international banks:

1. International banks add to the stock of money supply through credit creation and this way they encourage inflation.
2. These banks are sometimes responsible for bank failures that mar the interest of the depositors. This is because they siphon off suddenly a good amount of cash to other countries and create liquidity problem in the banking sector. This is also because they do not avail of the "lender of the last resort" facility.
3. They charge high interest rates causing unmanageable indebtedness among the borrowing governments.
4. They do not adhere to the credit allocation policy of the host government, which is based on the socio-economic environment there.

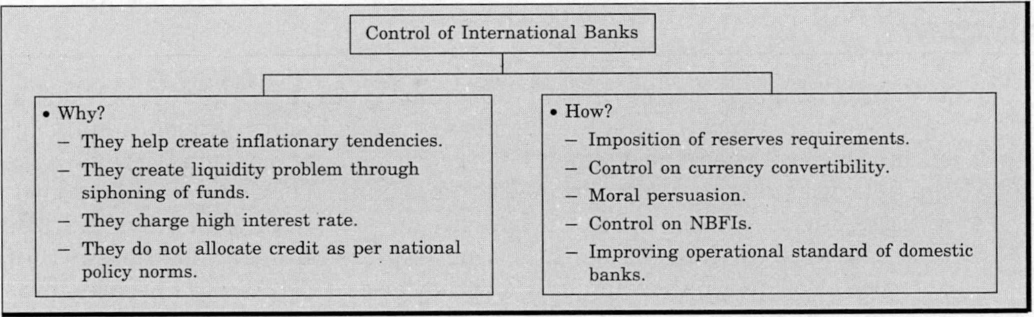

There are some counter arguments too. For example, it is said that the international banks are more efficient in maturity transformation and so they contribute more to liquidity in the banking system. It is also said that the share of international banks in total money supply in a country is not very large, which means that their activities do not easily lead to inflation. Again, it is a fact that they do not avail of the "lender of the last resort" facility, but in case of liquidity crisis, they get support from their parent organisation or from sister units. However, as experience shows, the arguments in favour of control of the international banks have been found to hold good on a number of occasions. This strengthens the case for control.

The "How" of Control

One way to control the activities of international banks is to impose statutory reserves requirements on them. This is expected to ensure equity between them and the domestic banks and to check disintermediation of funds. It will also improve the efficacy of national monetary policy so as to control money supply. It may also encourage business to be conducted on-shore, which may be advantageous for the national authorities. But at the same time, this provision will be taxing on international banking. Again, it will be possible to check disintermediation of funds, but international banks will try to find new ways, which may be more hazardous. Imposition of reserves requirements by a few government cannot be effective as international banks will move their offices to countries with lax regulations. So it is necessary to have a consensus on this issue among the host governments.

Secondly, there should be some control on the convertibility of currency. Hoffmeyer (1976) suggests that payments in foreign currency should be approved by the monetary authorities of the host country. But it is very difficult to police thousands of transactions.

The third way is *moral persuasion*. International banks should be periodically urged not take any step that dilutes the interest of the host country or the domestic banking sector.

Fourthly, some forms of control should be imposed on the non-banking financial institutions too. But such controls should be mild in nature.

Finally, the best way is to raise the operational standard of the domestic banking industry so that it can face the challenges posed by the international banks. Whatever be the measures, there should be consensus among different countries on these issues.

SUMMARY

- The international banks are of different types but their functions and operation are almost the same. Factors responsible for internationalisation of banks have been the tremendous growth in international trade and in the activities of the multinational corporations. They are manifest also in differing interest rates and in the benefits on account of global diversification. It is also viewed that the banks' ownership advantage, and the advantage on account of internalisation and location have led them to operate abroad.
- The international banks operate abroad through representative and correspondent offices, through branches and subsidiaries, and through acquiring a going concern. They set up a consortium when the size of business is large.
- The functions of international banks are: financial intermediation, credit creation, international cash management and intermediation in the foreign exchange market. These banks mobilise funds through deposits and borrowing and lend the funds to different units of the same firm, to different banks, to international traders, to non-trading companies and to governments. When the size of lending is large, they go for syndicated lending.
- International banks create credit, which means they lend more than what they receive as deposit. This provides additional liquidity in the banking industry as well as in other sectors.
- The international cash management function of these banks helps maintain liquidity among MNCs. International banks operate in foreign exchange market and participate in spot and forward deals, in arbitrage, and in the market for currency options.

- Since the functions of international banks are not strictly regulated, they are sometimes found not acting in the interest of the host country. There is need for control on their activities. There are different ways for regulating them, but they need collective effort among the host and home governments.

CASE STUDY

ABN AMRO BANK AND CORRESPONDENT BANKING IN INDIA

ABN AMRO bank has emerged as a major correspondent bank owing to a large network. In India, it operates in six major cities, viz. Baroda, Chennai, Kolkata, Mumbai, New Delhi and Pune. Being a correspondent bank, its product offerings are found primarily in the area of trade and clearing. It is doing well in these areas owing to strong tie-up with local Indian banks reaching 350 centres across the country. As a result, payments are effected speedily and effectively.

Cash Management

The customised products in the area of cash management include cheques payable at par at all its branches across the country, apart from traditional collection services, such as collection of outstation/upcountry cheques drawn on other banks.

ABN AMRO is a member of all major clearing centres in the major financial centres. It has an electronic delivery system and structures multilateral netting of cash.

Trade Services

Under trade services, the Bank offers a comprehensive range of products, such as:

1. LC reimbursement
2. Indian rupee trade payments
3. Handling documentary bills for collection
4. Bills negotiation
5. Letter of credit advising
6. Letter of credit confirmation
7. Guarantees

Treasury Services

Treasury services at ABN AMRO Bank (India) are available round-the-clock. Rupee funding at its treasury desk is provided at competitive rates along with advice on market trends and rates. It provides also advisory services on the request of financial institutions and corporates in the area of regulatory, economic and financial matters including depository services.

QUESTIONS

1. Describe the network of ABN AMRO Bank in India.
2. What role does it play for global cash management?
3. Name the Bank's products in the area of trade services.
4. What do you mean by treasury services? How does ABN AMRO (India) perform this job?

REVIEW QUESTIONS

Objective-Type Questions

1. State whether true (T) or false (F):

(a) In correspondent banking system, the host country bank acts as an agent of the international bank. ☐

(b) The ratio between the total deposit and original cash deposit is known as credit creation multiplier. ☐

(c) Sovereign risk arises when a private borrower is unable to repay debt. ☐

(d) Sovereign risk arises when the borrowing government refuses to repay debt. ☐

(e) Inter-bank transactions are an efficient tool for optimal allocation of liquidity in the banking sector. ☐

2. Choose the correct answer:

(a) Setting up a bank consortium means:

(i) an organisation of two or more banks
(ii) a single bank
(iii) none of these

(b) Financial intermediation function involves:

(i) accepting deposit and lending
(ii) participation in foreign exchange market
(iii) participation in the securities market

(c) Euro banks operate normally:

(i) on a narrow margin compared to domestic banks
(ii) on a wider margin
(iii) on a similar margin

Short-Answer Questions

1. What is recycling of petro-dollars?
2. Do international banks create credit?
3. Explain the different forms of lending risk.
4. What are the objectives of inter-bank transactions?

Long-Answer Questions

1. What are the motivating factors behind internationalisation of banks?
2. Describe the different modes of internationalisation of banks.
3. How do international banks intermediate in the foreign exchange market?
4. Should international banks be controlled? What are the ways of controlling them?

REFERENCES

Aliber, R.Z. (1984), International Banking: A survey, *Journal of Money, Credit and Banking*, XVI, 661–678.

Bell, G. (1973), *The Euro-Dollar Market and the International Financial System*, New York, Wiley, pp. 42–53.

Dunning, J.F. (1993), *The Globalisation of Business*, London and New York, Routledge, pp. 242–283.

Fielhke, N. (1977), The Growth of US Banking Abroad: An analytical survey, in Federal Reserve Bank of Boston, *Key Issues in International Banking*, Boston.

Fratianni, M. and P. Savons (1971), Euro-dollar Creation: Comments on Professor Machlup's Propositions and Developments, *Banca Nazionale del Lavoro Quarterly Review*, 13–22.

Goldberg, L.G. and A. Saunders (1980), The Causes of the US Banks' Expansion Overseas: The case of Great Britain, *Journal of Money, Credit and Banking*, XII, 630–643.

Grubel, H. (1977), A Theory of International Banking, *Banca Nazionale del Lavoro Quarterly Review*, 349–364.

Grubel, H. (1989), Multinational Banking, in P. Enderwick (Ed.), *Multinational Service Firms*, London and New York, Routledge, pp. 61–78.

Hewson, J. and E. Sakakibara (1974), The Euro-dollar Multiplier: A portfolio approach, *IMF Staff Papers*, XXV, 307–328.

Hoffmeyer, E. (1976), Monetary Cooperation and the Euro Markets, *Euromoney*, 70–74.

Johnston, R.B. (1982), *The Economics of the Euro-market: History, theory and policy*, New York, St. Martin's Press, pp. 217–243.

Khoury, S.J. (1980), *Dynamics of Development Banking*, New York, Praeger, Chap. 7.

Klopstock, F.H. (1988), The Euro-dollar Market: Some unresolved issues, *Princeton Essays in International Finance*, Princeton, Princeton University Press.

Lee, B.E. (1973), The Euro-dollar Multiplier, *Journal of Finance*, XXVIII, 867–874.

Levi, M.D. (1996), *International Finance*, New York, McGraw-Hill, Chap. 22.

Levich, R.M. (2001), *International Financial Markets: Prices and Policies*, Singapore: McGraw-Hill/Irwin.

Makin, J.H. (1972), Demand and Supply Functions for Stocks of Euro-dollar Deposits: An empirical study, *Review of Economics and Statistics*, LIV, 381–391.

Rugman, A.M. (1981), *Inside the Multinationals*, New York, Columbia University Press, pp. 89–103.

Walter, I. (1983), Country Risk in E.N. Roussakis (Ed.), *International Banking*, New York, Praeger, pp. 199–223.

SUGGESTED FURTHER READING

Dufey, G. and I. Giddy (1978), *The International Money Market*, Englewood Cliffs, Prentice-Hall.

Hultman, C.W. (1990), *The Environment of International Banking*, Englewood Cliffs, Prentice-Hall.

Park, Y.S. and J. Zwick (1985), *International Banking in Theory and Practice*, Readings, Massachusetts, Addison-Wesley Publishers.

CHAPTER 18

International Financial Market Instruments

Learning Objectives

International securities market being an important segment of international financial market makes available long-term, medium-term and short-term funds. The process is, of course, different. The borrower issues securities to obtain funds. The present chapter discusses the different types of securities to obtain funds. In particular, it attempts:

- To discuss how international equities are issued.
- To explain different kinds of bonds and how they are issued.
- To present the features of euro notes and euro commercial papers meant for short-term funds and medium-term euro notes meant for medium-term funds.

Funds are raised from the international financial market also through the sale of securities, such as international equities or Euro-equities, international bonds, and some structured products like equity-linked notes (ELNs), Credit-linked notes (CLNs) or Market linked Certificates of Deposit medium-term and short-term Euro notes and Euro commercial papers other than these there are some Derivatives viz., futures, options, swaps and forwards.

As mentioned in Chapter 15, the securities market began to grow on a big way after the international debt crisis of early 1980s. Presently, the use of securities is quite extensive. We shall therefore throw some light on the different aspects of these securities.

INTERNATIONAL EQUITIES

International equities or the Euro-equities do not represent debt, nor do they represent foreign direct investment. They are comparatively a new instrument representing foreign portfolio equity investment. In this case, the investor gets the dividend and not the interest as in case of debt instruments. On the other hand, it does not have the same pattern of voting right that it does have in the case of foreign direct investment. In fact, international equities are a compromise between the debt and the foreign direct investment. They are the instruments that are presently on the preference list of the investors as well as the issuers. This has enabled Euro-equity issues to surge to US $ 7.3 billion during 1990 to US $ 44 billion in 1995 (BIS, 1997) to US $ 59 billion in 2000 and to over 70 billion in 2004 and far greater at $ 496.2 billion during 2007 and $704.7 billion during 2010 (www.IFC.org) from a mere US $ 2.7 billion during 1985 (Chart 18.1). Chart 18.1 shows the distribution of the international equity issue during 2010 among different sets of countries.

Euro-equities are the ordinary shares sold to international investors in form of American/global depository receipt (ADRs/GDRs).

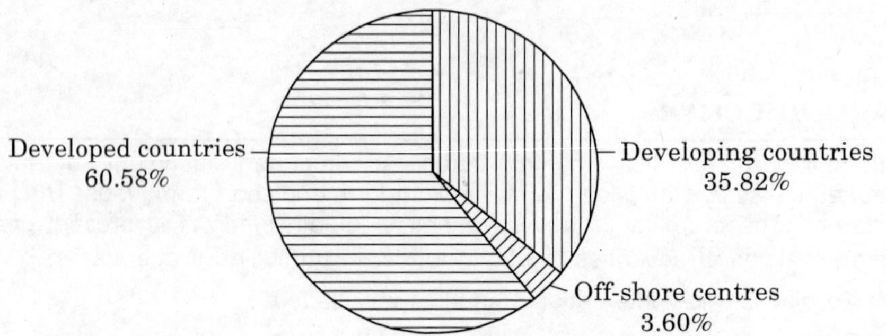

CHART 18.1 International equity issue during 2024.

Source: BIS Quartely Review, March 2024.

Procedure of Issue

Planning for the size and the governmental approval

When a company plans to issue international equity, it decides about the size of the issue, the market where the equities are to be issued, the price of the issue, and about many other formalities. It approaches the lead manager—normally an investment bank—which has a better knowledge of the international financial market. The lead manager examines the risk factor of the issue as well as its prospect. It suggests about the details of the issue as also whether the shares are to be routed through the American depository or through the global depository. When the lead manager gives a green signal, the issuing company prepares the prospectus, etc. and takes permission from the regulatory authorities.

Lead manager is often an investment bank that facilitates issue of the shares for a fee.

Role of custodian bank

After getting approval from the regulatory authorities, it deposits the shares to be issued with the custodian bank located in the domestic country. The custodian bank is appointed by the depository in consultation with the share-issuing company.

> Custodian bank gets the deposit of the equity shares as a security for the issue of the ADRs/GDRs.

When the shares are deposited with the custodian bank, the latter asks the depository located in a foreign country to issue depository receipts in lieu of the shares held. The ratio between the number of shares and the number of depository receipts is decided well before the actual issue. In fact, the fixing up of the issue price or the ratio between the depository receipts and the shares depends upon a host of economic variables. Generally, the issues are priced at discount insofar as the earning per share drops in proportion to the increase in capital. The market price of depository receipt in international market is largely dependent upon earnings potential, industry fundamentals, and macro-economic fundamentals.

Launching of the ADRs/GDRs

The depository, which is a bank or financial institution situated in an international financial centre, functions as a link between the issuing company and the investor. On getting information from the issuing company about the launch, the depository issues the depository receipts. The American depository issues American depository receipts (ADRs), while the depository in the international financial market outside the USA issues global depository receipts (GDRs).

> GDRs are issued by global depositories (often investment bank) located at international financial centres.

When GDRs are purchased by the investors, the proceeds flow from the depository to the custodian bank and from the custodian bank to the issuing company. The company enters the name of the investor in the register of the shareholders. The investor has the right to surrender GDRs and to take back the investment. For the surrender, the investor deposits the GDRs with the depository who in turn informs the custodian who will issue the share certificates in exchange for the GDRs. The proceeds from the sale of shares are converted into foreign exchange for the purpose of making payment to the foreign investors. It may be noted here that once the GDR is surrendered in exchange for the shares, such shares cannot be converted back into GDRs.

Again, the investors can sell the GDR back in the issuing company's domestic capital market. In order to discourage this practice, the issuer introduces a clause, known as *lock-in period*, during which this practice is prohibited.

In the process of the issue, the role of underwriting and listing is very important. The lead manager functions normally as an underwriter and charges underwriting fee. The listing agent, who is normally the lead manager, makes an application to the stock exchange for listing. The agent guides the issuing company and helps it file the required documents with the stock exchange. After the formalities are complete, GDRs are traded on the stock exchange. There are also international clearing houses, such as Euro-clear and CEDEL that facilitate the settlement of transactions.

> Euro-clear/ CEDEL is a clearing house facilitating settlement of transactions.

Voting rights

The question of voting rights is also important. Since GDR investors keep changing from time to time, they do not seem very much interested in the voting rights even though these cannot be denied to them. There are different procedures followed in this respect. One is that the issuing company and the overseas depository enter into an agreement which enables a depository to vote either with the majority voters or according to the wishes of the management. In the other procedure, it is understood that the depository votes in the same proportion as the rest of the shareholders do. Again, there is one more alternative where the depository votes in accordance with the instructions of a nominee of the management.

The cost of issue

The cost of international equity is normally not large, although commission, management fee, etc. are paid to the lead manager according to the different functions performed by it. The depository incurs some expenses. These approximate to 3–4 per cent of the issue amount.

Documentation

There are many documents used in the process of the issue of international equity. These are: 1. The *prospectus* containing detailed information about the issue and the issuer. 2. The *depository agreement*—the agreement between the issuing company and the depository—that contains, among other things, the rules followed for converting the shares into GDRs and back. 3. The *underwriting agreement* concluded between the issuing company and the underwriter, normally the lead manager, accompanies the issue. 4. A copy of the *agreement* concluded between the custodian and the depository is also enclosed. 5. A copy of the *trust deed* is enclosed which provides for the duties and responsibilities of the trustee regarding servicing of the issue. 6. A copy of the *agreement with the listing stock exchange* is annexed so that the investors are well aware of the secondary market for the issue.

Besides, a *subscription agreement* is also enclosed by means of which the lead manager and the syndicate members agree to subscribe to the issue.

INTERNATIONAL IPOS

An IPO refers to the process by which a private company first offers the shares of the company to the public by listing its stock in the stock exchange for sale. International IPO refers to listing of shares offered by a company in the public market of a foreign country or in several countries on foreign exchanges with the intent of raising access to a larger number of investors than the number present in their home country. This avails companies an opportunity to access international capital markets and raise funds from a diverse global investor base.

An international IPO is different from a domestic IPO where shares are listed on domestic exchanges and sold to the domestic investors. An international IPO usually involves listing of shares on the stock exchange of other regions, for example, NYSE, LSE, HKEX, so as to access global investors.

Some features of International IPOs:

- *Cross-Border Access to Capital*: By listing on multiple exchanges or targeting investors in different regions, companies will be in a position to raise capital from global investors, thereby increasing the total amount of funds they can generate through the IPO.
- Companies may seek access to the capital markets of various regions that have deep liquidity or low interest rates.
- *Dual Listings*: Companies may list their shares on more than one stock exchange. This provides them with an opportunity for raising capital from different parts of the world. This is known as a dual listing. A company can list in its home country so that access to local investors is possible and in other international markets, so that foreign capital inflow is attracted.
- *Global Investors*: An international IPO aims at a much broader, more diversified investor base, which covers institutional investors such as mutual funds, hedge funds, pension funds, and retail investors across the different regions of the world. It maximizes demand for the offering and a successful price discovery process.
- *International Underwriters:* Investment banks that sponsor an initial public offering can often be a global organization and may act as lead in multiple countries. These underwriters then go about marketing and operationalizing the issue within various regions while taking risk and distributing it. Large international investment banks, such as Goldman Sachs, JP Morgan, or Morgan Stanley, often lead international IPOs.
- *Access to a Larger Pool of Capital*: Listing on multiple exchanges or aiming at multiple markets increases capital available to the company. This is particularly useful for large companies that require significant funding for expansion, acquisition, or debt relief.
- *Higher Liquidity:* Listing on several international exchanges can increase the volume of trading and enhance the liquidity of its shares. Higher liquidity tends to bring in more institutional investors, thereby bettering the stock's stability.
- *Geographical Expansion*: International companies often prefer an international IPO to enhance their presence and reputation in key global markets. It also serves as a means of tapping into local investor bases where it conducts business operations.
- *Brand Recognition and Credibility*: An international IPO can enhance a company's global profile, creating brand recognition across different regions. It also signals to the market that the company is ready for the global stage, which can be important for long-term business growth.
- *Diversification of Investor Base*: Raising funds from investors in multiple countries helps diversify the shareholder base. This is advantageous if the company faces political, economic, or regulatory risks in any one region.
- *Strategic Partnerships and Acquisitions*: Listing on several markets can attract potential partners, customers, or acquisition targets from those markets. It also keeps companies competitive in cross-border markets.

For example: The Alibaba Group IPO is a classic example of an international IPO that could effectively tap into U.S. capital markets to access global investors, raise adequate funds, and enhance the company's profile in the global arena. In picking the NYSE, Alibaba was able to maximize the scale of its offering and set the stage for its future expansion around the world. This remains one of the largest and most publicized IPOs in history, detailing how globalization helped shape the futures of large multinational companies.

INTERNATIONAL BONDS

International bonds are a debt instrument. They are issued by international agencies, governments and companies for borrowing foreign currency for a specified period of time. The issuer pays interest to the creditor and makes repayment of capital. There are different types of such bonds. The procedure of issue is very specific. All these need some explanation here.

Types of International Bonds

Foreign bonds and Euro bonds

International bonds are classified as foreign bonds and Euro bonds. There is a difference between the two, primarily on four counts.

> Foreign bonds are denominated in the currency of the country where they are issued and so they are subject to regulations of that country. But euro bonds are not denominated in the currency of the country where they are issued; hence, they are not to abide by the rules and regulations of that country.

Firstly, in the case of foreign bond, the issuer selects a foreign financial market where the bonds are issued in the currency of that very country. If an Indian company issues bond in New York and the bond is denominated in US dollar, it will be called a *foreign bond*. On the contrary, in the case of Euro bonds, they are denominated in a currency other than the currency of the country where the bonds are issued. If the Indian company's bond is denominated in US dollar, the bonds will be issued in any country other than the USA. Then only it will be called *Euro bond*.

Secondly, foreign bonds are underwritten normally by the underwriters of the country where they are issued. But the Euro bonds are underwritten by the underwriters of multi-nationality.

Thirdly, the maturity of a foreign bond is determined keeping in mind the investors of a particular country where it is issued. On the other hand, the Euro bonds are tailored to the needs of the multinational investors. In the beginning, the Euro bond market was dominated by individuals who had generally a choice for shorter maturity, but now the institutional investors dominate the scene who do not seek Euro bond maturity necessarily to match their liabilities. The result is that the maturity of Euro bonds is diverse. In England, Euro bonds with maturity between 8 and 12 years are known as *intermediate Euro bonds.*

Fourthly, foreign bonds are normally subjected to governmental regulations in the country where they are issued. For example, in the case of *Yankee bonds* (the bonds issued in the USA), the regulatory thrust lies on disclosures. In some of the European countries, the thrust lies on the resource allocation and on monetary control. *Samurai bonds* (bonds issued in Japan) involved minimum credit-rating requirements prior to 1996. But the Euro bonds are free from the rules and regulations of the country where they are issued. The reason is that the currency of denomination is not the currency of that country and so it does not have a direct impact on the balance of payments.

Fifthly, queuing is not found in the case of euro-bonds, while it is a common practice in the issue of foreign bonds outside the USA. The reason is that the issue of foreign bonds is regulated largely by local authorities. The markets are smaller and bunching of issues is normally avoided. It may be noted that queuing is an effective policy instrument to avoid congestion in the market and to ensure better pricing of the bonds being at the head of the queue.

Global bonds

It is the World Bank which issued the global bonds for the first time in 1989 and 1990. Since 1992, such bonds are being issued also by companies. Presently, there are seven currencies in which such bonds are denominated, namely, the Australian dollar, Canadian dollar, Japanese yen, Swedish krona, Euro, US dollar and British pound sterling. The special features of the global bonds are:

- They carry high ratings.
- They are normally large in size.
- They are offered for simultaneous placement in different countries.
- They are traded on "home market" basis in different regions.

Straight bonds

The straight bonds are the traditional type of bonds. In this case, interest rate is fixed. The interest rate is known as *coupon rate*. It is fixed with reference to rates on treasury bonds for comparable maturity. The credit standing of the borrower is also taken into consideration for fixing the coupon rate.

Straight bonds carry fixed interest rate.

Straight bonds are of many varieties. *Firstly*, there is *bullet-redemption bond* where the repayment of principal is made at the end of the maturity and not in instalments every year. *Secondly*, there is *rising-coupon bond* where coupon rate rises over time. The benefit is that the borrower has to pay small amount of interest payment during early years of debt. *Thirdly*, there is *zero-coupon bond*. It carries no interest payment. But since there is no interest payment, it is issued at discount. It is the discount that compensates for the loss of interest faced by the creditors. Such bond was issued for the first time in 1981. *Fourthly*, in case of *bonds with currency options*, the investor has the right to receive payments in a currency other than the currency of the issue. *Fifthly*, *bull and bear bonds* are indexed to some specific benchmark and are issued in two tranches. The bull bonds are those where the amount of redemption rises with a rise in the index. The bear bonds are those where the amount of redemption falls with a fall in the index. *Finally*, *debt warrant bonds* have a call warrant attached with them (Warrants are zero-coupon bonds.) The creditors have the right to purchase another bond at a given price.

Floating-rate notes

Bonds, which do not carry fixed rate of interest, are known as *floating-rate notes* (FRNs). Such bonds were issued for the first time in Italy during 1970 and they have become common in recent times. The interest rate is quoted as a premium or discount to a reference rate which is invariably LIBOR. The interest rate is revised periodically, say, at every three-month or every six-month period, depending upon the period to which the interest

Floating rate notes carry floating interest rates.

rate is referenced to. For example, if the interest rate is referenced to one-month LIBOR, it would be revised every month.

FRNs are available in different forms. In the case of *perpetual FRNs*, the principal amount is never repaid. This means they are like equity shares. They were popular during mid-1980s, but when the investors began to ask for higher rate of interest, many issuers could not afford paying higher rates of interest. Such bonds lost their popularity.

Secondly, there are *minimax FRNs* where minimum and maximum rates are mentioned. The minimum rate is beneficial for the investors, while the maximum rate is beneficial for the issuer. If LIBOR rises beyond the maximum rate, it is only the maximum rate that is payable. Similarly, the minimum rate is payable even if LIBOR falls below the minimum.

The third form is the *drop lock FRN* where the investor has the right to convert the FRN into a straight bond. Sometimes the conversion is automatic if the reference rate drops below a mentioned floor rate.

Fourthly, there is *flip-flop FRN*. It was first issued by the World Bank. In this case, the investor has the option of converting FRN into a three-month note with a flat three-month yield. Again, the note can be converted into a perpetual note after the completion of the three-month period.

Fifthly, there are *mismatch FRNs*. In this case, the interest rate is fixed monthly, but interest is paid six-monthly. In such a situation, the investor may go for arbitrage on account of difference in interest rates. Such FRNs are also known *as rolling-rate FRNs*.

Sixthly, one of the recent innovations has come in form of *hybrid fixed rate reverse floating rate notes*. They were used in Deutsch mark segment of the market in 1990. These instruments paid a high fixed interest rate for a couple of years. The investors received the difference between LIBOR and even a higher fixed interest rate. They reaped profits with the lowering of LIBOR.

Convertible bonds

International bonds are also convertible bonds meaning that these variants are convertible into equity shares. Some of the convertible bonds have detachable warrants involving acquisition rights. In other cases, there is automatic convertibility into a specified number of shares.

Convertible bonds are convertible into equity shares.

Convertible bonds command a comparatively high market value because of the convertibility privilege. The value is the sum of the naked value existing in the absence of conversion and the conversion value. The conversion price per share is computed by dividing the bond's face value by the conversion factor, where the conversion factor represents the number of shares into which each bond could be exchanged. Suppose, a bond having a face value of \$ 1,000 can be exchanged for 15 shares, the conversion price will be equal to:

$$\$\ 1{,}000/15 = \$\ 66.66$$

Thus, if the market price of share is less than \$ 66.66, say \$ 60, bond-holders will not be interested in converting the bond into equity share. This is so because for a bond of \$ 1,000, a creditor will get 15 shares or \$ 900 only. But if the market price of share is \$ 80, the investors will convert the bond into equity shares and sell the equity shares in the market. This way each bond for \$ 1,000 will fetch \$ 1,200. In other words, the price of convertible bonds depends upon the price of the equity shares.

In the case of bonds with detachable warrants, the warrant can be detached from the bond and can be traded independently. The issuer has a double source of financing. The bonds remain outstanding even if the warrants are exercised.

From the viewpoint of the borrowers, convertible bonds cost less because they have lower coupon. They also help decrease the debt-equity ratio after conversion. From the investors' point of view, convertible bonds represent a better option as the investors get a fixed income in the form of interest prior to conversion. After conversion, they become the owner of the company.

Cocktail bonds

Bonds are often denominated in a mixture of currency. Such bonds are known as *cocktail bonds.* The SDR bonds represent a weighted average of four currencies. The investors purchasing the cocktail bonds get automatically the currency diversification benefits. The foreign exchange risk on account of depreciation of any one currency is offset by appreciation of another currency.

Documentation

Documentation requirements for a bond issue are complex. There are seven documents that are required. The first is the *prospectus*. It informs about the issuer, its management and about its past, present and future operation. It also covers the political and economic make-up of the country. The second is the *subscription agreement*. It comprises denomination, coupon rate, issue price, and maturity of the bond, underwriting commitments, details of selling arrangements, closing date and the terms of payment, names of the paying agents and trustees, details of listing, conditions under which agreement can be terminated, the legal jurisdiction and rules regarding compensation in case of misrepresentations or breach of warranties. The third important document is the *trust deed* which is an agreement between the issuer and the trustee for an orderly servicing of the bond. The fourth document is the *listing agreement* that shows listing centres. The fifth document is the *paying agency agreement* executed between the issuer and the bank that pays the agent for servicing of the bond. The sixth document is the *underwriting agreement* that brings in confidence among the investors. The last document is a copy of the *selling group agreement* that tells about the agencies involved in the sale of the bond. All these documents accompany the bond certificate.

Development of International Bond Market

Foreign bonds emerged on a substantial scale as early as in 1950s. The US dollar was then the strongest currency. In order to obtain US dollar, issuers from different countries issued bonds in the US financial market. These Yankee bonds were very popular. However, with weakening balance of payments, the US Government imposed restrictions on the issue of Yankee bonds in 1960s. The restrictions provided impetus for the emergence of Euro bonds. The first Euro bond was issued by an Italian borrower, Autostrade in 1963. Many other Euro bonds were issued subsequently. But since bank lending dominated the financial scene till early 1980s, sizeable growth in Euro bond market took place only thereafter. The total bond volume increased from US $ 38 billion in 1980 to US $ 169 billion in 1985 and to US $ 230 billion in 1990 (BIS, 1992).

During 1990s, owing to greater liberalisation in the international financial market, which was more apparent in Germany, France and Japan, the size of the bond market grew at a faster rate. By March 1995, the amount involved was over US $ 2,210 billion and it was over US $ 3,100 billion by 2,000 (www.IFC.org). In 1995, the straight bonds dominated the scene as they accounted for over three-fourths of the issue. FRNs accounted for around one-seventh. The rest was accounted for by convertible bonds. Again, it was found that Japanese yen-denominated bonds were mainly fixed-rate bonds, while floating-rate bonds were denominated mainly in British pound. The Swiss franc-denominated bonds were normally the convertible bonds (BIS, 1997). Yet again, around two-fifths of the total issue in 1995 were denominated in US dollar, a little less than one-fifth in Japanese yen, about one- seventh in DM, and the rest of the bonds were denominated in other currencies. In the case of bonds issued by the firms and governments of developing countries, 57 per cent of the issue was represented by US dollar and over one-quarter was denominated in Japanese yen. The share of DM was hardly one-tenth. The value of yen bonds increased during 1990s because many Latin American Brady bonds came to be denominated in yen in view of greater attraction for them among Japanese investors (BIS, 1997). Chart 18.2 shows the outstanding amount of international debt securities at the end of September 2024 from the viewpoint of nationality of issuers.

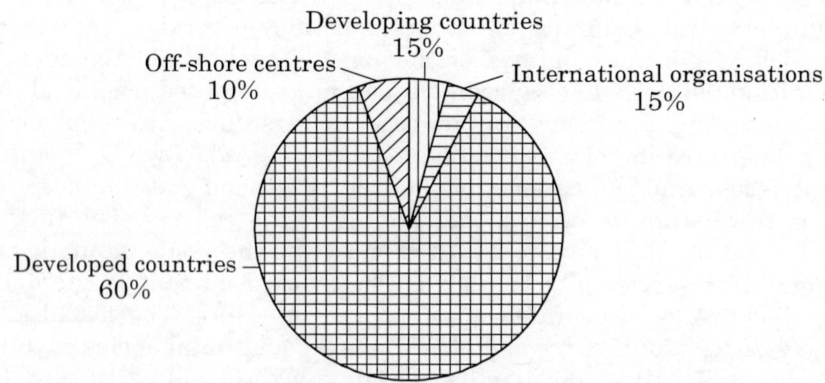

CHART 18.2 International debt Securities Outstanding at the end of June 2024.

Source: *BIS Quarterly Review*, June 2024.

In 1995 the average size of maturity of international bonds was 4.3 years, but subsequently, it rose due to longer-term bonds issued by many corporations. Again, after the Mexican crisis of 1994, some of the Latin American governments tried to re-establish benchmarks in international financial market and issued international bonds. This resulted in the growth of sovereign bonds during these years. In 1997, the borrowing of the developing countries through the issue of international bonds was as large as US $ 99 billion compared to only US $ 39 billion during 1995. The figure reached over $ 200 billion in 2004, $ 407.7 billion in 2007 and $42 trillion at the end of June 2024 (BIS, 2004, 2007 and 2024).

SECONDARY MARKET OPERATION OF INTERNATIONAL SECURITIES

Facilities do exist for secondary market operation for all types of euro issues. In the case of the foreign bonds, listing is done on a particular stock exchange in a particular country. But for Euro bonds, many financial centres are involved. This is why transactions take place in over-the-counter market. However, listing with international stock exchange helps Euro issues in determining their price, depending upon the performance of the issuer and the demand for the issue.

Sometimes, before the secondary market starts functioning, the particular Euro bond is in great demand. Such trading is known as *grey trading*, although such cases are rare.

For smooth operation of the clearing houses and operation of the secondary market, there is the International Securities Market Association (ISMA). ISMA has enrolled market makers who provide continuously two-way price quotations with a bid-ask spread of usually 50 b.p. and enable investors to buy and sell euro issues. The buyer pays the seller the agreed price along with interest accrued. The standard size of euro bond transaction is 100 bonds with $ 100,000 of face value.

The settlement is done usually within a week. The settlement instructions are routed through the clearing house. International securities clearing system was developed in 1968 at Brussels, known as *Euroclear*. Two years later, Cedel was set up in Luxembourg. These two provide settlement through book-keeping entries.

GAINS FROM INTERNATIONAL ISSUES

The international issues are beneficial for both the issuers and investors. The euro-issue market fits better into a firm's funding strategy. Kim and Stulz (1988) examined the impact of euro-bond issues on the value of the issuing firm based on 183 issues during 1975–1985 and found positive abnormal returns on equity within the two-day period of the announcement of the euro-bond offer. There are many more gains that are mentioned here at some length under two heads: primary market gains and secondary market gains.

The Primary Market Gains

First of all, the developmental outlay requires huge funds for investment, especially foreign exchange that may not be available domestically in the desired quantum. Euro issues are a right step because these issues help bring in foreign exchange.

Secondly, the funds from the international financial market are available at a lower cost. More specifically, in case of bonds to be issued in the international market, the rate of interest has normally been lower. The reason is that in a matured economy where market forces have a greater scope for a free play, interest rates tend to be lower.

Thirdly, the opening up of a route to international financial market helps diversification of the sources of funds and in turn lower the risk factor. It may be mentioned that the systematic risk can be reduced only internationally as the macro-economic variables tend to vary internationally. Thus the international issue of securities serves both the ends—lowering of the cost as well as lowering of the risk. The lowering of risk is significant also for the investors when they diversify their investments in different channels (Levy and Lerman, 1988).

Fourthly, the ADRs/GDRs are priced by the depositories normally at the average price of the related shares and so it is a source of gain when the share market is bullish.

Fifthly, it is not simply the advantage on account of price, it is also the convenience aspect. Since the international financial markets do not normally maintain stringent disclosure norms and so it is more convenient to raise funds there.

Last but not least, in many cases, it has been found that the company's presence in the international financial market helps elevate its image. It enjoys a higher rating. Choi and Stonchill (1982) confirm this view in the case of some Japanese and Korean firms.

The Secondary Market Gains

The significance of the euro-issues is not limited to the primary market. After the ADRs/GDRs are issued, they are also listed on the international stock exchanges and subsequently traded at the international stock exchanges. The trading brings in ample gains. The argument is that the international trading of shares reduces market segmentation and thereby reduces or eliminates risk premium and helps increase the share prices (Errunza and Losq, 1985). It may be noted here that capital market segmentation appears when the shares are traded simply in one market on account of restrictions imposed on international investment. The segmentation gets weaker with growing liberalisation of the foreign investment policy. The companies go for listing and trading of euro-issues that in turn puts a positive impact on the risk-return aspect of these issues. Kumar (2006) finds in case of 68 Indian firms going for listing their securities abroad in the form of depository receipts that the volatility of the underlying stocks reduced significantly. The investors at the international stock exchange too prefer to invest in the shares of the emerging market economies in view of growing stock market in these economies (Moel, 2000). The British investors in GDR of 20 Indian firms more than doubled in 2007 with a total turnover of $ 11.9 billion (*Financial Times*, 7.1.2008).

Again, it is also believed that the foreign listing of the securities enhances liquidity of a company's stock on account of informational linkages between domestic country and the foreign country where the shares are traded (Mittoo, 1992). Majumdar (2007) confirms that listing in the overseas markets raises the volume of trading in the respective securities at home and thereby boosts up the liquidity. Similar views were expressed by Hargis and Ramanlal (1998). Liquidity in the financial market gives, in turn, a boost to market credibility. It provides accurate price signal to investors and to the companies, which is essential for efficient risk-sharing strategies. Moreover, liquidity influences the cost of capital and makes the investment decision more effective.

Harris (1993) and Hamilton (1979) are of the opinion that multi-market trading stimulates competition between different markets which in turn forces market makers to provide the best possible bid-ask spread and thereby retains the existing traders and attracts the new investors.

Some of these views were empirically tested. Mittoo (1992), and Fanto and Karmel (1997) found an increase in liquidity as a result of multi-market trading of the shares of some Canadian firms. Pagano and Roell (1990) found that the French shares listed and marketed in London financial market had a lower bid-ask spread.

In short, the gains from euro-issues are sizeable. Hansda and Ray (2003) are of the opinion that given the volatility in the FIIs' investment in the secondary market, euro issues are a better way of approaching the international financial market.

Structured Products

The structured products are defined as the pre-packaged investments that are specifically designed to meet predefined/particular goals of investors. It combine the features of both the fixed-income securities as well as the derivatives. These securities provide a tailored solution that could align with some specific financial requirements and provide benefits and fulfill the investor's specific objectives like, protection of capital, market exposure, and enhance yields. With creating an opportunity for the risk-adjusted returns these hybrid products also bridge the gap between traditional and alternative investments.

Types of Structured Products

With the passage of time the various products emerges as it includes feature of both the Fixed-income securities and the derivatives. So, based on this there are some products that are available in the markets are:

- **Equity-Linked Notes (ELNs):** ELNs are those structured products that includes a combination of equity options as well as fixed-income instruments it enable investors to earn returns based on the performance of the particular equity that is linked to that product while retaining some downside protections.
- **Credit-Linked Notes (CLNs):** As the name only suggest that these products incorporate credit derivatives that transfers the credit risks to investors which provides returns linked to the creditworthiness of a specific entity or pool of entities.
- **Market-Linked Certificates of Deposit:** These products are linked to their returns to market indices or other benchmarks and that ensure the principal amount and protect the amount until maturity.

Application and Benefits

There are various applications and benefits of the structured securities, we will discuss them one by one for the clear understanding.

- **Portfolio Diversification:** Structured products enhance portfolio diversification, by providing access to non-traditional assets and strategies. With the help of these products one can diversify one's portfolio and can reduce the exposure to risk.
- **Hedging:** Hedging against the market volatility-specific risks, structured products allow investors to avoid risks of currency fluctuations and commodity price swings. For instance, investors who hold assets in foreign currencies can face significant losses if exchange rates move unfavorably. Structured products can be designed to provide protection against such adverse movements, ensuring that investors can maintain their purchasing power and investment value.

- **Enhance Yield:** Investors can attain higher returns than traditional investment methods, particularly in low-interest-rate environments. When interest rates are low, conventional fixed-income options, such as bonds and savings accounts, often yield inadequate returns that may not even keep up with inflation. Consequently, many investors explore alternative strategies, such as equities, real estate, and commodities, which offer greater growth potential. This shift encourages the creation of diversified portfolios that optimize investment results while managing risks associated with stagnant interest rates, highlighting the need for adaptive financial planning in today's economic climate.
- **Capital Protection:** Sometimes the investors have the perception in mind that they want to ensure the principal amount and safeguard the market performance. Some structured products are designed in that way that can protect the capital of investors and prevent it from possible risks.

Risks Associated with Structured Products

- **Complexity:** The structured products are designed in such a way that the intricacies of the product may become challenging for most of the investors to understand and comprehend they may need some professional and detailed guidance. Means without a proper financial literacy or professional advice, investors may not understand its intricacies.
- **Credit Risk:** The structured products are unsecured debt obligations of the issuer so the solvency of the issuing institutions becomes critical. There may be issuer default risk and investors may lose some or all the principal and promised returns. As these securities are not backed by the government insurance may cause some credit risk. Past crisis like Lehman Brothers collapse highlights the vulnerability of these products to issuer credit risks.
- **Illiquidity:** The market for structured products are often underdeveloped, that limit an investor's ability to exit the investment before maturity. But because of the niche market there is low demand and it is difficult to find buyers for structured products which makes it less liquid.
- **Market risk:** Dependence on underlying assets, market turbulence and complex correlations among multiple underlying assets cause market risks for the structured products. Market volatility lead to significant deviations from the expected returns.

Hence, we can say the the structured products offer some ways in achieving specific financial goals but with some risks that are needs a careful consideration. Before investing in these type of securities one should evaluate all the possible risks and understanding of the product before investing.

Derivatives

Derivative are financial instruments whose value is derived from the performance of underlying assets, it can be equity, bond, index or rates. Due to their versatility the derivatives are used in various way like managing risk, speculation, and arbitrage and hence these securities have become highly indispensable in modern financial markets. However there are some risks also associated with this.

Types of Derivatives:

- **Future Contract:** The future contract is a standardized agreement where a speculator buy or sell an asset at a predetermined price on a specified future date. These are traded on recognized stock exchanges (like., NSE, BSE, CME, NYSE.) and that is why it is highly regulated, which in turn reduces counterparty risk. It is commonly used for the purpose of hedging the price risk in certain goods, viz. commodities, oil, agriculture products and metals.
- **Forward Contract:** Unlike future contract the forward contracts are customized not standardized, these contracts are traded on OTC (over-the-counter) where speculator contract to buy or sell an asset at a predetermind price on a future date. These contracts are neither standardized nor traded on stock exchange hence they are having a high counterparty risk due to absence of clearing house. These are mainly used in foreign exchange and commodities markets.
- **Option Contracts:** In this contract the holder of the contract have the right, (either to sell or to buy) but not the obligation (to buy or sell). There are two types of option—one is called (call option) meaning the holder have right to buy at any point, and another is (put option) which means the holder has the right to sell at any future date. Key features of the option is that they have a limited downside risk as the premium is already paid and it has high flexibility for hedging or speculative strategies.
- **Swaps:** These are related to agreements between parties with term of exchanging the financial obligation at either fixed or floating interest rate of payments.

Some common types of swaps are interest rate swaps and currency swaps. These are commonly used by the corporations and financial institutions to manage the interest rate or currency risks.

Financial Engineering: Driving Market Innovation

Financial engineering means engineering of the financial instruments and come up with some transformative discipline that merges many types of instruments which indirectly merges finance, mathematics, statistics, and computational methods which innovate the financial products and strategies. The revolutionized ability of the financial engineering is having a greater impact on the financial industry by creating tools that enhance the market efficiency, that can meet complex financial needs. However, developing products like mortagage-backed securities, innovative risk management solution these instruments created with innovation and quantitative methods seems interesting but sometimes it becomes a double-edged sword, that may exacerbate the financial instability when misapplied.

Some examples of Financial innovation

As the core element in the financial engineering are using tools like Python, MATLAB, and R for finaicl modelling, or applying statistical models with algorithms to solve problems, which in turn integrate finance, economics and computational science. Now we will discuss some of the financial innovations.

- **Mortgage-Backed Securities (MBS):** These are created by pooling mortgages into an instrument that can be traded in the stock exchange to pay the underlying loans' interest and principal. It allows the lenders in managing risks by expanding the customer base of the particular underlying assets for generating more capital and more lending. It also provide access to diversified income streams to the investors. There was a great contribution of this instrument in creating bubble which cause 2008 financial crisis.
- **Inflation-Protected Bonds:** There are bonds designed to protect investors form inflation and reduce exposure of risk that may arise form inflation. One example is treasury Inflation-protected securities (TIPS). In this the principal value adjusts according to the inflation rates. It helps in maintaining the purchasing power at the time of inflationary periods. It also supported pension funds and insurance companies in meeting long-term liabilities.
- **Risk-Parity Portfolio:** This is a portfolio allocation strategy that balances the risk contribution of each assets rather than their capital weights. It helps in diversification by distributing risk more evenly, it gained a popularity among institutional investors that helps them to protect form market volatility.
- **Credit Default Swaps (CDS):** It is a type of derivative instrument that allows the investors in hedging or speculating on the credit risk of a bond, equity or any other securities. It have played a controversial role in amplifying the 2008 crisis.
- **Algorithmic Trading and ETFs:** This is also developed by using the financial engineering for some specific investment strategies. It increases market liquidity and transparency which made sophisticated investment strategies accessible to retail investors.

With understand the types or the innovations of the financial engineering we can also analyze some of the challenges in financial engineering. There are many challenges *Firstly*, over-complexity, these instruments are created with highly complex instruments which normal retail investors couldn't understand, the complexity of these institutions makes the pricing and risk assessment more difficult, and misunderstanding and misuse of such instruments have contributed to the 2008 global financial crisis.

Secondly, regulatory issues, as the innovative instruments have certain features of which the regulations have not yet been made so it outpaces the regulatory frameworks which leads in making gaps in oversight. It also creates moral hazard among financial institutions and regulators struggle to balance innovation with mitigating the systematic risks.

Third, is the ethical concern which mean that sometimes the priorities of profit over societal well-being is not good for the greater good and crates predatory financial products to exploit vulnerable consumers and also contributes in wealth inequality as there is an unequal access to complex financial tools.

Financial Engineering and Financial Crises

As the financial engineering can mitigate the risk and can also exacerbate the financial crises so it is a dual-edged sword and that totally depends upon how it is used. The products like ETFs and CDS help in diversification of risk and innovations like circuity breakers and high-frequency tradin algorithms can prevent market crash by quickly providing liquidity.

The financial engineering also exacerbate financial crisis and the cause of it is firstly, the opaque risk structure, many instruments like MBS and CDOs are not clearly identifiable and hence the underlying risks, this also contributed in the subprime mortgage crisis in 2008. Secondly, excessive leverage may also cause some of the participants to take disproportionate risks, and procyclicality may also affect based on past trends and may amplify the market cycles even worse.

Regulatory Frameworks and Standards on International Capital Markets

International capital markets require regulation and supervision in order to provide transparency, stability, and fairness in the financial markets. Regulatory bodies are national as well as international, and their work is to protect investors, ensure integrity of the market, and maintain financial stability. Major frameworks include IOSCO, IFRS, and national regulations such as MiFID II and Dodd-Frank with the same objective of creating a coherent framework on the international border. Challenges still arise from jurisdictional differences, market complexities, and technological innovations to constantly adapt and ensure international cooperation among regulators.

- **International Financial Reporting Standards (IFRS):** IFRS is an accounting standard developed by the International Accounting Standards Board (IASB). IFRS standards encourage openness, consistency, and comparability of financial statements across different jurisdictions. IFRS is adopted by over 100 countries, and therefore financial reporting through IFRS is considered a requirement in international markets.
- **The Dodd-Frank Act (U.S.):** The Dodd-Frank Wall Street Reform and Consumer Protection Act was enacted following the 2008 Global Financial Crisis and was directed towards comprehensive regulations meant to increase transparency, reduce risk, and protect consumers in U.S. financial markets. The Dodd-Frank Act has provisions pertaining to derivatives markets, systemic risk, consumer protection, and corporate governance that also impacts international investors and market participants.
- **MiFID II (Markets in Financial Instruments Directive II):** MiFID II is the European regulatory framework, aimed at creating harmonization and more transparent financial markets of the European Union (EU) together with better protection for investors. This regulation applies to investment firms, trading venues, and regulators in the EU.

  MiFID II seeks greater transparency in the markets, better functioning of financial markets, and enhanced protection for the investors in the EU. It has implications for global market participants trading with or within the EU.

Types of Regulatory Mechanisms in International Capital Markets

Disclosure Requirements: Public companies listed on the international capital market would, therefore be obligated to disclose much more comprehensive financial and operational information to the investors. The disclosure shall enhance the informed decision by the investors and reduce information asymmetry. The companies shall publish regular reports on the following; the financial performance, Material events, Executive compensation and Governance.

Market Surveillance: National regulators, usually in close coordination with the exchanges, operate surveillance systems to monitor the behaviour of trading activity and ensure adherence to the rules in the market.

Transborder Cooperation: The memoranda of understanding (MOU) and agreements between countries help exchange information and cooperate between jurisdictions' regulatory authorities. Such instruments ensure cross-border trade and investment complies with local regulations in a country. Coordination between regulators is essential for managing risks that arise from the global nature of capital markets, particularly in areas such as market manipulation, fraud, and money laundering.

Licensing and Registration: Investment firms, financial advisors, and asset managers must often be licensed or registered with relevant authorities in the jurisdictions where they operate. Such requirements ensure that only qualified and regulated entities participate in capital markets.

Issues in International Capital Markets Regulation

- *Cross-border and Cross-jurisdictional Complexity*: International capital markets are multi-country or multi-jurisdictional jurisdictions that have its respective own body of rules and regulations. It is complex and expensive to ensure that activities comply with various relevant jurisdictions.
- *Regulatory Arbitrage*: Some market participants may leverage differences in regulatory regimes, often by shifting operations or capital to jurisdictions with weaker regulations. This could lead to an uneven playing field as well as heighten investor risks.
- *Technological Disruptions*: Rise of new technologies such as blockchain, cryptocurrencies, and artificial intelligence will challenge regulators as these innovations often stay ahead of the curve of regulatory frameworks. There is a paradox between stimulating innovation and the need to maintain financial system integrity.
- *Global Financial Crises*: International regulatory frameworks can be very exposed at their weaknesses by financial crises, such as the global financial crisis in 2008. Systemic risks need to be prevented by constant adaptation of regulators to changing market conditions.

Key Trends in the International Capital Market

1. Technological Innovation and Digital Transformation

(i) Blockchain technology and cryptocurrencies have changed the face of international capital markets. New asset classes have been introduced, and blockchain promises to bring greater transparency, security, and efficiency into clearing and settlement systems as Bitcoin and Ethereum represent new asset classes.

(ii) Fintech and AI: There are companies in the fintech arena that are disrupting traditional capital market practices in areas such as payment processing, asset management, and trading. Algorithmic trading, risk management, and predictive analytics are increasingly being done through artificial intelligence (AI) and machine learning.

(iii) RegTech: Another important development is RegTech, or regulatory technology. This refers to the application of technology to improve the efficiency with which companies comply with regulatory requirements, particularly in the areas of AML, fraud detection and reporting, and so forth.

2. Rise in Sustainable and ESG Investments

(i) Sustainable Finance: Investment decisions are increasingly made with reference to environmental, social, and governance (ESG) factors. Rapid growth in sustainable investments covers green bonds, ESG-themed funds, and impact investing by both retail and institutional investors aimed at aligning portfolios with their values.

(ii) Green Bonds and ESG Funds: The issuance of green bonds and ESG investment funds has grown dramatically in the last few years. They offer financial instruments meant to fund environmental benefits projects like renewable energy or sustainable infrastructure projects, as well as those implemented to address social or governance goals.

(iii) Regulatory Drive toward ESG Disclosure: Most countries are now implementing regulations requiring disclosure of companies' ESG practices. The EU's Sustainable Finance Disclosure Regulation (SFDR) and guidelines from Task Force on Climate-related Financial Disclosures are examples. This regulatory drive for transparency integrates ESG factors into the analysis of capital markets.

3. Rising Cross-Border Investment and Globalization

(i) Global Capital Flows: Cross-border investment activity continued to expand with greater capital flowing between regions. Emergent market companies are increasingly going on global capital access through international IPOs, while international investors look at growth opportunities in developing economies.

(ii) Foreign Direct Investment (FDI): FDI remains a key driver of international capital flows. Multinationals invest in emerging markets to capture lower labor costs or entry into new consumer markets.

(iii) Globalisation of Financial Markets: The deepening of interconnectivity has led financial institutions to operate in various jurisdictions. This has led to more intense cross-border regulatory coordination, but also more complex market orders and potential risks.

4. Advent of Passive Investing and ETFs

(i) Exchange-Traded Funds (ETFs): ETFs have become among the most popular investment vehicles globally, with increasing demand for low-cost diversified exposure to international markets. ETFs allow investors to access global stock, bond, and commodity markets with ease.

(ii) Passive Investing: The shift toward passive investing (index-based strategies) has accelerated, as investors increasingly favor low-cost strategies that track broad market indices rather than actively managed funds. This trend has reshaped the landscape for fund managers and asset owners.

(iii) Smart Beta: Smart beta strategies, which use alternative weighting schemes for portfolio construction (e.g., by value, volatility, or dividends), are gaining traction, providing investors with a middle ground between active and passive management.

5. Rising Influence of Sovereign Wealth Funds (SWFs)

Sovereign wealth funds are growing significantly as a component of international capital markets. State-owned investment funds, for example, like the Norwegian Government Pension Fund or the Abu Dhabi Investment Authority, manage a broad portfolio of capital and are significant investors in global equities, real estate, and other asset classes. SWFs are very powerful in the emerging markets space, where they help stabilize economies and fund infrastructure projects while at the same time pushing global liquidity.

6. Democratization of Investment and Retail Investors

(i) Retail Investors Rise: A democratization of access to capital market by lowering fees and reducing entry barriers for retail investors to trade stocks, options, and other financial products, as propelled through new platforms such as Robinhood, eToro, Freetrade, among others.

(ii) Crowdfunding: The rise of equity crowdfunding platforms, such as Kickstarter and SeedInvest, has provided new opportunities for startups to access capital, bypassing traditional venture capital and private equity routes.

(iii) Retail Trading Boom: Particularly during the COVID-19 pandemic, retail investor participation surged, driven by the ease of access to trading platforms and the proliferation of commission-free trading. Retail investors are becoming an increasingly important force in the global capital market.

Key Challenges in the International Capital Market

1. Regulatory Fragmentation and Compliance

(i) Diverse Regulations: Capitals markets are regulated by a patchwork across different countries and regions. This creates hardships for various firms, which have to comply with multiple reporting standards, regulatory bodies, and tax rules if they operate across jurisdictions. For instance, MiFID II in the EU, Dodd-Frank in the U.S., and IFRS versus GAAP create complexity in cross-border transactions.

(ii) Cross-Border Coordination: There are challenges of cross-border coordination that regulatory bodies face in terms of oversight. International organizations such as IOSCO and the Financial Stability Board (FSB) seek to harmonize standards, but differences in country regulations could create barriers in international investment.

2. Geopolitical Risk and Market Volatility

(i) Political and Trade Tensions: Geopolitical risks, such as trade wars, sanctions, and political instability, can disrupt capital flows and affect market confidence. The example of the U.S.-China trade war has shown significant implications for global capital markets, where fluctuations in policy trade affected investor sentiment and market valuations.

(ii) Brexit: The UK's decision to leave the European Union has uncertainty in terms of market access, regulatory alignment, and capital flows between the UK and the EU.

(iii) Currency Volatility: Cross-border investments put firms and investors at increased currency risks, especially in volatile emerging market currencies. Sudden currency fluctuations may cause considerable loss to the international investor and affect corporate earnings for the multinational corporation.

3. Systemic Risks and Financial Crises

(i) Systemic Risk: The interconnectedness of global financial markets means that shocks in one market can quickly spread across borders. For example, the 2008 global financial crisis demonstrated how the collapse of major financial institutions in the U.S. triggered a global recession, affecting capital markets worldwide.

(ii) Liquidity Risks: There can be liquidity risks for financial institutions, particularly those in emerging markets, where it becomes difficult to access capital at will. This is portrayed by crisis events, including the COVID-19 pandemic, which influences capital market deep contractions that sometimes freeze liquidity.

(iii) Shadow Banking System: The "shadow banking" sector—non-bank financial intermediaries—is growing, posing a challenge to regulators. This is because this sector is often conducted outside the reach of traditional banking regulations, increasing systemic risk if not properly monitored.

4. Cybersecurity and Data Privacy Risks

(i) Cyber Threats: The risk of cyberattacks has been increasing as capital markets become more technology-dependent. A cyber breach could easily compromise the systems of an exchange, bank, or even an investor, leading to data breaches, financial losses, and damage to market integrity. A major cybersecurity incident could undermine investor confidence and disrupt trading.

(ii) Data Privacy: Data-driven technologies such as AI and big data analytics are proliferating, raising critical concerns around protection of sensitive financial information. Where risk created, regulations like General Data Protection Regulation (GDPR) by the EU are helping to mitigate these, but it is not easy for firms with a truly global scale and scope to ensure full compliance across borders.

5. Environmental, Social, and Governance (ESG) Integration

(i) ESG Disclosure: The growing prominence of ESG investing has generated an awareness and demand for standardized, transparent ESG reporting, but the existing inconsistency in global standards makes it a challenge for investors trying to gauge the real sustainability of companies and projects. There are many frameworks-like GRI, TCFD, and SASB-though global consensus on ESG reporting remains elusive.

(ii) Greenwashing: As ESG investing gains popularity, greenwashing has become a big concern wherein companies describe their environmental practices more positively than they actually are to attract ESG-sensitive investors. The regulators face pressure for the prevention and development of measures addressing such issues and ensuring the credibility of investments in ESG.

6. Liquidity and Market Fragmentation

(i) Market Fragmentation: The same globalization factor that has opened access to international markets also increases fragmentation of trading. The fragmentation of the execution process across various venues; that is, multiple exchanges, alternative trading systems, or over-the-counter markets can lead to reduced liquidity, costs, and even price differences between markets.

(ii) Liquidity Risk: Liquidity can dry up quickly, particularly in less liquid assets such as emerging market debt or high yield bonds. Market distress can thus readily trigger or enhance large price movements by making it difficult for an investor to exit positions without loss.

CASE STUDY

THE FINANCIAL CRISIS OF 2008

Overview

The most significant economic downturn since the Great Depression, the 2008 Financial Crisis, also referred to as the Global Financial Crisis (GFC), led to numerous bank collapses, a sharp decline in property values, and a worldwide economic slump. This event exposed fundamental flaws in the financial system, particularly within the housing and credit sectors. The crisis underscored the need for reforms in these areas and highlighted the interconnectedness of global financial markets.

Origins of the Financial Meltdown: Real Estate Inflation: The United States experienced a significant increase in property values in the early 2000s. Financial institutions extended high-risk loans to individuals with poor credit scores, anticipating continuous appreciation in real estate prices. Mortgage Repackaging: Home loans were consolidated into mortgage-backed securities (MBS) and distributed to global investors. These were subsequently transformed into complex financial instruments such as collateralized debt obligations (CDOs). Insufficient Oversight: Financial entities operated with minimal supervision, enabling hazardous practices to proliferate. Credit assessment agencies frequently assigned favorable ratings to high-risk securities. Housing prices began to decline in 2007, resulting in widespread loan defaults. The value of MBS and CDOs plummeted, inflicting substantial losses on banks and investors. Lehman Brothers: The collapse of this investment firm in September 2008 signaled the crisis's apex. AIG: This insurance conglomerate faced a liquidity crisis due to its involvement in credit default swaps (CDS). Governmental Bodies and Central Banks: These institutions were instrumental in addressing the crisis through financial interventions and monetary measures.

Global Ramifications: The interconnected nature of worldwide financial networks caused the crisis to extend beyond U.S. borders, impacting Europe, Asia, and other regions. 2007: Subprime mortgage defaults increased, weakening the housing market. March 2008: Bear Stearns, a major investment bank, was acquired by JPMorgan Chase to avert collapse. September 2008: Lehman Brothers filed for bankruptcy. The U.S. government provided an $85 billion rescue package to AIG. Global stock markets experienced sharp declines. October 2008: The U.S. Congress passed the Emergency Economic Stabilization Act, establishing the $700 billion Troubled Asset Relief Program (TARP). 2009: As the recession deepened, recovery measures, including fiscal stimulus packages, began to show results.

Impact

Economic Effects: Global GDP contracted, leading to widespread job losses and home foreclosures. Banks tightened lending practices, resulting in a credit crunch. Stock markets experienced significant losses.

Policy Changes: The U.S. implemented the Dodd-Frank Act, imposing stricter regulations on financial institutions.Central banks worldwide adopted unconventional monetary policies, such as quantitative easing.

QUESTIONS

1. What were the main causes of 2008 financial crisis?
2. How did subprime mortgages contribute to the housing buddle?
3. Explain the role of mortgage-backed securities (MBS) and collateralized debt obligations (CDOs) in exacerbating the crisis.
4. How did lax regulation and oversight contribute to the crisis?
5. How has the financial landscape changed since 2008?

SHORT-TERM AND MEDIUM-TERM INSTRUMENTS

Euro Notes

Euro notes are like promissory notes issued by companies for obtaining short-term funds. They emerged in early 1980s with growing securitisation in the international financial market. They are denominated in any currency other than the currency of the country where they are issued. They represent low-cost funding route. Documentation facilities are the minimum. They can be easily tailored to suit the requirements of different kinds of borrowers. Investors too prefer them in view of short maturity.

Financial intermediation function is related to deposits, borrowings and lending.

When the issuer plans to issue Euro notes, it hires the services of facility agents or the lead arranger. On the advice of the lead arranger, it issues the notes, gets them underwritten and sells them through the placement agents. After the selling period is over, the underwriter buys the unsold issues.

The Euro notes carry three main cost components:

1. underwriting fee;
2. one-time management fee for structuring, pricing and documentation; and
3. margin on the notes themselves. The margin is either in the form of spread above/below LIBOR or built into the note price itself.

The documentation is standardised. The documents accompanying notes are usually underwriting agreement, paying agency agreement, and information memorandum showing, among other things, the financial position of the issuer. The notes are settled either through physical delivery or through clearing.

In course of time, a few variants of Euro note issue system have evolved. The first is the *revolving underwriting facility* in which there is a sole placement agent who allocates the notes among investors at a uniform pre-set yield. The second is the *tender panel system* in which the placement agent forms a panel of banks for placing Euro notes on behalf of the issuer. The tender panel members submit tenders to the placement agent indicating the amount and price of notes they would like to acquire. In this case, price is set by open competition and so it goes in favour of the issuer. But the placement agent may not have the same level of commitment as it is found in the case of the sole placement agent. The third variant is *continuous tender panel* in which the underwriters constitute a tender panel for each draw-down of notes. They buy them, if left unsold, during the offer period. This system brings in competition among the underwriters.

Euro Commercial Papers

Another attractive form of short-term debt instrument that emerged during mid-1980s came to be known as *Euro commercial paper* (ECP). It is a promissory note like the short-term Euro notes although it is different from Euro notes in some ways. It is not underwritten, while the Euro notes are underwritten. The reason is that ECP is issued only by those companies that possess a high degree of rating. Again, the ECP route for raising funds is normally investor-driven, while the Euro note is said to be borrower-driven.

> Euro commercial papers are short-term fund instruments issued only by highly rated companies.

ECP came up on the pattern of domestic market commercial papers that had a beginning in the USA and then in Canada as back as in 1950s. The prefix "Euro" means that the ECP is issued outside the country in the currency in which it is denominated. Most of the ECPs are denominated in US dollars, but they are different from the US commercial papers in the sense that the ECPs have longer maturity going up to one year. Moreover, ECPs are structured on the basis of all-in-costs, whereas in US commercial papers, various charges, such as front-end fee and commission are collected separately.

The detailed features of ECPs vary from one country to another. They involve market-based interest rate, LIBOR. The issue is normally arranged through placement agents as in the case of Euro notes. The amount varies from US $ 10 million to US $ 1 billion or above. The ECPs are issued either in interest-bearing form or in a discounted form with interest built in the issue price itself. On completion of the maturity, they are settled generally at the clearing houses, such as Cedel (Luxembourg), Euroclear (Brussels), First Chicago (London) or Chase Manhattan (London) so that the physical delivery is avoided. The settlement is complete normally within two days.

ECPs face minimal documentation. Over and above, they are not underwritten. This is why their use has been large since their very inception. The outstanding amount of transactions through ECPs rose from US $ 13.9 billion in 1986 to US $ 79.6 billion in 1991. By March 1995, the amount was US $ 81.3 billion, over three-fourths of which were denominated in the US dollar (BIS, 1997). By 2007, this figure rose to $ 696.6 billion (BIS, 2007).

Medium-term Euro Notes

Medium-term Euro notes are just an extension of short-term Euro notes as they fill the gap existing in the maturity structure of international financial market instruments. They are a compromise between short-term Euro notes and long-term Euro bonds as their maturity ranges between one year and five to seven years.

Medium-term euro notes are medium-term fund instrument.

The short-term Euro notes are allowed to roll over repeatedly over five to seven years. Every three or six months, the short-term Euro notes are redeemed and a fresh issue is made. Alternatively, a medium-term Euro note is issued to get medium-term funds in foreign currency without any need for redemption and fresh issue.

Medium-term Euro notes are not underwritten, yet there is provision for underwriting. This is for ensuring the borrowers that they get the funds even if they lack sufficient creditworthiness. They are issued broadly on the pattern of US medium-term notes that are found there since early 1970s. Medium-term Euro notes carry fixed rate of interest, although floating rates are also there. In recent years, multicurrency structure has come up. The issuers are mainly banks, sovereigns and international agencies.

The medium-term Euro notes have been popular. The outstanding amount, which was just US $ 0.4 billion at the end of 1986, grew to US $ 9.6 billion by 1990 and to US $ 347.1 billion by March 1995 (BIS, 1997). The galloping growth in such issues shows the tremendous popularity of this instrument. By 2000, the amount crossed US $ 400 billion mark.

Of late, the Euro market has come up with global medium-term note issues. Under this programme, issues of different credit ratings are able to raise funds through accessing retail as well as institutional investors. This is a comparatively new programme.

SUMMARY

- International financial market represents the use of different types of securities. International equities and international bonds are the source of long-term capital, while Euro notes and ECPs are used for obtaining short-term funds. Medium-term Euro notes are used for obtaining medium-term funds.
- International equities are beneficial for both the issuer and the investor. The process of their issue is specific in which the global depository has a specific role to play. International bonds are either foreign bonds or Euro bonds. They are straight bonds, floating rate notes, convertible bonds, global bonds and cocktail bonds. The lead manager has a vital role in the issue of international bonds.
- Euro notes and ECPs vary in details. Medium-term notes are almost similar, although they are meant for raising medium-term finance.

STUDY TOPIC

Euro-issues of the Indian Firms

There are three instruments, viz. ADRs, GDRs and FCCBs that are known as euro-issues and through which Indian companies get funds from the international capital market. If the bank/depository is located in the USA, the receipt issued by it is known as ADR. ADRs are listed and traded in the US market. GDRs, on the other hand, are listed and traded elsewhere. ADRs/GDRs are issued and sold by the depositories in the international financial market on the basis of the shares deposited by Indian companies with a custodian bank located in India. The funds flow from ultimate investors to GDs, from GD to the custodian bank and from the custodian bank to the company. The ratio between the Indian shares and the depository receipts, the value of depository receipts, etc. are agreed upon between the custodian bank in India and the foreign depository before the issue of the depository receipts. An Indian company can sponsor an ADR/GDR issue. When a resident shareholder submits his shares back to the company, the latter can go for the issue of depository receipts on the basis of those shares.

There are three different types of ADR issues, although an alternative approach under Rule 144A is also there. In fact, the type depends upon the profile of the company sought by the investor, the choice of the accounting standards and the amount to be raised. At Level 1, the disclosure requirements to the US Securities and Exchange Commission (USSEC) are the minimum possible. Under this provision, the ADRs are traded in the US over-the-counter market. The issues are not listed on the national stock exchanges. In this case, the provisions of the Generally Accepted Accounting Principles (GAAP) are not applicable.

The Level 2 issue requires a greater amount of disclosures. The GAAP provisions are applicable. The ADRs are registered at NASDAQ or New York Stock Exchange.

At Level 3, ADRs represent public offerings to raise money. They need to be registered with the USSEC and need to comply with the listing requirements of the stock exchange. The GAAP provisions are also applicable.

Last but not least, under Rule 144 A, the issue is restricted to the qualified institutional buyers. No sales are effected in the first two years. The securities being unregistered or unsponsored are sold under very stringent procedures.

In September 2009, the Indian Government allowed the issue of Level 1 ADRs held by existing shareholders in the domestic market. It is true that there is no fresh accrual to the company, yet it is beneficial from other points of view.

As far as FCCBs are concerned, they, being a debt instrument, involve the repayment of the principal and interest payment in foreign currency. It is issued normally by high promoter shareholding companies which do not perceive any risk of losing management control even after the exercise of the conversion option. Such bonds are known by varying nomenclature in different countries, e.g. Yankee bonds in the USA, Bull-dog bonds in the UK and Samurai bonds in Japan. However, if these bonds are denominated in currency other than the currency of the country where they are issued, they are known as euro bonds. In such cases, there are multi-country investors.

The FCCB can be secured. However, in the Indian context, it is often unsecured. Normally, it is subordinated to the existing debt. The holder of the FCCB can sell a part or the whole of the holding or can convert it into American depository shares. It is often listed on the stock exchanges that helps improve its liquidity. There are many cases of listing of Indian companies' FCCBs at the Singapore Stock Exchange and Luxembourg Stock Exchange.

Governmental Guidelines

The euro issues are guided initially by the Scheme for Issue of Foreign Currency Convertible Bonds and Ordinary Shares (Through Depository Receipt Mechanism) 1993 (GOI, 1993) along with the guidelines issued from time to time by the Ministry of Finance, SEBI and RBI. They have also to abide by the provisions of the Foreign Exchange Management Act.

The Government of India treats euro issues as part of foreign direct investment for the purpose of sector-wise caps and some other purposes. The companies going for euro issues must have a consistent track record of good performance for a minimum period of three years, although relaxations can be made in case of infrastructural projects. Again, as per the SEBI regulations, companies not eligible for accessing to domestic securities market cannot go for the euro issues. The company must be a listed one. If not listed, simultaneous listing must be made along with the euro issue. Similarly, those overseas corporate bodies not eligible for investing in India through the portfolio route cannot participate in such issues. As per the guidelines issued by the Indian Government in May 1994, a company could go for a second issue only after a gap of twelve months at the minimum.

The issues are made either under automatic route or after the approval of the RBI. If they are related to the infrastructure sector or if they involve an amount up to US $ 500 million, they come under the automatic route. The eligible issuers under the automatic group are the companies except financial intermediaries, units in special economic zones, and non-governmental organisations in micro-finance activities.

In other cases, RBI's approval is mandatory. The eligible issuers under the approval route are: infrastructure/export finance companies, banks and financial institutions, non-banking financial companies, multi-state cooperative societies, and housing finance companies. As regards maturity of the FCCBs, the minimum average should be three years if the issue amount is up to US $ 20 million. Beyond this amount, the maturity must be at least five years. There is no maximum limit for the maturity. Pre-payment of FCCBs is permitted up to US $ 200 million subject to the compliance of the minimum average maturity period.

The raised funds can be used for the acquisition of foreign companies and direct investment in joint-ventures and wholly-owned subsidiaries abroad. They can be used for the modernisation/expansion of the existing projects or for refinancing of an existing FCCB issue. But the proceeds cannot be used for investment in the capital market, real estate, working capital or for repayment of a rupee loan. In fact, the FCCB issue proceeds are just like external commercial borrowings as far as end-use is concerned.

The euro issues are priced at not less than the higher of the two averages—one being the average of the high and low weekly prices of the related shares at the stock exchange during the past six months and the other being the average of high and low prices during the past fortnight. Although the companies going for simultaneous issue for the domestic and foreign markets or going for the foreign issue within 30 days of the domestic issue may not abide by the price guidelines. They have simply to get approval of the market regulator.

An Indian company can acquire an overseas company via the ADR/GDR share swap route, provided the total value of the ADR/GDR share swap transactions (undertaken in each financial year) should not exceed $100 million or 10 times the export earnings of the acquirer during the preceding year.

The guidelines have allowed for two-way fungibility since 2002. Prior to this provision, once a company issued ADR/GDR and if the ADR/GDR was converted back into underlying equity shares of the Indian company, it was not possible to reconvert the equity shares into ADR/GDR. But now the re-conversion is possible. The stock brokers in India are authorised to purchase shares of the Indian companies for re-conversion.

In 2008, in the wake of the international financial crisis, the RBI allowed FCCB buy-back under the approval route provided the buy-back was financed out of existing foreign currency resources or fresh external commercial borrowings. The policy was further liberalised through allowing the FCCB buy-back under automatic route and also permitting the use of Indian rupee proceeds for this purpose.

Funds Raised through ADRs/GDRs

Table ST18.1 shows the annual figures of the inflow of investment through the euro-issues—ADRs/GDRs. Since the policy was announced in the second half of FY 1992–93, there were only two issues: one being the GDRs of Reliance Industries in November 1992 and other being the GDRs of Grasim Industries both at Luxembourg collectively amounting to US $ 240 million during that financial year. The scheme was welcomed by the Indian companies with the result that in the following two financial years, it was as large as US $ 1,520 million and US $ 2,082 million respectively. But subsequently, the tempo could not be maintained. The annual figure moved in the range of US $ 270 million at the minimum and US $ 1,366 million at the maximum till FY 2004–05. However, with the growth rate of the Indian economy moving up thereafter and reaching 9.6 per cent during FY 2006–07 and also with procedural relaxations in international financial market, the figures of the euro-issues too moved up from US $ 2,552 million in FY 2005–06 to US $ 6,645 million in FY 2007–08.

The flow of investment under this mechanism was hit hard by the international financial crisis with the result that the figure plummeted to US $ 1,162 million during FY 2008–09. However, there was immediate revival in FY 2009–10 when this figure inflated to US $ 3,328 million but again, there was a drop down to US $ 2,049 million in the following year.

TABLE ST18.1 Investment Inflow through ADRs/GDRs

FYs	*Amount in US $ million*	*FYs*	*Amount in US $ million*
1992–93	240	2008–09	1,162
1993–94	1,520	2009–10	3,328
1994–95	2,082	2010–11	2,049
1995–96	683	2011–12	597

(Contd.)

FYs	*Amount in US $ million*	*FYs*	*Amount in US $ million*
1996–97	1,366	2012–13	187
1997–98	645	2013–14	20
1998–99	270	2014–15	1271
1999–00	768	2015–16	373
2000–01	831	2016–17	0
2001–02	477	2017–18	0
2002–03	600	2018–19	*
2003–04	459	2019–20	*
2004–05	613	2020–21	*
2005–06	2,552	2021–22	*
2006–07	3,776	2022–23	*
2007–08	6,645	2023–24	*

Source: SEBI Handbook of Statistics on Indian Securities Market

*SEBI did not publish any data of ADR/GDR in its Handbook from 2018-19 onwards

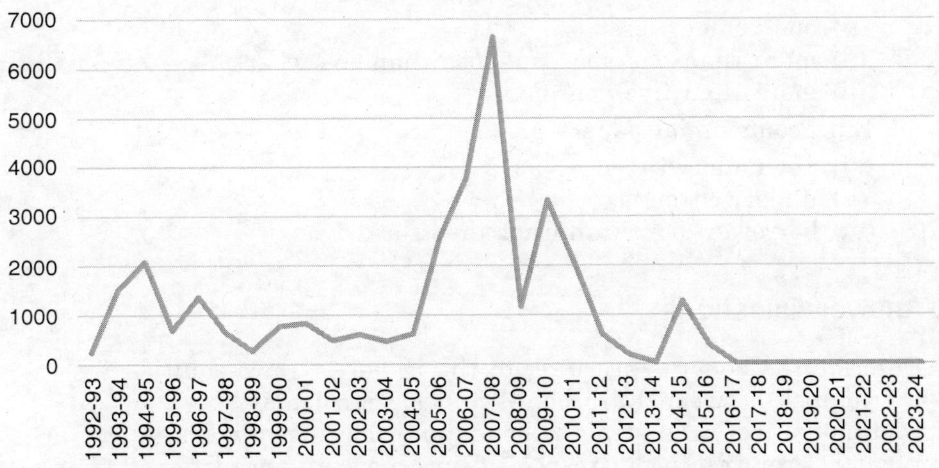

CHART 18.3 Foreign investment inflow under ADRs/GDRs Mechanism.

The ADRs/GDRs of Indian companies are listed and traded at the international stock exchanges. While ADRs are traded at NYSE and NASDAQ, GDRs are traded mainly at LSE. LuxSE, SSE, and a few others.

QUESTIONS

1. What do you mean by euro-issues? Are the governmental guidelines encouraging to such issues?
2. Comment on the trend of the funds raised by the Indian firms through euro-issues.

REVIEW QUESTIONS

Objective-Type Questions

1. State whether true (T) or false (F):
   (a) Euro bonds are denominated in the currency of the country where they are issued. ☐
   (b) Global bonds are large-size and have high rating. ☐
   (c) The value of ECP issues varies normally between US $ 10 million and one billion. ☐
   (d) ECP issues face nominal documentation. ☐
   (e) Euro notes have revolving underwriting facility. ☐
2. Choose the correct answer:
   (a) Cocktail bonds are denominated in:
      (i) US dollar
      (ii) Japanese yen
      (iii) Euro
   (b) Euro notes have a maturity of:
      (i) one year or less
      (ii) more than one year but less than five years
      (iii) more than five years
   (c) Euro commercial papers are:
      (i) not underwritten
      (ii) underwritten
      (iii) borrower-driven and not investor-driven

Short-Answer Questions

1. Describe the benefits accruing to the issuer of Euro-equities.
2. Distinguish between Euro bonds and foreign bonds.
3. Distinguish between straight bonds and floating-rate notes.
4. What is grey trading in respect of international securities?
5. Name important documents that accompany issue of international bonds.

Long-Answer Questions

1. What is the procedure of issuing Euro-equities?
2. Explain the procedure of the issue of international bonds.
3. What do you mean by Euro notes? How are they different from Euro commercial paper?
4. Write a note on the Euro-issues by Indian companies.

REFERENCES

Bank for International Settlements (1997), *Annual Report*, Basle.

Choi, F.D.S. and A.I. Stonehill (1982), "Foreign Access to US Securities Markets: The Theory, Myth and Reality of Regulatory Barriers", *Investment Analyst*, July, 17–26.

Errunza, V. and E. Losq (1985), "The Behaviour of Stock Prices in the LDC Markets", *Journal of Banking and Finance*, 9, 561–575.

Fanto, J.A. and R.S. Karmel (1997), "A Report with Attitudes of Foreign Companies regarding a US Listing", *Stanford Journal of Law, Business and Finance*, 3, 55–83.

Government of India (1993), *Scheme for Issue of Foreign Currency Convertible Bonds and Ordinary Shares (Through Depository Receipt Mechanism) 1993*, New Delhi, Ministry of Finance.

Hamilton, J. (1979), "Market Place, Fragmentation, Competition and the Efficiency of the Stock Exchanges", *Journal of Finance*, 34, 171–87.

Hansda, S.K. and P. Ray (2003), "Stock Market Integration and Dually Listed Stocks: Indian ADR and Domestic Stock Prices", *Economic and Political Weekly*, 38 (8), 741–754.

Hargis, K. and P. Ramanlal (1998), "When Does Internationalization Enhance the Development of Domestic Stock Markets?", *Journal of Financial Intermediation*, 7, 263–292.

Harris, L. (1993), "Consolidation, Fragmentation, Segmentation and Regulations", *Financial Markets, Institutions and Instruments*, 2, 1–28.

Kim, Y.C. and R.M. Stulz (1988), "The Euro-bond Market and the Corporate Financial Policy: A Test of the Clientele Hypothesis", *Journal of Financial Economics*, 22 (Dec.), 189–205.

Kumar, M. (2006), "The Impact of Indian Overseas Listings on the Volatility of the Underlying Shares", *SSRN Electronic Paper Collection.*

Levich, R.M. (2001), *International Financial Markets: Prices and Policies*, Singapore, McGraw Hill/Irwin.

Levy, H. and Z. Lerman (1988), The Benefits of International Diversification in Bonds, *Financial Analysts Journal*, Sept./Oct., 56–64.

Majumdar, S. (2007), "A Study of Internation Listing by Firms of Indian Origin", *Money and Finance (ICRA Bulletin)*, 6 (Feb.), 57–90.

Moel, A. (2000), "The Role of ADRs in the Development of Emerging Markets", *Harvard Business School Working Paper.*

Mittoo, U. (1992), "Managerial Perceptions of the Net Benefits of Foreign Listing: Canadian Evidence", *Journal of International Financial Management*, 4, 40–62.

Pagano, M. and A. Roell (1990), "Trading Systems in European Stock Exchanges: Current Performance and Policy Options", *Economic Policy*, 10, 65–115.

The Financial Times, 7th Jan. 2008.

The World Bank (2004), *Global Development Finance: 2004*, Washington D.C.

SUGGESTED FURTHER READING

Giddy, I.H. (1994), *Global Financial Markets*, Lexington, D.C. Heath.

Grabbe, J. Orlin (1996), *International Financial Markets*, Englewood Cliffs, Prentice-Hall.

CHAPTER 19 Financial Swaps

Learning Objectives

In the funds-raising process, there is every possibility that a firm needing fixed-rate loan is able to get floating-rate funds. Again, a firm is able to borrow in some other currency than the desired one. In such cases, the firm exchanges the borrowing from another firm in order to suit its needs. The exchange is called swap that is discussed in the present chapter. The chapter attempts:

- To discuss the features of an interest-rate swap and its variants.
- To discuss the features of a currency swap and its variants.
- To explain what is an equity swap.
- To show how the different parties to swap—the counter party and the swap dealer benefit from such deals.
- To explain the different kinds of risk borne by the swap dealer.

We have already discussed about the various sources of funds and fund-raising instruments. But there is every possibility that a borrower may not have an easy access to a particular segment of financial market of its own choice. For example, a firm needs fixed-rate funds, but has an easy access to floating-rate funds. Similarly, a firm needs borrowing from the US dollar market, but has an easy access to Euro market. In this case, it can borrow the funds from the easily available sources and then can exchange its liability into another form of liability of its own choice. This exchange is swap. In the above example, the borrowing firm can swap the floating-rate loan for fixed-rate loan, or it can swap the Euro loan for US dollar loan in the swap market. Thus swaps by themselves are not a funding instrument, but they represent a device or technique adopted for obtaining the desired form of financing in an indirect way that could otherwise be inaccessible or costly.

Swap deals are an extension of the parallel loans or the back-to-back loans that had emerged during 1970s while exchange control mechanisms were in operation. The international financial market turned a bit liberal in 1980s, but even then it was characterised with too much of segmentation. Access to desired sources of funds was not easy in all cases. The borrowers used parallel and back-to-back loans, but their use was limited because of their limitations in the form of finding a party with matched financing requirements. Naturally, the borrowers began using swaps on a large scale, which were an improvement over the back-to-back loans or parallel loans. The first interest-rate swap is believed to have been used in London in 1979. Immediately thereafter, the currency swap was used by the World Bank to obtain Swiss francs and Deutsch mark to finance its operations in Switzerland and Germany without borrowing these two currencies. The swap concept was extended by Chase Manhattan in 1986 to include commodity swap. In 1989, the Bankers Trust introduced the first reported equity swap. Presently, the swap deals have a heyday. In this chapter, we deal with the interest-rate swap, currency swap and equity swap in view of their important role in the international financial market.

How is currency swap different from interest-rate swap?

1. While interest-rate swap involves any single currency, currency swap involves different currencies.
2. In interest-rate swap, cash flows occurring on concurrent dates are netted. But since cash flow in a currency swap represents different currencies, it cannot be netted. Principal and interest payments are exchanged without netting.

INTEREST-RATE SWAP

Basic Features

Interest-rate swap involves the exchange of interest payments. It usually occurs when a person or a firm needs fixed-rate funds but is able to get floating-rate funds. It finds another party who needs floating-rate loan but is able to get fixed-rate funds. The two, known as the counter-party, exchange the interest payments and feel as if they are using the loans according to their own choice. It is the swap dealer, usually a bank, that brings together the two counter-parties for the swap. The essential condition for the interest-rate swap is that the amount of loan is identical in the two cases and periodic payment of interest takes place in the same currency. At the same time, there must be synchronisation of interest between the two parties—one getting cheaper fixed-rate funds and the other getting cheaper floating-rate funds.

Interest-rate swap involves exchange of interest payments.

Counter-party are the parties to the swap.

Leg of the swap is related to the interest payment.

Since the principals are identical in size, they are not exchanged. They are only notional. It is the interest payment that is exchanged on periodic payment dates. The interest payments are called the *legs of the swap* and the fixed rate is called the *swap coupon*. The process of interest-rate swap will be clear from a simple example.

Example: Suppose Firm A needs fixed-rate funds which are available to it at the rate of 10.50 per cent to be computed half-yearly, but it has access to cheaper floating-rate funds available to it at LIBOR + 0.3 per cent.

Firm B needs floating-rate funds available to it at 6-month LIBOR flat, but has access to cheaper fixed-rate funds available to it at the rate of 9.50 per cent to be computed half-yearly.

Both the principals are identical in size and maturity and are in the same currency. The interest-rate swap will take place in the following stages:

Stage 1: If Firm A has access to floating-rate loan market, it will borrow from floating-rate loan market. Similarly, Firm B having access to fixed-rate loan market, will borrow fixed-rate loan.

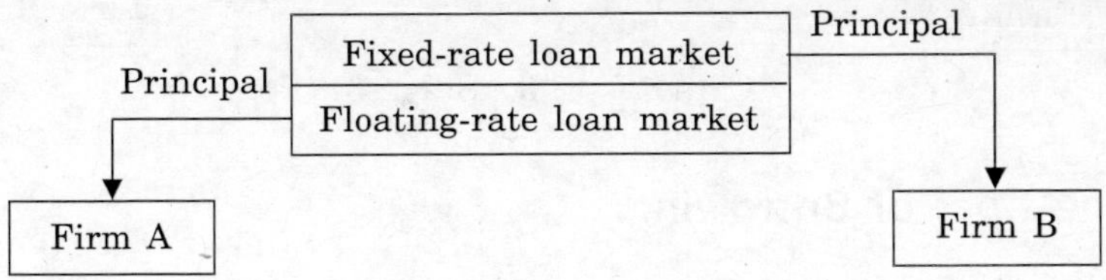

CHART 19.1 Stage 1.

Stage 2: Since both the firms have not borrowed according to their needs, they approach a swap dealer. Since Firm A needs fixed-rate loan, the swap dealer asks it to pay fixed-rate interest to it (swap dealer) as if it has borrowed fixed-rate loan. The fixed rate of interest payable through the swap dealer is higher than what Firm B has to pay to the lender in the fixed-rate loan market but lower than what Firm A has to pay to the lender if it had borrowed from the fixed-rate loan market. It is, say, 9.75 per cent. In exchange, the swap dealer pays Firm A the interest at 6-month LIBOR. Firm A pays LIBOR + 0.3 per cent to the lender on its floating-rate borrowing.

> Swap dealer is normally a bank that acts as an intermediary between the two counter-parties.

On the other hand, the swap dealer asks Firm B to pay 6-month LIBOR as if it has borrowed floating-rate loan. In exchange, the swap dealer pays Firm B fixed-rate interest which is higher than what Firm B has to pay to the ultimate lender. This is the interest rate what the swap dealer has received from Firm A minus its (swap dealer's) own commission. It is, say, 9.65 per cent. Here, Firm B gets interest from the swap dealer at 9.65 per cent and pays interest to the fixed-rate lender at 9.50 per cent.

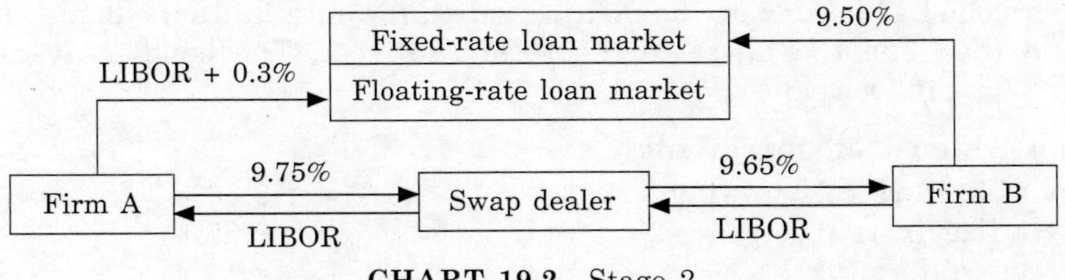

CHART 19.2 Stage 2.

Firm A is attracted for the swap deal not only because it uses the loan according to its own choice but also because the fixed rate of interest payable by it is lower than what it had to pay for borrowing from the fixed-rate loan market. Firm B is attracted for the swap deal not only because it is using the loan according to its own choice but also because it gets from the swap dealer an interest rate which is higher than what it has to pay to the ultimate lender. The swap dealer is attracted to the swap deal because it earns from such a deal.

Stage 3: At the maturity, the two firms repay the loan. Firm A repays the floating-rate loan and Firm B repays fixed-rate loan.

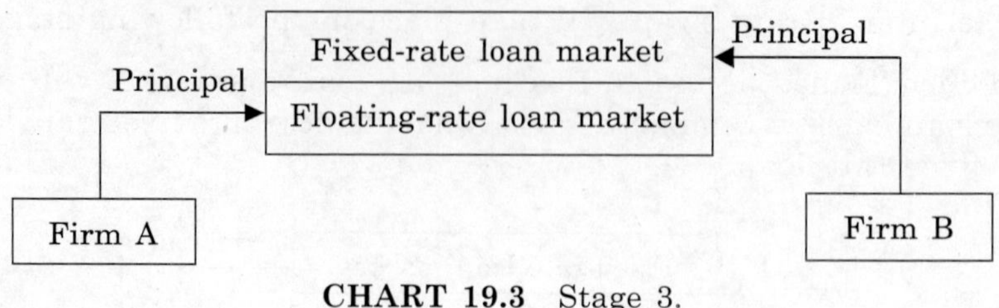

CHART 19.3 Stage 3.

Impact on the Cost of Borrowing

The benefit of the interest-rate swap is two-fold: the counter-parties use the borrowing according to their own choice, but it is also that it has a favourable impact on the cost of borrowing. Based on the above example, one can easily compute the cost of borrowing after the swap deal.

Firm A's cost of borrowing

Cost of floating-rate loan	LIBOR + 0.3%
Less floating interest rate received	LIBOR
Net cost differential	0.3%
Converting the cost differential from money-market yield to bond-equivalent yield	0.3% × 365/360 = 0.304%
Add swap coupon	9.75%
Total cost of borrowing	10.054%

Had Firm A borrowed fixed-rate loan which it actually needed, it would have to pay interest at the rate of 10.50 per cent. But as a result of swap deal, it has to pay interest only at 10.054 per cent. This means, it is saving interest payment at 0.446 per cent.

(*Note:* LIBOR is quoted as an annual money-market yield which involves 360 days a year. On the contrary, the fixed rate is quoted as semi-annual bond-equivalent yield. Here one has to convert the floating-rate differential into the bond-equivalent yield and then add the latter to the fixed rate cost. The bond-equivalent yield involves 365 days a year.)

Firm B's cost of borrowing

Cost of fixed-rate borrowing	9.50%
Less fixed-rate received	9.65%
Net cost differential	–0.15%

Converting the net cost differential from BEY to MMY	0.15% × 360/365 = –0.148%
Total cost of borrowing	LIBOR – 0.148%

Had Firm B taken floating-rate loan, it would have to pay LIBOR. But as a result of swap deal, it has to pay LIBOR – 0.148 per cent. This means that it has saved interest payment equivalent to 0.148 per cent.

Gain to Swap dealer

Interest rate received	9.75%
Interest rate paid	9.65%
Net gain	0.10%

Q. Why is interest-rate swap preferable to loan?

Ans: Interest-rate swap involves only exchange of interest payments. Principal is notional having no impact on the balance sheet.

Variants of Interest-rate Swap

The interest-rate swap has broadly five variants. *First*, commonly is the fixed-for-floating rate swap which is also known as generic or plain vanilla swap. In this case, one leg is fixed, while the other leg is floating. Sometimes, the fixed-rate leg represents zero-coupon loan where no interest payment is made, although repayment is made on maturity.

Secondly, *floating-for-floating rate swaps* are also available where both the legs are floating. Such swaps are of two kinds. One is known as *basis swap* where the two legs are tied to two different indices. For example, one leg is tied to 3-month LIBOR, while the other leg is tied to 6-month LIBOR. The other variant is the *yield-curve swap* where the two legs are tied to two long-term rates.

Thirdly, there is *fixed-for-fixed rate swap*. It is found when the cash flow stream of the firm opting for swap is highly volatile. When the cash flow of a particular firm is higher in a particular season than the average, the firm shall pay the swap dealer a fixed sum. On the other hand, the swap dealer pays a fixed sum to the firm in case the cash flow in a particular season is lower than the average.

Fourthly, in the case of *option swap*, the purchaser of swap has the right, and not the obligation, to enforce the deal. When the results of the deal are expected to be in favour of the purchaser, it enforces the deal. If the result is not favourable, it does not enforce the deal.

Fifthly, when the swap is terminated before maturity by the fixed interest rate payer, it is called a *callable swap*. When it is terminated by the floating interest rate payer, it is known as *putable swap*. When maturity is extended, it is known as *extendable swap*.

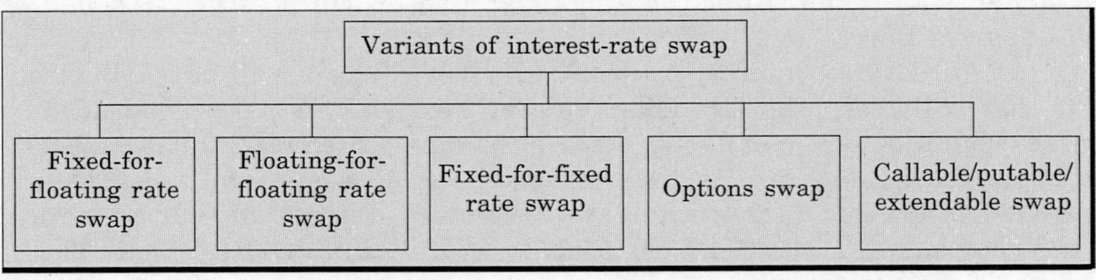

PROBLEM 19.1

A has fixed-rate debt on which it is paying T + 1 per cent. But it could borrow floating-rate funds at LIBOR. B has floating-rate debt on which it is paying LIBOR + 25 b.p. But it could borrow fixed-rate funds at T + 1.75 per cent. Can the two counter-parties go for interest-rate swap? If so, indicate the gains accruing to them.

Solution

Swap is arranged in such a way that:

A: Pays T + 1% to the debt market.
Pays to B: LIBOR – 25 b.p.
Receives from B: T + 1%
Net cost = LIBOR – 25 b.p.
Had A borrowed from the floating-rate market, it would have to pay LIBOR.
But because of the swap, it has to pay 25 b.p. less than LIBOR.

B: Pays LIBOR + 25 b.p. to the debt market.
Pays to A: T + 1%
Receives from A: LIBOR – 25 b.p.
Net cost = (LIBOR + 25 b.p.) – (LIBOR – 25 b.p.) + T + 1% = T + 1.50%
Had B gone to fixed-rate market, it would have to pay T + 1.75 per cent.
Thus swap makes it available cheaper fixed-rate funds.

CURRENCY SWAP

Basic Features

Currency swap involves the exchange of currency.

A currency swap is different from the interest-rate swap insofar as it (currency swap) involves two different currencies. This is the reason that the two currencies are exchanged in the beginning; again, at maturity, the two currencies are re-exchanged. The exchange of currencies is necessitated by the fact that one counter-party is able to borrow a particular currency at a lower interest rate than the other counter-party is able to borrow. Suppose Firm A can borrow Euro at a fixed rate of 8.0 per cent or it can borrow US dollar at a floating rate of one-year LIBOR. Firm B can borrow Euro at a fixed rate of 9.2 per cent and can borrow US dollar at one-year LIBOR. If Firm B needs fixed-rate Euro, it will approach the swap dealer provided Firm A needs floating-rate US dollar. The swap deal will be conducted in different stages as follows: In the *first stage*, Firm A borrows Euro at 8.0 per cent interest rate. Firm B borrows US dollar at LIBOR.

In the *second stage*, the two firms exchange the borrowed currencies with the help of the swap dealer. After the exchange, Firm A will possess US dollar. Firm B will possess Euro.

In the *third stage*, interest payment will flow. Firm A will pay LIBOR on US dollar that will reach the US dollar market through, first, the swap dealer and then through Firm B. Similarly, Firm B will pay fixed rate interest that will flow to the fixed rate Euro market through the swap dealer and through Firm A. Firm B will pay fixed rate of interest to the swap dealer that will be more than 8.0 per cent but less than 9.20 per cent. It will be, say, 8.60 per cent. The swap

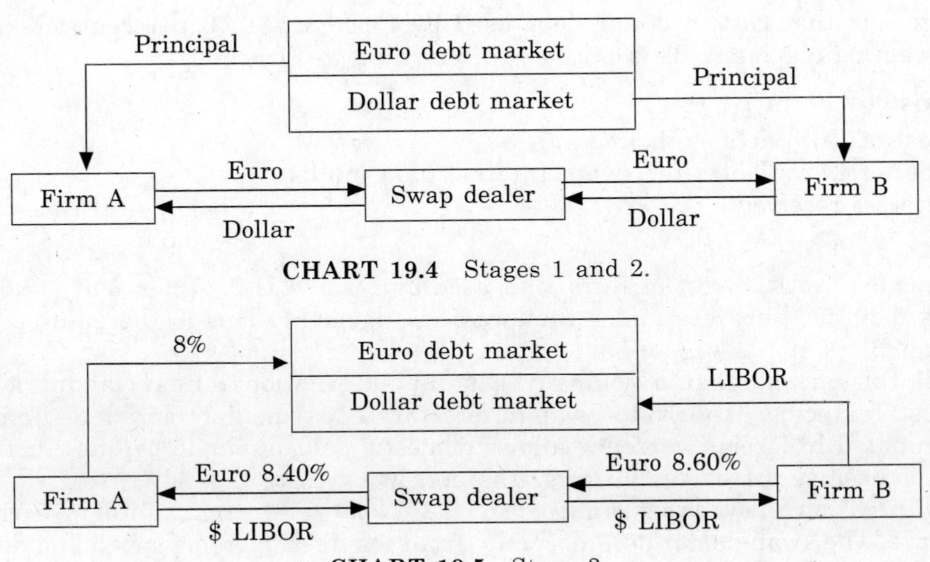

CHART 19.4 Stages 1 and 2.

CHART 19.5 Stage 3.

dealer will take its own commission and shall pay to Firm A in this case only, say, 8.40 per cent.

In the *fourth stage*, the two principals are again exchanged between the two counter-parties. Firm A gets back Euro and repays it to the lender. Firm B gets back US dollar and repays it to the lender.

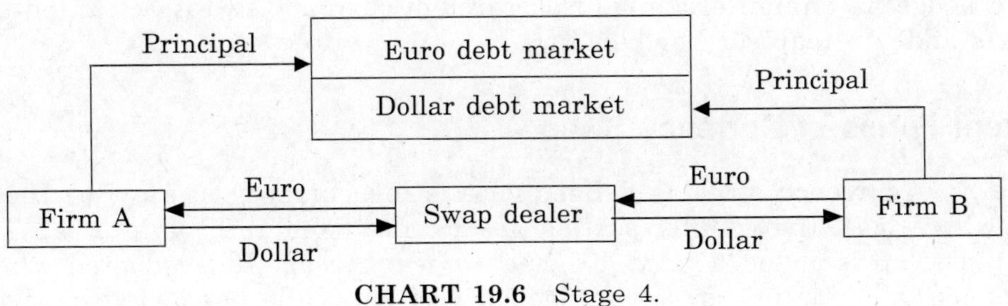

CHART 19.6 Stage 4.

Benefits from the Currency Swap

First, Firm A gets the currency of its own choice. Firm B gets the currency of its own choice.

Secondly, the cost of borrowings gets reduced, which brings in gains to Firm A as well as to Firm B.

Cost to Firm A

Cost of US dollar debt in absence of swap	LIBOR
Cost of US dollar debt after swap: Interest paid minus interest received	8.0% + LIBOR – 8.40% = LIBOR – 0.40%

This means that cost of dollar debt used by Firm A is 0.40 per cent less under the swap arrangement. This is the gain accruing to Firm A.

Cost to Firm B

Cost of Euro debt without swap	9.2%
Cost of Euro debt after swap: Interest paid minus interest received	8.60% + LIBOR – LIBOR = 8.60%

This means that the cost of Euro loan used by Firm B is 9.20 per cent – 8.60 per cent = 0.60 per cent less under the swap arrangement. This is the gain accruing to Firm B.

All this means that a company can tap international financial market for low-cost financing. Ability to swap interest rate payments related to financing denominated in foreign currency allows domestic debt issuer to tap new markets, expand the investor base and lower the borrowing cost.

Thirdly, currency swap can be used as a tool for hedging foreign exchange exposure. The swap dealer uses normally fixed-for-fixed currency swap and designs the interest rate in such a way that influences the cash flow of the counter-parties. It helps reduce the interest rate if the borrower is the loser on account of changes in the exchange rate. It may also help increase the interest rate if the borrower is the gainer on account of changes in exchange rate. This way the loss from the depreciation of a currency is offset considerably by the interest changes.

Reduction in the foreign exchange risk enables a firm to operate on a larger scale. The firm reaps in turn the economies of scale. Moreover, if the firm is able to hedge its foreign exchange risk through currency swaps, it can enter new markets and can reap further benefits.

Different Forms of Currency Swap

Normally, a currency swap is a fixed-for-floating currency swap. But there are cases where both the counter-parties are paying fixed rate of interest. In this case, the swap is called a *fixed-for-fixed currency swap*. It is adopted when one counter-party maintains an advantageous position while borrowing a particular currency. Suppose a German firm is able to borrow from the German market at a fixed rate of 8.50 per cent, while it can borrow from the US dollar market at a fixed rate of 10.50 per cent. On the other hand, an American firm is able to borrow at 10.75 per cent from the US dollar market, while it can borrow at 9.25 per cent from the German market.

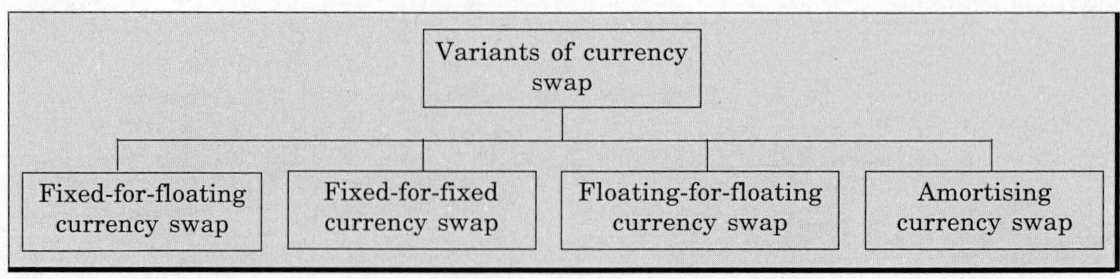

In this case, the German firm will borrow Euro from the German market. The American firm will borrow dollar from the dollar market. The two will exchange the currency through a swap dealer. After the exchange of the principal amount, the German firm possesses US dollar and the American firm possesses Euro. The German firm pays interest on the dollar loan to the American firm at 10.50 per cent. The American firm adds to it 0.25 per cent interest and pays 10.75 per cent interest rate to the lender. At the same time, the American firm pays to the swap dealer an interest at 8.80 per cent on the Euro loans. The swap dealer deducts its commission at 0.05 per cent and passes on the remaining interest at 8.75 per cent to the German firm. The German firm pays interest to the German lender at 8.50 per cent and saves 0.25 per cent. This means that the German firm uses dollar loan only at 10.50 per cent – 0.25 per cent = 10.25 per cent. Had it not swapped the currency, it would have to pay 10.50 per cent for the dollar loan. There is a distinct gain for 0.25 per cent.

Similarly, the American firm is paying 0.25 per cent more to the dollar market lender than what it receives from the German firm, but since it is saving 9.25 per cent – 8.80 per cent = 0.45 per cent on the Euro loan, its net gain on the borrowing is 0.45 per cent – 0.25 per cent = 0.20 per cent. Both the counter-parties are gainers on account of fixed-for-fixed currency swap.

The second form of currency swap is known as the *floating-for-floating currency swap*. In this case, both the counter-parties pay floating rate of interest. This type of swap can be achieved through a single swap agreement or through a double agreement. In the latter, it is combination of one fixed-for-floating currency swap and one fixed-for-floating interest-rate swap. The combination is usually known as a *circus swap*. The currency swap is used for the initial transaction, while the interest-rate swap is used for converting fixed-rate side to a floating rate. If the two fixed-rate payments equal, the net result is manifest in the flow of floating-rate interest.

> Amortising currency swap involves no exchange of currency but the amortization of the principal over the life of the swap.

The third variant is known as the *amortising currency swap*. In this case, principals amortise over the life of the swap and so there is no single re-exchange of currencies.

PROBLEM 19.2

A can borrow floating-rate funds from dollar market at 1-year LIBOR or it can borrow fixed-rate Euro at 7 per cent. B can borrow floating-rate funds from US dollar market at LIBOR + 25 b.p. or can borrow fixed rate funds from the Euro market at 8.25 per cent. B needs fixed-rate Euro. A needs floating-rate dollar. Can the currency swap be gainful to both of them?

Solution

1. A borrows euro and B borrows US dollar.
2. A will pass on euro to B in return for US dollar. It means there will be exchange of currency.
3. A will pay LIBOR to B. B will pay, say, 7.50 per cent fixed to A.
4. At the maturity, currencies are re-exchanged.

Cost of swap:

A: 7 per cent + LIBOR – 7.50 per cent = LIBOR – 0.5 per cent

B: LIBOR + 0.25 + 7.5 per cent – LIBOR = 7.75 per cent

Had A gone to floating-rate market, it would have to pay LIBOR. But after the swap, it is paying less by 0.5 per cent. Had B gone to the fixed-rate market, it would have to pay 8.25 per cent. But owing to swap, it is paying only 7.75 per cent.

EQUITY SWAP

Basic Features

Equity swap is used when the return from investment in equity is highly volatile. The recipients of the dividend go for swapping their receipt with the swap dealer. The fluctuating receipt of dividend is passed on to the swap dealer. The swap dealer in exchange pays a fixed rate of dividend to the shareholder.

Equity swap involves the exchange of dividend.

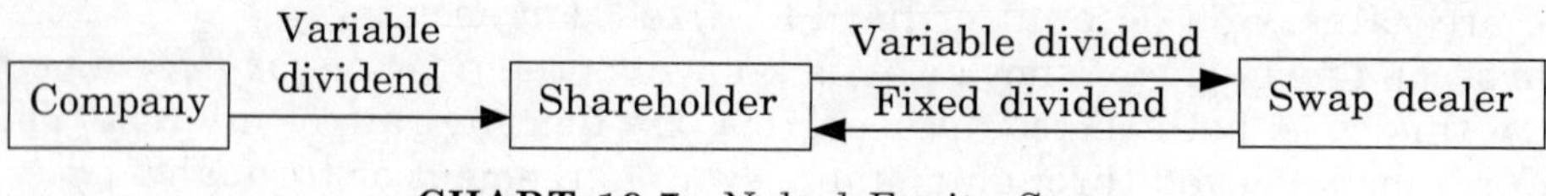

CHART 19.7 Naked Equity Swap.

In some cases, the swap dealer passes on its risk to those shareholders who are interested in higher dividend even if the risk is greater. In this case, swap dealer's position is not naked, rather it is covered. This can be shown in Chart 19.8.

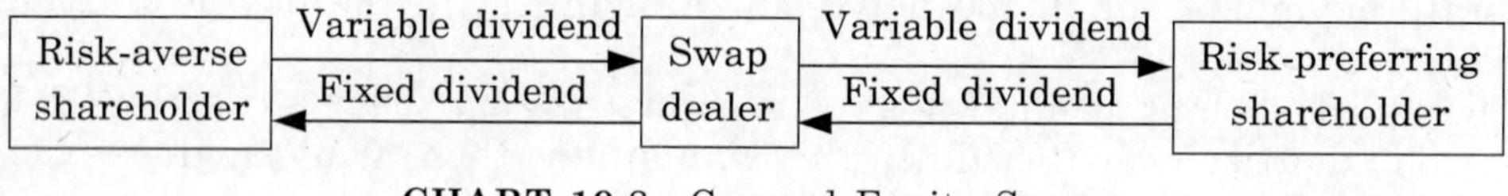

CHART 19.8 Covered Equity Swap.

Forms of Equity Swap

There are different forms of equity swap. One is known as *capped equity swap*. In this case, the end user's potential pay-out, that is the variable leg of the swap, is capped. If it has to pay more than the ceiling, the excess amount is paid by the cap dealer with which there is an agreement.

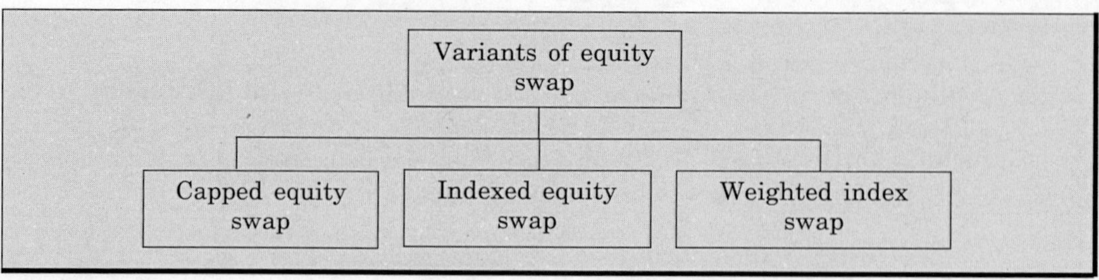

In the other form, the equity return or the variable leg of the swap is pegged to the greater of the two share indices. In yet other form, both of the two share indices are used. The counter-party pays the total return based on one index and receives the total return based on the other index. Sometimes there is one more form of the equity swap where the weighted average of two or more indices is used.

Swaps: Hedging and Speculation in Financial Markets

As we have had discussed all types of Swaps in the former part of this chapter such as interest-rate swaps, currency swaps, commodity swaps, and equity swaps. While the main purpose of making swaps is to hedge and manage risk. The swaps have also gained a significant importance in the speculation purposes and making the swaps profitable. We are going to discuss more about how the swaps are used as Hedging and Speculation in the international financial markets.

1. Use of Swaps for Hedging: With the use of this mechanism, the swap offers a way for the mitigation of the risks (viz., currency risk, interest-rate risk, and commodity price volatility) that are associated with the volatility in the financial market. This process allows any business to strategically align their financial decisions with more accuracy, and helps in avoiding the disruption in the market.

Let us discuss more on how each type of swap is used as a hedging instrument for the purpose of avoiding risks and fluctuations in the financial markets.

Interest-rate swaps: Corporations use this swap to protect against the possible uncertainty caused by the fluctuations of interest rates. A floating-rate loan can be converted into a fixed rate by using the interest rate swaps for a stable future interest payment.

Example: A company (A Ltd.) is having a floating rate loan which is based on LIBOR+2%. If the company fears a rise in the interest rate, that can also raise the interest expenses. Assessing this situation, the company (A Ltd.) is going to have an agreement for the interest rate swap with any bank, and agrees to pay a fixed interest rate of let say 4% in exchange of receiving payment based on LIBOR, now if LIBOR rises, the payments from the bank will increase that will offset the higher cost of the floating-rate loan.

Currency swaps help in managing exposure to fluctuation in exchange rate, it is prominently used by the companies operating internationally and having a debt in foreign currencies.

Example: Company X, a US-based company issued a bond in euros to attract European investors, but the revenue generated by them is mostly in $ (USD), so they faces a currency risk. To mitigate this risk the company enters into an agreement with a bank to exchange its euro-denominated payments for $ (USD) and hence it uses currency swaps as a hedging instrument. With this agreement the Company X hedges the risk of the euro appreciating against the dollar.

Commodity swaps allow businesses in mitigating the risk associated with the fluctuation of commodity prices. This type of swap especially relevant for the industries that rely more on the commodities transitions. Such as Airline fuel, Manufacturing metal, and agriculture grains.

Example: An alirline company (A) is more concerned about the rapid rising of the cost of jet fuel, that can impact its profitability. To hedge this risk the company entered into a commodity swaps with a Bank and agreed on terms that a fixed price for jet fuel over the next year will be paid to him. In return to this agreement Bank will pay the market price of jet fuel each payment date. And if by any chance the price of jet fuel rises, then the Airline company is going to receive the higher price, and can effectively keep its fuel cost stable by hedging this commodity risk of rising prices.

Equity swaps help investors in hedging exposure of volatile equity markets without actually buying or selling the underlying stock or index. In this swap two parties comes into an agreement to exchange returns on an equity index or stock for a fixed or a floating interest rate.

Example: An investor is holding a large portfolio position in any stock index but he is more concerned about the potential market volatility in the short term. He used the equity swaps as a hedging technique and enter into swap with a Bank, where the investor agrees to receive a fixed rate in exchange for paying the return on the stock index. Now if the stock index performs adversely the investor will be protected as he can still receive the fixed rate agreed in the swap.

To summarize, hedging facilitates the efficient planning of budgets and financial strategies within institutions. The utilization of swaps allows firms to mitigate risks associated with market fluctuations, thereby helping to avert the disruptive effects of volatility.

2. Use of Swap as Speculation: While swaps are used not only in hedging but also in speculative purpose by the investors, with a objective of profit motive from the movement prediction in the interest rates, exchange rates, or other underlying assets.

Let's discuss these speculation techniques that are done with the help of swaps there ways of speculation in each and every types of swaps that are as follows:

Firstly, **Interest-rate swaps** are used by speculators to take advantage of anticipated shifts in interest rates. If they can anticipate that the rate is going to rise, then they might enter in a interest rate swaps where they get a floating rate and pay a fixed rate, and hoping that the floating rate will increase beyond the fixed rate they have paid.

Example: A trader anticipated the short-term rise in the interest rate. The trader can enters into the interest rate swap, and agrees to receive a floating rate payments based on LIBOR and they pay a fixed rate of 3%. Now if the LIBOR rises to 5%, then trader can benefit from receiving the floating rate payments than the fixed rate that he paid, and hence generate a profit.

Secondly, in **Currency swaps** the speculators bet on the rise or fall in the exchange rates between two currencies. The speculators may exchange the interest payments in one currency for another, and makes a favorable cash flow from the currency movement differentials.

Example: An investor predicts that the euro is going to be strengthen against the $ (USD). Now the speculative investor is going to enter into a currency swap and pay $ (USD) and receive euro payments, and desires that Euro will appreciate. If the Euro get strengthen, then the euro-denominated payment becomes more valuable than the $ (USD), and this results in a significant profit when exchanged with the $ dollar.

Thirdly, **Commodity Swaps** allows speculators to predict on the commodity prices movement, such as oil or metals, without holding the physical commodity. The speculator can take a fixed price position when confident that commodity prices will fall, and a floating price position if they expect prices to rise.

Example: A trader expects that the oil prices are going to rise sharply in near future. Irrespective of buying and storing that commodity they are going to capitalize this prediction by entering into a commodity swap, and agrees to pay a fixed price of $60 per barrel while receiving a floating market price of oil. Now if the oil prices is going to increase to $80 per barrel, the trader will generate a profit with the difference between the floating rate and received and the fixed rate paid.

Fourthly, **Equity swaps** is also used by the speculator as they exchange the returns on equity indices or on individual stocks, with an aim to generate profit form such expected movements in equity markets. In this swap also, they are not going to buy or hold any such equity upon which the speculation is made.

Example: An investor expects that a particular stock index is going to perform well in the next year. So, to make this prediction profitable he enters into an Equity swap transaction, where he consents to receive compensation contingent upon the total return of the index, while simultaneously remitting a fixed interest rate. Now if the index performs as per the expectations of the investor then he make a profit from the difference, and gain exposure in the market without acutally holding that index itself.

Swaps serve as a crucial instrument for speculators, enabling them to articulate their perspectives on diverse market conditions without the obligation of holding the underlying assets. Nevertheless, the practice of speculation entails considerable risks and demands a comprehensive understanding of the markets along with robust risk management strategies. In conclusion, while swaps offer significant opportunities for speculation, a careful and informed approach is essential to navigate the inherent uncertainties they present.

SOME ASPECTS OF SWAP MANAGEMENT

Risks Borne by Swap Dealer

In the process of swap, the role of swap dealer is significant insofar as it brings together two counter-parties whose interests are complementary to each other. For this role, it takes a small part of the interest payment flow. Since the principal amount is large, even a small percentage of the interest payment adds considerably to its profit. But, on the other hand, the swap dealer has to face a variety of risks. It is a fact that the swap dealers are professional bodies and they anticipate almost with certainty the changes in interest rate or the exchange rate. But there is every possibility that their anticipation proves wrong. In that case, they have to bear the interest rate exposure or the exchange rate exposure. In addition to these two forms of risk, there are some other forms of risk that they are exposed to. These different forms of risk need some explanation here.

Interest-rate risk

Interest-rate risk arises when the interest rate on a particular loan fails to keep abreast of the movement of the market interest rate. Thus it can be said that the fixed rate loans under the swap carry higher risk. On the contrary, floating interest rate should not be risky because it changes with the changing profile of the money market. But it does carry risk at least between two reset dates when the interest rate of a particular loan may not be reset despite changes in the market interest rates.

The swap dealer is faced with the interest-rate risk, especially when it has a naked position in the swap. Suppose the swap dealer pays fixed-rate interest to the end-user or to the counter-party; and in exchange, it receives LIBOR. If LIBOR moves to the swap dealer's disadvantage, it will have to pay more in form of interest. But the risk can be reduced if the swap dealer does not have a naked position and passes on the risk to another counter-party.

Exchange-rate risk

Changes in the exchange rate are a common affair in the foreign exchange market. If the swap dealer pays fixed rate of interest on a loan denominated in a currency which is going to depreciate, it will have to pay a greater amount of interest to the end-user. Here it may be noted that if the swap dealer faces both the interest-rate risk and the exchange-rate risk simultaneously, the quantum of risk will be very large. If the two risks are positively correlated, the risk will be still higher. But if they are negatively correlated or uncorrelated, the risk will not be so high.

Credit risk

Credit risk arises when a counter-party defaults payment to the swap dealer. In such cases, the contract is terminated. However, termination of the contract does not protect the swap dealer from loss. This is because the contract is terminated only with one counter-party. The other needs payment which the swap dealer has to make.

Mismatch risk

There are occasions when it is difficult for the swap dealer to find a perfect match for a counter-party. When a perfect match is not available, the swap dealer offers concessions to attract suitable counter-party. Any such concession causes loss to it. Sometimes after giving concessions, perfect match is not available on different counts, such as notional principal, maturity, swap coupon, reset dates, etc. The swap dealer may have to pay more interest.

Sovereign risk

Sovereign risk arises when the government of a country to which one of the two counter-party belongs, puts restrictions on the flow of foreign exchange. This entails upon payments received by the swap dealer. It should not be called a default risk or credit risk because the counter-party is willing to make payments. It is the governmental restriction that comes in the way.

Delivery risk

Delivery risk arises when the two counter-parties are located in two different time zones so that the date of maturity differs by one day. However, the swap dealer is not very much affected by it.

Termination of the Swap Deal

A swap deal can be terminated even before maturity if a counter-party makes default, or it needs to change the very structure of the existing cash flow or it likes to go out of swap for some other reasons. The process of termination varies from one case to another. In the first process, the two counter-parties evaluate or assess the cash flow and settle the payments under an agreement after terminating the swap deal. In the other process, the two counter-parties agree for a reverse swap deal that may nullify the original deal. The new deal may not be carried out with the same swap dealer. Yet again in the other process, the counter-parties approach another swap dealer who buys out the original deal. The new dealer takes over the swap counter-party's position vis-à-vis the original swap dealer.

Documentation

Swap deal is agreed upon normally on telephones in over-the-counter market. So confusion may arise if the deal is not written subsequently. It is thus a normal practice to prepare the necessary documentation after the deal is finalised. In this context, the role of the International Swap Dealers' Association (ISDA) is very important. For the first time in 1982, it made distinct rules in this context. Subsequently, in 1987 and in 1992, the rules were made more comprehensive. The rules deal with the identification of the parties to the swap, payments, representations, agreements, default, termination, tax matters, jurisdictions, etc. Obviously, these rules provide the swap market a systematic structure.

Central Clearing Counter-parties (CCPs) and their Role in Risk Mitigation

The central clearing counter-parties (CCPs) play critical role in reducing the counter-party risks in the swap transactions, this is especially used in over-the-counter (OTC) markets. There are two parties involved in the swap contract and here the CCP is standing between to two that is buyer and the seller for giving guarantee to the swap transaction.

Functions of CCPs

The function of CCPs becomes considerable as this is the counter-parties that helps the transaction of swap and facilitate both the parties in easy conduct of the transactions. Some of the main functions are as under:

- **Risk Management:** CCPs act as a counter-parties to both sides of a transaction, to reduce the risk of defalult of either party. It puts a rigorous risk management practices, that include initial margin requirements and also daily variation margins, that helps ensure adequate collateral to support the parties position.

- **Transparency:** CCPs contribute to transparency in standardizing reporting and data requirements, which makes it easier to regulate and keep monitoring the market activity and intervene if needed.
- **Systemic Stability:** CCPs reduces systemic risk by putting itself in center of the counterparty exposure and mitigating the domino effect that can trigger across all the financial system. At the time of crisis the CCPs serves as a stabilized force in the derivatives market.

Challenges of CCPs

- It concentrates the risk by centralizing counter-party risk within CCPs that can lead to systemic risks if the CCP fails. When any large CCP fails it can have a catastrophic impact on the global financial system.
- The CCPs require a high level of liquidity so that they can meet the margin requirements, these requirements can surge during the volatile markets, and hence it comes with a challenge of liquidity for the market participants.

There are various other challenges also with the CCPs as it tries to combine parties and keep the system centralized to ensure easy and effective transactions.

Regulatory Challenges in the OTC Derivatives Markets

The over-the-counter (OTC) derivatives market has emerged as a central focus of regulatory reform, particularly in the aftermath of the 2008 financial crisis. Historically, this market has operated with less regulatory oversight compared to exchange-traded derivatives markets. Consequently, it presents distinct challenges for regulatory bodies seeking to enhance transparency and mitigate systemic risk.

- **Transparency and Disclosure:**
  - The key issue in OTC derivatives markets is the lack of transparency, and the current regulations stipulates the requiremtn for OTC trades to be reported to designated trade repositories. This facilitates regulatory oversight and monitoring of systemic risk. Neverthless, the enforecement of uniform reporting standards across diverse jurisdictions poses significant challenges.
- **Standardization and Central Clearing Mechanisms:**
  - Regulatory bodies have increasingly advocated for the standardization of OTC derivatives to render them more conducive to central clearing and to mitigate counter-party risk. However, the bespoke nature of certain contracts, designed to meet specific hedging objectives, limits the feasibility of standardization for all OTC derivatives.
- **Cross-border Regulatory Challenges and Compliance:**
  - The international character of the OTC derivatives market introduces complex regulatory challenges, as transactions frequently involve multiple jurisdictions. Achieving regulatory harmonization and compliance across varied legal frameworks is intricate, and different standards may lead to instances of regulatory arbitrage.

- **Regulatory Coordination:**
  - Initiatives such as the Basel III framework and Dodd-Frank Act in the United States strive to establish coherent global standards. However, discrepancies in enforcement and interpretation among different countries often persist.

Case Study: Managing Currency and Interest Rate Risk through Swaps

ABC Corp., a U.S.-based multinational corporation, recently expanded its operations to the European market by establishing a subsidiary in France. To finance its European expansion, ABC Corp. issued ₹ 40 million in Euro-denominated debt at a fixed interest rate of 2.5%. Since most of ABC's revenue is in USD, the company faces currency risk due to its Euro-denominated debt and potential fluctuations in the EUR/USD exchange rate.

ABC Corp. seeks to mitigate this exposure through a currency swap with a European company that holds USD-denominated debt and is interested in Euro exposure. Furthermore, ABC has a floating-rate loan in the U.S. with an interest rate of LIBOR + 1.8%, and due to anticipated rate hikes, ABC is considering a swap to lock in a fixed rate.

Swap Terms:

- **Currency Swap:** ABC Corp. would pay a fixed USD interest rate to the European counter-party and receive a fixed Euro interest rate, allowing it to effectively align its Euro debt obligations with its USD-based cash flows.
- **Interest Rate Swap:** ABC Corp. would swap its floating LIBOR-based loan for a fixed rate of 4.2% over a three-year term.

The company is analyzing these swap structures to determine if they would effectively address its currency and interest rate risk in line with its financial strategy and broader risk management goals, considering current market trends and forecasts.

This approach requires evaluating the potential impacts on cash flow stability, interest expense predictability, and overall financial resilience under varying economic scenarios.

Following questions with solution are given for the better understanding:

Calculate Interest Payments: ABC Corp. issued ₹ 40 million in debt at a fixed interest rate of 2.5%. What would be its annual interest payment on this Euro-denominated debt?

Calculate Currency Swap Payment: ABC Corp. decides to enter into a currency swap where it pays 3.5% fixed interest in USD and receives 2.8% fixed interest in Euro on a notional amount of ₹ 40 million. What are the annual USD payment ABC Corp. would make and the Euro payment it would receive each year under this swap arrangement?

Calculate Interest Rate Swap: ABC Corp. currently has a floating-rate USD loan of $25 million at a rate of LIBOR + 1.8%. If LIBOR is currently 2.5%, calculate ABC's annual interest expense on this loan.

Now, if ABC swaps this floating rate for a fixed rate of 4.2%, what would its new annual interest expense be?

What is the impact of Exchange Rate Changes: If the EUR/USD exchange rate shifts from 1.10 to 1.15, how does this change ABC Corp.'s Euro debt obligation in USD terms? Specifically, calculate the USD equivalent of ₹ 40 million under both exchange rates.

Give a comparative Analysis of Swaps: Assume ABC Corp. keeps its floating-rate loan and that LIBOR rises by 0.5% each year from its current level of 2.5%. Calculate ABC's total interest payments over three years with the floating rate, compared to a fixed rate of 4.2% through an interest rate swap. How much would ABC Corp. save or incur in additional interest costs with the swap over this period?

SWAPS IN INDIA

Interest-rate and currency swaps are widely used in India to hedge the interest rate risk. The RBI permits banks to arrange currency swaps with one leg being the Indian rupee and the other leg being a foreign currency, mainly US dollar. The swap is used not only for hedging the currency risk involved in foreign exchange trade but also for reducing the borrowing cost. Since the currency swap involves forward foreign exchange market also, such swaps cannot be thought of rolling beyond twelve months. Moreover, the banks are not allowed to take risk and run open swap books. They have to locate counter-parties with matching requirements —one desiring to swap dollar liabilities into rupee liabilities and the other wishing to exchange rupee debt obligation for dollar obligations. Corporates having huge rupee debt burden want foreign currency loans in their books, swap rupee loan into low-cost foreign currency loan through US $/INR swap route. However, in India, swap of foreign currency loans into rupee liabilities is common.

There are three kinds of currency swap available in India. One is the amortising currency swap where the notional principal is scheduled to decrease over the life of the swap. The other is accreting currency swap where the notional principal increases periodically. Still the other is known as floating-to-floating rate swap where the swap involves the exchange of a floating interest rate payment schedule in one currency against some other floating interest rate payment schedule in another currency.

The policy related to rupee-FC swap has been made more liberal over the years. Earlier, the open position on the swap book and the access to inter-bank spot market on account of swap transaction was restricted to US $ 10 million, which was gradually raised to US $ 25 million and US $ 50 million. In late November 2011, it was raised further to US 100 million so that greater amount of dollar could be sold in the market and rupee could not slide further.

On January 4, 2008, Japan and India signed a currency swap deal for US $ 6.0 billion to supply each other up to US $ 3.0 billion from their foreign exchange reserves for possible market intervention in the event of financial turmoil.

Interest rate swaps were first introduced in India in 1999. They are largely based on one of two benchmarks–overnight Mumbai Interbank Offer Rate (MIBOR), published by the National Stock Exchange, and the six-month Mumbai Interbank Forward Offer Rate (MIFOR), which is a rate implied from the dollar-rupee foreign exchange market. Swaps based on the overnight MIBOR are referred to as MIBOR swaps. On the other hand, MIFOR swaps are based on the six-month MIFOR. MIFOR rates exploit the availability of currency forward premia from a highly active domestic foreign exchange market and thus overcome the limitation of the lack of a developed term interbank market.

Although the two swap rates are based on different economic variables, there is an arbitrage possibility between them. If the 1 year MIFOR swap rate is lower than the 1 year MIBOR rate, a bank:

(a) Raises term rupee funds at a covered interest rate equal to the 1 year MIFOR swap rate through borrowing dollars at 6 month LIBOR and entering into a 6 month sell/buy dollar swap with the interest payment in dollars due 6 months later covered with a forward contract. It repeats this transaction after six months, and enters into a 1 year pay fixed, receiving floating MIFOR swap. The payments received every six months on the floating leg of the MIFOR swap will exactly offset the dollar payments to be paid every six months—the forward premium on the FX swap and interest payment on the foreign borrowing.

(b) Invests the rupee funds at the 1 year MIBOR swap rate through investing the funds in the Indian overnight money market, rolling the funds over on a daily basis, and entering into a 1 year receive fixed, pay floating MIBOR swap rate. Interest received from the rolled-over overnight investments will (more or less) offset the payment required to be made on the floating leg of the MIBOR swap. Of course, the offset may not be exact as it may not be possible to invest each day in the overnight market at exactly the same rate as the MIBOR fixing for the day.

SUMMARY

- Financial swaps emerging on a large scale in 1980s are now an important tool used in the international financial market. They are used for the purpose of reducing the cost of funds, for getting loan of a desired type or in a desired currency, and for hedging the interest-rate risk and foreign exchange risk.
- Financial swaps are interest-rate swap, currency swap and equity swap. Each of these three has different variants. However, in an interest-rate swap, principal is identical and notional, and it is not exchanged. It is the interest payment only that is exchanged. In currency swap, what are exchanged and re-exchanged are the currencies. In equity swap, variable return from equity is exchanged for a fixed return.
- All these exchanges are done through the help of a swap dealer who is normally a bank. It is a fact that the banks earn a lot out of the swap deals. But they face different forms of risks and so a perfect management of swap is necessary. The management includes not only the control of the risks but also following of the rules prescribed by the ISDA.
- Interest rate swaps and currency swaps are being widely used in India.

Review Questions

Objective-Type Questions

1. State whether true (T) or false (F):
   (a) Basis point is 1/10 of 1 per cent. ☐
   (b) In a capped equity swap, variable leg of the swap is capped. ☐
   (c) Sovereign risk and delivery risk—both are different from each other. ☐
   (d) In case of option swap, the purchaser of the swap has the right, and not the obligation, to enforce the deal. ☐
   (e) Money market deals involve 360 days a year. ☐
   (f) Bond-equivalent yield involves 360 days a year. ☐
2. Choose the correct answer:
   (a) Principals in interest-rate swap are:
      (i) identical in size and maturity
      (ii) identical in size only
      (iii) not identical in size and maturity
   (b) Swap dealer earns through:
      (i) difference in interest payments passing through him in two different directions
      (ii) charging a premium
      (iii) charging a special fee
   (c) In a basis swap, the two legs are tied to:
      (i) two indices
      (ii) two long-term rates
      (iii) the same index
   (d) In amortising currency swap:
      (i) principal amortises over the life of the swap
      (ii) there is single re-exchange of currencies
      (iii) none of these
   (e) In LIBOR-flat:
      (i) some basis points are added to LIBOR
      (ii) some basis points are subtracted from LIBOR
      (iii) the interest rate is equal to LIBOR

Short-Answer Questions

1. What do you mean by:
   (a) counter-party
   (b) leg of the swap
   (c) swap coupon
2. Explain zero-coupon swap.
3. What are the features of floating-for-floating rate swap?

4. What is fixed-for-fixed rate swap?
5. Explain callable swap.

Long-Answer Questions

1. Explain a plain interest-rate swap with a suitable example.
2. Explain a currency swap with a suitable example.
3. What are the characteristics of an equity swap?
4. What are the important variants of currency swap?
5. What kind of risk is borne by a swap dealer?

SUGGESTED FURTHER READING

Antl, B. (Ed.) (1986), *Swap Finance*, London, Euromoney Publications.

Marshall, J.F. and K.R. Kapner (1993), *The Swap Market*, Miami, Kolb Publishers.

CHAPTER

20 Management of Interest-Rate Risk

Learning Objectives

In a floating interest-rate regime, various forms of risk arise on account of changes in interest rate. These risks need to be managed in the interest of the borrowers and lenders/investors. The present chapter attempts:

- To discuss the various forms of interest-rate exposure.
- To discuss the impact of changes in the interest rate and the term structure on the value of bond that in turn influences the asset/liability position of a financial firm.
- To explain various techniques of interest-rate-risk management.

International financial transactions are fraught with ample risk not only because of changes in exchange rate but also because of changes in interest rate. With growing preference for floating interest rate since 1980s, the interest-rate risk or exposure has become more significant. Sometimes it moves in favour of the lender, but then the debt burden of the borrower gets bigger. When it moves in favour of the borrower, the lender has to suffer loss on account of interest. Again, it is not only the size of interest payment that causes exposure. It is also the fact that changes in interest rate influence the market price of the bond and the changes in the price of the bond are often the source of exposure.

The interest-rate exposure is no doubt large in the case of floating-rate, but it is present also in the case of fixed-rate loans. This is because a borrower borrows normally in different currencies and each currency has its own interest-rate structure. Moreover, the interest rate swings across countries are not necessarily correlated in favour of the borrower. Thus, whether the interest rate is fixed or floating, a firm involved in borrowing or lending needs to manage the interest-rate exposure. This chapter, therefore, discusses the nature of interest-rate exposure, the impact of interest rate changes on the value of the firm, and the techniques of managing such exposure.

NATURE OF INTEREST-RATE EXPOSURE

The nature of interest-rate exposure varies between a financial and a non-financial firm. For a non-financial firm, changes in interest rate lead to changes in financial cost and thereby to changes in earning before tax and the return from investment. However, for a financial firm, changes in interest rate affect the very asset and liabilities and thereby the very net worth of the firm.

Interest-rate risk may be grouped under four heads:

1. Credit risk
2. Liquidity risk
3. Basis risk
4. Optionality risk

Credit risk is concerned with the default risk when the borrower fails to make payment of interest and principal. In order to minimise this type of risk, the lender makes loans to only those borrowers who are financially sound and who have no record of default. The risk can be minimised also through diversification of lending among large number of borrowers.

> Credit risk is concerned with default risk when loans are not repaid.

Liquidity risk, which is also known as the gap risk, is more typical of a non-financial firm. Such risk is related to the timing mismatches between cash inflows and cash outflows on account of interest payment. A non-financial firm usually possesses a comparatively small amount of interest-sensitive asset, while interest-sensitive debt may account for a large segment of the total liabilities. In such a situation, if long-duration interest-sensitive assets are financed by short-duration interest-sensitive liabilities, liquidity risk is bound to arise. In order to ascertain the magnitude of gap risk, the firm divides the entire planning horizon into sub-periods. For each sub-period, the difference between the assets and the liabilities is assessed.

> Liquidity risk, often known as gap risk, is related to timing mismatch between receipt and payment of interest.

On the other hand, basis risk is related primarily to financial companies. It arises when interest-rate exposure on one instrument is offset by the interest-rate exposure on another instrument. It also happens when floating-rate financial assets tied to one index are funded by floating-rate liabilities tied to some other index. Financial companies, whose revenues and costs consist primarily of interest-rate payment flows, are more prone to such risks. This is because the net interest income, that is, the difference between receipt of interest on assets and interest payment on liabilities, matters much for such firms.

> Basis risk is typical of financial companies when floating-rate assets and liabilities are tied to different indices.

Last but not least, optionality risk arises when options are embedded in a financial company's assets and liabilities. Options may be exchange-traded options or over-the-counter contracts. They include various types of bonds and notes with call and put provisions and also loans giving borrowers the right to repay balances and various

> Optionality risk arises from the options embedded in a financial company's assets and liabilities.

types of non-maturity deposit instruments giving depositors the right to withdraw funds at any time. If all these are not managed properly, asymmetrical pay-off characteristics of instruments with optionality features may pose a problem for those who sell them. It is because the options are advantageous for the buyers and not for the sellers.

Whatever the type of risk may be, its magnitude depends also upon how the interest is calculated. This is initially so because practices differ from one country to another. In Switzerland, for example, 360 days make a year for calculating interest. On the contrary, the British practice involves 365 days. With the same amount of principal, the interest will vary in these two cases.

BOND YIELD, TERM STRUCTURE AND INTEREST-RATE RISK

The changes in interest rate influence the very asset-and-liability position of a firm, especially a financial firm. This is because the interest rate changes lead to the changes in the yield on the bond and thereby to changes in the value of the bond and the very asset-and-liability position of a financial firm. Similarly, the term structure too influences the value of the bond and thereby the asset-and-liability position of a financial firm. This is why it is of special significance to have at least some discussion of the concept of yield and term structure.

Concept of Yield

Yield is expressed in different ways. Let us first explain the *coupon yield*. The coupon yield of a coupon bond is simply the payment of coupon. If one-year coupon bond having a face value of $ 100 carries 8.0 per cent interest rate, the coupon yield will be 8.0 per cent. If interest is paid half-yearly, the coupon yield will be 4.0 per cent.

Coupon yield is related to the payment of interest.

In the case of a zero-coupon bond, the coupon yield depends upon the relationship between the face value and the discounted value of the bond. If a one-year zero-coupon bond having a face value of $ 100 has a discounted value of $ 92, the coupon yield is

$$100/92 - 1 = 1.0870 - 1 = 8.70\%$$

Current yield represents the ratio between interest payment and the market price of the bond.

The *current yield* of a coupon bond is the ratio of the annual coupon payment to the current market price of the bond. If the annual interest payment is $ 8 and the current market price of the bond is $ 104, the current yield is

$$8/104 = 7.7\%$$

Yield to maturity represents the discount rate equating present value of interest and amortization with the market value of bond.

The *yield to maturity* gives the bond's true actuarial yield. It represents the discount rate that equates the present value of future cash flows on account of interest and repayment of principal with the present market value of bond. In Eq. (20.1), yield to maturity is represented by r, the rate that equates the two sides of the equation.

$$B = \frac{CF_1}{1+r} + \frac{CF_2}{(1+r)^2} + \ldots + \frac{CF_n}{(1+r)^n} \tag{20.1}$$

where B is the present market value of bond, and CF is the cash flow inclusive of interest and principal during different periods till maturity.

If a two-year bond having a face value of $ 1,000 and coupon rate of 10.0 per cent per annum has a present market value of $ 1,027.50, the yield to maturity computed on a trial-and-error basis, assuming yearly repayment of principal in equal instalments, will be:

$$1{,}027.50 = (100 + 500)/1.0797 + (50 + 500)/1.07972 = 7.97\%$$

However, in the case of a bullet bond, which is very much common and where principal is repaid in a single lump sum amount only on the maturity and not in instalments every year along with the interest payment, the cash flow each year (other than the final cash flow) will be inclusive of only interest payment and the final cash flow will include the interest and the entire amount of principal. In such cases, the yield to maturity will be different. Based on the above example, the yield to maturity will be:

$$1{,}027.50 = 100/1.085 + 1{,}100/1.0852 = 8.50\%$$

PROBLEM 20.1

A bond with a face value of $ 1,000 has a coupon rate of 12 per cent. The maturity is two years and the interest is paid half-yearly. The current market price of the bond is $ 900. Find out the yield to maturity.

Solution

Applying Eq. (20.1), we get

$$R = \$\ 900 = 60/(1 + r) + 60/(1 + r)^2 + 60/(1 + r)^3 + 1{,}060/(1 + r)^4 = 0.0912$$

The YTM on a six-monthly basis = 9.12 per cent.

Again, applying Eq. (20.3), we get the annual YTM as

$$(1 + 0.0912)^2 - 1 = 0.1907 = 19.07 \text{ per cent}$$

Again, if the bond is sold in the market later after the issue, the buyer of the bond will be paying to the seller of the bond not only the market price of the bond but also the interest accrued for the fraction of the period. If a $ 1,000 bond is sold after six months of the issue, and if the coupon rate, as per the above example, is 10.0 per cent, the interest accrued will be: 180/360 × 100 = $ 50. The accrued interest is added to the market price of the bond while calculating the yield to maturity. Equation (20.1) can be rewritten after taking into account the interest accrued as

$$B + if = \frac{CF_1}{1 + r} + \frac{CF_2}{(1 + r)^2} + \dots + \frac{CF_n}{(1 + r)^n} \tag{20.2}$$

where *if* is the interest accrued for the fraction of the period. If it is so, the yield to maturity will be different in this case.

Yet again, if interest payments are made quarterly or half-yearly instead of annually, yield to maturity will change because it has to include the compounding over the year. In this case, the cash flow has to be discounted at the rate R, where

$$(1 + R)^T = (1 + r) \tag{20.3}$$

Here T represents the number of interest payments per annum. If interest payment is half-yearly and if R is equal to 5.0 per cent, then r will be

$$(1 + 0.05)^2 = 10.25\%.$$

Sometimes *yield to call* is calculated. When the prevailing interest is lower than the coupon rate, a company issues bonds with a call option. When its liquidity improves, it makes a call for the outstanding bond, pays it off and issues a new bond with a lower coupon rate. In such cases, the maturity will be equal to the time when call option actually takes place and not that mentioned in the bond. The process of calculating yield to call is the same as that of yield to maturity with the exception that the maturity changes to a lower value.

Yield and Price of the Bond

The foregoing discussion shows that there is close relationship between the yield and the market price of the bond. Thus, if there are changes in yield, the price of the bond has to change and, consequently, the buyer or the seller of the bond has to bear the risk. The relationship between yield and the bond price has been explained at length by Malkiel (1962). The entire explanation lies beyond the scope of this book and so we mention here only some of the main findings of this study. They are:

1. There is inverse relationship between yield and the bond prices. If yield increases, bond price decreases.
2. With a given change in yield, bonds with lower coupon lead to a greater proportionate change in price of the bond.
3. With a given change in yield, there will be proportionately greater change in the price of the bond which is issued at discount than that issued at premium.
4. A fall in yield will lead to a proportionately greater change in the price than a rise in the yield.

Duration and the Bond Price

It is not only the yield but also the duration of the bond that influences its price. Duration is nothing but the weighted average maturity of a bond where each date of interest plus instalment payment is weighted by the present value of cash flow. Mathematically, the duration, D can be represented as

Duration is the weighted average maturity of a bond where each date of interest plus instalment payment is weighted by the present value of cash flow.

$$D = \sum_{t=1}^{n} tCF_t(1+r)^{-t}/B \tag{20.4}$$

Example: Suppose a \$ 1,000 bond has a coupon rate of 10.0 per cent and a maturity of 2 years. The interest is paid annually. The principal is repaid on the maturity. The present market price of the bond is \$ 1,027.50. The yield to maturity is 8.50 per cent. The weighted average maturity will be calculated as follows:

(i) The sum of cash flow at t_1 and t_2 discounted at 8.5 per cent = 100/1.085 + $1{,}100/1.085^2$ = $ 1,027.50

(ii) The sum of the discounted flow shown in (i) after multiplying by

$$t = (100/1.085) \times 1 + (1{,}100/1.085^2) \times 2 = \$\ 1{,}960.97$$

(iii) The market price of the bond = $ 1,027.50

(iv) Duration = 1,960.97/1,027.50 = 1.9 years.

As already stated, since duration expresses the impact of changes in interest on the price of the bond, by rearranging the first derivative of Eq. (20.1) with respect to $(1 + r)$ and dividing by B, we get

$$(dB/B)/\{d\ (1 + r)/(1 + r)\} = -D \tag{20.5}$$

Based on Eq. (20.5), if the interest rate rises by 0.5 per cent and if the duration is 1.9 years, the price of the bond will change by:

$$dB/B = -1.9 \times 0.005 = -\ 0.0095 = -\ 0.95\%$$

It shows clearly that the extent of change in the price of bond as a sequel to a change in the interest rate depends upon the duration. The larger the duration, the greater will be the change in the price of the bond with the same percentage change in the rate of interest. For example, if the duration is 3 years, 0.5 per cent increase in the interest rate will reduce the price of the bond by 1.5 per cent.

PROBLEM 20.2

A $ 10,000 bond with a coupon rate of 5 per cent, a maturity of 4 years and yield to maturity of 9 per cent has a market price of $ 9,155.26. The interest is paid annually and the principal is repaid in equal annual instalments.

Find out (a) the duration and (b) the price of the bond if interest rate rises by 0.5 per cent.

Solution

1. Cash flow:

$$3{,}000/1.09 + 2{,}875/1.09^2 + 2{,}750/1.09^3 + 2{,}625/1.09^4 = \$\ 9{,}155.26$$

2. Cash flow multiplied by t = 21,400.96
3. Duration = 21,400.96/9,155.26 = 2.34 years.
4. Changes in interest by 0.5 per cent will lead to –2.34 × 0.005 = 1.17 per cent change in the price of the bond.

TECHNIQUES OF MANAGING INTEREST-RATE EXPOSURE

There are different techniques to hedge the interest-rate risk. A particular technique is practised, depending on the circumstances and the cost involved. Broadly speaking, the techniques can be grouped under three heads:

1. *Yield curve-based techniques* such as mismatched borrowings and forward rate agreement
2. *Derivative-based techniques*, for example, interest-rate futures and interest-rate swap
3. *Option-based techniques*, for instance, options on forward rate agreements, swaptions, caps, floors, collars and corridors.

One can also group the various techniques of interest-rate management on the basis of whether they are practised in over-the-counter market or they are adopted through the organised stock exchanges. In the first category come the mismatched borrowings, forward rate agreements, interest rate and currency swaps, caps, floors and collars; while the interest-rate futures come under the second category.

Mismatched Borrowings

The yield curve is normally supposed to be a forecast of future spot interest rates. Thus, if the yield curve is upward sloping, the future rate of interest will be more attractive for the investor. In this case, it is better to borrow short and invest long. The short-term borrowing will bring funds for long-term investment. At the same time, the cash inflow in the medium term on account of investment will cover the repayment of the short-term borrowing.

If, on the other hand, the yield curve is sloping downward, the firm can borrow long and invest short. The long-term borrowing will provide funds for making short-term investments. At the same time, the inflow from short-term investment will enable the firm to service the long-term borrowing.

Forward Rate Agreements

Forward rate agreements are a contract where interest rate is locked.

Forward rate agreements (FRAs) are a contract through which a borrower or a lender/investor locks the interest rate on its future borrowings or lending/investment and protects itself from the unfavourable changes in the interest rate.

FRAs and the borrower

Let us take the case of borrower who buys FRA when interest rate is expected to move up. Suppose a firm needs to borrow in the near future when it expects the interest rate to move up. This means that with rising interest rate, it will have to make larger interest payment. To protect itself from larger interest payment, it buys an FRA contract from its banker for an amount equivalent to its borrowing amount. The principal amount under the FRA deal will just be a notional amount. If the actual interest rate is greater than the locked interest rate, the bank will pay to the firm the present value of the difference of the interest payment between the pre-change rate mentioned in the deal or the locked interest rate and at the post-change rate prevailing at the time of maturity. The interest payment differential is discounted because FRA is settled in the beginning of the period and not at the end when interest is normally paid. The discount factor is the actual (post-change) interest rate. This payment would be rather a compensation that eliminates the interest-rate exposure faced by the firm.

Example: Suppose the present interest rate is 6 per cent p.a. The amount of future borrowing is $ 1,00,000. The maturity is three months. The risen interest rate is 7 per cent p.a. This means that at the risen rate, the borrowing firm will have to make interest payment equivalent to $ 1,769.44 or $ 252.77 more than that at the pre-change rate. The interest-rate exposure that the borrowing firm has to face is \$ 252.77. If it purchases FRA for an equivalent principal, it will get from its banker (seller of the FRA), the following amount as compensation:

$$\$\ [1{,}00{,}000 \times \{(0.07 - 0.06) \times (91/360)\}]/\{1 + (0.07 \times 91/360)\} = \$\ 248.39$$

The interest-rate exposure amounting to \$ 252.77 is completely eliminated through the receipt of \$ 248.39. It is because the seller of the FRA pays \$ 248.39 in the beginning of the period. If this amount is multiplied by [1 + (0.07 × 91/360)], it will be equal to \$ 252.77 at the end of the period when the excess interest is paid on account of interest rate escalation.

FRAs and the lender

A lender buys FRA when interest rate is expected to drop. Suppose the present rate of interest is 8 per cent. The amount of future borrowing is \$ 1,00,000. The maturity is three months. The fallen interest rate is 7 per cent. It means that the lender will get lesser interest equivalent to \$ 252.77. But if the lender buys an FRA, the loss will be compensated by the seller of the FRA. The seller will pay:

$$[1{,}00{,}000 \times \{(0.08 - 0.07) \times (91/360)\}]/(1 + (0.07 \times 91/360) = \$\ 248.39$$

FRA as a double-edged sword

Here it may be mentioned that forward rate agreement is like a double-edged sword. It is possible that contrary to the expectations of the borrower, the interest rate does not move up, rather it moves below the locked rate. If it is there, the borrower (the buyer of the FRA) will pay the interest rate difference to the seller of the FRA.

PROBLEM 20.3

A borrower borrows \$ 2.0 million for three months, six months from now at LIBOR flat. LIBOR is 7.5 per cent at present but is expected to rise to 9 per cent after three months. In order to hedge the rise in interest rate, the borrower buys an FRA. How much the borrower will receive from the seller of the FRA?

Solution

In the beginning of the FRA period, that is after three months from now, the borrower will receive from the FRA seller:

$$\$[20{,}00{,}000 \times (0.09 - 0.0750) \times (91/360)]/1 + [0.09(91/360)] = \$\ 7{,}415$$

The additional cost to the borrower on account of rise in interest payment during the FRA period will be 20,00,000 × (0.09 – 0.0750) = \$ 7,583, out of which he receives US \$ 7,415 in the beginning of the period. It means that at the end of the period when interest will be actually paid, the entire interest-rate risk is hedged. It is because the value of \$ 7,415 received in the beginning of the period will come to: \$ 7,415 × 1 + (0.09 × 91/360) = \$ 7,583.

Interest-Rate Swap

Interest-rate swap, already discussed in the preceding chapter, is used when floating interest rate is highly volatile. When the borrowers expect a rise in interest rates, they swap floating-rate loan for a fixed-rate loan. On the contrary, when they expect a fall in the interest rate, they swap fixed-rate loan for floating-rate loan. Suppose a firm borrows at floating interest rate and lends the borrowed amount at fixed rate of interest. So long as floating interest rate is lower than the fixed rate, the firm will earn a profit. But if LIBOR moves up beyond the fixed rate, there will be loss to the firm. This loss is known as *interest-rate risk.*

The use of interest-rate swap for hedging this kind of risk may be explained through the help of an example. Suppose a television manufacturing firm provides loan to its customers for financing the purchase of television at a fixed rate of 12 per cent. Such loans are financed by medium-term notes that the firm issues at LIBOR + 0.25 per cent. LIBOR is 7.0 per cent, and the administrative and other costs involved in borrowing/lending come to 2.0 per cent. If LIBOR does not fluctuate, the firm will enjoy a margin of 12.0 – 7.25 – 2.0 = 2.75 per cent. But if LIBOR moves upward, the margin will get squeezed. In order to check squeeze in the margin, the firm will go for a fixed-for-floating rate swap with a swap dealer. Under the swap arrangement, the firm will be paying fixed interest rate to the swap dealer and will be receiving floating interest rate from the swap dealer. Here the receipt of floating interest rate from the swap dealer will neutralise to a great extent the increase in LIBOR that the firm has to pay on its medium-term notes.

After the swap, the interest margin of the firm will be equal to the difference between the interest received from the customers as well as from the swap dealer, and the interest paid to the swap dealer and to the purchasers of the medium-term notes. If LIBOR is 7.0 per cent, the margin, assuming the cost involved to be zero, is

$$(12.0 + 7.0) - (7.0 + \text{LIBOR} + 0.25) = 4.75\%$$

If LIBOR rises to 8%, the interest margin is

$$(12.0 + 8.0) - (7.0 + 8.0 + 0.25) = 4.75\%$$

Had there been no swap, the margin would have squeezed to 3.75 per cent after increase in LIBOR to 8.0%. This means that swap could hedge the interest-rate risk completely.

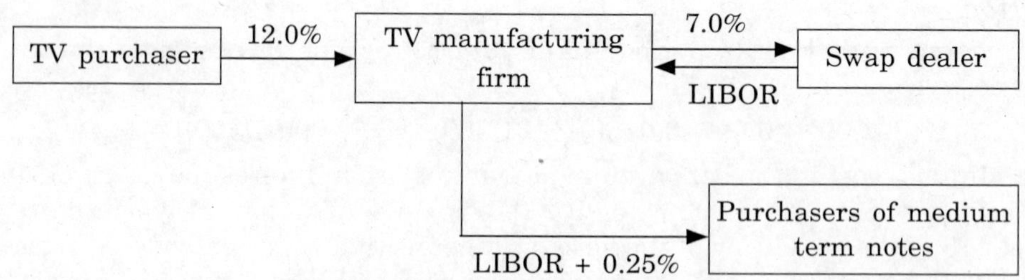

FIGURE 20.1 The Sinc Function.

Interest-Rate Futures

> Interest-rate futures are just like currency futures contracts bought and sold for hedging the interest-rate risk.

Interest-rate futures (IRFs) meant to hedge interest-rate risk evolved in mid-1970s in the US financial market. Presently, they are available in many other markets and in many other currencies. IRFs market is like currency futures market where contracts are made in the pit of the organised exchange through an authorised broker. Nominal amount of the contract is standardised. Maturity falls in March, June, September and December. There is a clearing house to record the transactions and to function as a counter-party. Margin money and margin call mechanisms are found. On the maturity, the contract is reversed.

IRFs are used both in the case of rising interest rate and falling interest rate. It may be mentioned that based on the earlier discussion in this chapter, the value of a bond diminishes with a rise in the interest rate and vice versa. Firms in a long position, that is, the firms holding bonds, incur loss with a rise in interest rates inasmuch as the value of the bond diminishes. When they expect loss, they go for IRFs. Suppose a company is having 10-year French Government bond for Euro 10,00,000. The interest rate, which is 10 per cent in July, is expected to move up to 11 per cent by December, as a result of which the price of the bond is expected to fall. The company would like to go for interest-rate futures for protecting itself from this loss. It will instruct its broker to sell interest-rate futures for the equivalent amount which is a notional amount. Since the standard size of Euro futures is Euro 5,00,000, two futures will be sold.

In December, interest rate rises to 11 per cent and, as a result, the value of the bond drops to Euro 9,91,000 (Euro 9,41,000 as the price of the bond plus Euro 50,000 as the interest accrued). The broker will then go for a reverse contract, that is, for buying December delivery futures at a price of Euro 9,41,000. By doing so, the broker will gain:

Price sold – Price bought

or Euro 10,00,000 – Euro 9,41,000 = Euro 59,000

Now,

1. After the future deals, the value of the company's portfolio at the end of December will be equal to:

   Euro 9,41,000 + 50,000 + 59,000 = Euro 10,50,000

2. If the bondholder does not opt for the IRFs, the value of the investment portfolio will be equal to:

   Euro 9,41,000 + 50,000 = Euro 9,91,000

3. If there is no interest rate change and no futures deal, the value of the investment portfolio will be equal to:

   Euro 10,00,000 as principal + Euro 50,000 as the interest
   = Euro 10,50,000

Thus, it is clear that with a rise in interest rate, the value of the investment portfolio diminishes and it puts the investors to loss. But if the investor goes for the interest-rate futures, the loss is hedged.

So far we have discussed that the interest rate rises as per expectation. But it may be that the rate of interest falls contrary to the expectation. In that case, there will be loss on the future contracts, but the loss would be compensated by an increase in the value of the bonds.

Again, if the bond-holder expects a fall in the interest rate, it will buy interest-rate futures for an equivalent notional amount that will be reversed on the maturity date. If the expectation comes true, the price of sale will be larger than the price of purchase and there will be net gain to the bond-holder. Here it must be noted that *hedging of interest-rate exposure through interest-rate futures is based primarily not on the changes in interest rate but on the value of the bond, which changes as a sequel to changes in the interest rate.*

PROBLEM 20.4

A company needs short-term funds and it plans to issue 90-day commercial paper for $ 20 million with expected yield of 12 per cent. But since it fears a rise in interest rate, it goes to hedge the interest-rate risk with the help of interest-rate futures. Explain how interest-rate futures cover the risk.

Solution

1. At 12 per cent yield, the company expects to realise the net proceed equal to:

   $ 2,00,00,000 – (2,00,00,000 × 0.03) = $ 1,94,00,000

2. If the yield rises to 12.5 per cent at the time of issue, the net proceeds will be equal to:

   2,00,00,000 – (2,00,00,000 × 0.03125) = $ 1,93,75,000

3. It means that the rise in interest rate reduces the net proceeds by $ 25,000
4. In order the hedge the risk, the company contracted to sell twenty 90-day treasury bills for $ 1.0 million each at then prevailing discount rate of 10 per cent.
5. At the maturity, the prevailing discount rate was 10.5 per cent. It means that selling the interest-rate futures on the maturity brought in gain for $ 25,000 and the entire risk on account of rise in interest rate could be covered.

Interest-Rate Caps

Interest-rate cap (IRC) is an option-based technique practised in over-the-counter market. This technique evolved in mid-1980s in the Euro-dollar market and now it is more frequently used.

When a firm borrowing floating-rate loan fears a rise in LIBOR, it may buy an IRC for the loan-equivalent amount that will help reduce the interest-rate exposure. It is because the seller of the IRC, normally a bank, reimburses the buyer's loss in the event LIBOR exceeds the cap's interest-rate level. In order to arrive at the net gain accruing to the buyer of the cap, the amount of premium paid by the buyer of the cap must be deducted from the amount of the reimbursement.

Interest-rate cap involves compensating the loss to borrowers if interest rate moves up beyond the cap.

The principal amount of the cap is notional. The total maturity is divided into a number of reset periods. Suppose the maturity is two years with reset period or tenor at three months, there will be seven three-month reset dates as no reset exists for the first three-month period.

Example: Suppose a firm borrows $ 1,00,000 for four years at 6-month LIBOR + 25 basis points. If the firm fears a rise in LIBOR, it buys IRC for an equivalent amount with the same maturity at a strike price of 7.0 per cent which is equal to the prevailing rate. The premium is 0.5 per cent for the reset period. If, at the end of the first reset, LIBOR rises to 10.0 per cent, the amount of the interest paid by the borrower will be equal to:

$$\$\ 1{,}00{,}000 \times 10.25\% \times \frac{180}{360} = \$\ 5.125$$

Moreover, the borrower will have to pay premium equivalent to:

$$\$\ 1{,}00{,}000 \times 0.005 = \$\ 500$$

On the other hand, the borrowing firm will receive from the bank, that is, from the cap seller, an amount equivalent to:

$$\$\ 1{,}00{,}000 \times (0.10 - 0.07) \times \frac{180}{360} = \$\ 1{,}500$$

As a result of the cap deal, the entire interest-rate exposure of the borrower is eliminated. However, the borrowing firm has to pay premium for the cap. But even after taking into account the amount of premium, we find that the interest-rate exposure is substantially reduced.

If, contrary to the expectation, LIBOR diminishes at the end of the first reset period or the other reset periods, the borrowing firm will have to pay a lower amount of interest but it will have to pay the premium. The net gain depends upon the extent of changes in LIBOR and the amount of premium. Here, it may be noted that sometimes the premium is paid in the very beginning in a single lump sum amount for the whole of the maturity. In this case, the premium is annualised for the purpose of computing the cost of capped payment. The fixed rate of interest at which the firm could borrow is used in the amortization of the cap premium over the maturity.

Suppose the lump sum premium is 1.0 per cent for the whole of the maturity of two years (with 4 reset periods) and the fixed rate of interest is 6.0 per cent per annum, the half-yearly premium will be

$$\frac{0.01}{\frac{1}{0.03} - \frac{1}{0.03} \times (1.03)^4} = 0.00269 = 0.269\%$$

Interest-Rate Floors

Interest-rate floor (IRF) is different from IRC inasmuch as the IRF protects against a fall in the interest rates. So, it is the investor or the depositor who buys IRF, whereas IRC, as we know, is bought by a borrower. However, many features of the two instruments are similar. IRF is also an over-the-counter market instrument. The seller of IRF compensates for the loss of the buyer on account of change (fall) in interest rates. For this privilege, the buyer pays premium to the seller.

> Interest-rate floors involve compensating the loss to lenders if interest rate falls below the floor.

Suppose a firm makes Euro-deposits for \$ 1,00,000 at 6-month LIBOR minus 25 basis points for one year. It fears a fall in LIBOR and so buys an IRF with a strike price of 6.0 per cent per annum, which is equivalent to the prevailing LIBOR. It pays a lump sum premium at 0.5 per cent for whole of the year. As expected, LIBOR moves down to 4.0 per cent after the six-month period.

If the depositor does not go for IRF, it will receive \$ 1,875 as interest for the six-month period which will be lower than that during the beginning of the deposit period by \$ 1,000. But if it goes for IRF, the bank will compensate this loss. The compensation is computed as

$$\$\ 1{,}00{,}000 \times (0.06 - 0.04) \times \frac{180}{360} = 1{,}000$$

However, the net gain accruing to the depositor will be lower by the amount of the premium. In this case, the premium, assuming fixed interest rate of 6.0 per cent, will be

$$\frac{0.005}{\dfrac{1}{0.03} - \left[\dfrac{1}{0.03} \times (1.03)^2\right]} = 0.002613 \times 100{,}000$$

$$= \$\ 261.30$$

Interest-Rate Collars

Interest-rate collars are a combine of interest rate caps and floors.

Interest-rate collar is a combination of caps and floors. It is just like a tunnel where an importer buys a call option and sells a put option simultaneously, or an exporter buys a put option and sells a call option. Similarly, a borrower buys a cap and sells a floor simultaneously or an investor or a depositor buys a floor and sells a cap simultaneously. This way the collar fixes a maximum and a minimum interest rate. A borrower limits risk owing to rise in interest rate but it also limits the opportunities of benefiting from fall in interest rate. An investor limits the risk owing to fall in interest rate and also limits the gains owing to rise in interest rates. The premium in both the cases is calculated in such a way that the premium received normally equals the premium paid.

Example: A simple example will make clear the distinctive characteristics of a collar. Suppose a firm borrows \$ 1,00,000 for two years at LIBOR plus 0.25 per cent. It purchases cap with a strike price of 7.0 per cent and sells a floor at a strike price of 5.0 per cent. If LIBOR varies between 5.0 per cent and 7.0 per cent, no payment is made on the collar. The borrower pays interest at LIBOR + 0.25 per cent. If the interest rate exceeds 7.0 per cent, the bank (seller of the cap) pays the difference. If the interest rate falls below 5.0 per cent, the borrowing firm pays the difference to the bank. The gain, however, depends on the size of premium vis-à-vis the extent in the fall of interest rate.

PROBLEM 20.5

A firm borrows \$ 2.0 million at six-month LIBOR + 25 basis points for a period of 2 years. It anticipates a rise in LIBOR and so it goes for (a) buying a cap, and (b) buying a collar, from a bank. The strike rate is 7%. LIBOR increases during different reset periods respectively to 8.00%, 8.50% and 9.00%. The lump sum premium is 1% for the whole of the three reset periods and the fixed rate of interest is 6% p.a. Find out how far interest-rate risk is hedged through (a) cap and (b) collar.

Solution

(a) If the borrower goes for buying a cap:

Reset period	*Additional interest payment due to rise in interest rate*	*Amount received from bank*	*Premium paid to bank*	*Net amount received from bank*
1	10,000	10,000	5,380	4,620
2	15,000	15,000	5,380	9,620
3	20,000	20,000	5,380	14,620
Total	45,000	45,000	16,140	28,860

Note: See the text in Chapter 20 for the calculation of premium payment.

The total interest-rate risk amounts to $ 45,000 which is reduced to $ 16,140 through the cap.

(b) If the borrower buys a collar:

The borrower receives the premium on the floor and the entire risk is eliminated.

Interest-Rate Corridors

While interest-rate collars present a combination of cap and floor, interest-rate corridors present a combination of two or more caps. A borrower buys one cap with a specific strike rate and, simultaneously, sells the other cap with a higher strike rate with a view to offsetting at least a part of the cost of the cap purchased.

The purchased cap protects from rising interest rates. On the contrary, the sold cap obligates the borrower to pay only when the second (sold) cap is activated. An example will make it clear. A borrower buys a two-year 6.0 per cent cap against a three-month LIBOR for 60 b.p. as premium and simultaneously, sells a two-year 7.0 per cent cap on which he receives 70 b.p. as premium. If interest rate rises to 6.75 per cent, the borrower will activate the first cap and will be compensated by the increased interest rate over and above the capped interest rate. The second cap will not be activated since the increase in interest rate has not crossed its strike rate. In respect of the second cap, the borrower has nothing to pay; rather he will receive the premium that covers more than fully the premium that he pays on the first cap. And this way, interest-rate corridor is better than a simple interest-rate cap.

Again, if interest rate rises to 9.0 per cent. Both the caps will be activated. In this case, the compensation the borrower will receive will be 3.0 per cent as against the compensation of 2.0 per cent the borrower has to pay. This means that the borrower is a net gainer by 1.0 per cent. Additionally, there will be gain on account of premium.

Options on FRAs

Options on the FRAs are normally used for short-term borrowing. A borrowing firm, when it is not sure of the direction of the interest rate changes, buys a call option on the FRA. If interest rate moves up, the firm exercises the call option and locks itself to the lower rate. If interest rate moves down, the firm prefers to let the call option expire and pays interest at the lower rate. But in both the cases, it has to pay the premium. On the contrary, a lending firm buys a put option on FRA. If interest rate moves up, it lets the option expire and receives interest at a higher rate. But if the interest rate moves down, option is exercised, as a result of which the lending firm locks itself to the higher rate. In both the cases, the interest inflow gets reduced by the amount of premium.

Options on Swaps

Option on swap is also called *swaption*. It is used in medium-term and long-term borrowing. This instrument confers the right to enter into an interest-rate swap either as the payer or as the recipient of the fixed side of the swap. When it is a payer swaption, it confers the right to pay the fixed rate in the swap. If the interest rate exceeds the swaption strike rate, the buyer exercises the option and locks itself to lower interest rate. The seller gets the fixed rate equal to the strike price and pays the floating rate. If the interest rate does not exceed the strike rate, swaption is not exercised.

In the case of receiver swaption, the buyer exercises the option and locks itself to higher rate when the interest rate falls below the swaption strike rate. If it is not, swaption is not exercised.

PROBLEM 20.6

A company plans to issue $ 20.0 million commercial papers at a current yield of 8.40 per cent. But it expects a rise in interest rate and so it goes for a swaption available at a strike rate of 8.50 per cent. Explain how swaption covers the risk if interest rate rises to 8.48 per cent and then to 8.52 per cent.

Solution

1. The company will pay a fixed rate of interest to the swaption dealer and will get a floating interest rate from the swap dealer. Till the interest rate does not change, the company will pay a fixed rate of 8.45 per cent and, in return, will get 8.45 per cent floating interest rate.
2. If interest rate rises to 8.48 per cent, the company will pay a fixed rate of interest at 8.45 per cent to the swaption dealer and, in return, will get 8.48 per cent from the swaption dealer. The interest-rate risk will be covered.
3. If interest rate rises to 8.52 per cent, the spot interest rate will be greater than the strike rate and the company as a buyer of the swaption will exercise the option. It will pay the strike rate in lieu of the swaption dealer paying the higher interest rate.
4. The swaption dealer will try to eliminate its loss through a reverse contract.

Interest Rate Hedging Strategies

The hedging strategies are being used to mitigate the exposure of the risk that may arise due to adverse price movements in the interest rates. It becomes very important for financial strategies, particularly for entities which has a large assets or liabilities prone to interest sensitivity.

- **Natural Hedging**
  - It involves aligning the interest rate characteristics of assets and liabilities of the company that my help in offsetting financial risk without relying on the external financial instruments.
  - This can be understood with an example, let say a company is earning revenues in a foreign currency might incur cost in the same currency. This offsets the risk of currency fluctuations. Similarly, we can also take an example of a company that earns a viable rate revenues may prefer financing its operations with viable-rate debt. In this way if the interest rates rise there will be an increase in revenue offsets which in turn rise the debt service costs.
  - Hence, we can say that there are some advantages of natural hedging lie it avoids the need for external instruments that make it cost effective. And it reduces the dependency on the market conditions for mitigating risks.
- **Synthetic Hedging**
  - Financial instruments like derivatives are used to manage risks when natural hedges are insufficient or unavailable to the speculators.
- **Dynamic Hedging**
  - To align with the changing market condition and exposures to risk this technique is actively used to monitor and adjust the risks. It require a close observation to market trends and positions to have a frequent monitoring and watch over the market movements, this strategy also ensures the hedging strategy to remain effective as company's exposure change over time.

Considerable Points in Hedging

- **Instrument Selection**
  - The instrument selection for hedging strategies totally depends upon the objective of risk exposure of the company. There are some of the strategies like Swaps, Options, futures. These strategies are selected based on the risk exposure. If a company is facing interest rate risk with predictable cash flow then they will select Swaps. If there is an issue of uncertainty of the direction of the exposure then in that case option will be a suitable strategy. And the future strategies are suitable for locking in prices but may not allow flexibility.
- **Cost-Benefit Analysis**
  - In the hedging, there might be some cost that a company may incur on a transaction, and If the cost to incur in hedging is less than the potential loss then the hedge is justified. For example if the cost in hedging currency risk is 2% and the potential loss is 5% then we can say it is worth to hedge then to wait for the loss. Therefore, the costs and benefits of hedging should be analyzed to select the most profitable and justified hedging strategy.
- **Basis Risk Management**
  - When the price movement of the hedging instrument does not correlate with the underlying exposure then a basis risk may arise. For example

a company may use a futures contract for hedging oil prices, but if the futures contract price diverges from the actual oil pirce, a residual risk remains. Hence, instruments should be closely aligned with the underlying exposure so that they can monitor the basis risk and adjust hedging positions as needed.

Impact of Monetary Policy on Interest Rate Dynamics

Monetary policy plays an important role in shaping the economic landscape, the influence of monetary policy is acutely felt through the interest rate dynamics. In this section we will understand the mechanisms, transmission channels, and real world examples which can help us understand the deep impact of the central banks' decisions on interest rates.

Central banks control nations' monetary systems, through monetary policy that ensures economic stability and growth. It influences the interest rates primarily through two mechanisms:

(a) **Policy Rate Adjustments:** The central banks in every monetary policy committee (MPC) meeting sets benchmark rates such as repo rate, reverse repo rate, bank rate, etc. which directly affects the short-term borrowing and cost for financial institution, which in turn controls the money supply.

(b) **Open Market Operations:** This technique is used to buy or sell the government securities, it influences the liquidity in the financial system, and hence it impacts the interest rates.

During the period of economic contraction, the European Central Bank (ECB) reduces the interest rates and injects liquidity into the market to stimulate borrowing and spending. It results in maintaining the monetary stability.

Transmission of Monetary Policy

Monetary policy plays a crucial role in determining interest rates, which in turn influence both short-term and long-term borrowing costs for consumers and businesses. By adjusting key rates, such as the federal funds rate, central banks aim to control inflation and stimulate economic growth. These adjustments impact not only immediate lending rates but also have a cascading effect on the broader yield curve. The yield curve, which represents the relationship between interest rates and different maturities of debt, reflects the market's expectations about future economic conditions. When monetary policy is accommodative, short-term rates may be low, encouraging borrowing and investment. Conversely, when policy becomes restrictive, higher rates can suppress economic activity. Thus, understanding how monetary policy shapes these rates is essential for analyzing economic trends and making informed financial decisions.

- **Short-term Rates:** Central banks directly impact instruments like treasury bills, certificates of deposit, and commercial paper. When short-term lending rates rise, the entire banking system's lending rates also increase.
- **Long-term Rates:** Market expectations regarding future policy actions and inflation influence bond yields. If investors anticipate prolonged high

inflation, they may require higher yields on long-term bonds, even when current short-term rates are low.

- **Yield Curve Dynamics:** The yield curve shows the relationship between bond yields and maturities. A steep curve typically indicates economic growth, while an inverted curve may signal fears of recession. These dynamics are significantly influenced by central bank policies.

During the post-COVID recovery, the Federal Reserve raised rates to curb inflation. This led to a flattening of the yield curve, as short-term rates rose sharply while long-term rates adjusted more slowly due to subdued growth expectations.

CASE STUDY

INVESTMENT DECISION BASED ON RISK-RETURN TRADEOFF (BALANCING RISK AND RETURN IN A RISING INTEREST RATE ENVIRONMENT)

Ms. Rupa, a 40-year-old investor, wants to strategize her portfolio where the interest rate are expected to rise sharply in the environment over the next few years. She has ₹ 20,00,000 to invest and there are three options she has selected: (a) A 10-year government bond with a fixed annual return of 6%. (b) A corporate bond with a 7% yearly return (duration 7 years) but higher sensitivity to interest rate changes. (c) A balanced mutual fund that allocates assets between stocks and bonds, offering an expected return of 10% with a standard deviation of 12%.

Interest rate environment (Current interest rate: 4%, Expected rise: 1% per year for the next three years).

Rupa's primary goal is to manage interest rate risk while achieving optimal returns. She is moderately risk-tolerant and open to diversification. And she decided to allocate her funds as follows: 50% in government bond, 30% in corporate bond, 20% in balanced fund.

Analyze how rising interest rates impact the risk-return tradeoff of different investment options and recommend an optimal portfolio for Rupa.

Solution:

Interest Rate Risk (Price Sensitivity):

Bond prices move inversely to interest rates. The price change can be estimated using the formula:

$$\Delta P \approx -D \cdot \Delta r$$

Where:

D = Duration of the bond

Δr = Change in interest rate

Option A (Government Bond):

$D = 10,\ \Delta r = 1\% = 0.01:$

$\Delta P \approx -10 \cdot 0.01 = -10\%$

A 1% rise in interest rates will reduce the bond's value by 10%.

Option B (Corporate Bond):

$D = 7,\ \Delta r = 1\% = 0.01$

$\Delta P \approx -7 \cdot 0.01 = -7\%$

A 1% rise in interest rates will reduce the bond's value by 7%.

Expected Returns and Risk:

Investment Option	*Expected Return (E[R])*	*Risk (Standard Deviation)*	*Interest Rate Sensitivity*
Option A	6%	Low	High (–10%)
Option B	7%	Moderate	Medium (–7%)
Option C	10%	High	Low (indirect impact)

Expected Portfolio Return (E(Rp)E(Rp)E(Rp)):

$$E(Rp) = w_A \cdot E(R_A) + w_B \cdot E(R_B) + w_C \cdot E(R_C)$$

Substituting the weights:

$$E(Rp) = (0.5 \cdot 6\%) + (0.3 \cdot 7\%) + (0.2 \cdot 10\%) = 3\% + 2.1\% + 2\% = 7.1\%$$

Portfolio Risk (Approximate Standard Deviation):

Assuming correlations among asset classes are low, the risk is reduced by diversification. A weighted estimate yields a portfolio standard deviation of approximately 5%.

Impact of Rising Interest Rates:

Bond Portfolio will lose value, but the diversified allocation to the balanced fund reduces the overall impact.

Balanced Fund equity exposure helps offset bond price declines during rising interest rates.

In conclusion, Rupa's portfolio is expected to achieve a return of 7.1% with moderate risk (5% standard deviation). Diversification mitigates interest rate risk while providing exposure to higher-return opportunities.

SUMMARY

- Borrowers and lenders have to face interest rate exposure on account of changes in interest rate. Such a change influences the earning position of a non-financial firm, while it affects the very asset-liability position of a financial firm. Interest-rate risk is grouped as credit risk, liquidity risk, basis risk and optionality risk.
- Changes in interest rate lead to changes in yield and thereby changes in the market price of the bond. The relationship between interest rate and the price of the bond is an inverse one. Yield may take different forms, such as coupon yield, current yield, call yield, and the yield to maturity. Yield to maturity is the most important which represents a discount rate equating the present value of the cash flow on account of interest and amortization with the market price of the bond.
- There are different techniques for management of interest-rate exposure. Most of them are found in over-the-counter market. Only a few of them are practised through the organised exchanges. They are grouped as yield-curve-based techniques, such as mismatched borrowing, forward rate agreement; derivative-based techniques, e.g. interest-rate swap and interest-rate futures; and yet again, option-based techniques, e.g. interest-rate caps, floors, collars, corridors, option on FRA, and swaption.

STUDY TOPIC

Forward Rate Agreements (FRAs) in India

In the wake of interest rate deregulation in India, the interest rate risk emerged on a big scale. In order to avoid the interest rate risk, RBI introduced the interest rate derivatives, such as interest rate swap and forward rate agreements in July 1999 and interest rate futures in 2003. Here it may be asserted that while interest rate futures are exchange-traded derivatives, the other two are over-the-counter derivatives. Since interest rate swap in India has already been discussed in Chapter 19, it would be worthwhile to throw some light here on FRAs in India.

FRAs in India are of the nature of plain vanilla where agreement is made between two contracting parties at a predetermined interest rate. It is exchanged for the market interest rate on the settlement date. The market interest rate is the reference rate which is based on:

1. Overnight call rate benchmark, known as Mumbai Inter-bank Offer Rate
2. Rupee rates implied in US dollar/Rupee foreign exchange market, known as Mumbai Inter-bank forward Offer Rate (MIFOR)
3. Rates prevalent in Government of India bond market

MIBOR and MIFOR

MIBOR launched on June 15, 1998 by the Committee for the Development of the Debt Market is an overnight rate. It is the interest rate at which banks borrow funds, in marketable size, from other banks in the Indian inter-bank market. The rate is calculated daily by the National Stock Exchange as a weighted average of lending rates of a specific group of banks on funds lent to Class 1 borrowers.

MIFOR is a rate related to setting of prices on forward rate agreements and other interest rate derivatives. It is normally a mix of LIBOR and a forward premium derived from Indian foreign exchange market. In view of avoiding speculative transactions, RBI allowed the use of MIFOR only in inter-bank-related transactions beginning from June 2005.

A borrower buys an FRA to protect itself against a rise in interest rate. The interest rate is computed on the basis of 360 days a year. On the settlement date, cash settlement is made between the two parties—the buyer and the seller, on the basis of the difference between the contract rate and the settlement rate. Since the principal is notional, no transfer of principal is made.

The participants are primarily the banks, although the primary dealers and the all-India financial institutions are also the participants. The Indian banks use FRAs under different circumstances. When the risk-sensitive assets are bigger than the risk-sensitive liabilities and a downward movement in the interest rates is expected that will ultimately help squeeze the net interest income, the banks sell FRAs. If the interest rate falls, the fall will approximately be compensated by FRA. In the reverse case, banks buy the FRA. Moreover, a bank uses FRA to lock-in its borrowing cost. If a bank is funding longer-term loans by rolling over its short-term liabilities, it buys FRA to lock-in its borrowing cost. Besides banks, corporates too use FRAs. If a company with a big issue of commercial paper fears a rise in funding cost, it makes use of FRAs.

In April 2007, RBI issued a comprehensive guideline making the entire process transparent. It defined the purpose of undertaking FRAs. Moreover, in order to maintain transparency, the banks and the primary dealers have to report the transactions on the trade-reporting platform created by the Clearing Corporation of India on a daily basis.

FRA Terminology

1. Forward contract rate is the forward rate of interest for the contract period as agreed between the parties.
2. British Bankers Association (BBA) means a panel of 12 banks or more.
3. Designated banks are the banks designated by the BBA from time to time for the purpose of establishing the BBA interest settlement rate.
4. BBA settlement rates are the rates quoted by specified reference banks for a given period.
5. Contract amount is the notional principal on which FRA is based.
6. Contract currency is the currency involved by the FRA.
7. Contract period is the period elapsing between the settlement date and the maturity date.

QUESTIONS

1. How is FRA different from interest rate swap?
2. Explain MIBOR and MIFOR.
3. Explain how does FRA help hedge interest rate risk.

REVIEW QUESTIONS

Objective-Type Questions

1. State whether true (T) or false (F):
   (a) A borrower not sure of the direction of changes in interest rate buys a call option on FRA. ☐
   (b) A lender buys a put option on FRA. ☐
   (c) Investors buy a cap. ☐
   (d) Investors buy a floor. ☐
   (e) Basis risk is caused when two indices are used for calculating interest rate. ☐
2. Choose the correct answer:
   (a) An investor expecting a fall in interest rate buys a:
      (i) cap and sells a floor
      (ii) floor and sells a cap
      (iii) floor and also a cap
   (b) A borrower apprehensive of rise in interest rate buys a:
      (i) cap and sells a floor
      (ii) floor and sells a cap
      (iii) floor and also a cap

(c) In a receiver swaption, the buyer exercises the option and locks itself to:
   (i) higher rate of interest
   (ii) lower rate of interest
   (iii) none of these

(d) Credit risk is concerned with:
   (i) liquidity risk
   (ii) default risk
   (iii) none of these

(e) The relationship between yield and the bond price is:
   (i) direct
   (ii) inverse
   (iii) non-existent

Short-Answer Questions

1. What is basis risk?
2. Explain gap risk.
3. What do you mean by coupon yield? Is it different from current yield?
4. How do you calculate yield to maturity (YTM)?
5. Explain mismatched borrowings.
6. What is swaption?
7. What is optionality risk?

Long-Answer Questions

1. "Duration is the weighted average maturity of a bond where each date of interest payment plus instalment is weighted by the present value of cash flow". Explain.
2. What do you mean by FRA? Is it a double-edged sword?
3. Explain interest-rate futures as a tool for interest-rate risk hedging.
4. Comment on the use of interest-rate swap for interest-rate risk hedging.
5. "Interest-rate collars are a combination of interest-rate caps and interest-rate floors". Discuss.
6. What do you mean by interest-rate corridors? How are they different from interest-rate collars?

Numerical Problems

1. A company issues zero-coupon bond which has to be redeemed after two years at a face value of \$ 100. The issue price is \$ 67.25. Find out the compounded annual interest yield.
2. The market price of 10.0 per cent coupon \$ 1,000 bond is \$ 975. Find out the current yield.
3. A bond with a face value of US \$ 1,000 has a coupon rate of 12 per cent. The maturity is two years and the interest is paid half-yearly. The current market price of the bond is US \$ 900. Find out the yield to maturity.

4. A borrower borrows US $ 2.0 million for three months, six months from now at LIBOR flat. LIBOR is 7.5 per cent at present but is expected to rise to 9.0 per cent after three months. In order to hedge the rise in interest rate, the borrower buys an FRA. How much will the borrower receive from the seller of the FRA?
5. A firm borrows $ 2.0 million at six-month LIBOR + 25 basis points for a period of two years, anticipating a rise in LIBOR during the following three reset periods to 6.0 per cent, 5.5 per cent, and to 5.0 per cent respectively, and goes for buying a floor with a strike rate of 7.0 per cent. The premium is 1 per cent for the whole of the maturity period, and the fixed rate of interest is 7 per cent. Find out whether floor is able to reduce the interest-rate risk. What will be the impact if he buys a collar?

REFERENCE

Malkiel, B. (1962), Expectations, Bond Prices and the Term Structure of Interest Rates, *Quarterly Journal of Economics*, LXXVI, 197–218.

SUGGESTED FURTHER READING

Andersen, T.J. (1993), *Currency and Interest Rate Hedging*, New York, New York Institute of Finance.

Antl, B. (1988), *Management of Interest Rate Risk*, London, Euromoney Publication.

PART 6

Management of Short-term Funds

CHAPTER 21

International Working Capital Management

Learning Objectives

MNCs attach great significance to the working capital management at the international level that helps them lower the operating cost and maintain adequate liquidity. The present chapter discusses the issues concerned with the international working capital management. In particular, it is:

- To refer to the basics of working capital policy and the complexities arising in case of international working capital management.
- To discuss how funds move intra-firm when the host governments impose restrictions on the outflow of funds.
- To analyse the different steps in the international cash management.
- To detail the issues concerning the investment of surplus cash, if any.
- To discuss the management of intra-firm and inter-firm receivables.
- To explain how inventory is managed at the international level.

Multinational enterprises raise funds not only for financing the fixed assets but also for financing the current assets so as to help start and maintain operation. This chapter, therefore, discusses the management of current assets or working capital in multinational firms spread over different countries. In the beginning, it will refer to the very concept of working capital; and then, it will deal with the management of different segments of the current assets.

WORKING CAPITAL POLICY

The Concept

Working capital refers to investment in current assets—the assets that are normally convertible into cash within one accounting year. The current assets are:

1. Cash
2. Near-cash assets, such as short-term marketable securities
3. Bill receivables
4. Inventory including raw material, semi-finished goods and finished goods.

The firm's current assets are known as *circulating assets* because the value represented by these assets circulates among themselves. Cash is used for buying raw material. Raw material is processed into finished goods. Finished goods are sold usually on credit that creates bill receivables. When the bills are honoured, the bill receivables are translated into cash. The cycle is thus complete. Similar cycles go on till the firm is in operation.

Working capital is often denoted in two ways. One is the *gross working capital* which is the sum of different current assets. The other is the *net working capital* which means current assets minus current liabilities. Current liabilities or short-term liabilities, or the sources of short-term funds, have already been discussed. Hence the discussion in this chapter will be related primarily to the management of current assets.

> Gross working capital means current asset. Net working capital is current assets minus current liabilities.

Before discussing about the management of various current assets, it is worthwhile to mention some of the major objectives of working capital management. *One objective is to determine the optimal size of current assets.* If the size is more than optimal, liquidity will be greater but profitability will be eroded insofar as part of the current assets will remain unutilised. If it is less than optimal, the operation will be affected for want of required current assets. This means it is the trade-off between liquidity and profitability that helps determine the size of current assets.

The other objective of working capital management is to see that there should be an optimal mix of long-term and short-term funds meant for financing the current assets. Long-term funds are liquid as compared to short-term funds but they involve greater cost. So again, it is the question of a perfect trade-off between profitability and liquidity.

In international working capital management when the current assets move across the border, there are many factors that influence their value. Changes in the exchange rate, changes in the inflation rate, exchange control mechanisms, and the political scenario in different countries are some of these important factors. The international manager has to see that the cost of holding the current assets is minimum on these counts without jeopardizing liquidity.

Here it would not be out of place to refer to a study conducted by Gentry, et al. (1979) in which 579 top executives working in different countries have been surveyed. The survey reveals that the most important objective of working capital management has been to support the expected sales. The objective has also been to minimise both the investment in current assets and the cost of short-term funds. In some cases, the objective has been to provide a financial cushion to absorb fluctuation in production and sales.

To sum up, the objectives of the working capital management in an international firm are:

1. Optimisation of cash holdings in different units through smoothening of the cross-border cash flows as well as in the firm as a whole.
2. Minimisation of finance and transaction cost.
3. Avoidance of foreign exchange losses.
4. Minimisation of the tax burden of the firm as a whole.
5. Avoidance of political and economic risk prevailing in different host countries.

To this end, the working capital policy in an international firm should be viewed from two angles: one based on the system/firm as a whole and the other based on the specific needs of different affiliates.

From the view point of the firm as a whole, profitability emerges as the prime consideration even if a particular unit may have to make sacrifice. Some of the subsidiaries, at a particular point of time, generate surplus funds for use elsewhere in the firm. The others with lower sales revenue vis-a-vis their investment requirements are the user of the funds. Again, there are financial co-ordinators that provide financial services in form of maintaining banking relationship, assisting currency risk hedge and promoting effective control over transaction cost. The working capital policy establishes an optimal linkage among them. The focus of this approach lies primarily on: creating and managing regional financial headquarters, managing centralised depositories, netting of payments, intra-firm loans, transfer pricing, dividend and remittances, reinvoicing centres, etc.

On the other hand, from the view point of an affiliate, international cash management strategy focuses more on its ability to budget and plan for more narrowly conceived objectives. Cash forecasting, leads and lags, local money market operations and local credit practices are some more important areas on which the focus lies.

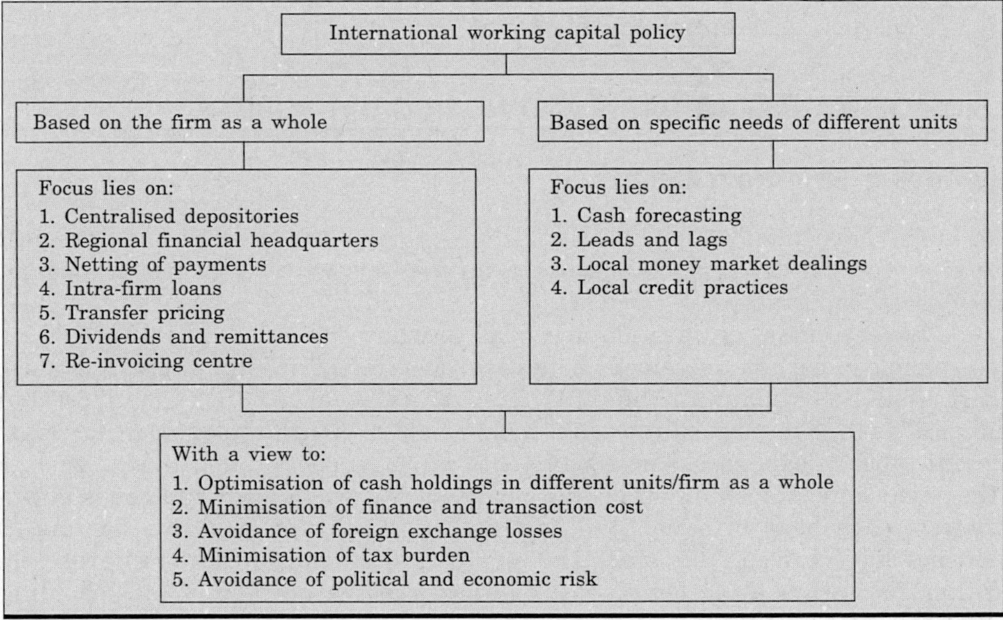

Complexity in International Firms

The management of working capital in an international firm is more complex than in a domestic firm. The reasons are:

1. A multinational firm has a wider option for financing of current assets. Host-country funds can be used. Funds can flow from various units of the same firm. International financial market can be approached. Domestic firms too can approach international financial market, but it is not easy for them to do so.
2. A multinational firm is often subjected to foreign exchange risk when the value of inflow and outflow of funds or the value of export and import is influenced by exchange rate changes. It also faces political risk when the home-country government or the host-country government imposes restrictions on the flow of cash or the flow of inventory. On the other hand, the operation of a domestic firm is normally confined to the national boundary.
3. Intra-firm flow of funds is very common among the multinational enterprises. Viewing from this angle, cash positioning as well as cash mobilisation is an important aspect of international working capital management. In a domestic firm, such questions do not arise.
4. A multinational manager finds it difficult to manage working capital of different units of the firm because he does not have a detailed idea of politico-economic conditions prevalent in different host countries. It is a fact that with the growth of international communication system, the problem has become easier to a great extent, but it still exists.
5. Interest rates and tax rates vary in different countries. A multinational manager has to take into consideration the interest-rate and tax-rate differentials while financing the current assets. In the case of a domestic firm, such differentials hardly count.

> Working capital management in MNCs is complex in view. of:
> 1. Multi-directional flow of funds,
> 2. Exchange rate risk,
> 3. Political risk,
> 4. Complexities of cash positioning,
> 5. Varying environment in host countries,
> 6. Varying interest and tax rates among countries.

BASICS OF MANAGING CASH AND NEAR-CASH ASSETS

Why does a Firm Hold Cash?

Cash is the most liquid asset. Its handling is complex in view of the complicated nature of cross-border financial transactions. This is why its proper management is of utmost importance.

At the very outset, a question arises as to what motivates a firm to hold cash. The principle of cash management believes in holding of minimum possible amount of cash that helps maintain liquidity. Keynes talks about three motives behind holding of cash. The first is the *transaction motive*. A firm holds cash for making different types of expenses. These payments cause a continual outflow of cash. But at the same time, sales and other incomes lead to cash inflow. Had the inflow and outflow of cash been of equal size and simultaneous, the need for holding cash would not have arisen. But since the size of inflow and outflow is hardly equal and there is always a lag between the inflow and the outflow of cash, holding of cash becomes essential.

The other motive behind holding of cash is known as *precautionary motive*. It explains that a firm holds cash for meeting exigencies that may arise. It may happen that when a big customer does not pay the bill or the raw material supplier eliminates the credit, the need for more cash will emerge suddenly without prior notice. Such needs are unforeseen but they are not a continual phenomenon. This is why a firm holds cash for this purpose in the form of near-cash assets. Whenever exigencies arise, near-cash assets are converted into cash.

Yet the other motive is the *speculative motive* that leads to additional requirements for cash. Sometimes unforeseen opportunities arise when it is profitable for the firm to invest. In order to exploit such opportunities, cash is required. Since such needs arise occasionally, the cash for this purpose is held in the form of near-cash assets.

In an international firm, cash holding is influenced also by *inter-firm* and *intra-firm flow of funds* and the various constraints influencing such flows. These flows are considerably influenced by the exchange control mechanisms adopted by different governments. Inter-firm flows are not solely within the control of a single multinational enterprise and so its manoeuvrability in this respect is very limited. On the other hand, the scope for its manoeuvrability in respect of intra-firm flows is quite large. The parent company can effect intra-firm flows even if there is exchange control and thereby it can manage the cash requirements. This is why it is worthwhile to mention the ways of intra-firm transfer of cash in the presence of exchange control.

Intra-firm Flow of Cash

Direction of flow

Intra-firm flow of funds manifests in funds moving (a) from parent to subsidiary, (b) from subsidiary to parent, and (c) among different subsidiaries.

The largest segment of the funds flowing from parent to subsidiaries is represented by initial and supplementary investment in working capital and transfer pricing. The reverse flow takes the form of dividend payment, payment of royalty and technical service fees, disinvestment by the parent company, interest and amortisation payments on loans given by the parent company, export proceeds, payment for imports, and transfer pricing. The flow from one subsidiary to another takes the form of export proceeds or the payment for import or transfer of funds for meeting the cash needs. Whatever the direction of the cash flow, it is very difficult to anticipate the timing and quantum of such flows, especially in view of exchange rate changes, exchange control mechanisms, and tax-rate differentials.

Forms of transfer of funds

When there is exchange control, a multinational enterprise adopts the following methods for transferring cash from one unit to another unit:

1. Transfer pricing
2. Parallel loans
3. Leads and lags
4. Changes in the rates of royalty and other fees
5. Changes in dividend pay-out ratio
6. Use of blocked funds.

Some of these modes have already been discussed. Transfer pricing is discussed in Chapter 23, on International accounting in Part VII. Parallel loans are covered in the chapter on the Management of Exchange Rate Exposure in Part III. Leads and lags have already been explained there, but they will be mentioned here exclusively from the view point of cash management. This will be followed by the discussion of other methods.

Leads and lags

Leading means shortening of credit terms in number of days, while lagging means extending or enlarging of the days of credit. Shortening of the period of credit causes greater flow of cash from the purchaser (importer) to the seller (exporter). Lagging, on the other hand, causes flow of cash from exporter to importer. Suppose Unit A is regularly supplying raw material to Unit B worth $ 2.0 million a month on 90-day credit. The average size of receivables will be $ 6.0 million. Suppose further that $ 4.0 million of cash has to be transferred from B to A, there will be a leading of the credit terms to 30 days. This will reduce the size of receivables to $ 2.0 million and it will result in the flow of cash worth $ 4.0 million from B to A. If, on the other hand, a sum of $ 6.0 million has to be transferred from A to B, the terms of credit will be lagged to 180 days. The average size of receivables will move up to $ 12 million. It will represent a cash flow of $ 6.0 million from A to B during the three-month period.

> Lead means advancing payments. Lag means postponing payments.

Leads and lags are practised in the face of exchange control insofar as the governments are less likely to interfere with the payment terms. However, benefit from this process cannot be thought of in isolation of the borrowing and the lending rate. Suppose due to leading, the importer has to pay more during a particular period of time. For the payment, it borrows from the market, whereas the exporter invests that amount in short-term marketable securities earning a particular rate of return. The leading will be beneficial only when the rate of return from investment is greater than the interest rate on borrowing. This means that the technique of leading and lagging must be viewed against the differential between the interest rate on borrowing and the rate of return from investment.

Changes in the rate of royalty and other fees

The rate of royalty and other fees is fixed by an agreement between the parent company and the subsidiary. But when possible, the parent company makes changes in these rates for the purpose of transfer of liquidity. If the subsidiary is cash-surplus and it has to remit the surplus to the parent company, the latter will raise the rate of royalty and other fees. On the contrary, the rates will be lowered if the subsidiary is cash-deficit. The lowering of rates will help the subsidiary to conserve cash. However, the host government does not like such changes.

Changes in the dividend pay-out ratio

As in the case of royalty, an increase in the dividend pay-out ratio helps the subsidiary to transfer the funds to the parent company. The lowering of the ratio leads to a reverse flow. This is a very common method as about one-half of total remittances to the US firms by their affiliates is represented by such payments.

However, in view of uniformity in the dividend pay-out ratio in line with that of the parent company, any wide deviation in this ratio is not possible. Moreover, liquidity transfer through changes in the dividend pay-out ratio depends to a considerable extent on the cost of alternative sources of funds. This ratio can easily and preferably be raised if the cost of borrowing is lower than the opportunity cost of the cash balance in the host country. Again, the changes in the ratio depend also upon the differential between tax rate on dividend pay-out and the tax rate on retained earnings. If the latter is higher, the parent company will prefer to raise the dividend pay-out ratio. Nevertheless, strict control on the dividend flow by the host government comes in the way of this practice. Besides, some firms relishing the idea of dividend stability do not permit abrupt changes in the dividend pay-out ratio.

Use of blocked funds

If there exist blocked funds in a host country as a sequel to restrictions on the transfer of funds, it is the motive of the parent company to use that amount either in that host country itself or in any other country. To this end, the company adopts a number of techniques such as the following:

1. Transfer pricing
2. Leading and lagging
3. Use of fronting loans
4. Creation of unrelated exports
5. Forced reinvestment

The first two methods, namely transfer pricing and leads and lags, have already been discussed. The other three methods will be explained here.

Fronting loan is a parent to affiliate loan channelled via a financial intermediary, usually an international bank. Suppose for the moment that a US subsidiary in India has blocked funds which could not be transferred to its US parent on account of exchange control prevalent in India. Now the US parent likes to use this fund. If it prefers to use a fronting loan, it will deposit that amount with an international bank which has an office in India. The bank will make a loan for that amount to the US subsidiary in India. In fact, it will simply front for the parent. After the lapse of a specified period, the subsidiary will repay the loan to the international bank and the repaid amount will be passed on to the parent. Here the bank will be interested in this function insofar as, first, the deposit made by the parent will serve as a collateral for the loan; and secondly, the interest paid by the bank on the deposit will be lower than the interest received on account of loan.

> Fronting loan is a parent-to-affiliate loan moving through a financial intermediary.

Creation of unrelated export is another method. Since the creation of additional export needs some amount of additional investment that will come out of blocked funds, the parent company emphasises on the creation of additional export by the subsidiary. Again, the additional export may be a barter deal in which the US subsidiary in India in our example may export normally those items that are not in demand abroad. This way the barter deal will not affect India's export to the general currency area; and at the same time, the blocked funds will be utilised for making exports.

Again, forced reinvestment of funds is made when blockage is only temporary. It is better to invest the blocked funds in the money market of that particular host country itself. If the money market is not well developed, the subsidiary can invest the blocked funds in some industries. If this channel too is not possible, the blocked funds can be used to purchase an asset, the value of which can rise with an increase in the inflation rate.

Thus, one finds that there are many ways for transfer of funds out of the host country circumventing the exchange control regulations. The choice of a particular method or a combination of methods depends upon the cost and benefit involved in them as well as on how far they are able to negate the restrictions imposed by the host government on the transfer of funds. The choice depends also upon the objectives that the different methods are going to serve. If the purpose is to avoid exchange control, the method will be different from that when the purpose is to save taxes.

Again, if the firm likes to reap the maximum advantage from the intra-firm transfer of funds, the parent should have a detailed information of the cash requirements of its different units and the cost of funds prevalent in the host country's financial market. It should possess also the knowledge of tax rates and the governmental regulations in the host countries.

STEPS IN MANAGEMENT OF CASH AND NEAR-CASH ASSETS

The management of cash and near-cash assets involves basically four steps:

1. Assessment of the cash requirements
2. Optimisation of cash need through restructuring of inflows and outflows
3. Selection of the sources from where cash could be brought in
4. Investment of surplus cash, if any, into near-cash assets

Selection of the sources of funds has already been discussed in Chapter 15. So in this chapter, we shall deal with the other three issues mentioned above.

Assessment of Cash Requirements

The first step in the international cash management is to establish the need for cash during a specific period which may be a week, a fortnight, or a month. It is computed on the basis of the expected amount of cash disbursements vis-à-vis expected inflow of cash during a particular period. The outflow and inflow of cash occur mainly on account of various transactions. The firm holds cash also to meet the precautionary and speculative needs, but as mentioned above, such needs are fixed, and the amount of cash for these purposes is determined on the basis of experience and the general trend of business environment.

For the assessment of cash needs, a *cash budget* is prepared for each of the subsidiaries. After assessing the cash need of each of the subsidiaries, the figures are consolidated in order to assess the cash need of the firm as a whole. This is so because in a multinational enterprise, it is the cash flow of the firm as a whole that is taken into account and it needs to be managed. The process of consolidation requires the translation of the host-country currency into the home-country currency which is always subjected to foreign exchange exposure. The readers are suggested to consult any book on corporate finance for the cash budget preparation. They are also suggested to consult Part VII of the text for an understanding of the translation of currencies. Here we present a simple illustration of how the cash budgets of different subsidiaries are consolidated.

Suppose a US parent company has two subsidiaries A and B in two different countries. The budget of the two subsidiaries shows the expected inflow and outflow of cash during all the four weeks of a particular month. The cash flows can be consolidated with the cash flow of the parent company. However, at the present juncture, we show the consolidation of the two cash budgets only.

The figures in Table 21.1 show the cash position of the two subsidiaries. In the beginning of the month, Subsidiary A is cash-deficit, while Subsidiary B is cash-surplus. In this case, the parent company can instruct the latter to transfer the

TABLE 21.1 Cash Inflow and Outflow

(US $ '000)

	Subsidiary A			*Subsidiary B*		
	Inflow	*Outflow*	*Net*	*Inflow*	*Outflow*	*Net*
Cash position in the beginning			–300			+250
Forecast: First week	180	50	+130	200	300	–100
Second week	160	180	–20	150	270	–120
Third week	300	140	+160	100	50	+50
Fourth week	100	200	–100	100	120	–20
Four weeks' total			+170			–190
Cash position at the month-end			–130			+60

TABLE 21.2 Consolidated Statement

(US $ '000)

	Subsidiary A	*Subsidiary B*	*Total*
Cash position in the beginning of the month	–300	+250	–50
Cash required (precautionary & speculative)	–100	–100	–200
	+150	–250	
Forecast: First week	+130	–100	+30
Second week	–20	–120	–140
Third week	+160	+50	+210
Fourth week	–100	–20	–120
Four weeks' total	+170	–190	–20
Cash balance at the end of the month	–230	–40	–270

surplus funds to Subsidiary A. The rest of the deficit can be met either by the parent company or by raising funds from outside the firm. Similarly, in the first week of the month, Subsidiary A will meet the deficit of Subsidiary B. But in the second week, both the subsidiaries are in deficit. In that case, the parent company, if it is in a surplus position, has to meet the deficit. It may also ask the subsidiaries to raise funds from outside the firm. Now the decision of the parent company whether to meet the deficit from the sources within the firm or to meet it by outside funds depends upon the cost of the funds to be raised from the market vis-à-vis the sum of the transaction cost involved in the intra-firm flow of the funds and the rate of return from the investment of the surplus funds in short-term marketable securities. If the former is higher than the latter, the parent company will insist on the intra-firm flow of funds. If the latter is higher, the parent company will prefer to raise funds from outside the firm.

In the third week, both the subsidiaries are in surplus position. In this case, the surplus funds will be invested in short-term marketable securities. When there is deficit in the subsequent week or weeks, the investment will be converted back into cash in order to meet the deficit. How to invest will be discussed in the subsequent section of this chapter.

Optimisation of Cash Needs

The required cash level can be minimised during a particular period through restructuring of the inflows and outflows. If, in the case of inter-firm payments, the inflows are accelerated and at the same time outflows are delayed, the cash needs at a particular point of time shall be lower. Again, if, in the case of intra-firm payments, netting of payments is adopted, the need for cash will reduce further. Yet again, the need for cash will be reduced if there is centralised holding and management of precautionary cash balance. Thus, after the assessment of cash needs for different subsidiaries individually and then for the firm as a whole, the firm steps into restructuring of the cash flows so as to minimise the cash need at a particular point of time. The restructuring includes three steps:

1. Accelerating inflows of cash and delaying disbursements
2. Netting of payments
3. Centralised management of precautionary cash balance.

Accelerating inflows and delaying outflows

There are two types of delays in the collection of cash. One is the mailing delay and the other is the processing delay. In collection from across the border, long procedural formalities and governmental restrictions too come in the way.

As regards *mailing delay*, the use of cable remittances is often suggested. The use of telex or cable transfers cuts short the mailing delay. In this respect, the Society for World-wide Inter-bank Financial Telecommunications (SWIFT) is doing a commendable job. It has brought into its fold around 1,000 banks among which funds are transferred electronically with ease. Again, the firm opens up regional mobilisation centres and instructs the customers to make their payments to the centres falling in their respective vicinity. Sometimes, the postal box with the post-offices falling in the customers' vicinity is set up. The postal box is operated by the local offices of the bank authorised by the firm. This method is commonly known as the *lock-box system*.

As far as *processing delay* is concerned, there are some multinational banks that provide "same-day-value" facilities. Under this facility, the amount deposited in any branch of the bank in any country is credited to the firm's account on the same day. This is done through electronic devices. Thus it is suggested that the firm should take help from such banks to cut short the processing delays.

Again, some of the firms adopt pre-authorised payment system in which they are authorised to charge a customer's bank account up to a specific limit.

Besides, disbursements are delayed in order to conserve cash at least for some time. But the firm should be careful that making such delay does not affect its creditworthiness. Again, when disbursements are delayed, there are chances for retaliatory measures. Thus the process of disbursements demands extra care.

Accelerating cash inflow and decelerating disbursements help improve the efficiency of cash management, but they do involve additional cost. Thus it is advisable for the company to adopt these techniques as long as their marginal returns exceed their marginal cost.

Netting of intra-firm payments

The other step towards lessening the requirements for cash is to encourage netting of intra-firm payments. There is usually a large volume of intra-firm payments. Such payments require not only huge amount of cash but they also involve transaction cost, inter-currency conversion cost and opportunity cost of float. Different units of a firm require cash, not only for making payments but also for meeting such costs. Netting is a solution to this problem.

> Netting of payments means payment of only the net amount. It may be bilateral/ multilateral.

Netting is, in fact, the elimination of counter payments. This means that only net amount is paid. For example, if the parent company is to receive US $ 3.0 million from its subsidiary and if the same subsidiary is to get US $ 1.0 million from the parent company, these two transactions can be netted to one transaction where the subsidiary will transfer US $ 2.0 million to the parent company. The cost of transfer too will be lower. If the amount of these two payments is equal, there will be no movement of funds, and the transaction cost will naturally be zero.

Netting can be bilateral involving two units. It may be multilateral involving more than two units. Suppose A, B and C are the three units of a firm. A has to receive US $ 15.0 million from B and US $ 12.0 million from C. B has to receive US $ 20.0 million from C and US $ 20.0 million from A. C has to receive US $ 30.0 million from A and US $ 6.0 million from B. In the absence of netting, there will be six transactions involving US $ 103 million. If it is bilateral netting, there will be three transactions involving US $ 37.0 million. If it is multilateral netting, there will be only two transactions involving only US $ 23.0 million.

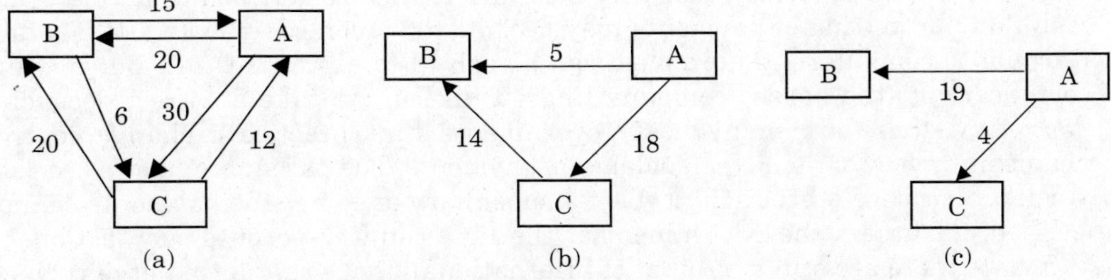

FIGURE 21.1 (a) No Netting; (b) Bilateral Netting; (c) Multilateral Netting.

However, for making netting successful, the parent company needs to maintain a close watch on all intra-firm transactions. The subsidiaries may not like it.

Again, for netting, the units of a firm located in different countries have to take permission from the monetary authorities. The monetary authorities may not allow them on the conditions of injury to the external balance of the country.

Centralised management of precautionary cash balance

The centralised holding and management of precautionary cash balance helps reduce the requirements for cash without impairing the ability of the firm to cover unforeseen expenses. The size of such cash balances depends on how safe the firm deserves to be in its ability to meet unexpected transactions. The larger the precautionary balance, the less is the risk of financial embarrassment and loss of credit standing.

The management of precautionary cash balance is based on the theory of probability which means that there is specific percentage of probability of running into cash shortage for different units. The risk of cash shortage is explained through standard deviation. In the case of decentralised holding of precautionary cash balance, each and every unit has some amount of standard deviation. But when the cash holding is centralised, the risk of the firm as a whole is explained through portfolio standard deviation. And as the theory of portfolio standard deviation suggests, the portfolio risk will certainly be lower than the sum of risk faced by different units. This is because there is possibility for a negative correlation between the risk of different units. In short, the centralised holding of precautionary cash balance lowers the risk and helps lower the cash requirements of the firm. In case a particular unit runs short of precautionary cash balance, the centralised depository comes to the rescue immediately.

Problems with the cash optimisation process

The problems coming in the way of accelerating and decelerating of cash flows or the netting process have already been pointed out in this section. Yet they may be grouped as:

1. Firm-related problems
2. Governmental restrictions
3. Deficiency in the banking system
4. Opposition by subsidiaries

When a multinational enterprise has a large number of subsidiaries and there is large fluctuation in the host-country currencies, the acceleration or deceleration of cash flows or netting of payments may become too much complicated. It is a fact that owing to computers, the problem can be solved to a great extent. But in view of complications, the parent company finds it difficult to take a correct decision.

Secondly, there are many host governments that practise exchange control mechanisms in view of their weak balance of payments. The parent company's decision to accelerate or decelerate cash flows of a subsidiary or to net the payments cannot be carried out unless the government of the host country permits such actions.

Thirdly, there are still a number of international banks that have not developed a sophisticated system of collections and payments. In these cases, acceleration of collection and netting of payments cannot be effective.

Fourthly, the acceleration or deceleration of cash flows may be beneficial for one unit or one firm, but it may not be beneficial for the other unit or the other firm. In such cases, those subsidiaries or firms that are at loss resent such a move. The firms may take retaliatory measures. The subsidiaries in which the parent company has very little control may come in the way of such moves.

Investment of Surplus Cash

It has already been mentioned that the cash balance for precautionary and speculative purposes is held in the form of near-cash assets. Surplus cash over the transaction purposes too is held in the form of near-cash assets or short-term marketable securities. The reason is that the near-cash assets earn something for the firm and are definitely better than holding of idle cash balance.

In this context, a couple of questions are involved that need some explanation. They are:

1. Whether the surplus cash balance of the entire firm should be centralised and then only it should be invested.
2. How much of the surplus cash balance should be invested in near-cash assets.

Forms of centralisation process

The process of centralisation of surplus cash can take two forms. One is the centralised control of the parent company over the surplus cash of different units. In this case, cash does not actually move to a centralised pool, but its movement to a cash-deficit unit or for investment in near-cash assets is strictly guided by the parent company. The other form manifests in the actual movement of cash to a centralised pool. Any investment into the near-cash assets takes place only out of the centralised pool.

> Centralised pool represents a pool of funds where the surplus cash of all the units of a firm is deposited.

Merits of the centralisation process

Since the working capital management among different units of a multi-national enterprise is designed to maximise the benefit of the firm as a whole, it is always better to have centralisation of decision. If the decision to invest the surplus cash is left to the individual units spread over different parts of the globe, the different units will think in their own terms only, and the objective of the maximisation of overall benefit will not be served. Moreover, it may happen that one unit does have surplus cash, while the other unit borrows at high interest rates from the external sources.

In the case of centralisation, the funds of the firm are invested in the most desirable fashion so as to avoid the weaknesses of some of the host-country currencies. Whenever any unit falls into liquidity distress, funds are immediately rushed to it.

> The centralisation process helps:
> 1. Meet global objective
> 2. Lower cost of funds
> 3. Avoid the impact of currency depreciation
> 4. Maintain firm's global liquidity
> 5. Achieve economies of scale.

Sometimes centralisation of surplus cash reaps the economies of scale. There are many investment avenues that need large sums of money. If investment is left to the individual units, the surplus may not be so large and the investment avenue can remain untapped. But that investment avenue can easily be tapped through centralised pool.

However, when the central pool is maintained, some precautions should be taken. *First*, each of the units should have smooth cash collection and disbursement procedures. *Secondly*, each of them should be aware of the quantum of cash inflow and cash outflow at a particular point of time. *Thirdly*, the system of movement of cash to and from the pool should not have any restrictions. *Fourthly*, the information system must be substantially improved.

Location of the centralised pool

The centralised pool may be located either in the host country or in the home country or in a third country. The location depends upon the following factors:

(a) *Strength of the currency of that country*. This means that the currency must be strong.
(b) *Strength of the money market*. The stronger and well developed the money market, the greater will be the investment avenues.
(c) *Tax rate*. Tax rate should be the lowest. In fact, this is the reason that most of the US multinationals locate their centralised cash pool in tax-haven countries, such as Panama, Cayman Islands, and the Bahamas.
(d) *Political stability*. The greater the political stability, the easier and safer it will be to locate the centralised pool of cash.
(e) *Attitude of the host government*. Pool is located only in those countries where the attitude of the government is congenial towards foreign companies.

How much of the surplus to be invested

Surplus cash should not lie idle. It should be invested. But the owner of the centralised pool must consider the benefit and cost of the investment. The larger the investment, the greater is the interest earned but at the same time greater is the risk of illiquidity. If the investment is lower, liquidity will improve but earning on the investment will be lower. Thus an *optimal division of funds between cash and near cash assets requires a trade-off between liquidity and profitability*.

The optimal ratio between cash and near-cash assets is influenced also by the transaction cost or the cost of conversion from cash to securities and back in the form of brokerage, etc. The larger the near-cash assets, the greater will be the transaction cost. On the contrary, larger cash balance does involve large opportunity cost in form of interest foregone that the near-cash assets could have earned. *The optimal level, therefore, represents a point where the sum of transaction cost and opportunity cost is the minimum.*

> Surplus cash is invested only to the extent where transaction cost = opportunity cost.

While making investment in near-cash assets, the international finance manager has to take care of a number of facts, of which the following are important:

1. Portfolio should be diversified so as to maximise yield for a given level of risk.
2. Portfolio should be reviewed daily so as to decide which particular investment has to be liquidated or which particular securities should remain undisturbed.
3. Investment should be made in those assets only where liquidity prevails.
4. Maturity structure of investment should coincide with the need for cash so that securities can be easily converted back into cash whenever need for fresh cash arises.

Currency of investment

An important question concerning the investment of surplus cash into near-cash assets is related to the choice of currency/country. Normally, the surplus cash is invested in a country where interest rate is higher as higher interest means higher return. However, the answer is not so simple as it looks at first sight. In fact, the firm has to take into account the effective yield/return that depends not only on the rate of interest but also on the changes in the exchange rate. If the currency of the country where the funds are invested depreciates vis-à-vis the home-country currency, the return in terms of home-country currency will be lower. Basing on Eq. (15.1), the effective return,

> Effective return from investment depends upon rate of interest and the exchange rate changes.

$$r = (1 + i_f)(1 + e_f) - 1 \tag{21.1}$$

where i_f is the interest rate on foreign currency investment, and e_f is the changes in the exchange rate.

Suppose a US company invests its cash in French securities where interest rate is 8.0 per cent as compared to 6.0 per cent in the USA. But French franc depreciates during the period by 5.0 per cent vis-à-vis the US dollar. The effective return will be:

$$(1 + 0.08)[1 + (-\ 0.05)] - 1 = 0.026 = 2.6\%$$

Thus the US company will not invest its surplus cash in French securities even when the interest rate is higher since the effective return is lower.

The above example is not very uncommon. For, as the Interest Rate Parity theory tells us, the currency with higher interest rate tends to depreciate over time. Thus, interest rate differential is a better guiding factor. With the elongation of the time period, impact of interest rate differential on the forward rate tends to become more apparent.

One can say that the interest rate differential normally matters because it is not very easy to anticipate the changes in the exchange rate. However, there are many exchange rate forecasting agencies that predict the movement in the exchange rate. Moreover, one can guess it on the basis of probability. Suppose there is 40 per cent probability for 5.0 depreciation, 20 per cent probability for 3.0 per cent depreciation, and the remaining 40 per cent probability for 2.0 per cent appreciation. The expected value can easily be calculated.

More often, a firm makes multiple-currency investment and reaps the benefit of diversification. Uncertainty in exchange rate changes is greatly reduced if there is negative correlation in the changes in the exchange rate of different currencies.

Thus whenever a firm has surplus of cash, it is better to have a centralised pool located in the most suitable place. The centralised funds should be translated into multiple-currency investment. However, care should be taken that the cost of investment does not exceed the benefits from investment. To be precise, investment of surplus cash should be made:

1. through a centralised pool located in the most suitable place;
2. through a perfect trade-off between liquidity and profitability;
3. at a point where the sum of conversion cost and opportunity cost is the minimum; and
4. in multi-currency investment channels.

MANAGEMENT OF RECEIVABLES

Credit sales lead to the emergence of account receivables. The management of receivables focuses on two important facts. One is that the cost of the credit sale should not exceed the benefit from the credit sales. The other is whether the sale is confined within different units of the firm or it is an inter-firm sale.

Benefits and Costs of Receivables

Greater sale volume is the benefit of credit sale. It is because customers get more time to pay for the goods. But, on the other hand, there are costs involved with the credit sale that need to be balanced against the benefits. The costs are:

> Receivables benefit in terms of greater sale. But the costs are: financing cost, administrative cost, collection cost, bad debt loss and loss owing to exchange rate changes.

1. Financing cost, that is, the interest on the funds tagged with receivables. The higher the interest rate or the longer the period of credit, the higher is the cost.
2. Administrative cost incurred on maintaining office for such sales. It includes the cost of maintaining records.
3. Collection cost which is incurred especially when the bills are not paid in time. Such costs move up with the gradual liberalisation of credit.
4. Bad debt loss when the sale proceeds are not realised in spite of best efforts.
5. Foreign exchange loss that arises if exchange rate changes against the exporter during the period of credit.

Thus the appropriate policy of managing account receivables should be that a firm extends credit only up to a point where the marginal profits on its increased sale are equal to the marginal cost of receivables.

If the size of credit sale is lower than this point or the optimal size, benefits shall be less than the maximum. On the other hand, if the size of the credit sale exceeds the optimal point, costs will turn higher to slash the benefit.

Selecting an Optimal Term of Credit

The terms of credit granted to the buyers influence the receivables' cost and the benefit. Liberal terms raise benefits but at the same time the costs too. Stringent terms, on the other hand, lower both the benefit and the cost. So the firm determines the optimal terms of credit that represents the maximum net benefit. The firm prepares proforma income statement assuming a particular size of sales and the size of different costs and then it arrives at the net profit. The term representing the maximum net profit is the optimal term of credit.

Credit Policy

Intra-firm sales

In case of intra-firm sales, the focus of receivables management is not on the quantum of credit sale or on the timing of payment but on the global allocation of firm's resources. There is often vertical integration among different units located in different countries. Different parts of the same product are manufactured in different units and exported to the assembly unit. In such cases, the size of receivables is very large. Similarly, early payment or late payment does not matter because the seller and the purchaser represent the same firm. A particular unit may delay the payment if it is suffering from cash shortage. The payment may be quick if the unit has surplus of cash. It is all a game of intra-firm allocation of resources. And to this end, leads and lags, explained earlier are frequently used. The readers are suggested to go through the explanation of this technique. It will be clear how far this technique is helpful in the intra-firm allocation of resources.

However, if a unit of the firm is located in a weak-currency country, it is asked to make a quick payment so that the cost of receivables borne by the firm as a whole may not be large. The impact of exchange rate changes may be illustrated here. Suppose credit period is 120 days. The financing cost is 1.0 per cent per month. The importer's currency is to depreciate by 2.0 per cent during the four-month period. The receivables are denominated in the importer's currency. The additional cost of receivables per unit of the exporter's currency, which is the product of the financing cost and the currency depreciation, is

Collection is expedited from a buying unit located in a weak-currency country.

$$1 - [(1 - 4 \times 0.01)(1 - 0.02)] = 0.059 = 5.9\%$$

Inter-firm sales

In the case of inter-firm sales or the sales to an outside firm, a couple of decisions are involved. One is about the currency in which the transaction should be denominated; while the other is about what the terms of payment should be.

As regards *currency denomination*, the exporter likes to denominate the transaction in a strong currency, while the importer likes to get it denominated in weak currency. In such a situation, it is the question of bargaining. However, the exporter may be ready to invoice the transaction in the weak currency even for a long period of credit if it has debt in that currency. It is because the sale proceeds can be used to retire the debt without any loss on account of exchange rate changes.

Inter-firm credit sale takes care of:
1. Currency of denomination
2. Terms of payment.

As regards the *terms of payment*, the exporter does not provide a longer period of credit and tries to get the export proceeds as early as possible if the transaction is invoiced in a weak currency. But sometimes, there is found deviation from this simple norm. The credit term may be liberal if the exporter is able to borrow from the bank on the basis of bill receivables and not on the basis of actual inventory. Again, the terms of credit may be liberal also in cases where competition in the market is tough forcing in turn the exporter to finance a part of the importer's inventory, and this act of the exporter is going to expand the sale significantly. But these conditions are not common.

MANAGEMENT OF INVENTORY

Complex Management in MNCs

Inventory accounts for the biggest share of the current assets. At the same time, it is the least liquid. This is why its management deserves sufficient care. To some extent, the management of inventory in an international firm is similar as in case of a domestic firm. But some additional factors are important in the case of an international firm. They are:

1. An international firm has to maintain inventory simultaneously in different countries.
2. Transit time is quite longer.
3. Customs procedures are quite lengthy.
4. Political risk along with exchange rate risk is there.

Based on these problems, there are some deviations from the simple norm of inventory management, which is practised in a domestic firm. These deviations are now explained at some length.

Deviation from the Economic Order Quantity

The economic order quantity (EOQ) is the optimal size of inventory that a firm orders at a particular point of time. The readers are suggested to consult any book on corporate finance where they will find an explanation of EOQ and the details about its calculation. However, it may be pointed out here that it is that quantity of order where the sum of the ordering cost and the carrying cost of inventory is the minimum. With the growth in the size of order, the number of orders in a particular period of time gets fewer and the ordering cost reduces. But, on the other hand, the carrying cost increases. Thus to arrive at the EOQ, the finance manager has to trade-off between the carrying cost and the ordering cost. The trade-off is complete where the sum of these two costs is the minimum.

> EOQ represents the size of an order for inventory where the sum of carrying cost and order cost is the minimum.

The domestic firms adhere to this norm strictly. But the international firms possess normally a bigger stock than the EOQ which is often known as *stockpiling*. The different units of a firm get a significant part of their inputs from sister units located in other countries. This is more common in a vertical set-up. In such cases, political risk and the exchange rate risk cannot be overlooked completely. If there is political disturbance, there will be obstruction in the import. If the currency of the importing country depreciates, the imports will turn costlier. Thus in order to avoid this problem, stockpiling is favoured.

> Stockpiling means inventory order for more than EOQ.

PROBLEM 21.1

Total demand for raw materials is 100 tonnes during time T. The carrying cost is \$ 10 per tonne of stock during time, T and the order cost is \$ 1 per order. Will you call it stockpiling if the firm makes an order for 6 tonnes of raw material?

Solution

First we have to find out the EOQ. EOQ lies where transaction cost is equal to order cost. In terms of an equation:

$$AQ/R = cTR/2$$

or $$2aQ/R^2 = cT$$

or $$R = (2aQ/cT)^{1/2}$$

Based on this equation,

$$EOQ = \{(2 \times 1 \times 100)/10\}^{1/2}$$
$$= 4.472 \text{ tonnes.}$$

If the firm makes an order for 6 tonnes, it is a clear case of stockpiling

However, stockpiling cannot be done indefinitely. The firm will have to decide against stockpiling if the cumulative carrying cost exceeds the expected increase in the price of the input on account of changes in the exchange rate. Nevertheless, if the probability of interruption in supply is very high, the firm may go for stockpiling even if it is not justified on the ground of higher cost.

Shifting of Re-order Point

The principle of financial management suggests that the next lot of inventory is to be ordered when the existing stock comes down to the sum of safety level of stock and the lead time—both expressed in terms of number of days. Suppose the existing stock based on the present usage rate can last for 30 days. If the firm maintains a safety level of stock for five days and if the lead time, that is, the time elapsed between making an order and the arrival of input is six days, the firm will make an order for the next lot only after 19 days of the arrival of the existing stock.

> Re-order point depends on:
> 1. Usage rate of inventory.
> 2. Lead time which is often geater in international procurement.

However, in the case of the international firms, the lead time is larger as the different units are located far-off in different parts of the globe. Even if goods reach the port, there are a lot of customs formalities. Because of all these factors, the re-order point for international firms lies much earlier.

Nevertheless, the decision regarding stockpiling or regarding re-order point depends on how much of the goods are to be imported and how much of them are locally available. Dependence on imports varies from one case to another, but it is definitely large for vertical set-up.

FINANCING OF CURRENT ASSETS

The discussion on international working capital management is not complete in absence of any explanation of how current assets are financed. It has already been pointed out that financing of the current assets involves essentially a perfect trade-off between liquidity and profitability. With this view in mind, the international managers finance the current assets with both the long-term and short-term funds.

But they rely more on short-term funds to finance the variable part of current assets and also a part of the permanent current assets. The process needs probe primarily into two issues. One is the source of the short-term funds to which an MNC can have the access. The other is the criterion on the basis of which an MNC selects a particular source. These two issues need some explanation.

> Short-term funds are required for financing the variable current assets and also a part of permanent current assets.

Sources of Short-term Funds

An MNC has wider options compared to a domestic firm. It can get funds from three sources. They are:

1. Funds from the cash-surplus units or from the centralised pool.
2. Borrowing from the international money market including euro-currency market and the international securities market.
3. Borrowing from the host-country sources of funds.

The channelling of the funds from the cash-surplus units/centralised pool has been discussed in the present chapter while discussing international cash management. Euro-currency market and international securities market are discussed in Chapter 17 and Chapter 18. Among the host-country sources, the most important source is the commercial bank, although the firms get funds also through promissory notes and commercial paper. Banks providing short-term and medium-term funds to the exporters and importers find a place in Chapter 22. Thus the focus of discussion in the present chapter falls on how an MNC selects a particular source of short-term funds.

Selection of a Particular Source of Funds

The process of selection is guided by the objective of a trade-off between liquidity and profitability. It means that the cost of funds is to be minimised but, at the same time, sufficient liquidity needs to be maintained. It is because the lack of liquidity mars smooth operation.

Selection of a particular source of funds is based on a perfect trade-off between liquidity and profitability.

In order to evaluate the cost of different types of funds, the finance managers compare between the costs of

(a) Internal funds and the external funds.
(b) International money market funds and the host-country funds.

As far as the former is concerned, a comparison is made between the opportunity cost of the internal funds and the interest rate of the external funds. If the opportunity cost of internal funds or, in other words, the rate of return from the investment of the surplus cash of the firm is higher than the interest rate on the borrowing from the external sources, it means that the firm's own resources are earning more than what is spent on paying interest on the borrowed funds. The firm finances the current assets with external funds.

Similarly, for comparison between the cost of host-country funds and the international money market funds, the finance manager of an international firm finds out the cost of the two types of funds in terms of the home-country currency for a more meaningful evaluation. This is primarily because: first, the exchange rate changes and that influences the cost of funds; second, the tax rate influencing the tax-adjusted cost of funds, varies among countries.

Changes in the exchange rate and tax rate influence the effective cost of funds.

Changes in exchange rate influence the cost of borrowing. Using Eq. 15.1, we find that the effective cost of funds is a product of interest rate and exchange rate. If a currency depreciates, the effective cost of borrowing it in terms of home-country currency will move down. If it appreciates, the opposite will be the case. Thus even if borrowing in a host country is costlier than in international money market but if the currency of the host country is expected to depreciate at a higher rate, it is advisable to borrow in the host country.

Similarly, the larger the tax rate, the lower is the cost of borrowing. Interest is tax-deductible and so the effective cost of borrowing is arrived at after multiplying the interest rate by one-minus-tax rate. Thus an MNC maintains care while selecting a source of funds and raises funds in a country where the tax rate is higher.

However, care is maintained to preserve liquidity. An MNC borrows from a source where availability of capital is easy and repayment terms are in tune with the liquidity norms. Liquidity cannot be ignored just in order to lower the cost of funds.

Supply Chain Finance (SCF)

The SCF is used to optimize the financial flows in supply chains, reducing the working capital burden on suppliers and buyers and improving overall supply chain efficiency. It is being used by the companies at the time when the demand spikes and dips. The supply chain finance works in many ways like a buyer who is having a strong creditworthiness can pay to the supplier for any approved invoices from the third-party financial institutions. Supplier get also benefited as there is an immediate cash flow, which in turn reduces the dependency on loans and enhances the stability in finance of the supplier. Summing up we can say that the supply chain finance provide benefit to both supplier and buyer.

SCF Products

1. **Reverse Factoring:** This strategy is used to generate finance by a third-party at a low cost for suppliers. In this the buyer approves invoices before the due date for the suppliers, then the supplier can approach to the financer and receive payment early. And now buyer pays the financer on the due date and supplier gets the finance with some minimum financing fee way before due payment. Hence, it benefits both the supplier and the buyers
2. **Inventory Financing:** It is a form of working capital loan wherein this business uses their inventory as collateral for securing the funding. This finance has been generated by the companies for meeting the operational expenses, purchasing the additional inventory, or meeting the cash flow gaps.
3. **Receivables Financing:** It is often called as factoring or invoice discounting, in this arrangement a supplier sells his account receivables to the third-party financer at a discount and receives the current cash (approximately 70–90% of the outstanding amount), which improves the liquidity and accelerates the flow of cash to the supplier. Once the buyer pays the outstanding amount to the financer, then supplier receives the remaining amount and deducting a service fee.

Dynamic Discounting

Dynamic discounting is a financial strategy that enables buyers to settle their invoices with suppliers ahead of the previously agreed payment terms, offering them the incentive of a discount in return. This approach provides flexibility, allowing both parties to benefit from improved cash flow; suppliers receive their payments sooner, while buyers can reduce their overall costs. The discount is typically calculated based on the number of days the payment is made in advance, encouraging timely transactions and fostering stronger relationships between buyers and suppliers. By leveraging dynamic discounting, organizations can optimize their working capital management while also enhancing supplier satisfaction.

Both the supplier and buyer gets benefits from this arrangement, supplier improves the cash flow without external financing. And buyers earn a retun on unused cash by saving through the negotiated discounts. The dynamic discounting platform enables real-time negotiation and implementation often integrated with enterprise resource planning (ERP) systems.

Blockchain Technology in Trade Finance

Blockchain is a revolutionary distributed ledger technology that enhances transparency, security, and efficiency in trade finance processes. By providing a decentralized and tamper-proof record of transactions, it effectively addresses long-standing challenges such as fraud, delays, and a lack of trust among parties involved in trade. With its ability to streamline documentation, automate verification processes through smart contracts, and enable real-time tracking of goods and payments, blockchain fosters a more reliable and collaborative trading environment, ultimately promoting greater confidence and efficiency in international trade.

Applications of Blockchain technology in trade finance:

(a) **Smart Contracts:** It automates the payment and trade processes, which trigger the payment if pre-defined conditions are met.

(b) **Document Digitization:** It replaces a huge paper-based documentation with the digital versions of recording and documenting. Example of such digitization are., letter of credit, bill of lading, etc.

(c) **Traceability:** It provides a real-time visibility of the goods and financial transactions that ease the traceability.

(d) **Fraud Prevention:** Unchanged ledgers reduce the duplication risk of financing and counterfeit goods.

The integration of Supply Chain Finance (SCF), dynamic discounting, and blockchain technology is revolutionizing the landscape of trade finance, representing a significant shift towards a more innovative and robust financial ecosystem. This convergence enhances efficiency and transparency, allowing businesses to streamline their operations and reduce costs. By leveraging these advanced technologies, companies can unlock substantial value, improving cash flow management and optimizing supplier relationships. Additionally, the implementation of blockchain introduces a higher level of security and traceability, helping to mitigate the risks traditionally associated with trade finance processes, such as fraud and discrepancies. Overall, this modern approach empowers organizations to navigate the complexities of global trade with greater resilience and confidence.

Challenges of Managing Working Capital in Global Supply Chains

The management of working capital at the global level is a complex task due to the interlinked of diverse factors across regions, industries, and stakeholders. Here are some of the key challenges with the strategies to address them.

- **Variability in Payment Terms**
  - In the global supply chain, industries adhere to distinct business practices, which lead to diverse payment terms and varying credit periods, that highlights the complexity and adaptability required in international commerce. Suppliers often experience delays in receiving payments, while buyers may require extended payment terms to better match their cash flow cycles. This dynamic can lead to inconsistencies and variability in payment schedules, creating challenges for both parties.

  Example: The disparity in payment terms between European buyers and Asian suppliers poses challenges for managing working capital cycles. European buyers often seek payment terms of up to 90 days, while Asian suppliers typically operate on 30-day terms. This mismatch can lead to cash flow issues for suppliers, as delayed payments may impact their liquidity.

  Solution: To address these challenges, effective coordination and communication between procurement and financial teams are essential for aligning working capital strategies. Implementing Supply chain finance (SCF) can also bridge payment term gaps. And using standardized payment term agreements also reduces variability.

- **Currency Exchange Rate fluctuations**
  - Currency volatility has a significant effect on cash flows, creating uncertainty in cross-border transactions. For instance, when the dollar strengthens, buyers sourcing from emerging markets may face higher costs, making imports more expensive. Conversely, suppliers in these markets could see their revenue decline when converted to their local currency, impacting their overall profitability.

  Example: A company that imports goods priced in USD while selling in a weaker local currency may face challenges due to exchange rate fluctuations. If the local currency depreciates against the dollar, the cost of imported goods rises in local terms, which can reduce profit margins and negatively impact financial stability. To mitigate these risks, the company may need to consider strategies such as hedging, adjusting prices, or diversifying currency exposures.

  Solution: To effectively manage currency risks, they can employ various hedging strategies, utilizing instruments such as forward contracts and options. These tools allow businesses to secure favorable exchange rates and protect against market fluctuations. Furthermore, establishing a multi-currency bank account can significantly minimize conversion losses, enabling more efficient financial transactions across different currencies and enhancing overall financial management.

- **Geopolitical risks and trade policies**
  - Political instability, along with tariffs and trade restrictions, significantly disrupts supply chain operations and affects cash flows. These factors create uncertainty that can lead to increased costs for businesses. Additionally, sudden changes in trade agreements or the imposition of new tariffs can result in delays both in payments and the delivery of goods. As a result, companies must navigate these challenges carefully to maintain operational efficiency and protect their financial health.

Example: The U.S.-China trade war has significantly impacted global commerce by imposing higher tariffs on goods exchanged between the two nations. These increased tariffs have altered payment terms for companies, making transactions more complex and costly. As a result, businesses are now faced with higher inventory holding costs, as they may need to stockpile goods to mitigate potential supply chain disruptions caused by fluctuating tariffs. This situation not only affects the financial performance of individual companies but also has broader implications for international trade dynamics and market stability.

Solution: To effectively address challenges associated with reliance on high-risk regions, businesses should diversify their supplier bases. By sourcing from various geographical locations, they can reduce the impact of political instability and other disruptions. Additionally, utilizing trade finance solutions, such as export credit, can provide financial protection and mitigate political risks. This combined strategy enhances supply chain resilience and ensures smoother operations in the global market.

- **Supply Chain Disruption**
  - Natural disasters, pandemics, and other unexpected events can significantly disrupt business operations, leading to delays in production, delivery, and revenue collection. These disruptions often increase working capital requirements, as businesses may be obligated to fulfill supplier payments or maintain inventory levels before receiving payments from customers. Such circumstances create cash flow gaps, placing pressure on liquidity and challenging the financial stability of firms. This phenomenon underscores the critical need for robust financial planning and risk mitigation strategies to address the increased unpredictability of operational cash flows during periods of crisis.

Example: The COVID-19 pandemic significantly disrupted global supply chains, leading to delays in production, transportation bottlenecks, and shortages of critical inputs. To mitigate these challenges, businesses were often required to prepay suppliers to secure essential materials and ensure continuity of operations. Additionally, firms resorted to holding excess inventory as a strategic response to supply chain uncertainties, thereby increasing their working capital requirements and exposing them to heightened financial pressures.

Solution: These disruptions underscored the fragility of global supply chains and emphasized the necessity for more resilient and adaptive supply chain management practices to address systemic risks during global crises.

CASE STUDY

MANAGING WORKING CAPITAL IN GLOBAL SUPPLY CHAINS

ABC Ltd., a global consumer electronics manufacturer with an annual revenue of approximately $1.9 billion, faces significant challenges in optimizing working capital while managing its complex global supply chain. The company sources raw materials from suppliers in China and South Korea, assembles products in Vietnam and Mexico, and distributes them through warehouses in Europe and the United States. These operations are impacted by variability in payment terms, currency fluctuations, geopolitical risks, rising financing costs, and sustainability pressures.

The company's CFO, Sumita Sharma, has identified key working capital issues. One major challenge is the mismatch between accounts receivable and accounts payable. European buyers request 90-day payment terms, while Asian suppliers demand payment within 30 days, creating a 60-day cash flow gap. To address this, ABC Ltd. could implement a Supply Chain Finance (SCF) program to provide early payments to suppliers while extending its payment terms with financial institutions. Negotiating dynamic discounting with distributors, offering discounts for early payments, could also help accelerate cash inflows. Additionally, standardizing global payment terms may simplify operations but requires careful consideration of its feasibility across regions.

Currency volatility, particularly a weakening euro, has further reduced profit margins on European sales. ABC Ltd. could hedge foreign currency exposure using forward contracts or options, establish multi-currency bank accounts to optimize foreign exchange transactions, and adjust pricing strategies to account for fluctuations. Rising global interest rates have also increased the cost of short-term loans used to finance working capital. Diversifying funding sources through peer-to-peer financing and green bonds, optimizing the cash conversion cycle, and incentivizing early payments from buyers could help mitigate these costs.

Inventory management poses another challenge. Overstocking of smartwatch components tied up approximately $4.8 million, increasing holding costs. Implementing just-in-time (JIT) inventory practices, leveraging AI-powered demand forecasting tools, and collaborating with suppliers for flexible order adjustments can help align inventory with consumer demand. Geopolitical risks, such as U.S.-China trade restrictions, threaten raw material costs and supply chain continuity. Diversifying suppliers, negotiating long-term contracts, and exploring nearshoring strategies could reduce geopolitical exposure while maintaining cost efficiency. Finally, sustainability pressures have necessitated an investment of nearly $9.5 million in renewable energy to meet investor expectations. ABC Ltd. could apply for green financing options, partner with suppliers to share sustainability costs, and quantify the ROI of these initiatives through long-term savings and enhanced brand value. Prioritizing investments that align with both sustainability goals and cash flow stability will be critical.

Sumita's team must develop a comprehensive working capital management strategy that balances short-term liquidity needs with long-term growth objectives. This plan should incorporate tools such as SCF, hedging mechanisms, JIT inventory systems, and green financing, alongside metrics like cash conversion cycles, inventory turnover, and ROI on sustainability investments to measure success and ensure financial stability.

QUESTIONS

1. How should ABC Ltd. structure its Supply Chain Finance (SCF) program to balance the costs of early supplier payments with the benefits of improved cash flow and supplier relationships?
2. What strategies can ABC Ltd. use to mitigate currency volatility risks in its European operations, and should it hedge its full euro exposure or maintain some flexibility?

3. What combination of funding sources should ABC Ltd. use to minimize reliance on short-term loans and reduce the impact of rising financing costs?
4. What inventory management practices and technological tools can ABC Ltd. implement to avoid overstocking and optimize working capital?
5. How should ABC Ltd. prioritize its sustainability investments, such as the $9.5 million renewable energy project, while maintaining cash flow stability and meeting investor expectations?

SUMMARY

- Working capital is concerned with the operational aspect of a firm. Gross working capital is represented by current assets, while net working capital is represented by current assets minus current liabilities.
- The objective of the working capital management is, among other things, to determine the optimal size of the current assets and to determine how current assets should be financed. In the case of international working capital management, a few complexities arise in view of proximity to international financial market, changes in exchange rate, tax rate differentials, etc. and so the objectives are tuned to suit both the individual units and the firm as a whole.
- As far as management of cash is concerned, a firm holds cash for transaction purposes, precautionary purposes, and speculative purposes. In an international firm, holding of cash is greatly influenced by intra-firm cash flows. Such flows are prominent despite exchange control regulations. They are then not direct but through transfer pricing, parallel loans, leads and lags, changes in various remittances and through the use of blocked funds.
- In the process of cash management, the important step is first to assess the need for cash, then to optimise the cash requirements through restructuring of inflows and outflows and through netting of intra-firm payments, and then to find the cheapest source of cash. The surplus cash, if any, is invested normally through a centralised pool and in the currencies where the effective return is the greatest.
- For management of receivables, the finance manager should create receivables only to the extent where marginal cost is equal to the marginal benefit. In the case of intra-firm sales, the size of receivables and timing of payment is not important. It is rather the intra-firm allocation of cash that is important. On the contrary, in the case of inter-firm sales, the currency of invoice and the terms of payments are important.
- As regards inventory management, international firms possess often larger stocks than the principle of EOQ permits. This is due to political risk and the exchange rate risk inherent in the transaction of goods. These firms have also a different re-order point in view of longer lead time.

REVIEW QUESTIONS

Objective-Type Questions

1. State whether true (T) or false (F):
   (a) Leads and lags are the tools to transfer funds among different units of a firm. ☐
   (b) Mailing delay lessens the need for cash. ☐
   (c) Netting increases the transaction cost. ☐
   (d) Investment of surplus cash depends upon a trade-off between liquidity and profitability. ☐
   (e) Effective return from investment of cash includes changes in the exchange rate. ☐
2. Choose the correct answer:
   (a) Stockpiling means:
      (i) size of inventory less than the economic order quantity
      (ii) size of inventory greater than the economic order quantity
      (iii) size of inventory equal to the economic order quantity
   (b) Lead time means:
      (i) time between making of order and arriving of goods at the factory
      (ii) time between arrival of the goods and complete use of the goods
      (iii) none of these
   (c) Centralised cash pool is located in a country where:
      (i) tax rate is very high
      (ii) tax rate is very low
      (iii) political instability is a big problem
   (d) Fronting loan:
      (i) is a parent to affiliate loan channelled through a financial intermediary
      (ii) is an inter-firm loan
      (iii) none of these
   (e) Current assets are financed normally by:
      (i) current liabilities only
      (ii) long-term liabilities only
      (iii) a mix of current and long-term liabilities

Short-Answer Questions

1. Do you agree that intra-firm flow of funds influences the cash holding in a particular unit?
2. Explain parallel loans.
3. Describe the concept of leads and lags.
4. Distinguish between bilateral netting and multilateral netting.
5. Mention the problems related to the process of cash optimisation.
6. Do you justify stockpiling in respect of international inventory management?
7. Name the main factors responsible for greater lead time in international inventory management.

Long-Answer Questions

1. Is international working capital management more complex than the domestic working capital management? Explain.
2. How is cash need assessed? Can it be optimised?
3. What do you mean by cash positioning? Should the surplus cash be centralised?
4. How much and in which currency should surplus cash be invested?
5. What should be the shape of optimal receivables policy?

Numerical Problems

1. Unit A has to pay US $ 20 million to Unit B and $ 15 million to Unit C. Unit B has to pay $ 15 million to Unit A and $ 10 million to Unit C. Unit C has to pay $ 5 million to Unit B and $ 9 million to Unit A. Find out what will be the amount of funds movement after multilateral netting.
2. If order cost is $ 2,000 per order, holding cost is $ 500 per order size, and if total demand is 300 tonnes, what will be the EOQ?
3. If the size of one order is 50 tonnes lasting for 30 days, if lead time is 10 days and two days are the safety level of stock, find out the re-order point.

REFERENCE

Gentry, J.A., et al. (1979), An International Study of Management Perceptions of the Working Capital Process, *Journal of International Business Studies*, X, 28–38.

SUGGESTED FURTHER READING

Soenen, L.A. (1986), International Cash Management: A study of practices of UK-based companies, *Journal of Business Research*, 345–354.

Smith, K.V., (Ed.) (1980), *Readings in the Management of Working Capital*, St. Paul (Minnesota), West Publ.

CHAPTER

22 Financing of Foreign Trade

Learning Objectives

Financing of foreign trade involving primarily short-term funds needs to be discussed in the present part of the book. The chapter proposes:

- To acquaint the readers with major documents used in international trade.
- To explain different modes of payment by the importer.
- To describe different methods of trade financing.
- To pinpoint the role of Export-Import Bank of India in foreign trade financing and allied activities.

After the discussion of working capital management of the multinational corporations, it would be worthwhile to discuss the financing of foreign trade activities. In this context, this chapter acquaints the readers with foreign trade documentation that facilitates trade payments, the modes of payments in foreign trade, and with the methods of foreign trade financing.

FOREIGN TRADE DOCUMENTATION

Objectives of Foreign Trade Documents

The basic objective behind foreign trade documentation is to assure the exporter to get the export proceeds and the importer to get the shipment in order. Since the exporters and importers are located quite at distance, they do not know much about each other. There is every possibility of either non-payment of export proceeds or non-receipt of goods according to specification. But the documents, such as letter of credit, draft, bill of lading, etc. overcome these problems. The exporter is confident about the receipt of export proceeds. The importer too is confident of receiving the goods according to order. All this means that proper documentation helps eliminate the non-completion risk.

Foreign trade documents help exporter to get payments and importer to get the shipment in order.

The foreign trade documents help both the exporter and the importer to hedge the foreign exchange risk in a better way because they assure the amount and the time of payments. In the absence of necessary documents, when the time and amount of the flow of funds are not known with certainty, it becomes difficult to practice any hedging technique.

The foreign trade documents facilitate payments from the importer to the exporter. In fact, they are the media through which payments are made. They are more significant when the importer's creditworthiness is not well known.

Thus, in short, foreign trade documentation is significant in the sense that it eliminates various types of risk the trading firms are exposed to, and at the same time, it facilitates payments. It is still more significant when foreign trade is episodic with no sustained relationship between the exporter and the importer.

Letter of Credit

A letter of credit (L/C) is an instrument signed by the importer's banker, wherein it promises the exporter to make payments if he abides by the conditions mentioned in the L/C, and if the specifications of the export tally with those mentioned in the L/C. It is a letter of promise but not a letter of guarantee of the underlying commercial transaction. The issuing bank receives a fee for issuing it. The document incorporates a specified expiration date and a specified amount of money. The bank's responsibility of making payments arises only after the presentation of specific documents. The importer's obligation to reimburse the bank is based on the same conditions on which the bank has paid the amount.

L/C is an instrument whereby the importer's bank promises the exporter to make payments if the latter abides by the conditions mentioned therein.

This instrument serves the interest of the exporter as well as of the importer. The exporter gets assurance for the payment even if credit risk or political risk is involved in the trade. Similarly, the importer has to make payments only when the goods of the shipment are in good conditions and the terms set in the L/C are met. However, the advantage accruing to the importer must be judged against the fee charged by the bank for issuing L/C. Sometimes the L/C reduces the importer's borrowing line of credit from its bank. This is another factor to be judged while estimating the benefits from the L/C.

How does L/C operate?

When an importer places a purchase order with the exporter, it (importer) requests its own banker to issue an L/C. The banker writes L/C and delivers it to the exporter's bank. The latter confirms it and passes it on to the exporter. The exporter ships the goods and deposits the L/C, draft and other export documents with its banker. The exporter's bank delivers L/C and other documents to the importer's bank. The latter accepts the draft and remits money or export proceeds to the exporter's bank if the contents of the shipment tally with those mentioned in the L/C. The exporter's bank credits the exporter's account. The exporter can get the money even earlier if it discounts the bill under L/C with its bank or when it raises loans on the strength of L/C.

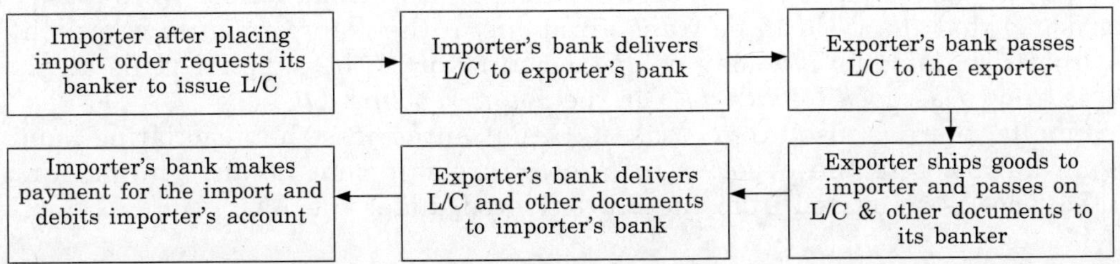

Variants of L/C

There are many variants of L/C. A clean L/C does not require the documents of title to goods or other documents to accompany the bills drawn under the L/C, while a *documentary L/C* does require them. In the case of clean L/C, the exporter sends the documents directly to the importer. After sending the documents, he does not retain control over the goods under transaction. As a result, he may have to face the risk of default. This is why a clean L/C is used only when the importer is highly creditworthy. On the contrary, a documentary L/C is normally used because it minimizes such risk.

Variants of L/C

- Clean and documentary L/C
- Revocable and irrevocable L/C
- Confirmed and unconfirmed L/C
- Fixed and revolving L/C
- Transferable and back-to-back L/C
- Red-clause L/C

Again, an L/C may be *revocable* or it may be *irrevocable*. The former may be cancelled or amended by the issuing bank at any time without prior notice to the beneficiary. An irrevocable one cannot be cancelled or amended. Thus a revocable credit does not provide guarantee for the payment of export proceeds. The exporters prefer naturally an irrevocable L/C.

When an L/C is advised to the exporter through a bank in the exporter's country, the exporter may request another bank to add its (the latter's) confirmation. With the added confirmation, the L/C becomes a *confirmed* one. In the absence of any such confirmation, the L/C remains an *unconfirmed* one. All this means that a confirmed L/C is always an irrevocable L/C because then only any bank dares to confirm it. A confirmed L/C gives an added guarantee of payment of export proceeds.

An L/C may be a *fixed* one or a *revolving* one. The former limits the amount of bill to be drawn under the L/C. On the contrary, under the revolving L/C, the limit of the bill amount is renewed automatically after the amount of the bill is paid. The Indian laws prohibit opening of revolving L/C against import of goods into the country.

Similarly, a *transferable L/C* is one where the exporter has the right to transfer the L/C to third parties. It normally happens when the exporter is simply an intermediary procuring goods from the producers or suppliers and exporting them. Normally, the entire amount involved is transferred. But sometimes, only a reduced amount is transferred as the exporter deducts its own commission. Here it may be mentioned that the L/C can be transferred only if the transfer clause is present in it. Otherwise, another L/C may be opened in favor of the supplier. This ancillary L/C is known as *back-to-back L/C* or the *countervailing L/C*.

Finally, there is also a *red-clause L/C* that authorizes the negotiating bank to extend advances to the exporter in form of pre-shipment credit. The amount of the advance is recovered from the bill tendered under the L/C.

Trade Credit Insurance

Foreign trade is one of most risky venture in business arena, there is always significant threat due to changing economic and political dynamics across borders. To have a booming business across borders there is a need for safe and secure payment system along with the certainty of payments. This problem can be solved through trade credit insurance, which not only solve the problem of importer and exporter rather it facilitates the international financial transactions, overseas loans and international banking system. This insurance product gives assurance to the other party in case of insolvency or default from the part of their client. It covers receivables and provide protection from insolvency of customers, default due to political or economic risks by providing compensations when required.

Key features

- **Domestic and International Coverage:** The trade credit insurance has coverage across borders which means if there is a case of default or risk generated either in domestic country or internationally or in the ocean it is covered by trade credit insurance based on the policy conditions.
- **Protection against Default:** The trade insurance gives coverage against any kind of default by importer whether aroused due to insolvency or domestic risks it is covered under insurance and in case of default the insurance company is liable to pay off losses.
- **Better Creditworthiness:** In case of international business availing credit is a difficult task but if there is a insurance coverage for credit default then banks or other financial institutions tends to give more loans and easy credit because of there low risk of default and risk mitigation tool.
- **Enhance Financing Options:** The insurers sometimes provide credit rating and worthiness monitoring systems, they also track the risk of default for individuals and countries which help the financers to provide loan and thus new avenues for loans can be traced.
- **Customization of Policy:** The insurance policy is customized according to the repaying capacity and creditworthiness of the client along with amount under risk is to be considered.

The coverage of risk

Economic Risks: Under the trade insurance the commercial risks like buyers insolvency and protracted risks are covered too , if the buyers goes insolvent before payment of debt or if the buyer fails to pay before due date then the insurance company is liable to pay in place of debtors. In the extreme if there is a refusal from the buyers side to pay after delivery of goods then also the loss is covered by insurance company.

Political Risks: The change in government regime lead to unfavorable conditions for the exporter which may pose a risk, this can be covered by the insurer. The importing country may go into war with exporting country or any other country which can hamper the trade relations between countries, thus there is a risk of non-payment or default from importers side, this risk can also be covered by the insurance company. Political economic problems or policy crisis like devaluation of currency or change in trade policies may lead to serious risk for the exporting country, this risk can be mitigated by insurance.

Uncertain Natural Calamity: Trading in global arena pose significant risk from catastrophic events and natural calamities like flood or tsunami in oceans lead to significant loss of man and material. These kinds of catastrophic events or calamities can be insured through trade insurance.

Documentary Collection

Documentary collection is one of the most popular type of trade financing tool, which is cheaper than letter of credit but less safe than it. The problem of transfer of documents from exporter to importer is well managed through this mechanism. Under this mechanism the banks act as intermediary in whole process of trade, exporter's bank collect receivables from importer's bank , the importer's bank has access to financial details of importer and based on which they decide how much credit can be given to the importer . The importer's bank transfer amount due to exporter's bank once they receive the required documents based on which the importer can take possession of goods, thus goods are transferred from exporters to importers and accordingly payment is made by bank.

Features of documentary collection

1. **Security of Payment:** The payment of exporter is secured under this mechanism as the payment is made in lieu of documents of export, thus with arrival of goods the payment is made to the exporter later settlement is made between importer and its bank.
2. **Intermediation by Banks:** The banks acts as intermediary in this whole process, where the transaction of amount as well as documents are done by banks of importers and exporter. Involvement of banks increase trust in international transactions, and help in promotion of trade between two parties.
3. **Professional Handling of Documents:** Handling of crucial trade related documents is very important in international trade, mishandling of these documents can lead to severe losses for companies, since these documents are managed by banks, and there profit kept in stake, they handle these documents with care.

Types of documentary collection

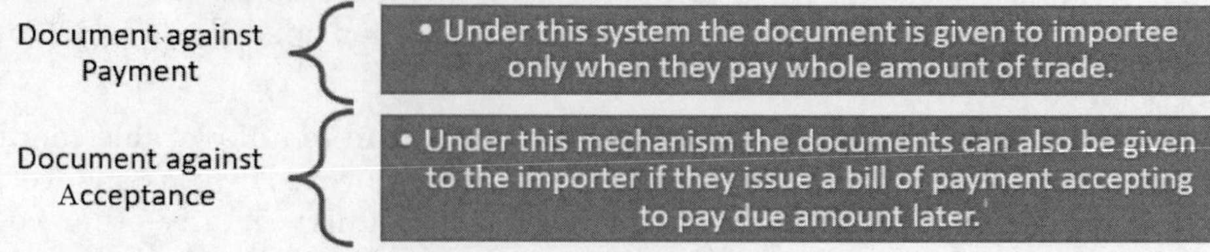

The Process of Documentary Collection

FIGURE 22.1 Process of Documentary Collection

Draft

A draft, also known as the bill of exchange, is an instrument through which an exporter instructs the importer or its agent to pay a specified amount of money at a specified time. In this case, the exporter, who initiates the draft, is known as the maker, originator or drawer. The importer, on the other hand, is known as the drawee. The amount mentioned in the draft may not necessarily be paid to the drawer. Sometimes it is paid to its agent, normally the bank. In this case, the drawer is not the payee, rather the payee is the bank.

> Draft is an instrument whereby an exporter instructs the importer to make payments.

A draft is normally a negotiable instrument if it is properly drawn. Properly drawn draft means that it should

1. be in writing and signed by the drawer;
2. incorporate an unconditional promise or order to pay a specified amount of money;
3. be payable either at sight or at a specified time; and
4. be payable to order or to bearer. (When it is payable to order, the payment is made to the person specified. When it is a bearer one, the amount can be paid to any person presenting the draft.)

Types of draft

When a draft is a *sight* or *demand draft*, payment is made immediately on the presentation of the draft. In case of non-payment, it is treated as dishonour of the draft. On the other hand, a *time draft* is a draft where payment is made after the lapse of a specified time. The specified time is known as *tenor* or *usance*. When a draft is drawn on, and accepted by, a bank, it turns to be a *bankers' acceptance*. Now it is the duty of the bank to honour the draft on maturity. The holder of such a draft, which is normally an exporter in international trade, may enjoy various options. It can hold it till maturity and get the specified amount of money minus the bank's acceptance commission. Alternatively, it can sell it or get it discounted in the money market where it receives immediately the face value of the draft minus the sum of acceptance commission and discount.

> A sight draft necessitates immediate payment on sight. But payment is made after a specified time in a time draft.

Again, draft is classified also as a *clean draft* and a *documentary draft.* In the case of a clean draft, no other document accompanies it. The other documents are sent directly by the exporter to the importer. Clean draft is normally in use in the case of intra-firm trade where the question of trust and credit is not involved. It is used also for non-trade remittances where collection of an outstanding amount is sought. On the contrary, shipping documents are enclosed with the documentary draft. In such cases, these documents are obtained by the importer only after making payments or on acceptance of the draft. In the former, that is, when documents are delivered to the importer only after payment, documentary draft is known as D/P. When it is delivered after the acceptance, the documentary draft is known as D/A.

Bill of Lading

A bill of lading is a shipping document issued by a carrier to the exporter or its banker. It can be treated simultaneously as a receipt, a contract and a document of title. It is a receipt because it shows that the carrier has received certain amount of goods for transportation. It is a contract because the carrier has to deliver the goods to the importer after charging a fee. It is a document of title because it establishes the ownership of goods. All this means that this document ensures payment before the goods are delivered.

> A bill of lading is a shipping document issued by the carrier.

Bill of lading may be *straight.* Also, it may be to *order.* The former stipulates that the carrier shall deliver the goods to the designated consignee but shall not provide it the title to the goods. So it is not a good collateral for loans. However, it is used when the goods have been paid for in advance or when it is an intra-firm transaction.

The order bill of lading, on the other hand, grants title to the goods only to the person to whom the document is addressed. The title of the goods remains with the exporter until payment is made. On payment, the exporter endorses the order bill of lading to the payment-making party which is normally the importer. The endorsed document can be used as a collateral for loans.

Bill of lading may be a *clean bill of lading* or *a foul bill of lading.* The former assumes that the goods have been received by the carrier in good conditions and the carrier is not obliged to check the goods. On the contrary, the foul bill of lading allows the carrier to check the goods.

Additional Documents

Besides the above three important documents, there are other documents too that are used in foreign trade. To mention some of them, the first is the *commercial invoice* incorporating the description of the goods and terms of sale. The second is the *insurance document* that gives the details of the insurance and the risk covered. The third is the *consular invoice* which is issued by the consulate of the importing country and which provides customs information. The fourth is the *packing list* which shows the contents of the container. Finally, there is also *export declaration* which is prepared by the exporter. It helps the government to prepare export statistics.

MODES OF PAYMENT IN INTERNATIONAL TRADE

Modes of payment vary from one transaction to another. What would be the mode in a particular transaction depends upon the bargaining power and creditworthiness of the exporter and importer and upon the requirements of the exchange control. The different modes are:

1. Cash in advance
2. Payment under consignment sale
3. Drafts
4. Letter of credit
5. Open account

The draft and the letter of credit have already been dealt with in the preceding section. Here in this section, the other three will be explained.

Cash in Advance

When cash is paid in advance by the importer to the exporter, that is prior to the shipment of the goods or before the arrival of the goods, the exporter does not need money to finance the receivables. Moreover, this mode negates any risk concerning payment to be borne by the exporter. But it is not a very common mode. It is normally adopted when the importing country is facing political instability, causing obstruction in transfer of funds. It is also common where the goods are specifically designed and manufactured to order from abroad. In India, facilities of advance remittances are allowed in specific cases.

Payment under Consignment Sale

When the goods are shipped by exporter on consignment, the title of the goods remains to lie with the exporter even after the goods are received by the importer. The importer remits money only after it sells the goods. This means that the exporter's capital is tied until goods are finally sold. In such cases, if importer defaults, it is difficult for the exporter to collect money. This is why consignment sale is found normally between related companies. In India, it is more frequently found in the export of traditional goods.

In consignment sale, title of the goods remains with the exporter even after consignee receives the goods.

Open Account

Open account is concerned with the credit sales when the importer makes payment on a pre-determined future date. The exporter ships the goods directly to the importer. The latter takes the delivery of the goods without making any payment. In this case, the entire risk is borne by the exporter; and so, it extends credit terms only to creditworthy importers. Experience shows that one or two per cent of the export proceeds turns out as bad debt loss. In such cases, the exporter hires an attorney or it avails of the services of a collection agency. In both the cases, cost is involved.

Open account is concerned with credit sales to the importer on a continuous basis.

METHODS OF TRADE FINANCING

Trade deals require finance. Availability of finance enables the exporter to export more and the importers to import more. In other words, availability of finance encourages trading activities. Here we discuss how the traders get finance from banks and other sources.

Bank Credit

Banks are the most important source of foreign trade finances. The importers do borrow from the banks, but the exporters are the major beneficiary. The different forms of credit are:

1. Pre-shipment credit
2. Post-shipment credit
3. Medium-term credit
4. Credit under duty draw-back scheme

Pre-shipment credit

Pre-shipment credit provided to the exporters is meant for procuring raw material, processing and packing of goods and for some other processes till the goods are really shipped. This type of credit is also known as *packing credit*. It is extended normally on the strength of letter of credit but sometimes also on the strength of purchase order. It is extended in the form of a loan amount. A separate account is maintained for each export order. Alternatively, it may be a running account, that is, a single cash credit account for all export orders. Inputs purchased out of such credits are hypothecated or pledged to the bank, although in exceptional cases, it may be a clean advance. The credit is extended not in a lump-sum amount but in stages, depending upon the need of the exporter.

> Pre-shipment credit is provided to the exporter for buying raw material, processing and packaging.

It is a short-term credit, normally not exceeding 180 days, but it can exceed up to 270 days in exceptional cases. If it exceeds 180 days, interest rate goes higher. Sometimes credit is partly given to the supplier and partly to the exporter if the supplier and the exporter are two different persons. But in this case, the period of 180 days does not exceed, rather it is divided between the two, say 90 days for the supplier and the remaining 90 days for the exporter.

As regards the size of the credit, it does not exceed the FOB price or the domestic cost of production, whichever is less. The bank may maintain a margin, depending upon the credit rating of the exporter or upon the nature of goods to be exported. In exceptional cases, it is more than the FOB price when the local cost of production is very high and the commodity is eligible for incentives from the government.

The packing credit is repaid out of export proceeds or partly out of export incentives like duty draw-back. If export does not materialise due to factors lying beyond the control of the exporter, the amount of the credit is adjusted with the proceeds of the subsequent export.

Pre-shipment credit is also provided in the form of foreign currency. The purpose is to finance the import of inputs for goods to be exported. In India, it is provided to the exporters having a turnover of ₹ 100 million and above and to those manufacturers whose 25 per cent of the output is committed for export. The amount of the credit is repaid out of export proceeds.

Interest Rates on Rupee Export Credits

Earlier, banks were charging interest rate not exceeding BPLR minus 2.5 percentage points on rupee pre-shipment credit up to 270 days and post-shipment credit up to 180 days. But now they charge interest rate not exceeding BPLR minus 4.5 percentage points on pre-shipment credit up to 270 days and post-shipment credit up to 180 days on the outstanding amount for the period April 1, 2010 to March 31, 2011 to specified sectors. However, the total subvention will be subject to the condition that the interest rate, after subvention, will not fall below 7 per cent, which is the rate applicable to the agriculture sector under priority sector lending. The banks may ensure that the benefit of the 2 per cent interest subvention is passed on completely to the eligible exporters.

Source: Based on RBI notification, April 23, 2010.

Post-shipment credit

Post-shipment credit is extended by the banks after the goods have been shipped and against the submission of export documents evidencing the shipment of the goods. It is also a short-term credit. The rate of interest is lower up to 90 days, but then it increases and it is still higher beyond 180 days. The purpose of progressive interest rate is to make this credit strictly a short-term one.

Post-shipment credits are extended after goods are shipped to the importer.

There are different ways to extend post-shipment credit. When bill is drawn not under L/C, that is when transaction is not covered by L/C, credit is available through the purchase of export documents. The bank takes special precaution before granting credit in such cases. It is because there is no guarantee for payment. If the importer refuses to pay and if the financial position of the exporter is not sound for the repayment of credit, the bank is put to loss. Even if it redirects the ship, it has to bear the additional freight and insurance charges. This is why the bank examines thoroughly the financial ratios of the importer and obtains a cover from an insurance company before extending such credits.

When bill is drawn under L/C, there is guarantee for payment. However, the bank examines whether the documents are exactly in tune with the terms and conditions mentioned in the L/C. When the bank is satisfied, it negotiates the document and extends credit to the exporter. The negotiating bank sends the documents and the bill for collection. There are sometimes cases when the export documents do not comply with the norms set in the L/C. In this case too, the bank extends credit but only to the creditworthy clients.

When the goods are exported on a consignment basis, it does not mean at all that the goods have been sold and the export proceeds will definitely be received. In such cases too, the bank provides credit but maintains a sufficient margin.

The bank extends post-shipment credit also in the case of deemed export or supplies made to international bodies. Since January 1992, the banks in India have been extending post-shipment credit also in foreign currency. The procedure is that the Indian exporter is paid in Indian rupees, but the liability of the exporter is denominated in US dollar. This way the exporters enjoy the benefits of low interest rate prevalent in the international financial market that normally conforms to LIBOR.

Medium-term credit

There are certain categories of export, such as engineering items, capital goods and project export, in case of which short-term finance does not meet the desired objective. It is because the importers normally withhold a part of the cost of goods/services towards guarantee of performance. Such withholding generally crosses the six-month mark and so the short-term finance is hardly of any use in these cases. It thus necessitates medium-term credit.

> Suppliers' credit involves payment by the importer to the exporter in instalments. Bank lends to the exporter meeting its working capital need.

Medium-term loans/credits may be *external commercial borrowing* (*ECB*) if the maturity exceeds three years. But with a maturity of three years or less, the credits are either suppliers' credit or they may be buyers' credit. For *suppliers' credit*, the exporter provides deferred-payment terms to the importer. This means that the importer makes payment for the import in instalments. And to meet the working capital requirements on account of deferred payment, the exporter borrows from the bank. The suppliers' credit is provided by the bank either at the pre-shipment stage or at the post-shipment stage, or at both the stages.

Besides extending credit to the exporter, the bank executes a performance guarantee on behalf of the exporter. The exporter too gives an undertaking to the bank to repay the debt. But this undertaking has no concern with the amount the importer has to pay to the exporter. Thus in such a situation, if the importer refuses to pay, the exporter will have to face the credit risk. Again, the bank lends to the exporter in local currency, while the exporter gets the export proceeds in foreign currency. This means that the exporter may have to face the risk on account of changes in exchange rate. Fortunately, in India, Export Credit and Guarantee Corporation covers the exchange risk.

> Buyers' credit involves importer making full payment to the exporter immediately and getting deferred-payment facilities from the exporter's bank.

In the case of *buyers' credit*, the exporter gets the export proceeds immediately, but the buyer or importer gets the deferred-term facilities from the exporter's bank. In other words, the importer makes the payment for import out of its borrowing from the exporter's bank. The bank's credit is repaid in instalments. The buyers' credit is extended both at pre-shipment and the post-shipment stages. At the pre-shipment stage, such credit normally takes the form of opening of red-clause L/C by the importer authorising the exporter's bank to extend pre-shipment finance. At the post-shipment stage, credit extended by the exporter's bank is used by the importer for making payment for import. However, in such cases, the importer's bank guarantees the repayment of loan by the importer.

Buyers' credit is different from the suppliers' credit. In the former, it is not the exporter but the exporter's bank that has to face the credit risk if the importer refuses to pay. In India, the banks need taking permission from the Reserve Bank of India if they like to extend buyers' credit to the importers abroad.

Guidelines for trade credits

Banks can approve trade credit up to US $ 20 million of imports. No roll-over is allowed beyond the permissible period. The interest rate would be LIBOR + 50 basis points for credits with a maturity up to one year. But for a maturity exceeding one year but less than three years, the interest rate would be LIBOR + 125 b.p. The banks can issue guarantee/letter of undertaking or letters of comfort in favour of overseas supplier, bank and the supplier up to US $ 20 million. The Government has issued certain guidelines in this respect.

Advances under duty drawback scheme

The duty drawback scheme provides that the duty paid by the exporter on the imported inputs or the excise duty paid on the goods produced for export are repaid to the exporter on the completion of the export. Since the exporter's cash is locked up during the period between the payment of duty and the completion of export, the exporter is given a cash advance by the banks for this period. Such an advance is given both at the pre-shipment stage and the post-shipment stage. At the pre-shipment stage, it is represented by additional amount of credit over and above the FOB value of the goods. It is because the credit up to the FOB value is purely the pre-shipment or packing credit. If the bank grants additional amount over and above the FOB value, it is nothing but an advance against the duty drawback. At the post-shipment stage, it is extended by the bank when an exporter makes a claim with the bank.

> Import duty paid by the importer/ excise duty paid by the exporter is repaid under duty drawback scheme.

The period of such advance is three months. It is the exporter's bank that gets the duty drawback from the government on behalf of the exporter. When it gets the amount, it adjusts the advance with this amount. There is no interest charged on such an advance.

Factoring

The exporter receives the payment normally after a number of days of the shipment. During this period, its export is treated as account receivables. Again, there is possibility of bad debt loss involved in the transaction. Thus, in order to avoid the bad debt loss, to avoid the collection expenses and to get immediate payment for export, the exporter sells its receivables without recourse to a bank. The process of the sale of receivables is known as *factoring*. Now it is the bank that has to collect the amount from the importer.

> Factoring is the sale of receivables to a bank by the exporter in order to shift the credit risk to the bank.

Since the bank has to bear the risk of non-payment, and at the same time, it has to pay the collection charges, it usually purchases the receivables at discount and receives a flat processing fee. It purchases only those receivables where the importer is found creditworthy. There is a network of factors in different countries, which helps in assessment of credit risk. Suppose a bank in India likes to buy receivables from an Indian exporter, it will assess the credit risk either with the help of the correspondent factor residing in the importer's country or through its own subsidiary, if residing in that country.

Forfaiting

Forfaiting is a non-recourse financing originated in Switzerland during 1950s. In the beginning, it was used largely in case of trade with the east European countries, but it is now commonly used throughout the globe.

Forfaiting is similar as factoring in the sense that it is the forfaiting agency, and not the exporter, that bears the credit risk. But in many respects, forfaiting is different. Forfaiting is done usually in large and long-term transactions. When the exporter exports capital goods, the amount involved is normally big and as a result of which the importer takes a longer time to repay. What happens is that the importer writes a promissory note to the exporter for a period ranging usually from three to seven years and the exporter sells that promissory note without recourse to the bank. This sale of promissory note is known as *forfaiting*.

Forfaiting is similar as factoring but related to long-term transactions extending normally to 3–7 years.

The buyer of the promissory note is known as *forfaiteur* which is normally the exporter's bank. The seller, who is the exporter, is known as *forfaitiste*. Since it is a non-recourse financing process, the forfaiteur cannot go to the exporter for money in case the importer fails to pay the amount.

The forfaiting transaction is normally covered by a guarantee from the importer's bank or by L/C issued by the importer's bank. This minimises the credit risk and helps the forfaiting agencies to forfait. Again, when the amount involved is quite large, a syndicate of forfaiting agencies buys the promissory note.

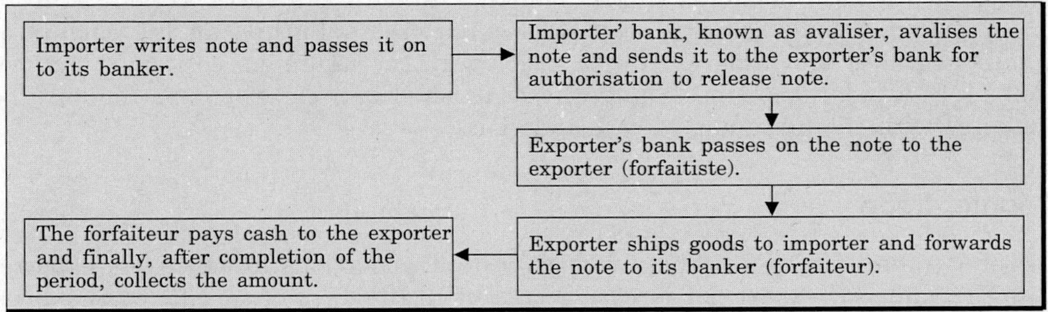

Forfaiting facilities are available to an exporter for a single shipment or for a series of shipment. But the rate of discount varies from one shipment to another depending upon the risk involved. The risk in turn depends upon the credit period, distance of the shipment, nature of trade and contractual terms, political and economic conditions prevailing in the importing country, etc.

Forfaiting is advantageous insofar as it helps quick funding without too much of documentation. Again, it is a good financing method for small and medium-size firms inasmuch as the transaction risk does not influence the balance sheet. It helps encourage trade as the credit terms are more attractive. But the problem is that the interest rate built into the discount rate is often very high. Moreover, the resolution of litigation is often difficult in view of varying rules in different countries.

In India, the sole agency for forfaiting has been the Export-Import (Exim) Bank of India, although since the announcement of the monetary policy in October 1997, banks are allowed to do forfaiting. The Exim Bank collaborates with foreign forfaiting agencies while doing this business. At the maturity, the bill is collected through the foreign forfaiting agency.

Forfaiting verses L/C

Whereas in the case of forfaiting, the exporter obtains the forfaiting commitment from a bank in its own country as a way of offering credit terms to the importer, an L/C involves the issue of documentary credit by a bank in the importer's country as a means of providing an assured payment to the exporter. Documentary credit provides in some cases short-term credit facilities, while forfaiting provides normally medium-term credit to the importer and, at the same time, gives the importer an assurance for payment through the forfaiting bank's commitment to negotiate without recourse. Again, while an L/C is available for acceptance or deferred payment, forfaiting involves commitment from a reliable forfaiting house to discount the L/C proceeds.

Although forfaiting is adopted in many cases in India, L/C is more popular. The reasons are that, first, while L/C is ubiquitous and indigenous, forfaiting is used primarily by big exporters. It is because the minimum transaction amount by foreign banks offering forfaiting services is too high for an Indian exporter, often one million US dollar. Secondly, an L/C possesses an advantage of irrevocability, transferability, assignment, negotiation and confirmation. Thirdly, post-shipment finance in the case of L/C is easier. Fourthly, an L/C can serve as collateral for pre-shipment finance, generally called packing credit. Fifthly, an L/C facilitates credit insurance providing maximum cover with the minimum cost. Last but not least, L/C stipulations can be mutually contracted between the exporter and the importer with the minimum of cost and risk.

Counter-trade

Counter-trade is related to those foreign trade transactions in which the exporter gets the value for export not in cash form but in the form of specific commodities as per an agreement concluded between the two trading parties. In other words, one can say that under the counter-trade mechanism, imports are financed through exports.

> Counter-trade is a bilateral barter not involving any immediate cash for import.

Counter-trade is commonly known as *barter*, *parallel trade*, *counter-purchase*, *buy-back*, etc. However, their details differ to some extent. Broadly speaking, the above-mentioned variants can be grouped as:

1. Counter-trade of purely commercial nature
   (a) Classical barter
   (b) Counter-purchase
   (c) Pre-compensation
2. Industrial counter-trade
   (a) Buy-back agreement
   (b) Framework agreement

Classical barter is a simple barter and involves a once-only exchange of goods on the terms agreed upon between the buyer and the seller. The quantum, quality and the value of the goods to be exchanged are well-defined. Consequently, trade flow in one direction is fully compensated by the flow in the reverse direction. The exchange of Jamaican bauxite for US powdered milk, the exchange of Iranian oil for New Zealand's lamb are some of the examples of classical barter (Banks, 1983).

In *counter-purchase*, which is also known as *parallel barter*, there is no mention of specific goods to be exported or to be imported. Moreover, there are separate contracts for export and import. The only thing required is to balance the trade during a period of three to five years. If any gap between export value and import value remains to exist, it is met by cash payment.

In the case of *pre-compensation*, imports are paid for immediately. The amount to be paid is entered into an evidence account and it is balanced completely by the export of specific goods. If any amount remains left after balancing, it is paid in cash.

Buy-back agreements do not represent purely commercial transactions. Being a form of industrial counter-trade, they involve normally a larger amount corresponding to the sale of industrial equipment or turn-key plants in exchange for the products manufactured by the industrial plant. The contract period is larger ranging sometimes up to 20 years. An example of this type of counter-trade could be found in Austria's sale of oil pipeline equipment and related material to the former Soviet Union in exchange for piping oil back to Austria (UNECE, 1979).

For *framework agreements*, there is a long-term bilateral clearing agreement, normally between two governments. The nature and prices of goods and the timing of shipment are decided upon in the beginning. The contract period is renewed from time to time. The difference between the export and import at the end of the contract period is paid in cash. A classic example of this type of counter-trade was found in the case of Malaysia-Mexico trade. When Malaysia had a trade surplus, Mexico sold cocoa in the United States and paid Malaysia in dollars (*Far Eastern Economic Review*, 1983).

Counter-trade is nothing new. East European countries practised it for a long time. In other regions too, it was practised occasionally and in a few cases. It is estimated that counter-trade accounts for five to six per cent of the world trade (Miramon, 1985; Banks, 1983; Yoffie, 1984). However, the percentage varies widely among different regions of the world.

Counter-trading by Indian Firms

Bharat Heavy Electricals Ltd. being India's largest power generation equipment manufacturer, along with State-owned mineral trading company, MMTC Ltd. underwent a counter-trade arrangement for importing palm oil from Malaysia worth one billion US dollar in exchange for setting up of a hydropower project there. MMTC had a similar arrangement along with State-owned Ircon International Ltd., where Ircon set up a railway line in Malaysia and MMTC got palm oil.

Source: Based on reports of Mint, May 11, 2010.

There are some problems with the counter-trade. For instance, it is opposed to the multilateral trading system. The stronger trading partner mars the interest of the weak trading partner, grabbing a lion's share of gains from trade. Lack of double coincidence as well as price rigidity is found. The settlement of trade is often difficult. Micro-level settlement is often more difficult than the macro-level settlement. Nevertheless, there are some justifications for the counter-trade. The developing countries that usually suffer from trade deficit on account of price differences, world recession, tariff and non-tariff barriers, take resort to counter-trade. Counter-trade resolves the problem of instability in export earnings and helps the developing countries in chalking out a sustained and stable development plan. Settlement of the trade accounts is done after a gap of long time; and so, the countries can import even larger amount of goods without making necessary payments.

EXPORT-IMPORT BANK OF INDIA

Any discussion on the financing of foreign trade in India cannot be made in isolation of the Export-Import (Exim) Bank of India. This is so because it is the apex body in the country for the provision of direct finance or for refinance facilities for encouraging foreign trade. There are also other important functions of this body, such as making guarantee, and promotional and advisory activities.

The Exim Bank is a public sector financial institution established in January 1982 by an Act of Parliament. Its funds for operation come from different sources, viz. share capital, loan from the Government and from the Reserve Bank of India, loan from foreign sources, public deposits and funds from capital market. It provides funds to Indian companies engaged in foreign trade, to foreign governments and foreign companies and to Indian banks in the form of refinancing credits.

Main Functions

The Bank supports financially the domestic entities, the overseas entities, and the commercial banks. However, its functions are not limited to financing. They incorporate advisory and promotional contents too. To the *Indian entities*, it provides suppliers' credit, pre-shipment, post-shipment and medium-term credits, export marketing finance, export vendor development finance, funds to finance rupee expenditure in relation to project export contracts, consultancy and technology services, and deemed export. The importers get import lines of credit and bulk import finance. The Bank provides equity finance for joint ventures, underwrites the issues and does forfaiting.

To the foreign entities, the Bank provides credit for import that includes mainly the buyers' credit.

To the commercial banks in India, it provides refinancing facilities in relation to various types of credits meant for the exporters and importers. It rediscounts the export bills and confirms L/C.

Performance

The Exim Bank has performed well from the very beginning. Here we focus on its performance, highlighting broadly three areas: approval of export bids, loans, and guarantees.

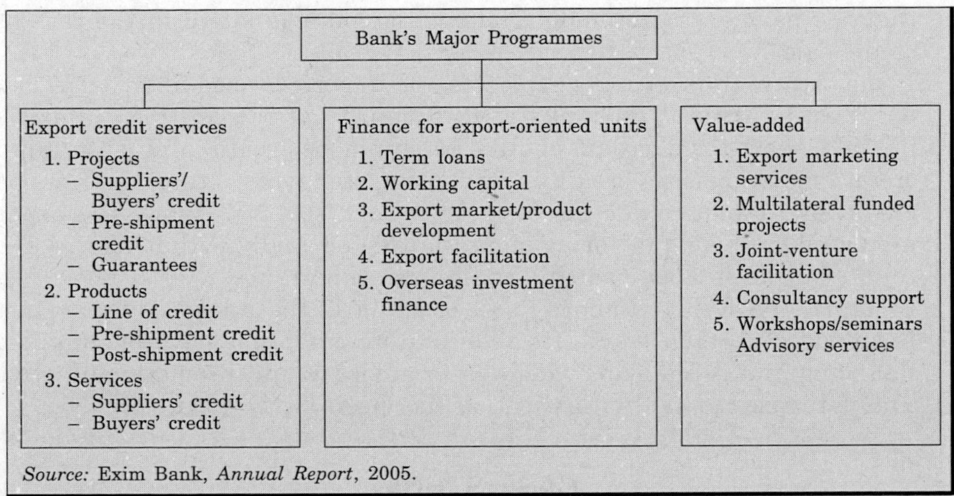

Source: Exim Bank, *Annual Report*, 2005.

TABLE 22.1 Performance of Export-Import Bank of India

(Amount ₹ billion)

Activities	*1990–91*	*2000–01*	*2009–10*	*2023–24*
Loans				
Sanction	10.4	21.7	388.430	980.14
Disbursements	8.6	19.0	332.485	436.95
Outstanding	13.1	56.4	390.357	543.19
Guarantees				
Sanction	1.1	2.1	13.580	90.1372
Issued	0.3	1.7	3.875	22.5314*
Outstanding	6.1	10.7	22.736	67.6058*

Source: Export-Import Bank of India, *Annual Report*, various issues. (* approximate value)

The performance has been commendable. The Bank sanctioned loans worth ₹ 10.4 billion in FY 1990–91, the amount of which shot up to ₹ 21.7 billion in FY 2000–01 and to ₹ 388.430 billion in FY 2009–10. The disbursements rate was very high in these years showing a very high rate of efficiency. The Bank provided guarantees too, the amount of which surged up from ₹ 1.1 billion to ₹ 2.1 billion and to ₹ 13.6 billion during the respective years.

SUMMARY

- Foreign trade documentation helps in minimising non-completion risk and exchange rate risk as well as facilitates payment. The major documents are letter of credit, draft and bill of lading supplemented by some additional documents.
- Payments in international trade are made through different modes. In some cases, payment is made in advance. But normally, it is made through draft under the very framework of the terms of the letter of credit. In the case of consignment sale, it is only after the sale of the goods by the importer

that the payments are made. The open account is found in the case of the credit sales.

- In majority of the cases, the exporters and importers need financial assistance for effecting trade. The banks have a significant role in this context. They provide short-term credit—both pre-shipment credit and post-shipment credit, medium-term credit in the form of buyers' credit and suppliers' credit, and credit under the duty draw-back scheme. Again, the exporters are found practising factoring and forfaiting normally with banks. Moreover, counter-trade is also a means to finance import.
- In India, the Export-Import Bank of India is the apex body in respect of financing of foreign trade. Its role is quite comprehensive beginning from financing and refinancing facilities to advisory and promotional activities. The performance of this institution has been fairly good.

CASE STUDY

FORFAITING AGREEMENT BETWEEN GHANA COMMERCIAL BANK AND VIKAS INTERNATIONAL

Vikas International has been engaged in export-import business for the last 10 years. The company exports spare parts of cars, scooters, cycles to African countries. The company's export turnover has been to the tune of USD 50 million for the last 3 years.

The company enjoys export credit limits with their bankers but the limits have been fully utilised. Meanwhile the company won a contract to supply car spare parts to Ghana. Export order is valued at US $ 2,00,000 involving credit period of one year from the date of shipment. The company was able to buy the material on credit due to their good reputation, therefore, no need of packing credit loan was felt by the exporter.

Since their export credit limits were fully utilised and the banker was not keen on exposure to Ghana, the company contacted Forfaiter and obtained the following quote from the Forfaiter based upon the underlying trade:

Invoice	:	US $ 2,00,000
Purpose	:	Export of car spare parts to Ghana
Shipments	:	Single in July 2023
Commitment date	:	20th June 2023
Credit period	:	One year from the date of shipment in two semi-annual instalments
Availability	:	Latest by 20th September 2023
Evidenced by	:	Avalised Promissory Notes
Avalising bank	:	Ghana Commercial Bank, Ghana
Documentation Required	:	Promissory Notes duly avalised by Ghana Commercial Bank, Ghana including confirmation of payment without deductions at maturity
	:	Certified true copy of invoice
	:	Certified true copy of Bills of lading

Indication Rate

Rate	:	Average life US $ LIBOR + 5% p.a. DTY, 365/360 basis semi-annually compounded
Grace period	:	5 days
Commitment fee	:	3 per cent p.a. from the date of commitment till drawn

The company makes shipment on 20th July 2023 and documents presented for discounting on 20th August 20023.

The forfaiter has sent the Note giving basis of pricing as under

Currency	:	US Dollar
Bill rate	:	US $ 2,00,000
Number of bills	:	Two Bills
Method of interest calculation	:	365/360 days
Commitment date	:	20th June 2023
Interest date/shipment date	:	20th July 2023
Notes available on	:	20th August 2023
Commit fee	:	3% p.a.
Grace period	:	5 days
Discount rate	:	LIBOR + 5% p.a. = 8% p.a.

The method of pricing for arriving at net proceeds given as under:

Bill no.	*Maturity date*	*Principal (US $)*	*Discount (US $)*	*Net value of proceeds*
1.	20.01.2024	1,00,000	3,392.02	96,607.98
2.	20.07.2024	2,00,000	7,147.28	92,852.72
		2,00,000	**10,539.30**	**1,89,460.70**

Net value of bills forfaited	:	US $ 1,89,460.70
Less commitment fee (61 days)	:	US $ 1,016.64
Net proceeds	:	US $ 1,88,444.06

The company received cheque USD 188,444.06 through their bankers from the forfaiter.

QUESTIONS

1. Why the company opted for forfaiting instead of pursuing with their bankers for Bill Discounting?
2. What are the merits and demerits of forfaiting?
3. What is Aval and what is the role of Avalising Bank?
4. Should Vikas International obtain ECGC cover?

REVIEW QUESTIONS

Objective-Type Questions

1. State whether true (T) or false (F):
   (a) Classical barter involves a once-only exchange of goods on the terms agreed upon between buyer and seller. ☐
   (b) Counter-purchase involves separate contracts for export and import. ☐
   (c) Buy-back agreements represent purely commercial transactions. ☐
   (d) Interest is charged on the advances under the duty drawback scheme. ☐
   (e) Post-shipment credit is a medium-term credit. ☐
2. Choose the correct answer:
   (a) Pre-shipment credit is meant for:
      (i) short-term
      (ii) medium-term
      (iii) long-term
   (b) Under consignment sales title of the goods lies:
      (i) with the exporter
      (ii) with the importer
      (iii) neither with the importer nor with the exporter
   (c) Foul bill of lading:
      (i) assumes that goods have been received in order
      (ii) permits the carrier to check the goods
      (iii) none of these
   (d) Framework agreements involve:
      (i) long-term bilateral clearing agreements between the two trading governments
      (ii) immediate payments for imports
      (iii) none of these

Short-Answer Questions

1. Describe any three objectives of foreign trade documentation.
2. What is L/C? Is it useful for the traders?
3. What are the characteristics of a properly drawn draft?
4. Distinguish between factoring and forfaiting.
5. Distinguish between straight bill of lading and order bill of lading.

Long-Answer Questions

1. What are the different variants of L/C? How does an L/C operate?
2. Who are the drawer and the drawee of a draft in international trade? Distinguish between demand draft and time draft and between clean draft and documentary draft.
3. Explain the different modes of payment in international trade.

4. Explain different types of credit meant for financing foreign trade.
5. What is counter-trade? What are its different forms?
6. What are the functions of the Export-Import Bank of India? Comment on its performance.
7. Distinguish between buyer's credit and supplier's credit.

REFERENCES

Banks, G. (1983), The Economics and Politics of Counter-trade, *The World Economy*, VI, 159–182.

Far Eastern Economic Review (1983), 27th Jan.

Miramon, Jacques de (1985), Counter-trade: An illusory solution, *The OECD Observer*, May, pp. 24–25.

United Nations Economic Commission for Europe (1979), *Counter-trade Practices in the ECE Region*, Geneva, Trade R. 385, p. 22.

Yoffie, D. (1984), Barter: Looking beyond the short-term pay-offs and long-term threat, *International Management*, August, p. 36.

SUGGESTED FURTHER READING

Citibank (1991), *An Introduction to Letters of Credit*, New York. Export-Import Bank of India, *Annual Report*, latest issue.

Korth, C., (Ed.) (1985), *International Counter-trade*, New York: Quorum.

Rentzmann, W.F. and T. Teichman (1975), Forfaiting: An alternative technique of export financing, *Euromoney*, December.

PART 7

Miscellaneous Issues

CHAPTER 23

International Accounting

Learning Objectives

International financial accounting is a part of IFM. So the present chapter discusses some more common aspects of it. The objective is:

- To acquaint the readers with very concept of international accounting and the factors making it more significant.
- To discuss how the parent unit consolidates the financial statements of the subsidiaries in order to know the global profit/financial position.
- To explain how functional currency is translated into the reporting currency.
- To explain how inflationary trends are accounted for.
- To show how financial statements of different units are analysed.
- To discuss the concept of transfer pricing and how transfer prices are set.
- To narrate the motivations behind adopting transfer pricing.
- To explain the benefits and costs and also regulation of transfer pricing.

GLOBALISATION OF THE CONCEPT OF ACCOUNTING

The Motivating Factors

There was a time when the principles of accounting were being practised for domestic operation of the firms. But with growing globalisation, that is, with increasing linkages among different countries, the principles of accounting attained international dimensions. There are three major factors that have led to the emergence of international accounting:

1. Growth in international trade
2. Growth in the activities of multinational corporations
3. Expansion in international financial market

Growing international trade has caused multiplicity of international payments in terms of their number, size and pattern. When there was fixed parity system of exchange rate, the problem was not very complex. The exporters and importers knew in advance how much payments were to be effected. But with floating exchange-rate regime since mid-1970s, the problem has become complex as volatility in exchange rate is a usual phenomenon. All this requires a more complex accounting technique on the global level.

Again, it is the phenomenal growth of multinationals that has given accounting an international dimension. These firms are one of the best tools for an efficient resource allocation among different countries. The parent company tries to evaluate its overall performance; and to this end, it prepares a consolidated financial statement. Intermediate goods flow from one unit to another, which require specific pricing for the maximisation of overall profitability or the maximisation of net aggregate output. All this cannot be done in the absence of international accounting. Even if centralised control is not given importance, the parent company tries to evaluate the performance of the affiliates so as to be sure whether its involvement in a foreign country is viable or not. In this context, the national accounting system of the host country has greater say, but at the same time, evaluation remains an integral part of international accounting.

Yet again, sizeable expansion of international financial market has added to the importance of international accounting. Emergence of international financial activities at some of the national financial centres and Euro markets has led to the necessity of a comparable and reliable market information regarding variables prevalent in different markets. Moreover, it requires proper accounting of the flow of funds from one market to another or from lender to borrower. The procedures of accounting in this respect automatically become international.

Dimensions

International accounting refers to:
1. Accounting principle and practices followed in different countries;
2. Harmonisation among varying accounting practices; and
3. Accounting principles for evaluating parent-subsidiary financial relationship.

The concept of international accounting is interpreted in different ways that broaden its coverage. *First*, international accounting refers to the principles and practices of accounting followed in different countries. The studies reveal that there is wide diversity in accounting principles and procedures among different countries. The study is not feasible within the limited space of the present chapter, although passing references will be made wherever necessary.

Secondly, international accounting refers to the harmonisation between varying accounting practices prevalent in different countries. This means that a globally accepted set of accounting principles should develop so that the hurdles coming in the way of international transactions on account of varying accounting practices are eliminated and international accounting linkages get stronger. In many cases, international norms have evolved over a period of time. The European Union has issued directives and framed regulations for intra-Union payment accounting. In January 1990, a conference was held in Brussels on the future of harmonisation of accounting standards in the European Union. The United Nations Commission on Trans-national Corporations has done at least something about accounting standards and disclosures of financial information. But still, there is a long way to go, particularly in view of various impediments to standardisation, such as different legal systems, lack of strong professional accounting bodies, and the varying objectives of financial reporting.

Thirdly, international accounting embraces the principles of accounting that are practised for studying and evaluating the financial relationship between a parent company and a subsidiary company or between two or more subsidiaries of a single multinational firm. This is really a more important aspect of international accounting that will be discussed in the present chapter at some length. Our focus will be on how:

- a parent company consolidates the financial statements of subsidiaries with those of its own;
- the figures of financial statements shown in different currencies are translated into those of the home-country currency;
- the inflation factor is taken into account and, more importantly;
- the transfer pricing is practised for maximising profitability or net aggregate output.

CONSOLIDATION OF FINANCIAL STATEMENTS

If a firm sets up its network abroad through opening up of subsidiaries, it will like to evaluate its overall performance. It is done through combining the financial statements of the subsidiaries along with its own. The process of combining of financial statements is known as *consolidation*.

Techniques of Consolidation

There are two ways for consolidating financial statements. One is known as *gross consolidation*. The other is known as *net consolidation*. Under the process of gross consolidation, all the assets and liabilities of the subsidiary are added to the respective values of the balance sheet of the parent company irrespective of the share of the parent company in the equity of the subsidiary. However, the value of the minority interest is shown on the liabilities side of the consolidated balance sheet. Suppose the minority interest accounts for 20 per cent of the subsidiary's equity which amounts to $ 80,000. The minority interest, which is $ 16,000 in this case, will be entered on the liabilities side of the consolidated balance sheet. The minority interest in reserves will be indicated similarly on the liabilities side. The entire profit of the subsidiary is added to the profit of the parent company, but the profit accruing to the minority interest is identified and adjusted against the consolidated profit.

> Gross consolidation refers to adding up of liabilities and assets of various units and then making adjustment for the minority interest. Net consolidation involves adding up of only the net figures excluding the minority interest from the very beginning.

Procedure of Consolidation of Financial Statements: Some Provisions of Accounting Standard 21

For a consolidated financial statement, it is necessary that the financial statements of the parent and the subsidiaries are combined on a line-to-line basis by adding together the items of liabilities, assets, income and expenses. In this process:

1. The cost to the parent of its investment in each subsidiary and the parent's position of equity of each subsidiary should be eliminated.
2. Any excess of such costs over the parent's portion of equity in subsidiary is known as *goodwill* and is recognised as an asset in the consolidated statement.
3. If such costs are less than the parent's portion of equity in the subsidiary, the difference is regarded as capital reserve in the consolidated statement.
4. Minority interest in the net assets of the consolidated subsidiaries is presented in the consolidated balance sheet separately from the liabilities and equity of the parent's shareholders.
5. Unrealised profit/loss resulting from intra-group transactions is eliminated.
6. If subsidiaries' statements have different reporting dates, necessary adjustments are made to bring them in line with the parent's one.
7. If a subsidiary has outstanding cumulative preference shares held outside the group, the parent computes its share of profit/loss after making adjustments for the subsidiary's preference dividends, whether or not dividend has been declared.

Under the net consolidation method, the long procedure of adding up of the whole of the subsidiary's value and then making adjustments for the minority interest is avoided. Instead, the net figures, which depend upon the parent company's share in the subsidiary's equity, are added. This means that the minority interest is excluded from the very beginning.

Whatever may be the method of consolidation of financial statements, the profits of intra-firm transactions are excluded. If it is not done, the profits will remain overstated. Again, if the entire amount of intermediate goods supplied by the parent company to the subsidiary is sold by the latter, there is no accounting problem. But if only a part of it is sold, proportionate share of intra-firm profit is eliminated.

One problem that often arises in this context is when the date of financial year closing differs between the parent and the subsidiary, the span of the period is taken into account and adjustments are made for significant transactions that occur between the two reporting dates.

A simple example will illustrate how consolidation is done. Suppose a parent company has 80 per cent share in the equity capital of the subsidiary. At the year-end, the balance sheet items of the parent and the subsidiary are as follows:

Assets	*Parent company* $	*Subsidiary* $
Investment in subsidiary	48,000	–
Plant and machinery	3,00,000	25,000
Current assets	1,75,000	30,000
Total	**5,23,000**	**55,000**

Liabilities	*Parent company* $	*Subsidiary* $
Equity shares	2,00,000	40,000
Reserves	3,23,000	15,000
Total	**5,23,000**	**55,000**

In the consolidated balance sheet, the fixed and the current assets of the two units will be clubbed together. The fixed assets will be valued at $ 3,25,000 and the current assets will amount to $ 2,05,000. The amount of goodwill will be equal to investment in subsidiary minus parent company's share in subsidiary's equity, that is $ 48,000 – 80% of 40,000 = 16,000.

On the liabilities side, the share capital will be $ 2,00,000. The reserves will be equal to $ 3,23,000 plus 80% of $ 15,000 or $ 3,35,000. The minority interest will be shown as 20% of $ 40,000 + 20% of $ 15,000 or $ 11,000.

Consolidated Balance-sheet (Gross consolidation method)

Assets	$
Plant and machinery	3,25,000
Current assets	2,05,000
Goodwill	16,000
Total	**5,46,000**
Liabilities	
Equity capital	2,00,000
Reserves	3,35,000
Minority interest	11,000
Total	**5,46,000**

The above is an example of gross consolidation method. If the balance sheet is prepared on the basis of net consolidation method, the fixed assets and the current assets of the consolidated balance sheet will embrace only those of the parent company. The amount of investment will be equal to the sum of investment and the proportionate share in the reserves of the subsidiary. This proportionate share will be clubbed with the reserves of the parent company. There will be no mention of the minority interest. The consolidated balance sheet under the net consolidation method will be as follows:

Consolidated Balance-sheet (Net consolidation method)

Assets	*$*
Fixed assets	3,00,000
Current assets	1,75,000
Investments ($ 48,000 + 80% of $ 15,000)	60,000
Total	**5,35,000**
Liabilities	
Share capital	2,00,000
Reserves ($ 3,23,000 + 80% of $ 15,000)	3,35,000
Total	**5,35,000**

Treatment of the Consolidation Differences

In many cases, the date of acquisition of the subsidiary by the parent company does not coincide with the closing date of the financial year. Again, in many cases, profit/loss prior to acquisition is taken into account. In these cases, consolidation differences arise. This means that in such cases, there may be disparity between the purchase cost and the amount of capital to be consolidated. If disparity arises, it needs adjustment.

The difference may be positive, meaning that the purchase price is greater than the amount of capital to be consolidated. It is found normally on account of taking over of undisclosed reserves or of goodwill. In such cases, the difference is added to the respective assets and is gradually adjusted through raising of the value of depreciation or writing-off of the goodwill. On the contrary, there may be negative difference when the purchase price is lower than the amount of capital to be consolidated. Such a possibility is only rare, but it arises when a firm acquires another firm with overvalued assets or with consistently low earnings. In such cases, the difference is adjusted through providing a spread of depreciation on the assets or through opening of a subsidy account which is gradually written back over a specified period.

Consolidation Provisions in Different Countries

The US companies were the pioneers in this area. In the USA, all the parent companies have to practise consolidation except where their control over the subsidiaries is only temporary or where the control does not rest with the majority owners. In the UK, the Companies Act of 1989 makes consolidation compulsory, except in some cases where consolidation is not practical and where it involves undue expenses and time. Exemptions are also allowed in cases where consolidated figures are misleading. The German law makes consolidation compulsory, especially where the parent company has a major stake in the subsidiary. In Japan too, consolidated financial statements are compulsory although exemptions are allowed where the sales of the subsidiary account for less than 10 per cent of those of the parent company or where the total assets of the subsidiary are less than 10 per cent of those of the parent company.

In India, Section 212 of the Companies Act provides that the balance sheet of the subsidiary has to be attached with that of the parent company if the financial year closing of both of them coincides. In other cases, the holding company has to submit a copy of the profit and loss account, the Director's report and the Auditor's report of the subsidiary along with its own.

PROBLEM 23.1

Prepare the consolidated balance sheet as on 31.3.2024 with the figures given below:
(Amount in US $)

Liabilities	*Parent*	*Subsidiary*	*Assets*	*Parent*	*Subsidiary*
Share capital			Fixed assets	1,00,000	60,000
(Shares of $ 10 each)			Current assets	1,15,000	20,000
Equity shares	1,20,000	50,000	Cash	70,000	10,000
Preference shares	40,000	10,000			
Profit & loss	25,000	10,000			
Creditors	1,00,000	20,000			
Total	**2,85,000**	**90,000**		**2,85,000**	**90,000**

The figures of the subsidiary are the translated values in terms of the US dollar. On 1.1.2020, the parent acquired 90 per cent of the shares in the subsidiary at $ 15 per share.

Solution

Consolidated Balance sheet of the Parent and Subsidiary as on 1.4.2024

Liabilities			*Assets*		
Equity share capital		1,20,000	Cost of control		13,500
Preference share capital		40,000	Fixed assets:		
Profit & loss		25,000	Parent	1,00,000	
Minority interest		16,000	Subsidiary	60,000	1,60,000
Creditors:			Current assets:		
Parent	1,00,000		Parent	1,15,000	
Subsidiary	20,000	1,20,000	Subsidiary	20,000	1,35,000
			Cash:		
			Parent	2,500	
			Subsidiary	10,000	12,500
		3,21,000			**3,21,000**

Note: 1. Assessment of cost of control:

Purchase of 4,500 shares @ $ 15 per share		$ 67,500
Less paid-up value of 4,500 shares	$ 45,000	
90% of pre-acquisition profit	9,000	54,000
		$ 13,000

2. Minority interest:

Paid-up value of 500 equity shares @ $ 10 each	= $ 5,000
Paid-up value of preference shares	= 10,000
10% of profit and loss	= 1,000
	$ 16,000

ACCOUNTING OF FOREIGN CURRENCY TRANSLATION

Consolidation of financial statements is a right step in the direction of the evaluation of overall financial performance of an MNC. But the problem arises when the figures of the financial statements of the subsidiaries are expressed in different currencies. This would not have been serious, had there been fixed exchange rate between different currencies. But in a floating-rate regime, volatility of rates creates a problem for translation of figures in different currencies into those of domestic currency of the parent company.

In a volatile exchange-rate regime, the procedure of translation takes into account three types of exchange rate. One is pre-change or historical rate. The other is post-change or current rate. Still another is the average of historical and current rates. Use of different rates gives different results. There is every possibility of loss or gain with changes in exchange rate. In such a situation, two important questions arise. One is which rate should be used for a particular type of transaction. The other is how the translation loss or gain should be treated.

Use of Foreign Exchange Rates

There are four approaches that explain which of the rates should be used for a particular type of transaction. They are current-rate approach, current/non-current-rate approach, monetary/non-monetary approach, and temporal approach. All these approaches have already been discussed in Part III while dealing with translation exposure. However, it may be mentioned that the use of a particular method depends upon whether the finance manager treats the subsidiary as an integral part of the firm or simply as a semi-independent unit. In the former case, for example, the temporal method is normally used; while in the latter, the current method is preferably used, although none of the methods are fool-proof.

Treatment of Translation Gains or Losses

There are broadly three approaches for the treatment of translation losses or gains:

1. Deferral approach
2. Immediate recognition approach
3. Deferral and amortisation approach

The *deferral approach* suggests that since the translation gains or losses are 'unrealised' having no effect on the cash flow between the parent and the subsidiary, they are not shown in the consolidated income statement. Rather, they accumulate separately as a part of consolidated equity.

The *immediate recognition approach* suggests that the translation gains or losses should immediately be shown in the income statement. The rationale is that the immediate inclusion will enable the financial statement to show the impact of changes in exchange rate.

The *deferral and amortisation approach* is a mixture of the above two approaches. Under this approach, the gain or loss is amortised over the life of the related balance-sheet items.

Which of the three approaches should be used depends upon the objective of translation. If it is viewed from the parent company's point of view, the gain or loss is adjusted in the income statement. But if the subsidiary's interest prevails, gain or loss is reflected through increase or decrease in equity in terms of domestic currency of the parent company.

Translation Practices in Different Countries

In the USA, Financial Accounting Standards–8 (FAS–8) was implemented in 1975 which recommended the use of the temporal method. FAS–8 was subsequently substituted by FAS–52 which recommended the use of the temporal method only in those cases where the US dollar happened to be the primary currency. But where foreign currency was the functional currency, FAS–52 was in favour of the use of the current method. Similarly, in Canada, the temporal method is used where subsidiaries are an integral part of the firm. In other cases, the current method is used. The Swedish Companies Act permits the use of current-rate method in normal cases, but the monetary/non-monetary method is used in the case of high inflation country subsidiaries. In France, current rate is used on a wide scale. In the UK, both the current method and the temporal method are widely used.

In India, it was for the first time in 1976 that the Institute of Chartered Accountants of India (ICAI) presented a guideline. It was primarily in favour of the use of current/non-current method, although Section 212 of the Indian Companies Act did not necessitate consolidated statements. In 1988, the practice became mandatory, although the compliance rate was very low. Again, a revised guideline Accounting Standard 11 came into force from April 1995 which was amended again in 2004. But it is restricted to accounting for transactions in foreign currencies and to translation of financial statements of foreign branches. For the purpose of translation: (a) revenue and cost, other than the depreciation, are translated at average rates; (b) inventory is translated at rates prevalent at the time of acquisition; (c) depreciation is translated at historical rates; (d) current rate is applied to monetary items, while historical rate is applied to non-monetary items and fixed assets; and (e) contingent liabilities are translated at current rates.

> In India, the use of current/ non-current rate method is favoured.

ACCOUNTING FOR INFLATIONARY TRENDS

Consolidation of accounts faces the problem of not only translation but also of inflation prevalent in the host country. If the inflation factor is not taken into account, the profits of the subsidiary will stand overstated and the consolidated picture will be different. This is why adjustment for inflation differential is essential.

Inflation-adjustment Techniques

Creation of reserves

A part of profit is transferred to reserves which may be used for meeting the increased cost of asset replacement. Reserves eliminate the problem of asset replacement as well as reduce the overstated profits. The technique is very simple and so it is used in many countries. But it is often an arbitrary decision as to how much of the profit should be transferred to reserves. The transfer may not help adjust completely the inflation factor.

Devaluation of assets

The book value of assets is revised, which helps the cost of fixed assets to conform to the current price and thereby provides a realistic measure of capitalisation. Depreciation is charged on the revised value which is able to meet the replacement cost of the assets. The overstatement of profits is also checked. It is a common method used in many countries.

LIFO method of inventory valuation

Inventory is valued in such a way that helps match current revenue with current cost of goods. Income statement shows a collection of the most recent purchase cost. However, this method is useful in those cases where raw material is purchased at frequent intervals and where all the goods produced are sold during the same period. In many countries, this method of inventory valuation is not allowed as it understates the profit and thereby the tax liability.

Historical cost accounting

Under this method, various items of income statement and the balance sheet are adjusted for inflation. In this context, the items are bifurcated into monetary and non-monetary ones. This is because monetary items, like cash, bill receivables, fixed earnings on investment, bill payables, and fixed-rate long-term obligations, are not adjusted for inflation. Adjustment is made for non-monetary items only, such as inventory, fixed assets, and share capital. The rationale is that the monetary items are fixed by contract regardless of changes in the purchasing power of the involved currency. Even in the case of non-monetary items where adjustment is made, the index for adjustment varies. For example, if sales spread over the whole year, the revenue is adjusted for inflation by the average of the index. If inventory is purchased in the beginning of the year, it is adjusted by the year-end index/initial price index. Suppose an inventory for \$ 100 is put into operation and the output is sold for \$ 150. If the price level is stable, the income will amount to \$ 50. But if the price index moves up from 100 in the beginning of the year to 121 in the end of the year, the revenue is adjusted as

$$\$\ 150 \times 121/100 = 181.50$$

The cost of inventory is adjusted as

$$\$\ 100 \times 121/100 = 121$$

Then, the inflation-adjusted operating income is

$$\$\ 181.50 - 121 = \$\ 60.50$$

Current value accounting

This method is applied in the case of price rise of specific commodities. Since a firm is continually replacing its assets, it is the replacement cost, and not the historical cost, that should be taken into account while preparing the income statement or the balance sheet. If the value of inventory rises by 40 per cent, the equity needs upward revaluation by the same percentage so that the risen cost of inventory is met by increased liabilities.

Accounting for Foreign Inflation

The accounting for foreign inflation is required when the subsidiary is operating in an inflationary environment. There are two methods in this respect. One is known as *restate-translate* method. The other is *translate-restate* method. In the former case, the figures of the financial statement of the subsidiary are first adjusted for inflation and then translated into the currency of the parent company. On the other hand, in the latter method, the figures are first translated into the currency of the parent company and then are adjusted for inflation.

ANALYSING FOREIGN FINANCIAL STATEMENTS

Normally, investors like to invest in foreign securities to reap the diversification benefits. Prior to investment, they need analysing the financial statements of those companies in which they think to invest. Similarly, the parent company goes through the financial statements of the subsidiaries in order to evaluate their performance. The analysis of financial statements of foreign companies is the subject-matter of international accounting.

Techniques of Analysing Financial Statements

There are three approaches for the analysis of financial statements:

1. Horizontal
2. Vertical
3. Combination of the above two.

In the case of horizontal approach, the financial data of a company is compared for two or more years from which the trend becomes clear. On the basis of the trend, the investor takes a decision. The vertical approach, on the other hand, shows the relationship between two or more financial items within a single time period. It is done in two ways: one through the preparation of common-size financial statement, and the other through the financial ratio analysis.

> Horizontal approach represents comparison of data on a time-series basis. Vertical approach represents comparing the financial variables of two or more firms for the same period.

The common-size financial statement shows the relationship between different items of financial statement in percentage terms. Suppose, in the income statement, sales amount to $ 5,00,000 and the cost of goods sold amounts to $ 4,00,000. The gross profit on sales will be 20 per cent.

Similarly, operating income, profit before-tax, net profit, etc. are expressed in percentage terms.

Financial ratio analysis gives a broader view of financial performance. Broadly, four types of ratios are computed: liquidity ratios, profitability ratios, solvency ratios, and market performance ratios. The readers are suggested to consult any textbook on financial management for the calculation of ratios.

Problems in the Analysis

Reliability and timeliness of information

In developed countries, there are specialised agencies for providing information to the corporate world. Moody's Investor Services and Computer Data Bank of the USA are well known all over the world. In developing countries, such facilities are not well developed. The study of Choi and Mueller (1992) reveals that information delays ranged on an average from 30 to 60 days for Brazilian and Canadian companies and from 60 to 90 days for companies domiciled in Australia, Finland, the Netherlands and Norway. It was as high as 90 to 120 days in the case of companies domiciled in Belgium, France, Germany, India, Malaysia and the UK.

Language and terminology

In many countries, financial statements are published in English. But in some countries, they are published in local language which is unintelligible for analysis. Moreover, the same item is termed differently in different countries. For example, ordinary shares are known as *common stock* in the USA. All this causes difficulty for the analysis.

Forms and contents of annual reports

Forms and contents of financial statements too vary in different countries. For example, the annual reports of some of the public sector enterprises in India embrace also non-statutory information, such as human resource accounting, social balance sheet, etc. The format of the balance sheet in India is quite different from that in the USA.

Varying practices of accounting

Accounting practices too differ among countries. There are different methods and mechanics of consolidation of financial statements. Treatment of affiliates' investment varies among different countries. In Australia, France, Germany, India, Japan and the USA, investment in affiliates is carried on the basis of cost, while the cost plus par value of stock dividends received form the basis of investment in some Latin American countries. Differences in tax laws, stock valuation, depreciation and other legal requirements exist among different countries.

Extent of disclosures

The level of disclosure is high in the UK, the USA and the Netherlands. But it is very low in Austria that comes in the way of obtaining the desired information.

Environmental differences

High debt ratio and greater collection period are common among Japanese firms, while they are low in US companies. If one looks at the US companies from

Japanese viewpoint, the judgement will be misleading. An analyst must be aware of the differing environment.

TRANSFER PRICING CONCEPT

Transfer pricing is basically the pricing of intra-corporate transactions. Different units of an MNC operate in different countries on the basis of vertical and horizontal linkages. Varieties of goods, especially intermediate goods, are bought and sold among different units. Prices charged on such sales take normally the form of transfer prices. Transfer prices have assumed importance in view of the fact that they are normally lower or higher than the arm's-length prices and they are charged through underinvoicing and overinvoicing of transactions. It may be noted that the *arm's-length prices* are those prevailing in transactions between unrelated parties engaged in similar or the same trade under similar conditions in the open market. It is a fact that transfer prices are set with reference to arm's-length price, but setting is quite arbitrary depending upon the subservience of the objectives of the firm. However, argues Rugman (1981), an MNC cannot charge arbitrary prices for intermediate goods produced by one unit and transferred to the other one. This is essentially so because it will influence the price of the final product. The final product may be price-uncompetitive and it may be suicidal for the MNC.

> Transfer pricing is intra-corporate transaction pricing where the prices are above/below the arm's-length price. Arm's-length prices are uncontrolled market price found in case of unrelated firms.

Rugman's argument holds good where the objective of the firm is the decentralised profit maximisation. This means, that each unit of the firm is independent for maximising its profit. But when the objective of the firm is to maximise the centralised profit without caring for a particular unit's profit, transfer pricing may be arbitrary, quite different from the arm's-length price. The profit before tax of a unit located in a high-tax country is shifted to another unit of the same firm located in a low-tax country. This is done through designing accordingly the prices of the intermediate goods flowing from one unit to another; or in other words, through designing the transfer prices quite different from the arm's-length prices. Diewert (1985) calls it *money transfer prices*.

> Money transfer prices aim at shifting pre-tax profits from a high-tax country to a low-tax one.

Again, if the objective is to maximise the aggregate net output of the firm in terms of constant reference price (excluding the intermediate goods), the price of intermediate goods is designed to boost up the production multiplier so as to facilitate production in different units. Such designing of prices, quite different from the arm's length prices, is known as *efficient transfer prices*. Thus the difference between the income (or money) transfer prices and the efficient transfer prices is that the former aims at maximum centralised profit, while the latter focuses on the maximum net output (Diewert, 1985).

> Efficient transfer prices aim at maximising output.

The Diewertian income transfer prices are, in a way, similar to the *fiscal transfer prices* explained by Horst (1971), Copithorne (1971), and Elam and Henaidy (1980). They are meant to minimise the tax-cum-tariff burden and to mitigate the effects of barriers to capital flows. But, on the contrary, Hirschleifer (1956) sees transfer price as *shadow price* aimed at optimum allocation of resources among various units of a firm, which leads to optimum liquidity adjustment. It emphasises on liquidity rather than on profitability. Funds are transferred from cash-surplus units to cash-deficient units of a firm through transfer pricing devices.

Setting of Transfer Prices

Since transfer prices are set on the basis of arm's-length prices, the process embraces two elements. These elements are:

1. The arm's-length price determined by
   (a) market price, or/and
   (b) cost of production.
2. The element of arbitrariness which is influenced by the desire to achieve a particular corporate objective.

Arm's-length price

When open market exists, arm's-length price is normally equal to the market price. Here one must distinguish between the uncontrolled market price and the resale price. The comparable *uncontrolled market price* method offers the most direct way of determining the arm's-length price. Uncontrolled sales are those sales made to an unrelated party outside the firm's own network. For the prices of goods to be comparable, it is essential to look at the prices of goods sold in those markets that are economically comparable. It is an important condition in view of the fact that market conditions differ from one country to another. Economic and social structures, geographical situations, consumers' habits, etc. are different in different countries. Again, for prices to be comparable, it is necessary to compare goods sold at the same point of distribution channel. This is due to difference between wholesale and retail prices of a commodity. If retailer's mark-up of prices is easily ascertainable, there will be no problem in making necessary adjustments. But if goods are non-standardised or if they are not completely processed or are differentiated on account of trademark, quality, monopoly element, etc., it will not be easy to find comparable uncontrolled prices.

The *resale price*, on the other hand, is the price at which a product, which has been purchased from a related seller, is resold to an independent purchaser. From this price, the margin (cost and profit) of the reseller is deducted to arrive at the arm's-length price. This method is useful where the margin of the reseller is not substantial or where the evidence of comparable uncontrolled sales does not exist. But this method is not suitable where the original product undergoes substantial transformation in the hands of the reseller. It is not suitable also where the time elapsed between the original sale and resale is significantly large so as to be exposed to changes in exchange rate or in market conditions, or still in the cost structure.

The other method for ascertaining arm's-length price, which is known as the *cost-plus method*, is more useful when semi-finished products are sold between related parties, although it is not often easy to determine the cost as well as the profit. The cost accounting concepts and practices vary from one set of countries to another and from one set of business to another. It is often the vendor's cost that is calculated. The purchasers too incur some expenses that need to be considered. As regards profit, any specific amount cannot be guaranteed. The cost-plus method generally overemphasises historical cost. If the cost is unnecessarily high due to inefficiency at the seller's point, the inefficiency may be transmitted to the buyer.

The two methods—market price and cost-plus—do not necessarily arrive at the same result in view of their specific limitations. In such cases, therefore, it is necessary to make additional calculation to cross-check the results with the cost/profit structure of similar firms in the same industry. These two methods find still further limitations if the transfer of intangible property, such as technical know-how, has to be priced. In such cases, the usual practice is to base the price on those prices that are related to transferring of similar technology or on the cost incurred on research and development.

Despite limitations, the two methods are normally used. In this respect, Hirschleifer (1956) believes that market price should form the basis when the market for traded items is perfectly competitive. If not, the marginal manufacturing cost should form the basis. From a survey conducted by Business International (1982), it is clear that both these methods are employed. The cost-plus method was employed mostly by US MNCs, whereas the market price method was adopted generally by non-US MNCs. Large-size firms preferred market-based transfer prices probably because of their greater visibility of different governments, tax and other systems. Similarly, market-based price was adopted mainly by decentralised units of MNCs, while more centralised units adopted cost-plus methods (Benvignati, 1985). Arpan (1972) has found that the US, French, British and Japanese MNCs preferred cost-oriented methods, while Canadian, Italian and Scandinavian firms opted for market-based methods. Lecraw (1985) has found that the non-market-based factor accounted for 58 per cent of the transfer-pricing decisions. It was as low as 32 per cent in the case of US MNCs and as high as 75 per cent in the case of Japanese firms.

Element of arbitrariness

After the arm's-length price is set, the element of arbitrariness follows as to how much of the deviation—plus or minus—from the arm's-length price should be brought in. This decision depends upon the firm's objectives to be achieved. The degree of arbitrariness is high in those cases where market does not exist. For example, when an MNC gathers a particular knowledge on account of experience or research and development which it does not like to part with any other firm, there does not exist an open market for transfer of knowledge. If such a knowledge is transferred within the firm, prices can be charged either very high or very low compared to arm's-length price. Richman and Copen (1972) have found a price mark-up of imports in India's drugs and chemical sector to the extent of 400 per cent in general and, in special cases, as high as 1,000 per cent.

Motivations behind Transfer Pricing

The existing literature on the subject mentions broadly three factors that motivate a firm to employ transfer pricing. *One* is that a huge amount of money is spent on research and development for the creation of an intermediate product. Thus the transfer of that product must be charged at a high price so that the cost could be recovered. The firm is able to charge a high price till such an ownership advantage is the exclusive monopoly of the firm and there does not exist any market price for it.

Secondly, there are various market imperfections. Different national markets are segmented on account of tax rate, tariff rate, exchange-rate control, currency risk, restrictions on investment, etc. Transfer pricing is used for doing away with these imperfections and thereby maximising the profits of a firm.

Thirdly, transfer pricing is used for liquidity adjustment among different units of a firm. It helps the liquidity-deficit units to get funds from liquidity-surplus units. The working capital management becomes smooth.

Some of the motivations or the objectives need further explanation.

Reducing tax burden

Minimisation of income-tax liability for the maximisation of overall profit is a pressing factor behind transfer pricing (Kim and Miller, 1979). The MNC transfers a good part of profit before tax from a unit facing higher rate of taxes to a unit subjected to lower rate of taxes. This is done through over-invoicing of import of the former unit from the latter or under-invoicing of export to the latter.

Suppose an MNC has its subsidiary in Country A and in Country B. Corporate tax in Country A is 10 per cent and 25 per cent in Country B. The unit in Country A produces intermediate goods exported to Country B unit. In the absence of transfer pricing, the unit in Country A exports 50,000 units of the component at the rate of \$ 10 per unit. But owing to higher tax rate in Country B, the MNC likes to siphon off before-tax profit from unit in Country B to the unit in Country A. This export is overpriced, say, by 20 per cent. As a result of transfer pricing, total profit of both the units taken together increases as the total tax liability of the two units taken together decreases. Assuming a fixed ratio between operating expenses and revenue, we get the following data:

Income Statement (without transfer pricing)

	Unit A *\$*	*Unit B* *\$*
Revenue	5,00,000	8,00,000
Cost of material	3,00,000	5,00,000
Gross margin	2,00,000	3,00,000
Operating expenses	50,000	80,000
Profit before tax	1,50,000	2,20,000
Tax	15,000	55,000
Net profit	1,35,000	1,65,000

Total net profit (A + B) = \$ 3,00,000
Total tax liability (A + B) = \$ 70,000

Transfer pricing by 20 per cent leads to an increase in profit by \$ 15,000 as the tax liability shrinks by \$ 15,000.

Income Statement (after transfer pricing)

	Unit A $	*Unit B* $
Revenue	6,00,000	8,00,000
Cost of material	3,00,000	6,00,000
Gross margin	3,00,000	2,00,000
Operating expenses	50,000	80,000
Profit before tax	2,50,000	1,20,000
Tax	25,000	30,000
Net profit	2,25,000	90,000

Total net profit (A + B) = $ 3,15,000
Total tax liability (A + B) = $ 55,000

However, if there is tax-avoidance treaty between the two countries or if administrative machinery is slack in evaluating taxes, the need for transfer pricing loses its significance.

Reduction of tariff burden

Lowering of tariff burden is another factor motivating for transfer pricing. A survey made by Kim and Miller (1979) reveals this factor being more significant than reducing of tax burden. However, it is only the ad valorem tariff burden that can be reduced. Quantitative restrictions do not lend themselves to transfer pricing gambits because their impact is on the quantities and not on the price of import. Similarly, if there are specific duties on import structured according to physical characteristics of imports, transfer pricing would not be of much use. above example a tariff rate of 30 per cent and at the same time equalise the corporate tax rate at 10 per cent in the two countries.

Income Statement (without transfer pricing)

	Unit A $	*Unit B* $
Revenue	5,00,000	8,00,000
Cost of material	3,00,000	6,50,000
Gross margin	2,00,000	1,50,000
Operating expenses	50,000	80,000
Pre-tax profit	1,50,000	70,000
Tax	15,000	7,000
Net profit	1,35,000	63,000

Duty paid = $ 1,50,000
Tax paid = $ 22,000
Net profit = $ 1,98,000

Income Statement (after transfer pricing)

	Unit A $	*Unit B* $
Revenue	4,00,000	8,00,000
Cost of material	3,00,000	5,20,000
Gross margin	1,00,000	2,80,000
Operating expenses	50,000	80,000
Pre-tax profit	50,000	2,00,000
Tax	5,000	20,000
Net profit	45,000	1,80,000

Duty paid = $ 1,20,000
Tax paid = $ 25,000
Net profit = $ 2,25,000

Since the transfer price is less than the arm's-length price, the size of duty paid plummets by $ 30,000. The amount of tax increases marginally by $ 3,000. Profit increases by $ 27,000. The profit increases because the company has to pay lower amount of duty. However, one has to take care of the fact that the issue of reducing tariff burden cannot be thought of in isolation of other factors, such as the tax liability. In the above example, tax burden has risen marginally, but since the tariff burden has diminished substantially, the net profit has increased considerably. But it may be that the tax burden increases significantly to eat away the benefits from tariff reduction. In that case, transfer pricing will lose its significance. Suppose that the tax rate in Country A and in Country B are respectively 10 per cent and 25 per cent. In the absence of transfer pricing, tariff burden will be $ 1,50,000; tax burden will be $ 32,500, and the net profit will be $ 1,87,500. After underinvoicing of export to Unit B, the amount of duty will shrink to $ 1,20,000, but the tax burden will increase to $ 55,000, and the profit will increase only marginally by $ 7,500. A greater tax differential between the two countries will lead to a reduction in total profit. This means, while adopting transfer-pricing devices, a balance has to be maintained between reducing tariff burden and reducing tax burden.

Controlling currency risk

Transfer pricing cannot prevent changes in exchange rate between currencies, but it can minimise the adverse impact of such changes through reshuffling cash balances and profits among different units of a firm located in weak and strong currency countries. If large cash balances of the firm are held with the unit located in a strong-currency country, any weakening of the currency in other countries will not matter much. Rather, it is possible that the firm could gain from such changes. This is the reason for an MNC preferring to shift the surplus cash from units situated in weak-currency country to the units located in strong-currency country. For this shifting of cash balances, the firm uses transfer pricing. The goods exported by the weak-currency unit to a strong-currency country will be under-invoiced.

Joint-venture constraints

Sometimes the host government imposes restrictions on foreign participation in corporate equity. In such cases, the parent company charges greater prices for the transfer of technology or for other supplies if such supplies are translated into equity shares.

Similarly, when the host government puts restrictions on the remittances of dividend and other payments, the parent company uses transfer pricing so as to effect such remittances.

Liquidity adjustments

When the different units of a firm are well-knit, the parent unit maintains a centralised control on the management of cash. Surplus cash of one unit is either sent to the cash-deficit unit or to a centralised pool for the purposes of its investment in the near-cash assets. When the government of the cash-surplus unit imposes restrictions on such movement of cash, the parent company uses the transfer-pricing technique.

Fostering competition

The parent unit likes its subsidiary to possess an edge over the local firms and, to this end, it supplies the intermediate products at much lower than the arm's-length price or without any charge. It enables the subsidiary to sell the final product at a lower price and compete with the local firms.

Benefits and Costs of Transfer Pricing

In the views of Aliber (1985), transfer pricing leads to economic welfare. The main contention of his argument is that tax and tariff differentials lead to sub-optimal allocation of resources, which leads to loss of economic welfare. Resources move away from a country where tax and tariff are high to a country where they are low despite the fact that the use of capital in the latter group of country may not be so effective. But the use of transfer pricing technique enables the firm to shift the pre-tax profit to those locations where the funds could be put to an effective use and thereby checks any sub-optimal use of the resources.

However, if the MNCs begin producing too much of the intermediate goods in lure of huge profits through transfer pricing, the use of the scarce resources will be sub-optimally tilted, which lowers in turn the economic welfare.

Moreover, transfer pricing minimises the benefits reaped by the host country from the operation of the firm. It lowers the revenue of the government from taxes and tariff. It also entails upon the balance of payments in the form of higher import bill and lower export receipt. It is often a source of conflict between the MNC and the host government. However, the adverse effects of transfer pricing can be checked to a great extent through regulations.

Regulation of Transfer Pricing

One school of thought favours complete deregulation where no government shall apply exchange control. Naturally, no MNC will be compelled to adopt transfer-pricing technique. The play of market forces will foster optimal allocation of resources. But complete deregulation is a utopian and hence transfer pricing is quite prevalent. Because of its prevalence, there is need for its regulation which may be direct or indirect.

Direct regulation

Direct regulation includes the measures replacing directly a particular transfer price by another set of prices determined by the host government. There are the cases when the government has set a particular price at which intra-firm transactions take place. For the first time, legislation was enacted to this end in the USA in 1973. The United Nations published a similar report in 1978. However, there are problems in following such a move. Kyrouz (1975) finds that out of 900 cases reviewed by the US Internal Revenue Service, arm's-length standards were completely unsuitable in over 40 per cent of the cases. In many cases, comparable uncontrolled prices were not available. In many other cases, cost-plus method was not feasible. In many developing countries, the government has fixed a ceiling on the royalty payment, but that irks the MNCs. Nevertheless, direct regulation is possible. In many cases, intermediate products are standardised. In many cases, expert arbitration is available.

> Direct regulation involves alternative prices set by the government.

Indirect regulation

Indirect regulation may be manifest in different forms. First, harmonisation of tax and tariff differential between home country and host country may be thought of. Kim and Miller (1979) find that profit tax consideration is comparatively less relevant than what is popularly believed. Yet this factor needs harmonisation. The system of tax holiday may be encouraged. Treaties for avoidance of double taxation may also be helpful.

> Indirect regulation means
> 1. harmonisation of tax and tariff differential;
> 2. taxation of intra-firm payments; and
> 3. apportioning of the consolidated profits among the units of the firm on the basis of assets, etc.

The second form of indirect regulation is to tax royalty and other intra-firm transfer payments that compensates for the loss of corporate tax revenue on account of transfer pricing. A few countries are found to disallow deduction of intra-firm royalty altogether as a business expense for the purpose of taxation. This is because they treat royalty payment as the remittances of profit. This measure checks transfer pricing through higher rate of royalty payment. But other forms of transfer pricing remain unchecked.

The third form of indirect regulation is to apportion the consolidated profit of the MNC among the relevant jurisdictions usually on the basis of total assets, sales and labour and capital employed. But this measure goes against the very fundamental notion that the MNC is interested in maximising global profits. Moreover, when different subsidiaries are inter-dependent, especially in a vertical set-up, any such apportionment is difficult to be justified on the ground of the contribution of different subsidiaries to the total profit. If the apportionment is based on the amount of labour employed, differences in productivity of labour in different countries cannot justify it.

The regulatory measures—direct and indirect—are not fool-proof. The host governments need taking a mix of measures supplemented by a series of negotiations with the parent company of the units operating in their country.

Transfer Pricing and Indian Tax Provisions

For the first time, it was the Indian Finance Act, 2001 that incorporated the detailed provisions relating to transfer pricing by the multinational companies. This was done through inserting two sub-sections, 92A and 92F and also the two relevant rules, 10A and 10E. The purpose is to compute reasonable and fair tax and profits in India and also the income from international transactions with reference to arm's-length price. The rules are based on the OECD guidelines, but the Indian rules stress on the computation of arm's-length price rather than considering an arm's-length range. The Central Board of Direct Taxes prescribes five methods to compute the arm's-length price. They are:

1. Comparable uncontrolled price method
2. Resale price method
3. Cost-plus method
4. Profit-split method
5. Transactional net margin method

The adoption of a particular method depends on the nature of transaction.

Again, it is the taxpayer that has to prove that the transactions have taken place in accordance with the norms of arm's-length pricing. It has to obtain the Accountant's Certificate in respect of the international transactions. Any violation of the norms is subject to stiff penalty. The penalty goes up to 100–300 per cent of tax on addition to income on account of concealment of details. Again, it may be 2.0 per cent of the value of international transactions if proper documents are not furnished with the tax authorities. The penalty can be equal to ₹ 1,00,000 if the Accountant's Certificate is not obtained.

After the submission of the documents, the tax officer forwards them to specially appointed Transfer Pricing Officer to review the entire matter. The latter finalises the assessment proceedings.

ACCOUNTING FOR FINANCIAL INSTRUMENTS

Concepts

The change in latest update in IFRS-9 (International Financial Reporting Standards) discuss about the accounting for financial assets. The IFRS-9 effective from 1st January 2018 laid down rules for classification and treatment of financial assets and liabilities and in cases it laid down rule for treatment of few contracts which is of financial nature. The IFRS-9 specifies that any entity can recognizes any financial assets or instrument only when the entity becomes a party to the contract.

Valuation of Financial Assets

The financial assets are not recognized as the normal assets which are valued based on its fair value or profit or losses which can be derived from the assets or liabilities, rather IFRS-9 has directed a rules for classification and valuation of financial assets based on model of business the entity is following.

Amortized cost: If the objective of the business model is to hold financial assets and collect cash after contractual period, then the valuation of financial assets will be based on amortized cost for the period of time assets are being hold along with that, the asset should be a income generating asset whose cash flow is due on a specified date and principal remains intact.

Fair value through comprehensive income: The financial assets are valued by fair value with comprehensive income if the model of business for that entity is to sell financial assets or collect cash of the contract for specified period time.

Fair value through profit and losses: The assets are valued at fair value with considering profit or losses, in case the assets do not falls under any of the above category states above.

Impact on International Finance

The change in valuation of financial assets based on business models, the MNCs often have financial assets across border, with change in IFRS and standard valuation based on business model may need those firms to change there classification and valuation of financial assets. This can also help MNCs to consolidate there financial asset's position under one framework. The IFRS-9 classifies hedging activities with risk management activities which will impact those firm which deals with cross-country exchange rate risk, changing interest rate risk and risk in commodity prices, it will help those firm to reduce the volatility from there books of accounts.

REVENUE RECOGNITION FROM CONTRACTS

Concept

The IFRS-15 deals with recognition of revenue and cashflow into the business out of any contract. Under the principles laid down under IFRS-15 the entity recognizes the revenue which is consideration arising out of the contract between two parties of transfer of goods or services. The amount of consideration for the fulfillment of contract is considered to the revenue of the entity once the goods or services are transferred to the other party.

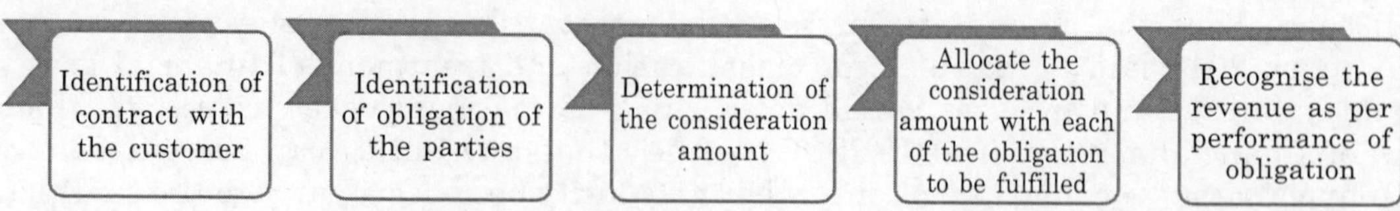

FIGURE 23.1 Process of Revenue Recognition

The revenue recognition is matched with performance of related obligation of the contract, where the entire contract is not considered as whole rather it is sub-grouped into smaller unit of obligation and amounts were allocated to them as according to the obligation of other party.

CHALLENGES OF FINANCIAL REPORTING IN MULTINATIONAL CORPORATIONS

The multinational corporations need to work in the economic domain of various nations with different laws and accounting practices, where the translation cost is very high and translating accounting information from one country to another is really a difficult job. There is need for professionals who understand accounting language of more than one country, but with the application of common IFRS system, things are going to be easy for accountants and finance managers. We are going to see what are the potential challenges faced by the MNCs in case of international accounting.

- **Multiple Compliances:** Working in international markets needs to follow a lot of compliances of different countries regarding accounting rules and regulations along with the compliance for doing trade. Thus there is a challenge for MNCs to follow different set of compliance for each country they are doing business, they need to prepare separate accounting information for each of the countries, and comply according to the local laws but at the end they need to compile all relevant information according to the need of domestic authorities and stake holders of the company.
- **Exchange Rate Risk:** While having international business and accounting for different countries, there is always a problem of currency exchange rate fluctuation. This means at the time of recording of transaction the true value of currency might be different with respect to the currency of parent company's home country, where as it might get fluctuated in the due course at the time of reporting of the accounting information to the parent company, or closing of books of accounts. Due to change in exchange rate the valuation of revenue and profit might change, which may lead to deviation from actual profit and hard to discover true revenue or profit of the firm.
- **Multiple Tax Compliance:** The tax laws in different countries are very different and there are other complexities like double tax avoidance, etc. too which make the reporting of tax payment complex. This may lead to confusing accounting information and make books of accounts of two subsidiaries difficult to compare.
- **Varying Inflation across Economies:** In the international arena there are certain countries who are having very high inflation and other are having very low. Due to inflation the price or revenue shown in the books of accounts are very high but in reality this is not the case thus leads to unrealistic accounting information.
- **Transfer Pricing:** Transfer pricing one of the most important thing in international reporting of accounting information. Most often the companies are involved in intercompany transactions, which is carefully scrutinize by tax authorities to avoid tax evasion and profit shifting, if there will be any error in proper reporting of transfer pricing this may lead to high penalties and other legal actions.
- **Valuation of Assets:** Different country follows different style for valuation of assets, whether tangible or intangible also while valuating the assets we need to consider the exchange rates and inflation to get true value in domestic currency.

- **ESG Compliances:** A lot of modern countries made it mandatory to have ESG compliance for their companies but the ESG norms are not same for all of them and they differ on various aspects, thus in international accounting, companies need to prepare separate ESG accounting for each of the countries in which they are working.
- **Consolidation of Accounting Information:** A lot of segments and subsidiaries of a MNC prepare there accounting records in different manner but for taking decisions at the center level there is a need for uniform and consolidated books of accounts by the parent company. The consolidation of subsidiaries is a difficult jobs in its own because of high translation complexities and different accounting norms, thus companies lose a lot of value due to this error.

ROLE OF TECHNOLOGY IN AUTOMATION OF ACCOUNTING PROCESSES

The development in modern technologies has affected almost all dimensions of business operations but the advantage of having big data analysis tools and modern artificial intelligence can change the whole scenario of preparation and management of accounting data. The role of information technology in management of accounting information can be seen in eight dimensions as follows:

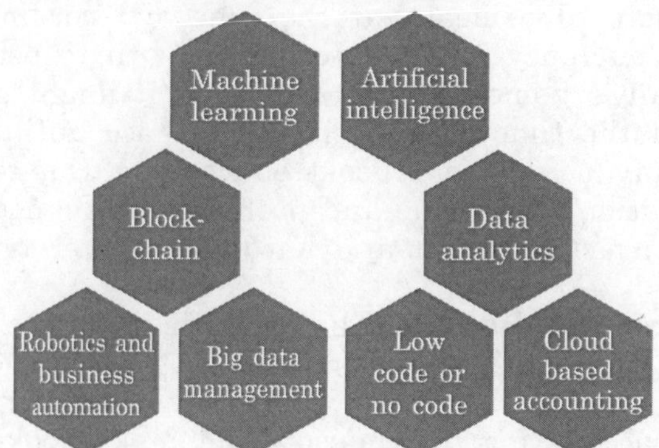

FIGURE 23.2 Technology and Automation in Accounting Process

Machine Learning: Machine learning one of the modern tool used for processing of big data sets and find meaningful inferences out of it. The machine learning can be used in the accounting process for processing of large financial transactions and high frequency data. The machine learning tools can be used for pattern recognition and fraud detection, accounting data and financial transactions can be modeled with machine learning leads to easy analysis and quick management of these data, without using machine learning this task can be tedious and time consuming, for example if we feed the data of companies having fraud in its books and then we feed the data of any company then the machine will learn by itself, the hidden pattern in books of accounts which lead a company to fraud, thus identifies the irregularities in books of accounts using machine learning.

Artificial Intelligence: The artificial intelligence is comprehensive term for machine learning, deep learning, neural networks and other such tools. The artificial intelligence tools can be used for automation of accounting processes and preparation of financial statements seamlessly. The AI tools can be developed to automate the task of trailer or bill manager, where the computer will itself do the billing entry by scanning of QR code by customer, based on that data the computer will itself able to prepare financial statements by following all the accounting processes. Artificial intelligence can also be deployed for audit process in which fraud detection and anomaly in books of accounts can be easily detected.

Cloud based Computing: With the expansion of multinational companies and growth of big giant companies, storage of financial and accounting information has posed a problem for modern managers. There is need of big computers for storage and analysis of these data which can be solved through the use of cloud based computing system. Under cloud based computing system, the data is stored in clouds or specially created data centers, which can be accessed from anywhere or anytime. The data can be analyzed using cloud computers where computation can be performed even without a need for dedicated person for it or any specialized infrastructure, because these computations are performed in dedicated computers which are situated at some specific place.

Robotic Process Automation: Robotics process automation is a powerful tool for doing the task with definite process and structured data, basic accounting tasks like invoice generation can be completely automated, cross referencing from diverse sources of data and there assimilation along with analysis and interpretation can be automated using robotic process automation.

Big Data: Big data processing one of the leading domain in the area of data science engineering is gaining its popularity in the domain of accounting too. Big business with too many of transactions at the same time need big data analytics tool for data processing. Online services companies, E-Commerce websites, giant MNCs, etc. need big data analytics tools for processing of their financial data and establish the interlinkages or intra-linkages between variables for flawless and easy processing of accounting data.

Data Analytics and Business Intelligence: The data analytics and business intelligence tools automate the process of accounting, it helps in decision-making based on the given information. This tool is specifically useful for managers who need to take decisions based on given accounting information. This tool helps in cutting short the time required for analysis of financial information to reach at common decision. These tools helps us by summarizing the data and presenting it in more clear and easy way. Data analytics tools are used for complex decision-making because of its utility in millions of computations at the same time and giving decisions based on all available probability.

Blockchain: The blockchain technology is leveraged in accounting process for distributed and more secure storage of accounting data. The blockchain technology is based on the distribution of information into several computers, with a secured key or passcode. The accounting information is highly sensitive from a business point of view, thus security of these information is very important which can be easily secured through blockchain ledgers. Individual ledger for each of the accounts can also be created on different locations which may make reduce load on a single computer and helps in fast computation of accounting information.

Low Code or No Code: Developing a software from scratch can be a costly as well as tedious job, thus there is problem with individual software development. This problem is solved by low code or no code software, a standard software suitable for every business entity is developed by the developer which customized according to the use of individual business with very less coding which is easy to replicate and scale. In no code accounting software, there is no need for customization, a basic software is developed with extended utilities which is fit for all business of same kind, software like Tally ERP or Busy are examples of no code software.

SUMMARY

- International accounting is concerned with the accounting practices followed in different countries, with harmonisation among those practices and with the financial relationship between a parent and its subsidiary. It has attained significance in recent decades in view of massive growth in the activities of MNCs, in international trade and in international financial market.
- Consolidation of financial statements of the parent and subsidiaries through gross method/net method is an important area of international accounting, especially in view of legal compulsion of doing it. In this respect, the translation of foreign currency into the currency of the parent unit is significant in view of changing exchange rate. There are different exchange rates and different methods used for this purpose. The results of different methods differ and there are different ways to treat the variations. There are sets of guidelines in this respect in different countries.
- Similarly, for consolidation of accounts, inflation differentials between the host country and the home country are taken into account. There are various methods for making adjustment for inflation factor.
- International accounting is employed also for evaluating financial statements of the foreign companies for the purpose of foreign investment. There are many problems in this respect that need to be considered.
- Transfer pricing is the most significant aspect of international accounting. It is an intra-firm transaction price which is equal to arm's-length price plus arbitrary addition or subtraction that depends upon the fulfilment of the corporate objectives. Transfer price is interpreted in terms of income transfer price, efficient transfer price, fiscal transfer price or shadow price. The purpose is to recover the huge expenditure incurred on the development of intermediate products, to maximise profit through minimising tax and tariff burden, and to make optimum liquidity adjustments among the different units of a firm. Transfer pricing leads to economic welfare but at the same time it creates problems for the host country. This needs regulation, which may be direct or indirect.

REVIEW QUESTIONS

Objective-Type Questions

1. State whether true (T) or false (F):
   - (a) Transfer pricing is a means to liquidity adjustments among different units of a firm. ☐
   - (b) Transfer price is different from arm's length price. ☐
   - (c) Money transfer prices do not involve liquidity adjustment among different units of a firm. ☐
   - (d) Efficient transfer prices are the same as the money transfer prices. ☐
   - (e) Language is the main problem involved in analysing foreign financial statement. ☐
2. Choose the correct answer:
   - (a) Common-size financial statement shows:
     - (i) relationship between two items of financial statement in percentage terms
     - (ii) financial data for two or more years
     - (iii) none of these
   - (b) High inflation in the host country:
     - (i) overstates the profit of the firm as a whole
     - (ii) understates the profit of the firm as a whole
     - (iii) none of these
   - (c) Under deferral approach to treat translation gains/losses, such gains/losses are:
     - (i) shown in the income statement
     - (ii) not shown in the income statement
     - (iii) amortised over the life of related balance sheet items

Short-Answer Questions

1. How are the consolidation differences treated?
2. Explain the various approaches to treat translation gains or losses.
3. Can transfer pricing be regulated? Describe the ways to do it.

Long-Answer Questions

1. What are the factors contributing to the growing importance of international accounting? Explain the dimensions of international accounting.
2. Distinguish between gross and net consolidation methods.
3. What are the different methods of currency translation?
4. Explain different techniques for adjustment of inflation for international accounting.
5. Describe the techniques of analysing foreign financial statements. What are the problems involved therein?

6. What do you mean by transfer pricing? How are transfer prices set?
7. Is it correct to say that transfer pricing is done for minimising the tax and tariff burden of the firm as a whole?

Numerical Problems

1. Find out the inflation-adjusted operating income if:
   (a) inventory put into operation is valued at $ 200,
   (b) the output is sold for $ 300, and
   (c) price index moves from 100 to 125.
2. The following are the balance sheet of Andrew Boyce, the parent company of the USA and its Indian subsidiary, Ashoka Floorings as on 31st March 2024. The figures of the subsidiary are the translated value in US dollars.

(Amount in US $)

Liabilities	*Parent*	*Subsidiary*	*Assets*	*Parent*	*Subsidiary*
Equity capital (share of $ 10 each)	90,00,000	30,00,000	Fixed assets	90,00,000	40,00,000
			Investment	60,00,000	–
General reserves	50,00,000	3,00,000	Debtors	16,00,000	9,00,000
Profit & loss A/c	60,00,000	20,00,000	Inventory	21,00,000	12,00,000
Sundry creditors	10,00,000	17,00,000	Cash	23,00,000	9,00,000
Total	2,10,00,000	70,00,000	Total	2,10,00,000	70,00,000

The parent acquired 75 per cent of the subsidiary's share at $ 60,00,000 on 1 July 2023. The subsidiary had an opening balance of $ 10,00,000 in Profit & Loss A/c from which it had paid dividend for 2023–24 at 20 per cent at the end of September 2023. The dividend received by the parent stands included in its Profit & Loss A/c. Again, inventory of the parent includes $ 2,00,000 out of purchases of $ 5,00,000 made from the subsidiary in January 2024. Credit period is 90 days. The subsidiary sold these items at a margin of 25 per cent on cost. There is no change in the reserves of the subsidiary during 2023–24.

Prepare a consolidated balance sheet as on 31 March 2024.

REFERENCES

Aliber, R.Z. (1985), Transfer Pricing: A taxonomy of impacts on economic welfare, in Rugman, A.M. and L. Eden (Eds.), *Multinationals and Transfer Pricing*, New York: St. Martin's Press, 1985, pp. 82–97.

Arpan, J.S. (1972), International Intra-corporate Pricing: Non-American systems and views, *Journal of International Business Studies*, III, 18.

Benvignati, A.M. (1985), An Empirical Investigation of International Transfer Pricing by US Manufacturing Firms, in Rugman and Eden, *op.cit.*, pp. 193–211.

Business International (1982), *Assessing Foreign Subsidiary Performance: Systems and practices of leading multinational corporations*, New York, p. 59.

Choi, F.D.S. and G.G. Mueller (1992), *International Accounting*, Englewood Cliffs (NJ), Prentice-Hall, pp. 432–469.

Copithorne, L.W. (1971), International Corporate Transfer Prices and Government Policy, *Canadian Journal of Economics*, IV, 321–341.

Diewert, W.E. (1985), Transfer Pricing and Economic Efficiency in Rugman and Eden, *op.cit.*, pp. 47–81.

Elam, R. and H. Henaidy (1980), Transfer Pricing for the Multinational Enterprise, *International Journal of Accounting*, Spring, 49–65.

Hirschleifer, J. (1956), On the Economics of Transfer Pricing, *Journal of Business*, XXIX, 172–184.

Horst, T. (1971), Theory of the Multinational Firm: Optimal behaviour under differing tariff and tax rates, *Journal of Political Economy*, LXXIX, 1059–1072.

Kim, S.H. and Stephen W. Miller (1979), Constituents of International Transfer Pricing Decisions, *Columbia Journal of World Business*, XIV, 65–77.

Kyrouz, M.E. (1975), Foreign Tax Rates and Tax Bases, *National Tax Journal*, 61–80.

Lecraw, D.J. (1985), Some Evidence on Transfer Pricing by Multinational Corporations, in Rugman and Eden, *op. cit.*, pp. 223–246.

Richman, B.M. and M. Copen (1972), *International Management and Economic Development*, New York, McGraw Hill, p. 603.

Rugman, A.M. (1981), *Inside the Multinationals*, New York, Columbia University Press, p. 84.

SUGGESTED FURTHER READING

Rathore, S. (1996), *International Accounting*, New Delhi, Prentice-Hall of India.

Rugman, Alan M. and L. Eden, (Eds.) (1985), *Multinationals and Transfer Pricing*, New York, St. Martin's Press.

Yunker, Penelope J. (1982), *Transfer Pricing and Performance Evaluation in Multinational Corporations: A survey study*, New York, Praeger.

CHAPTER 24

International Indebtedness

Learning Objectives

External indebtedness has been a major problem among developing countries borrowing large without their commensurate capacity to repay loans. The present chapter discusses the concept, magnitude, causes and management of external indebtedness. In particular, it attempts:

- To examine how external resources do contribute to the process of economic development in the developing countries.
- To show the magnitude of external debt.
- To explain the factors behind the debt crisis of 1980s and beyond.
- To discuss the management of external indebtedness.

External borrowing does help achieve faster rate of growth through bridging the investment-saving gap or import-export gap, but it is not an unmixed blessing: if the terms are hard, the burden of servicing will be larger, and if the borrowed funds are not utilised effectively, enough savings will not be generated to a level to repay the debt. Indebtedness will then attain unmanageable proportions that may adversely affect the process of growth.

A few countries have quickened the pace of economic development with the help of foreign borrowings and there are a number of others where growing indebtedness has posed a serious problem. The management of external indebtedness, especially since the early 1980s when it had turned alarming, has achieved international dimensions and has become an integral part of international finance.

EXTERNAL RESOURCES AND DEVELOPMENT

In a less developed economy, saving is normally too low to allow the warranted rate of investment. The country, therefore, borrows funds from external sources to bridge the investment-saving gap and make investment possible. The proponents of the "dual gap" approach are of the view that it is not the existence of the investment-saving gap alone that compels a country to borrow from abroad. There is also an import-export gap or foreign exchange gap that needs to be bridged to activate the process of development. The foreign exchange gap exists because the development outlay normally embraces a foreign exchange component and the export earnings are not sufficient to finance those imports.

Dual gap approach explains that external resources meet not only the investment-saving gap but also the foreign exchange gap that arises on account of deficit balance of trade.

From the viewpoint of national accounting, the two gaps are of equal value. A surplus of import over export allows a country to invest more than it saves. On the contrary, if a country invests more than it saves, a balance of deficit will emerge because the excess of investment over saving will be financed through raised imports.

The national income equation can be written from the expenditure side as

$$Y = C + I + X - M$$

Since saving is equal to income minus consumption,

$$S = Y - C$$

then

$$S = I + X - M$$

or

$$I - S = M - X \tag{24.1}$$

However, it is not necessary that the two gaps should always be equal. It may be that the income generation and thereby the saving generation is sufficient for permitting the warranted rate of investment, but the country is not able to export to an extent that could finance the import content of the investment. In such cases, the foreign exchange gap appears without any savings gap. This was perhaps the reason that Reddaway (1962) found the foreign exchange gap more crucial than the saving gap in some of the Asian countries.

If the two gaps are not equal *ex ante*, there will be wastage of resources. This is why, when the foreign exchange gap is wider, efforts should be directed to the use of savings to raise export. On the contrary, if the saving gap is greater, efforts should be directed to raise the saving rate. Again, if the two gaps are not equal *ex ante*, they may turn equal *ex post* either through a fall in the productivity of capital or through a fall in the productivity of imports.

The "dual gap" approach stresses the role of foreign borrowings in bridging the larger of the two gaps and thereby allowing the warranted rate of investment. If the growth rate is faster, that will ease the repayment of the external debt as well as meeting of the resource gap and the process of development will be self-sustaining. Dragoslav Avramovic (1964) divides the process of growth into three phases. The first phase is characterised by heavy inflow of foreign loans to meet the required investment as well as to make service payments and the magnitude of external indebtedness keeps on growing very fast. In the second phase, domestic savings as also the export surplus grow to equal the investment. The country then no longer needs external resources for domestic investment, but it still borrows to meet the interest and amortisation payments. So indebtedness does not rise as fast as in the first phase, but it does go up because the new borrowings necessary for honouring the service obligations on older loans also carry an interest and repayment burden. In this process, the country's indebtedness grows rather slowly and reaches its peak at the end of the second phase. In the third phase, domestic resources grow to a magnitude that is sufficient not only to meet current investment needs but also to service past loans. Debt then begins to lessen and in the end, indebtedness disappears and the entire investment is made of domestic resources. The process of growth then becomes self-sustaining. This is an optimal path of growth process that may not be always feasible. Attainment of self-reliant growth may be delayed if domestic resources are not generated either because of changes in international economic environment or owing to defective economic policies and weak implementation of plan programmes in the borrowing country. It may be delayed also if the terms of loans are hard enough to make servicing difficult.

The magnitude of the servicing burden depends upon the amount of the loan, the rate of interest it carries and on the repayment period including the grace period. It is true that the total outflow on account of repayment and interest payment gets larger if the repayment period is longer, but the loans with longer repayment period and longer grace period are soft loans in that the borrowing country gets more time to generate resources for the purpose of meeting servicing obligations. If quick and high pay-off is expected, short-term loans can be accepted. In other cases, long-term loans are preferable. Again, long-term loans are not desired where marginal propensity to consume is high but if marginal propensity to consume is expected to drop in the long run, long-term loans are desirable.

As regards the rate of interest, a high interest rate swells the outflow on this account. To illustrate, a country gets each year a loan of a specific amount repayable in ten annual instalments with a specific rate of interest. The grace period is two years during which interest is paid. If interest rate is 5.0 per cent, outflow will exceed the inflow after the 8th year. If interest rate is 3.0 per cent, the net outflow will begin from the 11th year and if interest rate comes down to 1.0 per cent, net outflow will begin from the 12th year.

A high rate of interest may not matter much if income is generated at a desired rate and the marginal propensity to save is high and if export earnings are generated satisfactorily. Lewis (1966) seems to be of a similar view when he prescribes that for attaining a self-reliant growth, there should be a diminution in personal consumption from 80 per cent to 70 per cent of gross domestic product. In his opinion, it can be achieved by having output rise faster than consumption. But in view of incentive to work and maintaining a better living standard, the ratio of consumption should not fall by more than 0.5 per cent per annum so that the process to be complete should take 20 years.

In this context, marginal saving rate should be considered in per capita terms because if population growth is faster than growth rate of income, per capita income will contract diminishing in turn the volume of saving. Similarly, the volume of required investment will be larger if the population is growing fast. Fies and Paauw (1965) developed a growth model in the Harrod-Domar tradition with reasonably realistic values of parameters. In their view, domestic efforts involving a per capita marginal saving rate of 35 per cent were essential for self-sustaining growth. They also viewed that in cases where saving rate was low or population growth rate was high or where target growth rate was high, the termination date of debt was infinite.

It is necessary for the attainment of self-sustaining growth that the output generated is exported to finance the import bill and to repay the debt. One can argue along the comparative cost lines of neo-classical economics that if both the markets of developed and less developed countries were perfectly free and competitive, the country's exportable surplus would eventually adjust to a product and price combination that could be fully sold abroad, but the argument does not hold good since the markets are not perfectly free and competitive.

Experience shows that the various conditions necessary for attaining self-sustaining growth could not be met and that led to a serious external debt crisis in a number of developing countries.

International Debt Terminology

Debt forgiveness: It occurs when the lender writes off a part or the entire of the principal and the accrued interest on an outstanding loan.

Debt provisioning: It means putting funds into reserves by lending banks to cushion themselves against default of loan.

Debt rescheduling: It occurs when the repayment of principal along with the interest payment due on outstanding loans are postponed to a future date. The borrower gets some time to breathe.

Debt-service ratio: It is the sum of amortization and interest payment as percentage of export.

Default: It occurs when the borrower fails to service debt.

Moratorium: It occurs when the borrower refuses to service debt till a fresh agreement with the lender. It is different from default in the sense that the borrower has the intention to service debt whereas in the case of default, it does not intend to service debt.

Official development assistance (ODA): It is the loan extended by governments at a very low interest rate and with a very long maturity. It is a soft form of loan where the grant element is greater.

Paris club: It is an organisation of official lenders.

Public and publically guaranteed debt: Public debt is owed by the government. Publically guaranteed debt is related to loans extended to private sector enterprises but guaranteed by the government of that country in view of greater risks involved.

NATURE AND MAGNITUDE OF EXTERNAL DEBT

At the very outset, it should be made clear that external indebtedness is primarily a problem of the developing countries. The developed countries have attained a stage where their own resources are capable of generating a sustained growth process. Over past one half of a century, external loans have been flowing to developing countries in order to bridge their resource gap. The huge flow with inappropriate terms in many cases and with its sub-optimal use at the recipients' end in some cases has led to the problem of external debt. Chart 24.1 reveals that the external debt of the developing countries moved up from a bare figure of $ 5,712.60 billion in 2013 to $ 8,836.50 billion in 2023.

(US $ billion)

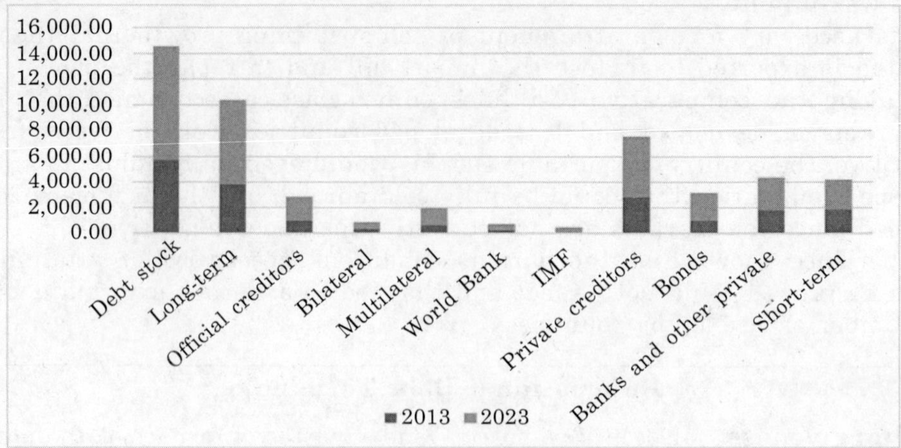

CHART 24.1 External Debt Stock of Low- and Middle-income countries, 2013–23.

TABLE 24.1 External Debt Stock of Low- and Middle-Income Countries, 2013–2023

(US$ billion)

Year	*2013*	*2023*
Debt stock	5,712.60	8,836.50
Long-term	3,850.80	6,495.90
Official creditors	998.5	1,822.90
Bilateral	367	499
Multilateral	631.5	1,323.90
World Bank	264.3	437.2
IMF	106.1	382.8
Private creditors	2,852.30	4,673.00
Bonds	1,017.30	2,140.70
Banks and other private entities	1,835.00	2,532.30
Short-term	1,861.80	2,340.60

Source: World Bank International Debt Report, 2024

From 2013 to 2023, the total debt stock in the country has increased significantly, with a 54.67% increase. The long-term debt component has seen a 68.83% growth, indicating a more stable debt profile. The debt owed to official creditors, bilateral creditors, international creditors, private creditors, and banks has also increased. The issuance of bonds has also seen a significant increase, with a 38.02% growth. Short-term debt has also increased, with a 25.46% growth.

The debt stock has risen, indicating heightened borrowing activity. The transition to long-term debt is favorable for debt sustainability, and the expansion of debt to official creditors has accelerated, indicating a heightened dependence on government financing sources. The substantial expansion in bonds signifies a transition towards market-oriented financing.

To better understand the debt position, additional factors such as debt service expenses, the debt-to-GDP ratio, and economic growth can be considered. A comprehensive evaluation of debt sustainability and associated risks can be conducted by examining these aspects. The study relies on the data provided, but additional economic and financial statistics are essential for a more nuanced view.

FACTORS BEHIND THE DEBT CRISIS

It would be interesting to refer to the factors responsible for the international debt crisis of early 1980s. These factors can be grouped broadly under two heads, namely the changes in the international economic environment and the defective policies pursued by the borrowing countries themselves.

Changes in the International Economic Environment

First oil shock

The most significant change in the international economic environment was the first oil shock of 1973–74. The balance of payments position of the non-oil-producing donor countries worsened. Their ability to lend as well as to replenish the IDA's resource pool was badly affected and weakened the flow of multilateral and bilateral resources. The ODA was the worst victim. The flow of ODA as percentage of total official lending dropped from 67 per cent in 1970 to 60 per cent by 1980. This means that the share of non-concessional official loans got larger and resulted in greater interest burden on the developing borrowers. The aftermath of the oil shock was evident not only in the risen official non-concessional loans but also in the rapidly expanding international bank loans. In fact, the surplus cash inflow of the oil-exporting countries was deposited with these banks thus enabling them to lend more. At the same time, growing current account deficit of the net oil-importing countries forced them to borrow more. In the absence of sizeable official flow, they had to approach the international banks for loans even at higher rates of interest. They preferred borrowing from these banks as these loans carried the least of restrictive covenants. Greater lending was facilitated by the introduction of a cross-default clause covering publicly guaranteed debt. If a developing country borrower defaulted, the cross-default clause would ensure that all bank lenders would be affected. A borrower confronting a debt-service problem had a strong incentive to reschedule the debt rather than to default on a loan. All this made lending less risky. Moreover, many industrialised countries eased their exchange control mechanism that encouraged the banks to lend abroad. The growth of off-shore banking was a further stimulus in this respect. The banks stressed balance-sheet growth through greater lending even without careful screening of the projects' viability and the borrowers' creditworthiness. The size of international bank lending rose at an annual average of 28 per cent—from US $ 8.0 billion in 1973 to US $ 53.0 billion in 1981 (The World Bank, 1985). In some quarters, it was called "over-lending" by banks. Over-lending at high interest rates and with shorter maturity caused greater servicing burden.

Oil shock means rising prices of oil causing strains on the balance of payments of the oil-importing countries.

Abrupt cutback of lending

Over-lending was followed by an abrupt cutback of lending. The debt problem would not have been serious had there been regular flow of loans and the borrowing countries could have got new loans to repay the older ones. But unfortunately, this did not happen and some of the oil-exporting countries turned net borrowers by 1982. The obvious result was that the supply of funds with the international banks was squeezed all of a sudden. Moreover, in the absence of proper screening of projects, the loans in many cases proved bad debt losses. The borrowing countries began defaulting on the loans. As a sequel of these facts, the banks went for an abrupt cutback of lending and so the borrowing countries did not get loans for servicing of past loans and the debt problem turned grave.

Transition from inflation to disinflation

Apart from the activities of the international banks, it was the transition from inflation to disinflation that aggravated the problem of indebtedness. Funds were borrowed in the 1970s when inflation was high and real interest rate was low or, in some cases, negative, but during the 1980s when the industrialised countries adopted restrictive monetary policies, disinflation began to appear. In the absence of a falling nominal interest rate the real interest rate began to shoot up. The second oil shock of 1979–80 failed to stop the upsurge in real interest rates, and repayment of loans became a costly affair.

Emerging recession

The 1980s decade dawned with emerging recession among many of the industrialised countries. In the face of recession, the developing countries were struggling hard to augment their export. Simonsen (1985) explains that during 1974–80, the floating rate of interest on loans to net oil-importing developing countries had averaged 10.7 per cent, but the debt problem was not serious because exports of these countries had expanded at 21.1 per cent. During 1981–82, however, the growth rate of export plummeted to 1.0 per cent against the upsurge in interest rate to 16.3 per cent and the debt burden turned serious as a consequence.

Deteriorating terms of trade

The deteriorating terms of trade of the net oil importing developing countries during 1980–82 caused the debt crisis. In the first half of the 1970s there was a commodity boom. The prices of many primary commodities in real terms rose which in turn lowered the cost of borrowing. The lower cost of borrowing motivated the developing countries to jack up expenditure and to borrow more but when the export prices fell during the 1980s, the borrowing countries suffered severely and found it difficult to repay external loans (Cline, 1984).

Defective Policy of the Borrowing Countries

The borrowed funds can be utilised in two ways: they can be spent and that cannot help the borrowing country to repay its debt, or they can be invested which leads to generation of income and saving and builds up the ability to repay the debt. However, as Dornbusch and Fischer (1986) point out, many Latin American countries adopted a defective policy and financed primarily consumption and government deficit rather than investment. Kharas and Levinsohn (1988) find that in case of 12 out of 26 countries, the level of consumption rose with an increase in borrowings in which case, external debt problem was bound to emerge. Even if the foreign borrowings were used for investment, profitability of investment was always doubtful. Diaz-Alejandro (1984) argues that many of the Latin American countries suffered from a deterioration in investment productivity after 1973 which was an important factor behind the debt problem.

The reasons for fall in investment productivity in case of low-income and least developed countries were different. They were perhaps weak administrative and managerial capabilities. To quote a few instances, World Bank funds were not used effectively in Nepal on account of administrative laxity (Dhungel and Tips, 1987). In Nigeria, the concerned personnel officials from the managing director to the lowest rank were found to see the organisation as a legitimate source of additional private income (Reilly, 1987).

Defective policy was evident in improper foreign exchange rate management policy. Cuddington (1987) finds that during 1976–83, faulty policy of exchange rate management led in many Latin American countries to appreciation in the real exchange rate of their currency and to black market premia on foreign exchange. The overvalued exchange rate contributed to the debt crisis insofar as it lowered the export competitiveness and thereby affected the current account and also the ability to repay the debt.

Defective policy was evident also in the form of outward trade orientation without requisite economic strength. Balassa (1984) feels that countries having an outward orientation had to suffer greater external shock as their economies were more open to changes in the external economic environment. The losses they suffered weakened their capacity to repay the debt.

Structural economic rigidities too, especially in the low-income countries came in the way of policy changes designed to overcome indebtedness. These rigidities manifested in lack of economic diversification, a concentrated export base, high population growth, lack of basic facilities, and poor living conditions, etc. They adversely affected the incentive to save and invest and to generate the income necessary for repaying debt.

Additional Factors during the 1990s and thereafter

Some of the significant factors behind the external debt problem during the early and mid-1980s, continued into the 1990s and thereafter. There were some additional factors operating during this period. The first, was the break-up of the erstwhile USSR. The economy of most of the countries coming out of the USSR bondage was so weak that their trade with the rest of the developing world came to be at the lowest ebb. The export earning of most of the developing borrowers from Eastern Europe declined and this eroded their repaying ability. The Gulf War led to rise in oil import bills of many developing borrowers. In the sequel, their ability to repay debt turned lower. The financial crisis in East Asia adversely affected the debt repaying capacity of not only the countries gripped by the crisis but also many others that were indirectly affected by the crisis. The turmoil in global fixed-income markets in the summer of 1998, problems in high-yield markets following slowdown of 2001, and fall in debt flows in East Asia, Russian Federation and Latin America were some of the additional factors behind the continuance of international debt problem during 2000s. However, many developing countries adopted economic reforms that helped them to revive their economy and to come out of the debt problem. Moreover, the debt-relief measures on a wide scale were no less important in mitigating the external debt problem.

It is true that the economic reforms initiated by many of the developing countries helped them ease their external indebtedness. The process of globalisation did yield good results in the sense that the size of trade and investment flows rose sizeably. But when the financial crisis emerged in the developed countries during 2008 or when the US debt crisis turned significant during 2010, or when some countries of the European Union witnessed financial crisis during 2010s, the effects permeated to the developing world. The process of permeation was made smooth by the process of globalisation. The developing countries could not be free from the pressures of rising external indebtedness. Thus, the issue of external indebtedness needs to be looked at from the view of the latest developments in the world economy.

MANAGEMENT OF EXTERNAL INDEBTEDNESS

Debts are owed either to official lenders or to private lenders, mainly international banks. The tools of management of these two forms of debts are alike to a great extent, but as they differ as to details, let us discuss the techniques and plans of management separately.

Management of Official Debt

The problem of debt was foreseen long ago and, with this in view, the Paris Club was set up in 1956. It took concrete shape in 1961 and since then, various types of negotiations have been taking place for implementing debt relief measures. Broadly speaking, relief measures under the aegis of the Paris Club comprise cancellation; refinancing and rescheduling of debts.

> Paris Club is an organisation of the official lenders that takes account of lending to developing countries and of managing their debt.

Sometimes they are implemented separately, but often simultaneously. Cancellation of an entire debt or a part of it brings maximum relief to the borrower. In case of refinancing, softer forms of loans or grants are extended to borrowers through which costlier loans can be repaid. Again, in case of rescheduling of debts, repayment is postponed to a later date and the borrower gets time to generate income to repay debt. Between 1980 and 1988 rescheduling alone reduced the debt service payments of low-income African countries by over US $ 10 billion (Humphreys and Underwood, 1989).

In October 1988 the Paris Club introduced what were called the Toronto Terms making special arrangements for heavily indebted low-income countries on a case-by-case basis. However, these provisions were limited to IDA-only countries. Between October-1988 and June-1991, debt-relief was extended to 20 countries under the Toronto Terms. Highly concessional assistance was provided for debts relating to ODA, while a menu approach was followed in case of non-ODA debts.

In December 1991 the Toronto Terms were revised and renamed Enhanced Toronto Terms. They were intended for the same group of countries but the role of cancellation of debt was enhanced: one-half of the debt was to be written off and the other half was to be rescheduled to a 23-year maturity including a 6-year grace period and at market-related rates. Between December 1991 and December 1993, this benefit was availed by 16 countries. On the whole, between 1981 and 1993, on an average, 18 countries availed of debt relief under the aegis of the Paris Club every year (Klein, 1994).

The *Houston Terms* were adopted almost simultaneously with the Toronto Terms, in September 1990. Their approach was almost similar to the menu approach where ODA debts and non-ODA debts were treated differently. Under the London Terms that were prevalent between December 1991 and December 1994 the net present value (NPV) of debt was to be reduced by 50 per cent. The Naples Terms that became effective from January 1995 went in for a drastic cut in the size of debt. They were meant for 67 per cent NPV reduction on eligible non-concessional debt (50 per cent in case of Cameroon, Guinea and Honduras). The debt-relief measures under the Lyon Terms that were initiated in January 1996 were even more beneficial for the borrowers as they stressed on 80 per cent NPV reduction.

One of the latest moves of the Paris Club has been to initiate the Heavily Indebted Poor Countries (HIPC) Initiative in 1996. It is proposed as a comprehensive solution to the unsustainable level of debt owed by the 40 poorest countries in the world. The purpose is to focus resources on countries with a solid track record of performance with the help of the adjustment programmes of the World Bank and the IMF. During the first two years of this scheme, 31 out of 40 countries fulfilled the eligibility criteria for debt-relief assistance and they availed of the facilities under this scheme (World Bank, 1999). According to an IMF study, the effective NPV debt reduction under the HIPC Initiative was to be 95 per cent by July 1998 (IMF, 1998). Concessional assistance for debt relief is provided by different bilateral sources. The World Bank has a special debt-reduction facility that has benefited many, especially the sub-Saharan countries.

According to the World Bank figures, 26 countries—being two-thirds of the eligible HIPCs began to get relief from all creditors in 1990s that amounted to around \$ 40 billion. The HIPC unit of the World Bank is working along with the Low Income Countries Under Stress Initiative. The outstanding debt of the HIPCs came down from over \$ 62 billion in 1999 to \$ 27 billion by 2002 and to \$ 21 billion by 2004. Debt-service ratio during this period fell from 14.7 per cent to 9.9 per cent and to 7.3 per cent.

In 2005, the HIPC Initiative was supplemented with the Multilateral Debt Relief Initiative (MDRI) in which IMF, IDA and ADB provided additional debt relief. Inter-American Development Bank too began providing debt relief to Latin American and Caribbean HIPCs.

At the end of 2010, thirty-two out of the forty countries eligible or potentially eligible for HIPC Initiative assistance were receiving full debt relief from the IMF and other creditors after reaching their completion points. Out of the remaining eight, four countries had reached their decision points and some of them started receiving interim debt relief. Four countries, which had been identified as potentially eligible for HIPC Initiative assistance, did not reach their decision points.

Before the HIPC Initiative, eligible countries were, on an average, spending slightly more on debt service than on health and education combined. Now, they have increased markedly their expenditures on health, education, and other social services. On an average, such spending is about five times the amount of debt-service payments. For the 36 countries receiving debt relief, debt service paid, on an average, has declined by about two percentage points of GDP between 2001 and 2009. Their debt burden is expected to be reduced by about 80 per cent after the full delivery of debt relief (including under the MDRI).

Debt relief has improved the debt position of post-completion point countries, bringing their debt indicators down below those of other HIPCs or non-HIPCs. However, many remain vulnerable to shocks, particularly those affecting exports as seen during the recent global economic crisis. To reduce their debt vulnerabilities decisively, countries need to pursue cautious borrowing policies and strengthen their public debt management.

The total cost of providing assistance to the 40 countries was estimated at $ 75 billion in end-2009 net present value terms. A little less than one-half came from the IMF and other multilateral institutions, and the remaining amount came from bilateral creditors.

Nevertheless, some challenges are still there. Many of the 8 countries failed to complete the requirements for full debt relief face common challenges, such as lack of stability and good governance. There is need to strengthen policies and institutions, and support from the international community. Another challenge is to ensure that eligible countries get full debt relief from all their creditors. Smaller multilateral institutions, non-Paris Club official bilateral creditors, and commercial creditors, which together accounted for about one-quarter of the total HIPC Initiative costs, delivered a small share of their expected relief. Non-Paris Club bilateral creditors as a whole had delivered close to two-fifths of their share of HIPC Initiative debt relief, but about half of these creditors did not deliver any relief at all.

The delivery of debt relief by commercial creditors has increased markedly in recent years through a few large operations. A number of commercial creditors have initiated litigations against highly indebted countries, raising significant legal challenges to burden sharing among all creditors, including the multilateral institutions (IMF Fact Sheet, 6.9.2011).

Management of Non-official Debt

Short-leash approach

As far as non-official debt is concerned, in the early 1980s the international banks adopted a "short-leash" approach when they rescheduled and rolled over debt service due from debtors over a short period ranging from one year to two years. Following this approach, they adopted multiyear rescheduling arrangement that offered consolidation of debt with longer maturity. The IMF and the World Bank guided these moves and at the same time provided finance to the borrowing countries for taking up adjustment measures. Debt reduction measures were thus combined with economic development programmes.

> Short-leash approach concerned primarily with rescheduling of debt.

The short-leash approach was found yielding positive results. There was a buoyant recovery in 1984. The growth rate in the industrialised countries averaged

5.0 per cent. At the same time, interest rates, LIBOR ebbed from 19 per cent in 1981 to 11 per cent in 1984. Thus the two factors behind the crisis of early 1980s—recessionary trends and high interest rates—disappeared automatically by the mid-1980s. Some of the key debtors ran current account surpluses. Economic growth in Latin American countries again turned positive to 3.7 per cent in 1984 compared to (–) 1.2 per cent in 1982 and (–) 2.6 per cent in 1983 (Cline, 1989).

The Baker plan

The success of debt management of 1983–84 was short-lived. In 1985 the mood began to swing once again to pessimism. Argentina and Brazil moved from military to civilian rule and in this process, the IMF-led adjustment programme was temporarily suspended. Mexico had to face fiscal erosion, rising inflation and weakening oil prices. It needed fresh loans, but the banking community was hesitant to give them. In such cases, a medium-term management of debt was required. Fortunately, the then Secretary of the Treasury in the US government, James Baker drafted a medium-term plan in 1985 that was implemented subsequently.

Baker plan relied on increased lending to cover the exposure.

The Baker plan called for banks to provide new lending of US $ 20 billion over a three-year period between 1986 and 1988 to 15 (later on to 17) highly indebted countries. The amount was to cover 2.5 per cent of then existing exposure every year. The target was conceived on a net disbursement basis, that is over and above the repayment of principal but not the interest payment.

The plan expected the official creditors to extend an equal amount and this way symmetry was brought between the official and the private lenders. The onus of lending among the official creditors fell mainly upon the multilateral development banks. The governments of the industrialised countries were to support the multilateral development banks' resource pool through an enhanced flow of about US $ 3.0 billion annually or US $ 9.0 billion for the whole of the three-year period.

The plan suggested that the economic adjustment programmes be adopted by the debtor countries but it rejected the idea of aid cancellation because that would cut off the borrowers from the capital markets. It was a medium-term plan and so the responsibility for providing new money shifted from the IMF to the World Bank. However, the Baker Plan did not turn out to be as effective as it was expected because the envisaged size of the debt-relief flow was lower than the requirements and the actual flow was even lower than the envisaged size. The official creditors provided only US $ 15.75 billion and the banks provided only US $ 12.8 billion against the envisaged amount of US $ 20.0 billion each. Probing deeper, one finds that it was not entirely the fault of the creditors and in many cases the borrowers failed to implement the economic adjustment programmes suggested by the creditors which debarred them from getting the loans. The growth rate in the Latin American countries fell during the Baker Plan period. Thus the debt relief measures under the Baker plan neither reduced the debt burden as desired nor pushed up the growth rate in the debtor countries.

Market-based menu approach

Baker himself was not happy with the outcome of his plan and so in 1987, he introduced an improved version of the plan, known as the *market-based menu approach*. The improved plan adopted a case-by-case approach and tuned each financial package to the specific needs of each debtor country and to the specific constraints of the banks. It stressed upon the need for axing the net outflow of funds from the debtor countries to US $ 15.0 billion annually during 1989–1991 from a level of US $ 28.6 billion annually during the Baker plan period.

Market-based menu approach stressed on case-by-case approach and introduced variety of debt conversion plans.

The plan sought to introduce instruments that could make the banks' increasing exposure more attractive. Debt conversion programmes, relending rights, new money bonds, etc. were some of the new features. Capitalisation of interest was allowed, although Baker admitted that it was not a permanent solution. Its debt conversion plan included primarily debt-equity swap, debt-for-development swap and buy-backs. In debt-equity swap, the banks buy debt at a discount, the central bank of the debtor country redeems the debt to the new creditor in local currency and the local currency is invested in the equity. In debt-for-development swap, an international organisation, normally an NGO purchases the debt at a deep discount and exchanges the debt with the central bank of the debtor country for domestic bonds. Again, in buy-backs, the debtor country buys back its debt at deep discount for cash (Rogoff, 1992).

The plan expected official contribution to the extent of US $ 14.0 billion during 1989–1991, out of which the World Bank was to contribute US $ 8.0 billion, the IMF US $ 2.0 billion and the remaining US $ 4.0 billion was to be contributed by the bilateral lenders. The banks were to contribute to an extent of US $ 9.0 billion and a sum of US $ 10.0 billion was expected in the form of foreign direct investment (Cline, 1989).

The Brady plan

The Brady plan, named after Nicholas Brady, the US Secretary of the Treasury, stressed voluntary debt reduction through increasing the role of official lenders and through forgiveness. Brady-type deals involved the exchange of loans for agreed financial instruments followed by the deposit of collateral and the necessary payments in cash. Principal collateral was normally provided by the US treasury zero-coupon bonds. Short-term US treasury bills were used for interest collateral.

Brady plan stressed voluntary debt reduction through increasing role of official lenders and forgiveness.

Some of the countries were prompt in repayment of principal but defaulted on interest payment, while some others paid the interest and defaulted on principal repayment. A huge balance of arrears of interest was converted into post-due interest bonds that involved comparatively short maturity and grace period. Normally, such bonds yielded market rate of interest, LIBOR plus a few percentage points.

The World Bank and the IMF were expected to provide funds for debt and debt-service reduction at a higher level, that is between US $ 20.0 and $ 25.0 billion over a three-year period from 1989 to 1991. Among the bilateral donors, Japan was ready to provide US $ 10.0 billion over the next several years. The commercial bank debt, including interest arrears, of the middle-income countries amounted to US $ 194.0 billion at the end of 1995, out of which a sum of US $ 40.0 billion was eliminated in nominal terms through different measures suggested by Brady (World Bank, 1996).

Recently, during 2000s, many countries have gone for rescheduling of loans and for debt swap and have managed their external debt burden. But, at the same time, in this period, there have been more cases of default. In 2002, Argentina defaulted foreign currency debt for US $ 95 billion. Gabon and Maldova defaulted on debt respectively for US $ 30 million and US $ 75 million. Such specific cases should be taken care of by implementing proper economic management and by ensuring coherent trade and aid policies.

CHALLENGES AHEAD

Efforts are on to ease the external indebtedness problem of the developing world. But there are some major problems coming in the way. It is true that the size of the ODA has increased since 2000, but it is not sufficient. The United Nations report presented to the General Assembly has estimated that ODA should increase by at least $ 50 billion a year. But it seems to be distant possibility viewed against the current trend.

Secondly, a number of the low-income countries do not possess the required aid-absorptive capacity. The problem lies at different levels. The national economic policy is defective. The public budget management is poor. Economic and social infrastructure is not yet developed. A committee assessed the aid absorptive capacity of 18 well-performing low-income countries and found considerable variation in the absorptive capacity (*World Bank, 2005a*).

> Aid absorptive capacity means the ability to make an efficacious use of aid.

Thirdly, aid fragmentation still remains high among developing countries. It means that donors either extend small-size loans for too many projects in a country or target many countries with limited funds. The index constructed in this respect is very high meaning that fragmentation is very high and it can have negative implications for the quality of aid in terms of high transaction cost for recipients. The recipients cannot achieve the economies of scale and thereby cannot benefit to the desired extent. (*World Bank, 2005a*)

> Fragmentation of aid means small pieces of loans spread over many projects/countries)

Fourthly, tying of aid to the purchases in the donor's country, which is rampant among the donors, slashes the real value of aid. It is because the suppliers in the donor countries charge higher price of the supplies. A recent OECD study finds that untied aid could be beneficial 50 per cent more than the tied aid. (*World Bank, 2005a*)

Fifthly, the quantum of aid flows has been volatile and unreliable undermining the very budget management in the recipient countries. Cross-country data reveal that aid has continued to be more volatile than fiscal revenue. Moreover, the index of volatility is on the rise as the measure of aid volatility relative to revenue in 2000–2003 was almost twice the median value of 1995–98. (*World Bank, 2005a*)

Thus the international community has to find ways to meet these challenges and then only the problem of international indebtedness can be tackled.

SUMMARY

- External borrowing helps bridge the savings gap and the foreign exchange gap and thereby permits warranted rate of investment and growth. There is no serious problem of debt if the terms of loans are soft and sufficient income, saving and export surpluses are generated for making the process of development self-reliant.
- Till the 1970s there was no debt problem. It tended to build up during the 1970s and turned unmanageable by the 1980s. The debt problem of middle- income countries has been different from that of the low-income countries. In the former, commercial debt is significant, while the latter face problems primarily related to the official debt. The different ratios indicating indebtedness have, however, been improving.
- The factors behind the debt crisis include changes in international economic environment on the one hand, and the defective economic policies pursued by the borrowing governments, on the other. The oil shock of the 1970s, abrupt cut-back of lending by the international banks in the 1980s, transition from inflation to disinflation, and recession among aid-giving countries and deteriorating terms of trade of the primary goods-exporting borrowers were some features of the international economic environment that aggravated the debt problem. Some of these factors were present in the 1990s but there were additional factors during this period, such as the break-up of the erstwhile USSR, the Gulf war and the financial crisis in East Asia. In 2000s, it was a general slow-down in high-yield markets that delayed any improvement in the debt crisis.
- As far as management of debt is concerned, the Paris club negotiations under different terms have a significant role in cancellation and refinancing of debt and rescheduling of repayment so as to lower the burden of external debt among developing countries, mainly the low-income countries. For commercial debt, the short-leash approach of early 1980s, the Baker plan in its earlier version and in the revised one known as the market-based menu approach, and the Brady initiative are of special significance. Though they were not entirely successful, they did something positive in this respect.
- Despite various efforts, there are a few challenges that need solution for tackling the problem of external indebtedness.

CASE STUDY

INDIA'S GROWING EXTERNAL INDEBTEDNESS

At end-March 2024, India's external debt was placed at US$ 663.8 billion, an increase of US$ 39.7 billion over its level at end-March 2022.

The provided information offers a comprehensive assessment of India's external debt scenario from March 2022 to March 2023. During this era, the nation's total external debt rose substantially from $618.8 billion to $663.8 billion. This signifies an increase of $45 billion, corresponding to a percentage rise of 6.4%.

The General Government sector significantly contributed to this growth, with its external debt rising from $130.8 billion to $148.7 billion, marking a notable increase of 15.4%. A detailed analysis of the data indicates that the industry emerged as a substantial contributor. The Deposit-taking Corporations sector experienced a notable rise in external debt, escalating from $160.4 billion to $186.8 billion, signifying a growth of 23.4%. This transpired simultaneously with the preceding sector. The Other Sectors category witnessed a little decrease in external debt, declining from $299.9 billion to $296.7 billion. Direct investment experienced a 1.9% increase, predominantly in intercompany loans, rising from $27.6 billion to $31.4 billion. This indicates a little increase from the prior data.

The examination of percentage variance reveals that the General Government sector experienced the highest percentage increase in foreign debt, totaling 15.4%. Nonetheless, it is crucial to recognize that this increase is predicated on a comparatively low initial value, even if the Central Bank also reported a substantial growth rate of 77%. The Deposit-taking Corporations sector ranks second, exhibiting a notable percentage increase of 23.4%.

The data collectively indicate a steady increase in India's external debt, predominantly propelled by the General Government and Deposit-taking Corporations sectors. This increase can be attributed to various factors, including heightened borrowing for infrastructure projects, trade deficits, and government expenditure. It is crucial to note that India's debt-to-GDP ratio remains very low relative to other emerging nations, which mitigates immediate concerns.

It is essential to explore additional factors to attain a comprehensive understanding of India's external debt status. This encompasses the expenses associated with debt servicing, including interest payments and principal repayments, together with the rate of economic growth in the nation, which directly influences its capacity to generate revenue and fulfill debt obligations. The volume of foreign exchange reserves possessed by the nation is a crucial determinant of its capacity to service external debt. To undertake a thorough assessment of India's external debt sustainability and associated risks, an examination of these factors is feasible.

External Debt–Outstanding and Variation

(US$ billion, unless indicated otherwise)

Outstanding as at end-March				Absolute Variation		Percentage Variation	
Sector	*2022 R*	*2023 PR*	*2024 P*	*March 2023 over March 2022*	*March 2024 over March 2023*	*March 2023 over March 2022*	*March 2024 over March 2023*
I. General Government	130.8	133.3	148.7	2.5	15.4	1.9	11.5
II. Central Bank	0.1	0.1	0.2	0.1	0.1	77	56.3
III. Deposit-taking Corporations, except the Central Bank	160.4	163.4	186.8	3	23.4	1.8	14.3
IV. Other Sectors	299.9	297.8	296.7	−2.1	−1.1	−0.7	−0.4
IV.1. Other financial corporations	51.1	55	48.5	3.9	−6.5	7.7	−11.8

(Contd.)

External Debt–Outstanding and Variation

(US$ billion, unless indicated otherwise)

Sector	Outstanding as at end-March			Absolute Variation		Percentage Variation	
	2022 R	*2023 PR*	*2024 P*	*March 2023 over March 2022*	*March 2024 over March 2023*	*March 2023 over March 2022*	*March 2024 over March 2023*
IV.2. Non-financial corporations	248.8	242.8	248.1	−6	5.4	−2.4	2.2
IV.3. Households and nonprofit institutions serving households (NPISHs)	0	0	0	0	0	−23.7	−16.5
V. Direct Investment: Intercompany Lending	27.6	29.4	31.4	1.8	1.9	6.6	6.6
Total Debt (I to V)	618.8	624.1	663.8	5.3	39.7	0.9	6.4

QUESTIONS

1. Analyse the trend in India's external indebtedness, especially from the viewpoint of different types of external debt.
2. What is rupee debt? Why has it declined during the past decade?
3. Do you feel that the debt burden is still in a sustainable stage?

REVIEW QUESTIONS

Objective-Type Questions

1. State whether true (T) or false (F):

(a) A very high GNP/external debt ratio is a symptom of severe debt problem. ☐

(b) A low export/debt ratio is an indicator of severely indebted countries. ☐

(c) ODA flows carry larger proportion commercial borrowings. ☐

(d) IBRD loans are channelled to extremely poor countries. ☐

(e) Improvement in terms of trade further aggravates the external debt problem. ☐

2. Choose the correct answer:

(a) Baker plan was concentrated on:

(i) official debt

(ii) non-official debt

(iii) both official and non-official debt

(b) The market-based menu approach:
   (i) coincided with the original Baker plan
   (ii) followed the original Baker plan
   (iii) preceded the Baker plan

(c) HIPC Initiative was initiated in:
   (i) 1996
   (ii) 1990
   (iii) 1984

(d) International debt problem turned severe:
   (i) after the first oil shock
   (ii) after the second oil shock
   (iii) during the second half of 1990s

(e) Paris Club was set up:
   (i) after the international debt crisis of 1980s
   (ii) during 1950s
   (iii) during 1990s

Short-Answer Questions

1. Is the saving-investment gap equal to export-import gap?
2. Do you suggest that maturity of loan should be shorter?
3. Distinguish between external debt/export ratio and debt-service ratio.
4. What do you mean by short-leash approach of external debt management?

Long-Answer Questions

1. What were the factors behind the international debt crisis of 1980s?
2. Explain Baker plan for alleviating international debt problem.
3. How far was market-based menu approach different from the original Baker plan?
4. Explain Brady Initiative.
5. What have been the measures adopted for reducing official debt?

REFERENCES

Avramovic, D. (1964), *Economic Growth and External Debt*, Baltimore, Johns Hopkins Press, pp. 47–84.

Balassa, B. (1984), *The Problem of the Debt in Developing Countries*, Washington, D.C., The World Bank.

Cline, W.R. (1984), *International Debt: Systemic risk and policy response*, Cambridge (Mass.), MIT press.

———(1989), The Baker Plan and Brady Reformulation: An evaluation, in Ishrat Hussain and Ishac Diwan (Eds.), *Dealing with the Debt Crisis*, Washington, D.C., The World Bank, 176–196.

Cuddington, John T. (1987), *Capital Flight: Estimates, issues and expectations*, Princeton University Studies in International Finance, No. 58.

Dhungel, Y.N. and W.E.J. Tips (1987), Rural Development Management in Nepal, *Public Administration and Development*, VII, 43–58.

Diaz-Alejandro, C. (1984), Latin American Debt: I don't think we are in Kansas anymore, *Brookings Paper on Economic Activity*, II, 335–403.

Dornbusch, R. and S. Fischer (1986), Third World Debt, *Science*, CCXXXIV, 836–841.

Fies, J.C.H. and D.S. Paauw (1965), Foreign Assistance and Self-help: A reappraisal of development finance, *Review of Economic and Statistics*, XLVII, 251–267.

Humphreys, C. and J. Underwood (1989), External Debt Difficulties of Low-income Africa, in Hussain and Diwan, *op. cit.*, 45–63.

IMF (1998), *World Economic Outlook*, Washington D.C., September.

Kharas, H.J. and J. Levinsohn (1988), LDC Savings Rates and Debt Crisis, *World Development*, XVI, 779–786.

Klein, Thomas M. (1994), *External Debt Management*, Washington, D.C., The World Bank, Technical Paper No. 245.

Lewis, W.A. (1966), Allocating Foreign Aid to Promote Self-sustained Economic Growth, *Development Digest*, IV, 81–84.

Reddaway, W.B. (1962), *The Development of the Indian Economy*, London, George Allen & Unwin, Appendix D.

Reilly, W. (1987), Management and Training for Development: The Hombe Thesis, *Public Administration and Development*, VII, 25–42.

Rogoff, K. (1992), Dealing with Developing Countries Debt in 1990s, *World Economy*, XV, 480.

Simonsen, M.H. (1985), The Developing Country Debt Problem in Gordon W. Smith and John T. Cuddington (Eds.), *International Debt and the Developing Countries*, Washington, D.C., The World Bank.

The World Bank (1985), *World Development Report*, Washington, D.C.

———(1996), *World Debt Tables*, Washington, D.C.

———(1999), *Global Development Finance*, Washington, D.C.

———(2005), *Global Development Finance*, Washington, D.C.

———(2005a), *Global Monitoring Report: 2005*, Washington, D.C.

SUGGESTED FURTHER READING

Klein, Thomas M. (1994), *External Debt Management*, Washington, D.C., The World Bank, Technical Paper No. 245.

Ohlin, Goran (1966), *Aid and Indebtedness*, Paris, OECD.

CHAPTER

25 International Taxation

Learning Objectives

Taxes influence the size of profits reaped by MNCs. So the discussion of international taxation is an important segment of IFM. The purpose of the present chapter is:

- To explain the basic principles of international taxation.
- To explain major types of taxes.
- To acquaint the readers with the tax haven countries.
- To discuss the modes of double taxation relief.
- To examine the international tax management strategy of the MNCs.
- To focus on Indian tax scenario.

Taxation plays a vital role in international operation of firms. It is the core of various financial decisions, such as international investment decisions, international working capital decisions, funds raising decisions and the decisions concerning dividend and other payments. It is true that the tax issue is relevant to such decisions also in respect of domestic firms. But the management of taxation is a highly complex issue for international corporations. The reasons are very obvious. *First*, these firms have to operate in many tax jurisdictions where tax rates are different and also the administration of tax system is not uniform. *Secondly*, the ultimate burden of tax in the context of international firms is determined by a more complicated interplay of varying definitions of tax base. *Thirdly*, the varying tax treatment in different countries can lead to distortions in international trade and investment. The firms located in a low-tax country can have an edge over other firms in international market. Similarly, investment can be diverted to those countries having lower tax rates. *Fourthly*, the international firms often straddle different tax jurisdictions, exploit the arbitrage opportunities and maintain an edge over the domestic firms. This chapter, therefore, discusses some more significant issues related to international tax environment and some of the provisions of the Indian Income Tax Act in this context.

BASES OF INTERNATIONAL TAX SYSTEM

It is expected that the international tax system should be neutral, meaning that it should not affect economic efficiency. At the same time, it has to be equitable ensuring equal sacrifice by different tax payers. Besides, a firm should not be taxed twice for the same income. These three concepts need more explanation.

Tax Neutrality

Neutrality of international taxation is based on the concept of economic efficiency. It means that tax should not come in the way of optimal allocation of capital among different countries. If tax is neutral, it does not affect either the location of the investment or the nationality of the investor. Capital will move from a country with lower return to a country with higher return. Consequently, resources may be allocated efficiently, and the gross world output in turn will be higher.

> Tax neutrality refers to a tax structure favouring optimal allocation of capital among countries.

Tax neutrality may be explained in terms of capital-export neutrality and capital-import neutrality (Horst, 1980). Capital-export neutrality means that the rates of taxes should be the same between domestic investment and foreign investment. It implies that investors are indifferent between domestic and foreign investment. It is possible when pre-tax and post-tax returns on capital are the same between capital exporting country and the capital importing country. But uniformity of this kind is difficult to be achieved in practice. This is so because accounting norms vary in different countries. The tax policy of different governments is also heterogeneous.

> Capital export neutrality means that the taxes should not discriminate between domestic investment and foreign investment.

> Capital import neutrality means that taxes should not discriminate between firms operating in a particular capital importing country.

Capital-import neutrality, on the other hand, occurs when the same tax rate is applied to the income of all firms competing in the same capital-importing country so that no firm—domestic or foreign—enjoys any competitive advantage. But since tax bases are different, it is not easy to achieve capital-import neutrality. Some of the capital-exporting companies are found making reconciliation between two forms of neutrality, and they follow a mix of the two. For example, the taxes on their subsidiaries' earnings are credited against their own taxes.

Tax Equity

The principle of tax equity rests on the belief that all similarly situated tax payers should participate in the cost of operating the government according to the same rules. The concept of equity can be interpreted in two ways. One is that the contribution of each tax payer should be in conformity with the amount of public services he or she receives. The other is that each tax payer should pay taxes according to his or her ability to pay. The *ability to pay* means a person with greater ability has to pay a greater amount of tax. However, it is difficult to define the concept of equity when the tax jurisdiction is more than one. We cite a simple example. There are two Indian residents. The first individual is deriving his entire income from domestic source. The second person has the same amount of income, but a part of his income is derived from foreign sources. Now the second person has to pay a greater amount of taxes as he pays taxes also in the foreign country where the income is generated. The same income from the foreign source is taxed twice. Thus, if the principle of equity has to be ensured, something needs to be done in this respect.

Equity means that everyone should pay taxes according to his/her ability to pay. Alternatively, tax amount should be in proportion to the amount of public services a tax-payer receives.

Avoidance of Double Taxation

The corporate income tax is levied when a firm earns income. But if the post-tax income is remitted to foreign countries, the recipient of such income is taxed again. It means the same income is subject to double taxation. Double taxation dampens the incentive to invest. And so it needs to be avoided. For this purpose, the entire income from foreign sources may be exempted from tax. Alternatively, the provisions of foreign tax credits may be created in the domestic tax system. In a subsequent section, these relief provisions are discussed at some length.

Avoidance of double taxation means that no one should be taxed twice for the same income.

Additionally, there may also be treaties for the avoidance of double taxation between the home government and the host government. For the first time, it was the League of Nations that had drafted a model for double tax avoidance treaty in 1929. The OECD developed its own model in 1963 and revised it in 1974. In 1967, the United Nations set up a Group of Tax Experts on Tax Treaties, and on its recommendations, issued in 1974 "Guidelines on Tax Treaties" between developed and developing countries. India is a party to such treaties with a number of countries. These treaties provide, among other things, for full exemption from tax in the country in which a minor activity is carried on. The cumulative figure of such treaties by the end of 1997 was 2730. In 2007 alone, 69 treaties were concluded, out of which 17 were signed between the developed countries; 8 were signed between the developing countries and the rest 44 were concluded between the developed and the developing countries (UNCTAD, 2008). The rate of conclusion of agreements has gone up fast during the recent past. Between October 2010 and 15th January 2011, some 32 agreements were signed between 58 countries, of which 23 were double tax avoidance treaty (UNCTAD, 2011).

TYPES OF TAXES

The international operation of a firm is subjected broadly to three kinds of taxes:

1. Income tax
2. Withholding tax
3. Value-added tax

Income Tax

A significant part of the tax revenue in a country is represented by tax on personal income as well as corporate income tax. The tax is levied on income arising out of a firm's operation—whether the operation is a manufacturing one or it is concerning the provision of services. However, the rate of the tax varies widely among different countries or different tax jurisdictions with the result that the concept of neutrality or equity is hard to be adhered to.

Withholding Tax

Withholding tax is a tax levied on passive income earned by an individual or a corporate body. The word "passive" is used because the income arises, or is generated, in some other country. Suppose a corporate body in India gets dividend from its subsidiary operating in some other country and pays tax on the dividend income to the Indian Government. The dividend income is a passive income as it is generated abroad. The tax on such income is known as *withholding tax* because the corporate body receiving the dividend withholds the tax borne by the tax payer (shareholder) and passes on the tax amount to the tax authorities.

Withholding tax is a tax levied on passive income.

The passive income takes many forms, such as dividend income, income from royalty and technical service fees, and income from interest. It has been observed that the rate of taxes varies from one form of passive income to the other and from one country to the other. For example, the USA withholds 5 per cent of interest income from tax payers residing in a large number of countries, but the rate moves up to 30 per cent for those residing in Pakistan. Similarly, in the USA, the withholding tax rate in respect of portfolio investment is higher than that in the case of direct investment (Eun and Resnick, 1998).

Value-added Tax

A value-added tax (VAT) is a tax levied on the value added at different stages of production of a commodity or services. VAT is an indirect tax and is often preferred to direct income tax insofar as it discourages unnecessary consumption, fosters national savings, and is easier to be collected. However, this tax too faces the same problem, that is to say, the rates are different in different tax jurisdictions.

TAX HAVENS

A tax-haven country is one that has zero rate or a very low rate of income tax and withholding tax. In addition, there are some non-tax factors that make a country tax haven. Gordon (1981) mentions them as (1) strict rules on secrecy and confidentiality in respect of business transactions, (2) relative importance of banking and other financial activities, (3) lack of currency controls, and (4) governmental measures promoting tax haven status. Alworth (1988) groups the tax havens into four types:

Tax havens are those countries that have no, or a very low rate of, taxes; or allow special provisions to exempt income from taxes.

1. Those having no income or capital gains tax
2. Those having a very low rate of tax

3. Those exempting from tax all income from foreign sources
4. Those allowing special tax privileges in specific cases

In the first group are Bahamas, Bermuda, the Cayman Islands, Nauru, New Hebrides and Turks and the Caicos Islands. In these countries, the Government does not impose any specific rate of taxes but has fixed a small amount of tax. The manufacturing companies get a long-term guarantee against taxes.

In the second group of countries are British Virgin Islands, the Netherlands Antilles, Montserrat, Gersey, Guernsey and Isle of Man, where tax rates are very low and special tax privileges are provided to shipping, aviation and to holding companies.

Costa Rica, Hong Kong, Liberia and Panama represent the third group. In these countries, the Government taxes only locally generated income and not any income flowing from foreign sources.

In the fourth group are Luxembourg, the Netherlands, Switzerland, Liechtenstein, Gibraltar, Barbados and Grenada. In the first four of these countries, special tax privileges are provided to qualified holding companies, while in the latter three countries, low rates of taxes are applicable to special status companies or to international business companies.

The OECD has published a list of 35 tax havens (see the box). The World Investment Report (2004) mentions that the size of offshore havens grew from 30 jurisdictions with $ 200 billion in assets in 1983 to 60 jurisdictions with $ 5.0 trillion of assets by 2001.

It is found that small countries with poor economic background use tax-haven status to attract international banking and such other commercial activities. Tight secrecy laws support such activities. Moreover, the growth of internet services has given impetus to these activities. MNCs maintain their centralised cash pool in these countries in order to evade taxes.

However, the OECD feels that the tax havens have distorted the natural flow of international funds. It is for this reason that it has asked the tax havens to match their tax rates with those of the OECD members. In the past four to five years, emphasis was laid on legislation to achieve the goal, but now on-the-spot checks and issuing warnings are common.

List of Tax Haven Countries

Alderney	BVI	Guernsey	Liechtenstein	Nauru	Singapore
Anguilla	Barbados	Hong Kong	Luxembourg	Netherlands	St. Vincent
Antigua	Campione	Grenada	Madeira	Netherlands Antilles	Switzerland
Aruba	Cayman Islands	Ireland	Malta	Nevis	Turks & Caicos
Austria	Cook Islands	Isle of Man	Marshall Islands	Niue	United Kingdom
Bahamas	Costa Rica	Jersey	Mauritius	Panama	Uruguay
Belize	Cyprus	Labuan	Melilla	Sark	Vanuatu
Bermuda	Gibraltar	Liberia	Monaco	Seychelles	Western Samoa

As per an estimate of Global Financial Integrity, poor countries "lose" more than $ 1 trillion a year to tax havens, around ten times the aid they receive. Two-thirds of this is tax evasion and avoidance, the group says, the rest transfers by criminals and the corrupt. Tax Justice Network (TJN) is of the view that global off-shore deposits amount to at least $ 9 trillion, some $ 2 trillion more than the total held at home by American banks. Mauritius is the largest investor in India. British Virgin Islands is one of the biggest in China. Tax havens make it harder to gain a true picture of where debt and risk lie, for example in hedge funds trading exotic derivatives. Enron's finances were obscured by its habit of hiding debt in its hundreds of subsidiaries in the Caribbean.

Some latest moves are that Switzerland has agreed to tax money held in its banks by British residents up to 34 per cent as well as, from 2013, a withholding tax that could bring the British treasury around £ 5 billion or $ 7.8 billion. It is based on the premise that even if a company's profits are higher as a result of using a tax haven, that money needs to be taxed similarly as dividend tax. The offshore finance skews the global distribution of wealth, away from poor countries and those that levy taxes to pay for public goods (including the ones that benefit companies).

It would be proper to place onus on companies to explain what profits they make where. That would help prevent the worst abuses of transfer pricing scams, in which tax havens play a handy role. The muddled Dodd-Frank reforms, passed by Congress in America and now being implemented by regulators, supposedly go some way towards this; so does legislation being drafted in the EU.

Automatic exchange of tax information on non-residents is a good idea. Bilateral tax treaties normally require such exchanges only on request. This works if the government seeking information knows precisely what it is looking for and if the host government can obtain it. On the whole, resistance to change remains strong, not least in big Western financial centres such as Wall Street and in the City of London, which see the flexibility offered by tax havens as an essential part of their business model. Political support for reforms is still patchy. France wanted to discuss tax havens at next month's G-20 meet but other countries were less keen.

MODES OF DOUBLE TAXATION RELIEF

Double taxation relief is normally granted by the country in which the parent company has its legal residence. The modes are:

1. Credit system without deferral
2. Credit system with deferral
3. Tax Exemption
4. Deduction of tax paid abroad as expenditure
5. Investment credit

Credit System without Deferral

Taxes paid in the host country are allowed as a credit against the tax liability in the home country. Suppose the tax rate in India is 35 per cent and a foreign subsidiary of an Indian company pays taxes on its profit at the rate of 40 per cent foreign tax jurisdiction as an offset against the amount of tax paid within its own jurisdiction.

The tax credit without deferral is based on the principle of capital-export neutrality, which means that the income generated either domestically or in a foreign country should be taxed at the same rate. Bearing this principle in mind, the profits earned by the foreign branch or the subsidiary are clubbed with those of the parent company and all eligible taxes levied in the host country are allowed as credits. This means that the foreign investment is taxed at the rate prevalent in the home country. However, in practice, consolidation is not common in most of the countries as it is expected to raise a host of administrative problems. When losses occur, the credit system operates as if double taxation relief were provided as an exemption.

Tax Credit with Deferral

In this case, taxation in the home country is deferred until earnings are repatriated by the subsidiary to the parent company. It is similar to the case of a holding company whose subsidiaries are located within the national boundary or the same tax jurisdiction. Profits of the subsidiary are taxed at the rate prevalent in the host country. They are subject to home-country taxes only when they are repatriated.

Tax Exemptions

In this case, if the profits of the subsidiary are taxed in the host country, they are exempted from any taxation in the home country. In some cases where the host-country government provides tax holiday for specific number of years, dividend distribution by the parent company is normally taxed in the home country. This type of relief is based on the principle of territoriality where profits of the multinational corporation are taxed only in one tax jurisdiction. Such provisions are found in France and the Netherlands.

Deduction of Tax Paid Abroad as Expenditure

In this case, the amount of tax paid in a foreign country is treated as an expenditure and so it is deducted from the total income arising in the country. It is similar to the exemption although the procedure is different.

Investment Credit

In this method, the amount of capital invested abroad is deducted from the income arising in the country of residence. The purpose is to encourage capital export through reducing the burden of taxes.

EQUALIZATION LEVY OR DIGITAL TAX

Equalization levy or Digital tax is the taxation strategy aligning with BEPS to tax those digital companies who are significantly present in a country but have headquarter situated somewhere else, this helps them to evade tax from various countries.

In the year 2016 India has introduced this tax system for the advertising companies like google and meta which are not headquarters in India but having significant business in India. The government imposed 6% of tax on the payment made by Indian residents for these advertising services.

In the second phase of development in digital tax in the year 2020, the government expanded the scope of this tax to non-resident E-commerce companies too. Government of India imposed a 2% tax on the income generated from India by non-resident E-commerce companies having revenue exceeding INR 20 million.

In the budget of year 2024, the government of India announced to abolish EL-2.0, or second phase of Equalization levy to align with OECD commitments and due to certain compliance complexities.

The equalization levy will impact the business of digital companies in a negative manner because this may charge a high amount from there pocket but it will be a benefit for state exchequer and ensure payment of taxes by companies who are taking benefit of Indian market.

This tax is essentially for non-resident companies, thus our domestic companies are out of the purview of this tax, domestic companies are taxed according to the corporate tax laws. The equalization levy will provide a level playing field for our domestic companies too in front of non-resident companies and promote our domestic industry.

Challenges

The equalization levy may be unfavorable for big American as well Chinese companies and giants like Amazon, google, etc. thus the challenge for India is to present this tax in global arena and get is accepted by international fraternity.

There is a challenge of uniform accounting and proper determination of tax liability, the MNCs tends to manipulate there accounts, making it difficult for authorities to determine liability. In case of online service companies it becomes difficult to determine origin source of the revenue, thus compliance pose a challenge for the authorities.

INTERNATIONAL TAX MANAGEMENT STRATEGY

The minimization of the overall tax burden so as to maximize the overall profit is the strategy of international firms. A number of activities are directed to this end.

First, a firm has to take a decision whether the profits of the subsidiaries should lie with them and their repatriation to the parent unit delayed in order to evade taxes at home. If this is adopted, the profits would be reinvested in profitable channels and the corporate wealth of the subsidiary will increase. However, if repatriation is delayed, the parent unit will not witness a net cash inflow and the basic purpose of investment in subsidiary is marred. Thus, there should be a trade-off between the repatriation of dividend and retention of earning with the subsidiary.

Secondly, the objective of minimisation of tax burden depends on the cost allocation between different units of the firm. If a firm allocates cost more in a high-tax country and shows greater profits in a low-tax country, total tax burden would greatly be reduced. However, there are limits to cost allocation, to overcome which, a firm adopts transfer-pricing devices. Chapter 23 explains how funds move intra-firm through transfer pricing. Profits shift from one subsidiary to the other through the movement of funds that depends in turn on the successful operation of transfer pricing. However, there are limits to transfer pricing. When tariff is imposed on the imports, transfer pricing can be used only to a limited extent. It is because tariff influences the profits and thereby the taxes.

> International tax management strategy aims at maximising profit and involves:
> 1. Trade-off between retention and repatriation of profits, by subsidiaries;
> 2. Cost allocation among subsidiaries facing varying tax rates;
> 3. Decision to operate through either branches or subsidiaries.

Thirdly, the tax management strategy incorporates the decision whether the foreign operation should take the form of either a branch or a subsidiary. If it is anticipated that foreign operation will incur huge losses in some of the years, it is better to operate through branches. Branches do not represent an independent entity and so the loss incurred by one branch will absorb the profits earned by other units and the total tax burden will be lower.

Whatever the strategy, a firm needs considering the tax provisions in the home country as well as in the host country. Any strategy should be implemented only in view of this.

INDIAN TAXATION SCENARIO

The foreign investors operating in India are subject to Indian tax rules and regulation. The taxes are both direct and indirect. Some of the major provisions relating to taxes on corporate income, on the income of the expatriates working in India and also the customs duty are discussed here.

From the viewpoint of taxes, it is necessary to identify whether:

1. The assessee company is a domestic or a foreign company
2. The assessee company is resident assessee or a non-resident assessee
3. The assessee company's income is Indian or foreign

A domestic company is a company registered in India under the provisions of the Indian Companies Act and that declares its dividend in India. Others are treated as a foreign company. Again, a domestic company is treated as a resident assessee. On the contrary, a foreign company is treated as a resident assessee only when its entire operation, and not a part of it, is located in India.

The income is compartmentalised into (1) Indian income, and (2) Foreign income. Indian income is an:

1. Income that accrues/arises in India and is received/deemed to be received in India.

2. Income that accrues/arises outside India but is received/deemed to be received in India.
3. Income that accrues/arises in India but is received/deemed to be received outside India.

On the contrary, foreign income is an income that accrues/arises outside India and is received/deemed to be received outside India.

A resident assessee is taxed on both its Indian income and foreign income. But a non-resident/foreign company is not taxed on its foreign income. There are, of course, some foreign incomes which are treated as Indian income. Income of a business process out-sourcing (BPO) units in India, even if they are a permanent establishment of a non-resident foreign company, specific cases of interest, dividend, technical fees, royalty, etc. are apposite example. However, many of them are exempted from tax.

Taxes on Corporate Income

As per the Finance Act 2011, the corporate income tax is 30.0 per cent in the case of domestic companies plus an education cess at 3.0 per cent. If the income exceeds ₹ 10 million, there will be a surcharge of 5.0 per cent. Foreign companies have to pay corporate income tax at 40.0 per cent along with the education cess. If the turnover exceeds ₹ 10 million, surcharge has to be paid at the rate of 2.0 per cent. This means that the effective tax rate is 32.445 per cent in the case of a domestic company and it is 42.024 per cent in the case of a foreign company. In order to bring zero-tax companies into the tax net, minimum alternate tax (MAT) is levied at the rate of 18.5 per cent.

A dividend distribution tax of 16.22 per cent is applicable to domestic companies. In case of short-term capital gains, the normal base rate is applicable but long-term capital gains are subject to tax at a rate varying between 10.0 and 20.0 per cent. Short-term profits out of selling of equity shares are taxed at 15.0 per cent but long-term profits are exempted from taxes.

The above taxes are followed by withholding tax which is as follows:

1. Interest income: 20.0 per cent
2. Technical services fees: 10.0 per cent
3. Royalty: 20.0 per cent
4. Other services: 40.0 per cent

Taxes on Expatriates' Income

Those expatriates working in embassies/consulates are exempted from any tax. From the viewpoint of income tax, there are two categories of expatriates: one working in the companies coming into operation in India, while the other being of the general category concerning foreigners operating in any Indian/foreign company. Since their salary accrues and arises in India, it is taxed at a rate applicable to "salary"-class income. When the salary is paid in foreign currency, the amount is converted into the Indian currency on the last day of the month.

Indirect Taxes

Customs duty is the most important among the indirect taxes. It is imposed on the imports. It is either *ad valorem* or specific. The rate is amended from time to time. In the past one and a half decades, the rate has been slashed significantly.

Besides the basic customs duty, there is countervailing duty. The purpose is to ensure that the protection provided by the basic customs duty to the domestic manufacturers is not eroded.

Again, additional duty is levied at 4.0 per cent in order to counter the local sales tax./Vat, etc.

The manufacturers of goods in India have also to pay excise duty normally at 16.0 per cent. However, the foreign investors operating in India get some credit in specific cases.

Assuming the basic customs duty at 10.0 per cent, countervailing duty at 16.48 per cent, education cess at 3.0 per cent, additional duty at 4.0 per cent and allowing for credit at 10.84 per cent, the impact of these indirect taxes comes to around 23.29 per cent.

Tax Incentives

The Indian tax authorities have provided tax holiday in order to attract the foreign investment. Any profit from the industrial establishment located in backward area or any establishment related to power generation is exempted entirely from taxes for the first five years. For the next five years, the exemption rate comes down to 30 per cent. The profit from commercial oil production is completely exempted from taxes for the first seven years. There is 100 per cent tax exemption related to research and development activities for the first five years. Last but not least, export processing zones/special economic zones are also exempt from taxes for the first ten years.

Double Tax Avoidance Agreements in India

Section 90 of the Income Tax Act empowers the Indian government to enter into an agreement with a foreign government for the purpose of avoidance of double taxation. The Indian government signed such a treaty for the first time in 1965 with the Austrian government. Presently, there are such treaties with 75 governments. The treaties are either comprehensive, partial, or specific. Comprehensive treaties cover all items of income, while partial treaties cover income only from specific sources such as air transport, shipping, and so on.

> Comprehensive treaties cover all items of income, while partial treaties cover income only from specific sources.

However, this does not mean that in cases where any treaty is absent, there is no relief. An Indian resident will get tax relief under Section 91 and he shall be entitled to deductions under the Indian Income Tax Act. The income is subjected to Indian tax rate as well as to the tax rate of a specific foreign country. The lower of the two amounts is considered for relief. If both are equal, any of the two may be considered.

List of Countries having Double Tax Avoidance Treaty with India			
1	Afghanistan	40	Nepal
2	Armenia	41	Netherlands
3	Australia	42	New Zealand
4	Austria	43	Norway
5	Bangladesh	44	Oman
6	Belarus	45	Philippines
7	Belgium	46	Poland
8	Brazil	47	Portuguese Republic
9	Bulgaria	48	Qatar
10	Canada	49	Romania
11	China	50	Russian Federation
12	Cyprus	51	Singapore
13	Czech Republic	52	Slovenia
14	Denmark	53	South Africa
15	Egypt	54	South Korea
16	Finland	55	Spain
17	France	56	Sri Lanka
18	Germany	57	Sudan
19	Greece	58	Sweden
20	Hungary	59	Swiss Federal Council
21	Iceland	60	Switzerland
22	Indonesia	61	Syria
23	Ireland	62	Tanzania
24	Israel	63	Thailand
25	Italy	64	Trinidad & Tobago
26	Japan	65	Turkey
27	Jordan	66	Turkmenistan
28	Kazakhstan	67	Uganda
29	Kenya	68	Ukraine
30	Kingdom of Saudi Arabia	69	United Arab Emirates
31	Kuwait	70	United Arab Republic
32	Kyrgyz Republic	71	United Kingdom
33	Libya	72	United States of America
34	Malaysia	73	Uzbekistan
35	Malta	74	Vietnam
36	Mauritius	75	Zambia
37	Mongolia		
38	Morocco		
39	Namibia		

Source: Ministry of Finance (Govt. of India) documents.

SUMMARY

- Taxes play an important role in international financial decisions. An international tax system has three bases: neutrality, equity, and avoidance of double taxation. Neutrality may be viewed as capital-export neutrality and capital-import neutrality. The principle of equity is based on the principle of equal sacrifice. It is in consonance with the principle of neutrality. Double taxation is avoided through relief either under treaty or even without any treaty.
- An international firm is usually subjected to income tax, withholding tax and VAT. There are tax-haven countries that have zero/a very low rate of taxes. In some cases, they exempt foreign income from tax or, alternatively, they provide specific tax privileges.
- There are different modes of relief measures provided for the avoidance of double taxation. They are tax credit with or without deferral, tax exemptions, treating foreign paid tax as expenditure and investment credit.
- MNC, do focus on specific tax strategy in order to minimise the total tax burden.
- Under Indian tax laws, various kinds of incentives are provided to the residents on their income from foreign sources. Specific forms of income of the foreign enterprises in India are also exempted from tax. Last but equally important, the Indian Government has signed treaties for the avoidance of double taxation. Even in cases where treaty has not been signed, relief is provided to the assessee.

REVIEW QUESTIONS

Objective-Type Questions

1. State whether true (T) or false (F):

(a) Capital-import neutrality means the same rate of tax for residents as well as non-residents. ☐

(b) Ability-to-pay principle means the same amount of tax for varying income-group tax payers. ☐

(c) Income from foreign sources may be exempted from tax for avoidance of double taxation. ☐

(d) VAT is a direct tax. ☐

(e) Tax havens vary among themselves in respect of rates of taxes. ☐

2. Choose the correct answer:

(a) Comprehensive treaties for double tax avoidance include

(i) all aspects of income

(ii) specific income

(iii) none of these

(b) Section 91 of the Indian Income Tax Act provides for:
  (i) double taxation relief under the framework of treaties
  (ii) double taxation relief even without any tax treaty
  (iii) none of these

(c) Any new EPZ unit gets tax deductions if its export accounts for:
  (i) 50% of total sales
  (ii) 75% of total sales
  (iii) none of these

Short-Answer Questions

1. Distinguish between capital-export neutrality and capital-import neutrality.
2. Explain the two bases of the principle of equity.
3. Name any three measures for avoiding double taxation.
4. What are the different forms of tax-haven countries?
5. Distinguish between tax credit with deferral and without deferral.

Long-Answer Questions

1. Explain the different bases of international tax system.
2. What are the major forms of taxes an international firm is subjected to?
3. Describe the different modes of double taxation relief.
4. What are the tax incentives provided to the foreign enterprises in India?

REFERENCES

Alworth, J.S. (1988), *The Finance, Investment and Taxation Decisions of Multinationals*, Oxford, Basil Blackwell.

Eun, C.S. and B.G. Resnick (1998), *International Financial Management*, Boston, Irwin-McGraw-Hill, 509.

Horst, T. (1980), A Note on the Optimal Taxation of International Investment Income, *Quarterly Journal of Economics*, XCIV, 793–99.

Gordon, R. (1981), *Tax Havens and Their Use by United States Taxpayers: An overview*, Washington, D.C., US Department of the Treasury, 15–19.

UNCTAD (2004), *World Investment Report: 2004*, Geneva.

UNCTAD (2008), *World Investment Report: 2008*, Geneva & New York.

SUGGESTED FURTHER READING

Bhargave, U.K. and R. Bhargave (2000), *Income Tax Act*, New Delhi, Taxmann Publications.

Grundy, M. (1984), *The World of International Tax Planning*, Cambridge, Cambridge University Press.

CHAPTER

26 Fintech and Digital Transformation in International Finance

Learning Objectives

In the present of digital transformation, even finance is rapidly changing its dynamics to the digital world. Financial technology or Fintech is a reality now, financial managers need to be dealt with all these changing technologies and thus after reading this chapter, students will be equipped with:

- Understanding of financial technology.
- Understanding of dynamics of financial technology.
- How to leverage technology for financial development.
- Understand dynamics of international finance and fintech.

Humanity has consistently endeavored to comprehend the system of exchange of goods or services more effectively. This pursuit of understanding led to the study of subjects such as economics and commerce, which subsequently contributed to the development of finance. With the advent of the Renaissance in Europe and advancements in scientific development, human progress has spanned from the steam engine to artificial intelligence. However, individuals still face challenges in understanding and managing money. While we have created money as an artificial medium of exchange, the storage and convenient transport of money posed difficulties, limiting transactions and consequently, the growth of business and commerce. Various financial institutions, such as banks, and instruments like checks and bills of exchange, were established to facilitate

The Renaissance (14th–17th century) was a cultural revival in Europe, emphasizing humanism, art, and science, bridging the medieval and modern eras.

transactions. Nevertheless, obstacles persisted in this rapidly evolving world, leading to the invention of NEFT and RTGS, among other innovations. Beyond transactions, issues related to information dissemination and awareness were encountered. Challenges arose in the proper maintenance of financial data records and their reporting to authorities, resulting in system glitches. This manual involvement created certain vulnerabilities that were exploited by fraudulent actors. The lack of technology in the financial sector and excessive human intervention led to delays in operations and occasional misappropriation.

NEFT: A batch-based electronic fund transfer system in India.

RTGS: A real-time, high-value fund transfer system.

Without modern technology, it was nearly impossible for businesses to conduct international transactions in such an efficient and seamless manner. The path to international finance without technological involvement presented more challenges than opportunities. The biggest challenge was transfer of virtual money from one country to other within less time and timely communication of transfer of funds. Thus, there were limited scope for investors to park their additional funds and it was hard for corporates to procure funds from across borders which posed a serious challenge for development of under developed nations.

Technologies like blockchain, digital banking, and cryptocurrencies have removed geographical constraints in financial operations.

With the involvement of technology in financial sector made this mammoth task child's play. With unlimited number of transactions happening in and around globe within no time, it is virtually impossible for manual system to facilitate this high frequency transactions and take record of that, it is only the creation of technology that even we can take record of unlimited number of transactions at any place from any entity to any entity just by sitting at one place of world.

The word fintech includes both finance and technology, which translates that it is the system in which we use technology for facilitating financial events. Fintech is a major contributor for facilitating transaction without limitation of borders and distance, but fintech do not limit itself only up to that rather its purview and dimensions are very dynamic and fintech is involved in a lot things which is other than just transaction facilitation. In the present era we are way ahead of our need for transfer of funds, we moved into the realm of digital currency and blockchain technology, which is way ahead of just storing of financial data rather facilitates cross-country transaction very well.

Fintech (Financial Technology): The use of technology to improve and automate financial services.

More advanced technologies of digital currency, blockchain, digital banking, cryptocurrencies are opening new dimension for financial managers. Now they have more option for supply of funds, maintaining liquidity is easy as well as efficient. Technology has significantly reduced time gap in procurement of funds. But at the same time involvement of technology has opened new dimensions of business too in the financial sectors for management of these technologies, financial frauds are also very common these days and misappropriation is very common.

FINTECH IN THE REALM OF INTERNATIONAL FINANCE

Financial innovation has gone through a slow process to reach its present form, with increase in technological innovations financial sector has also experienced something new.

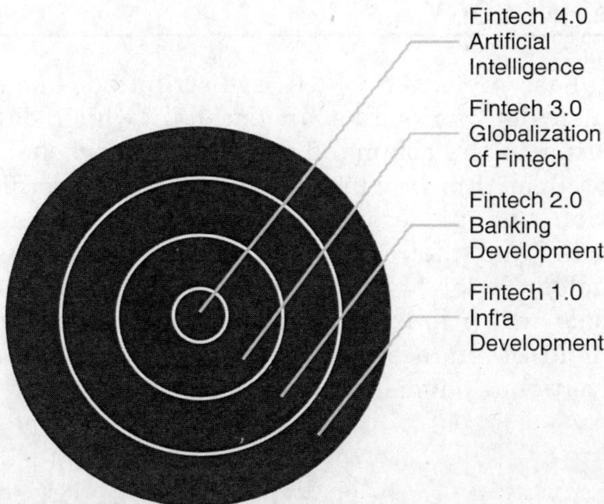

FIGURE 26.1 Stages of Financial Information Revolution.

Stage I Fintech 1.0: This was the phase which started with the transmission of financial information across borders using telegraph and transmission lines, this idea started our idea of global finance.

Stage II Fintech 2.0: This was the second revolution in the field of financial development which embedded computer technology with finance. From the use of hand-held calculator to digitization of banking and stock exchanges were happened in this period. In true sense, this era established a solid foundation for modern developments. Banks became interconnected through computer network, the records got digitalized as well as consumer also have access of all this information. Increase in financial inclusion and access to information connected investors to the market and increased availability of capital in market and made people connected which was earlier a small market.

> Fintech 1.0: Cross-border financial communication began via telegraphs.
> Fintech 2.0: Finance integrated with computers, enabling digital banking.
> Fintech 3.0: Blockchain and digital currencies revolutionized transactions.
> Fintech 4.0: AI drives data-driven finance and consumer-focused innovations.

Stage III Fintech 3.0: What we today see as fintech was actually developed in this era where the startups and corporates exploited newly developed blockchain technology, digital currencies were developed like bitcoin and dogecoin. Development of Unified payment system and common gateway system helps in easy secure and rapid transaction which is expanded the purview of financial development.

Stage IV Fintech 4.0: This era is embarked by involvement of Artificial Intelligence (AI) tools in financial sector. The technology like AI is now integral part of almost every financial development and changing dynamics of finance. This era focuses on behavior of consumer and investors towards use of internet and its products. New financial products are developed keeping in mind this behavior of investors and consumers.

BLOCKCHAIN TECHNOLOGY

Blockchain is a database or ledger which is distributed among a lot of multiple computers which basically works like an excel in which database is managed automatically according to the command given. The blockchain technology works on the cryptographic algorithm in which each transaction is divided into multiple blocks for verification and procession, each block is connected through main network through nodes and their distinct transaction history and time stamps. In blockchain technology a lot of multiple ledgers are created and each having a similar identity code which is to be matched to alter and access the data base altogether. In the field of finance, it is used for crypto transaction as well as settlements of international payments, trade finances, etc.

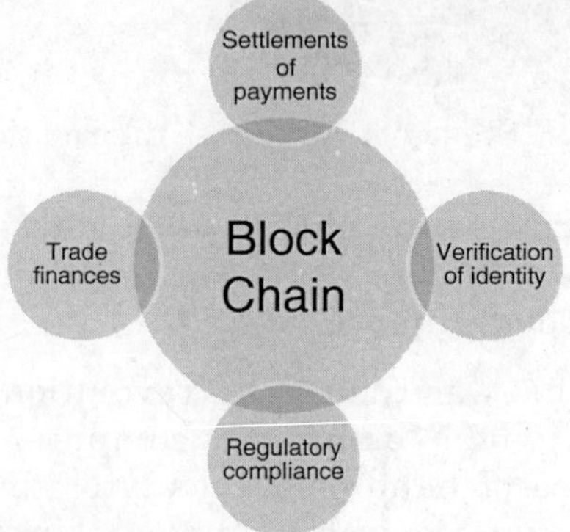

FIGURE 26.2 Elements of Blockchain.

Blockchain Technology in Cryptocurrencies

The blockchain technology facilitates and mainly used for cryptocurrencies because crypto are based on the network of ledgers maintained separately. High security feature of blockchain technology makes it useful for cryptocurrencies.

Blockchain Technology in International Payments

The blockchain technology helps in automation of transaction processes, which is very useful for international payment system. Leveraging blockchain technology and smart contract system we can easily and securely perform international transactions because it eliminates cross-border settlement problems of identification and multiple processes by doing it in real time.

CRYPTOCURRENCIES AND INTERNATIONAL FINANCE

Cryptocurrencies are the digital currencies which is basically a computer program which has a distinct identity and unique access code, which can be easily exchanged between two parties and it uses blockchain technology for maintaining its data and ledgers. Famous cryptocurrencies are bitcoin, Ethereum, dogecoin, etc.

Cryptocurrencies provide new alternative for the currency system where we can transact digitally without use of physical cash or going through the banking system. The cryptocurrencies are not governed by central banks rather it is automated through blockchain technology and it is created by "crypto mining" which makes its availability in limited quantity but at the same time makes it difficult to control as a "money" because its flow cannot be managed.

> Cryptocurrency: A decentralized digital currency secured by blockchain technology, enabling peer-to-peer transactions without intermediaries.

In case of international transactions, cryptocurrencies are very beneficial because due to its cryptographic technology and use of blockchain it is very secure and nearly impossible to breach. The use of crypto can bypass the normal international banking system and information swapping system which makes it efficient and cost effective. This acts as a globally accepted common currency which bypass the problem of multicurrency system in which translation cost is very high and currency exchange is a major hindrance for international transactions in traditional methods.

Now the introduction of cryptocurrencies in international finance will change the dynamics of the game because it can shake the foundation of international finance by eliminating the problem of exchange rates and time lags in international settlements, which will facilitate the development of international businesses.

FINTECH AND INTERNATIONAL FINANCE

In the domain of international finance, innovation in financial technology serves as both a disruptor and facilitator of trade. Particularly in the case of international transactions, it has proven to be advantageous. The implementation of international swap systems has created new opportunities for interbank transactions and payment systems. The exchange of banking information has become more efficient and time-effective. Through the utilization of NOSTRO and VOSTRO accounts, these transactions can be executed with ease.

> Nostro Account: A bank's account in a foreign bank, in foreign currency. (our account in their bank)
>
> Vostro Account: A foreign bank's account in a domestic bank, in local currency. (their account in our bank)

The application of artificial intelligence and international transaction platforms such as PayPal, Wise, and Remitly has enabled instantaneous and seamless international transactions. This financial technology innovation has significantly streamlined international finance processes.

AI and blockchain technology make it super easy to automate huge international data management and keep track of global transactions. Blockchain technology uses multiple nodes and data points which is a boon for data security and management of data.

When we talk about the modernity in global monetary system, then cryptocurrency will be the champion in this field. Introduction of cryptocurrency has eliminated the problems related to international transaction like exchange rate, multiple currency system and translation cost, etc. Nonetheless it will impact the global markets in a different way because it will also eliminate the issues of spillovers and volatility, which is generally transferred from one country to other due to multiple currency system and exchange rate system.

The introduction of AI and Blockchain technology in the field of international finance has proved to be a tool for regulatory compliance and more stringent monitoring of transactions because of end to end connectivity of transactions and nodal accounting records. The algorithm used by blockchain will give a big push to the regulatory compliance framework worldwide and information will be accessible to the authorities with minimum lag of time. The use of this structure will make the code system resilience towards threats and make it difficult for the hackers to breach into system for stealing information. Fintech and blockchain will be proved as a biggest facilitator in transfer of financial information and funds effortlessly and efficiently.

SUMMARY

- The use of fintech and blockchains in the world of international finance has not only benefitted the transfer and storage of information and funds, rather it has facilitated trade too. Use of these tech-based solution can lead to diametric change in the way international transactions are done, it will enhance the regulatory framework for international transactions and eliminate administrative hurdles for execution of deals. Global financial system will be more facilitating in terms of trade and development. But the most significant change it may carry with it is that with elimination of currency and translation risk whole accounting and financial management scenario along with portfolio diversification can be changed.

CASE STUDY

FINTECH AND DIGITAL TRANSFORMATION IN INTERNATIONAL FINANCE

BACKGROUND

The change is a constant process, fits apt in the dimension of international finance. The constant struggle of man with money and its charm has persuaded mankind to experiment with technology in the area of finance and the present scenario of emerging technology like Fintech and digital transformation in the area of international finance is no amazement. With intermingling Fintech and digital advancement we are able to revolutionize cross-border transactions, foreign exchange, international investment flows and global trade. Blockchain, Artificial Intelligence and big data analytics is leading this change.

We can take the example of ripple, a blockchain-based payment protocol, which enables near real time cross-border money transfer with a cheaper alternative to the old school banking system.

PayPal a leading company in the industry of payment gateway, has enhanced its operations by leveraging artificial intelligence since 2022. The artificial intelligence has improved its fraud detection abilities and optimized currency conversions. The same model is used by other companies in the industry like Wise money and Revolut. Integrating Artificial intelligence with international payment has served a lot of purpose from fraud detection to easy and cheap operations, which has boosted the growth of these companies and helped them to capture more market share compared to other competitors.

Although we are swiftly integrating tech solution to more real world financial problems still we have to tackles the burning issues of cyber security risks and financial inclusion and wrestle with regulatory compliance which a tough task in itself. The plus side in this scenario is that every stakeholder from government to financial institutions and even small participating agents are joining hands to develop frameworks to address these challenges and harness the best out of this transformation.

Case Scenario

XYZ, a leading name in the global banking system is doing business with traditional methods. In the present scenario, the bank is not able to keep its head held high because its rivals like fintech platforms are attracting more customers due to their efficient, fast, transparent and more cheaper solutions, which makes the whole plethora hard to beat. To address this, the CEO decided to adopt blockchain technology for cross-border payments and AI for risk management. However, some stakeholders are worried about the cybersecurity risks and high implementation costs associated with these changes. The CEO is now looking for ways to innovate while managing risks and complying with regulations.

QUESTIONS

1. Analyze the primary advantages and challenges XYZ Global Bank may encounter while integrating blockchain technology into its cross-border payment system.
2. In what ways can artificial intelligence enhance risk management in international finance for XYZ Global Bank? Provide practical examples.
3. What measures should the bank take to overcome resistance from internal stakeholders regarding digital transformation?
4. Evaluate the potential impact of regulatory frameworks on XYZ Global Bank's fintech adoption. How can the bank ensure compliance while innovating?

REVIEW QUESTIONS

Objective-Type Questions

1. State whether true (T) or false (F):

(a) Fintech 2.0 introduced blockchain technology and digital currencies. ☐
(b) The introduction of AI and blockchain has improved regulatory compliance and transaction monitoring in international finance. ☐
(c) Cryptocurrency eliminates exchange rate issues and reduces translation costs in international transactions. ☐
(d) The first phase of fintech (Fintech 1.0) began with the integration of computers into banking. ☐
(e) NOSTRO and VOSTRO accounts facilitate seamless international transactions between banks. ☐
(f) Fintech and blockchain technology have made global financial transactions more secure and efficient. ☐

2. Choose the correct answer:

   (a) What is the primary objective of fintech in international finance?
      (i) Increasing the use of manual transactions
      (ii) Facilitating high-frequency transactions across borders
      (iii) Limiting the use of digital currencies
      (iv) Reducing access to financial records

   (b) Which stage of fintech introduced blockchain and digital currencies?
      (i) Fintech 1.0
      (ii) Fintech 2.0
      (iii) Fintech 3.0
      (iv) Fintech 4.0

   (c) Blockchain technology's security is primarily attributed to its use of:
      (i) Manual ledger entries
      (ii) Cryptographic algorithms
      (iii) Centralized database management
      (iv) Hand-held calculators

   (d) Which technology is a defining characteristic of Fintech 4.0?
      (i) Telegraph-based communication
      (ii) Blockchain technology
      (iii) Artificial intelligence tools
      (iv) Digital calculators

   (e) What challenge does cryptocurrency aim to address in international finance?
      (i) Increase in manual intervention
      (ii) High transaction costs due to multicurrency systems
      (iii) Requirement for physical cash
      (iv) Reduced financial fraud

   (f) How does artificial intelligence contribute to fintech in international finance?
      (i) Increases manual data handling
      (ii) Automates international regulatory compliance
      (iii) Replaces blockchain technology
      (iv) Eliminates digital currencies

   (g) Which of the following is NOT an advantage of fintech in international finance?
      (i) Elimination of exchange rate problems
      (ii) Faster cross-border transactions
      (iii) Vulnerability to financial frauds
      (iv) Increased automation in data handling

Short-Answer Questions

1. What is the role of blockchain technology in international finance, especially in the areas of cryptocurrency and international payments?
2. What are the four stages of fintech evolution, and how has each stage impacted the current landscape of international finance?
3. How have digital currencies, including cryptocurrencies, affected traditional international financial systems?

Long-Answer Questions

1. What are the main challenges that fintech poses to international finance, and what are some potential solutions?
2. How can artificial intelligence be utilized to automate regulatory compliance and transaction processes within the realm of international finance?
3. In what ways has fintech disrupted traditional banking systems? Provide examples using technologies such as PayPal, Wise, or Remitly.
4. What are the major vulnerabilities of fintech systems in regard to cyberattacks and financial fraud? What measures can be implemented to improve security?

REFERENCES

Arner, D. W., Barberis, J., and Buckley, R. P. (2016), *The Evolution of Fintech: A New Post-Crisis Paradigm?, Georgetown Journal of International Law.*

Böhme, R., Christin, N., Edelman, B., and Moore, T. (2015), *Bitcoin: Economics, Technology, and Governance, Journal of Economic Perspectives.*

Brynjolfsson, E., and McAfee, A. (2017), *The Business of Artificial Intelligence,* Harvard Business Review.

Chui, M., Manyika, J., and Miremadi, M. (2018), *What AI Can and Can't Do (Yet) for Your Business, McKinsey Quarterly.*

Claessens, S., Frost, J., Turner, G., and Zhu, F. (2018), *Fintech Credit Markets Around the World: Size, Drivers, and Policy Issues, BIS Quarterly Review.*

King, B. (2018), *Bank 4.0: Banking Everywhere, Never at a Bank*, Wiley.

Kshetri, N. (2017), *Can Blockchain Strengthen the Internet of Things?*, IT Professional, IEEE Computer Society.

Liang, B., and You, J. (2020), *Cybersecurity in Fintech: Issues and Challenges, Journal of Cyber Policy*, Taylor & Francis

Nakamoto, S. (2008), *Bitcoin: A Peer-to-Peer Electronic Cash System*, https://bitcoin.org/bitcoin.pdf

Schueffel, P. (2016), *Taming the Beast: A Scientific Definition of Fintech, Journal of Innovation Management.*

Stallings, W. (2018), *Cryptography and Network Security: Principles and Practice,* Pearson.

Tapscott, D., and Tapscott, A. (2016), *Blockchain Revolution: How the Technology Behind Bitcoin and Other Cryptocurrencies is Changing the World*, Portfolio/ Penguin.

Yermack, D. (2015). *Is Bitcoin a Real Currency? An Economic Appraisal*, National Bureau of Economic Research (NBER).

Zalan, T., and Toufaily, E. (2017). *The Promise of Fintech in Emerging Markets: Not as Disruptive*, Contemporary Economics, University of Economics and Human Sciences in Warsaw.

SUGGESTED FURTHER READING

Chishti, S., and Barberis, J. (Eds.) (2016), *The FINTECH book: The financial technology handbook for investors, entrepreneurs, and visionaries*, Wiley.

Lee, K.F. (2018), *AI superpowers: China, Silicon Valley, and the new world order*, Houghton Mifflin Harcourt.

Skinner, C. (2014), *Digital bank: Strategies to launch or become a digital bank*, Marshall Cavendish International.

Vigna, P., and Casey, M. J. (2015), *The age of cryptocurrency: How Bitcoin and digital money are challenging the global economic order*, St. Martin's Press.

CHAPTER

27 Global Financial Crisis: From International Financial Management Perspective

Learning Objectives

Financial crisis is one of the very important component of global financial dynamics as it disturbs whole financial system and demand special attention and policies for the same. Thus by reading this chapter the students will be able to:

- Get an overview of the causes of financial crisis.
- Develop understanding about the dynamics of financial crisis.
- Deal with various risk posed by financial crisis.
- Learn lesson out of financial crisis for international financial management.

The global financial system is one the complex orders which is dynamic in its own sense and works efficiently and flawlessly based on the assumptions of its stakeholders. When there is disruption in any one component of this system, it got amplified and trigger a domino effect which results in the disruption in the system as whole. Whole financial system is supported by power of banking system in assisting flow of liquidity and magical tool of money creation which makes it vulnerable to failures because value of money depends upon the demand and supply of money which indeed depends upon perception of people towards money. Financial crisis is an exaggerated situation of financial system disruption which is very common because of a lot of factors but the economy has an intrinsic tendency to rebound to original position but when the economy fails to do so, we call it a situation of crisis. Global financial crisis is declared when the impact of this event can be seen globally. The global financial system is complexly interwoven thus adverse event in one place of globe cannot save other part leading to global financial crisis.

> Domino effect refers to a chain reaction where one event sets off a sequence of similar events, like falling dominoes.

The most recent of the global financial crisis which the world has seen is the global financial crisis of year 2008, which is trigged by the failure of US housing market and spread to the world through serial banking failures who were mainly bailed out by government aids and created a situation of fear in the eyes of investors leading to recession in most of advanced economies. The global financial crisis was mainly caused by neglected reckless lending by banks due favorable macro-economic conditions, leads to accumulations of non-performing assets which leads to bad financial health of banks, and thus trigger bank failure and bank runs.

Bank run occurs when many depositors withdraw their money simultaneously, fearing the bank's failure, which can lead to its collapse.

In the situations of financial crisis, the economic system went into turmoil, leads to volatility in exchange rate which results in uncertainty in external sector financing. The crisis creates a situation of economic distrust due to investors tends to change premium for additional risk taken by them. The situation of global financial crisis not only pose a critical situation for financing from foreign sources from the perspective of corporate rather it posed critical situation for investors also because due to excessive volatility in economic system it is very difficult for investors to take decisions.

The risk premium increases which tends to increase the cost of financing from external sources adding on to that it becomes very difficult to discover true value to currency of any economy because the valuation of dollar also becomes unstable. This situation leads to instability in external trade of any nation and affects BOP of that country. In worst case to remain solvent the governments often open their coffers to support foreign reserves, accumulate deficits which is balanced by increasing tax collections, sucking liquidity from the market. This chain reaction of monetary and fiscal polity leads to vicious cycle of low demand and fearful behavior of the investors, in this critical condition role of International financial management becomes crucial.

BOP (Balance of Payments): A country's record of international trade and financial transactions.

GLOBAL FINANCIAL CRISIS: CONTEXT AND CAUSES

Any financial crisis is manifestation of lack of regulatory efforts and raptures in economy, but there must be an ignition point. In case of GFC 2008 the crisis started with the breaking down of US housing market. During 2006, the US market was very optimistic for increasing private income and demand for houses due to increasing population of new age IT professionals and increasing employment. Due to its credit driven structure of economy, and high optimism among business men and investors, cost of credit was low which facilitated a lot of real estate businesses for construction of houses at large scale, but the actual fault laid in using these homes as mortgage for getting further loans. The houses were overvalued compared to actual market valuation in that area. The central problem in this scenario was that there were weak demand of homes compared to what was estimated by most of the real estate companies. Due to weak demand the houses remained unsold which made it difficult for debtors to pay back bank loans and either they tended to default on there loans or they managed to get another loan keeping those houses as mortgage.

A mortgage is a loan secured by property, where the borrower repays over time, and the lender can seize the property if payments are not made.

This faulty practices by the investors on the assumption of strong demand in future led to a complex bubble in which one asset was dependent on another and there was negligible underlying backing behind all these loans. Thus this system was more of a domino effect which was about to create a chain reaction in future by moving just one brick. Since there were no such true backing behind these loans, (because the valuation of houses were not true and that can only be realized when houses were sold off which was not possible due to weak demand), most of these assets of the banks were in distress. The moving brick of this domino was failure of Lehman brothers' (bank).

> The Subprime Mortgage Crisis (2007–2008) was a financial meltdown caused by risky lending practices, excessive subprime mortgage loans, and the collapse of the U.S. housing bubble. It led to a global recession, massive bank failures, and widespread economic turmoil.

Due to high non-performing assets and turning up of a lot of assets into bad assets, Lehman brothers failed to honor its financial obligations and filed bankruptcy. As Lehman brothers fell, a chain reaction of bank run and high risk premium got triggered. People lost confidence in banks as most of the banks had invested in the real estate industry because of bubble. When banks started failing it became difficult for the government to bail out every bank. This situation not only concentrated in US change in valuation of dollar and fear among American investors exported this crisis to other countries as investors started sucking out liquidity from the market in wake of uncertainty and volatility, market became more volatile, strengthening prediction of investors. Thus capital markets started crashing in wake of outward movement of FPI and FII.

The crisis was so big that it was compared with great depression of 1930, in which the world had seen change of orders. The lack of strong consumer demand led to unemployment and situation got worsen.

There were mainly three main reason for Global financial crisis:

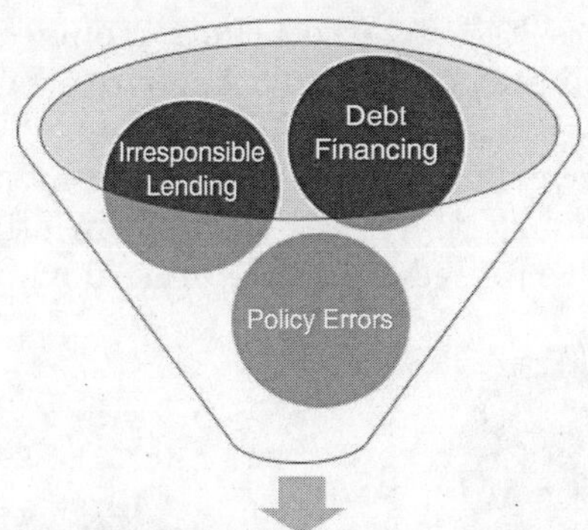

FIGURE 27.1 Subprime Mortgage Crisis.

1. **Irresponsible Lending:** In the year 2006–7, the macro-economic variables like GDP growth rate was good, unemployment and inflation were under control, the investors sentiments got boosted in the market. Due to increase in employment the rate of houses and rents also increased. High returns from good assets enhanced their assumptions and motivated the investors to deep dive into this market in US as well as Europe. The banks started giving loans to low wealth individuals which was highly risky in the hope of high returns from these borrowers. Due to high competition among lenders

to siege this opportunity they failed to deeply scrutiny the potential of borrower to payback this loan moreover they even didn't paid attention to the quality of mortgaged assets, which often found to be faulty and fictitious. This irresponsible lending by banks in hope of profit led to compilation of huge NPAs which led to this crisis.

2. **Borrowings by Banks and Investors:** In hope of higher profit gains the banks started taking loans from the market to fund these housing projects, the loan was upon banks which they hade to pay to the lender, earlier the motive was to get the benefit of arbitrage but when assets started turning bad then it became a problem for the banks to honor their obligations and banks came into distress about loan servicing. To save banks from bank failure, the government infused external assistance.
3. **Faulty Policy Measures:** There was a serious gap in case of policy for creation and regulation of mortgage backed securities, which was used by the borrowers to create opaque and fraudulent securities, they sold them to the investors. Such a large loans were distributed to the borrowers, that they were unlikely to payback those debts. Thus they were tended to fail in debt repayment which could be a serious issue from banks perspective. Due to lack to strong policy measures fraudulent activities were prevalent and borrowers with mala fide intentions were likely to get loans easily without due diligence.

IMPACT OF GFC ON GLOBAL ECONOMY

The global financial crisis or generally known as subprime mortgage crisis was not only centered in USA rather it had a vast expansion across the globe. The foreign banks and investors had invested their money in US market due to hype in housing market and demand of loan by American banks to fund their housing market. Due to default by these banks and falling of a lot of banks, the global investors and banking networks were loosing their money, making it difficult for them to play in domestic market. There was a twin effect of this global financial crisis on the market which rippled into economic downturn globally.

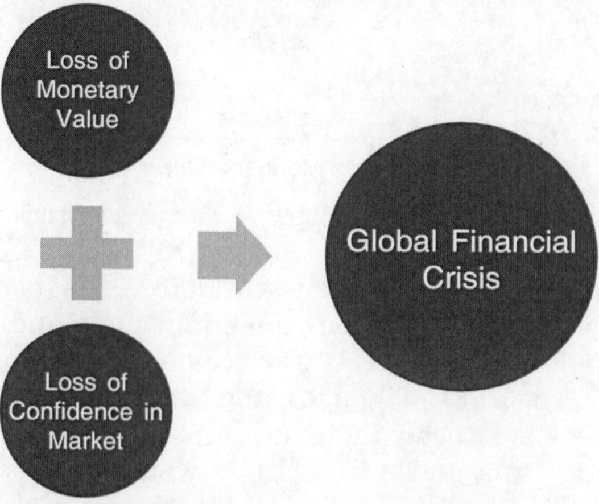

FIGURE 27.2 Global Financial Crisis.

Due to loss of value of currency and bank failure in US, investors lost confidence in the market and sucked there money from the market. US dollar had special status of medium exchange in global market and there was no central bank at global level to maintain monetary policy globally. Any problem with US dollar got amplified in other countries too creating a contagion effect and affected global economy.

Due to GFC, there was a problem of liquidity in the market which resulted in less money for production as well as demand in market. Due to weak demands in the market, business started firing their employees who were an additional cost for them at the time of cash crunch. Increasing unemployment did no good rather worsen the situation to further decrease demand in the market and we got stuck into this vicious cycle. 8.8 million of people lost their jobs. $ 17 trillion of household wealth lost, $ 7.4 trillion of valuation in stock market got evaporated. S&P 500 got down by 38%.

> The Subprime Mortgage Crisis (2007-2008) triggered the Global Financial Crisis by causing massive losses in the banking sector due to bad mortgage-backed securities. As major financial institutions collapsed or required bailouts, panic spread worldwide, leading to a severe credit crunch, stock market crashes, and a global economic recession.

LESSON LEARNED FROM GFC

1. **Banking Institutions Need to Always be Supervised:** The regulators and central banks had created a notion of "too big to fail" for big banks and using this notion they bailed out these banks from failing because they were systematically important institution requiring help. The regulators and governments learned a lesson that banks, especially big banks need to be supervised always, because the tendency of the business is to chase profits, in wake of this they tend to move towards riskier zone of lending from where they are unable to recover. Secondly due to lack of clear and strong policy about lending this all happened, thus clear guidelines for lending and due diligence are ensured. The borrowing behavior of banks are to be supervised because in this case we have already seen that the situations got amplified because of external borrowings by the banks to fund housing projects.

> Bank Supervision–Prevents excessive risk-taking.
>
> Stock Market Control–Limits speculative banking.
>
> Market Overheating–Prevents asset bubbles.
>
> Regulatory Coordination–Ensures financial stability.

2. **Not to be Risky at Stock Market:** When banks see rally in the stock market due to good macro-economic indicators or market bull run, they tend to go into riskier side to earn more and more profits infusing capital of their clients. This practice is against clients interest which is to be controlled and presence of banks in stock should be scrutinized. Fraudulent practices to book stock prices by banks artificially is to be checked otherwise this bubble can create a hype of "all good situation" in the economy, when this bubble investors loose there money mainly retail and small investors.

   During the crisis, banks tend to reduce their capital requirement in books, to show good health of the institution, and move from leverage to another sources of funds. This practice not only worsen the situation rather pose serious concern for banks. This situation should be regulated and a minimum capital requirement at all times is to be decided and strictly implemented.
3. **Overheating of Markets:** We have seen that the main cause of global financial crisis was overheating of housing markets and serious mismatch

between demand-supply in starting led to high hopes of the investors but in actual case this was castles of sand. Overheating of any market whether housing or other attract unnecessary attention of investors for earning more profits. This situation is starting point for any turmoil in the market. Overheating and serious mismatch between demand and supply is to be checked. The regulators should be more cautious during such a situation.

4. **Collective Efforts and Failure of Many Agencies:** The situations like global financial crisis is not something which happens in solace or one day. It is failure of a lot of interconnected institution who didn't have proper coordination or intent to stop such a situation thus collective responsibility should be ensured inside and across the borders. There should be proper coordination among regulatory agencies and regular meeting should be conducted to look into global economic conditions.

SUMMARY

The chapter examines the 2008 Global Financial Crisis (GFC) as a case of systemic economic failure rooted in irresponsible lending, excessive risk-taking by banks, and policy gaps. Triggered by the US housing market collapse, the crisis spread globally due to interlinked financial systems, leading to liquidity shortages, unemployment, and economic downturns. It highlights lessons like regulatory vigilance, minimizing risk exposure, and ensuring market stability through coordinated global efforts.

REVIEW QUESTIONS

Objective-Type Questions

1. State whether true (T) or false (F):
   (a) The 2008 Global Financial Crisis was triggered by the collapse of the U.S. housing market. ☐
   (b) Debt financing reduces financial vulnerability during economic downturns. ☐
   (c) Lehman Brothers' collapse had no significant impact on global financial markets. ☐
   (d) Banks should always be supervised to prevent excessive risk-taking and financial instability. ☐
   (e) Overheating of markets occurs when there is a serious mismatch between demand and supply. ☐

2. Choose the correct answer:
   (a) What was the primary cause of the 2008 Global Financial Crisis?
      (i) High interest rates globally
      (ii) Subprime mortgage lending and US housing market collapse
      (iii) Overregulation of financial institutions
      (iv) Lack of foreign investment in the US

(b) Which financial institution's failure is often seen as the catalyst for the 2008 GFC?
 (i) Lehman Brothers
 (ii) Bear Stearns
 (iii) Merrill Lynch
 (iv) AIG

(c) What is the term for investors withdrawing funds due to fear of market instability?
 (i) Market overheating
 (ii) Bank run
 (iii) Capital infusion
 (iv) Asset appreciation

(d) What economic indicator was significantly impacted during the 2008 crisis, leading to global downturns?
 (i) Exchange rate stability
 (ii) Global employment levels
 (iii) Inflation rates
 (iv) Government expenditure

(e) What lesson from the GFC emphasizes supervision of large banking institutions?
 (i) Encouraging speculative investments
 (ii) Supporting unlimited borrowing
 (iii) Avoiding the "too big to fail" notion
 (iv) Eliminating stock market participation by banks

Short-Answer Questions

1. Explain the role of subprime mortgage lending in the 2008 Global Financial Crisis.
2. What is the significance of the 'domino effect' in the context of the GFC?
3. How did the crisis affect international trade and currency valuation?

Long-Answer Questions

1. Discuss the three main causes of the 2008 Global Financial Crisis as outlined in the chapter.
2. Analyze the impact of the GFC on global employment and economic stability.
3. What lessons can regulatory bodies and financial institutions learn from the GFC to prevent future crises?

REFERENCES

Gorton, G. (2008), The panic of 2007, NBER Working Paper No. 14358, https://doi.org/10.3386/w14358

Kindleberger, C. P., and Aliber, R. Z. (2011), *Manias, panics, and crashes: A history of financial crises* (6th ed.), Palgrave Macmillan.

Mishkin, F. S. (2019), *The economics of money, banking, and financial markets* (12th ed.), Pearson.

Reinhart, C. M., and Rogoff, K.S. (2009), *This time is different: Eight centuries of financial folly*, Princeton University Press.

Stiglitz, J. E. (2010), *Freefall: America, free markets, and the sinking of the world economy*, W.W. Norton and Company.

SUGGESTED FURTHER READING

Allen, F., and Gale, D. (2007), *Understanding financial crises*, Oxford University Press.

Minsky, H.P. (2008), *Stabilizing an unstable economy*, McGraw-Hill.

Rajan, R.G. (2010), *Fault lines: How hidden fractures still threaten the world economy*, Princeton University Press.

Shiller, R. J. (2015), *Irrational exuberance* (3rd ed.), Princeton University Press.

CHAPTER

28 Sustainable Finance and ESG Investing

Learning Objectives

Socially responsible corporate governance, and environmental awareness are gaining momentum in business arena and it is expected from the business to be more financially sustainable. In this chapter we have explored:

- Various dynamics of International finance and sustainability.
- Factors influencing ESG.
- Impact of sound of ESG policy on the growth of corporates.
- Various challenges for the ESG of corporates.

In today's world scenario the Sustainability in finance and investing in ESG is becoming important as peoples are now worried about the environmental disorder, and more aware of the business malpractices. This threat has changed the thinking of all the stakeholders being it an investor, regulator, or financial institution. There is a behavioral shift and a slight shift from concept of money making to environmental awareness and taking care of the society. Sustainability in finance and considering ESG investing can support economic growth and benefit the future generations without exploiting much of today's resources.

ESG Investing–Investing with a focus on environmental, social, and governance factors.

ESG (Environmental, Social and Governance) investment is that branch of sustainable finance which considers the financial decision-making that involves investment in those sectors which does the operation considering ESG components. This can also generate the long-term value for both the investors as well as the society. The traditional finance and investment were primarily talks shareholder returns and the short-term gains while sustainable finance talks about the broader perspective and emphasizes the minimization of carbon footprint, advancing social equity, and ensuring ethical business practices too.

Some important aspects of sustainable financial inclusion are as follows:

Green Finance– Funding eco-friendly projects like renewable energy and green bonds.

- **Green Finance:** This concentrates on investments that promote environmental sustainability, such as renewable energy projects and green bonds.
- **Social Finance:** This encompasses investments in projects that yield positive social impacts, including affordable housing, education, and healthcare.
- **Impact Investing:** This strives to generate measurable social or environmental benefits in addition to financial returns.

The transition towards sustainable finance has been propelled by various global challenges, such as climate change, biodiversity loss, and social inequality. There is a growing recognition of the principle that collaboration is essential for achieving collective goals. Various stakeholders, including governments, large corporations, and financial institutions, are increasingly engaging in cooperative efforts to promote a more equitable and sustainable global economy.

THE RISE OF ESG INVESTING

What is ESG investing? This includes one's moral aspect of thinking! Investors who thinks morally for the world and have values in their behavior may make a positive shift towards the aspects of ESG that may impact the society and the environment in a better way.

- **Environmental Factors**? Think about a company's carbon footprint, how they handle waste, and if they're doing their part to save the planet.
- **Social Factors**? The social aspect talks about how the company treats its stakeholders (i.e., employees, customers, suppliers, and the communities) around them. They also focus on some key questions like, Are they fair? Do they respect human rights?
- **Governance Factors**? It's all about leadership and how a company is run. Is the board diverse? How's executive pay? Do shareholders have a voice?

A boom in ESG investing! In 2020, due to growing investment in ESG the assets size were valued at $40 trillion globally, everyone from assets management to pension funds and insurers are jumping to the ESG bandwagon.

The Increasing Significance of ESG Factors in Financial Decision-making are given below.

- **Risk Management:** It's simple. The risk management is really important, when we talk about the companies having bad environmental practices may face fines or could damage their reputation. It leads to financial losses, while sustainable companies are likely to be more profitable in the long run.
- **Regulatory Requirements:** Governments are making companies disclose their ESG performance, so investors can make informed decisions. This also pushes companies to be more sustainable.

- **Investor Preferences:** Especially younger generations are looking for sustainable investments. Companies that follow ESG principles are more likely to attract their money.
- **Reputation and Brand Equity:** Sustainability is beneficial for businesses! Customers tend to trust and remain loyal to companies that prioritize Environmental, Social, and Governance (ESG) principles.
- **Global Challenges:** Such as climate change and inequality are significant issues. Investors and companies are increasingly recognizing their role in addressing these problems. Sustainable finance and ESG investing provide a way to generate profit while contributing positively to society.

ESG is crucial in investment as it helps assess long-term risks, sustainability, and ethical impact, leading to more resilient and responsible portfolios. Investors increasingly prioritize ESG to mitigate financial risks, enhance returns, and align with regulatory and societal expectations.

ESG INVESTMENT STRATEGIES

If you're an investor looking to incorporate sustainability into your portfolio, there are several ESG (Environmental, Social, and Governance) strategies you can consider:

Negative Screening– Avoids ESG non-compliant sectors.
Positive Screening– Invests in ESG-leading companies.
Impact Investing– Funds businesses with social impact.
Shareholder Engagement– Investors push for ESG reforms.
Thematic Investing– Focuses on sustainable sectors.

1. **Negative Screening:** Under this approach we exclude those companies or sectors which are not level up in case of ESG standards and show negative impacts to the environment. The prominent examples of these sectors include tobacco or fossil fuels in which investors should refrain from investing.
2. **Positive Screening:** Contrary to above-mentioned approach, in this approach companies are sorted based on their involvement and contribution in the ESG practices. We follow certain parameters like low carbon footprints, strong labor practices or diverse leaderships to select these companies and motivate investors to invest in these companies being more sustainable in the long run.
3. **Impact Investing:** "Business model should not be only able to earn more rather it should be going and help society". This is the underlying principle of this kind of investment philosophy in which companies and sectors are selected based on their ability to create an impact on the society, additional to the return fetched by them. Affordable housing, clean water and renewable energy are such examples.
4. **Shareholder Engagement:** Under this strategy, the owner of the companies, the shareholders take more interest in insuring that, there should be more concern for ESG in company. They may took voting mechanism on ESG reports or indirect route of pressure through board of directors and ultimately management.
5. **Thematic Investing:** Under this strategy, specific sectors are identified whose goals and operations align with the sustainability goals like clean and green energy, financial inclusion, etc. The portfolio is charted out based on the theme chosen for investment.

Using these strategies we can build a more sustainable investment portfolio.

CHALLENGES IN SUSTAINABLE FINANCE AND ESG INVESTING

- **Lack of Standardization:** The absence of common parameter for testing sustainability is a major hurdle in this dimension. Adding on to it, there is a lack of standard method for reporting and comparison of ESG-related information which makes it difficult for investors and regulators to fix this problem.

No Standard Metrics–ESG reporting lacks uniformity.
Greenwashing–Fake sustainability claims.
Low Transparency–Unreliable ESG disclosures.
Short-termism–Profit over sustainability.
Regulatory Uncertainty–Frequent policy shifts.

Sustainable finance integrates ESG factors into financial decisions to promote long-term economic growth while protecting the planet. It includes green investments, ethical banking, and policies that support a sustainable future.

- **Greenwashing:** Companies often involves in the malpractice of exaggerating, their sustainability efforts, to gain more attention and report themselves as eco-friendly which boost their sustainability graph.
- **Lack of Transparency and Reliability:** The disclosure of ESG-related information is not mandatory in various countries and for various companies which act as a loophole and create a grey area where companies try to hide itself. This problem creates a lack of transparency and reliability on the data given.
- **Short-term Focus:** Many of the investors prioritize gain from short-term arbitrage over long-term sustainability which is a challenge for the company. They juggle between going green and being profitable because at the end of the day wealth of shareholders and valuation of company depends upon its growing share prices.
- **Regulatory Challenge:** Changing political dynamics and uncertainty regarding ESG-related reforms is prominent across globe. Constant reforms in this field make it difficult for investors as well as company to keep up with change.

THE FUTURE OF SUSTAINABLE FINANCE AND ESG INVESTING

The future of ESG (Environmental, Social and Governance) is bright. It seems positive from perspective of investor. Increasing awareness towards environmental issues will fetch more attraction of government, investors, financial institutions and companies towards this burning issue. This may lead to better regulation and policies.

Globally, sustainable finance is growing rapidly, with ESG assets expected to exceed $50 trillion by 2025, making up more than one-third of total assets under management.

- **Stricter regulatory frameworks** are adopted and implemented by governments by some of the countries across globe, they have issued guidelines for ESG investing, expenditure and disclosure which is strictly monitored. Most prominent of them is taxonomy regulation implemented by European Union, which classifies economic activities based on the environmental sustainability.
- **Advancements in technology**, like introduction of Artificial intelligence and block chain have not only enhance the efficiency of this area rather with advent of time, they will prove to be a significant tool for making ESG reporting more transparent and reliable. Using these advanced tools we can better track the development of companies in terms of ESG metrics.
- **Integration of ESG factors into mainstream finance** is becoming increasingly prevalent, as ESG investing transitions from a niche approach to a widely accepted strategy. Institutional investors are progressively

adopting sustainable finance practices, which positions ESG considerations as a fundamental aspect of contemporary financial decision-making.

- **Growing demand for impact investing** is for the investors who are balancing between profit generation and social welfare, if they tend to create a positive impact on the ground of social and environmental sustainability of corporates they can opt for these investment strategies which surely will be investment for future.

SUMMARY

This chapter examines sustainable finance and ESG investing, emphasizing the incorporation of environmental, social, and governance factors into financial decision-making. It highlights the significance of these factors for risk management, regulatory compliance, and long-term profitability. The chapter also discusses various ESG investment strategies, challenges, and the future of sustainable finance.

REVIEW QUESTIONS

Objective-Type Questions

1. State whether true (T) or false (F):

(a) ESG investing focuses only on financial returns and ignores social and environmental factors. ☐

(b) Greenwashing refers to companies falsely claiming to be environmentally sustainable. ☐

(c) AI and blockchain can improve ESG transparency and reporting. ☐

(d) Negative screening involves selecting companies that excel in ESG practices. ☐

(e) Frequent changes in ESG regulations create uncertainty for investors and companies. ☐

2. Choose the correct answer:

(a) What is the primary focus of sustainable finance?

(i) Maximizing short-term profits
(ii) Aligning financial goals with societal and environmental objectives
(iii) Ignoring environmental concerns
(iv) Promoting only financial returns

(b) Which of the following is a key element of ESG investing?

(i) Focus solely on financial returns
(ii) Investment in companies with strong environmental practices
(iii) Ignore social and governance factors
(iv) Avoid any involvement in renewable energy

(c) What is the main challenge in ESG investing?

(i) Excessive government regulation
(ii) Lack of standardized metrics and reporting frameworks

(iii) Too much investment in green projects
(iv) Unclear consumer demand for ESG products

(d) Which of the following is an example of positive screening in ESG investing?
(i) Excluding companies involved in fossil fuels
(ii) Investing in companies with strong labor practices
(iii) Avoiding companies with low stock market returns
(iv) Focusing on short-term gains

(e) What is "greenwashing" in the context of sustainable finance?
(i) Genuine investments in renewable energy
(ii) Companies misrepresenting their sustainability efforts
(iii) Strict regulatory compliance for ESG companies
(iv) Encouraging banks to invest in green bonds

Short-Answer Questions

1. What are the key factors evaluated in ESG investing?
2. Explain the concept of impact investing.
3. Why is regulatory uncertainty a challenge for sustainable finance?

Long-Answer Questions

1. Discuss the role of ESG investing in risk management and long-term financial returns.
2. Examine the challenges and solutions for ensuring reliable and standardized ESG data.

REFERENCES

Clark, G. L., Feiner, A., and Viehs, M. (2015), From the stockholder to the stakeholder: How sustainability can drive financial outperformance, University of Oxford and Arabesque Partners.

Eccles, R. G., and Klimenko, S. (2019), The investor revolution: Shareholders are getting serious about sustainability, *Harvard Business Review*.

Fatemi, A., Fooladi, I., and Tehranian, H. (2015), Valuation effects of corporate social responsibility, *Journal of Banking & Finance*, 59, 182–192, https://doi.org/10.1016/j.jbankfin.2015.04.028

Khan, M., Serafeim, G., and Yoon, A. (2016), Corporate sustainability: First evidence on materiality, *The Accounting Review*, 91(6), 1697–1724, https://doi.org/10.2308/accr-51383

Schoenmaker, D., and Schramade, W. (2019), *Principles of Sustainable Finance*, Oxford University Press.

United Nations Environment Programme Finance Initiative (2019), Changing course: A comprehensive investor guide to scenario-based methods for climate risk assessment in response to the TCFD.

SUGGESTED FURTHER READING

Elkington, J. (2018), *Green swans: The coming boom in regenerative capitalism*, Fast Company Press.

European Commission, (2020), *The EU taxonomy regulation: A framework for sustainable investments*, Official Publication of the European Union.

Friede, G. (2021), *ESG and financial performance: Aggregated evidence from more than 2000 empirical studies*, Springer.

Giese, G., Lee, L-E., Melas, D., Nagy, Z., and Nishikawa, L. (2019), *Foundations of ESG investing: How ESG affects equity valuation, risk, and performance, MSCI Research.*

Glossary

Absolute Purchasing Power Theory: A version of PPP theory explaining that the ratio between domestic and foreign price levels under floating exchange rate regime equals the equilibrium exchange rate between the two currencies.

Absorption: A nation's total expenditure on final goods and services net of exports.

Absorption approach: It states that, for improvement in the balance of trade, either total income needs to be raised or the total absorption needs to be lowered.

Acceleration: Earlier repayment of loan necessitated by lender when default is anticipated.

Accounting exposure: Gain/loss arising on account of translation of currency at changed exchange rates.

Adjustable peg: Fixed exchange rates with provision for devaluation/upward revaluation of currency.

African Development Bank: Regional Development Bank serving the African region.

Adjusted present value: The net present value of an investment proposal using different rates as a discount rate.

Agency costs: Cost arising from the conflict between the shareholders and the managers.

All-equity rate: The discount rate reflecting only the business risk of a project. It abstracts from the effects of financing.

American depository receipt: Depository receipt denominated in US dollars and issued by US-based depository.

American option: Options exercised even before maturity.

Amortization: The repayment of loan in more than one instalment.

Announcement effect: A change in private market interest rates/exchange rates that results from changes in market conditions signaled by the central bank policy.

Appreciation: Rise in the external value of currency in a floating exchange-rate regime.

Arbitrage: A risk-free trading in which the same currency/instrument is bought and sold simultaneously in two different markets in order to profit out of divergence between the two markets.

Arm's length price: The price at which a seller transacts with an unrelated buyer. Normally, it is based on cost/market price.

Asian Development Bank: Regional Development Bank meant for the Asian member countries.

Ask rate: The selling rate of a currency.

Asymmetric information: Information available to one party in a financial transaction that is not available to any other party.

At the money: It denotes a position in the options market where strike rate is equal to the spot rate.

Average options: The options in which the average exchange rate during the life of the option serves the purpose of strike rate. The average is calculated either arithmetically or geometrically and the rates are tabulated with a variety of frequencies.

Back-to-back loan: One of the two loans of the same value and the same maturity but in different currencies made by one party to the other in different countries.

Baker Plan: Plan devised by James Baker for alleviating external indebtedness during 1980s.

Balance of trade: The difference between the value of export and import of merchandise.

Balance of payments: A macro-level statement showing inflow and outflow of foreign exchange on different accounts.

Balance-sheet hedge: A technique to hedge translation exposure.

Base money: Currency plus commercial bank reserves held against deposits.

Basis point: 1/100 of one per cent.

Basis risk: Related primarily to financial companies, it arises when interest rate exposure on one instrument is not fully offset by the interest rate exposure on the other instrument on account of varying index.

Basis swap: An interest-rate/cross-currency swap in which the payment obligation of each of the parties is determined by the floating-rate index.

Bells and whistles: The additional features of a security intended to attract investors or to reduce the issue cost.

Benchmark security: The choice of a security that may serve as a guide for other securities especially from the viewpoint of return.

Beta: It is a measure of sensitivity of an asset to changes in the market portfolio.

Bid-ask spread: Difference between buying and selling rates of a currency expressed as a percentage.

Bill of exchange: A negotiable instrument where drawer asks the drawee to pay an amount within specified period.

Bill of lading: A document involving contract between the exporter and a carrier for the shipment of goods. It serves as a receipt for the exporter.

Bimetallism: Two metals, viz. gold and silver forming the money supply.

Black-Scholes model: A model developed in 1973 for measuring the value of currency options.

Blocked currency: A currency that is not convertible/transferable across the border due to exchange control.

Blue chip: Highly rated equity share.

Bond: An instrument through which a company or government borrows funds for a specified period.

Bond basis: Method to compute accrued interest assuming one year being equal to 365 days.

Branch: An operating unit in foreign country having no separate entity from the parent unit.

Bretton Woods Agreement: An agreement concluded at Bretton Woods (USA) in 1944 establishing IBRD and IMF.

Bridge finance: A loan linking a short-term loan and a medium-term loan, normally in form of renewable overdrafts.

Bulldog bond: A bond issued in the UK by a non-resident.

Bullet repayment: Repayment of principal in one instalment at the end of the maturity.

Butterfly spread: A compound option strategy consisting of a combination of a bull spread and a bear spread in respect of either calls or puts.

Call option: An option where option buyer agrees to buy the underlying currency.

Callable bond: A bond with a call provision where the issuer can redeem it even before maturity.

Cap: A limit on the upward movement of interest rate.

Capital account: That part of balance of payments showing flow of foreign exchange on account of foreign investment and borrowing and lending and also short-term capital transactions mostly by banks.

Capital asset pricing model: A model explaining pricing risk associated with holding of securities. It means that rate of return is directly related to the return on market portfolio adjusted for non-diversifiable risk.

Capital budgeting: Long-term investment decision concerning selection of the investment proposals.

Capital market: Market for medium and long term funds.

Capital structure: A company's capital consisting of owners' fund and borrowed fund.

Clean float: Independent floating exchange-rate regime.

Clearing house automated payments system (CHAPS): A network of UK banks with computer-operated payments settlement system.

Clearing house inter-bank payments system (CHIPS): A computerised system used by over 120 US banks for international payments settlements.

Closing rate: See current rate method.

Collar: A combination of cap and floor. See cap and floor.

Commitment fee: A charge on the undrawn balance of the loan.

Consolidation exposure: See accounting exposure or translation exposure.

Convertible bond: Bonds convertible into equity shares on a future date.

Correspondent bank: A bank handling the business of a foreign bank.

Coutertrade: Bilateral cross-border trade where commodities are exchanged for commodities.

Country risk: A trading risk emerging from a government's interference in the foreign exchange markets.

Coupon: The fixed interest rate of a bond.

Covenant: An obligation in writing related normally to lending and borrowing.

Covered interest arbitrage: A process where a currency is borrowed and then exchanged for another currency, investing the exchanged currency for the period of the loan, and after taking off the forward cover on maturity, re-exchanging the currency and repaying the original loan. The process helps arbitrageurs reap profit.

Covered position: A particular position in respect of a security is matched by a counter position in respect of another security neutralising the ultimate effect.

Crawling peg system: An exchange rate arrangement in which a country pegs its currency with another currency but allows the parity value to change at regular intervals.

Cross default clauses: A clause in the loan agreement allowing the lender to ask for immediate repayment.

Cross rate: The exchange rate between two currencies established through a common currency.

Currency arbitrage: See arbitrage

Currency call option: See call option.

Currency fixings: An open auction executed on a daily basis in some of the European countries foreign exchange market.

Currency futures contract: A specific type of forward outright deal with standard size and maturity performed in the currency futures market which is also known as the market for derivatives.

Currency put option: A type of currency options where the option buyer contracts to sell the underlying currency.

Currency risk-sharing: The gain or loss arising on account of changes in the exchange rate is shared by the transacting parties in specified proportions.

Currency swap: One borrowed currency is exchanged for the other in order to avail of the desired currency. This is done through the swap dealer.

Current account: It is a part of balance of payments statement where the trade in goods and invisibles are entered and the inflow and outflow of foreign exchange on these accounts are balanced.

Current-rate method: Translation of currency at the current exchange rate.

Current/non-current method: It is method of currency translation where some of the items of the financial statements are translated at historical rate of exchange and the others are translated at current rate of exchange.

Current yield: The coupon return on a bond divided by the bond's market price.

Daylight position limit: The maximum amount of a currency a trader is allowed to carry at any single time during the regular trading hours.

Debt-equity swap: Inter-bank trading of sovereign debt for the purpose of alleviating the external debt problem of developing countries.

Debt factoring: Purchase of account receivables for the purpose of providing short-term finance on a continuing basis.

Debt-service ratio: The ratio between debt service and exports.

Debt relief: Ways to lower the burden of indebtedness.

Deep discount bond: A low-/zero-coupon bond issued at discount.

Delta: (a) The change of the currency options price relative to a change in the currency price; (b) the hedge ratio between the options contracts and the currency futures contracts in order to establish a neutral hedge.

Depreciation: The fall in the external value of a currency in a floating-rate regime.

Devaluation: In a fixed exchange rate regime, the monetary authorities lower the external value of the currency. The process is known as *devaluation*.

Diagonal spread: A compound options strategy where two calls/two puts are combined with varying maturity and varying strike price.

Direct quote: The exchange rate quote where the amount of domestic currency per unit of foreign currency is shown. The domestic currency is on the numerator while quoting exchange rate.

Dirty float: A floating exchange rate regime where the monetary authorities (central bank of the country) intervenes in the foreign exchange market through the purchase and sale of foreign currency for the purpose of stabilising the exchange rate. It is also known as *managed float*.

Disintermediation: The process of bypassing the normal financial intermediaries.

Double dip lease: A cross-border lease where different rules in the two countries treat both the parties as the owner of the leased equipment for the tax purposes.

Draft: An unconditional order signed by the exporter and addressed to the importer for making the payment of the export value either on sight or on a fixed date.

Drop-lock bond: A bond having, first, floating rate of interest and then a fixed rate of interest when the market interest rate drops below a certain limit.

Duration: It is the weighted average of maturities of the payments in respect of a bond where the weights are the discounted present value of payments.

Economic exposure: The effects of exchange rate changes on the firm's future cash flows.

Effective exchange rate: The weighted average of a currency's value in terms of selected currencies.

Efficient market: It exists when spot and forward exchange rates reflect, and adjust quickly to, new and relevant information.

Elasticities approach: It states that devaluation or upward revaluation of a currency influences the magnitude of export and import and thereby influences the balance of trade.

Euro: The currency of the European Monetary Union.

Euro banks: International banks making financial intermediation in any currency other than the currency of the country where they are located.

Euro bond: Bonds issued in any currency other than the currency of the country where they are issued.

Euro commercial paper: Instrument issued by companies for getting short-term funds. It is denominated in any currency other than the currency of the country where it is issued.

Eurocurrency: The Euro bank deposits and lending.

Euro dollars: Dollars deposited with the Euro banks outside the USA.

Euro equity issue: Equity shares converted into global depository receipts and sold for raising funds from the Euro-currency market.

Euro note: Promissory note issued by companies for getting short-term funds. It is denominated in any currency other than the currency of the country where it is issued.

Euroclear: Clearing house of the Euro-currency market based in Brussels.

European currency unit: It was a monetary unit of the European Monetary Union prior to the emergence of Euro.

European monetary system: Now known as the European Monetary Union. It is a monetary integration scheme among some European countries.

Exchange rate risk: Gains/losses arising on account of changes in exchange rate.

Exposure netting: Offsetting exposure in one currency with exposure in the same or other currency. It results in offsetting the loss in one currency transaction by the gains in other.

European option: Options to be exercised only at the maturity.

European Union: Economic integration scheme among 25 European countries.

Exercise rate: See strike rate

Factor: Factor is usually a firm to which borrowers sell receivables as collateral security. Factor assumes the responsibility of collecting them at the maturity.

Fiat money: Non-convertible paper currency.

Fisher effect: The closed version of the theory explaining that nominal interest rate combines both the real interest rate and the rate of inflation; while the open version of the theory explaining that inflation rate differential between the two countries equals the nominal interest rate differential between them.

Fixed exchange rate: The exchange rate between the two currencies is fixed.

Floating exchange rate: The exchange rate is determined by the market forces of supply and demand.

Floating rate note: A debt instrument having floating interest rate, normally some basis points above LIBOR.

Floor: The minimum interest rate.

Foreign bond market: The bond issued and marketed in the foreign countries. Such bonds are denominated in the currency of the country where they are issued.

Foreign direct investment: Foreign investment that possesses the essence of control of the host country enterprise.

Foreign tax credit: Home country tax credit given against domestic tax in respect of foreign taxes already paid on foreign income.

Forfaiting: Discounting bills of exchange at fixed rate of interest without recourse to the drawer.

Forward contract: Sale and purchase of currency where currencies are delivered at a future date at a rate mentioned in the contract.

Forward differential: The difference between the spot and the forward rates expressed as annualised percentage.

Forward/Forward swap: A pair of forward contracts involving a forward purchase and a forward sale of a currency simultaneously entered into but for varying maturities.

Forward premium (discount): Greater forward rate of a currency than the spot rate is forward premium, while the reverse is forward discount.

Forward rate: The exchange rate at which currencies are delivered under the forward contract.

Franchise: A form of technical collaboration providing for the use of trade marks, patents, etc. by the host country unit.

Free float: Exchange rate depending entirely on the market forces.

Front-end fee: The fee paid in the very beginning of a financial arrangement.

Functional currency: It is the operational currency of different units of a multinational firm.

Fundamental analysis: The future movement of the exchange rate based on the macro-economic variables.

Futures contract: The contract for buying and selling a currency in the market for currency futures.

G-7 nations: Seven major industrialised countries, viz. Germany, France, Italy, the UK, Canada, Japan and the USA.

Gamma: The rate of change of an option's delta with respect to the underlying price.

General arrangement to borrow (GAB): It is an arrangement under which IMF borrows from the industrialised countries to support its needy members.

Global fund: A mutual fund investing anywhere in the world.

Gold standard: A monetary arrangement under which currency is backed by gold and gold is used for international payments.

Hard currency: A freely convertible currency not easily expected to depreciate.

Hedging: It is a process to make the net position for a given currency at a given date equal to zero. It is normally adopted in forward market and the market for derivatives.

Hot money: Speculative bank deposits moving around the international money market for the purpose of reaping profits on account of exchange rate and interest rate movements.

In the money: A position with positive intrinsic value when spot rate is greater than the strike rate in a call option and when strike rate is greater than the spot rate in a put option.

Indirect quote: It is an exchange rate quote when the amount of foreign currency is expressed per unit of domestic currency.

Interest rate differential: Also known as interest rate spread. It is the difference between short-term interest rate prevailing at any two money centres.

Interest rate futures: Futures contracts relating entirely to the level of interest rates.

Interest rate parity theory: The theory explaining parity between interest rate differentials and forward rate differentials.

Interest rate swap: Exchange of loans—between fixed-rate and floating-rate, normally through a swap dealer.

Interest tax shield: The value of tax write-off on interest payment.

Internal rate of return: The rate of return equating the present value of future cash flows to the initial investment.

International Bank for Reconstruction and Development (IBRD): It is an international development bank emerging under the Bretton Woods agreement.

International diversification: Reducing risk through investing in two or more nations.

International Fisher effect: See Fisher effect (open version).

International Monetary Fund: An international agency created under the Bretton Woods agreement for surveillance of exchange rate system, international liquidity and other international monetary issues.

Intrinsic value: It is a value of options that exists when they are in the money. At the at-the-money position, intrinsic value of an option is zero.

J-curve theory: The theory explains that the immediate impact of devaluation manifests in worsening of the balance of trade, but after some time, balance of trade begins improving and reaches the surplus zone.

Joint venture: An agreement between two firms where one firm supplies capital or technology or both to the other firm.

Junk bond: A high-yield bond deemed to be below the investment grade once became popular for financing corporate take-overs.

Law of one price: See absolute version of PPP theory.

Lead manager: The main organiser of a new issue which is normally a commercial bank/investment bank or a broker. It provides advice, sells the securities and underwrites them. It can appoint co-managers.

Leads and lags: Lead means prepaying debt. Lag means postponing the repayment of debt. They are adopted to hedge the exchange rate risk or to improve the working capital position among different subsidiaries.

Leaning against/with the wind: The purpose of central bank intervention in the foreign exchange market may be either to reverse the current trend (leaning against the wind) or to support the current trend (leaning with the wind).

Letter of credit: A letter issued by the importer's bank indicating that payments to the exporter will be made if goods are in accordance with those mentioned in documents.

Licensing: A form of technical collaboration where technology is transferred to the host country unit.

Link financing: See back-to-back financing.

Listed security: A security listed on the stock exchange for trading.

Loan syndication: When two or more banks join hands to serve a borrower.

Lombard rate: The interest rate charged by Bundesbank or the Swiss central bank for a loan against the security of a pledged promissory note. It is normally 0.5 above its discount rate.

London inter-bank bid rate (LIBID): The interest rate at which major banks in London bid to accept deposit from one another for a given maturity.

London inter-bank mean rate: The average of LIBID and LIBOR.

London inter-bank offer rate (LIBOR): The interest rate at which major banks in London offer deposit to the other among them.

Long position: Having greater inflow than the outflow of a given currency or holding greater assets than the liabilities of a given currency.

Louvre accord: A meeting of the central banks of G-7 nations (except Italy) in 1987 announcing the value of US dollar consistent with the economic fundamentals.

Managed float: Floating exchange rate regime where the monetary authorities intervene in the foreign exchange market for stabilising the exchange rate. See dirty float.

Management contract: A form of technical collaboration where management expertise is transferred to the host country unit.

Marking to market: The process of revaluing a security, or futures contract according to current market price.

Mismatch: When securities or cash inflow and outflow do not match in size and maturity.

Monetary base: Central bank holdings of domestic securities and loans plus foreign exchange reserves or the sum of currency and bank reserves.

Monetary/non-monetary method: It is a method of translating functional currency into reporting currency. Non-monetary assets/liabilities are translated at historical rates, while monetary items are translated at current exchange rate.

Money market: Financial institutions dealing in short-term funds.

Money market basis: The method to calculate accrued interest on the basis of 360 days a year.

Money market hedge: Borrowing and lending in foreign currency is used to lock in the domestic currency value of a foreign currency transaction.

Multi-currency clause: The clause giving the Eurocurrency borrowers the right to switch from one currency to another when the loan is rolled over.

Multilateral Investment Guarantee Agency (MIGA): It is a sister institution of the World Bank meant for insuring against non-commercial risk.

Mumbai Interbank Forward Offer Rate (MIFOR): It is a rate related to setting of prices on forward rate agreements and other interest rate derivatives.

Mumbai Interbank Offer Rate (MIBOR): It is the interest rate at which banks borrow funds, in marketable size, from other banks in the Indian inter-bank market.

Netting: A process through which payments are adjusted with receipts and only the net amount is paid or received.

Nominal effective exchange rate: It is the weighted average of the nominal exchange rates of a currency where weight is based on the trade with specific countries.

Nominal exchange rate: The actual exchange rate fixed by the monetary authorities.

Note issuance facility: A syndicate of banks allowing borrowers to issue short-term notes that are then placed by the syndicate providing such a facility.

Offer rate: See ask rate.

Off-shore banking centres: It is that type of international banking centres which deal only in foreign currency and only with the non-residents.

Official reserves: Holdings of gold, SDRs and foreign currency assets by the monetary authorities, normally the central bank in a country.

Open market operation: Sale and purchase of securities by the government for regulating the size of credit in an economy.

Open position: It represents either a long position or a short position in respect of a currency.

Operating exposure: When the changes in exchange rate influences the future cash flows, such an exposure arises. It is also known as real operating exposure as the changes in cash flow are adjusted for inflation.

Optimum currency area: The largest economic unit having the same currency.

Option swap: Also known as swaption. A right to enter into a swap on or before a particular date.

Optional date forward contract: A forward contract with open maturity.

Out of the money: It is a situation when the exercise of the option is not beneficial for the option buyer and so it is not exercised. It is just the reverse of in-the-money position.

Outright forward quote: The forward rate of a currency. It is different from the swap quote.

Outsourcing: Purchase of large amount of inputs from a foreign source.

Par value: Under the Bretton Woods fixed parity system of exchange rate, the value of a currency was denoted in terms of gold or US dollar. This was known as par value.

Parallel loan: Simultaneous borrowing and lending involving four related parties in two countries.

Parity grid: It is the matrix of bilateral par values for the members' currencies in a target-zone arrangement. It establishes the intervention prices between the members' currencies.

Payments netting: Minimising intra-firm funds transfer only to a netted amount.

Pip: The most junior digit in a currency quotation.

Plaza agreement: At a meeting of the central banks of G-5 in 1985, it was announced to drive down the value of dollar through joint intervention.

Political risk: Uncertainty in governmental/political environment leading to changes in the value of a firm.

Pooling: It is the centralized positioning of cash by different subsidiaries usually in a tax-haven country.

Portfolio balance approach: It states that the quantities demanded and supplied of the domestic and foreign financial assets have an influence on the exchange rate and the balance of payments.

Portfolio investment: It is the investment in foreign financial assets simply for return and not for controlling foreign operations.

Price-specie flow mechanism: It states that disturbances in the price level in one country is offset by the flow of gold coins. This forms the basis for automatic adjustment in the balance of payments under gold standard.

Product cycle: The time taken to bring new and improved products to the market.

Project finance: A financing arrangement under which funds are provided by banks for specified projects against the security of the project's cash flow.

Protectionism: A policy of restricting imports.

Put option: See currency put option.

Rational expectation: A concept explaining that the prices of a currency or other financial assets in the market represent an average of all investors' expectation.

Real effective exchange rate: Nominal effective exchange rate adjusted for price level.

Real exchange rate: Value of a currency based on its real purchasing power. It measures the price competitiveness of the domestic products in the international market.

Reinvoicing centre: A subsidiary taking title to all goods sold by one unit to other unit or to an outsider. It is the centre that pays to the seller and gets the sale proceeds from the buyer.

Relative Purchasing Power Parity theory: It is the inflation rate differential between the two countries that determines the exchange rate between their currencies.

Reporting currency: The currency in which the figures of the financial statement of the subsidiaries are translated or reported to the parent unit.

Rescheduling: Renegotiation of the terms of loans or restructuring of the repayment of the loan.

Reserve currency: The currency commonly used for settling international debts and to express the exchange value of other nation's currencies.

Samurai bond: Yen-denominated bonds issued in Japanese financial market by the non-Japanese residents.

Securitisation: It represents the packaging of assets and liabilities through sale and purchase of securities in the market.

Seigniorage: The difference between the cost involved in the issue of money and the real resources acquired by the issuer.

Settlement date: The date when the sale/purchase of a currency is settled and the currency is actually delivered under the spot/forward market transactions.

Short position: A position when the anticipated inflow of a foreign currency is less than the anticipated outflow.

Sight deposit: Overnight deposits or money at call.

Sight draft: A bill of exchange that is due on presentation.

Society for Worldwide Inter-bank Telecommunications: An electronic message transmission service designed to effect the transfer of funds internationally.

Soft currency: A weak currency whose convertibility is highly restricted.

Sovereign risk: It arises when the borrowing government defaults on a loan.

Special drawing rights: It is international reserves asset created by International Monetary Fund in 1969 in order to improve international liquidity. Its value is based on the weighted average of four major currencies.

Spot rate: The rate of exchange applicable to the spot market transaction. In the spot market transactions, currency is delivered within two working days.

Spread: The difference between the buying and selling rates of a currency. It is normally shown in percentage terms.

Stabilising intervention: When the intervention by the monetary authorities in the foreign exchange market for the purpose of stabilising exchange rate does not lead to the loss of foreign exchange, it is known as stabilising intervention.

Sterilised intervention: When the central bank intervenes in the foreign exchange market for the purpose of stabilising exchange rate, there is possibility for increase in money supply and thereby for inflation. But when the increase in money supply is managed through open market operation, the whole process is known as sterilised intervention.

Strike price: A price at which a currency is bought or sold under options contract. It is also known as exercise price.

Subsidiary: A foreign-based affiliate that is incorporated under the host country law.

Suppliers' credit: A type of the credit arrangement where the customer issues a promissory note to the supplier of the goods. The note is guaranteed by governmental authorities.

Swap rate: The difference between spot and forward rates expressed in terms of points, e.g. 0.0001 of British Pound or any other currency unit.

Swaption: See option swap.

Systematic risk: The fluctuation in the rate of return from specific portfolio of assets in relation to the overall rate of return in the market. The rate of return is influenced by the same macro-economic variables with the result that any diversification in the portfolio of assets is not expected to reduce the risk.

Target-zone arrangement: An exchange rate arrangement among a group of countries where intra-group exchange rate is fixed.

Tax haven: A country imposing no tax/very low tax on profit routed through that country.

Technical analysis: Forecasting future movements of exchange rates on the basis of past trends.

Temporal method: It is a method for translating foreign currency where items stated at historical cost are translated at historical rate and the items stated at replacement cost/market value are translated at current rate.

Terms of trade: The weighted average of a country's export prices relative to the import prices.

Trade acceptance: A draft accepted by a commercial entity. See draft.

Trade draft: See draft.

Transaction exposure: Changes in exchange rate causing changes in the present cash flow.

Transfer price: Arbitrarily determined price normally for intra-firm transfer of goods and services which is quite different from arm's-length price and which is done for the purpose of reducing overall tax and tariff burden as also for the working capital management.

Translation exposure: Exchange rate risk arising on account of consolidation of financial statements of foreign subsidiaries.

Uncovered interest arbitrage: It is different from the covered interest arbitrage insofar as forward contracts are not involved. It involves the impact of interest rate differential on the future spot rate.

Unilateral transfer: Movement of funds only in one direction.

Unsystematic risk: The risk associated with a particular security which is not in tandem with that of the market portfolio.

Value-added tax: Indirect tax where tax is levied at each stage of value addition in respect of a product.

Value additivity principle: It states that the net present value of a set of independent projects is the sum of the NPVs of the individual projects.

Value date: It is the day on which the deal is settled and the currency is delivered in the foreign exchange market.

Vehicle currency: A currency most often used for international transactions.

Warrant: It is a negotiable instrument the holder of which possesses an option to subscribe for new equity in the issuing company at a predetermined rate.

World Bank: It is an amalgam of the International Bank for Reconstruction and Development and its sister institution, International Development Association.

Yankee bond: A bond issued in USA by a non-US resident.

Yield: The amount of interest payment shown as percentage of the loan value.

Yield curve: A graphical presentation of interest rates prevailing in case of similar but differing-maturity securities.

Yield to maturity: It is the discount rate equating the present value of interest payment and repayment of principal with the market price of the bond.

Zero-coupon bond: It is a bond carrying no interest charge. It is sold at discount. The discount serves the purpose of interest.

Zero-coupon swap: It is a swap in which one counterparty makes a single payment on the maturity, while the other counterparty makes periodic payment.

Country and Currency

1. Afghanistan (Afghani)
2. Albania (Lek)
3. Algeria (Dinar)
4. Angola (Kwanza)
5. Antigua & Barbuda (East Carr. dollar)
6. Argentina (Peso)
7. Armenia (Dram)
8. Aruba (Florin)
9. Australia (Dollar)
10. Austria (Euro)
11. Azerbaijan (Manat)
12. Bahamas (Dollar)
13. Bahrein (Dinar)
14. Bangladesh (Taka)
15. Belgium (Euro)
16. Bermuda (Dollar)
17. Bhutan (Ngultrum)
18. Bolivia (Boliviano)
19. Bosnia-Herzegovina (Marka)
20. Botswana (Pula)
21. Brazil (Cruzeiro Real)
22. Brunei (Dollar)
23. Bulgaria (Lev)
24. Cambodia (Riel)
25. Canada (Dollar)
26. Cayman islands (Dollar)
27. Central African Republic (Eq. CFA franc)
28. Chad (Eq. CFA franc)
29. China (Mainland, Yuan)
30. Chile (Peso)
31. Colombia (Peso)
32. Comoros (Franc)
33. Congo (Eq. CFA franc)
34. Costa Rica (Colon)
35. Croatia (Kuna)
36. Cuba (Peso)
37. Cyprus (Pound)
38. Czech Republic (Koruny)
39. Denmark (Kroner)
40. Ecuador (Sucre)
41. Egypt (Pound)
42. Eritrea (Nakfa)
43. Estonia (Krooni)
44. Ethiopia (Birr)
45. Finland (Euro)
46. France (Euro)
47. Gambia (Dalasis)
48. Georgia (Lari)
49. Germany (Euro)
50. Ghana (Cedi)
51. Great Britain (Pound)
52. Greece (Euro)
53. Guatemala (Quetzale)
54. Haiti (Gourde)
55. Honduras (Lenipira)
56. Hong Kong (Dollar)

57. Hungary (Forint)
58. India (Rupee)
59. Indonesia (Rupiah)
60. Iran (Rial)
61. Iraq (Dinar)
62. Ireland (Punt)
63. Israel (New Sheqalim)
64. Italy (Euro)
65. Jamaica (Dollar)
66. Japan (Yen)
67. Jordan (Dinar)
68. Kazakhstan (Tenge)
69. Kenya (Shilling)
70. Kirgistan (Som)
71. Korea, Rep. (Won)
72. Kuwait (Dinar)
73. Laos (New Kip)
74. Latvia (Lat)
75. Lebanon (Pound)
76. Lesotho (Maloti)
77. Liberia (Dollar)
78. Libya (Dinar)
79. Luxembourg (Euro)
80. Macao (Pataca)
81. Madagascar (Ariary)
82. Malawi (Kwacha)
83. Malaysia (Ringgit)
84. Maldives (Ruffiya)
85. Malta (Liri)
86. Mauritius (Rupee)
87. Mexico (Peso)
88. Mongolia (Togrog)
89. Morocco (Dirham)
90. Mozambique (Metical)
91. Myanmar (Kyat)
92. Namibia (Dollar)
93. Nepal (Rupee)
94. Netherlands (Euro)
95. New Zealand (Dollar)
96. Nicaragua (Cordoba Oro)
97. Nigeria (Naira)
98. North Korea (Won)
99. Norway (Kroner)
100. Oman (Rial)
101. Pakistan (Rupee)
102. Panama (Balbao)
103. Papua New Guinea (Kina)
104. Paraguay (Guarania)
105. Philippines (Peso)
106. Peru (Nuevo Sol)
107. Poland (Zloty)
108. Portugal (Euro)
109. Quatar (Riyal)
110. Romania (Lei)
111. Russia (Rouble)
112. Samoa (Tala)
113. Saudi Arabia (Riyal)
114. Senegal (West CFA franc)
115. Seychelles (Rupee)
116. Singapore (Dollar)
117. Slovakia (Koruny)
118. Slovania (Tolar)
119. Somalia (Shilling)
120. South Africa (Rand)
121. South Korea (Won)
122. Spain (Euro)
123. Sri Lanka (Rupee)
124. Sudan (Dinar)
125. Swaziland (Emalangeni)
126. Sweden (Kroner)
127. Syria (Pound)
128. Taiwan (Dollar)
129. Tanzania (Shilling)
130. Thailand (Baht)
131. Trinidad & Tobago (Dollar)
132. Tunisia (Dinar)
133. Turkey (Lira)
134. Uganda (New Shilling)
135. USA (Dollar)
136. Uruguay (Peso)
137. UAE (Dirham)
138. Vanuatu (Vatu)
139. Venezuela (Bolivar)
140. Vietnam (New Dong)
141. West Indies (Dollar)
142. Yemen (Rial)
143. Zaire (New Zaire)
144. Zambia (Kwacha)
145. Zimbabwe (Dollar)

Answers to Objective Type Questions

CHAPTER 1

1. (a) F, (b) F, (c) F, (d) F, (e) F
2. (a) i, (b) ii, (c) ii

CHAPTER 2

1. (a) F, (b) F, (c) T, (d) F, (e) F (f) F
2. (a) i, (b) ii, (c) i, (d) ii, (e) ii (f) i

CHAPTER 3

1. (a) F, (b) F, (c) F, (d) T, (e) F
2. (a) i, (b) i, (c) iii, (d) ii, (e) i

CHAPTER 4

1. (a) T, (b) T, (c) T, (d) F, (e) T
2. (a) ii, (b) i, (c) i, (d) i, (e) ii

CHAPTER 5

1. (a) F, (b) T, (c) T, (d) F, (e) F
2. (a) ii, (b) i, (c) ii

CHAPTER 6

1. (a) T, (b) F, (c) T, (d) F, (e) F
2. (a) ii, (b) i, (c) i, (d) i, (e) i

CHAPTER 7

1. (a) F, (b) F, (c) T, (d) T, (e) T, (f) T
2. (a) i, (b) ii, (c) i, (d) i, (e) i

CHAPTER 8

1. (a) T, (b) T, (c) T, (d) F, (e) T
2. (a) ii, (b) i, (c) i,

CHAPTER 9

1. (a) F, (b) T, (c) F, (d) F, (e) F
2. (a) iii, (b) ii, (c) iii, (d) i, (e) ii

CHAPTER 10

1. (a) F, (b) F, (c) T, (d) F, (e) F
2. (a) i, (b) i, (c) ii, (d) i

CHAPTER 11

1. (a) T, (b) T, (c) T, (d) F, (e) T
2. (a) i, (b) i, (c) ii, (d) i, (e) i

CHAPTER 12

1. (a) F, (b) T, (c) T, (d) F
2. (a) ii, (b) i, (c) i, (d) i, (e) ii

CHAPTER 13

1. (a) F, (b) F, (c) T, (d) T, (e) T
2. (a) i, (b) i, (c) ii

CHAPTER 14

1. (a) F, (b) T, (c) F, (d) T, (e) T
2. (a) i, (b) i, (c) i

CHAPTER 15

1. (a) F, (b) F, (c) F, (d) F, (e) F
2. (a) iii, (b) i, (c) i

CHAPTER 16

1. (a) F, (b) F, (c) T, (d) F, (e) F
2. (a) i, (b) ii, (c) i

CHAPTER 17

1. (a) T, (b) T, (c) F, (d) T, (e) T
2. (a) i, (b) i, (c) i

CHAPTER 18

1. (a) F, (b) T, (c) T, (d) T, (e) T
2. (a) iii, (b) i, (c) i

CHAPTER 19

1. (a) F, (b) T, (c) T, (d) T, (e) T, (f) F
2. (a) i, (b) i, (c) i, (d) i, (e) iii

CHAPTER 20

1. (a) T, (b) T, (c) F, (d) T, (e) T
2. (a) ii, (b) i, (c) i, (d) ii, (e) ii

CHAPTER 21

1. (a) T, (b) F, (c) F, (d) T, (e) T
2. (a) ii, (b) i, (c) ii, (d) i, (e) iii

CHAPTER 22

1. (a) T, (b) T, (c) F, (d) F, (e) F
2. (a) i, (b) i, (c) ii, (d) i

CHAPTER 23

1. (a) T, (b) T, (c) T, (d) F, (e) T
2. (a) i, (b) i, (c) ii

CHAPTER 24

1. (a) F, (b) T, (c) F, (d) F, (e) F
2. (a) iii, (b) ii, (c) i, (d) ii, (e) ii

CHAPTER 25

1. (a) T, (b) F, (c) T, (d) F, (e) T
2. (a) i, (b) ii, (c) ii

CHAPTER 26

1. (a) T, (b) T, (c) T, (d) T, (e) T (f) T
2. (a) ii, (b) ii, (c) ii, (d) iii, (e) ii,
   (f) ii, (g) iii

CHAPTER 27

1. (a) T, (b) F, (c) F, (d) T, (e) T
2. (a) ii, (b) i, (c) ii, (d) ii, (e) iii

CHAPTER 28

1. (a) F, (b) T, (c) T, (d) F, (e) T
2. (a) ii, (b) ii, (c) ii, (d) ii, (e) ii

Answers to Numerical Problems

CHAPTER 2

1. Balance of trade = \$ – 17,098
   Balance of current account = \$ – 4,164
   Overall balance of payments = \$ 6,024

CHAPTER 4

1. \$ 0.02/₹
2. (a) \$ 0.02469 – 0.2500/₹ (b) 1.23%
3. BF 15.23 – 15.36 ? DM
4. Theory of one price holds good, but absolute version of PPP theory does not.
5. ₹ 41.17/\$
6. 8.49%
7. 5%
8. ₹ 46.33/\$
9. Nominal exchange rate = 50%; Real exchange rate 13.63%

CHAPTER 5

1. 27th and 28th February respectively.
2. Buying US \$ one-month forward, selling US \$ two-month forward and again buying US \$ three-month forward.
3. Selling pound in New York and buying pound in London to get \$ 0.0300 per pound
4. Forward deal will cause loss to the importer to the extent of ₹ 0.20 per dollar.

CHAPTER 6

1. Yes, the futures contract successfully hedged the currency risk. Even though the Euro appreciated from $ 0.60 to $ 0.65, the futures contract locked in the rate at $ 0.63, so the importer effectively paid $ 0.63/∈, thus avoiding a loss of $ 2,500 due to exchange rate movement.
2. • Futures Price = 0.5985 USD/Euro
   • Basis = 0.0015 USD/Euro
3. $ 5,550

CHAPTER 7

1. (a) Call option = $ 0.08/Pound; Put option = zero
   (b) Call = Gain is $ 0.03 per pound; Put = Loss is $ 0.05 per pound
   (c) Call = Loss is $ 0.03 per pound; Put = Gain is $ 0.05 per pound
2. The importer buys the first call with X = $ 1.60 and reduces the risk by $ 0.02/pound.
   If he goes for a tunnel with the same option, total risk will be covered.

CHAPTER 8

1. –2.44%

CHAPTER 9

1. Based on different methods of translation, the translation exposure will be as follows:
   (a) Current rate method ($ 2.30 million)
   (b) Current/non-current rate method ($ 0.90 million)
   (c) Monetary/non-monetary method $ 5.27 million
   (d) Temporal method $ 4.24 million
2. ₹ 300.25 million

CHAPTER 10

1. Forward market hedge provides the maximum risk coverage.

CHAPTER 12

1. $ 17 million is the initial investment from the viewpoint of the parent unit.
2. $ 18 million
3. $ – 0.70 million
4. The project's cost of capital is 20.5%.
5. WACC is 10.33%
6. Gain to Firm A = $ 2,650

CHAPTER 14

1. Portfolio return 14.25%
   Portfolio risk 0.595%
2. Indian investors will make investment in UK securities as the ratio of excess return to risk is higher.

CHAPTER 15

1. The firm will borrow from dollar market as effective interest is lower.
2. 6.70%

CHAPTER 20

1. 21.94%
2. 10.26%
3. 9.10%
4. $ 7,415
5. The borrower will not go for floor. As regards collar, cap reduces the risk to $ 16,140. The premium on selling floor along with cap will eliminate the risk.

CHAPTER 21

1. A will pay $ 11 million to C.
2. 48.99 tonnes
3. Re-order lies at a point when the inventory will come down to 20 tonnes.

CHAPTER 23

1. $ 125.

Index